W9-BFM-300

JavaScript™

- In an Instant -

by Michael Toot and Kelly L. Murdock

Visual

From
maranGraphics®
&

Hungry Minds™

Best-Selling Books • Digital Downloads • e-books • Answer Networks
e-Newsletters • Branded Web Sites • e-learning
New York, NY • Cleveland, OH • Indianapolis, IN

JavaScript™ In an Instant

Published by
Hungry Minds, Inc.
909 Third Avenue
New York, NY 10022
www.hungryminds.com

maranGraphics, Inc.
5755 Coopers Avenue
Mississauga, Ontario, Canada
L4Z 1R9
Library of Congress Control Number: 2001098184
ISBN: 0-7645-3659-1
Printed in the United States of America
10 9 8 7 6 5 4 3 2
1B/RT/RS/QR/IN
Distributed in the United States by Hungry Minds, Inc.
Distributed by CDG Books Canada Inc. for Canada; by Transworld Publishers Limited in the United Kingdom; by IDG Norge Books for Norway; by IDG Sweden Books for Sweden; by IDG Books Australia Publishing Corporation Pty. Ltd. for Australia and New Zealand; by TransQuest Publishers Pte Ltd. for Singapore, Malaysia, Thailand, Indonesia, and Hong Kong; by Gotop Information Inc. for Taiwan; by ICG Muse, Inc. for Japan; by Intersoft for South Africa; by Eyrolles for France; by International Thomson Publishing for Germany, Austria and Switzerland; by Distribuidora Cuspide for Argentina; by LR International for Brazil; by Galileo Libros for Chile; by Ediciones ZETA S.C.R. Ltda. for Peru; by WS Computer Publishing Corporation, Inc., for the Philippines; by Contemporanea de Ediciones for Venezuela; by Express Computer Distributors for the Caribbean and West Indies; by Micronesia Media Distributor, Inc. for Micronesia; by Chips Computadoras S.A. de C.V. for Mexico; by Editorial Norma de Panama S.A. for Panama; by American Bookshops for Finland.
For corporate orders, please call maranGraphics at 800-469-6616 or fax 905-890-9434.
For general information on Hungry Minds' products and services please contact our Customer Care Department within the U.S. at 800-762-2974, outside the U.S. at 317-572-3993 or fax 317-572-4002.
For sales inquiries and reseller information, including discounts, premium and bulk quantity sales, and foreign-language translations, please contact our Customer Care Department at 800-434-3422, fax 317-572-4002, or write to Hungry Minds, Inc., Attn: Customer Care Department, 10475 Crosspoint Boulevard, Indianapolis, IN 46256.
For information on licensing foreign or domestic rights, please contact our Sub-Rights Customer Care Department at 212-884-5000.
For information on using Hungry Minds' products and services in the classroom or for ordering examination copies, please contact our Educational Sales Department at 800-434-2086 or fax 317-572-4005.
For press review copies, author interviews, or other publicity information, please contact our Public Relations department at 317-572-3168 or fax 317-572-4168.
For authorization to photocopy items for corporate, personal, or educational use, please contact Copyright Clearance Center, 222 Rosewood Drive, Danvers, MA 01923, or fax 978-750-4470.
Screen shots displayed in this book are based on prereleased software and are subject to change.

Trademark Acknowledgments

Permissions

U.S. Corporate Sales
Contact maranGraphics at (800) 469-6616 or fax (905) 890-9434.

U.S. Trade Sales
Contact Hungry Minds at (800) 434-3422 or fax (317) 572-4002.

Some comments from our readers...

"I have to praise you and your company on the fine products you turn out. I have twelve of the *Teach Yourself VISUALLY* and *Simplified* books in my house. They were instrumental in helping me pass a difficult computer course. Thank you for creating books that are easy to follow."

–Gordon Justin (Brielle, NJ)

"I commend your efforts and your success. I teach in an outreach program for the Dr. Eugene Clark Library in Lockhart, TX. Your *Teach Yourself VISUALLY* books are incredible and I use them in my computer classes. All my students love them!"

–Michele Schalin (Lockhart, TX)

"Thank you so much for helping people like me learn about computers. The Maran family is just what the doctor ordered. Thank you, thank you, thank you."

–Carol Moten (New Kensington, PA)

"I would like to take this time to compliment maranGraphics on creating such great books. Thank you for making it clear. Keep up the good work."

–Kirk Santoro (Burbank, CA)

"I write to extend my thanks and appreciation for your books. They are clear, easy to follow, and straight to the point. Keep up the good work!"

–Seward Kollie (Dakar, Senegal)

"What fantastic teaching books you have produced! Congratulations to you and your staff. You deserve the Nobel prize in Education in the Software category. Thanks for helping me to understand computers."

–Bruno Tonon (Melbourne, Australia)

"Over time, I have bought a number of your 'Read Less, Learn More' books. For me, they are THE way to learn anything easily."

–José A. Mazón (Cuba, NY)

"I was introduced to maranGraphics about four years ago and YOU ARE THE GREATEST THING THAT EVER HAPPENED TO INTRODUCTORY COMPUTER BOOKS!"

–Glenn Nettleton (Huntsville, AL)

"Compliments To The Chef!! Your books are extraordinary! Or, simply put, Extra-Ordinary, meaning way above the rest! THANK YOU THANK YOU THANK YOU! for creating these."

–Christine J. Manfrin (Castle Rock, CO)

"I'm a grandma who was pushed by an 11-year-old grandson to join the computer age. I found myself hopelessly confused and frustrated until I discovered the Visual series. I'm no expert by any means now, but I'm a lot further along than I would have been otherwise. Thank you!"

–Carol Louthain (Logansport, IN)

"Thank you, thank you, thank you...for making it so easy for me to break into this high-tech world. I now own four of your books. I recommend them to anyone who is a beginner like myself. Now... if you could just do one for programming VCRs, it would make my day!"

–Gay O'Donnell (Calgary, Alberta, Canada)

"You're marvelous! I am greatly in your debt."

–Patrick Baird (Lacey, WA)

maranGraphics is a family-run business located near Toronto, Canada.

maranGraphics

At maranGraphics, we believe in producing great computer books — one book at a time.

Each maranGraphics book uses the award-winning communication process that we have been developing over the last 25 years. Using this process, we organize screen shots and text in a way that makes it easy for you to learn new concepts and tasks.

We spend hours deciding the best way to perform each task, so you don't have to!

Our clear, easy-to-follow screen shots and instructions walk you through each task from beginning to end.

We want to thank you for purchasing what we feel are the best computer books money can buy. We hope you enjoy using this book as much as we enjoyed creating it!

Sincerely,

The Maran Family

CREDITS

Major Contributors
Michael Toot
Kelly L. Murdock

Project Editor
Dana Rhodes Lesh

Acquisitions Editor
Jen Dorsey

Product Development Supervisor
Lindsay Sandman

Copy Editor
Tim Borek

Technical Editor
Angela Murdock

Editorial Manager
Rev Mengle

Editorial Assistant
Amanda Foxworth

Book Design
maranGraphics®

Production Coordinator
Maridee Ennis

Layout
LeAndra Johnson
Kristin McMullan
Jill Piscitelli

Screen Artists
Ronda David-Burroughs
Mark Harris
Jill A. Proll

Proofreaders
Andy Hollandbeck
Joanne Keaton

Indexer
Liz Cunningham

GENERAL AND ADMINISTRATIVE

Hungry Minds Technology Publishing Group: Richard Swadley, Vice President and Executive Group Publisher; Bob Ipsen, Vice President and Group Publisher; Joseph Wikert, Vice President and Publisher; Barry Pruett, Vice President and Publisher; Mary Bednarek, Editorial Director; Mary C. Corder, Editorial Director; Andy Cummings, Editorial Director

Hungry Minds Manufacturing: Ivor Parker, Vice President, Manufacturing

Hungry Minds Marketing: John Helmus, Assistant Vice President, Director of Marketing

Hungry Minds Production for Branded Press: Debbie Stailey, Production Director

Hungry Minds Sales: Michael Violano, Vice President, International Sales and Sub Rights

TABLE OF CONTENTS

TABLE OF CONTENTS

ENTER JAVASCRIPT STATEMENTS IN THE URL FIELD

JavaScript is composed of statements that when executed perform a desired function. For example, the JavaScript statement `document.write("hello")` displays the word *hello* in the browser. A semicolon (;) should be placed at the end of a JavaScript statement. You can include several different statements together in the Address box by separating them with semicolons.

ENTER JAVASCRIPT STATEMENTS IN THE URL FIELD

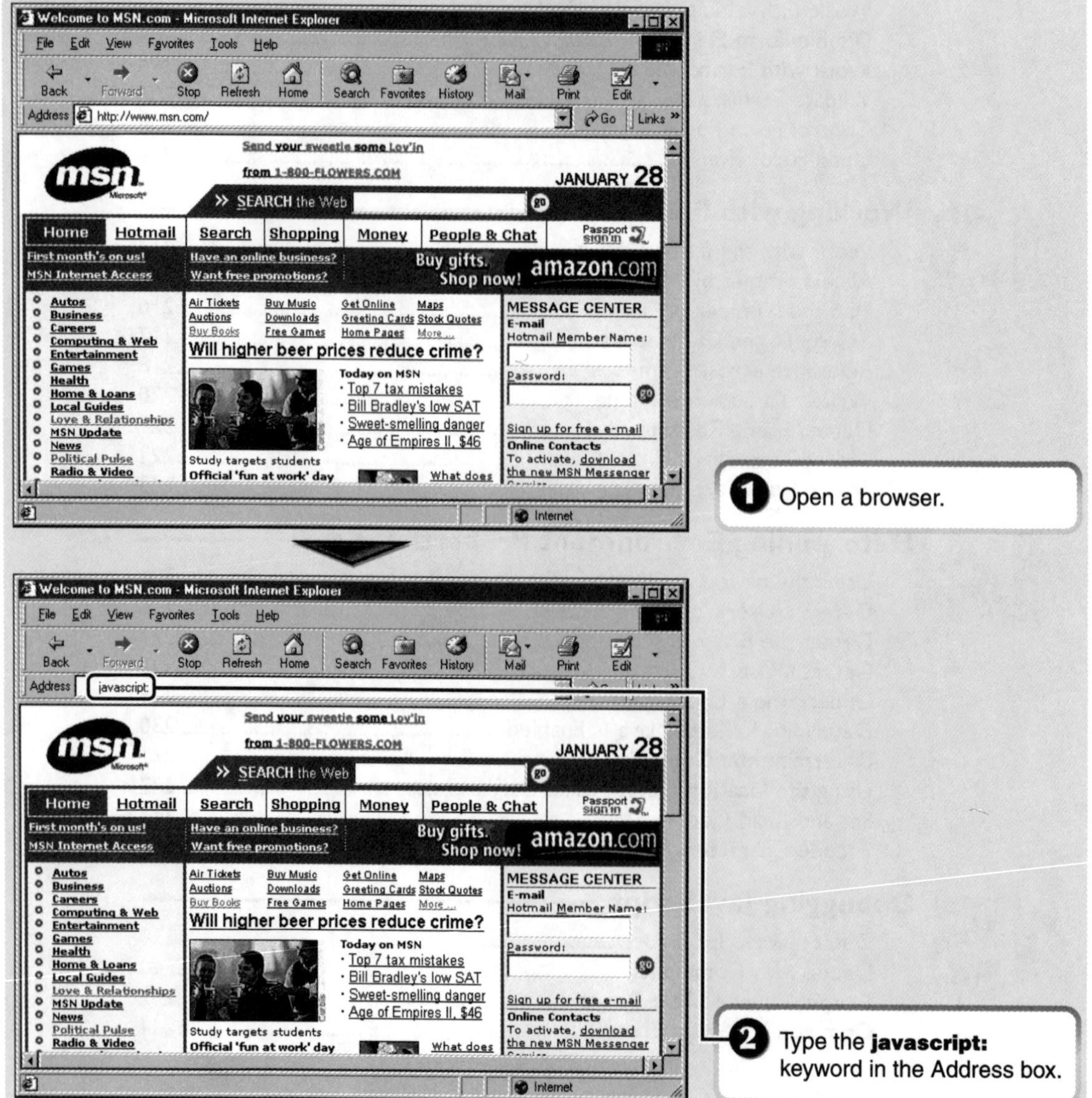

Welcome to MSN.com - Microsoft Internet Explorer
http://www.msn.com/
javascript:

1 Open a browser.

2 Type the **javascript:** keyword in the Address box.

in an instant

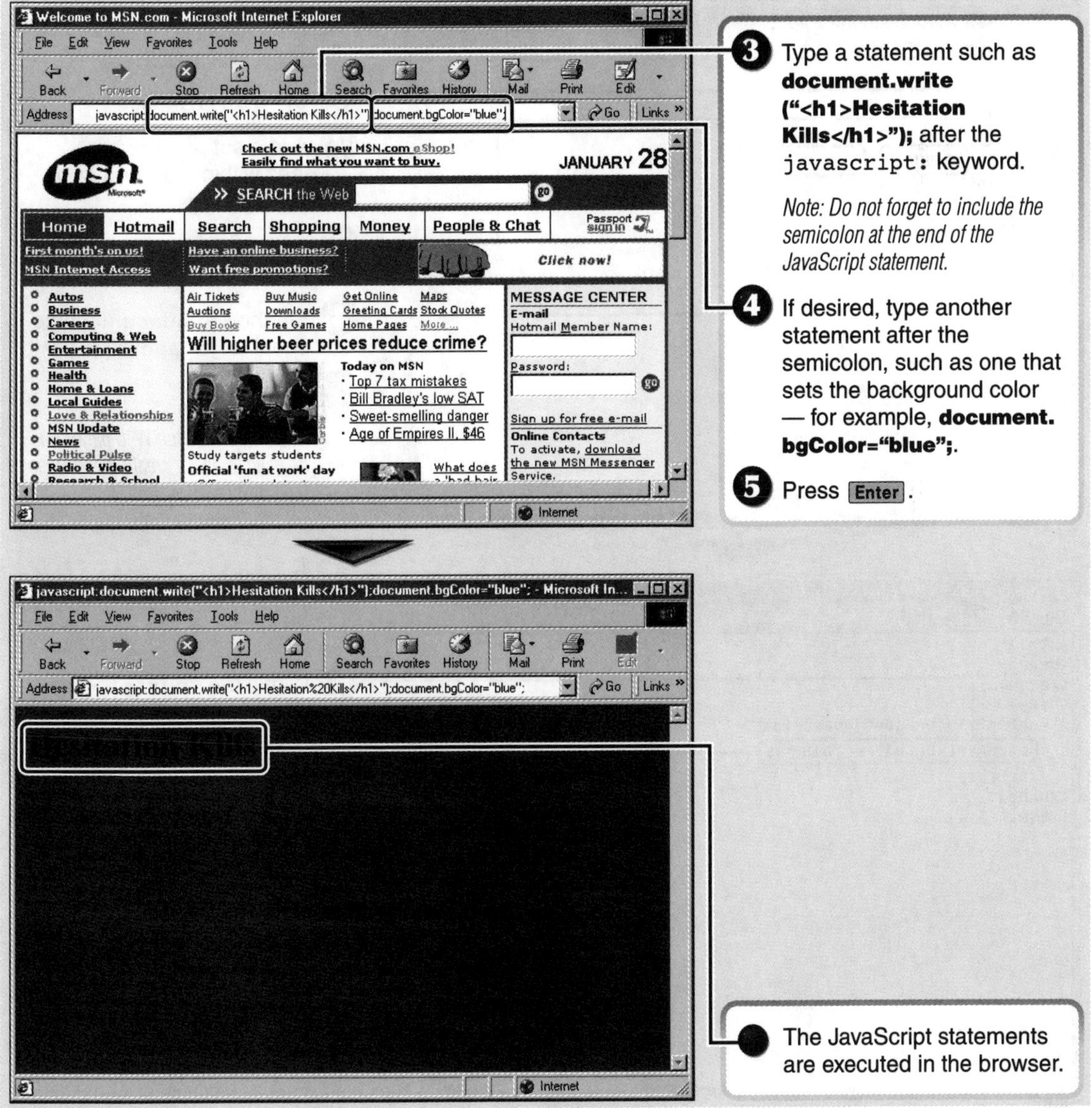
Welcome to MSN.com - Microsoft Internet Explorer
javascript:document.write("<h1>Hesitation Kills</h1>");document.bgColor="blue";
javascript:document.write("<h1>Hesitation Kills</h1>");document.bgColor="blue"; - Microsoft In...
javascript:document.write("<h1>Hesitation%20Kills</h1>");document.bgColor="blue";

3. Type a statement such as **document.write ("<h1>Hesitation Kills</h1>");** after the `javascript:` keyword.

   Note: Do not forget to include the semicolon at the end of the JavaScript statement.

4. If desired, type another statement after the semicolon, such as one that sets the background color — for example, **document.bgColor="blue";**.

5. Press Enter.

- The JavaScript statements are executed in the browser.

EMBED JAVASCRIPT WITHIN AN HTML DOCUMENT

You can include JavaScript in a Web page by using `<script>` tags, which can appear anywhere within the `<head>` or `<body>` tags. The `<script>` tag accepts the `type` and `language` attributes. `type` can be set to a recognized MIME type, such as `text/javascript`, and `language` is used to specify the scripting language, such as setting it to simply `javascript`.

EMBED JAVASCRIPT WITHIN AN HTML DOCUMENT

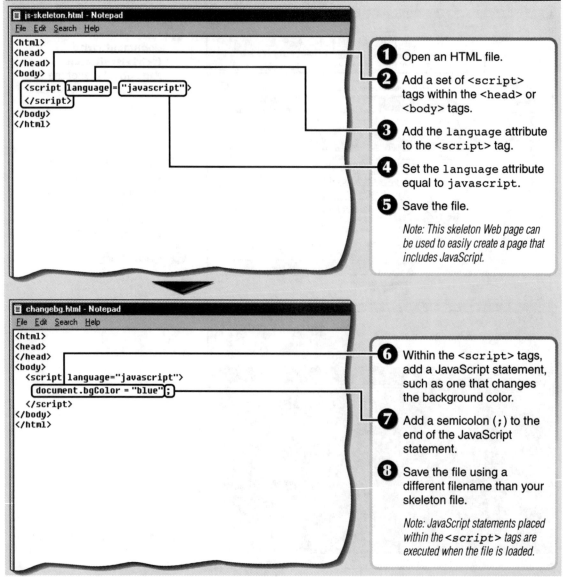

js-skeleton.html - Notepad

```
<html>
<head>
</head>
<body>
  <script language="javascript">
  </script>
</body>
</html>
```

1. Open an HTML file.
2. Add a set of `<script>` tags within the `<head>` or `<body>` tags.
3. Add the `language` attribute to the `<script>` tag.
4. Set the `language` attribute equal to `javascript`.
5. Save the file.

Note: This skeleton Web page can be used to easily create a page that includes JavaScript.

changebg.html - Notepad

```
<html>
<head>
</head>
<body>
  <script language="javascript">
    document.bgColor = "blue";
  </script>
</body>
</html>
```

6. Within the `<script>` tags, add a JavaScript statement, such as one that changes the background color.
7. Add a semicolon (`;`) to the end of the JavaScript statement.
8. Save the file using a different filename than your skeleton file.

Note: JavaScript statements placed within the `<script>` tags are executed when the file is loaded.

in an instant

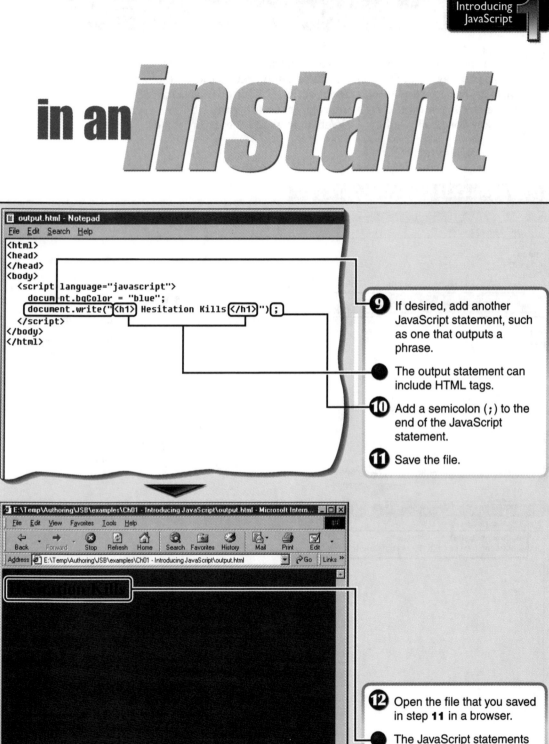

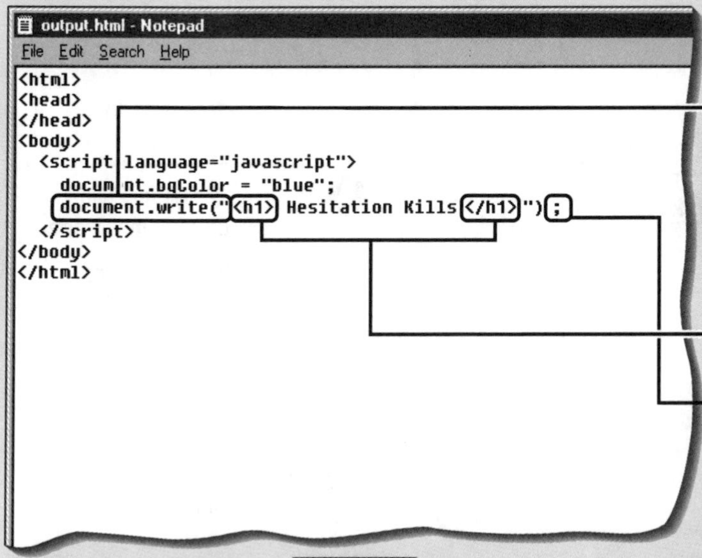

```
<html>
<head>
</head>
<body>
  <script language="javascript">
    document.bgColor = "blue";
    document.write("<h1> Hesitation Kills</h1>");
  </script>
</body>
</html>
```

9. If desired, add another JavaScript statement, such as one that outputs a phrase.

- The output statement can include HTML tags.

10. Add a semicolon (;) to the end of the JavaScript statement.

11. Save the file.

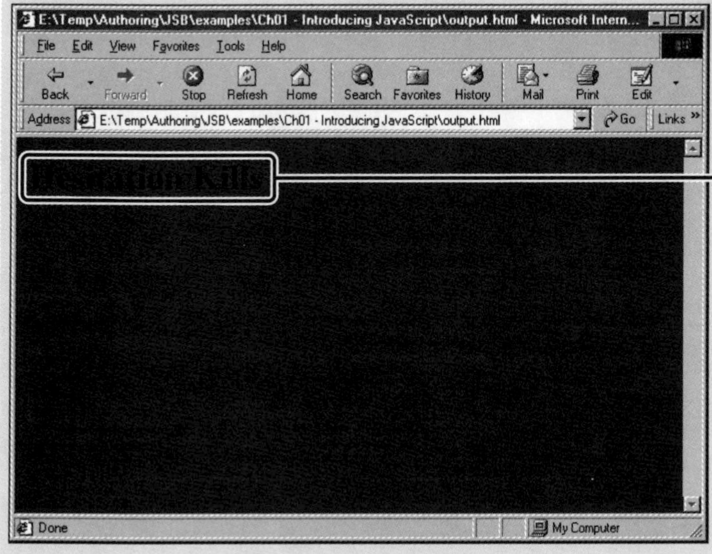

Hesitation Kills

12. Open the file that you saved in step **11** in a browser.

- The JavaScript statements are executed in the browser.

LINK TO AN EXTERNAL JAVASCRIPT FILE

In addition to `type` and `language`, you can use another attribute with the `<script>` tag: `src`. The `src` attribute can be set to the URL of an external file that contains the JavaScript script. The external JavaScript file can be anywhere on the Web and referenced using the `http://` protocol keyword, followed by the Web address for the external file.

LINK TO AN EXTERNAL JAVASCRIPT FILE

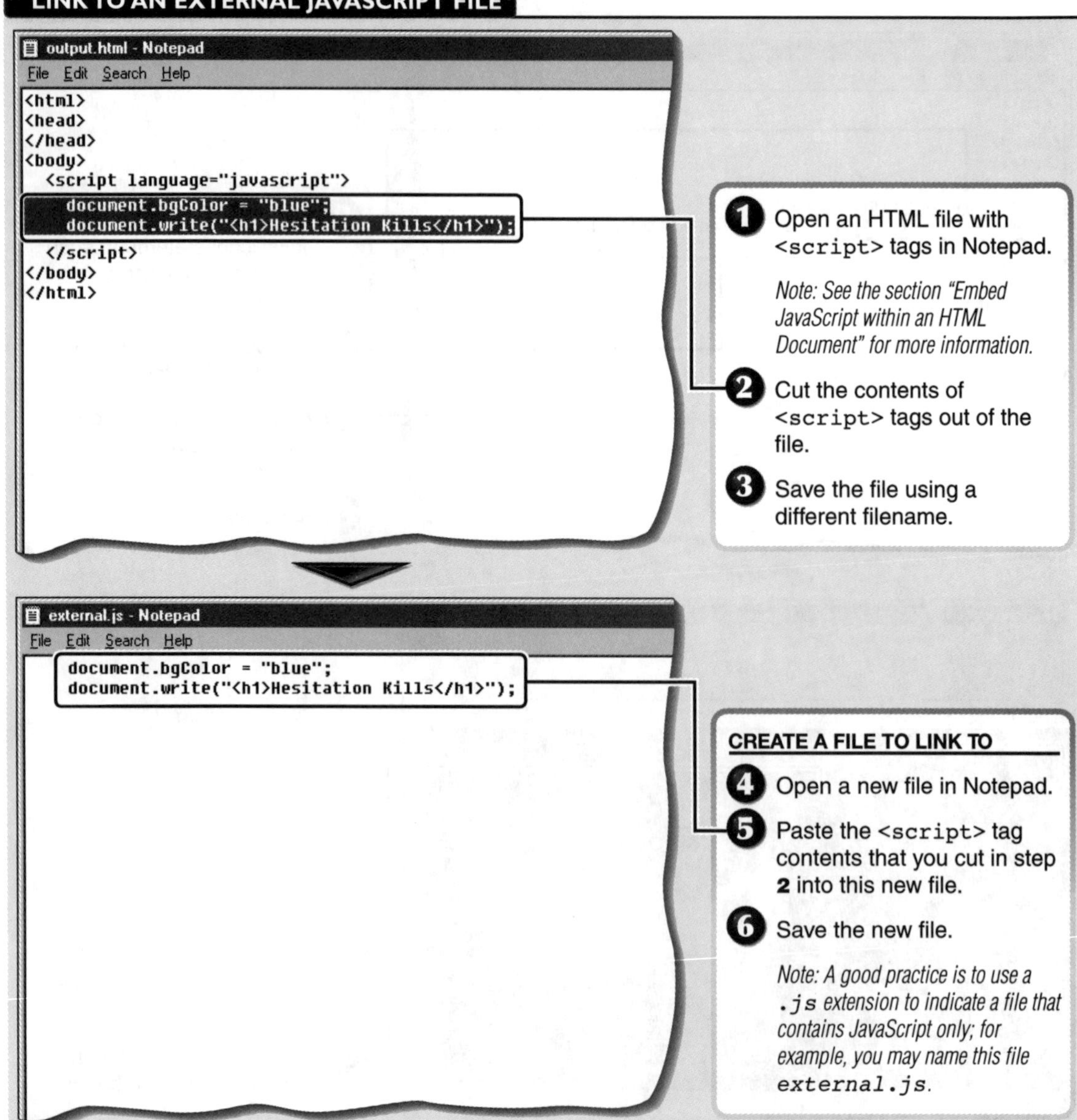

output.html - Notepad
File Edit Search Help
<html>
<head>
</head>
<body>
<script language="javascript">
document.bgColor = "blue";
document.write("<h1>Hesitation Kills</h1>");
</script>
</body>
</html>
external.js - Notepad
File Edit Search Help
document.bgColor = "blue";
document.write("<h1>Hesitation Kills</h1>");

1. Open an HTML file with `<script>` tags in Notepad.

   Note: See the section "Embed JavaScript within an HTML Document" for more information.

2. Cut the contents of `<script>` tags out of the file.
3. Save the file using a different filename.

CREATE A FILE TO LINK TO

4. Open a new file in Notepad.
5. Paste the `<script>` tag contents that you cut in step **2** into this new file.
6. Save the new file.

   Note: A good practice is to use a `.js` extension to indicate a file that contains JavaScript only; for example, you may name this file `external.js`.

in an instant

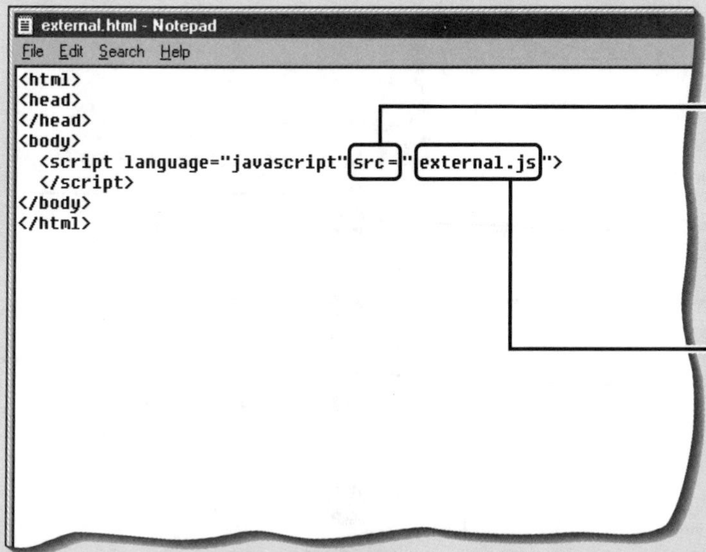

```
<html>
<head>
</head>
<body>
  <script language="javascript" src="external.js">
  </script>
</body>
</html>
```

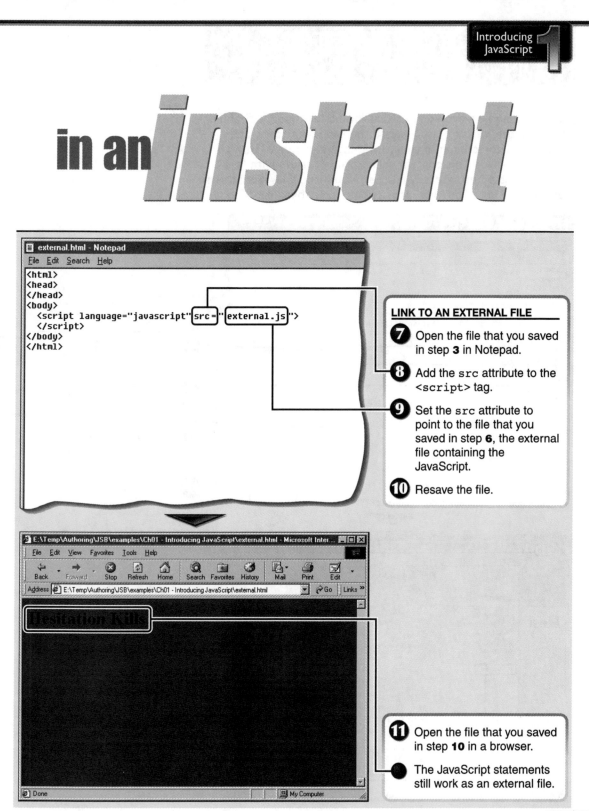

LINK TO AN EXTERNAL FILE

7 Open the file that you saved in step **3** in Notepad.

8 Add the `src` attribute to the `<script>` tag.

9 Set the `src` attribute to point to the file that you saved in step **6**, the external file containing the JavaScript.

10 Resave the file.

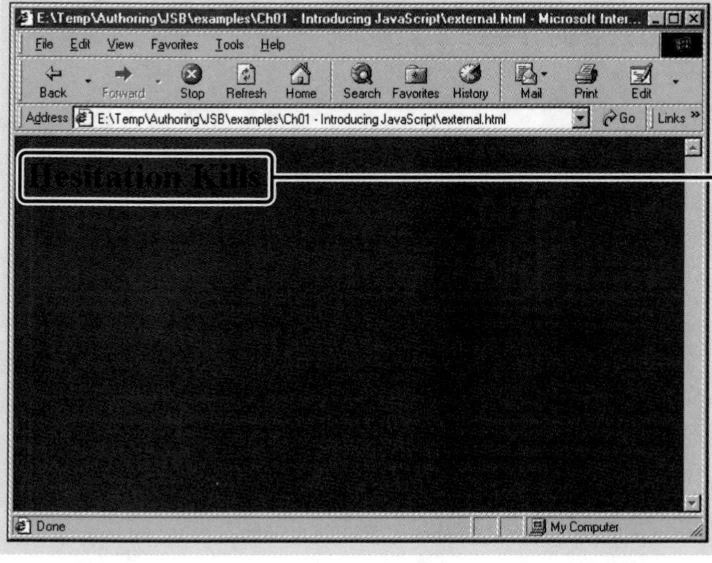

11 Open the file that you saved in step **10** in a browser.

- The JavaScript statements still work as an external file.

PRESENT CONTENT TO NON-JAVASCRIPT BROWSERS

You can handle a browser that has JavaScript support disabled by using the `<noscript>` tags. If the JavaScript cannot be processed, the content included within the `<noscript>` tags is displayed. This content can explain to users with Java Script-disabled browsers what they would see if JavaScript were enabled, or it can provide instructions on enabling JavaScript.

PRESENT CONTENT TO NON-JAVASCRIPT BROWSERS

```
<html>
<head>
</head>
<body>
  <script language="javascript">
    document.bgColor = "blue";
    document.write("<h1>Hesitation Kills</h1>");
  </script>
  <noscript>
    This web page uses JavaScript. To see the full page, make sure that
    JavaScript is enabled.
  </noscript>
</body>
</html>
```

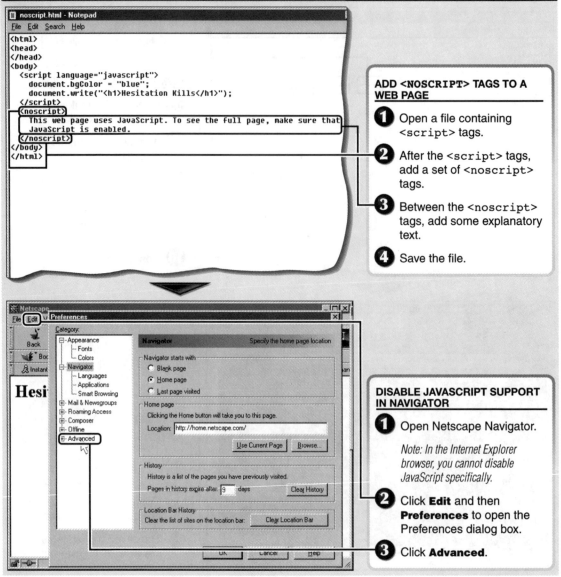

ADD <NOSCRIPT> TAGS TO A WEB PAGE

1. Open a file containing `<script>` tags.
2. After the `<script>` tags, add a set of `<noscript>` tags.
3. Between the `<noscript>` tags, add some explanatory text.
4. Save the file.

DISABLE JAVASCRIPT SUPPORT IN NAVIGATOR

1. Open Netscape Navigator.

   Note: In the Internet Explorer browser, you cannot disable JavaScript specifically.

2. Click **Edit** and then **Preferences** to open the Preferences dialog box.
3. Click **Advanced**.

in an instant

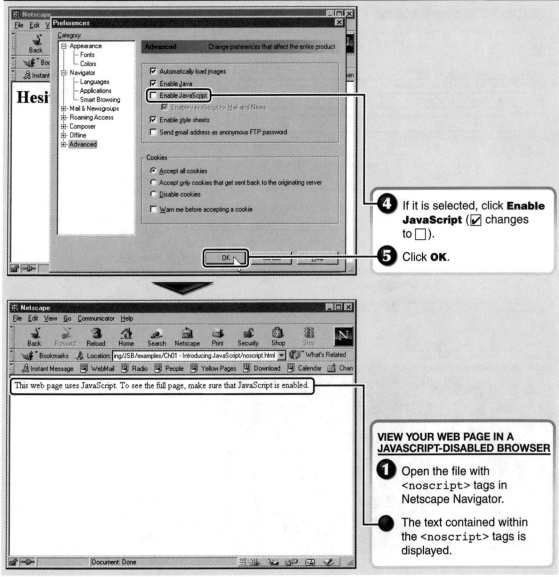

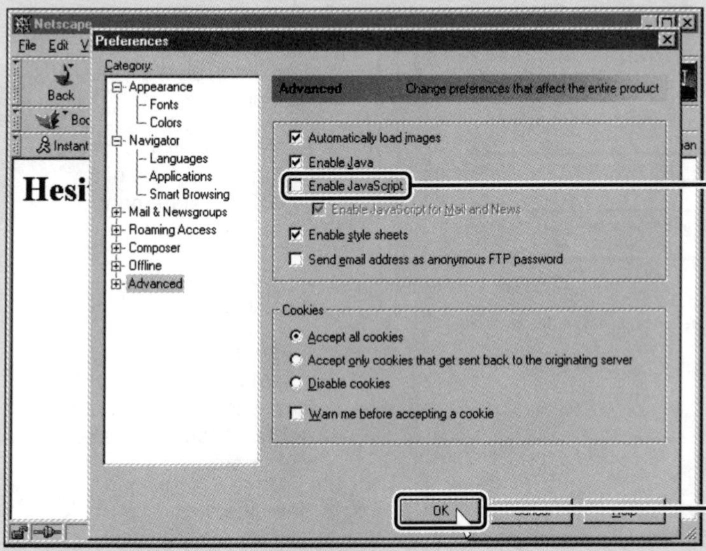

4 If it is selected, click **Enable JavaScript** (☑ changes to ☐).

5 Click **OK**.

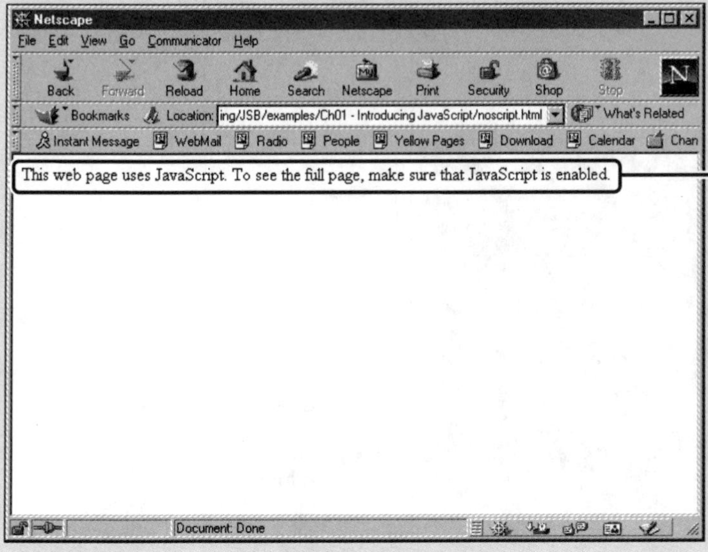

VIEW YOUR WEB PAGE IN A JAVASCRIPT-DISABLED BROWSER

1 Open the file with <noscript> tags in Netscape Navigator.

- The text contained within the <noscript> tags is displayed.

ADD COMMENTS TO JAVASCRIPT

You can use blocks of comments to document what a section of code does. Comments are ignored by the browser and are visible only in the actual file. You can designate a single-line comment with two forward slashes (//). Multiple-line comments start with a forward slash and an asterisk (/*) and end with the opposite (*/). You cannot nest multiple sets of comments. All statements included within the comment symbols are ignored.

ADD COMMENTS TO JAVASCRIPT

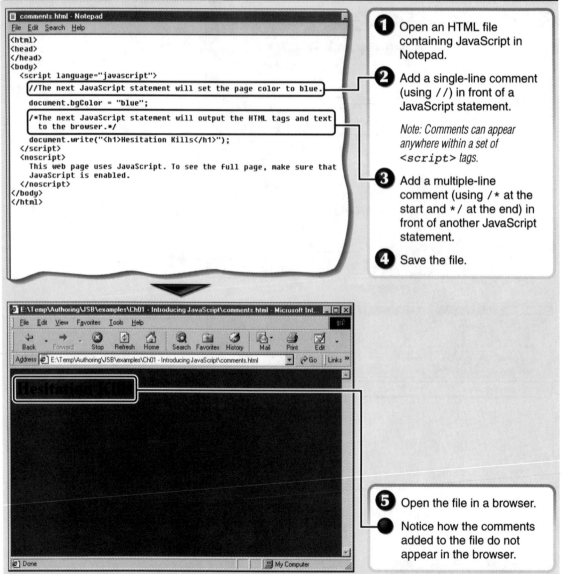

```
<html>
<head>
</head>
<body>
  <script language="javascript">
    //The next JavaScript statement will set the page color to blue.
    document.bgColor = "blue";
    /*The next JavaScript statement will output the HTML tags and text
      to the browser.*/
    document.write("<h1>Hesitation Kills</h1>");
  </script>
  <noscript>
    This web page uses JavaScript. To see the full page, make sure that
    JavaScript is enabled.
  </noscript>
</body>
</html>
```

1. Open an HTML file containing JavaScript in Notepad.
2. Add a single-line comment (using //) in front of a JavaScript statement.

Note: Comments can appear anywhere within a set of <script> tags.

3. Add a multiple-line comment (using /* at the start and */ at the end) in front of another JavaScript statement.
4. Save the file.
5. Open the file in a browser.

- Notice how the comments added to the file do not appear in the browser.

in an instant

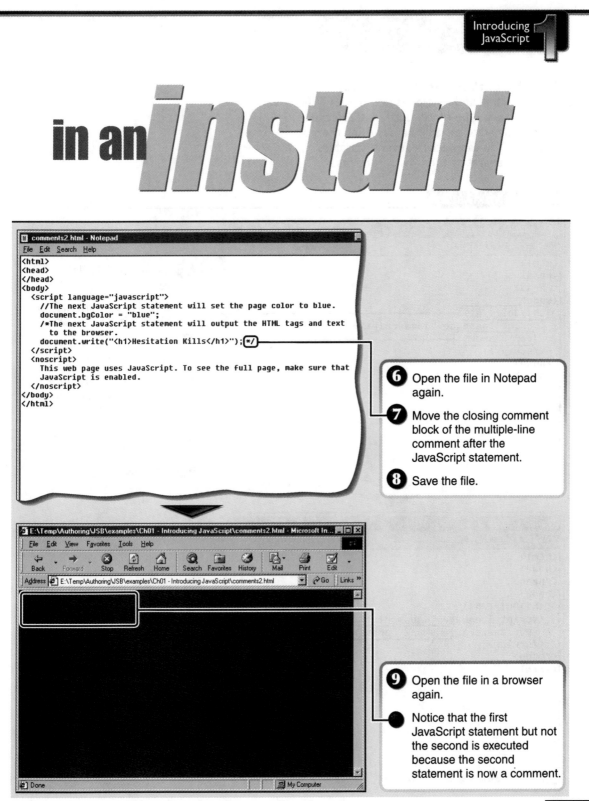

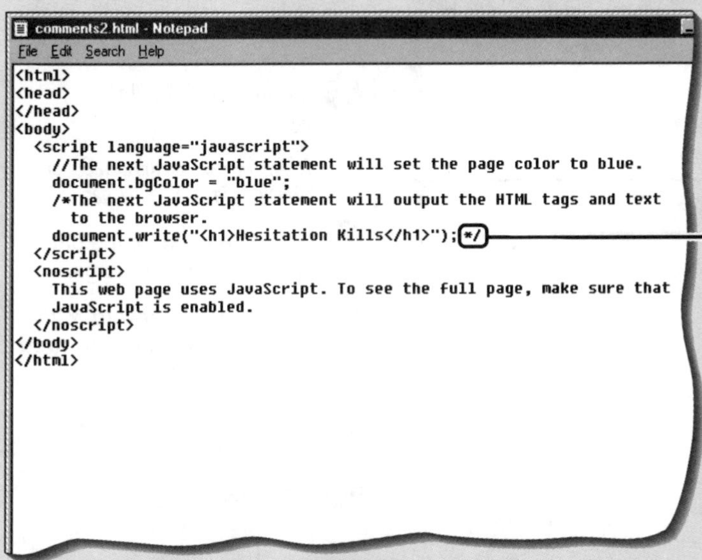

```
<html>
<head>
</head>
<body>
  <script language="javascript">
    //The next JavaScript statement will set the page color to blue.
    document.bgColor = "blue";
    /*The next JavaScript statement will output the HTML tags and text
      to the browser.
    document.write("<h1>Hesitation Kills</h1>");*/
  </script>
  <noscript>
    This web page uses JavaScript. To see the full page, make sure that
    JavaScript is enabled.
  </noscript>
</body>
</html>
```

6. Open the file in Notepad again.
7. Move the closing comment block of the multiple-line comment after the JavaScript statement.
8. Save the file.

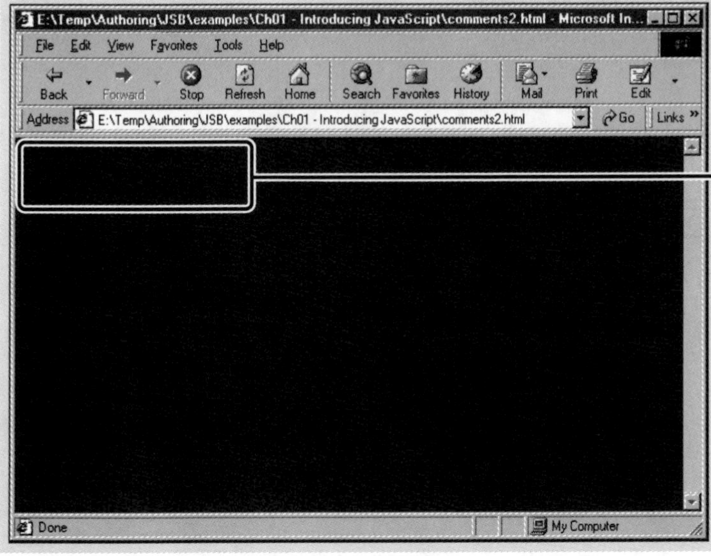

9. Open the file in a browser again.

- Notice that the first JavaScript statement but not the second is executed because the second statement is now a comment.

DECLARE VARIABLES

In JavaScript, all you need to do is type a variable name and its type is automatically set based on the type of value it holds. You can also specifically state variable names using the `var` keyword. You can declare several variables at once by separating them with commas.

DECLARE VARIABLES

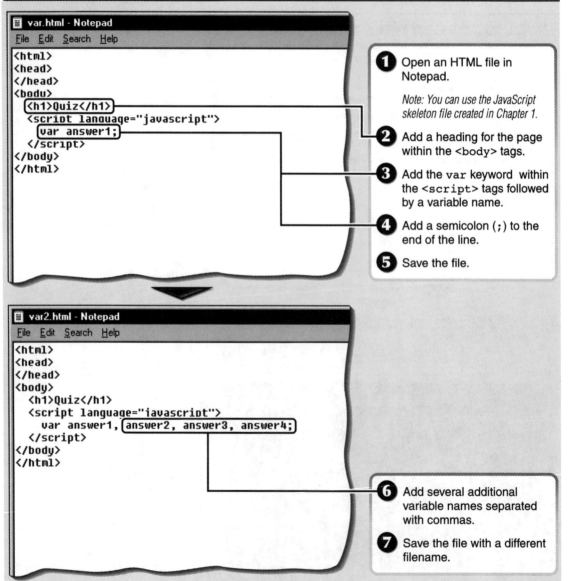

```
var.html - Notepad
File Edit Search Help
<html>
<head>
</head>
<body>
  <h1>Quiz</h1>
  <script language="javascript">
    var answer1;
  </script>
</body>
</html>
```

1. Open an HTML file in Notepad.

   Note: You can use the JavaScript skeleton file created in Chapter 1.

2. Add a heading for the page within the `<body>` tags.
3. Add the `var` keyword within the `<script>` tags followed by a variable name.
4. Add a semicolon (`;`) to the end of the line.
5. Save the file.

```
var2.html - Notepad
File Edit Search Help
<html>
<head>
</head>
<body>
  <h1>Quiz</h1>
  <script language="javascript">
    var answer1, answer2, answer3, answer4;
  </script>
</body>
</html>
```

6. Add several additional variable names separated with commas.
7. Save the file with a different filename.

ASSIGN VALUES TO VARIABLES

After a variable is declared, you can assign a value to it by using the equals sign (=). The value should always be placed on the right side of the equals sign with the variable name on the left. Strings can be assigned to a variable name if they are included in quotation marks (" "). Any string without quotation marks is considered a variable name.

ASSIGN VALUES TO VARIABLES

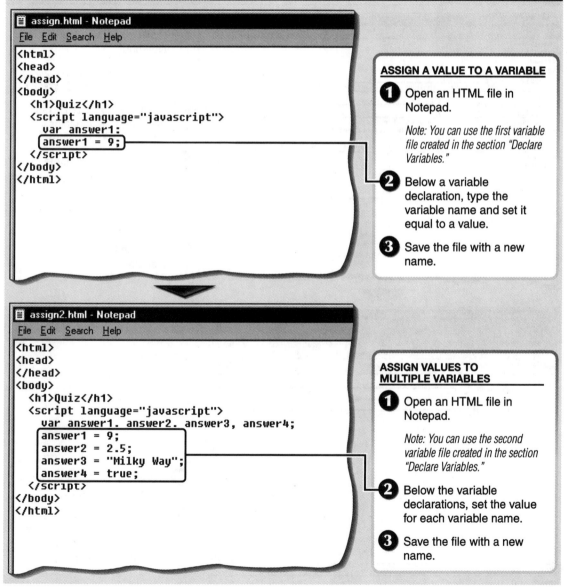

assign.html - Notepad

File Edit Search Help

```
<html>
<head>
</head>
<body>
  <h1>Quiz</h1>
  <script language="javascript">
    var answer1;
    answer1 = 9;
  </script>
</body>
</html>
```

ASSIGN A VALUE TO A VARIABLE

1. Open an HTML file in Notepad.

   Note: You can use the first variable file created in the section "Declare Variables."

2. Below a variable declaration, type the variable name and set it equal to a value.

3. Save the file with a new name.

assign2.html - Notepad

File Edit Search Help

```
<html>
<head>
</head>
<body>
  <h1>Quiz</h1>
  <script language="javascript">
    var answer1, answer2, answer3, answer4;
    answer1 = 9;
    answer2 = 2.5;
    answer3 = "Milky Way";
    answer4 = true;
  </script>
</body>
</html>
```

ASSIGN VALUES TO MULTIPLE VARIABLES

1. Open an HTML file in Notepad.

   Note: You can use the second variable file created in the section "Declare Variables."

2. Below the variable declarations, set the value for each variable name.

3. Save the file with a new name.

USING INTEGERS

Integers are values without a decimal point. These are typically referred to as the "counting numbers" and may be either positive or negative. Negative integer values have a minus sign (–) in front of them. Integer values can be either decimal, hexadecimal, or octal.

USING INTEGERS

integer.html - Notepad

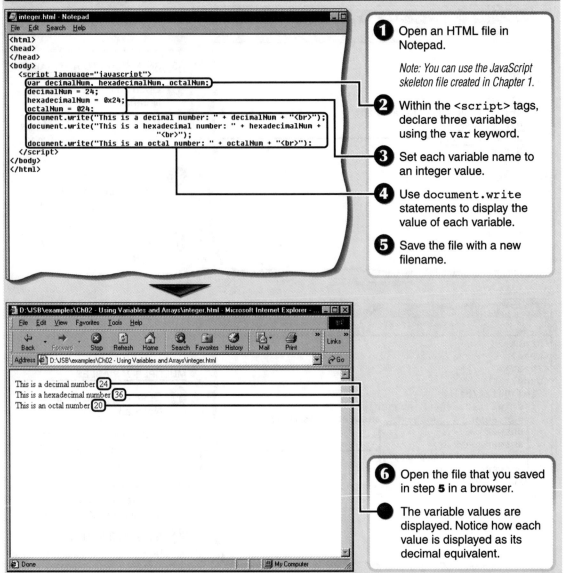

```
<html>
<head>
</head>
<body>
  <script language="javascript">
    var decimalNum, hexadecimalNum, octalNum;
    decimalNum = 24;
    hexadecimalNum = 0x24;
    octalNum = 024;
    document.write("This is a decimal number: " + decimalNum + "<br>");
    document.write("This is a hexadecimal number: " + hexadecimalNum +
                                        "<br>");
    document.write("This is an octal number: " + octalNum + "<br>");
  </script>
</body>
</html>
```

1. Open an HTML file in Notepad.

   Note: You can use the JavaScript skeleton file created in Chapter 1.

2. Within the `<script>` tags, declare three variables using the `var` keyword.

3. Set each variable name to an integer value.

4. Use `document.write` statements to display the value of each variable.

5. Save the file with a new filename.

D:\JSB\examples\Ch02 - Using Variables and Arrays\integer.html - Microsoft Internet Explorer

This is a decimal number: 24
This is a hexadecimal number: 36
This is an octal number: 20

6. Open the file that you saved in step **5** in a browser.

- The variable values are displayed. Notice how each value is displayed as its decimal equivalent.

USING FLOATING-POINT NUMBERS

Floating-point values are fractional numbers that include a decimal point. These numbers can be either positive or negative. You can express very large or very small numbers by using scientific notation. Scientific notation places the letter *E* within the number, followed by the number of places the decimal point is moved.

USING FLOATING-POINT NUMBERS

```
<html>
<head>
</head>
<body>
  <script language="javascript">
    var largeNum, veryLargeNum, smallNum, verySmallNum;
    largeNum = 1234567890000000000000.0;
    veryLargeNum = 5.14e52;
    smallNum = 0.000000123;
    verySmallNum = 6.023e-23;
    document.write("This is a large number: " + largeNum + "<br>");
    document.write("This is a very large number: " + veryLargeNum + "<br>");
    document.write("This is a small number: " + smallNum + "<br>");
    document.write("This is a very small number: " + verySmallNum + "<br>");
  </script>
</body>
</html>
```

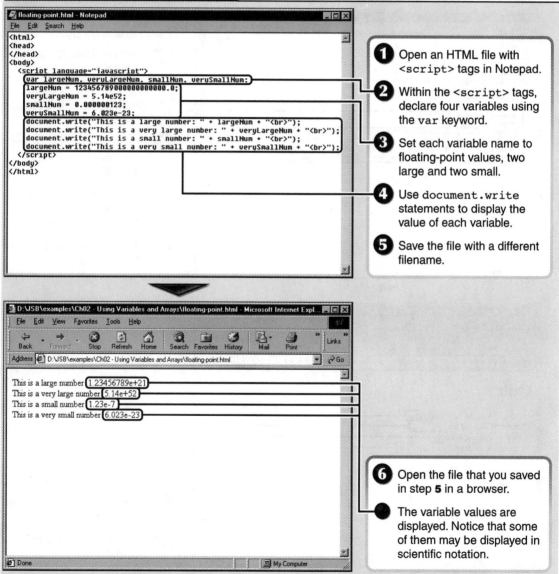

1. Open an HTML file with `<script>` tags in Notepad.
2. Within the `<script>` tags, declare four variables using the `var` keyword.
3. Set each variable name to floating-point values, two large and two small.
4. Use `document.write` statements to display the value of each variable.
5. Save the file with a different filename.

```
This is a large number 1.23456789e+21
This is a very large number 5.14e+52
This is a small number 1.23e-7
This is a very small number 6.023e-23
```

6. Open the file that you saved in step **5** in a browser.

- The variable values are displayed. Notice that some of them may be displayed in scientific notation.

USING BOOLEAN VALUES

Boolean values can be either `true` or `false`. In addition to the actual words, the values can be set to 0 or 1, with 0 representing `false` and 1 representing `true`. Because Boolean values can be only `true` or `false`, they make good conditional statements. You can use a conditional statement to determine the flow of the program. See Chapter 4 for more information on flow control.

USING BOOLEAN VALUES

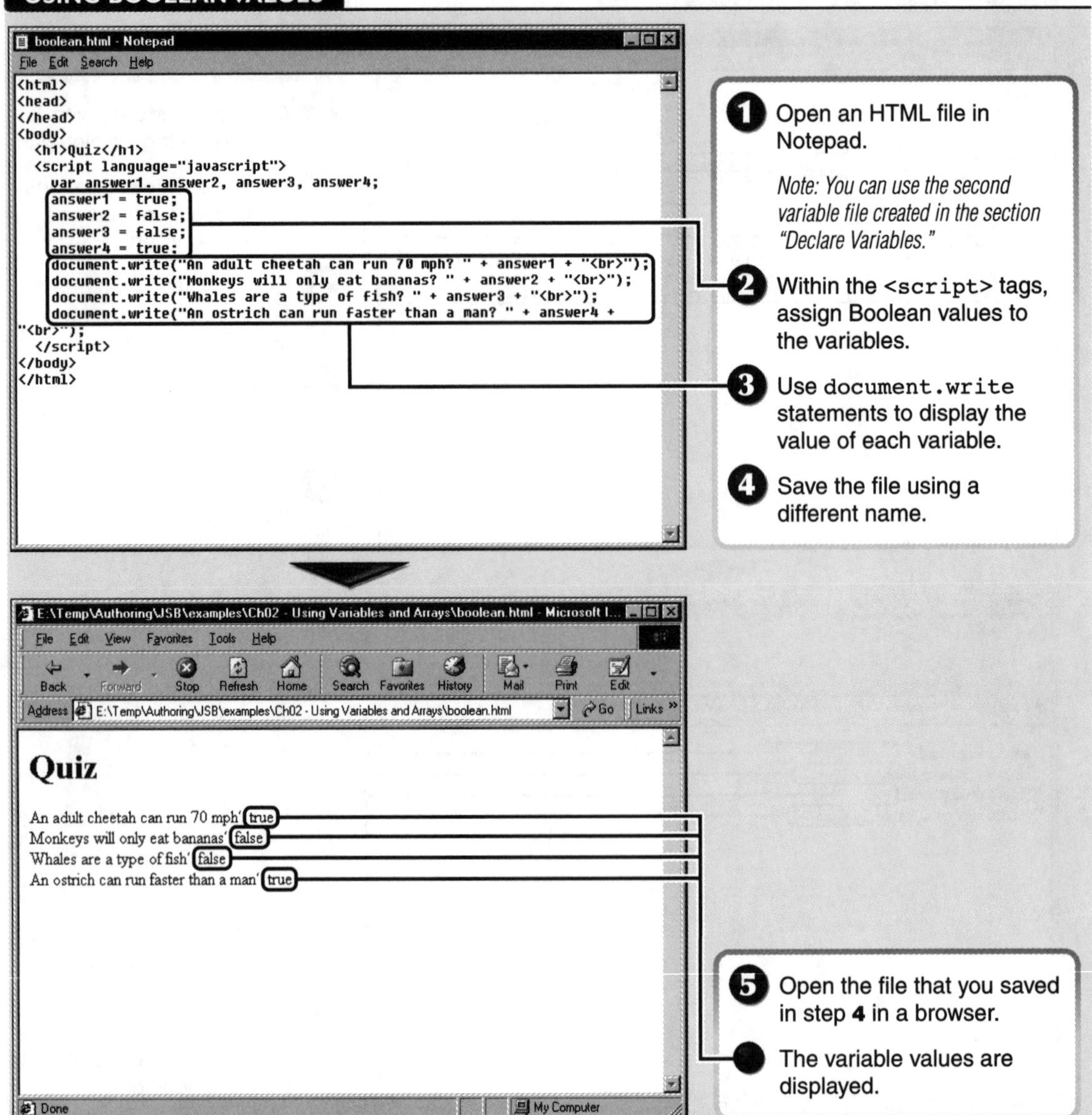
boolean.html - Notepad
File Edit Search Help
<html>
<head>
</head>
<body>
<h1>Quiz</h1>
<script language="javascript">
var answer1, answer2, answer3, answer4;
answer1 = true;
answer2 = false;
answer3 = false;
answer4 = true;
document.write("An adult cheetah can run 70 mph? " + answer1 + "<br>");
document.write("Monkeys will only eat bananas? " + answer2 + "<br>");
document.write("Whales are a type of fish? " + answer3 + "<br>");
document.write("An ostrich can run faster than a man? " + answer4 +
"<br>");
</script>
</body>
</html>
E:\Temp\Authoring\JSB\examples\Ch02 - Using Variables and Arrays\boolean.html - Microsoft I...
File Edit View Favorites Tools Help
Back Forward Stop Refresh Home Search Favorites History Mail Print Edit
Address E:\Temp\Authoring\JSB\examples\Ch02 - Using Variables and Arrays\boolean.html
Go Links
Quiz
An adult cheetah can run 70 mph? true
Monkeys will only eat bananas? false
Whales are a type of fish? false
An ostrich can run faster than a man? true
Done
My Computer

1. Open an HTML file in Notepad.

   Note: You can use the second variable file created in the section "Declare Variables."

2. Within the `<script>` tags, assign Boolean values to the variables.

3. Use `document.write` statements to display the value of each variable.

4. Save the file using a different name.

5. Open the file that you saved in step **4** in a browser.

- The variable values are displayed.

USING STRINGS

String values are composed of characters within a set of quotation marks, using either single quotation marks (') or double-quotation marks ("). To include a quotation mark as part of a string value, place a backslash symbol (\) in front of the quotation mark. You can use the `document.write()` method to include HTML tags within your string values. The browser then interprets the strings.

USING STRINGS

string.html - Notepad

File Edit Search Help

```
<html>
<head>
</head>
<body>
  <script language="javascript">
   var str1, str2;
   str1 = "Why did the chicken cross the road?<br>";
   str2 = 'Because there weren\'t any connecting flights.<br>';
   document.write(str1)
   document.write(str2)
  </script>
</body>
</html>
```

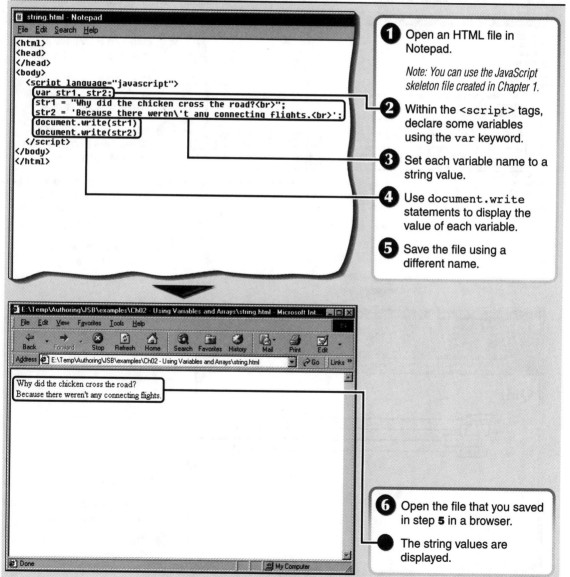

1. Open an HTML file in Notepad.

   Note: You can use the JavaScript skeleton file created in Chapter 1.

2. Within the `<script>` tags, declare some variables using the `var` keyword.

3. Set each variable name to a string value.

4. Use `document.write` statements to display the value of each variable.

5. Save the file using a different name.

E:\Temp\Authoring\JSB\examples\Ch02 - Using Variables and Arrays\string.html - Microsoft Int...

File Edit View Favorites Tools Help

Back Forward Stop Refresh Home Search Favorites History Mail Print Edit

Address E:\Temp\Authoring\JSB\examples\Ch02 - Using Variables and Arrays\string.html Go Links

Why did the chicken cross the road?
Because there weren't any connecting flights.

Done My Computer

6. Open the file that you saved in step **5** in a browser.

- The string values are displayed.

DETERMINE VARIABLE TYPE

JavaScript includes a keyword that you can use to check a variable's type — `typeof`. When the `typeof` keyword is placed in front of a variable name, the variable type is returned as a string. Returned values include `number` for integer and floating-point variables, `string` for string variables, `boolean` for Boolean variables, and `undefined` if the variable type cannot be determined.

DETERMINE VARIABLE TYPE

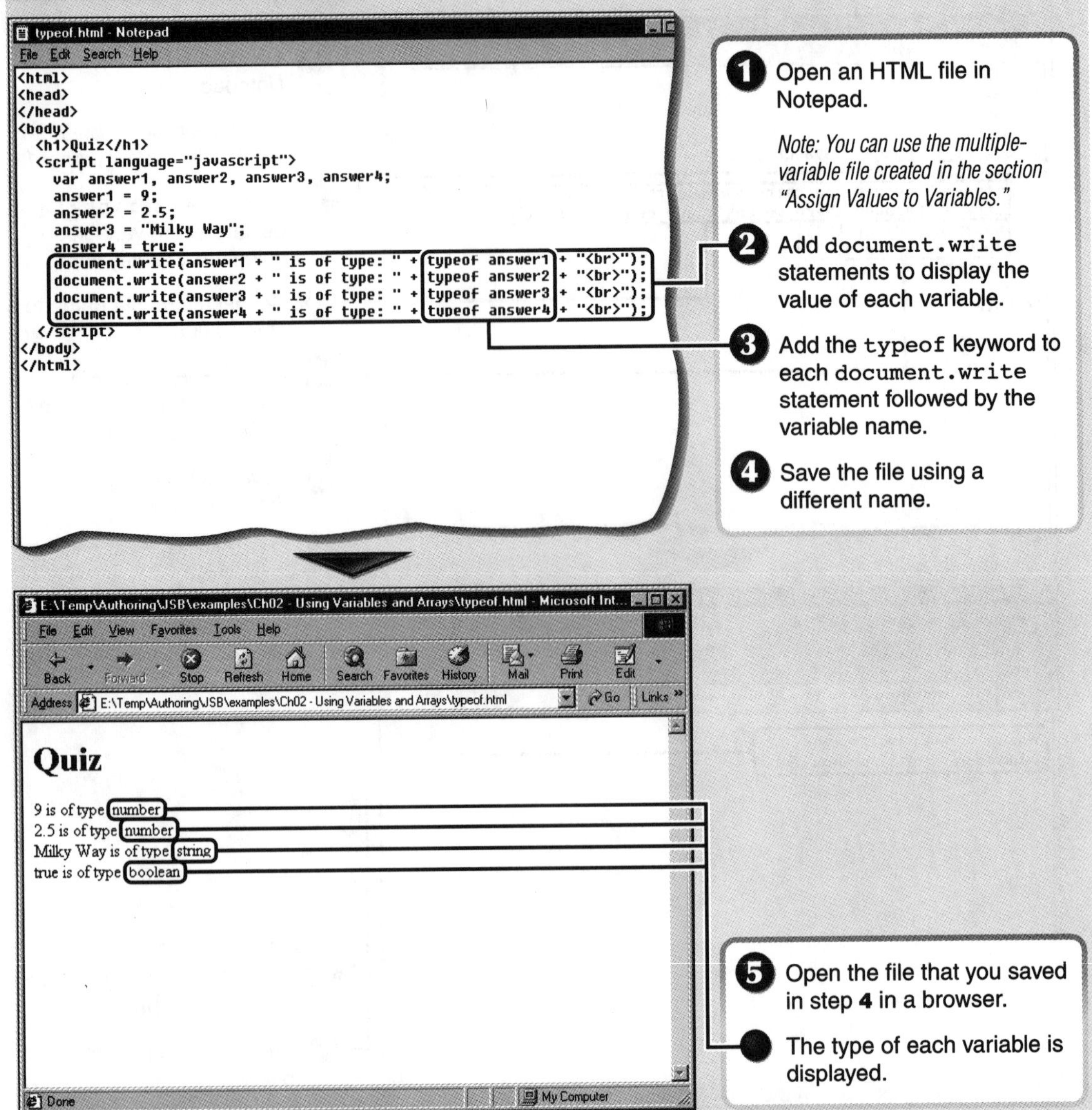
typeof.html - Notepad
File Edit Search Help
<html>
<head>
</head>
<body>
<h1>Quiz</h1>
<script language="javascript">
var answer1, answer2, answer3, answer4;
answer1 = 9;
answer2 = 2.5;
answer3 = "Milky Way";
answer4 = true;
document.write(answer1 + " is of type: " + typeof answer1 + "<br>");
document.write(answer2 + " is of type: " + typeof answer2 + "<br>");
document.write(answer3 + " is of type: " + typeof answer3 + "<br>");
document.write(answer4 + " is of type: " + typeof answer4 + "<br>");
</script>
</body>
</html>
E:\Temp\Authoring\JSB\examples\Ch02 - Using Variables and Arrays\typeof.html - Microsoft Int...
Quiz
9 is of type number
2.5 is of type number
Milky Way is of type string
true is of type boolean
Done
My Computer

1. Open an HTML file in Notepad.

   Note: You can use the multiple-variable file created in the section "Assign Values to Variables."

2. Add `document.write` statements to display the value of each variable.

3. Add the `typeof` keyword to each `document.write` statement followed by the variable name.

4. Save the file using a different name.

5. Open the file that you saved in step **4** in a browser.

- The type of each variable is displayed.

in an instant

DETERMINE UNASSIGNED VARIABLES

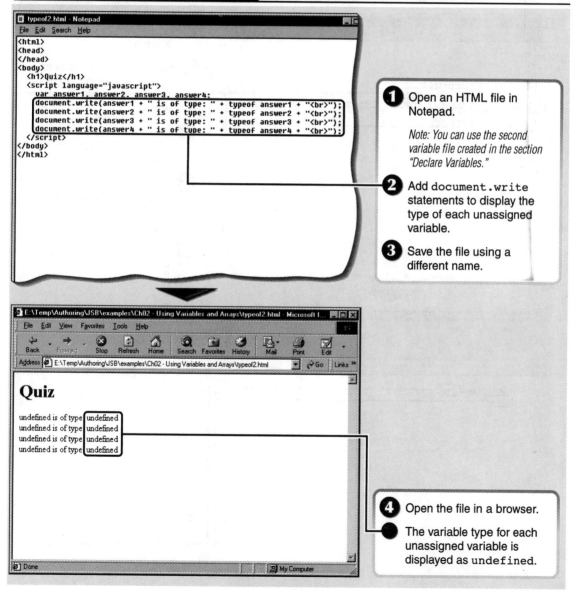

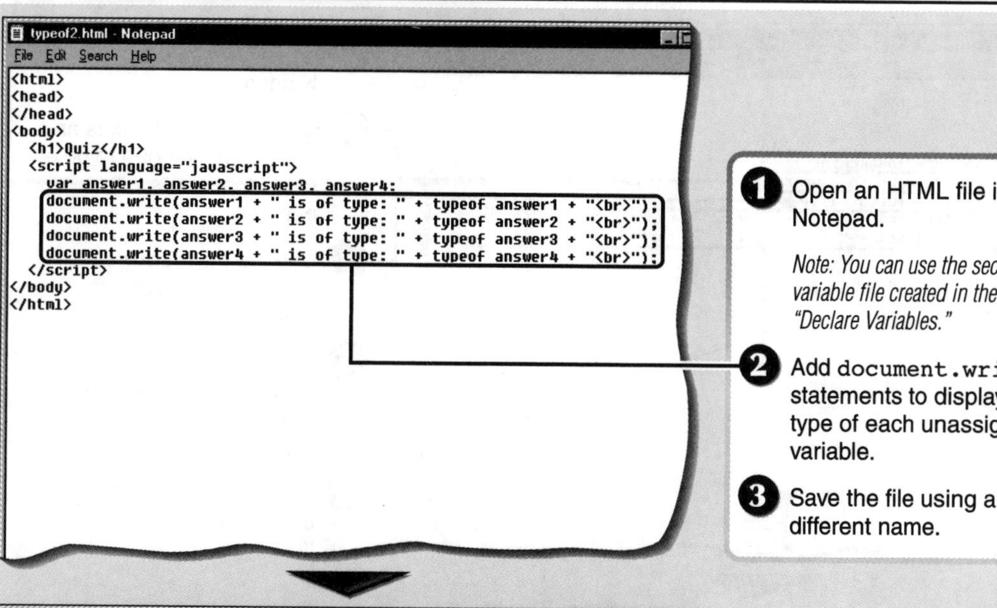
typeof2.html - Notepad
File Edit Search Help
<html>
<head>
</head>
<body>
<h1>Quiz</h1>
<script language="javascript">
var answer1, answer2, answer3, answer4;
document.write(answer1 + " is of type: " + typeof answer1 + "<br>");
document.write(answer2 + " is of type: " + typeof answer2 + "<br>");
document.write(answer3 + " is of type: " + typeof answer3 + "<br>");
document.write(answer4 + " is of type: " + typeof answer4 + "<br>");
</script>
</body>
</html>

1. Open an HTML file in Notepad.

   Note: You can use the second variable file created in the section "Declare Variables."

2. Add `document.write` statements to display the type of each unassigned variable.
3. Save the file using a different name.

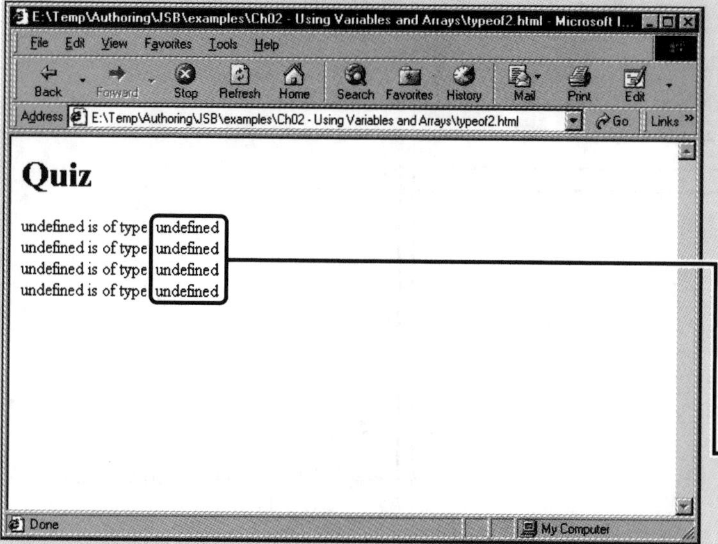
E:\Temp\Authoring\JSB\examples\Ch02 - Using Variables and Arrays\typeof2.html - Microsoft I...
File Edit View Favorites Tools Help
Back Forward Stop Refresh Home Search Favorites History Mail Print Edit
Address E:\Temp\Authoring\JSB\examples\Ch02 - Using Variables and Arrays\typeof2.html Go Links
Quiz
undefined is of type undefined
undefined is of type undefined
undefined is of type undefined
undefined is of type undefined
Done
My Computer

4. Open the file in a browser.

- The variable type for each unassigned variable is displayed as `undefined`.

CONVERT STRINGS TO NUMBERS

Before you can perform arithmetic operations between numbers, you have to make sure that you are dealing with number variable types and not strings. Strings that begin with numbers can be converted into a number variable type by using `parseInt()` for integers and `parseFloat()` for floating-point numbers. The variable name that holds the string should be placed within the parentheses.

CONVERT STRINGS WITH INTEGERS TO NUMBERS

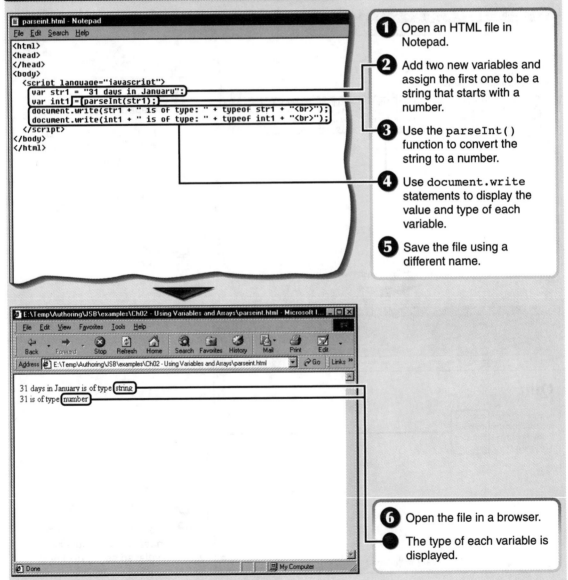

parseint.html - Notepad

```
<html>
<head>
</head>
<body>
  <script language="javascript">
   var str1 = "31 days in January";
   var int1 = parseInt(str1);
   document.write(str1 + " is of type: " + typeof str1 + "<br>");
   document.write(int1 + " is of type: " + typeof int1 + "<br>");
  </script>
</body>
</html>
```

1. Open an HTML file in Notepad.
2. Add two new variables and assign the first one to be a string that starts with a number.
3. Use the `parseInt()` function to convert the string to a number.
4. Use `document.write` statements to display the value and type of each variable.
5. Save the file using a different name.

E:\Temp\Authoring\JSB\examples\Ch02 - Using Variables and Arrays\parseint.html - Microsoft I...

31 days in January is of type string
31 is of type number

6. Open the file in a browser.

- The type of each variable is displayed.

in an instant

CONVERT STRINGS WITH FLOATING-POINT VALUES TO NUMBERS

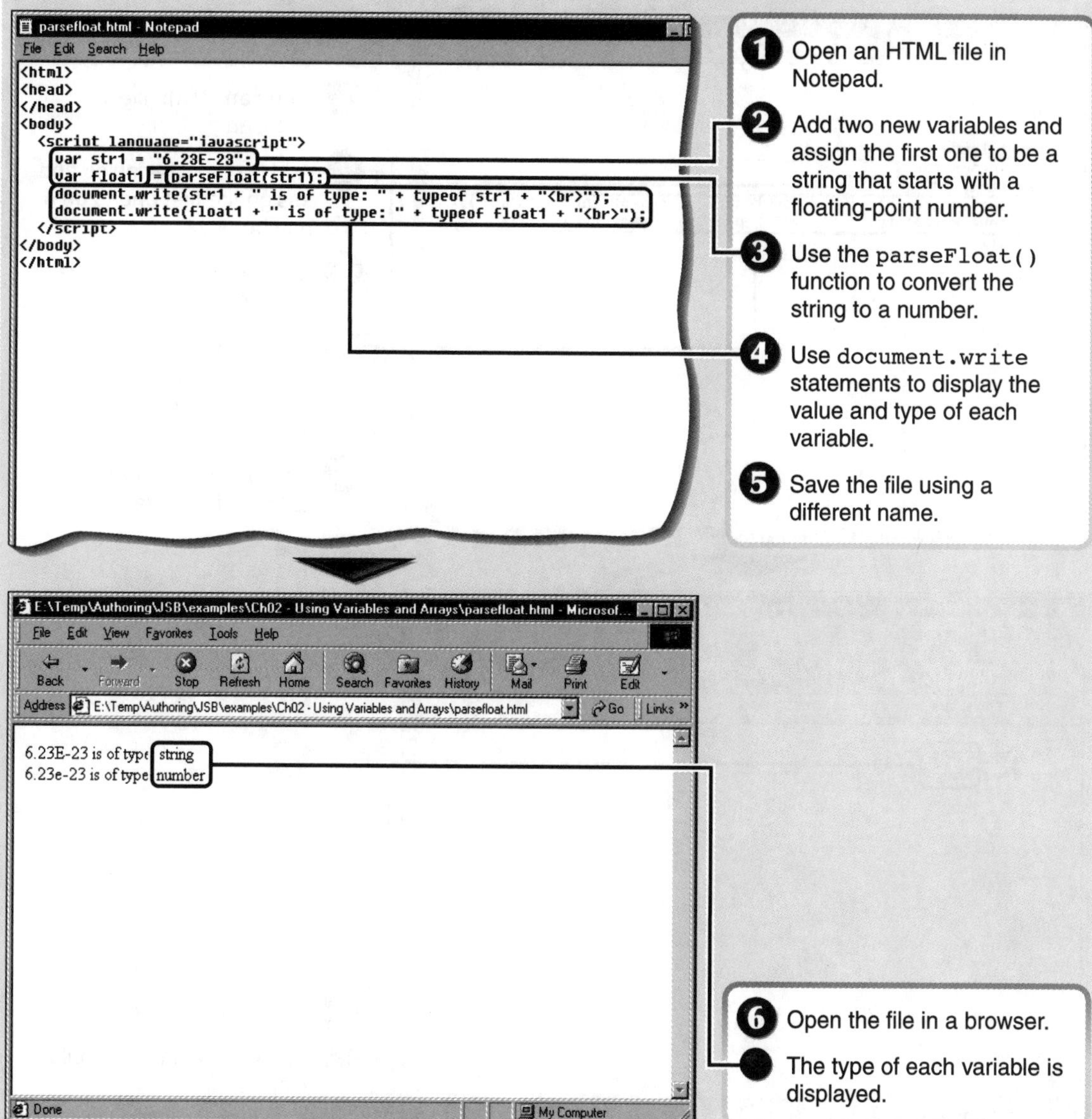
parsefloat.html - Notepad
File Edit Search Help
<html>
<head>
</head>
<body>
<script language="javascript">
var str1 = "6.23E-23";
var float1 = parseFloat(str1);
document.write(str1 + " is of type: " + typeof str1 + "<br>");
document.write(float1 + " is of type: " + typeof float1 + "<br>");
</script>
</body>
</html>
E:\Temp\Authoring\JSB\examples\Ch02 - Using Variables and Arrays\parsefloat.html - Microsof...
6.23E-23 is of type: string
6.23e-23 is of type: number
Done
My Computer

1. Open an HTML file in Notepad.
2. Add two new variables and assign the first one to be a string that starts with a floating-point number.
3. Use the `parseFloat()` function to convert the string to a number.
4. Use `document.write` statements to display the value and type of each variable.
5. Save the file using a different name.
6. Open the file in a browser.

- The type of each variable is displayed.

CONVERT NUMBERS TO STRINGS

You can easily convert numbers to strings by adding quotation marks or a space in front of the number. Another way is using the `toString()` method. To use this method, attach the method name to the end of the variable name with a period in between; for example, to convert a variable named `temp2` holding the value `36` to a string, you can use the statement `temp2.toString();`.

ADD A SPACE BEFORE THE NUMBER

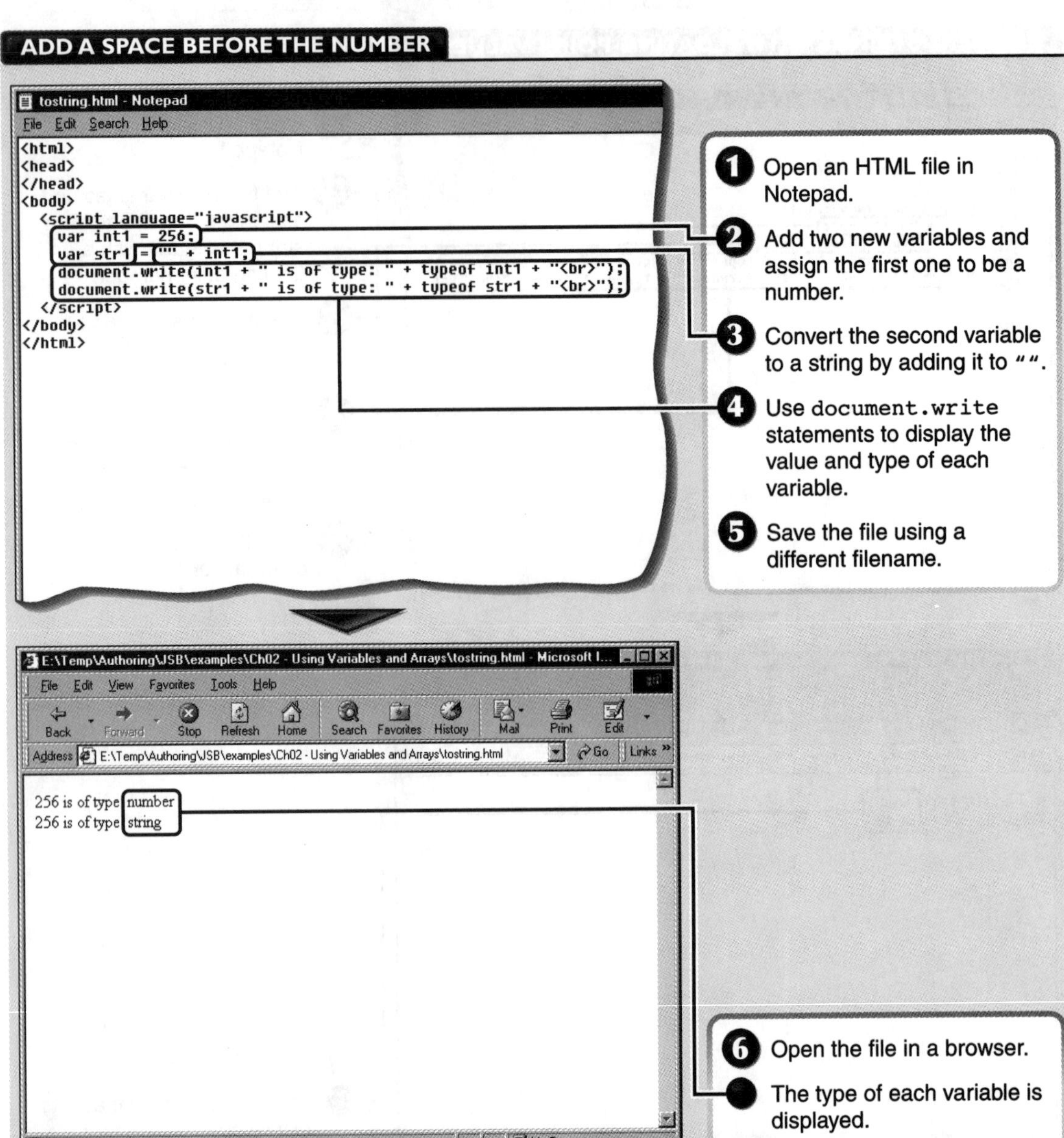

tostring.html - Notepad
File Edit Search Help
<html>
<head>
</head>
<body>
<script language="javascript">
var int1 = 256;
var str1 = "" + int1;
document.write(int1 + " is of type: " + typeof int1 + "<br>");
document.write(str1 + " is of type: " + typeof str1 + "<br>");
</script>
</body>
</html>
E:\Temp\Authoring\JSB\examples\Ch02 - Using Variables and Arrays\tostring.html - Microsoft I...
File Edit View Favorites Tools Help
Back Forward Stop Refresh Home Search Favorites History Mail Print Edit
Address E:\Temp\Authoring\JSB\examples\Ch02 - Using Variables and Arrays\tostring.html
Go Links
256 is of type number
256 is of type string
Done
My Computer

1. Open an HTML file in Notepad.
2. Add two new variables and assign the first one to be a number.
3. Convert the second variable to a string by adding it to `""`.
4. Use `document.write` statements to display the value and type of each variable.
5. Save the file using a different filename.
6. Open the file in a browser.

- The type of each variable is displayed.

in an instant

USING THE TOSTRING() METHOD

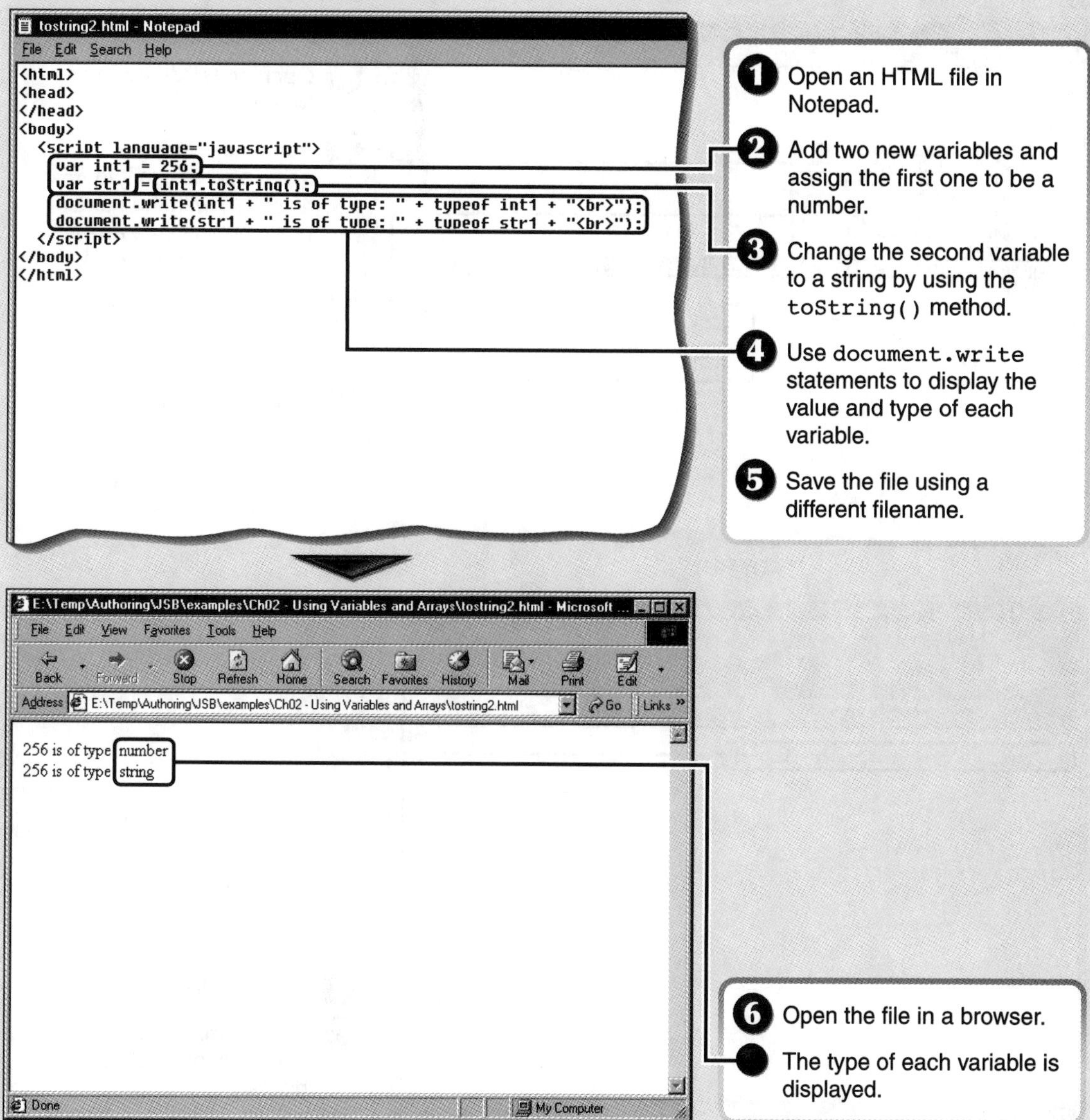
tostring2.html - Notepad
File Edit Search Help
<html>
<head>
</head>
<body>
<script language="javascript">
var int1 = 256;
var str1 = int1.toString();
document.write(int1 + " is of type: " + typeof int1 + "<br>");
document.write(str1 + " is of type: " + typeof str1 + "<br>");
</script>
</body>
</html>
E:\Temp\Authoring\JSB\examples\Ch02 - Using Variables and Arrays\tostring2.html - Microsoft ...
File Edit View Favorites Tools Help
Back Forward Stop Refresh Home Search Favorites History Mail Print Edit
Address E:\Temp\Authoring\JSB\examples\Ch02 - Using Variables and Arrays\tostring2.html
Go Links
256 is of type number
256 is of type string
Done
My Computer

1. Open an HTML file in Notepad.
2. Add two new variables and assign the first one to be a number.
3. Change the second variable to a string by using the `toString()` method.
4. Use `document.write` statements to display the value and type of each variable.
5. Save the file using a different filename.
6. Open the file in a browser.

- The type of each variable is displayed.

DECLARE AN ARRAY

Arrays are variables grouped together as a numbered index. You create arrays by assigning a variable name to `new Array()`, where the number of elements in the array is included within the parentheses. All the variables within an array use the same name but a different index number placed after the array name in square brackets (`[]`). Array index values always start with 0.

CREATE AN ARRAY OF STRING VARIABLES

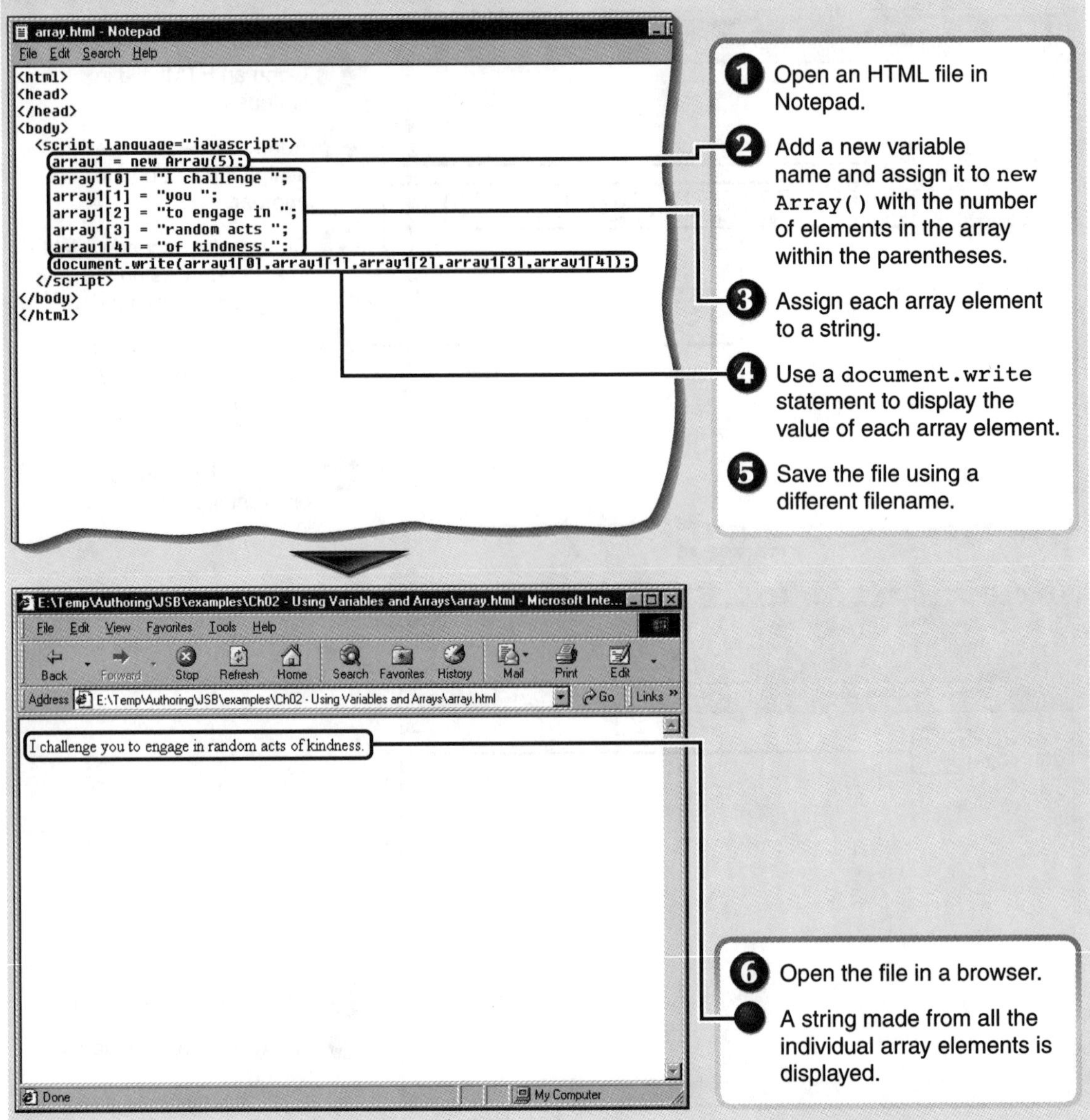

array.html - Notepad
File Edit Search Help
<html>
<head>
</head>
<body>
<script language="javascript">
array1 = new Array(5);
array1[0] = "I challenge ";
array1[1] = "you ";
array1[2] = "to engage in ";
array1[3] = "random acts ";
array1[4] = "of kindness.";
document.write(array1[0],array1[1],array1[2],array1[3],array1[4]);
</script>
</body>
</html>
E:\Temp\Authoring\JSB\examples\Ch02 - Using Variables and Arrays\array.html - Microsoft Inte...
File Edit View Favorites Tools Help
Back Forward Stop Refresh Home Search Favorites History Mail Print Edit
Address E:\Temp\Authoring\JSB\examples\Ch02 - Using Variables and Arrays\array.html
Go Links
I challenge you to engage in random acts of kindness.
Done
My Computer

1. Open an HTML file in Notepad.
2. Add a new variable name and assign it to `new Array()` with the number of elements in the array within the parentheses.
3. Assign each array element to a string.
4. Use a `document.write` statement to display the value of each array element.
5. Save the file using a different filename.
6. Open the file in a browser.

- A string made from all the individual array elements is displayed.

in an instant

CREATE AN ARRAY OF INTEGER VARIABLES

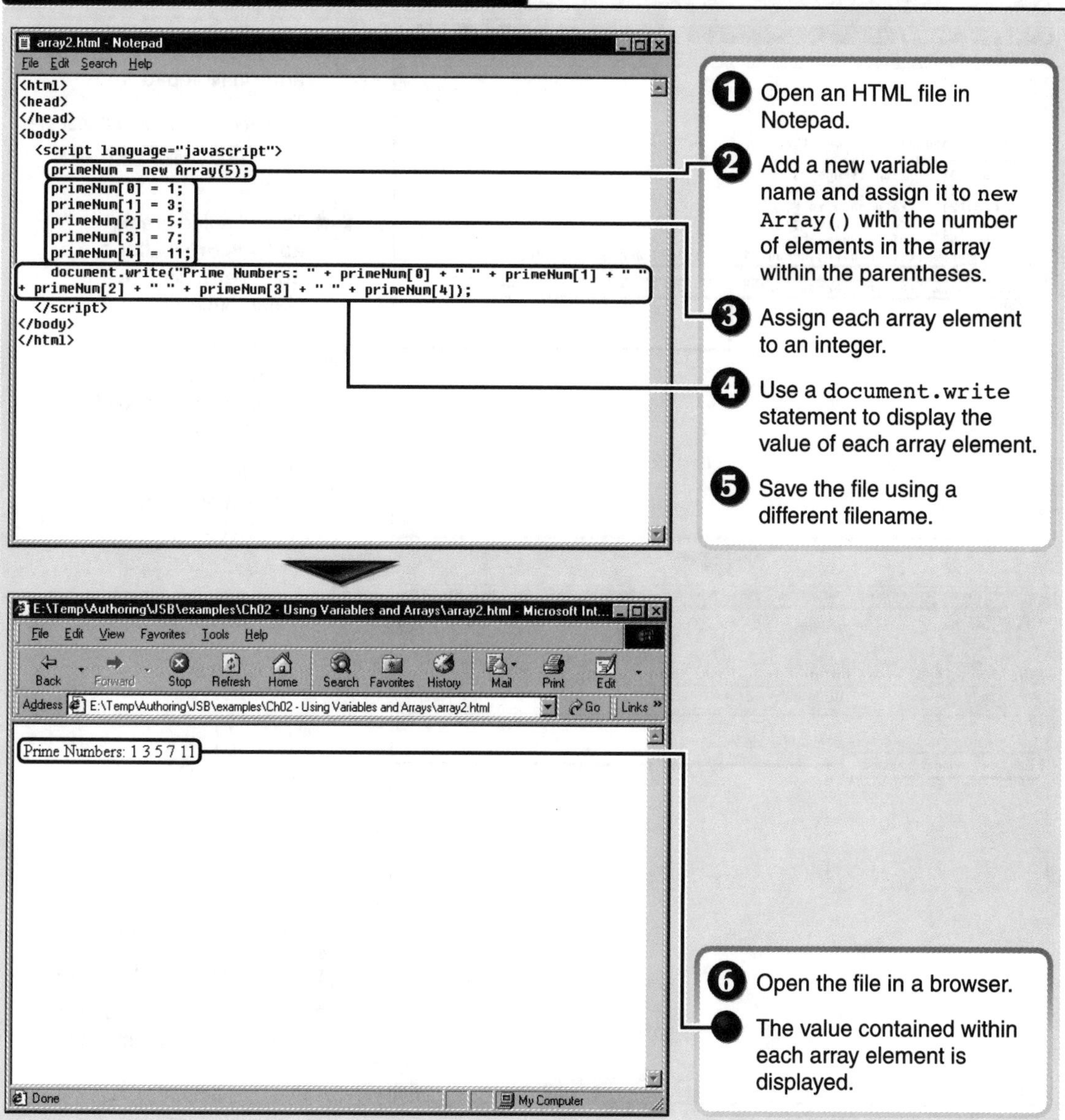
array2.html - Notepad
File Edit Search Help
<html>
<head>
</head>
<body>
<script language="javascript">
primeNum = new Array(5);
primeNum[0] = 1;
primeNum[1] = 3;
primeNum[2] = 5;
primeNum[3] = 7;
primeNum[4] = 11;
document.write("Prime Numbers: " + primeNum[0] + " " + primeNum[1] + " " + primeNum[2] + " " + primeNum[3] + " " + primeNum[4]);
</script>
</body>
</html>
E:\Temp\Authoring\JSB\examples\Ch02 - Using Variables and Arrays\array2.html - Microsoft Int...
File Edit View Favorites Tools Help
Back Forward Stop Refresh Home Search Favorites History Mail Print Edit
Address E:\Temp\Authoring\JSB\examples\Ch02 - Using Variables and Arrays\array2.html
Go Links
Prime Numbers: 1 3 5 7 11
Done
My Computer

1. Open an HTML file in Notepad.
2. Add a new variable name and assign it to `new Array()` with the number of elements in the array within the parentheses.
3. Assign each array element to an integer.
4. Use a `document.write` statement to display the value of each array element.
5. Save the file using a different filename.
6. Open the file in a browser.

- The value contained within each array element is displayed.

DETERMINE THE NUMBER OF ELEMENTS IN AN ARRAY

The `array` object includes a property named `length` that can be used to return the number of elements in the array. The `length` property is a statement just like a variable. You create it by placing the `length` property name with a period after the array name — for example, `array1.length`.

DETERMINE THE LENGTH OF A PREDEFINED ARRAY

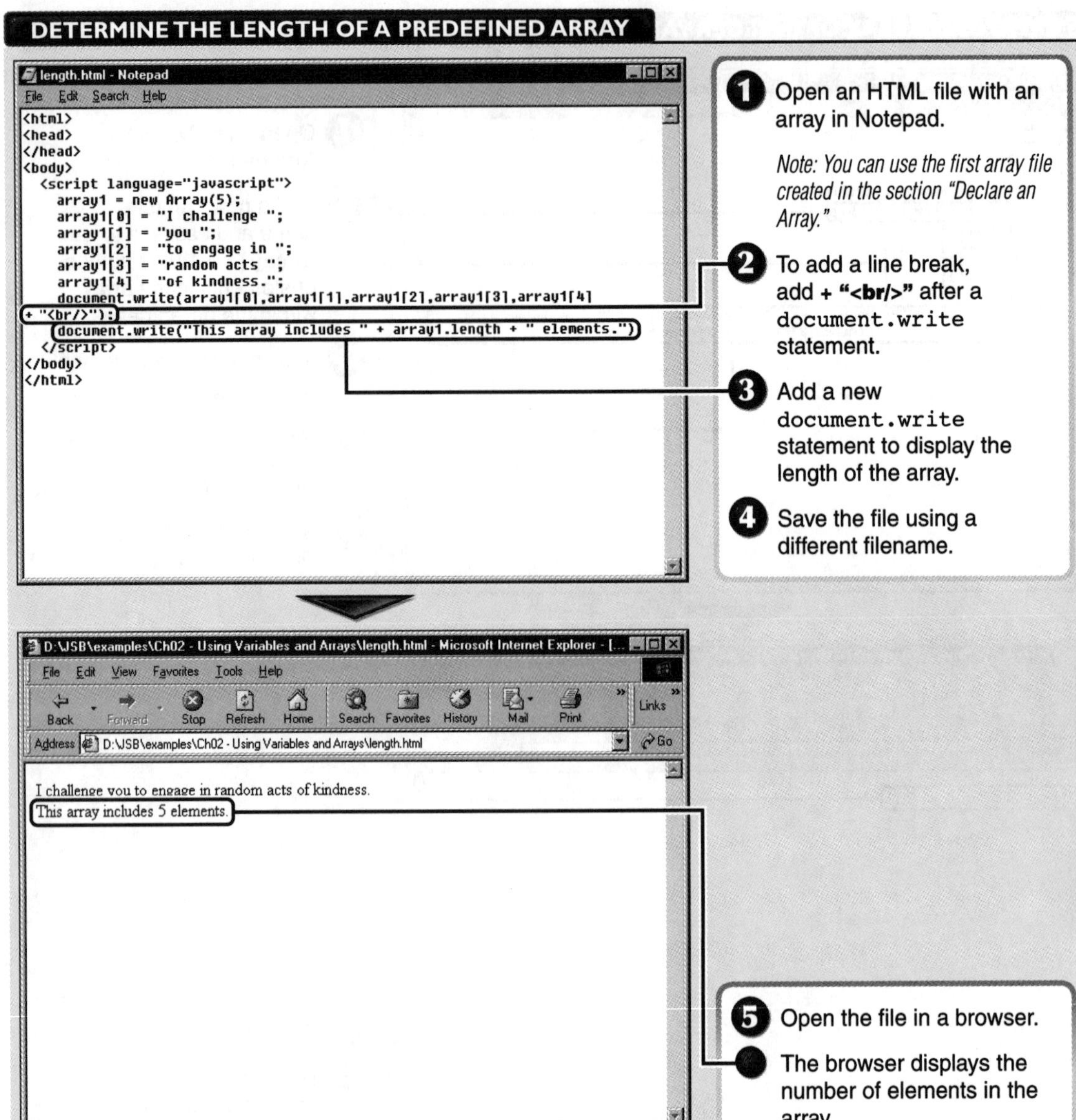
length.html - Notepad
File Edit Search Help
<html>
<head>
</head>
<body>
<script language="javascript">
array1 = new Array(5);
array1[0] = "I challenge ";
array1[1] = "you ";
array1[2] = "to engage in ";
array1[3] = "random acts ";
array1[4] = "of kindness.";
document.write(array1[0],array1[1],array1[2],array1[3],array1[4]
+ "<br/>");
document.write("This array includes " + array1.length + " elements.")
</script>
</body>
</html>
1 Open an HTML file with an array in Notepad.
Note: You can use the first array file created in the section "Declare an Array."
2 To add a line break, add + "<br/>" after a document.write statement.
3 Add a new document.write statement to display the length of the array.
4 Save the file using a different filename.
D:\JSB\examples\Ch02 - Using Variables and Arrays\length.html - Microsoft Internet Explorer
File Edit View Favorites Tools Help
Back Forward Stop Refresh Home Search Favorites History Mail Print
Links
Address D:\JSB\examples\Ch02 - Using Variables and Arrays\length.html
Go
I challenge you to engage in random acts of kindness.
This array includes 5 elements.
Done
My Computer
5 Open the file in a browser.
The browser displays the number of elements in the array.

in an instant

DETERMINE THE NUMBER OF ELEMENTS IN AN ARRAY

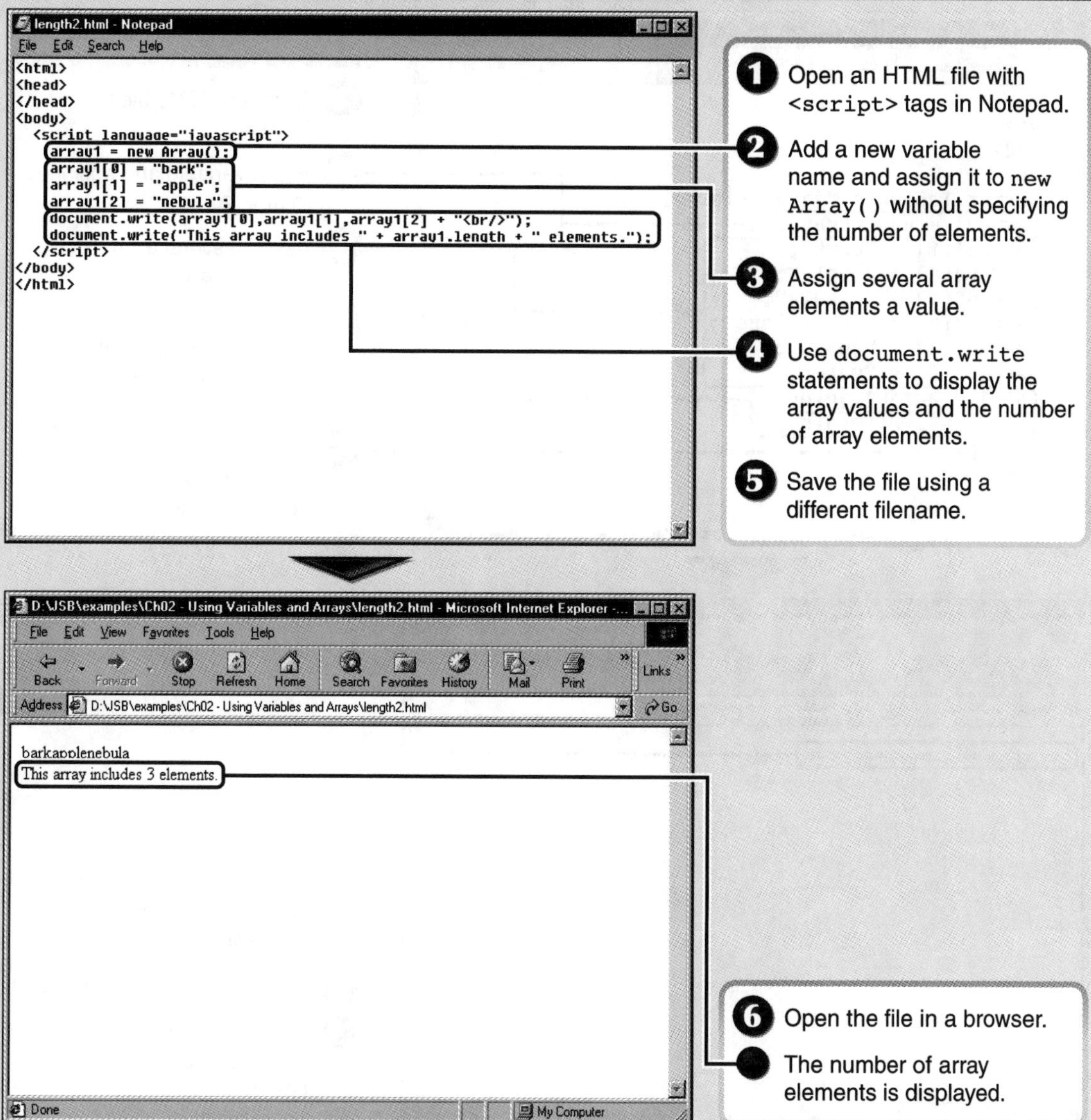
length2.html - Notepad
```
<html>
<head>
</head>
<body>
  <script language="javascript">
    array1 = new Array();
    array1[0] = "bark";
    array1[1] = "apple";
    array1[2] = "nebula";
    document.write(array1[0],array1[1],array1[2] + "<br/>");
    document.write("This array includes " + array1.length + " elements.");
  </script>
</body>
</html>
```
D:\JSB\examples\Ch02 - Using Variables and Arrays\length2.html - Microsoft Internet Explorer
barkapplenebula
This array includes 3 elements.
1 Open an HTML file with <script> tags in Notepad.
2 Add a new variable name and assign it to new Array() without specifying the number of elements.
3 Assign several array elements a value.
4 Use document.write statements to display the array values and the number of array elements.
5 Save the file using a different filename.
6 Open the file in a browser.
The number of array elements is displayed.

CONVERT AN ARRAY INTO A STRING

The `array` object includes a method called `join()` that converts the array elements to a string. The `join()` method accepts a single string as a parameter. This string is inserted between each separate array element as it is converted to a string. The default separator is a comma (,), but you can use a different separator if you specify one.

CONVERT AN ARRAY INTO A STRING

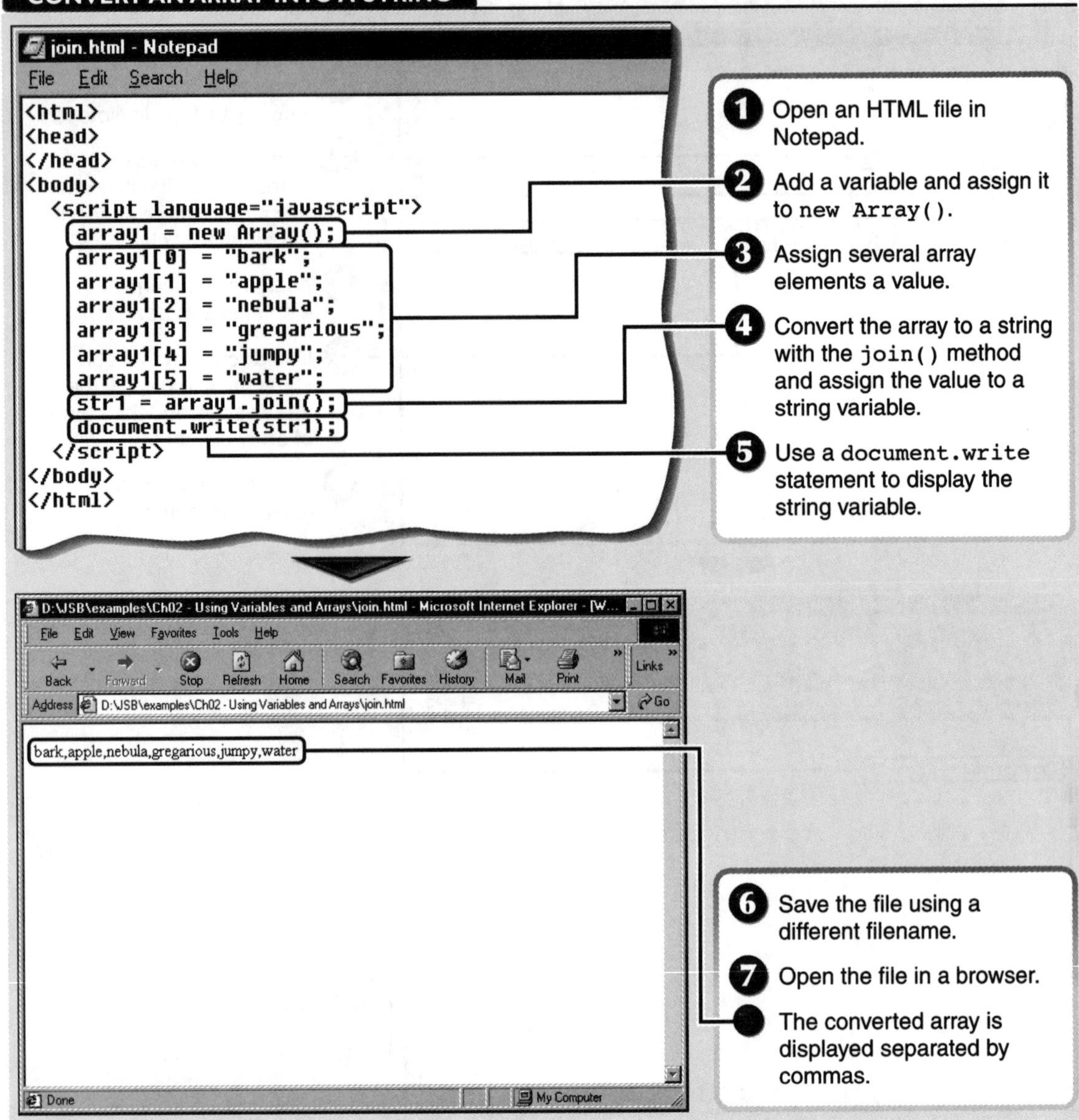

join.html - Notepad
File Edit Search Help
<html>
<head>
</head>
<body>
<script language="javascript">
array1 = new Array();
array1[0] = "bark";
array1[1] = "apple";
array1[2] = "nebula";
array1[3] = "gregarious";
array1[4] = "jumpy";
array1[5] = "water";
str1 = array1.join();
document.write(str1);
</script>
</body>
</html>
1 Open an HTML file in Notepad.
2 Add a variable and assign it to new Array().
3 Assign several array elements a value.
4 Convert the array to a string with the join() method and assign the value to a string variable.
5 Use a document.write statement to display the string variable.
D:\JSB\examples\Ch02 - Using Variables and Arrays\join.html - Microsoft Internet Explorer - [W...
bark,apple,nebula,gregarious,jumpy,water
6 Save the file using a different filename.
7 Open the file in a browser.
The converted array is displayed separated by commas.

in an instant

SPECIFY A UNIQUE SEPARATOR

join2.html - Notepad

File Edit Search Help

```
<html>
<head>
</head>
<body>
  <script language="javascript">
    array1 = new Array();
    array1[0] = "bark";
    array1[1] = "apple";
    array1[2] = "nebula";
    array1[3] = "gregarious";
    array1[4] = "jumpy";
    array1[5] = "water";
    str1 = array1.join(" ");
    document.write(str1);
  </script>
</body>
</html>
```

1. Open the file that you saved in step **6** of the preceding steps in Notepad.
2. Add a string with a space as a parameter to the `join()` method.

*Note: In step **2**, you are specifying to use a space as a separator rather than the default comma, so a space will appear in between each array element.*

3. Save the file using a different name.

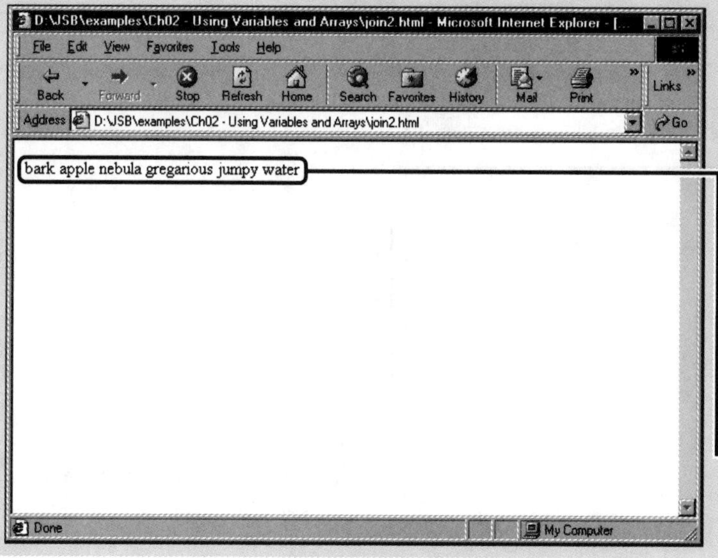
D:\JSB\examples\Ch02 - Using Variables and Arrays\join2.html - Microsoft Internet Explorer - [...
File Edit View Favorites Tools Help
Back Forward Stop Refresh Home Search Favorites History Mail Print
Links
Address D:\JSB\examples\Ch02 - Using Variables and Arrays\join2.html
Go
bark apple nebula gregarious jumpy water
Done
My Computer

4. Open the file in a browser.

- The converted array is displayed separated by spaces.

SORT AN ARRAY

The `array` object includes a method that sorts the array elements in ascending alphabetical order before converting them into strings — `sort()`. Note that if the `sort()` method is used on an array of numbers, the numbers are sorted alphabetically instead of in numerical order. For example, an array containing 1, 2, 10, 12 would be sorted as 1, 10, 12, 2.

SORT AN ARRAY OF WORDS

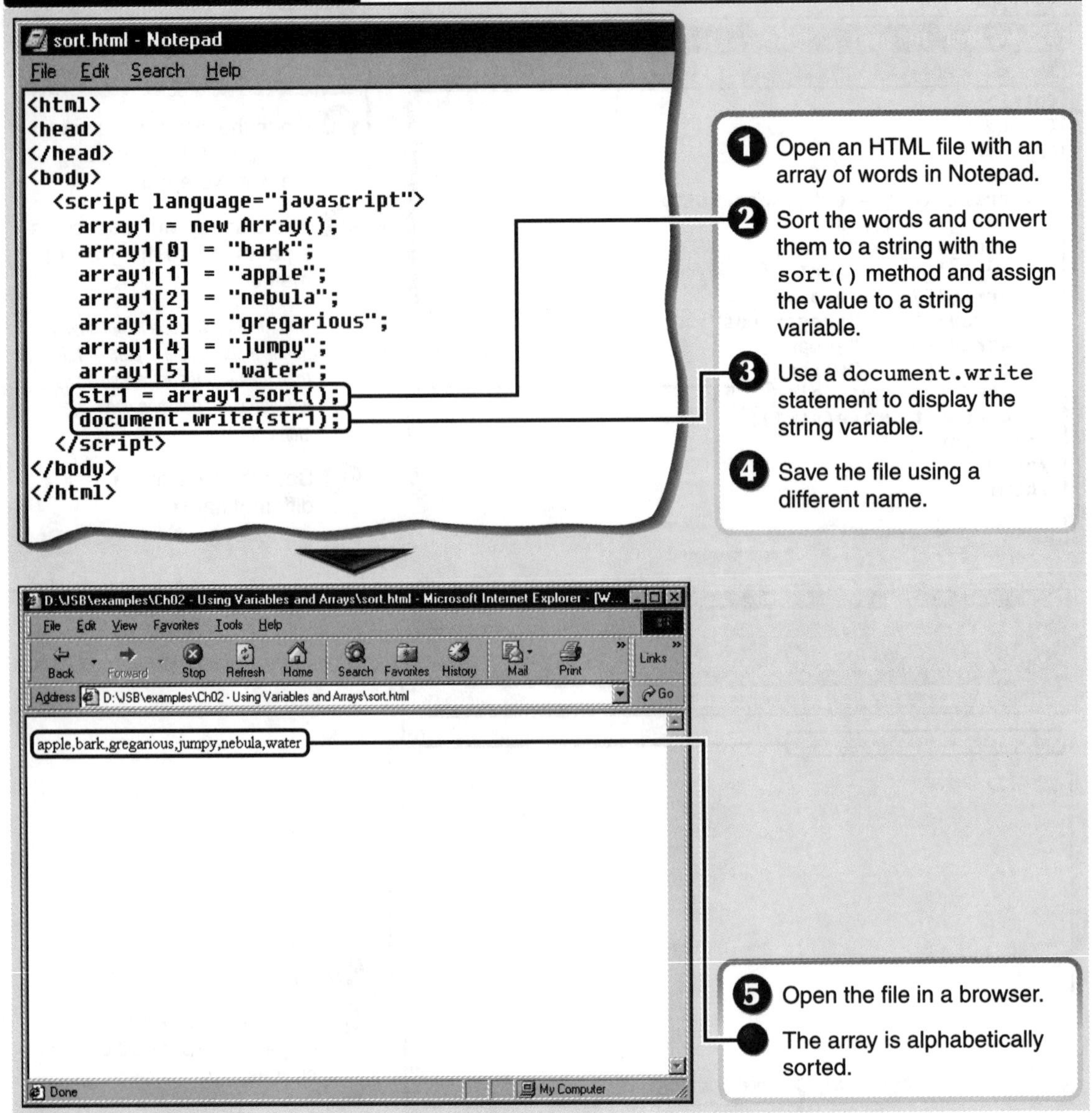

sort.html - Notepad
File Edit Search Help
<html>
<head>
</head>
<body>
<script language="javascript">
array1 = new Array();
array1[0] = "bark";
array1[1] = "apple";
array1[2] = "nebula";
array1[3] = "gregarious";
array1[4] = "jumpy";
array1[5] = "water";
str1 = array1.sort();
document.write(str1);
</script>
</body>
</html>
D:\JSB\examples\Ch02 - Using Variables and Arrays\sort.html - Microsoft Internet Explorer - [W...
File Edit View Favorites Tools Help
Back Forward Stop Refresh Home Search Favorites History Mail Print Links
Address D:\JSB\examples\Ch02 - Using Variables and Arrays\sort.html Go
apple,bark,gregarious,jumpy,nebula,water
Done
My Computer

1. Open an HTML file with an array of words in Notepad.
2. Sort the words and convert them to a string with the `sort()` method and assign the value to a string variable.
3. Use a `document.write` statement to display the string variable.
4. Save the file using a different name.
5. Open the file in a browser.

- The array is alphabetically sorted.

in an instant

SORT AN ARRAY OF NUMBERS

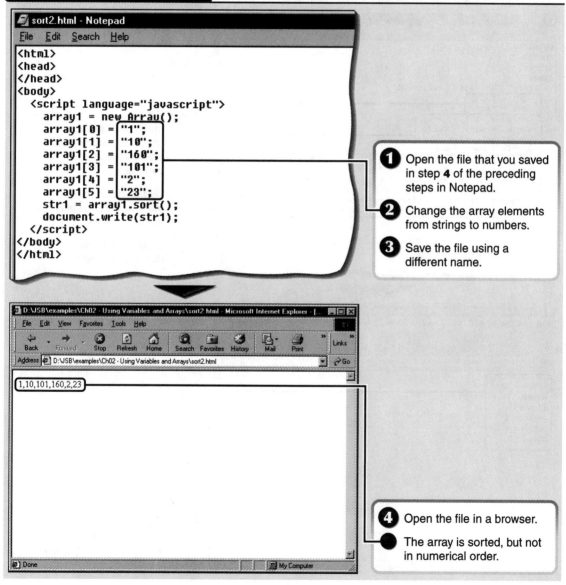

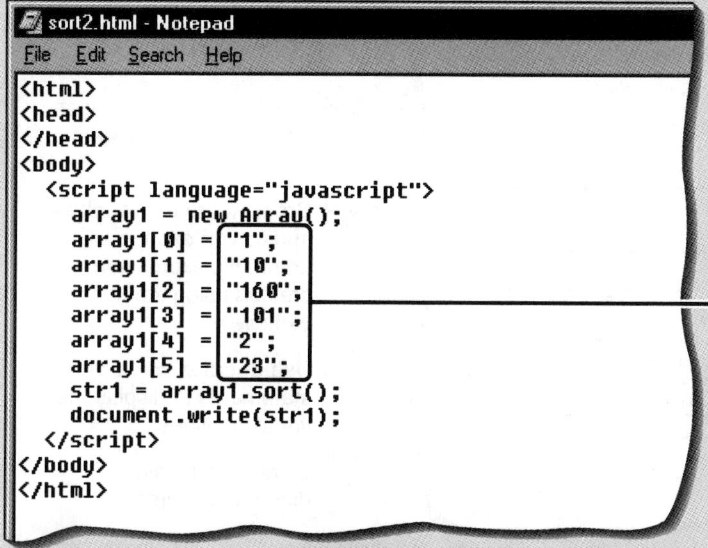
sort2.html - Notepad
File Edit Search Help
<html>
<head>
</head>
<body>
<script language="javascript">
array1 = new Array();
array1[0] = "1";
array1[1] = "10";
array1[2] = "160";
array1[3] = "101";
array1[4] = "2";
array1[5] = "23";
str1 = array1.sort();
document.write(str1);
</script>
</body>
</html>

1. Open the file that you saved in step **4** of the preceding steps in Notepad.
2. Change the array elements from strings to numbers.
3. Save the file using a different name.

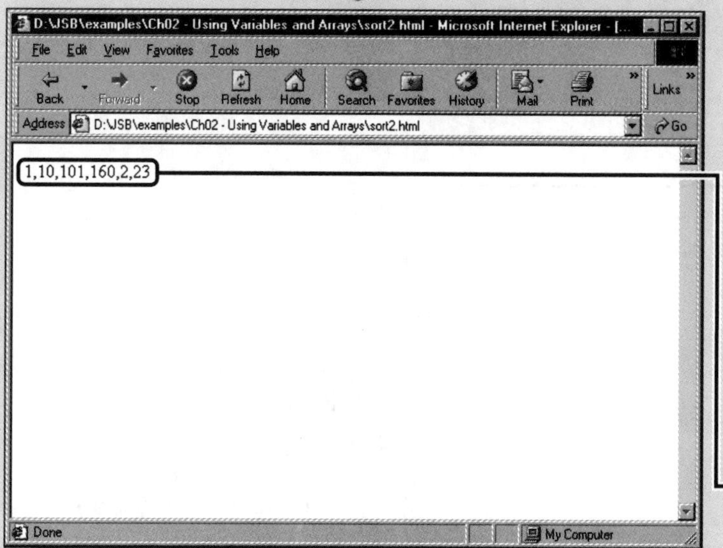
D:\JSB\examples\Ch02 - Using Variables and Arrays\sort2.html - Microsoft Internet Explorer - [...
File Edit View Favorites Tools Help
Back Forward Stop Refresh Home Search Favorites History Mail Print
Links
Address D:\JSB\examples\Ch02 - Using Variables and Arrays\sort2.html
Go
1,10,101,160,2,23
Done
My Computer

4. Open the file in a browser.

- The array is sorted, but not in numerical order.

USING ARITHMETIC OPERATORS

Expressions are used to compose mathematical equations. The easiest expressions to create use arithmetic operators. The four standard arithmetic operators are addition (+), subtraction (–), multiplication (*), and division (/). A less frequently used operator is the modulus operator (%), which returns the value of the remainder after dividing two numbers.

USING ARITHMETIC OPERATORS

arithmetic.html - Notepad

File Edit Search Help

```
<html>
<head>
</head>
<body>
  <script language="javascript">
    var1 = 12;
    var2 = 10;
    varAdd = var1 + var2;
    varSub = var1 - var2;
    varMult = var1 * var2;
    varDiv = var1 / var2;
    document.write("Variable 1: " + var1 + "<br>");
    document.write("Variable 2: " + var2 + "<br>");
    document.write("Addition: " + varAdd + "<br>");
    document.write("Subtraction: " + varSub + "<br>");
    document.write("Multiplication: " + varMult + "<br>");
    document.write("Division: " + varDiv + "<br>");
  </script>
</body>
</html>
```

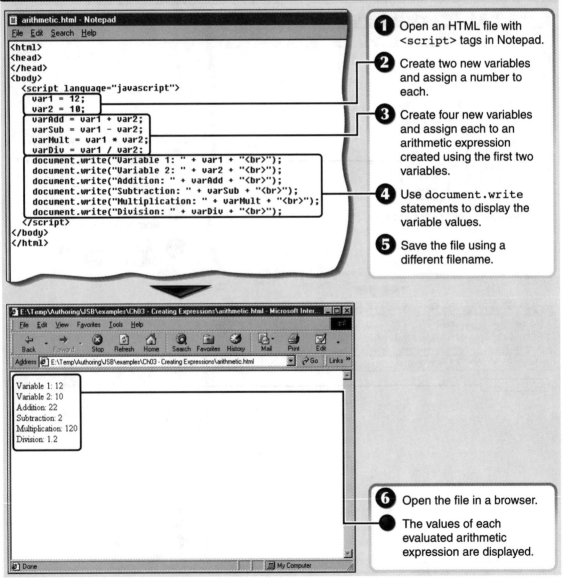

1 Open an HTML file with `<script>` tags in Notepad.

2 Create two new variables and assign a number to each.

3 Create four new variables and assign each to an arithmetic expression created using the first two variables.

4 Use `document.write` statements to display the variable values.

5 Save the file using a different filename.

E:\Temp\Authoring\JSB\examples\Ch03 - Creating Expressions\arithmetic.html - Microsoft Inter...

File Edit View Favorites Tools Help

Back Forward Stop Refresh Home Search Favorites History Mail Print Edit

Address E:\Temp\Authoring\JSB\examples\Ch03 - Creating Expressions\arithmetic.html Go Links

Variable 1: 12
Variable 2: 10
Addition: 22
Subtraction: 2
Multiplication: 120
Division: 1.2

Done My Computer

6 Open the file in a browser.

- The values of each evaluated arithmetic expression are displayed.

in an instant

USING THE MODULUS OPERATOR

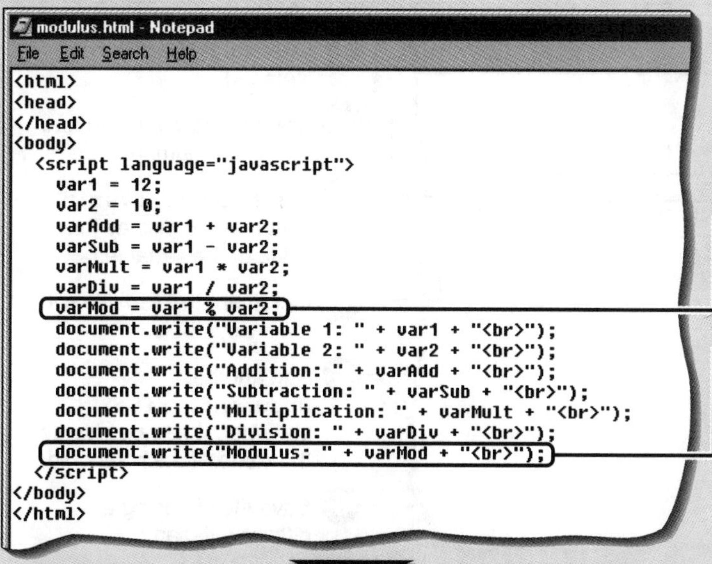

```
<html>
<head>
</head>
<body>
  <script language="javascript">
    var1 = 12;
    var2 = 10;
    varAdd = var1 + var2;
    varSub = var1 - var2;
    varMult = var1 * var2;
    varDiv = var1 / var2;
    varMod = var1 % var2;
    document.write("Variable 1: " + var1 + "<br>");
    document.write("Variable 2: " + var2 + "<br>");
    document.write("Addition: " + varAdd + "<br>");
    document.write("Subtraction: " + varSub + "<br>");
    document.write("Multiplication: " + varMult + "<br>");
    document.write("Division: " + varDiv + "<br>");
    document.write("Modulus: " + varMod + "<br>");
  </script>
</body>
</html>
```

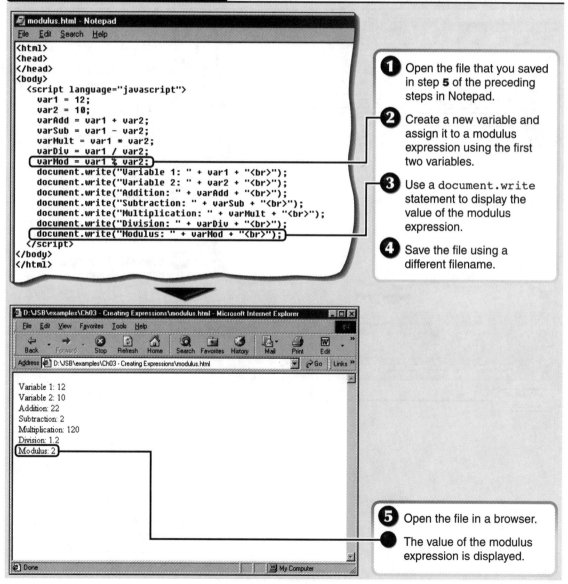

1. Open the file that you saved in step **5** of the preceding steps in Notepad.
2. Create a new variable and assign it to a modulus expression using the first two variables.
3. Use a `document.write` statement to display the value of the modulus expression.
4. Save the file using a different filename.

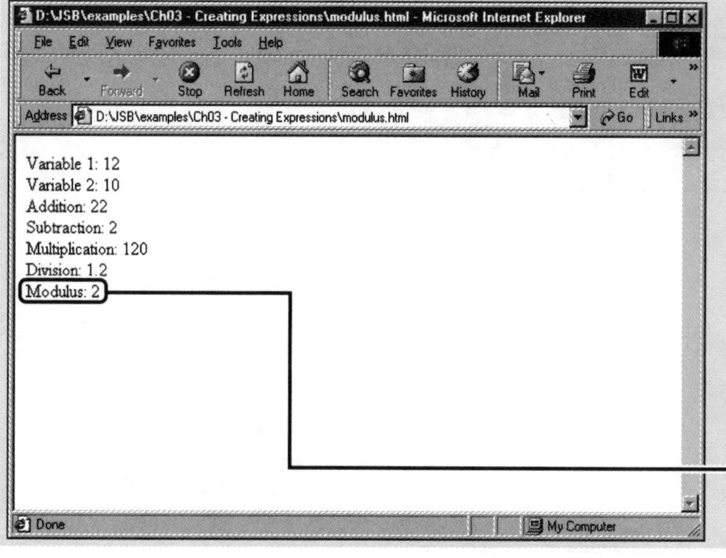
D:\JSB\examples\Ch03 - Creating Expressions\modulus.html - Microsoft Internet Explorer
Variable 1: 12
Variable 2: 10
Addition: 22
Subtraction: 2
Multiplication: 120
Division: 1.2
Modulus: 2

5. Open the file in a browser.

- The value of the modulus expression is displayed.

INCREMENT AND DECREMENT VARIABLES

One of the simplest expressions is one that increments or decrements a variable. Incrementing variables are often used as counters in `for` loops. JavaScript offers an easy way to increment variables using two plus symbols (++) attached to the variable. You can decrement variables by using two minus signs (––). This character set causes the variable to be decreased by 1.

INCREMENT VARIABLES

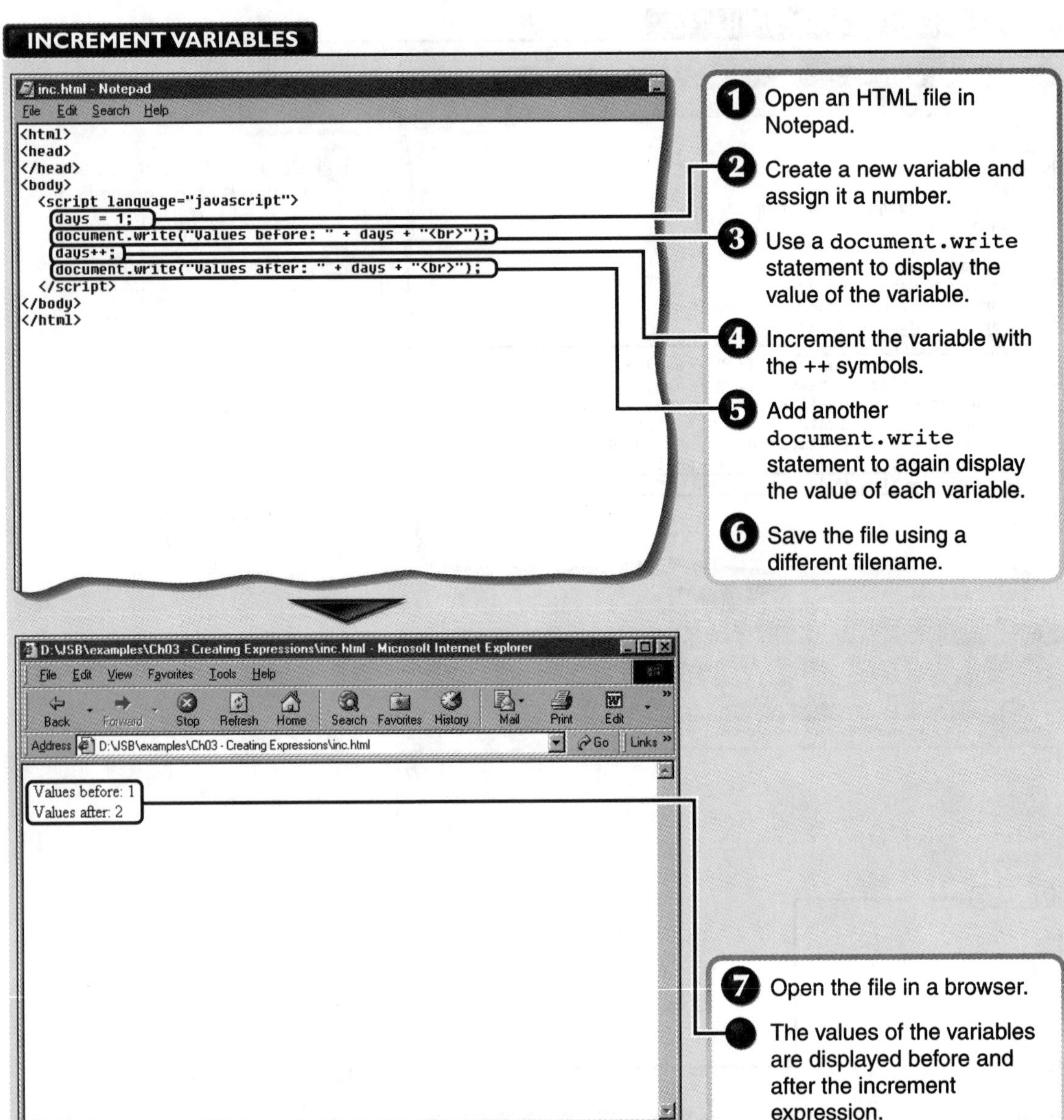

inc.html - Notepad
File Edit Search Help
<html>
<head>
</head>
<body>
<script language="javascript">
days = 1;
document.write("Values before: " + days + "<br>");
days++;
document.write("Values after: " + days + "<br>");
</script>
</body>
</html>
D:\JSB\examples\Ch03 - Creating Expressions\inc.html - Microsoft Internet Explorer
File Edit View Favorites Tools Help
Back Forward Stop Refresh Home Search Favorites History Mail Print Edit
Address D:\JSB\examples\Ch03 - Creating Expressions\inc.html
Go Links
Values before: 1
Values after: 2
Done
My Computer

1. Open an HTML file in Notepad.
2. Create a new variable and assign it a number.
3. Use a `document.write` statement to display the value of the variable.
4. Increment the variable with the ++ symbols.
5. Add another `document.write` statement to again display the value of each variable.
6. Save the file using a different filename.
7. Open the file in a browser.

- The values of the variables are displayed before and after the increment expression.

in an instant

DECREMENT VARIABLES

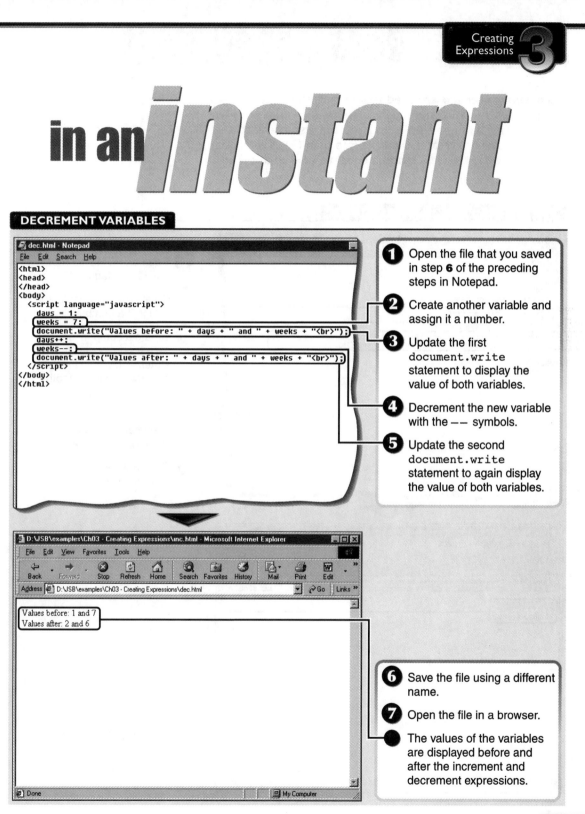

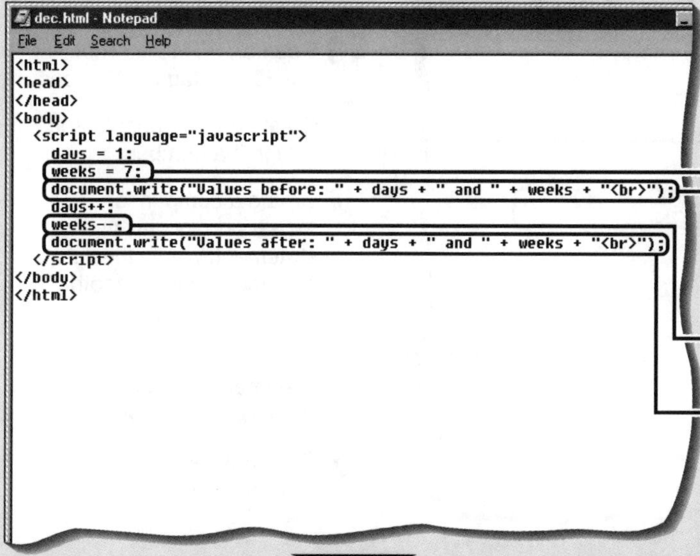

dec.html - Notepad

```
<html>
<head>
</head>
<body>
  <script language="javascript">
    days = 1;
    weeks = 7;
    document.write("Values before: " + days + " and " + weeks + "<br>");
    days++;
    weeks--;
    document.write("Values after: " + days + " and " + weeks + "<br>");
  </script>
</body>
</html>
```

1. Open the file that you saved in step **6** of the preceding steps in Notepad.
2. Create another variable and assign it a number.
3. Update the first `document.write` statement to display the value of both variables.
4. Decrement the new variable with the –– symbols.
5. Update the second `document.write` statement to again display the value of both variables.

D:\JSB\examples\Ch03 - Creating Expressions\inc.html - Microsoft Internet Explorer

Address D:\JSB\examples\Ch03 - Creating Expressions\dec.html

Values before: 1 and 7
Values after: 2 and 6

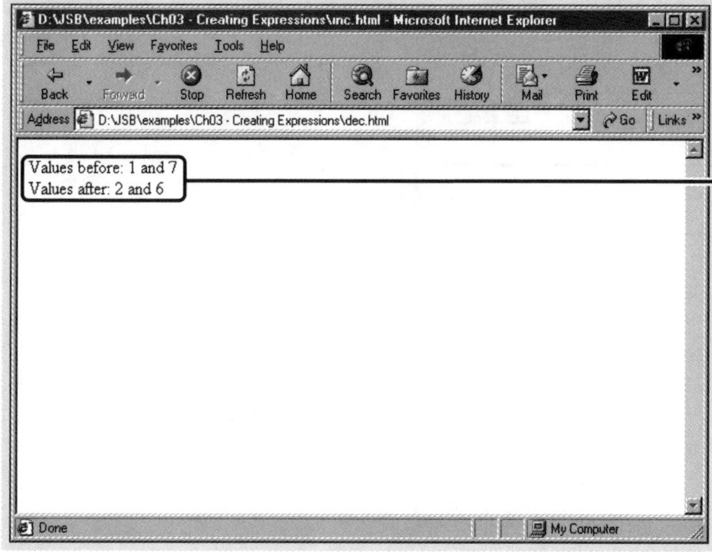

6. Save the file using a different name.
7. Open the file in a browser.

- The values of the variables are displayed before and after the increment and decrement expressions.

CREATE COMPARISON EXPRESSIONS

Comparison operators are used to compare the values of two variables in an expression, such as equals (==) (note the two equals signs) and not equals (!=). You can also check to see if two variables are greater than (>), less than (<), greater than or equal to (>=), or less than or equal to (<=) each other.

CREATE COMPARISON EXPRESSIONS

comp.html - Notepad

```
<html>
<head>
</head>
<body>
  <script language="javascript">
    daysOfMonth = 28;
    if (daysOfMonth == 28)
      month = "February";
    document.write("Days of Month: " + daysOfMonth + "<br>");
    document.write("Month: " + month + "<br>");
  </script>
</body>
</html>
```

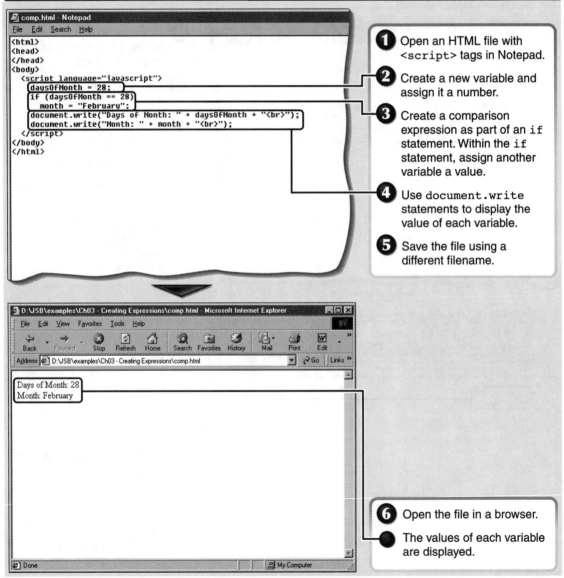

1. Open an HTML file with `<script>` tags in Notepad.
2. Create a new variable and assign it a number.
3. Create a comparison expression as part of an `if` statement. Within the `if` statement, assign another variable a value.
4. Use `document.write` statements to display the value of each variable.
5. Save the file using a different filename.

D:\JSB\examples\Ch03 - Creating Expressions\comp.html - Microsoft Internet Explorer

Days of Month: 28
Month: February

6. Open the file in a browser.

- The values of each variable are displayed.

in an instant

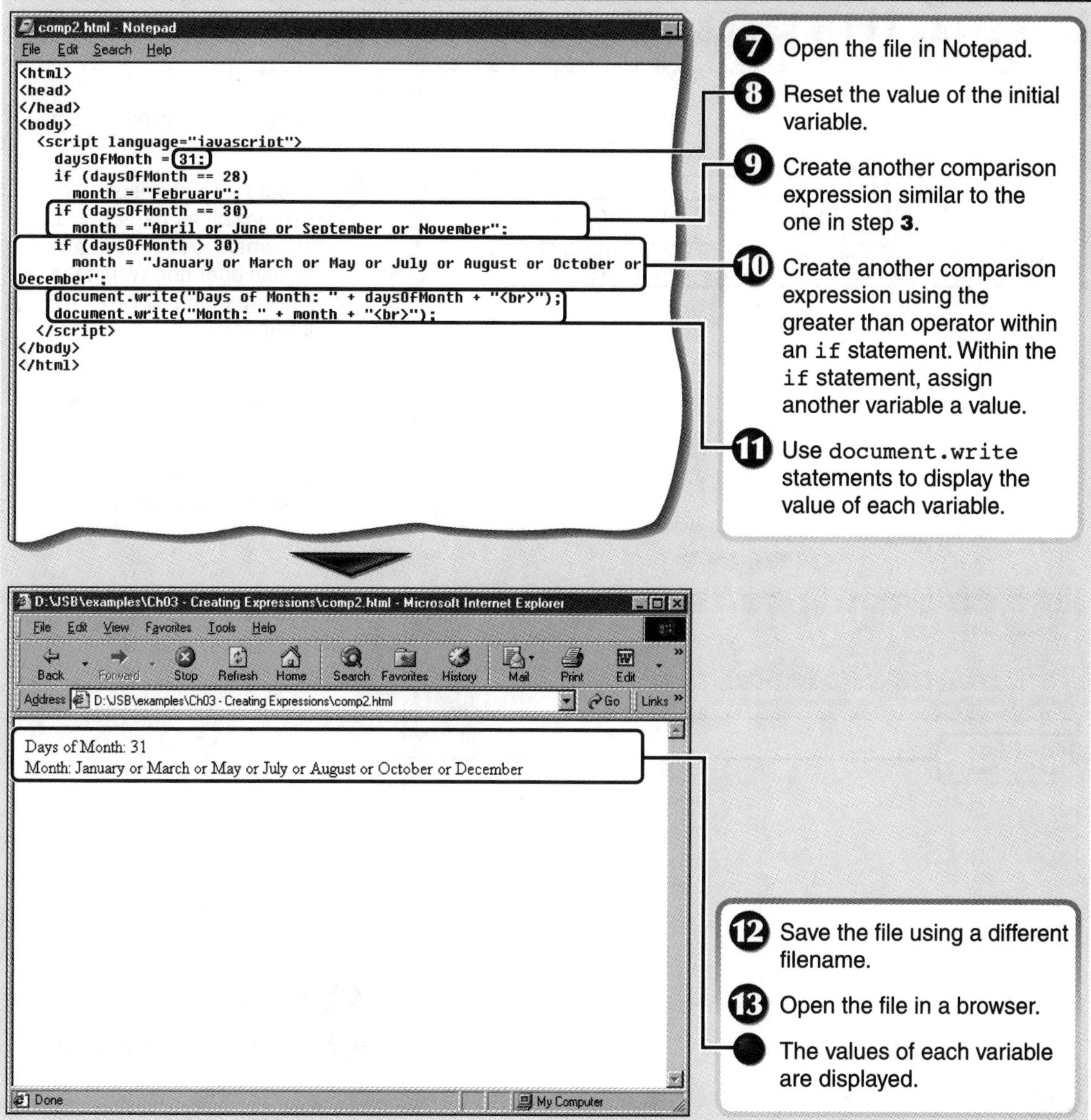
comp2.html - Notepad
File Edit Search Help
<html>
<head>
</head>
<body>
<script language="javascript">
daysOfMonth = 31;
if (daysOfMonth == 28)
month = "February";
if (daysOfMonth == 30)
month = "April or June or September or November";
if (daysOfMonth > 30)
month = "January or March or May or July or August or October or December";
document.write("Days of Month: " + daysOfMonth + "<br>");
document.write("Month: " + month + "<br>");
</script>
</body>
</html>
D:\JSB\examples\Ch03 - Creating Expressions\comp2.html - Microsoft Internet Explorer
File Edit View Favorites Tools Help
Back Forward Stop Refresh Home Search Favorites History Mail Print Edit
Address D:\JSB\examples\Ch03 - Creating Expressions\comp2.html
Go Links
Days of Month: 31
Month: January or March or May or July or August or October or December
Done
My Computer

7. Open the file in Notepad.
8. Reset the value of the initial variable.
9. Create another comparison expression similar to the one in step **3**.
10. Create another comparison expression using the greater than operator within an `if` statement. Within the `if` statement, assign another variable a value.
11. Use `document.write` statements to display the value of each variable.
12. Save the file using a different filename.
13. Open the file in a browser.

- The values of each variable are displayed.

CREATE LOGICAL EXPRESSIONS

Logical operators create logical expressions that can be used to control program flow. Logical operators include and (&&), or (| |), and not (!). The and operator produces a true value if both sides of the expression are true. The or operator produces a true value if either side of the expression is true. The not operator simply reverses the Boolean value.

CREATE LOGICAL EXPRESSIONS

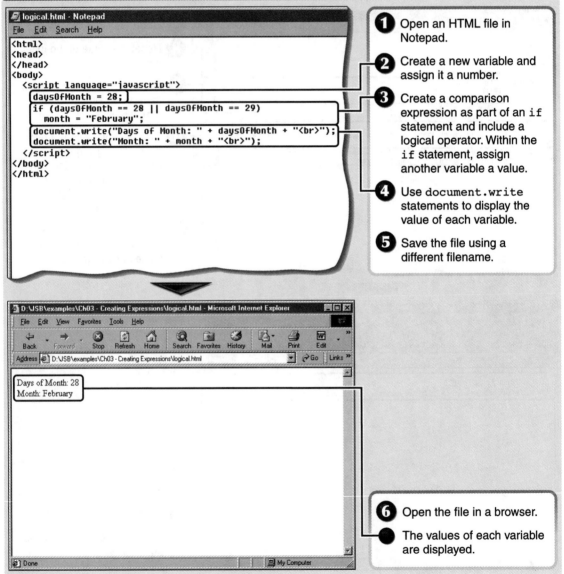

logical.html - Notepad
File Edit Search Help


```
<html>
<head>
</head>
<body>
  <script language="javascript">
    daysOfMonth = 28;
    if (daysOfMonth == 28 || daysOfMonth == 29)
      month = "February";
    document.write("Days of Month: " + daysOfMonth + "<br>");
    document.write("Month: " + month + "<br>");
  </script>
</body>
</html>
```

1. Open an HTML file in Notepad.
2. Create a new variable and assign it a number.
3. Create a comparison expression as part of an if statement and include a logical operator. Within the if statement, assign another variable a value.
4. Use document.write statements to display the value of each variable.
5. Save the file using a different filename.

D:\JSB\examples\Ch03 - Creating Expressions\logical.html - Microsoft Internet Explorer
File Edit View Favorites Tools Help
Back Forward Stop Refresh Home Search Favorites History Mail Print Edit
Address D:\JSB\examples\Ch03 - Creating Expressions\logical.html
Go Links
Days of Month: 28
Month: February
Done
My Computer

6. Open the file in a browser.

- The values of each variable are displayed.

in an instant

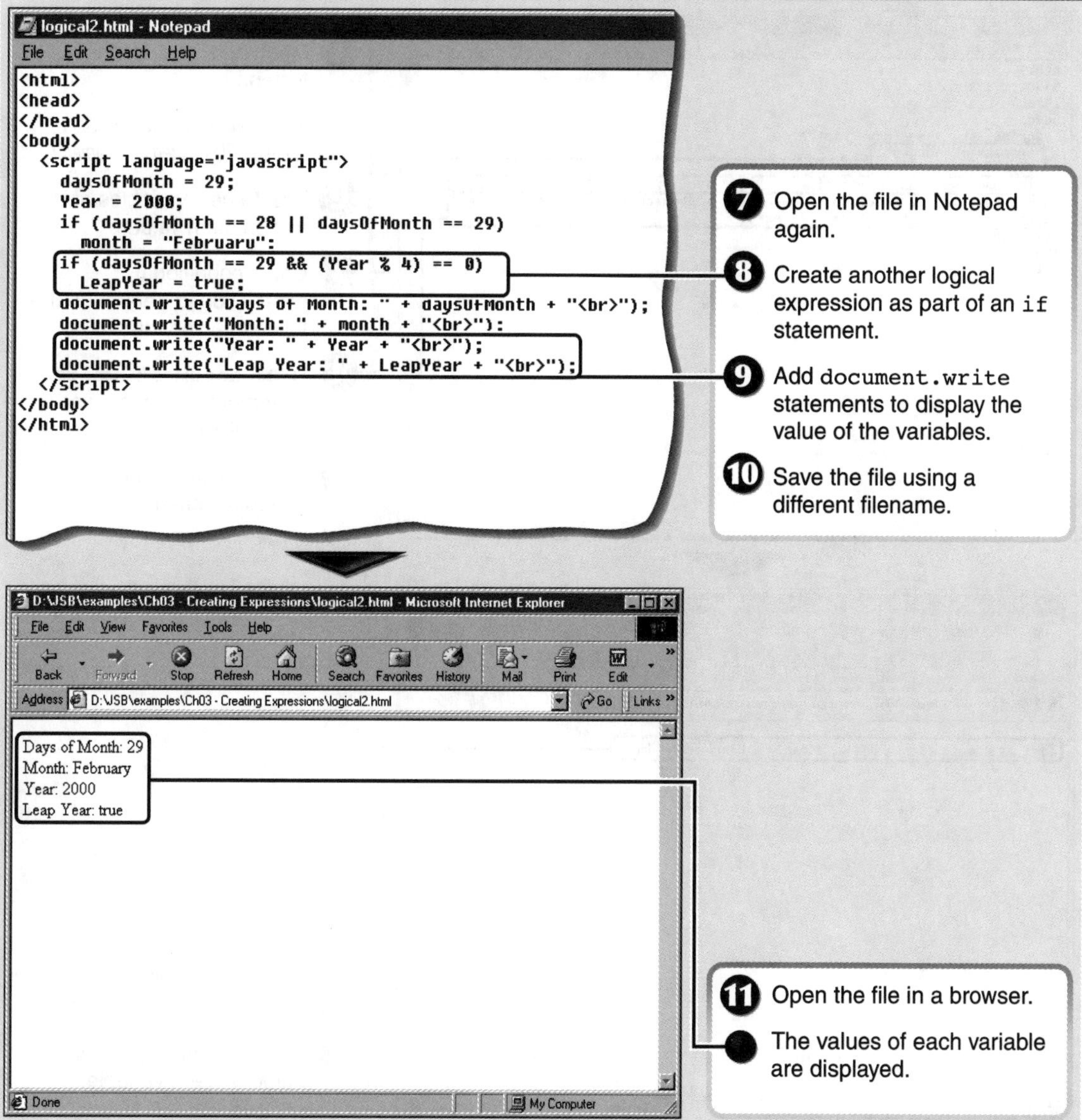
logical2.html - Notepad
File Edit Search Help
<html>
<head>
</head>
<body>
<script language="javascript">
daysOfMonth = 29;
Year = 2000;
if (daysOfMonth == 28 || daysOfMonth == 29)
month = "February";
if (daysOfMonth == 29 && (Year % 4) == 0)
LeapYear = true;
document.write("Days of Month: " + daysOfMonth + "<br>");
document.write("Month: " + month + "<br>");
document.write("Year: " + Year + "<br>");
document.write("Leap Year: " + LeapYear + "<br>");
</script>
</body>
</html>
D:\JSB\examples\Ch03 - Creating Expressions\logical2.html - Microsoft Internet Explorer
Days of Month: 29
Month: February
Year: 2000
Leap Year: true

7. Open the file in Notepad again.
8. Create another logical expression as part of an `if` statement.
9. Add `document.write` statements to display the value of the variables.
10. Save the file using a different filename.
11. Open the file in a browser.

- The values of each variable are displayed.

USING CONDITIONAL OPERATORS

A *conditional operator* is a shortcut for an `if-else` statement and consists of a question mark (`?`) and a colon (`:`). A conditional statement appears to the question mark's left. If the statement is true, the expression to the question mark's right is evaluated. If the conditional statement is false, JavaScript evaluates the statement that follows the colon.

USING CONDITIONAL OPERATORS

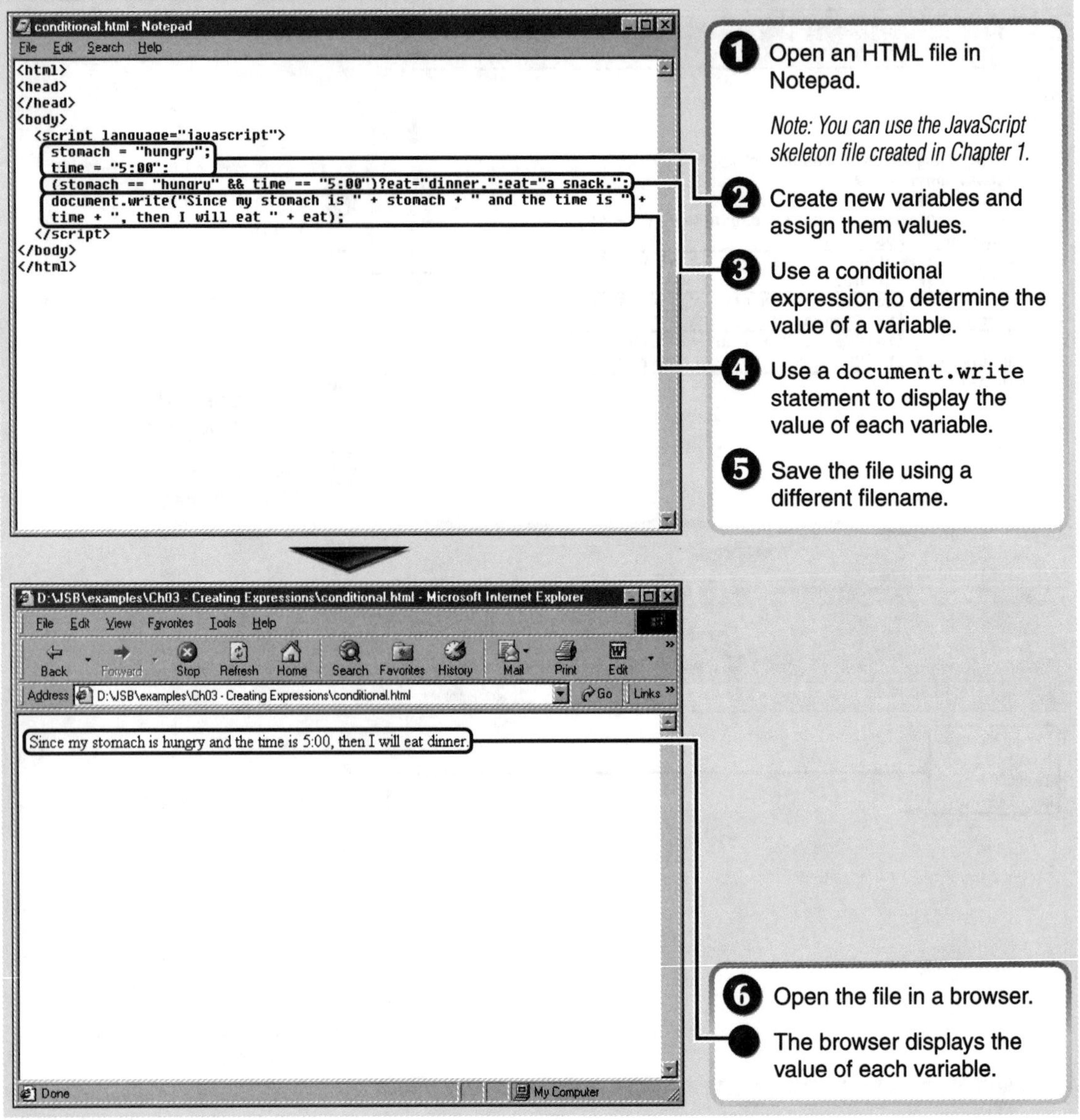

conditional.html - Notepad
File Edit Search Help
<html>
<head>
</head>
<body>
<script language="javascript">
stomach = "hungry";
time = "5:00";
(stomach == "hungry" && time == "5:00")?eat="dinner.":eat="a snack.";
document.write("Since my stomach is " + stomach + " and the time is " +
time + ", then I will eat " + eat);
</script>
</body>
</html>
1 Open an HTML file in Notepad.
Note: You can use the JavaScript skeleton file created in Chapter 1.
2 Create new variables and assign them values.
3 Use a conditional expression to determine the value of a variable.
4 Use a document.write statement to display the value of each variable.
5 Save the file using a different filename.
D:\JSB\examples\Ch03 - Creating Expressions\conditional.html - Microsoft Internet Explorer
File Edit View Favorites Tools Help
Back Forward Stop Refresh Home Search Favorites History Mail Print Edit
Address D:\JSB\examples\Ch03 - Creating Expressions\conditional.html Go Links
Since my stomach is hungry and the time is 5:00, then I will eat dinner.
Done
My Computer
6 Open the file in a browser.
The browser displays the value of each variable.

in an instant

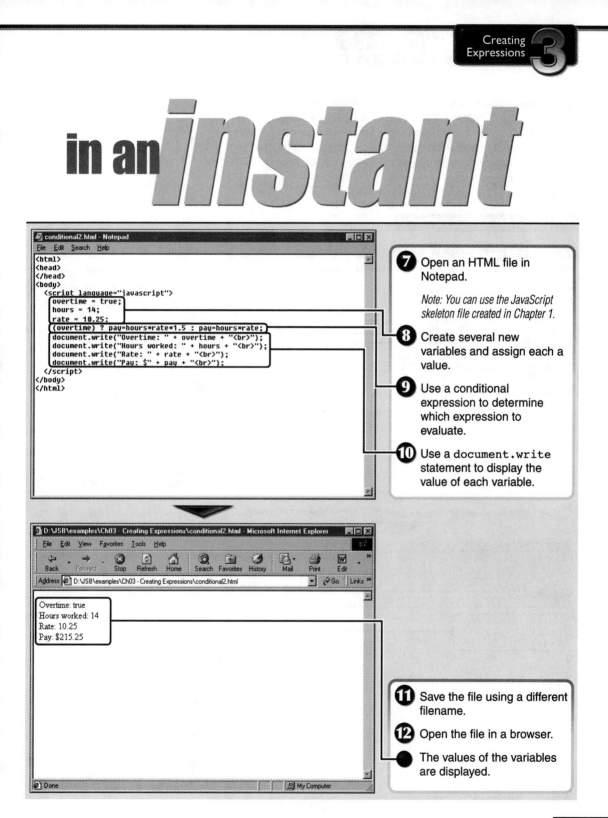

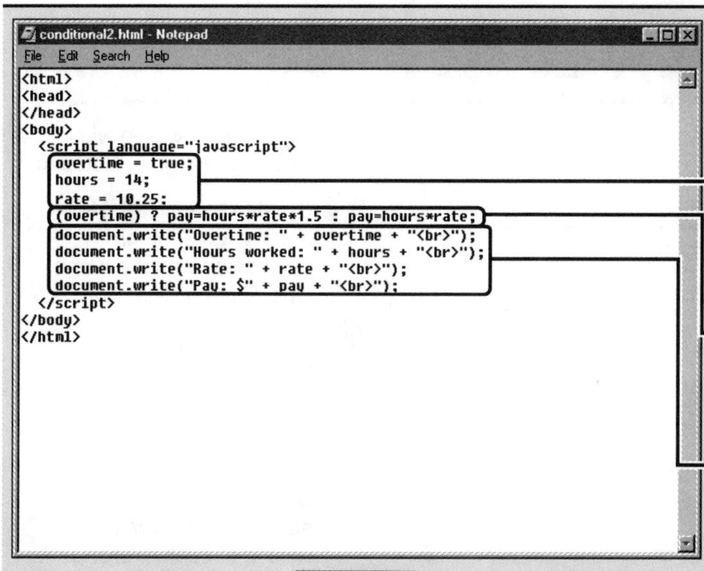

conditional2.html - Notepad

```
<html>
<head>
</head>
<body>
  <script language="javascript">
    overtime = true;
    hours = 14;
    rate = 10.25;
    (overtime) ? pay=hours*rate*1.5 : pay=hours*rate;
    document.write("Overtime: " + overtime + "<br>");
    document.write("Hours worked: " + hours + "<br>");
    document.write("Rate: " + rate + "<br>");
    document.write("Pay: $" + pay + "<br>");
  </script>
</body>
</html>
```

7. Open an HTML file in Notepad.

   Note: You can use the JavaScript skeleton file created in Chapter 1.

8. Create several new variables and assign each a value.

9. Use a conditional expression to determine which expression to evaluate.

10. Use a `document.write` statement to display the value of each variable.

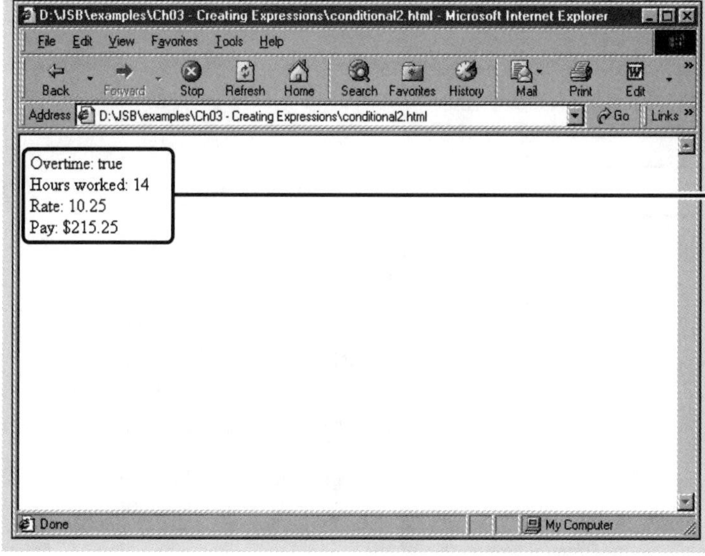

D:\JSB\examples\Ch03 - Creating Expressions\conditional2.html - Microsoft Internet Explorer

```
Overtime: true
Hours worked: 14
Rate: 10.25
Pay: $215.25
```

11. Save the file using a different filename.

12. Open the file in a browser.

- The values of the variables are displayed.

UNDERSTAND PRECEDENCE

JavaScript evaluates operators in a specific order. This order is known as *operator precedence*. The operators with the highest precedence get evaluated first. Parentheses have the highest precedence. After parentheses, the order is the following: unary operators — ++, – –, –, !; arithmetic — *, /, %, +, –; comparison — >, <, >=, <=; logical — &&, | |; conditional — ? :; and assignment — =.

UNDERSTAND PRECEDENCE

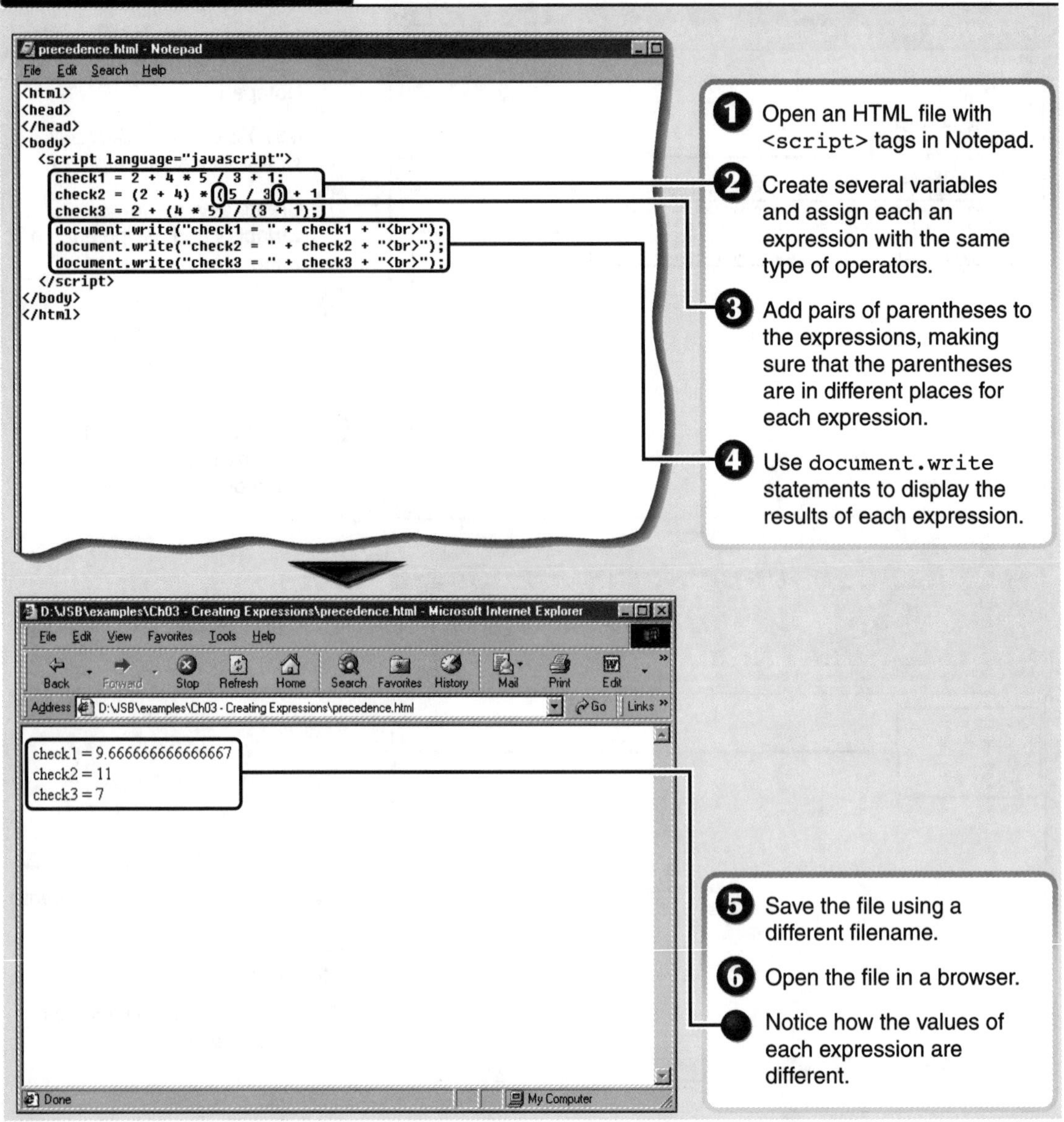
precedence.html - Notepad
File Edit Search Help
```
<html>
<head>
</head>
<body>
<script language="javascript">
check1 = 2 + 4 * 5 / 3 + 1;
check2 = (2 + 4) * (5 / 3) + 1
check3 = 2 + (4 * 5) / (3 + 1);
document.write("check1 = " + check1 + "<br>");
document.write("check2 = " + check2 + "<br>");
document.write("check3 = " + check3 + "<br>");
</script>
</body>
</html>
```
D:\JSB\examples\Ch03 - Creating Expressions\precedence.html - Microsoft Internet Explorer
File Edit View Favorites Tools Help
Back Forward Stop Refresh Home Search Favorites History Mail Print Edit
Address D:\JSB\examples\Ch03 - Creating Expressions\precedence.html
Go Links
check1 = 9.666666666666667
check2 = 11
check3 = 7
Done
My Computer

1. Open an HTML file with `<script>` tags in Notepad.
2. Create several variables and assign each an expression with the same type of operators.
3. Add pairs of parentheses to the expressions, making sure that the parentheses are in different places for each expression.
4. Use `document.write` statements to display the results of each expression.
5. Save the file using a different filename.
6. Open the file in a browser.

- Notice how the values of each expression are different.

EVALUATE STRING EXPRESSIONS

Sometimes expressions are contained within a string, such as when enabling the user to input to an expression in a form field. Using the `eval()` function, you can instruct JavaScript to evaluate the string as an expression.

EVALUATE STRING EXPRESSIONS

eval.html - Notepad

```
<html>
<head>
</head>
<body>
  <script language="javascript">
    hoursPerYear = "365 * 24";
    document.write("To compute the number of hours in a year, you can use
this expression: " + hoursPerYear + "<br>");
    document.write("The result of this expression is: " +
eval(hoursPerYear));
  </script>
</body>
</html>
```

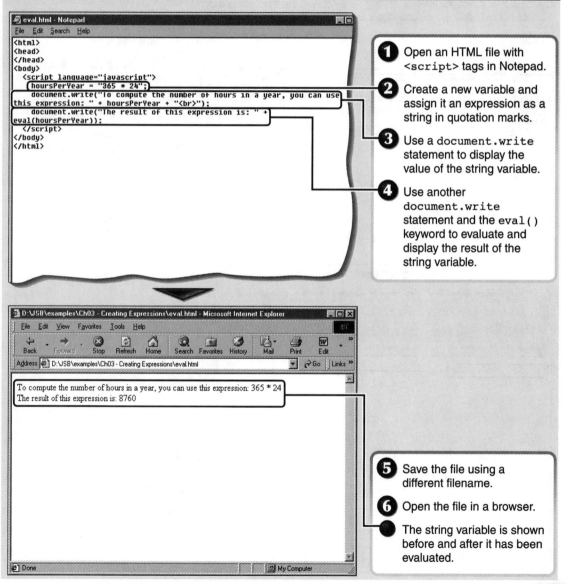

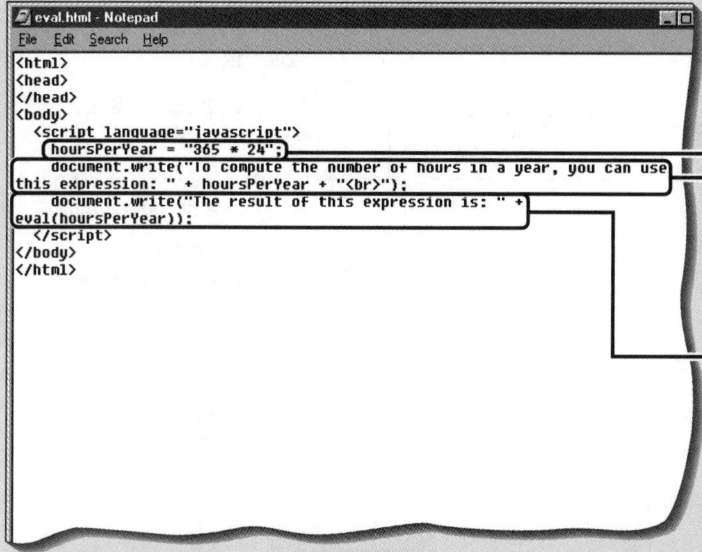

1. Open an HTML file with `<script>` tags in Notepad.
2. Create a new variable and assign it an expression as a string in quotation marks.
3. Use a `document.write` statement to display the value of the string variable.
4. Use another `document.write` statement and the `eval()` keyword to evaluate and display the result of the string variable.

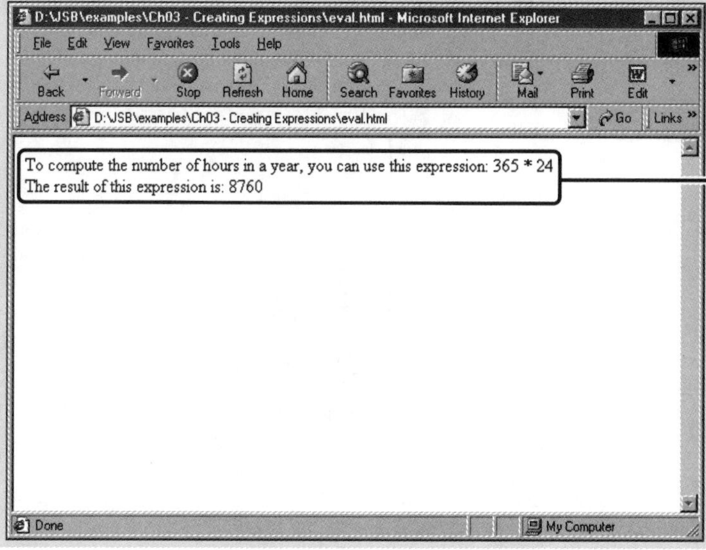

D:\JSB\examples\Ch03 - Creating Expressions\eval.html - Microsoft Internet Explorer

To compute the number of hours in a year, you can use this expression: 365 * 24
The result of this expression is: 8760

5. Save the file using a different filename.
6. Open the file in a browser.

- The string variable is shown before and after it has been evaluated.

IDENTIFY NUMBERS

JavaScript includes a unique method that can be used to identify variables as numbers — `isNaN()`, which accepts a single parameter that is checked. If the variable sent to the method is a number, the method returns a `false` value (because the method technically checks to see if the variable is *not a number*); if the variable is not a number, a `true` value is returned.

IDENTIFY NUMBERS

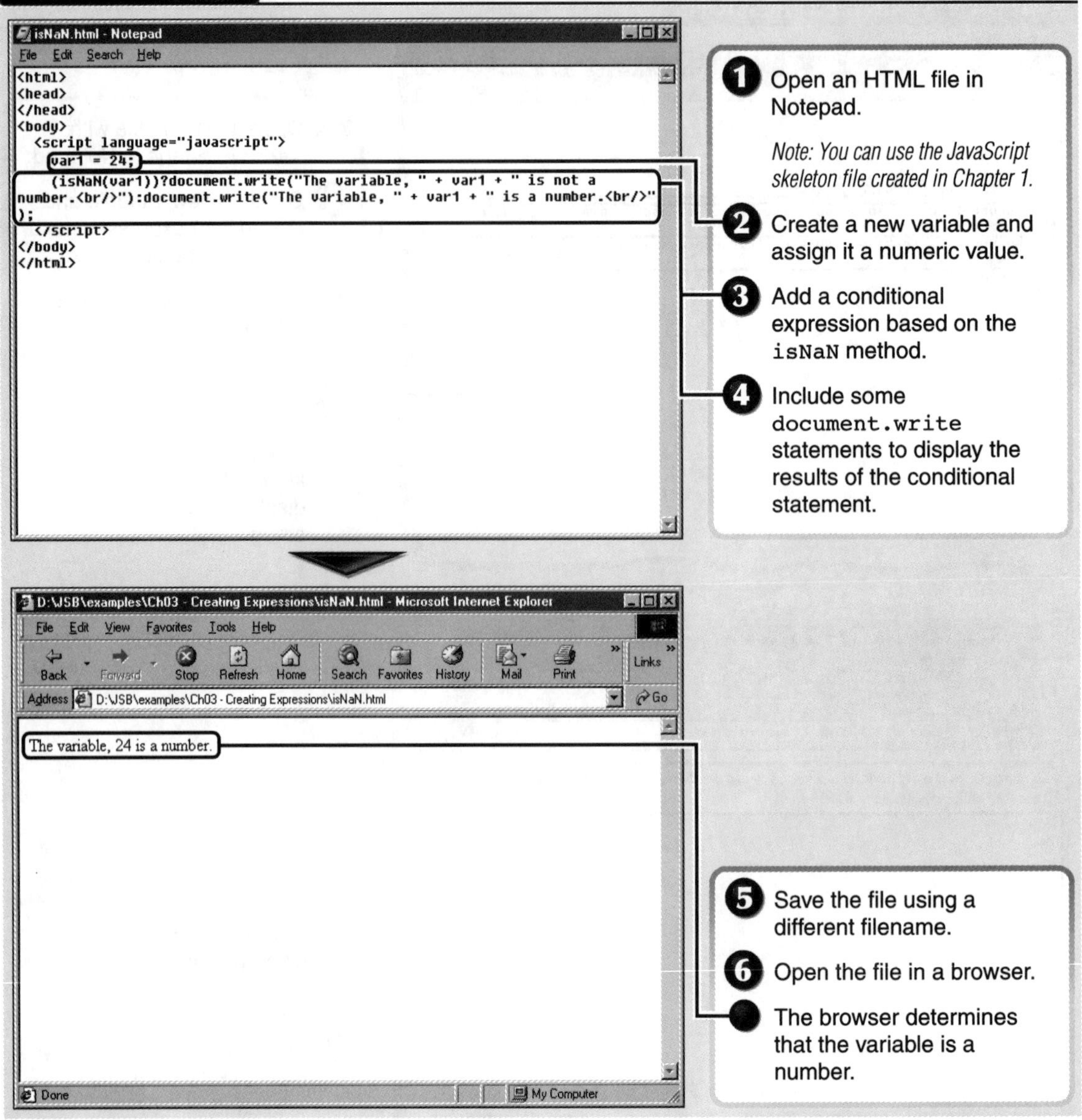

isNaN.html - Notepad
File Edit Search Help
<html>
<head>
</head>
<body>
<script language="javascript">
var1 = 24;
(isNaN(var1))?document.write("The variable, " + var1 + " is not a number.
"):document.write("The variable, " + var1 + " is a number.
");
</script>
</body>
</html>
D:\JSB\examples\Ch03 - Creating Expressions\isNaN.html - Microsoft Internet Explorer
File Edit View Favorites Tools Help
Back Forward Stop Refresh Home Search Favorites History Mail Print
Links
Address D:\JSB\examples\Ch03 - Creating Expressions\isNaN.html
Go
The variable, 24 is a number.
Done
My Computer

1. Open an HTML file in Notepad.

   Note: You can use the JavaScript skeleton file created in Chapter 1.

2. Create a new variable and assign it a numeric value.
3. Add a conditional expression based on the `isNaN` method.
4. Include some `document.write` statements to display the results of the conditional statement.
5. Save the file using a different filename.
6. Open the file in a browser.

- The browser determines that the variable is a number.

in an instant

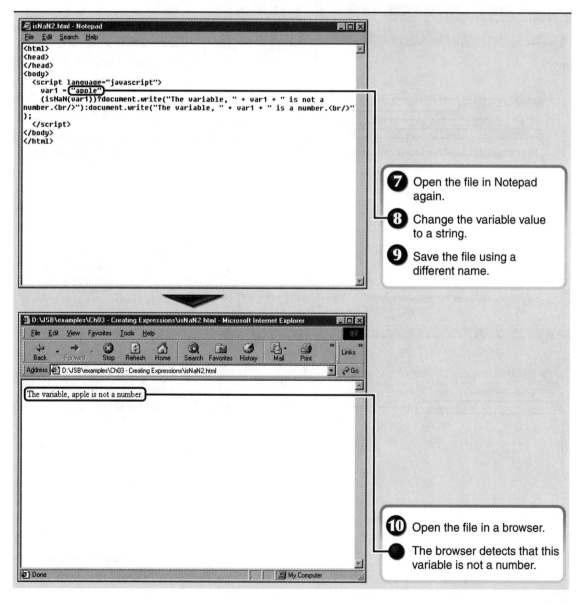

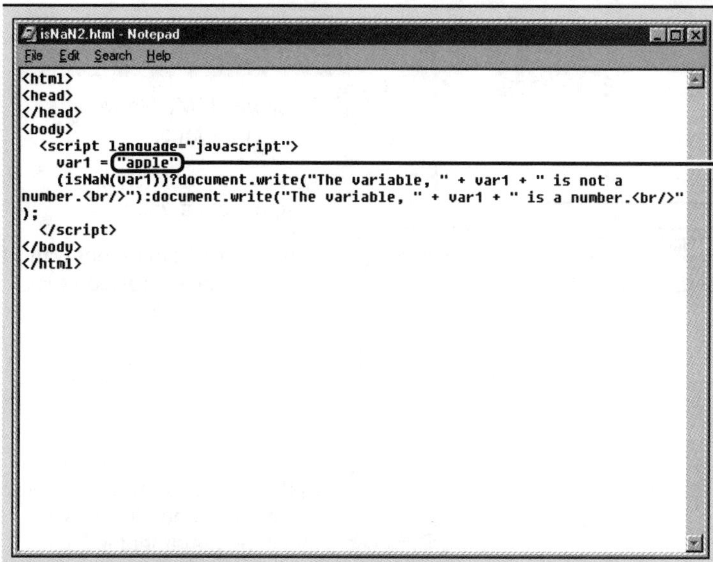

isNaN2.html - Notepad

File Edit Search Help

```
<html>
<head>
</head>
<body>
  <script language="javascript">
    var1 = "apple"
    (isNaN(var1))?document.write("The variable, " + var1 + " is not a
number.<br/>"):document.write("The variable, " + var1 + " is a number.<br/>"
);
  </script>
</body>
</html>
```

7. Open the file in Notepad again.
8. Change the variable value to a string.
9. Save the file using a different name.

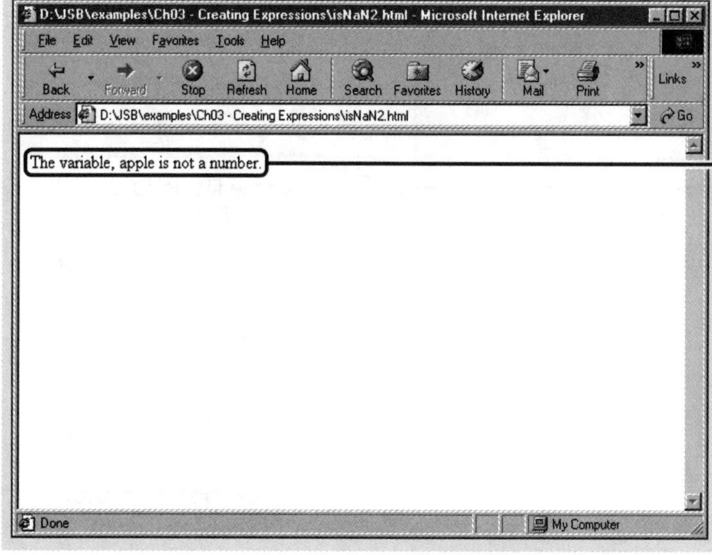

D:\JSB\examples\Ch03 - Creating Expressions\isNaN2.html - Microsoft Internet Explorer

File Edit View Favorites Tools Help

Back Forward Stop Refresh Home Search Favorites History Mail Print Links

Address D:\JSB\examples\Ch03 - Creating Expressions\isNaN2.html Go

The variable, apple is not a number.

Done My Computer

10. Open the file in a browser.

- The browser detects that this variable is not a number.

USING IF-ELSE STATEMENTS

An `if` statement includes the `if` keyword followed by a conditional statement within parentheses. The alternative statement is positioned below the `if` statement as part of an `else` statement. If the `if` condition is false, the statements in the `else` statement are executed. A single `if` statement can be followed by several `else if` statements, but the final `else` statement should not include the `if` keyword.

USING IF-ELSE STATEMENTS

```
<html>
<head>
</head>
<body>
  <script language="javascript">
   Month = "December";
   Date = 25;
   if (Month == "December" && Date == 25)
     document.write("Today is Christmas and the store is closed.");
   else
     document.write("Welcome. We are open until 5:00 pm.");
  </script>
</body>
</html>
```

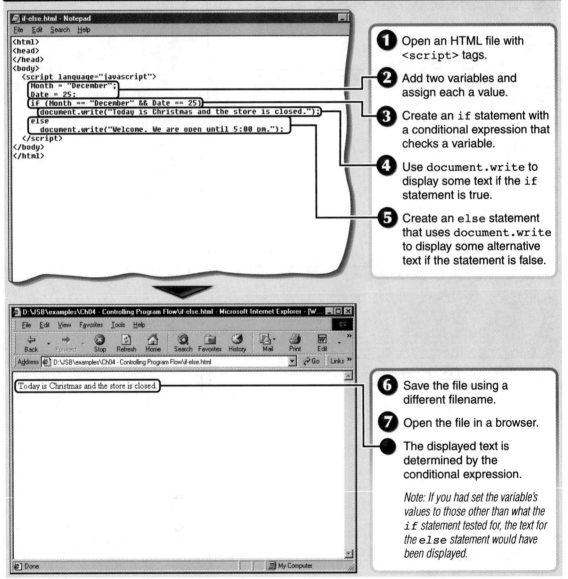

1. Open an HTML file with `<script>` tags.
2. Add two variables and assign each a value.
3. Create an `if` statement with a conditional expression that checks a variable.
4. Use `document.write` to display some text if the `if` statement is true.
5. Create an `else` statement that uses `document.write` to display some alternative text if the statement is false.

Today is Christmas and the store is closed.

6. Save the file using a different filename.
7. Open the file in a browser.

- The displayed text is determined by the conditional expression.

Note: If you had set the variable's values to those other than what the `if` statement tested for, the text for the `else` statement would have been displayed.

in an instant

USING MULTIPLE ELSE STATEMENTS

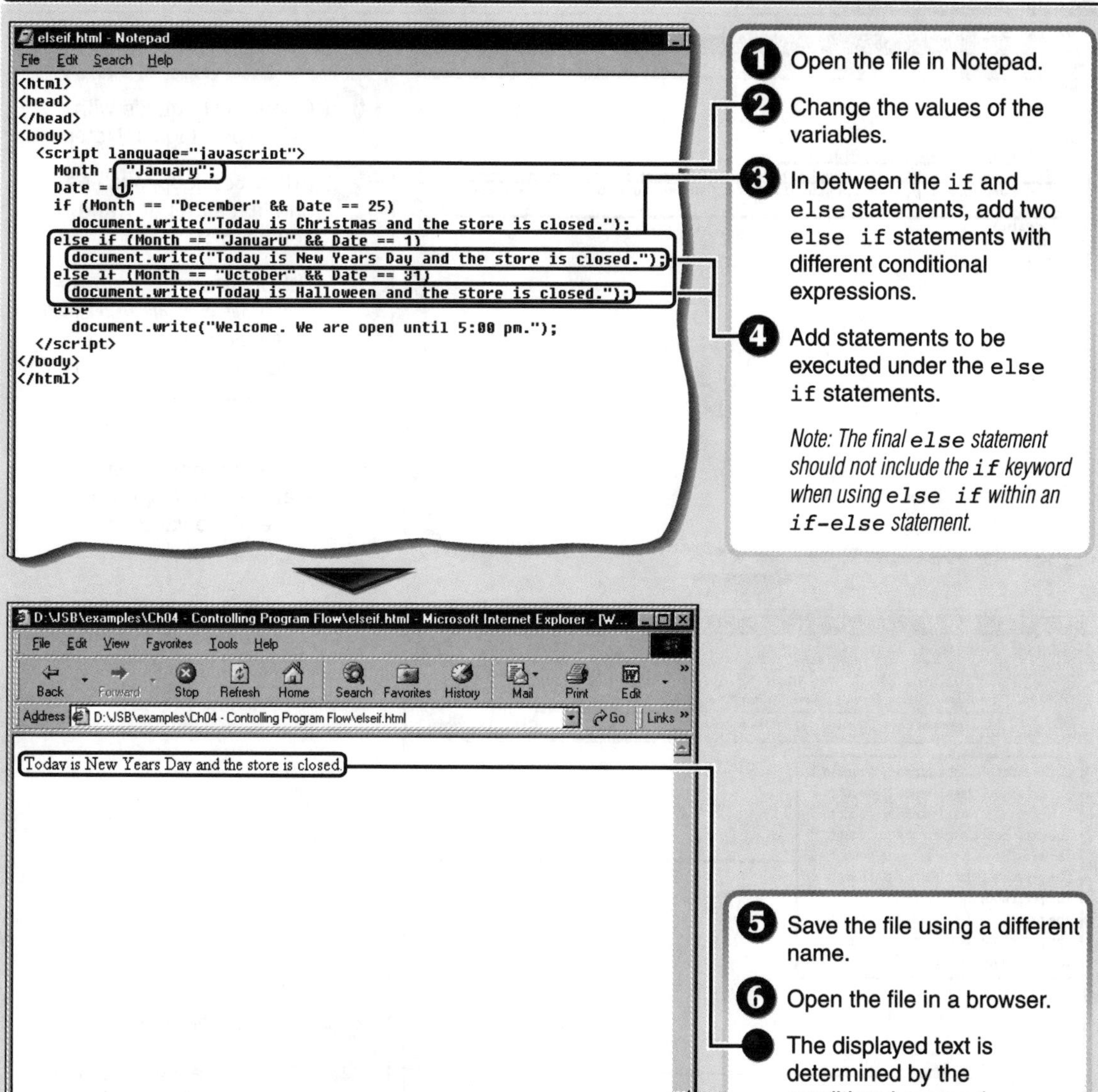
elseif.html - Notepad
File Edit Search Help
<html>
<head>
</head>
<body>
<script language="javascript">
Month = "January";
Date = 1;
if (Month == "December" && Date == 25)
document.write("Today is Christmas and the store is closed.");
else if (Month == "January" && Date == 1)
document.write("Today is New Years Day and the store is closed.");
else if (Month == "October" && Date == 31)
document.write("Today is Halloween and the store is closed.");
else
document.write("Welcome. We are open until 5:00 pm.");
</script>
</body>
</html>
D:\JSB\examples\Ch04 - Controlling Program Flow\elseif.html - Microsoft Internet Explorer - [W...
File Edit View Favorites Tools Help
Back Forward Stop Refresh Home Search Favorites History Mail Print Edit
Address D:\JSB\examples\Ch04 - Controlling Program Flow\elseif.html
Go Links
Today is New Years Day and the store is closed.
Done
My Computer

1. Open the file in Notepad.
2. Change the values of the variables.
3. In between the `if` and `else` statements, add two `else if` statements with different conditional expressions.
4. Add statements to be executed under the `else if` statements.

Note: The final `else` statement should not include the `if` keyword when using `else if` within an `if-else` statement.

5. Save the file using a different name.
6. Open the file in a browser.

- The displayed text is determined by the conditional expression.

USING FOR LOOPS

A `for` statement consists of three distinct parts within parentheses that are separated by semicolons: the loop's initial condition, the terminating condition, and how the loop is incremented. The `for` loop begins at the defined initial condition and continually executes the statement or statements that follow the `for` statement until the termination condition is met. The `for` loop variable is incremented each time through the loop.

USING FOR LOOPS

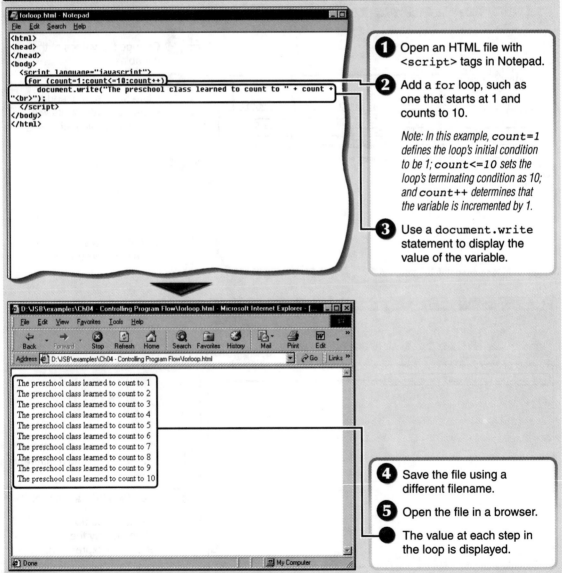

forloop.html - Notepad

```
<html>
<head>
</head>
<body>
  <script language="javascript">
   for (count=1;count<=10;count++)
     document.write("The preschool class learned to count to " + count +
"<br>");
  </script>
</body>
</html>
```

1. Open an HTML file with `<script>` tags in Notepad.
2. Add a `for` loop, such as one that starts at 1 and counts to 10.

   Note: In this example, `count=1` *defines the loop's initial condition to be 1;* `count<=10` *sets the loop's terminating condition as 10; and* `count++` *determines that the variable is incremented by 1.*
3. Use a `document.write` statement to display the value of the variable.

D:\JSB\examples\Ch04 - Controlling Program Flow\forloop.html - Microsoft Internet Explorer

The preschool class learned to count to 1
The preschool class learned to count to 2
The preschool class learned to count to 3
The preschool class learned to count to 4
The preschool class learned to count to 5
The preschool class learned to count to 6
The preschool class learned to count to 7
The preschool class learned to count to 8
The preschool class learned to count to 9
The preschool class learned to count to 10

4. Save the file using a different filename.
5. Open the file in a browser.

- The value at each step in the loop is displayed.

in an instant

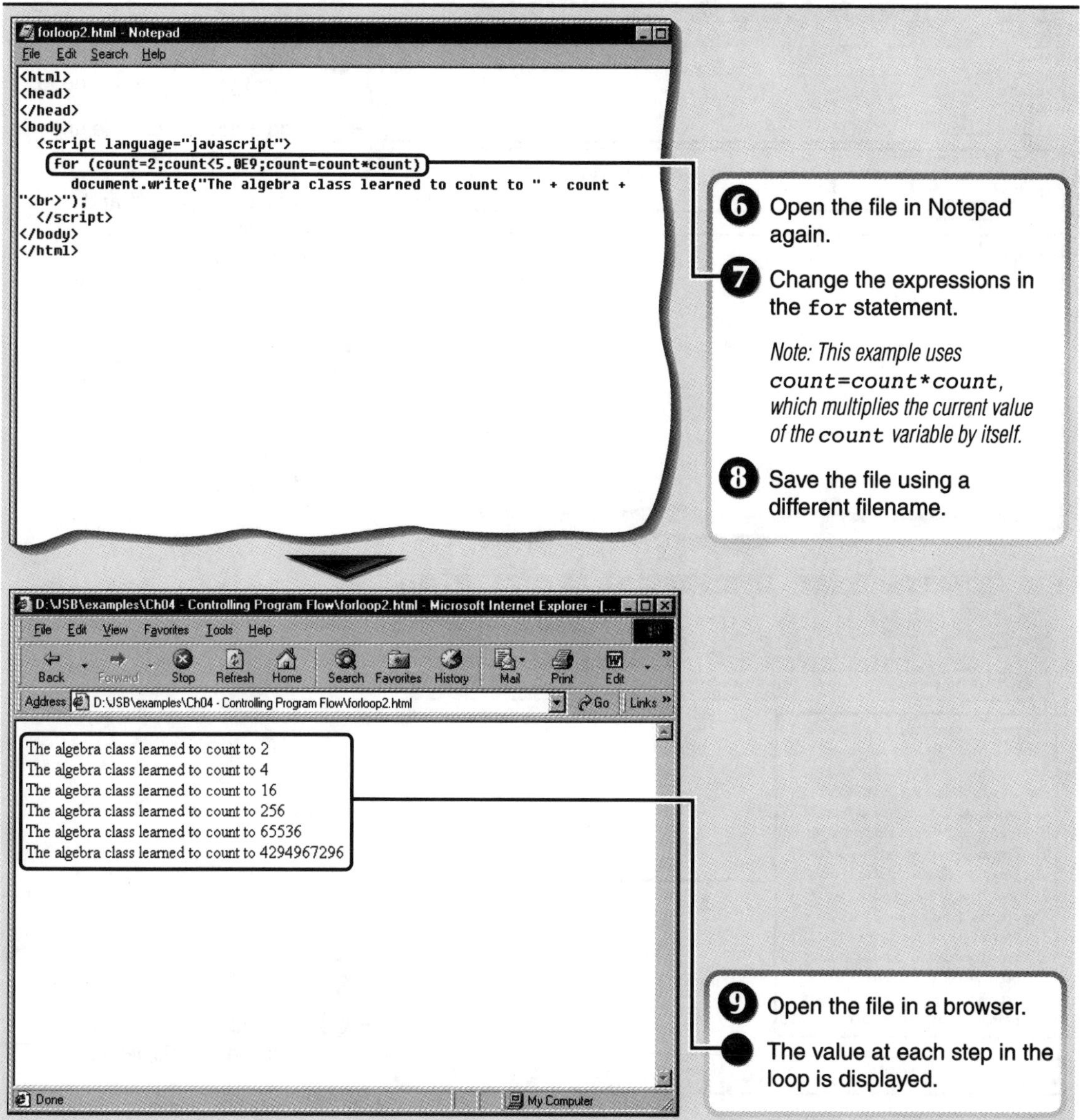
forloop2.html - Notepad
File Edit Search Help
<html>
<head>
</head>
<body>
<script language="javascript">
for (count=2;count<5.0E9;count=count*count)
document.write("The algebra class learned to count to " + count +
"<br>");
</script>
</body>
</html>
6 Open the file in Notepad again.
7 Change the expressions in the for statement.
Note: This example uses count=count*count, which multiplies the current value of the count variable by itself.
8 Save the file using a different filename.
D:\JSB\examples\Ch04 - Controlling Program Flow\forloop2.html - Microsoft Internet Explorer
File Edit View Favorites Tools Help
Back Forward Stop Refresh Home Search Favorites History Mail Print Edit
Address D:\JSB\examples\Ch04 - Controlling Program Flow\forloop2.html
Go Links
The algebra class learned to count to 2
The algebra class learned to count to 4
The algebra class learned to count to 16
The algebra class learned to count to 256
The algebra class learned to count to 65536
The algebra class learned to count to 4294967296
Done
My Computer
9 Open the file in a browser.
The value at each step in the loop is displayed.

USING WHILE LOOPS

A `while` loop is different from the `for` loop because it does not count to an end result. It simply continues to loop through the statements contained within the brackets until a conditional expression evaluates to `false`. When using a `while` loop, you need to be sure that the conditional statement will eventually become false, or the loop will continue indefinitely.

USING WHILE LOOPS

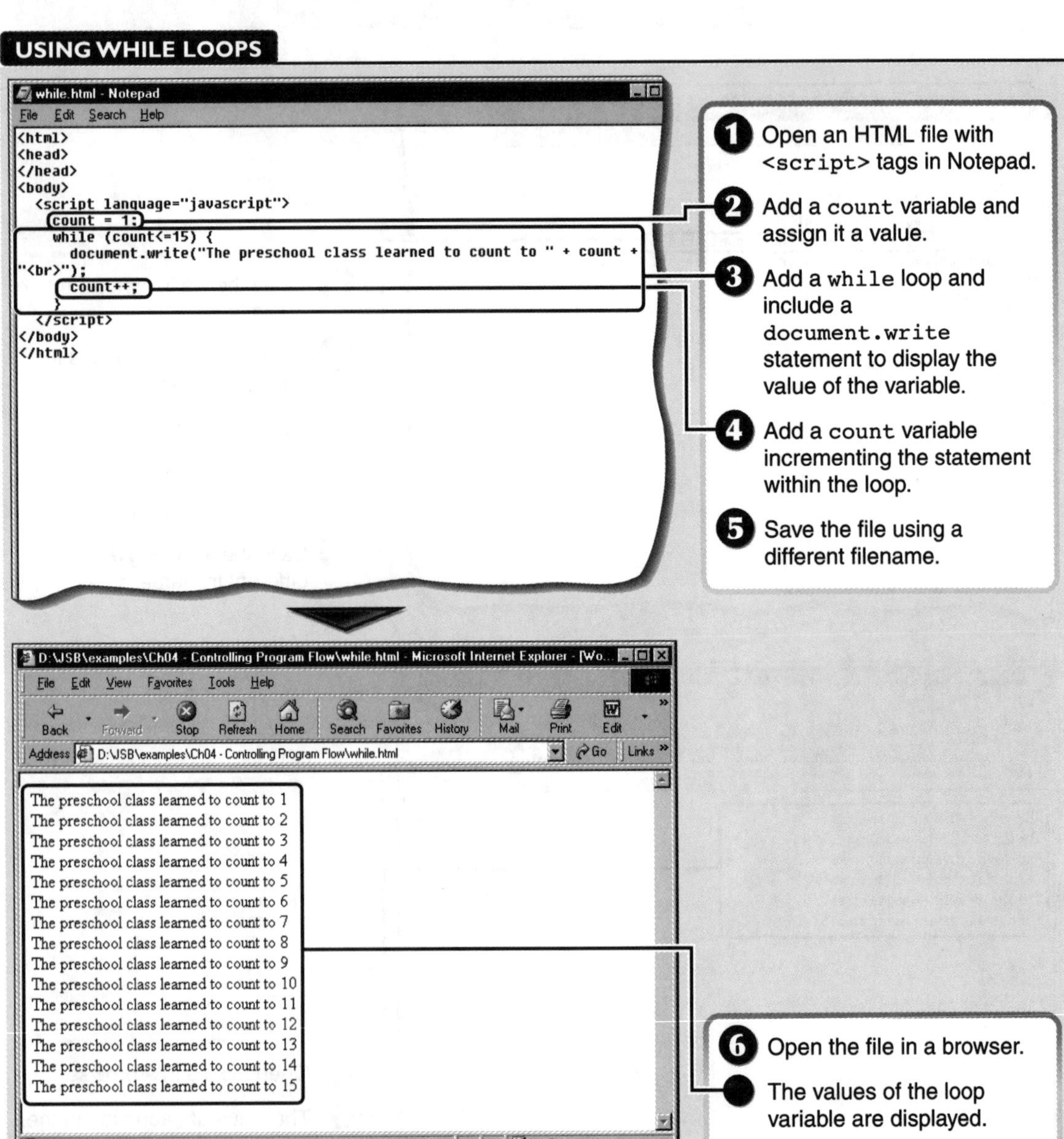

while.html - Notepad
File Edit Search Help
<html>
<head>
</head>
<body>
<script language="javascript">
count = 1;
while (count<=15) {
document.write("The preschool class learned to count to " + count + "<br>");
count++;
}
</script>
</body>
</html>
D:\JSB\examples\Ch04 - Controlling Program Flow\while.html - Microsoft Internet Explorer
The preschool class learned to count to 1
The preschool class learned to count to 2
The preschool class learned to count to 3
The preschool class learned to count to 4
The preschool class learned to count to 5
The preschool class learned to count to 6
The preschool class learned to count to 7
The preschool class learned to count to 8
The preschool class learned to count to 9
The preschool class learned to count to 10
The preschool class learned to count to 11
The preschool class learned to count to 12
The preschool class learned to count to 13
The preschool class learned to count to 14
The preschool class learned to count to 15

1. Open an HTML file with `<script>` tags in Notepad.
2. Add a `count` variable and assign it a value.
3. Add a `while` loop and include a `document.write` statement to display the value of the variable.
4. Add a `count` variable incrementing the statement within the loop.
5. Save the file using a different filename.
6. Open the file in a browser.

- The values of the loop variable are displayed.

in an instant

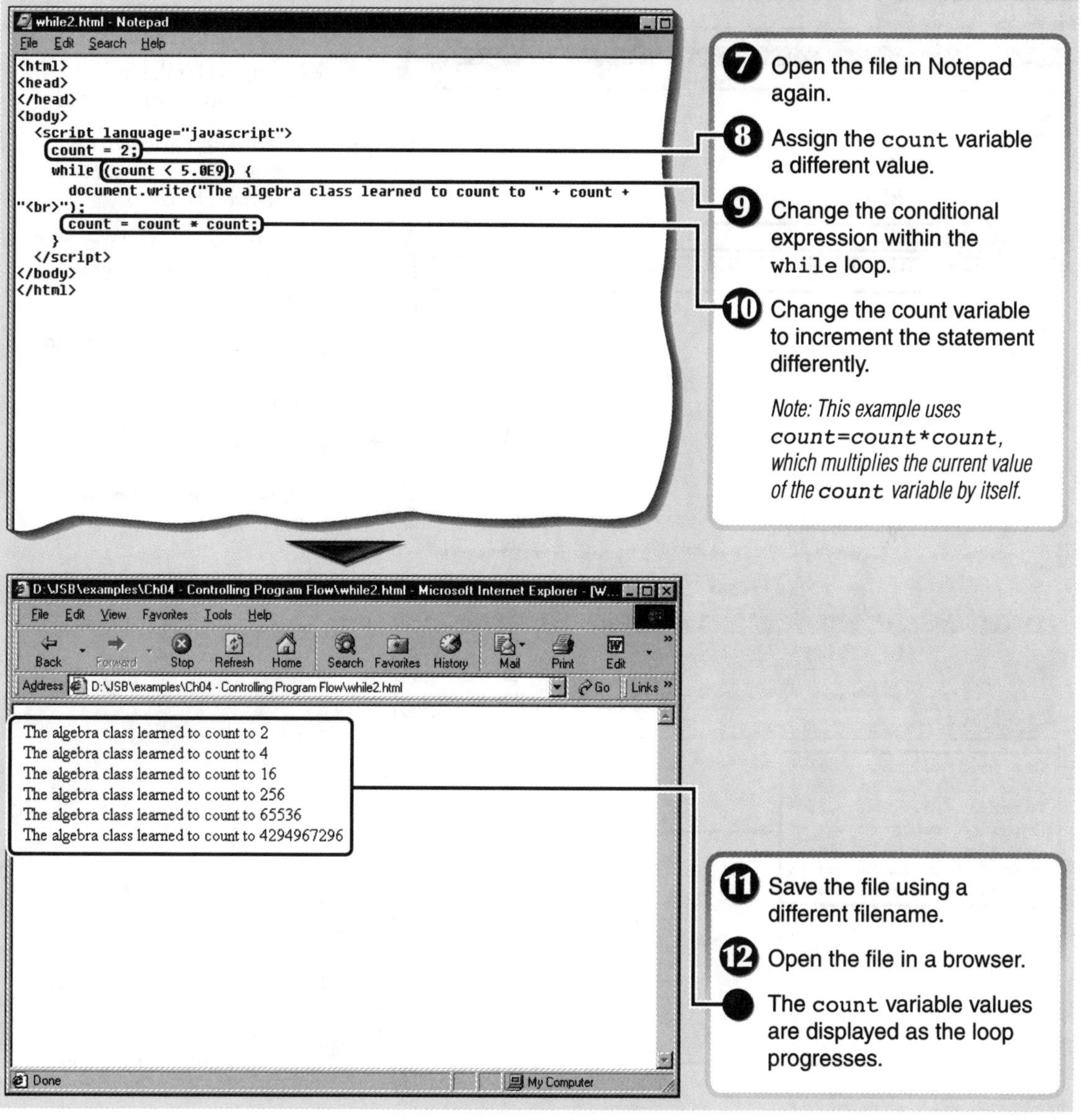
while2.html - Notepad
File Edit Search Help
<html>
<head>
</head>
<body>
<script language="javascript">
count = 2;
while (count < 5.0E9) {
document.write("The algebra class learned to count to " + count + "<br>");
count = count * count;
}
</script>
</body>
</html>
D:\JSB\examples\Ch04 - Controlling Program Flow\while2.html - Microsoft Internet Explorer
File Edit View Favorites Tools Help
Back Forward Stop Refresh Home Search Favorites History Mail Print Edit
Address D:\JSB\examples\Ch04 - Controlling Program Flow\while2.html
Go Links
The algebra class learned to count to 2
The algebra class learned to count to 4
The algebra class learned to count to 16
The algebra class learned to count to 256
The algebra class learned to count to 65536
The algebra class learned to count to 4294967296
Done
My Computer

7 Open the file in Notepad again.

8 Assign the `count` variable a different value.

9 Change the conditional expression within the `while` loop.

10 Change the count variable to increment the statement differently.

Note: This example uses `count=count*count`, which multiplies the current value of the `count` variable by itself.

11 Save the file using a different filename.

12 Open the file in a browser.

- The `count` variable values are displayed as the loop progresses.

BREAK LOOPS

Sometimes you can get stuck in a loop. This scenario is called an *infinite loop*. To break out of an infinite loop, you can use the `break` keyword. When JavaScript encounters the `break` keyword within a loop, it automatically terminates the loop and executes the first statement that comes after the loop.

BREAK LOOPS

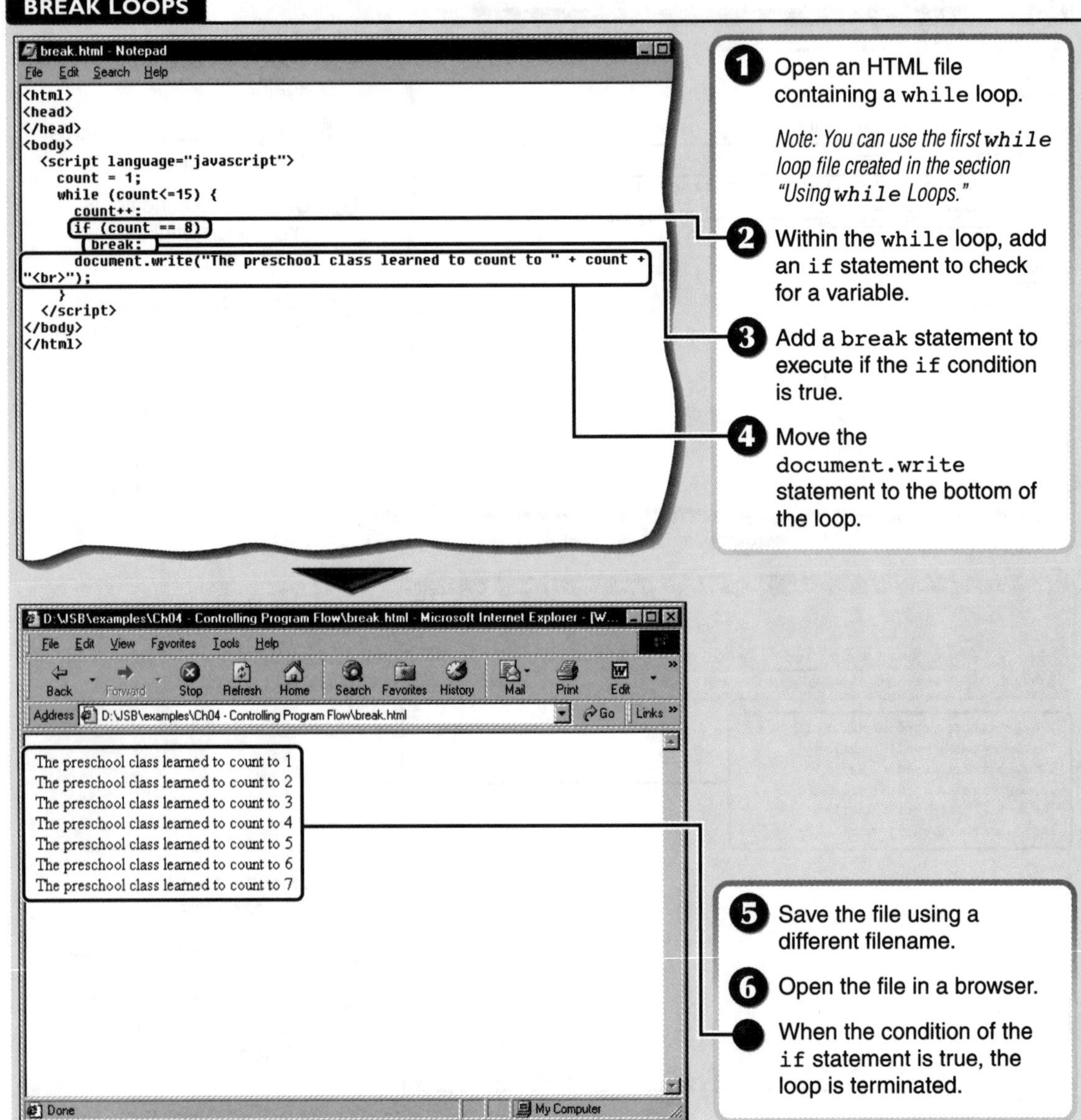
break.html - Notepad
File Edit Search Help
<html>
<head>
</head>
<body>
<script language="javascript">
count = 1;
while (count<=15) {
count++;
if (count == 8)
break;
document.write("The preschool class learned to count to " + count + "<br>");
}
</script>
</body>
</html>
D:\JSB\examples\Ch04 - Controlling Program Flow\break.html - Microsoft Internet Explorer - [W...
File Edit View Favorites Tools Help
Back Forward Stop Refresh Home Search Favorites History Mail Print Edit
Address D:\JSB\examples\Ch04 - Controlling Program Flow\break.html
Go Links
The preschool class learned to count to 1
The preschool class learned to count to 2
The preschool class learned to count to 3
The preschool class learned to count to 4
The preschool class learned to count to 5
The preschool class learned to count to 6
The preschool class learned to count to 7
Done
My Computer

1. Open an HTML file containing a `while` loop.

   Note: You can use the first `while` loop file created in the section "Using `while` Loops."

2. Within the `while` loop, add an `if` statement to check for a variable.

3. Add a `break` statement to execute if the `if` condition is true.

4. Move the `document.write` statement to the bottom of the loop.

5. Save the file using a different filename.

6. Open the file in a browser.

- When the condition of the `if` statement is true, the loop is terminated.

CONTINUE LOOPS

The `continue` statement stops the execution of a loop and returns to the top of the loop as if all the statements had been executed. Any statements that follow the `continue` statement will not be executed for this time through the loop. This enables you to check for special exceptions within the loop and skip them without interrupting the normal flow of the loop.

CONTINUE LOOPS

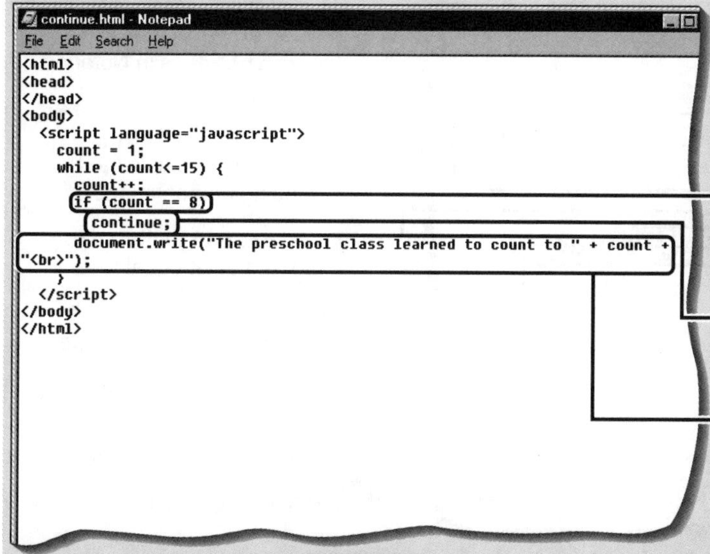

continue.html - Notepad

```
<html>
<head>
</head>
<body>
  <script language="javascript">
    count = 1;
    while (count<=15) {
      count++;
      if (count == 8)
        continue;
      document.write("The preschool class learned to count to " + count +
"<br>");
    }
  </script>
</body>
</html>
```

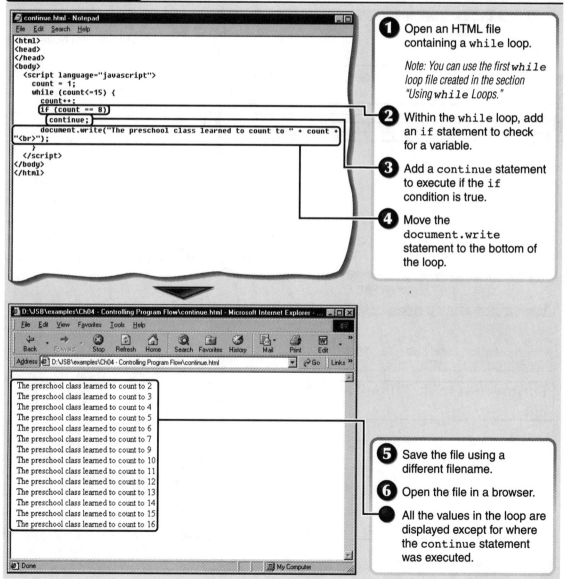

1. Open an HTML file containing a `while` loop.

   Note: You can use the first `while` loop file created in the section "Using `while` Loops."

2. Within the `while` loop, add an `if` statement to check for a variable.
3. Add a `continue` statement to execute if the `if` condition is true.
4. Move the `document.write` statement to the bottom of the loop.

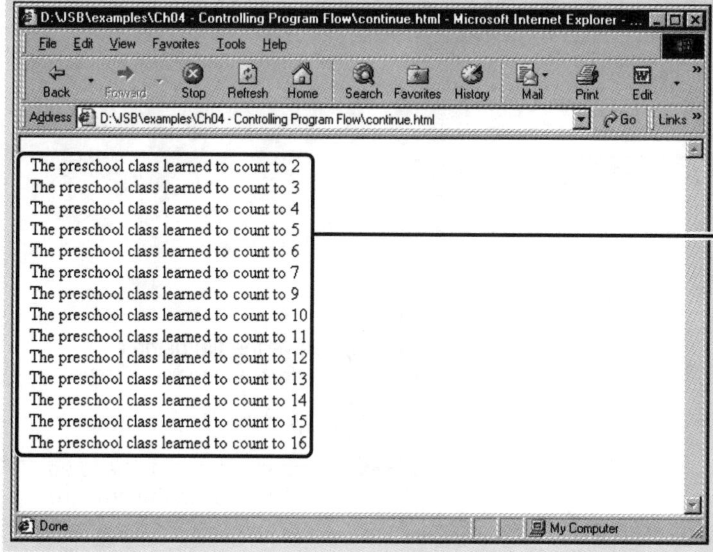

D:\JSB\examples\Ch04 - Controlling Program Flow\continue.html - Microsoft Internet Explorer

The preschool class learned to count to 2
The preschool class learned to count to 3
The preschool class learned to count to 4
The preschool class learned to count to 5
The preschool class learned to count to 6
The preschool class learned to count to 7
The preschool class learned to count to 9
The preschool class learned to count to 10
The preschool class learned to count to 11
The preschool class learned to count to 12
The preschool class learned to count to 13
The preschool class learned to count to 14
The preschool class learned to count to 15
The preschool class learned to count to 16

5. Save the file using a different filename.
6. Open the file in a browser.

- All the values in the loop are displayed except for where the `continue` statement was executed.

USING JAVASCRIPT TIMERS

You can set up timers in JavaScript by using the `window.setTimeout()` function, which accepts two parameters. The first parameter is a JavaScript statement or statements to execute, enclosed within quotation marks. The second parameter is the `time` value in milliseconds to wait before the statement executes. For example, a value of `5000` waits 5 seconds.

USING JAVASCRIPT TIMERS

timeout.html - Notepad

```
<html>
<head>
  <script language="javascript">
    function rabbit() {
      document.write("<h1>Oops, that's not a rabbit.</h1><br/><img
src='dudley.gif'/>");
    }
  </script>
</head>
<body onload="window.setTimeout('rabbit()', 5000)">
  <h1>For my next trick, I'll pull a rabbit out of a hat.</h1>
</body>
</html>
```

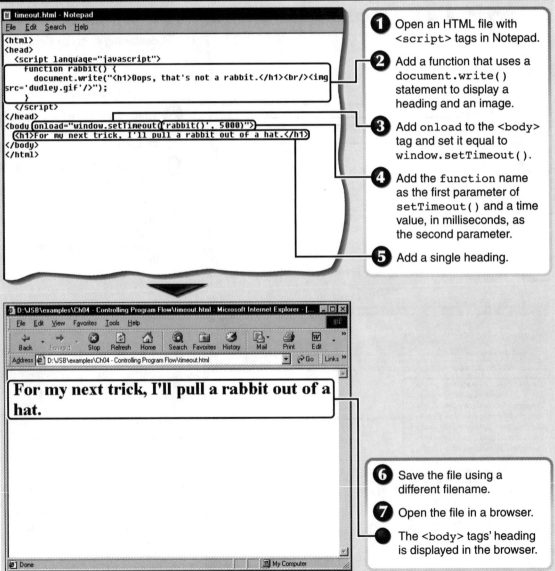

1. Open an HTML file with `<script>` tags in Notepad.
2. Add a function that uses a `document.write()` statement to display a heading and an image.
3. Add `onload` to the `<body>` tag and set it equal to `window.setTimeout()`.
4. Add the `function` name as the first parameter of `setTimeout()` and a time value, in milliseconds, as the second parameter.
5. Add a single heading.

D:\JSB\examples\Ch04 - Controlling Program Flow\timeout.html - Microsoft Internet Explorer

For my next trick, I'll pull a rabbit out of a hat.

6. Save the file using a different filename.
7. Open the file in a browser.

- The `<body>` tags' heading is displayed in the browser.

in an instant

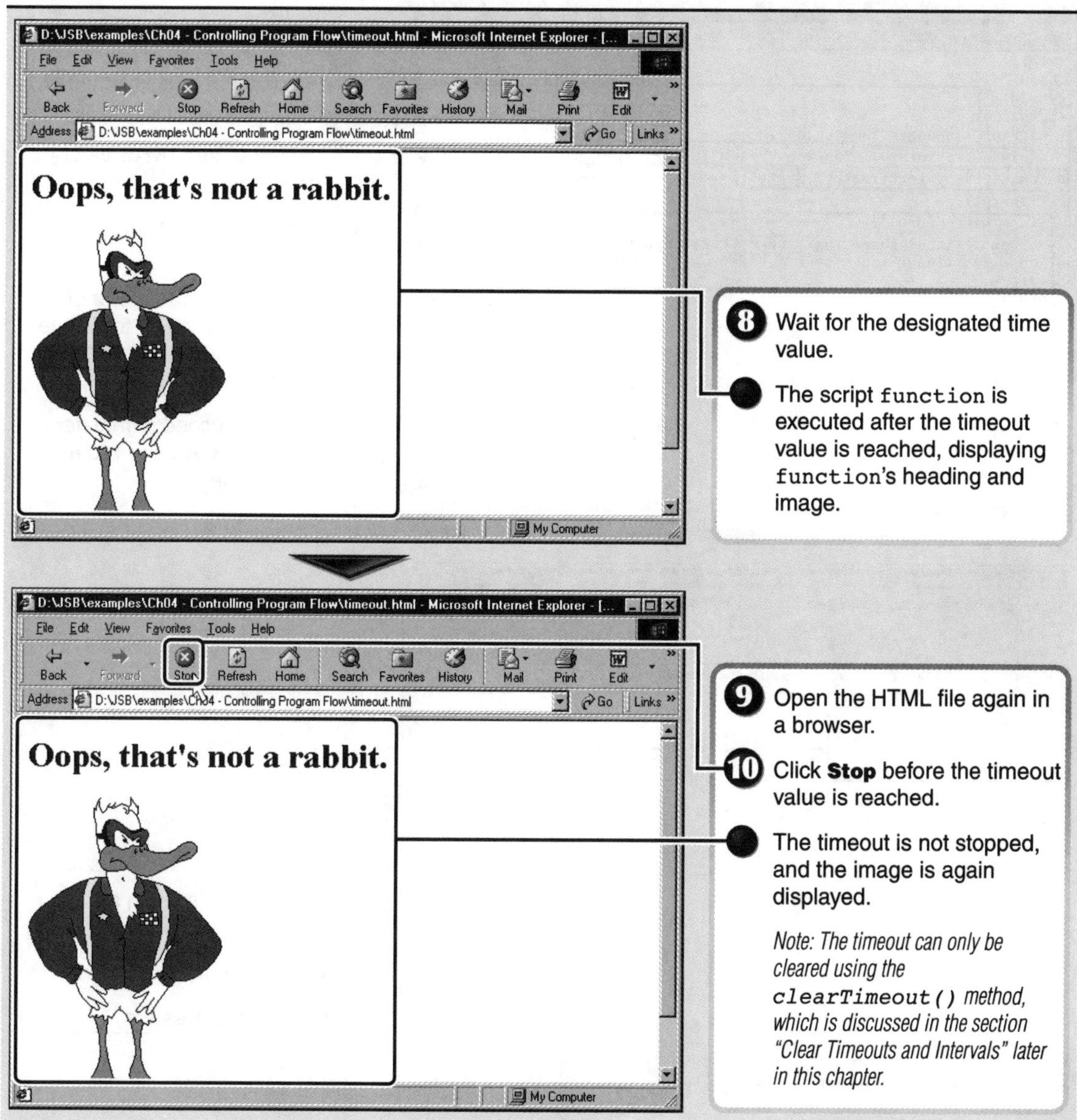
D:\JSB\examples\Ch04 - Controlling Program Flow\timeout.html - Microsoft Internet Explorer
Oops, that's not a rabbit.
My Computer

8. Wait for the designated time value.

- The script `function` is executed after the timeout value is reached, displaying `function`'s heading and image.

9. Open the HTML file again in a browser.

10. Click **Stop** before the timeout value is reached.

- The timeout is not stopped, and the image is again displayed.

Note: The timeout can only be cleared using the `clearTimeout()` *method, which is discussed in the section "Clear Timeouts and Intervals" later in this chapter.*

SET REGULARLY TIMED INTERVALS

You can use the `setInterval()` method to execute a statement, function, or group of statements at regular intervals. The method accepts two parameters: The first is the statement to execute, and the second is the time in milliseconds until the statement is executed. You must enclose the first parameter within quotation marks.

SET REGULARLY TIMED INTERVALS

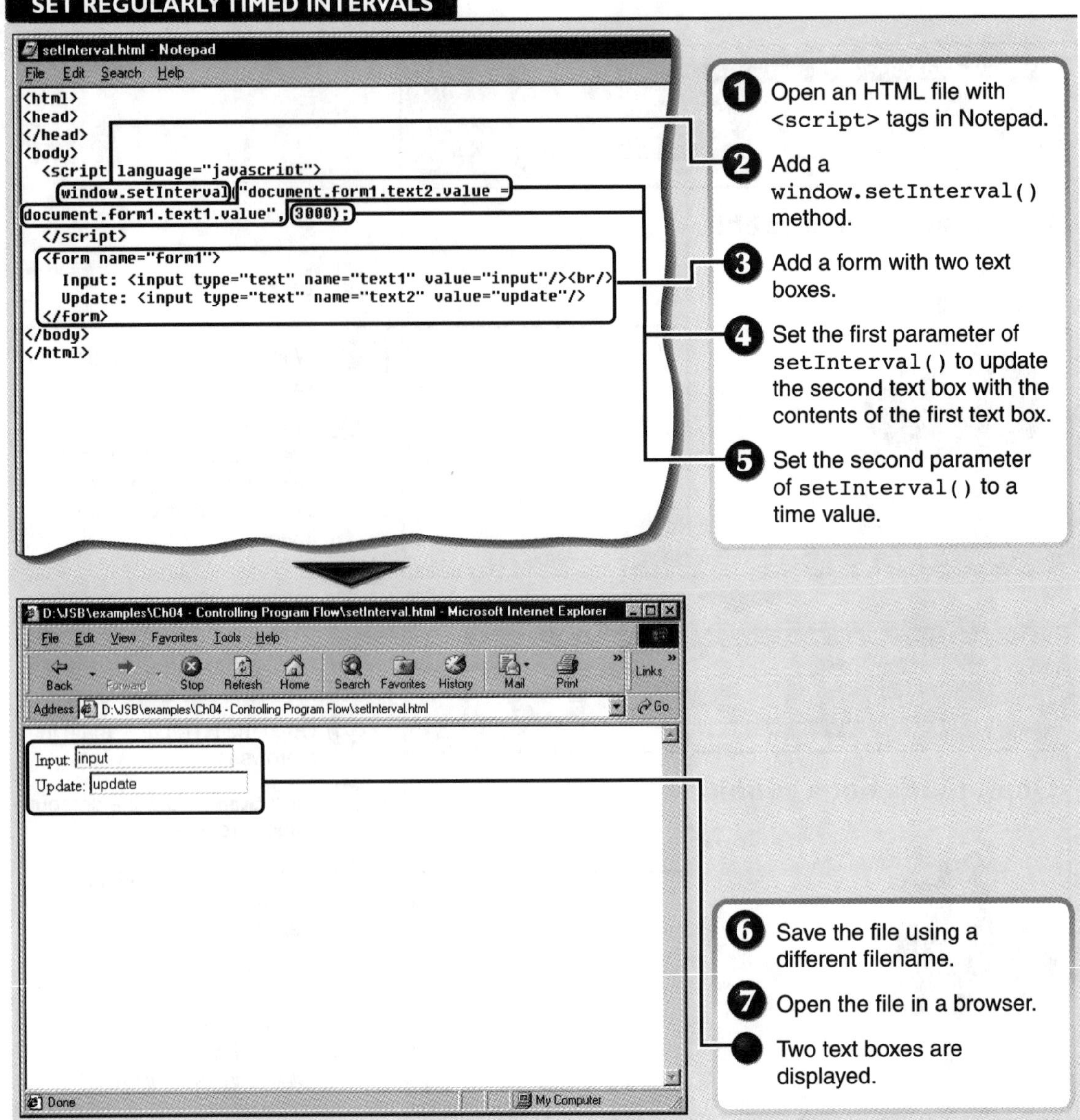

setInterval.html - Notepad
File Edit Search Help
<html>
<head>
</head>
<body>
<script language="javascript">
window.setInterval("document.form1.text2.value =
document.form1.text1.value", 3000);
</script>
<form name="form1">
Input: <input type="text" name="text1" value="input"/>
Update: <input type="text" name="text2" value="update"/>
</form>
</body>
</html>
D:\JSB\examples\Ch04 - Controlling Program Flow\setInterval.html - Microsoft Internet Explorer
File Edit View Favorites Tools Help
Back Forward Stop Refresh Home Search Favorites History Mail Print
Links
Address D:\JSB\examples\Ch04 - Controlling Program Flow\setInterval.html
Go
Input: input
Update: update
Done
My Computer

1. Open an HTML file with `<script>` tags in Notepad.
2. Add a `window.setInterval()` method.
3. Add a form with two text boxes.
4. Set the first parameter of `setInterval()` to update the second text box with the contents of the first text box.
5. Set the second parameter of `setInterval()` to a time value.
6. Save the file using a different filename.
7. Open the file in a browser.

- Two text boxes are displayed.

in an instant

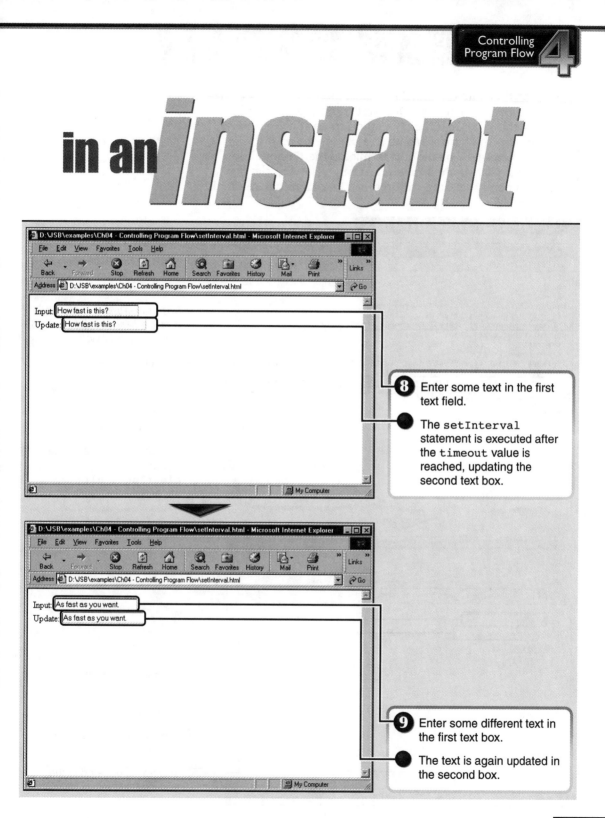

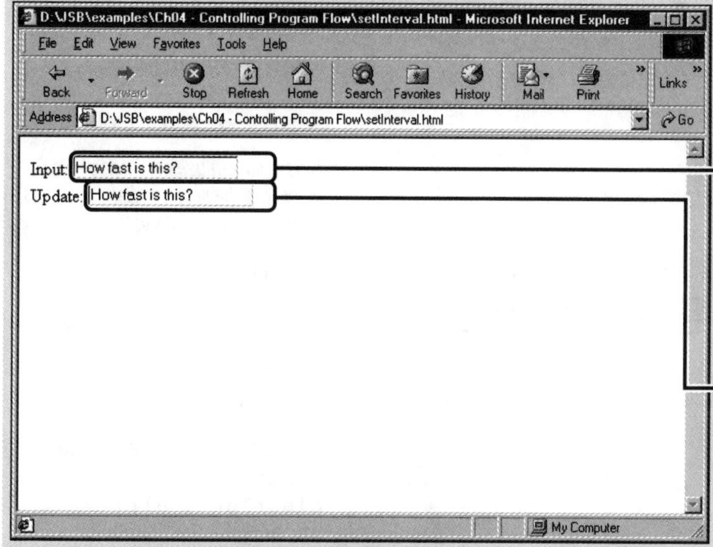

8. Enter some text in the first text field.

- The `setInterval` statement is executed after the `timeout` value is reached, updating the second text box.

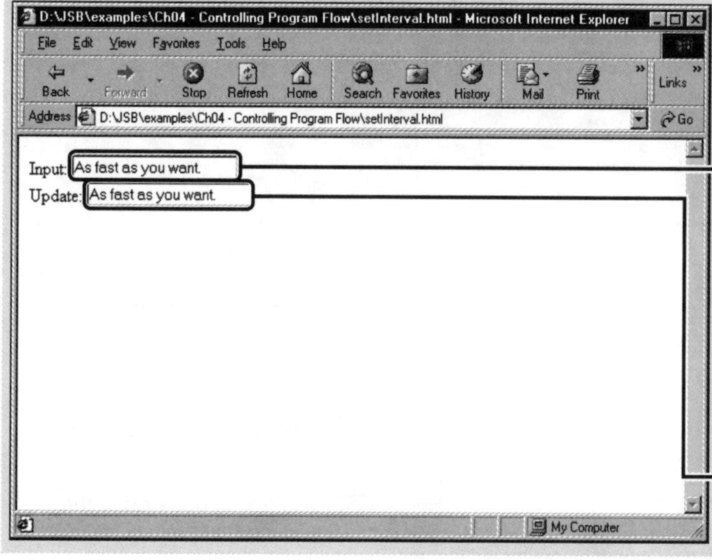

9. Enter some different text in the first text box.

- The text is again updated in the second box.

CLEAR TIMEOUTS AND INTERVALS

JavaScript timeouts can only be cleared internally by using the `clearTimeout()` method. You first name the timeout by assigning the `setTimeout()` method to a variable name; you then use this variable name as a parameter to the `clearTimeout()` method to terminate the timeout. You can use a similar method, `clearInterval()`, for clearing interval timeouts created with the `setInterval()` method.

CLEAR TIMEOUTS AND INTERVALS

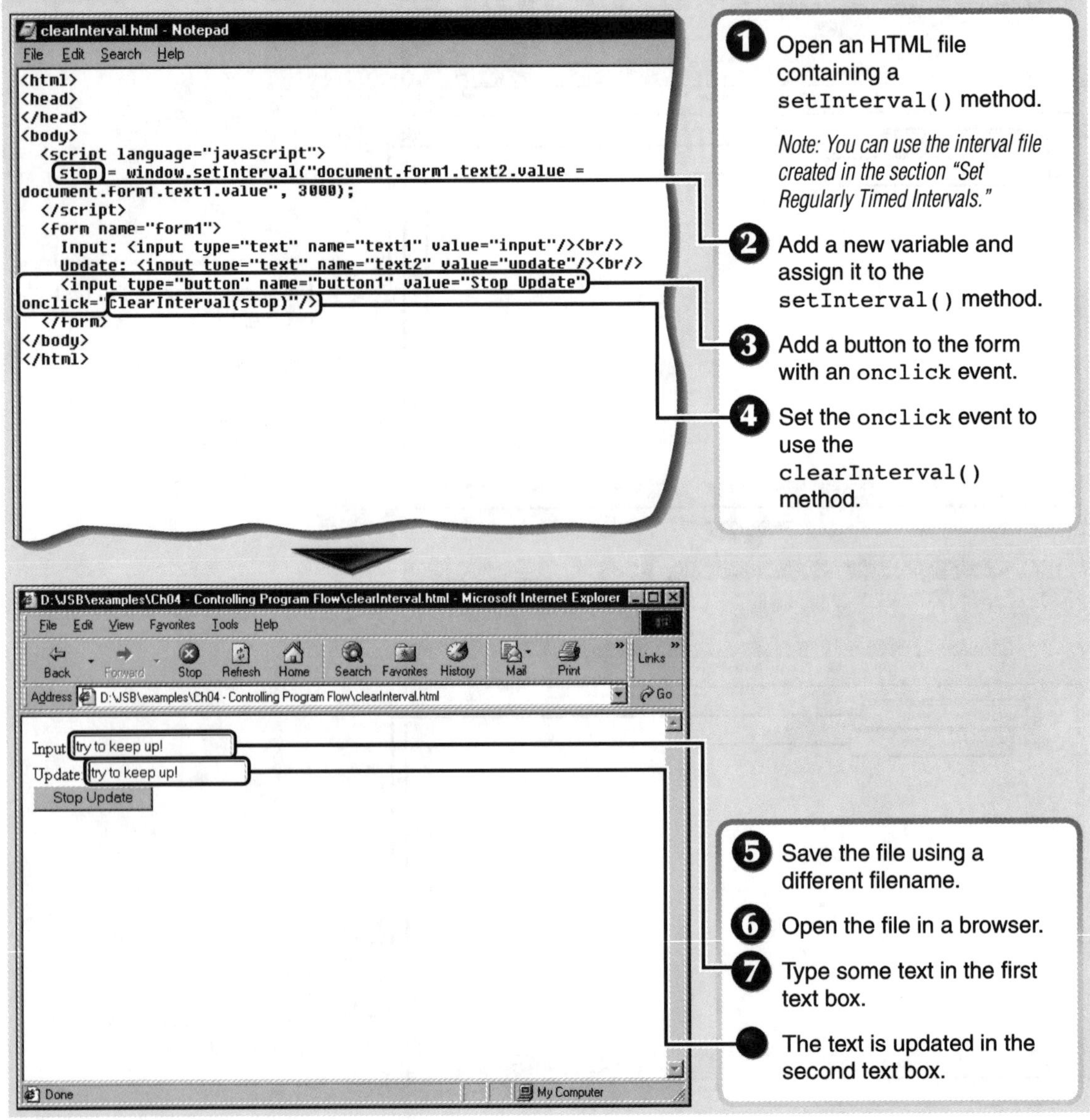

clearInterval.html - Notepad
File Edit Search Help
<html>
<head>
</head>
<body>
<script language="javascript">
stop = window.setInterval("document.form1.text2.value = document.form1.text1.value", 3000);
</script>
<form name="form1">
Input: <input type="text" name="text1" value="input"/>
Update: <input type="text" name="text2" value="update"/>
<input type="button" name="button1" value="Stop Update" onclick="clearInterval(stop)"/>
</form>
</body>
</html>
D:\JSB\examples\Ch04 - Controlling Program Flow\clearInterval.html - Microsoft Internet Explorer
File Edit View Favorites Tools Help
Back Forward Stop Refresh Home Search Favorites History Mail Print Links
Address D:\JSB\examples\Ch04 - Controlling Program Flow\clearInterval.html
Go
Input try to keep up!
Update try to keep up!
Stop Update
Done
My Computer

1. Open an HTML file containing a `setInterval()` method.

   Note: You can use the interval file created in the section "Set Regularly Timed Intervals."

2. Add a new variable and assign it to the `setInterval()` method.

3. Add a button to the form with an `onclick` event.

4. Set the `onclick` event to use the `clearInterval()` method.

5. Save the file using a different filename.

6. Open the file in a browser.

7. Type some text in the first text box.

- The text is updated in the second text box.

in an instant

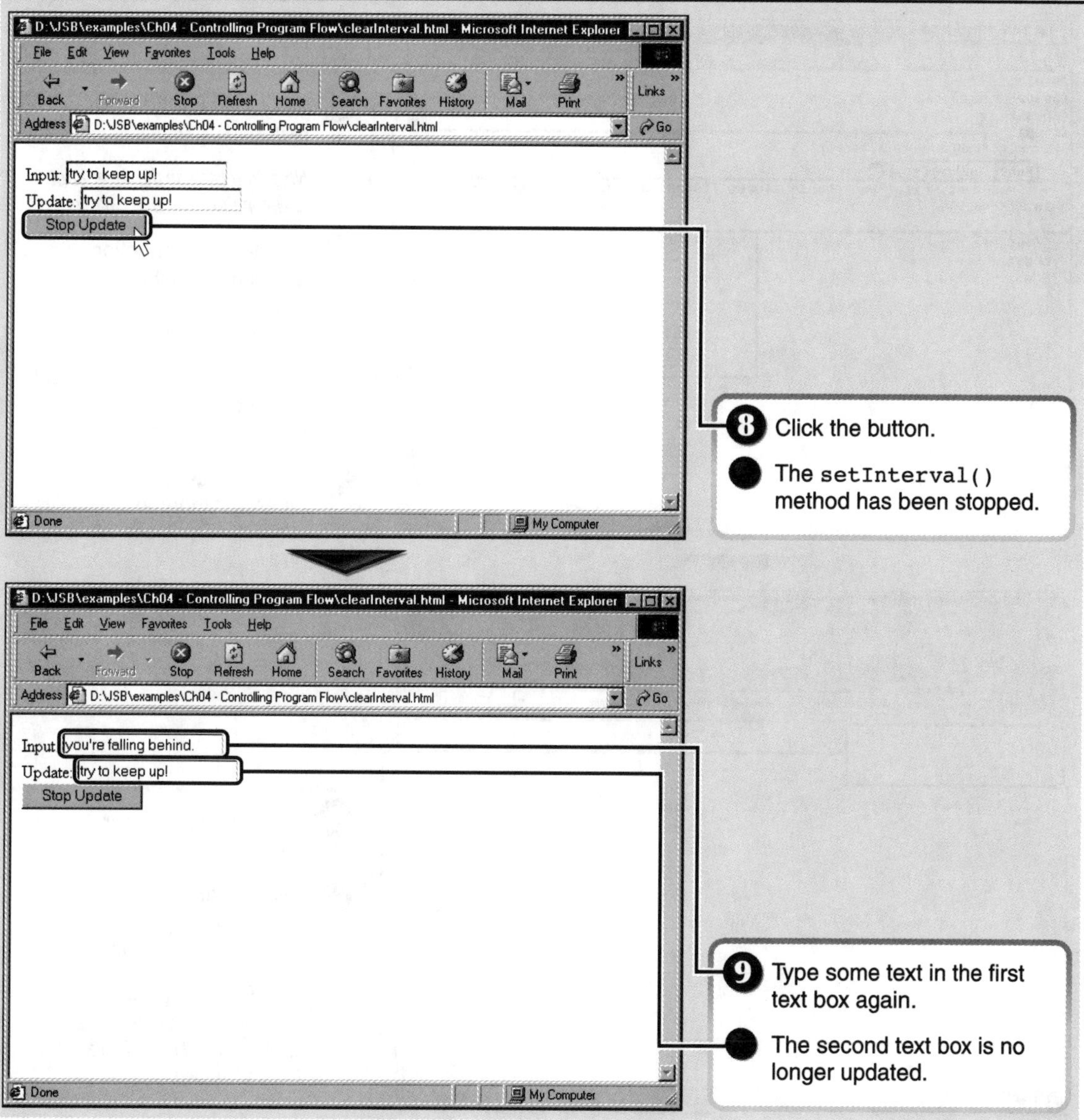
D:\JSB\examples\Ch04 - Controlling Program Flow\clearInterval.html - Microsoft Internet Explorer
Input: try to keep up!
Update: try to keep up!
Stop Update
Input: you're falling behind.
Update: try to keep up!
Stop Update

8 Click the button.

- The `setInterval()` method has been stopped.

9 Type some text in the first text box again.

- The second text box is no longer updated.

DECLARE A FUNCTION

You declare functions with the `function` keyword followed by the function name and parentheses. Parameters for the function are contained within these parentheses, but parameters are not required. All JavaScript statements within the function should be contained within braces after the function declaration. The function statements will not be executed until the function is called.

DECLARE A FUNCTION

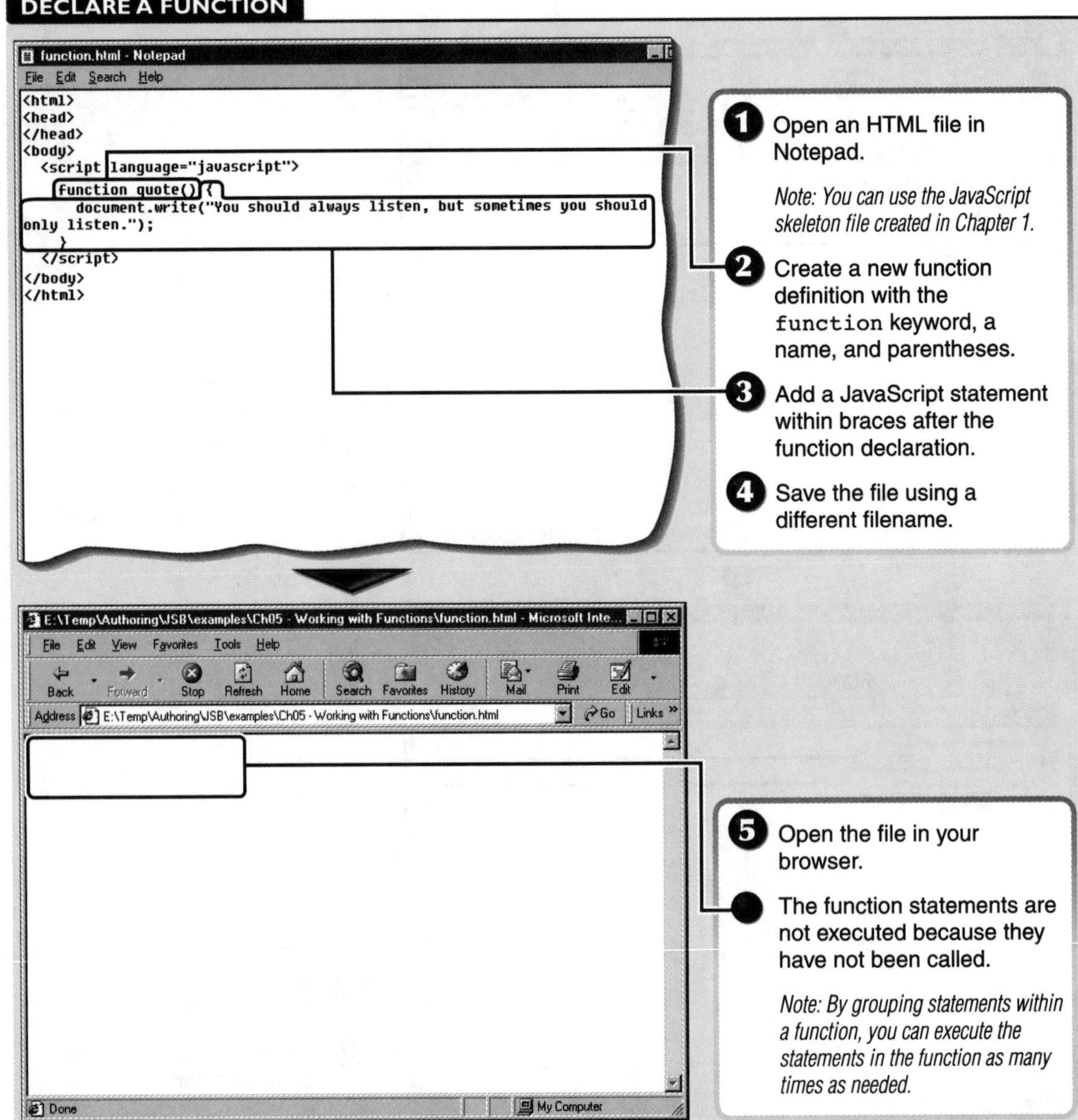

function.html - Notepad
File Edit Search Help
<html>
<head>
</head>
<body>
<script language="javascript">
function quote() {
document.write("You should always listen, but sometimes you should only listen.");
}
</script>
</body>
</html>
E:\Temp\Authoring\JSB\examples\Ch05 - Working with Functions\function.html - Microsoft Inte...
File Edit View Favorites Tools Help
Back Forward Stop Refresh Home Search Favorites History Mail Print Edit
Address E:\Temp\Authoring\JSB\examples\Ch05 - Working with Functions\function.html
Go Links
Done
My Computer

1. Open an HTML file in Notepad.

   Note: You can use the JavaScript skeleton file created in Chapter 1.

2. Create a new function definition with the `function` keyword, a name, and parentheses.

3. Add a JavaScript statement within braces after the function declaration.

4. Save the file using a different filename.

5. Open the file in your browser.

- The function statements are not executed because they have not been called.

Note: By grouping statements within a function, you can execute the statements in the function as many times as needed.

CALL A FUNCTION

After you declare a function, you can execute it at any time from anywhere within the document by listing the function name. You need to include parentheses when calling a function whether or not the function has parameters. For example, if a function is defined as `function hello()`, you can execute the function with the statement `hello();`.

CALL A FUNCTION

function-call.html - Notepad

File Edit Search Help

```
<html>
<head>
</head>
<body>
  <script language="javascript">
    function quote() {
      document.write("You should always listen, but sometimes you should
only listen.");
    }
    quote();
  </script>
</body>
</html>
```

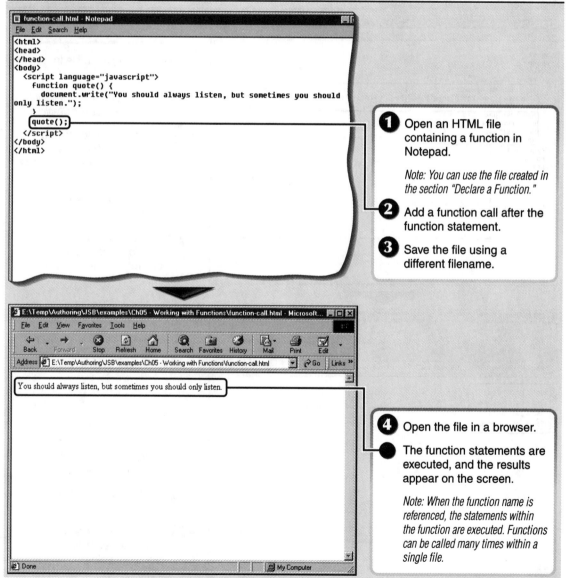

1 Open an HTML file containing a function in Notepad.

Note: You can use the file created in the section "Declare a Function."

2 Add a function call after the function statement.

3 Save the file using a different filename.

E:\Temp\Authoring\JSB\examples\Ch05 - Working with Functions\function-call.html - Microsoft...

You should always listen, but sometimes you should only listen.

4 Open the file in a browser.

- The function statements are executed, and the results appear on the screen.

Note: When the function name is referenced, the statements within the function are executed. Functions can be called many times within a single file.

PASS PARAMETERS TO A FUNCTION

You can pass parameters into a function within the parentheses that follow the function name. The calling statement should include the values, and the function definition should include the variable name. You can then use these variable names within the function. The number of values in the function call should match the number of variables in the function definition.

PASS A SINGLE PARAMETER

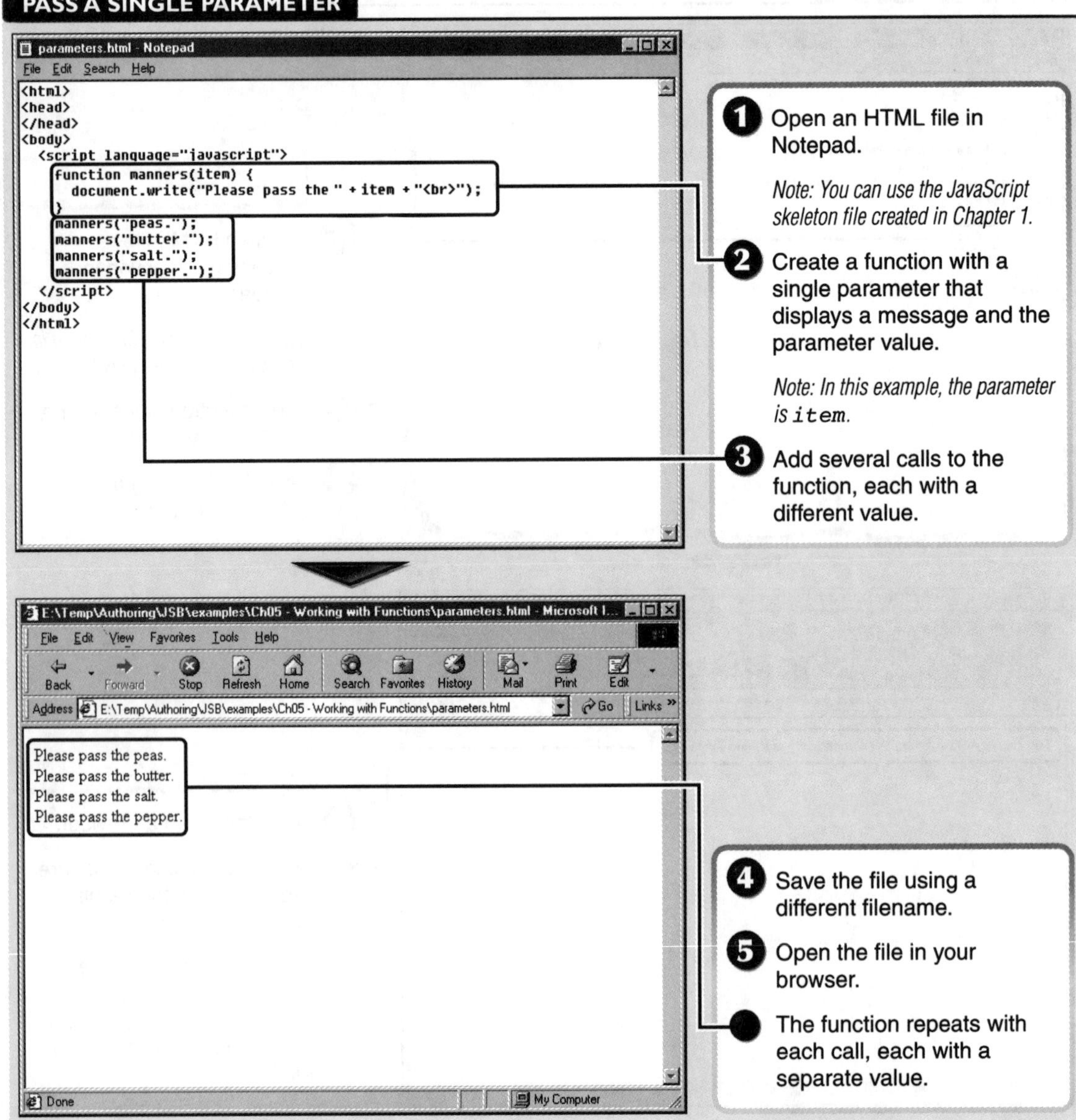
parameters.html - Notepad
File Edit Search Help
<html>
<head>
</head>
<body>
<script language="javascript">
function manners(item) {
document.write("Please pass the " + item + "<br>");
}
manners("peas.");
manners("butter.");
manners("salt.");
manners("pepper.");
</script>
</body>
</html>
E:\Temp\Authoring\JSB\examples\Ch05 - Working with Functions\parameters.html - Microsoft I...
File Edit View Favorites Tools Help
Back Forward Stop Refresh Home Search Favorites History Mail Print Edit
Address E:\Temp\Authoring\JSB\examples\Ch05 - Working with Functions\parameters.html
Go Links
Please pass the peas.
Please pass the butter.
Please pass the salt.
Please pass the pepper.
Done
My Computer

1. Open an HTML file in Notepad.

   Note: You can use the JavaScript skeleton file created in Chapter 1.

2. Create a function with a single parameter that displays a message and the parameter value.

   Note: In this example, the parameter is `item`.

3. Add several calls to the function, each with a different value.

4. Save the file using a different filename.

5. Open the file in your browser.

- The function repeats with each call, each with a separate value.

in an instant

PASS SEVERAL PARAMETERS

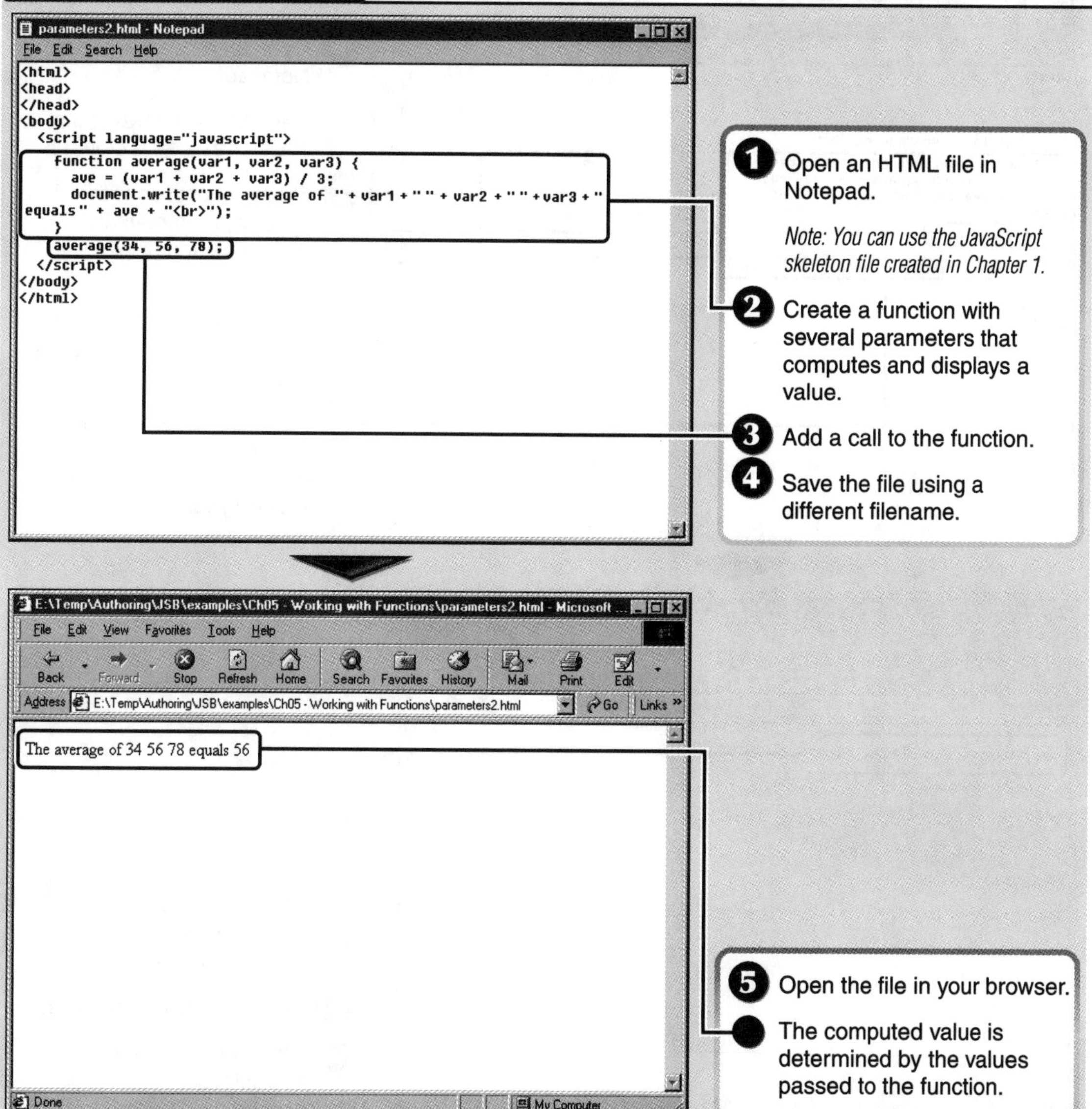
parameters2.html - Notepad
File Edit Search Help
<html>
<head>
</head>
<body>
<script language="javascript">
function average(var1, var2, var3) {
ave = (var1 + var2 + var3) / 3;
document.write("The average of " + var1 + " " + var2 + " " + var3 + " equals " + ave + "<br>");
}
average(34, 56, 78);
</script>
</body>
</html>
E:\Temp\Authoring\JSB\examples\Ch05 - Working with Functions\parameters2.html - Microsoft ...
File Edit View Favorites Tools Help
Back Forward Stop Refresh Home Search Favorites History Mail Print Edit
Address E:\Temp\Authoring\JSB\examples\Ch05 - Working with Functions\parameters2.html Go Links
The average of 34 56 78 equals 56
Done
My Computer

1 Open an HTML file in Notepad.

Note: You can use the JavaScript skeleton file created in Chapter 1.

2 Create a function with several parameters that computes and displays a value.

3 Add a call to the function.

4 Save the file using a different filename.

5 Open the file in your browser.

- The computed value is determined by the values passed to the function.

RETURN VALUES FROM A FUNCTION

You can return values from a function by using the `return` keyword. The type of data returned from a function can be a string, number, or any other value. Because a value is being returned to the function, the function call needs to be a statement that uses the returned value.

RETURN VALUES FROM A FUNCTION

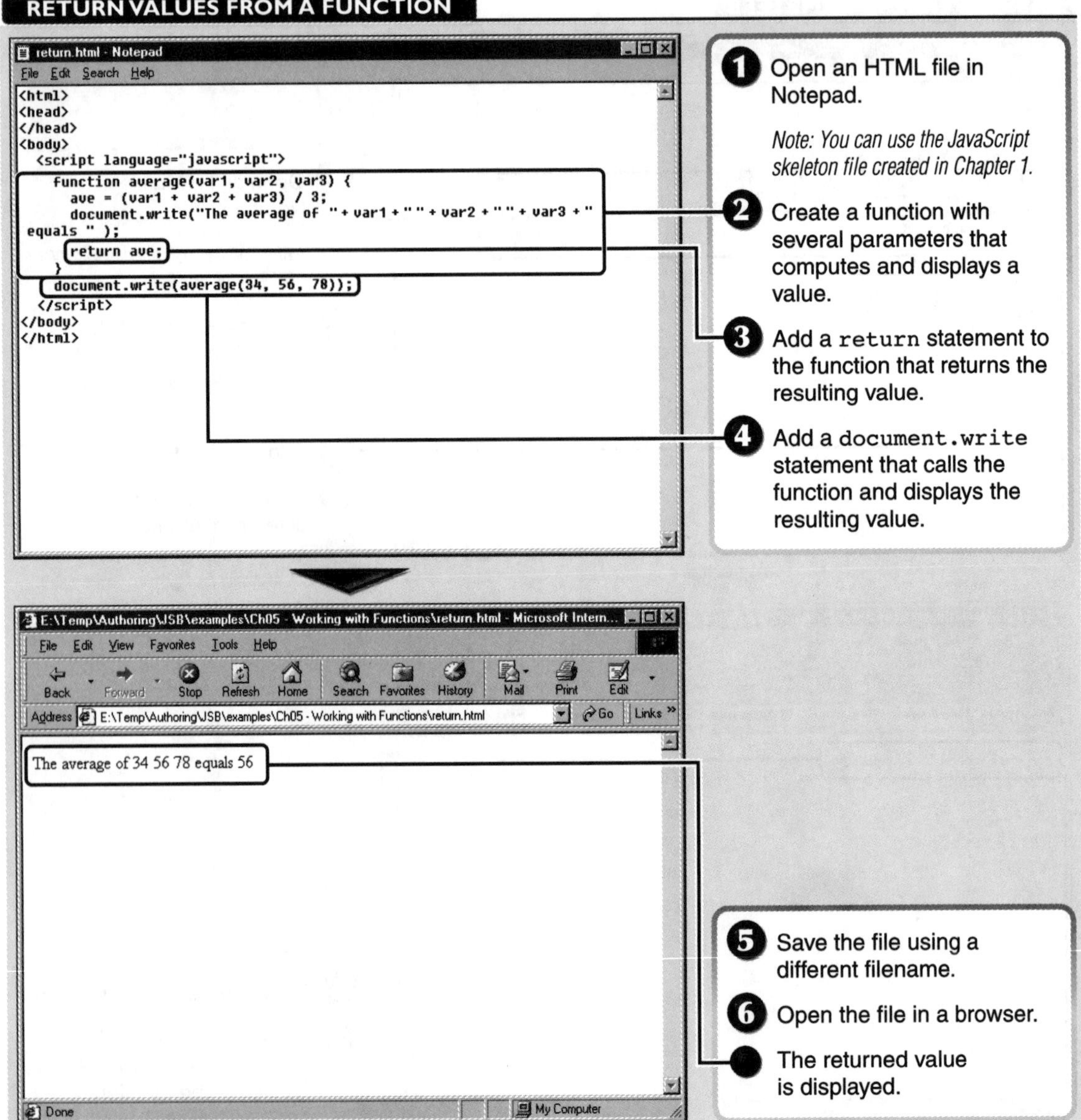

return.html - Notepad
File Edit Search Help
<html>
<head>
</head>
<body>
<script language="javascript">
function average(var1, var2, var3) {
ave = (var1 + var2 + var3) / 3;
document.write("The average of "+ var1 + " " + var2 + " " + var3 + " equals ");
return ave;
}
document.write(average(34, 56, 78));
</script>
</body>
</html>
E:\Temp\Authoring\JSB\examples\Ch05 - Working with Functions\return.html - Microsoft Intern...
File Edit View Favorites Tools Help
Back Forward Stop Refresh Home Search Favorites History Mail Print Edit
Address E:\Temp\Authoring\JSB\examples\Ch05 - Working with Functions\return.html
Go Links
The average of 34 56 78 equals 56
Done
My Computer

1. Open an HTML file in Notepad.

   Note: You can use the JavaScript skeleton file created in Chapter 1.

2. Create a function with several parameters that computes and displays a value.
3. Add a `return` statement to the function that returns the resulting value.
4. Add a `document.write` statement that calls the function and displays the resulting value.
5. Save the file using a different filename.
6. Open the file in a browser.

- The returned value is displayed.

in an instant

RETURN HTML VALUES

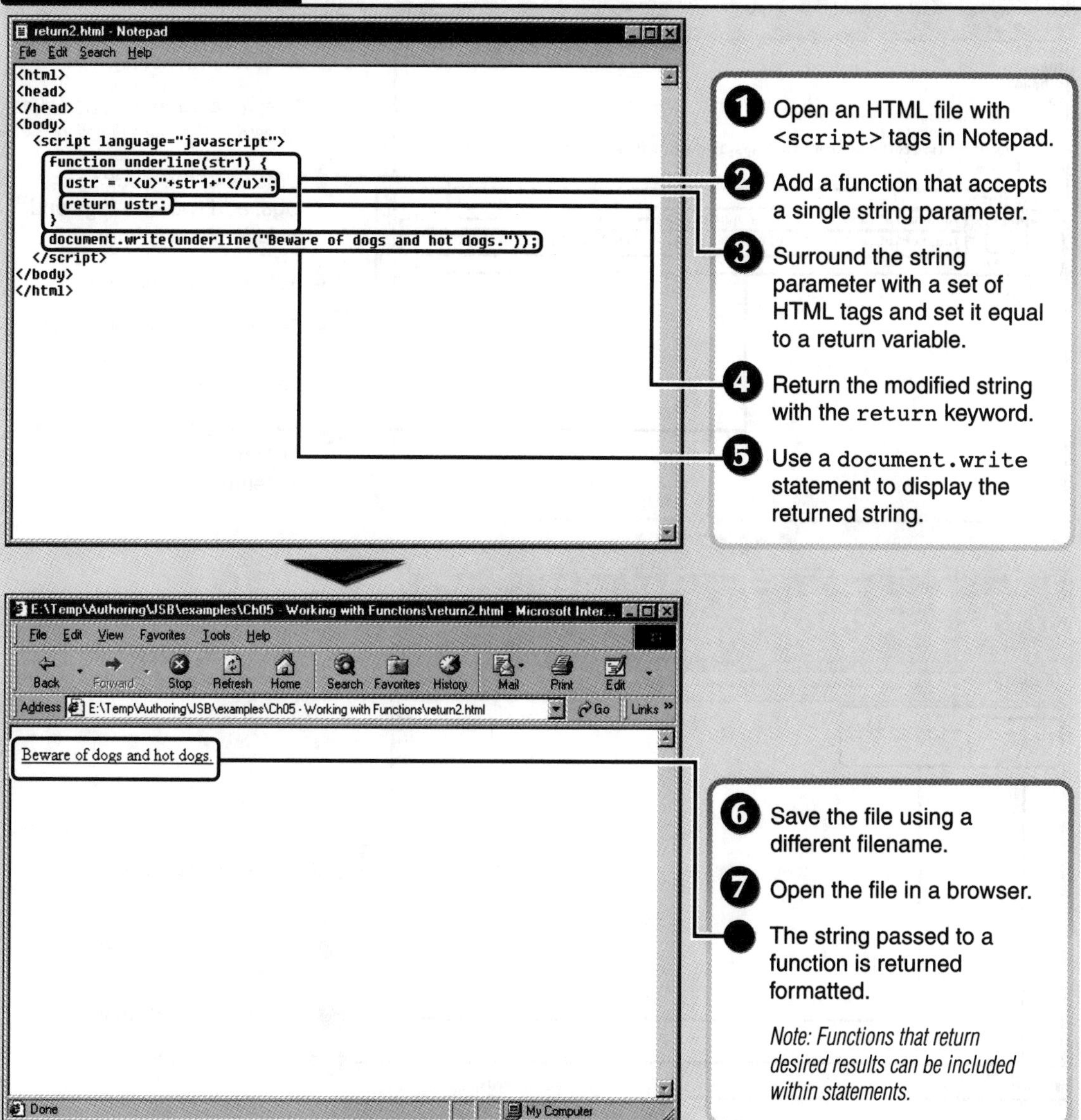
return2.html - Notepad
File Edit Search Help
<html>
<head>
</head>
<body>
<script language="javascript">
function underline(str1) {
ustr = "<u>"+str1+"</u>";
return ustr;
}
document.write(underline("Beware of dogs and hot dogs."));
</script>
</body>
</html>
E:\Temp\Authoring\JSB\examples\Ch05 - Working with Functions\return2.html - Microsoft Inter...
File Edit View Favorites Tools Help
Back Forward Stop Refresh Home Search Favorites History Mail Print Edit
Address E:\Temp\Authoring\JSB\examples\Ch05 - Working with Functions\return2.html
Go Links
Beware of dogs and hot dogs.
Done
My Computer

1. Open an HTML file with `<script>` tags in Notepad.
2. Add a function that accepts a single string parameter.
3. Surround the string parameter with a set of HTML tags and set it equal to a return variable.
4. Return the modified string with the `return` keyword.
5. Use a `document.write` statement to display the returned string.
6. Save the file using a different filename.
7. Open the file in a browser.

- The string passed to a function is returned formatted.

Note: Functions that return desired results can be included within statements.

CALL A FUNCTION FROM AN HTML LINK

You can call functions by referencing the function name within an HTML link. This is done using the `javascript` keyword followed by a colon and the function name. You can also use this format to call a function from a browser's Address field. If you type in **javascript:** and the function name, the function will be executed.

CALL A FUNCTION FROM AN HTML LINK

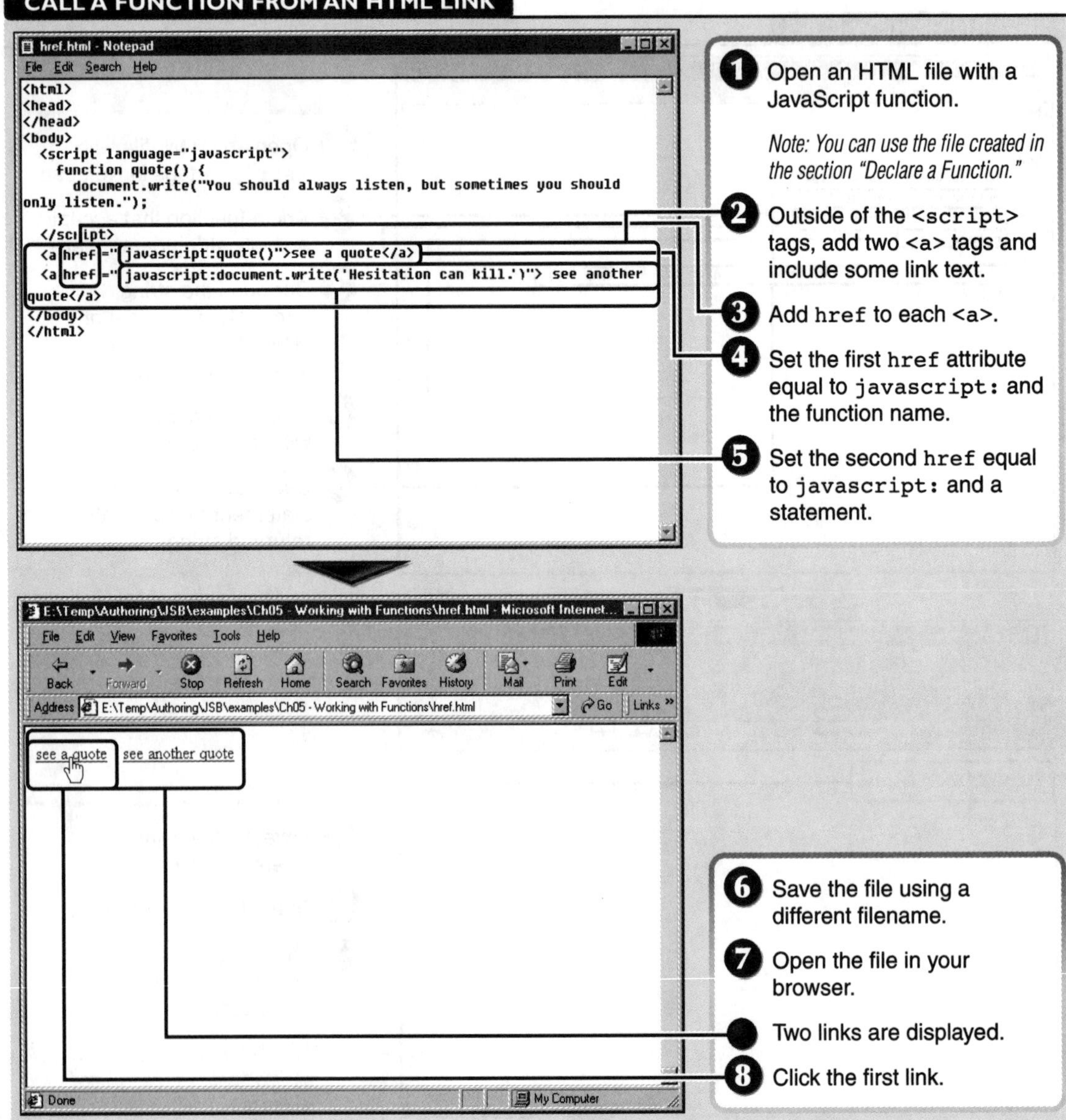
href.html - Notepad
File Edit Search Help
<html>
<head>
</head>
<body>
<script language="javascript">
function quote() {
document.write("You should always listen, but sometimes you should only listen.");
}
</script>
<a href="javascript:quote()">see a quote</a>
<a href="javascript:document.write('Hesitation can kill.')"> see another quote</a>
</body>
</html>
1 Open an HTML file with a JavaScript function.
Note: You can use the file created in the section "Declare a Function."
2 Outside of the <script> tags, add two <a> tags and include some link text.
3 Add href to each <a>.
4 Set the first href attribute equal to javascript: and the function name.
5 Set the second href equal to javascript: and a statement.
E:\Temp\Authoring\JSB\examples\Ch05 - Working with Functions\href.html - Microsoft Internet...
File Edit View Favorites Tools Help
Back Forward Stop Refresh Home Search Favorites History Mail Print Edit
Address E:\Temp\Authoring\JSB\examples\Ch05 - Working with Functions\href.html
Go Links
see a quote see another quote
Done My Computer
6 Save the file using a different filename.
7 Open the file in your browser.
Two links are displayed.
8 Click the first link.

in an instant

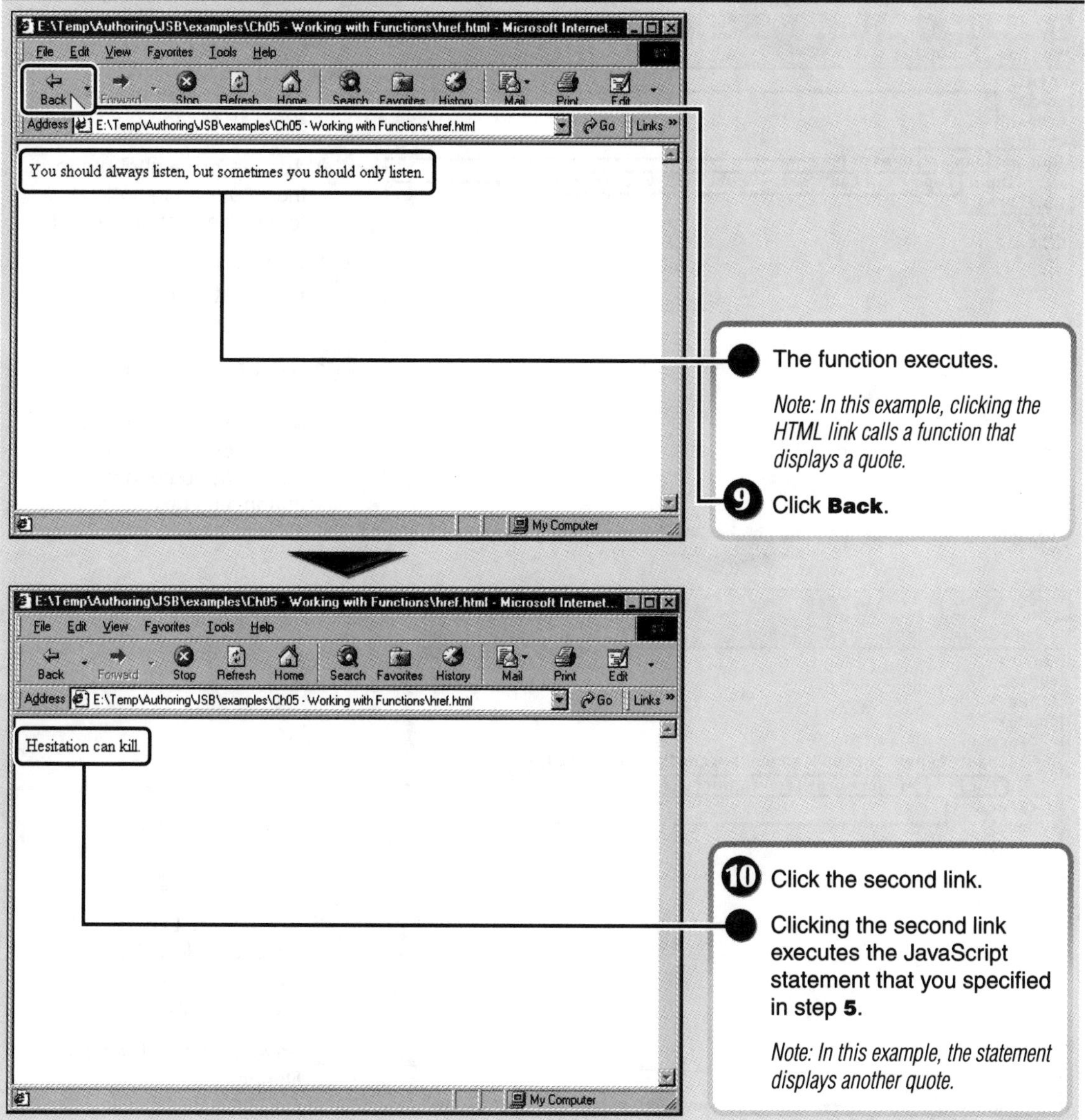
E:\Temp\Authoring\JSB\examples\Ch05 - Working with Functions\href.html - Microsoft Internet...
File Edit View Favorites Tools Help
Back Forward Stop Refresh Home Search Favorites History Mail Print Edit
Address E:\Temp\Authoring\JSB\examples\Ch05 - Working with Functions\href.html
Go Links
You should always listen, but sometimes you should only listen.
My Computer
E:\Temp\Authoring\JSB\examples\Ch05 - Working with Functions\href.html - Microsoft Internet...
File Edit View Favorites Tools Help
Back Forward Stop Refresh Home Search Favorites History Mail Print Edit
Address E:\Temp\Authoring\JSB\examples\Ch05 - Working with Functions\href.html
Go Links
Hesitation can kill.
My Computer

- The function executes.

Note: In this example, clicking the HTML link calls a function that displays a quote.

9. Click **Back**.

10. Click the second link.

- Clicking the second link executes the JavaScript statement that you specified in step **5**.

Note: In this example, the statement displays another quote.

DETECT A MOUSE CLICK

A single mouse click can be detected by using the onclick event. This event can then trigger an effect using JavaScript. The onclick event is typically added to form buttons such as submit and reset buttons, created using the <input/> and/or <button> tags. You can also use the onclick event within the <a> tag.

DETECT A MOUSE CLICK

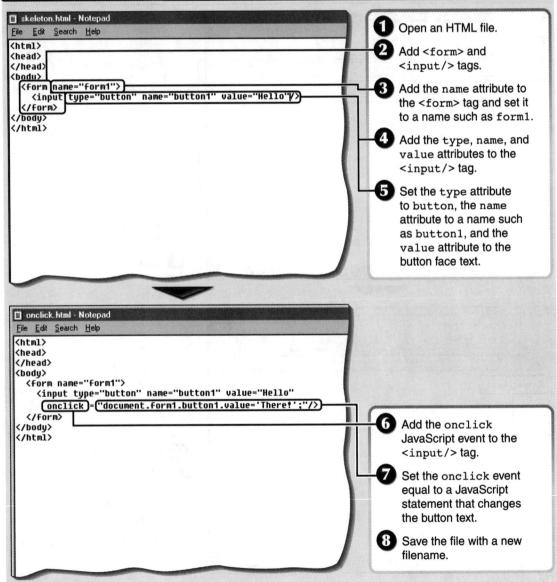

skeleton.html - Notepad

```
<html>
<head>
</head>
<body>
  <form name="form1">
    <input type="button" name="button1" value="Hello"/>
  </form>
</body>
</html>
```

1. Open an HTML file.
2. Add <form> and <input/> tags.
3. Add the name attribute to the <form> tag and set it to a name such as form1.
4. Add the type, name, and value attributes to the <input/> tag.
5. Set the type attribute to button, the name attribute to a name such as button1, and the value attribute to the button face text.

onclick.html - Notepad

```
<html>
<head>
</head>
<body>
  <form name="form1">
    <input type="button" name="button1" value="Hello"
     onclick="document.form1.button1.value='There!';"/>
  </form>
</body>
</html>
```

6. Add the onclick JavaScript event to the <input/> tag.
7. Set the onclick event equal to a JavaScript statement that changes the button text.
8. Save the file with a new filename.

in an instant

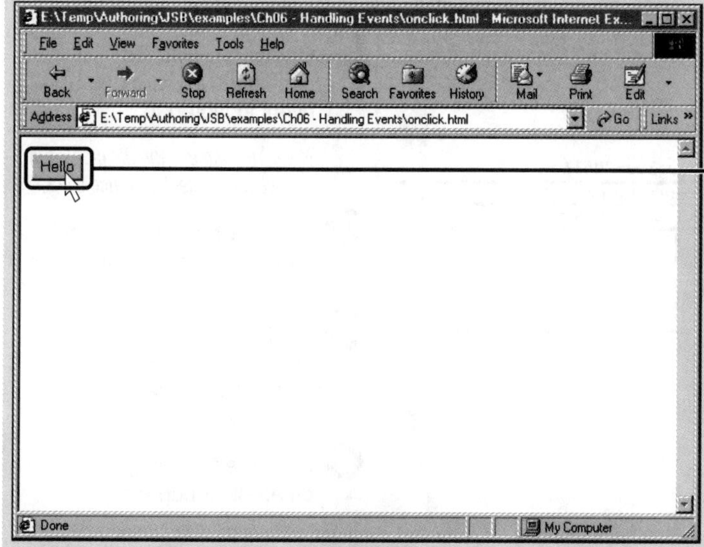

E:\Temp\Authoring\JSB\examples\Ch06 - Handling Events\onclick.html - Microsoft Internet Ex...

Hello

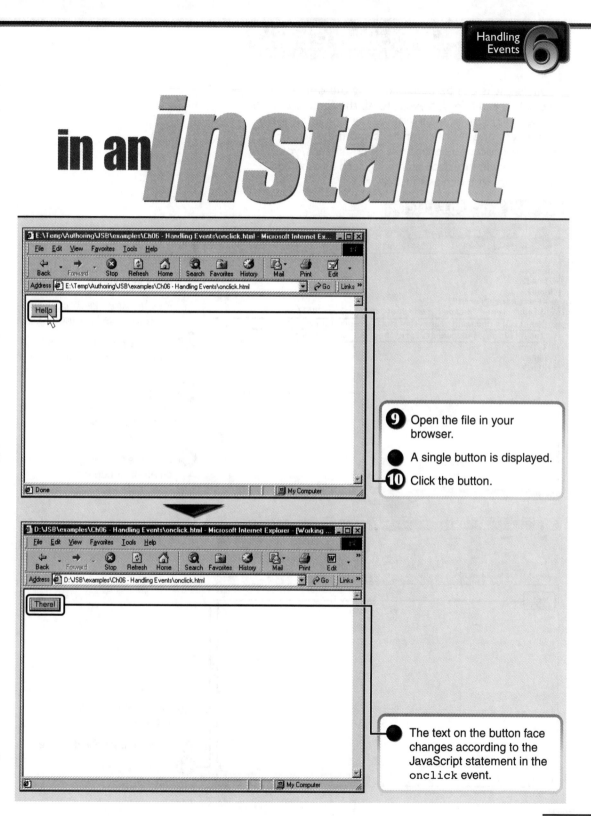

9 Open the file in your browser.

● A single button is displayed.

10 Click the button.

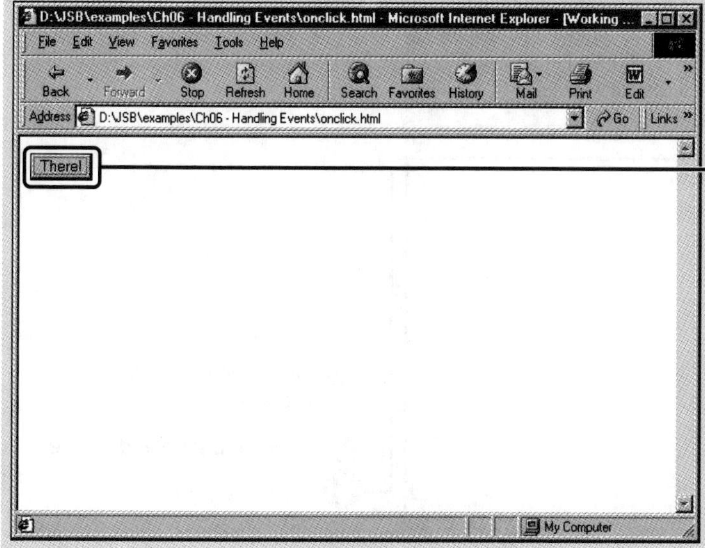

D:\JSB\examples\Ch06 - Handling Events\onclick.html - Microsoft Internet Explorer - [Working ...

There!

● The text on the button face changes according to the JavaScript statement in the `onclick` event.

DETECT A DOUBLE-CLICK

Double-clicks can be detected using the `ondblclick` event. You can add this event to all the same elements as the `onclick` event. If you set the `onclick` event to process one set of commands and the `ondblclick` event to process a second set of commands, you can use single interface elements, such as a button, to accomplish twice as much work.

DETECT A DOUBLE-CLICK

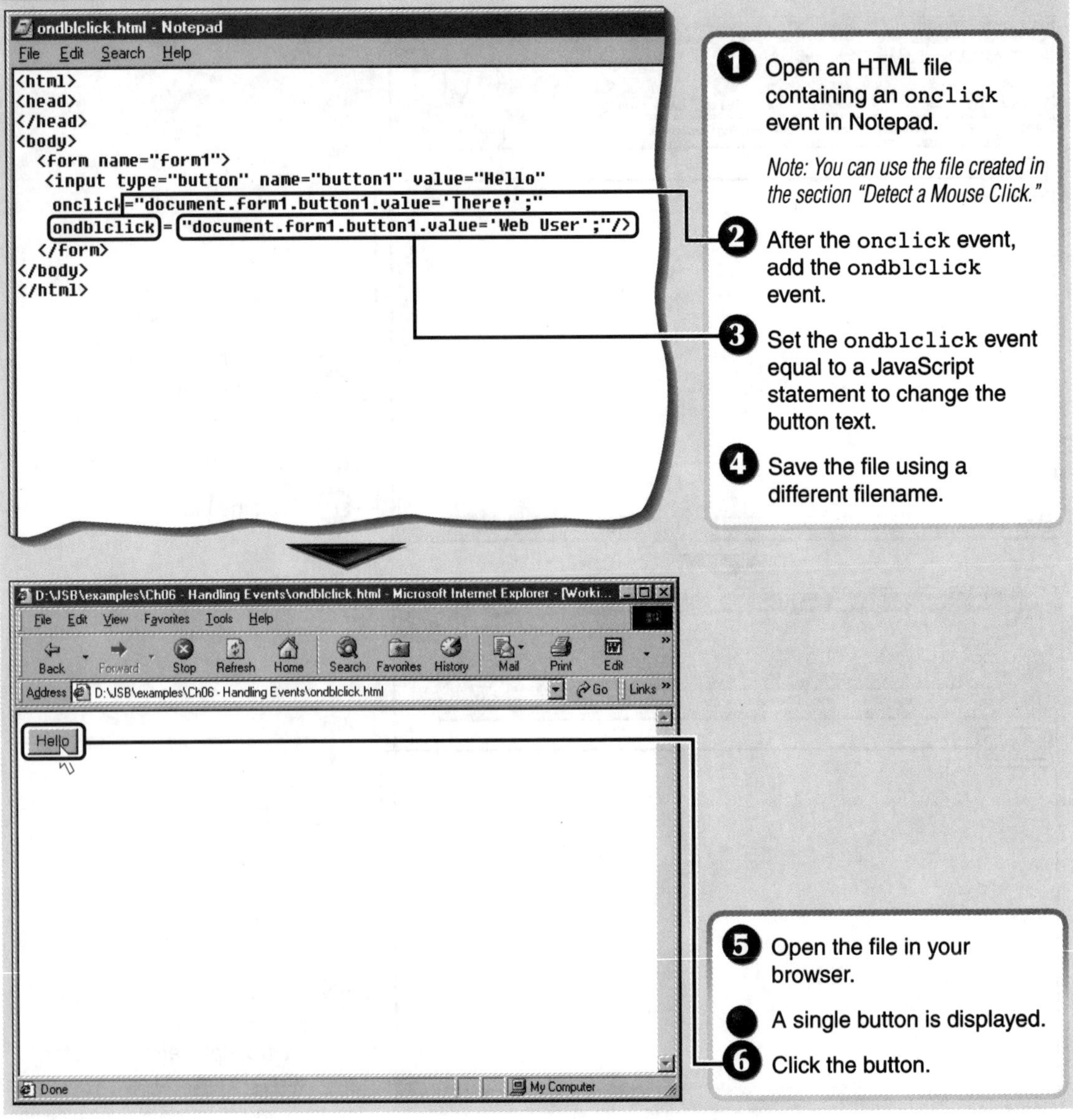

ondblclick.html - Notepad
File Edit Search Help
<html>
<head>
</head>
<body>
<form name="form1">
<input type="button" name="button1" value="Hello"
onclick="document.form1.button1.value='There!';"
ondblclick="document.form1.button1.value='Web User';"/>
</form>
</body>
</html>
D:\JSB\examples\Ch06 - Handling Events\ondblclick.html - Microsoft Internet Explorer - [Worki...
File Edit View Favorites Tools Help
Back Forward Stop Refresh Home Search Favorites History Mail Print Edit
Address D:\JSB\examples\Ch06 - Handling Events\ondblclick.html
Go Links
Hello
Done
My Computer

1 Open an HTML file containing an `onclick` event in Notepad.

Note: You can use the file created in the section "Detect a Mouse Click."

2 After the `onclick` event, add the `ondblclick` event.

3 Set the `ondblclick` event equal to a JavaScript statement to change the button text.

4 Save the file using a different filename.

5 Open the file in your browser.

- A single button is displayed.

6 Click the button.

in an instant

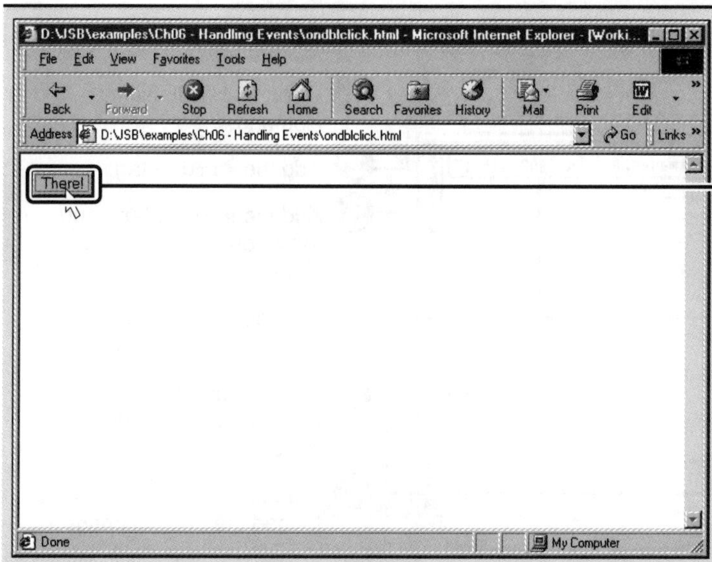

D:\JSB\examples\Ch06 - Handling Events\ondblclick.html - Microsoft Internet Explorer - [Worki...
There!
Done
My Computer

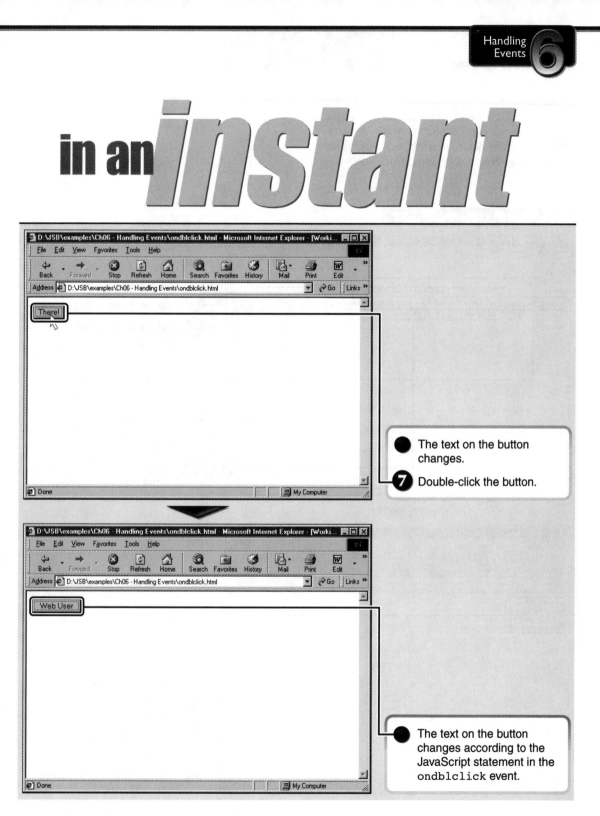

- The text on the button changes.
- 7 Double-click the button.

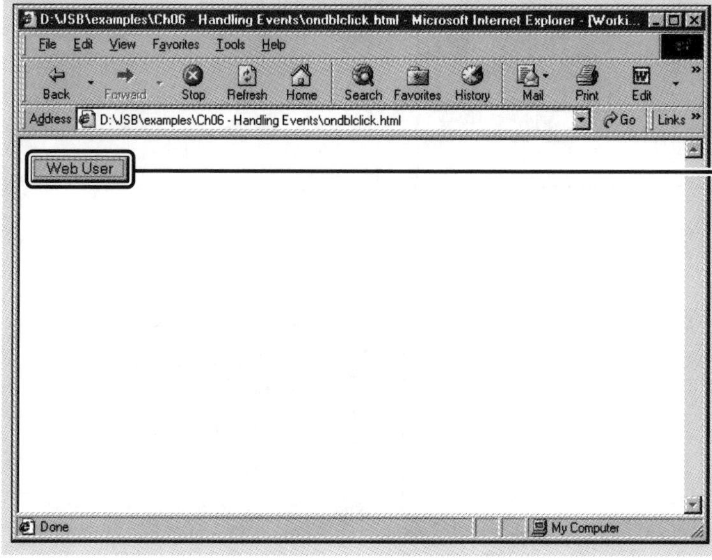

D:\JSB\examples\Ch06 - Handling Events\ondblclick.html - Microsoft Internet Explorer - [Worki...
Web User
Done
My Computer

- The text on the button changes according to the JavaScript statement in the `ondblclick` event.

CREATE ROLLOVER OBJECTS

You can create rollover objects by using the `onmouseover` and `onmouseout` events. These events display a new image in place of the original, such as buttons, hypertext links, image maps, and navigation bars.

CREATE ROLLOVER OBJECTS

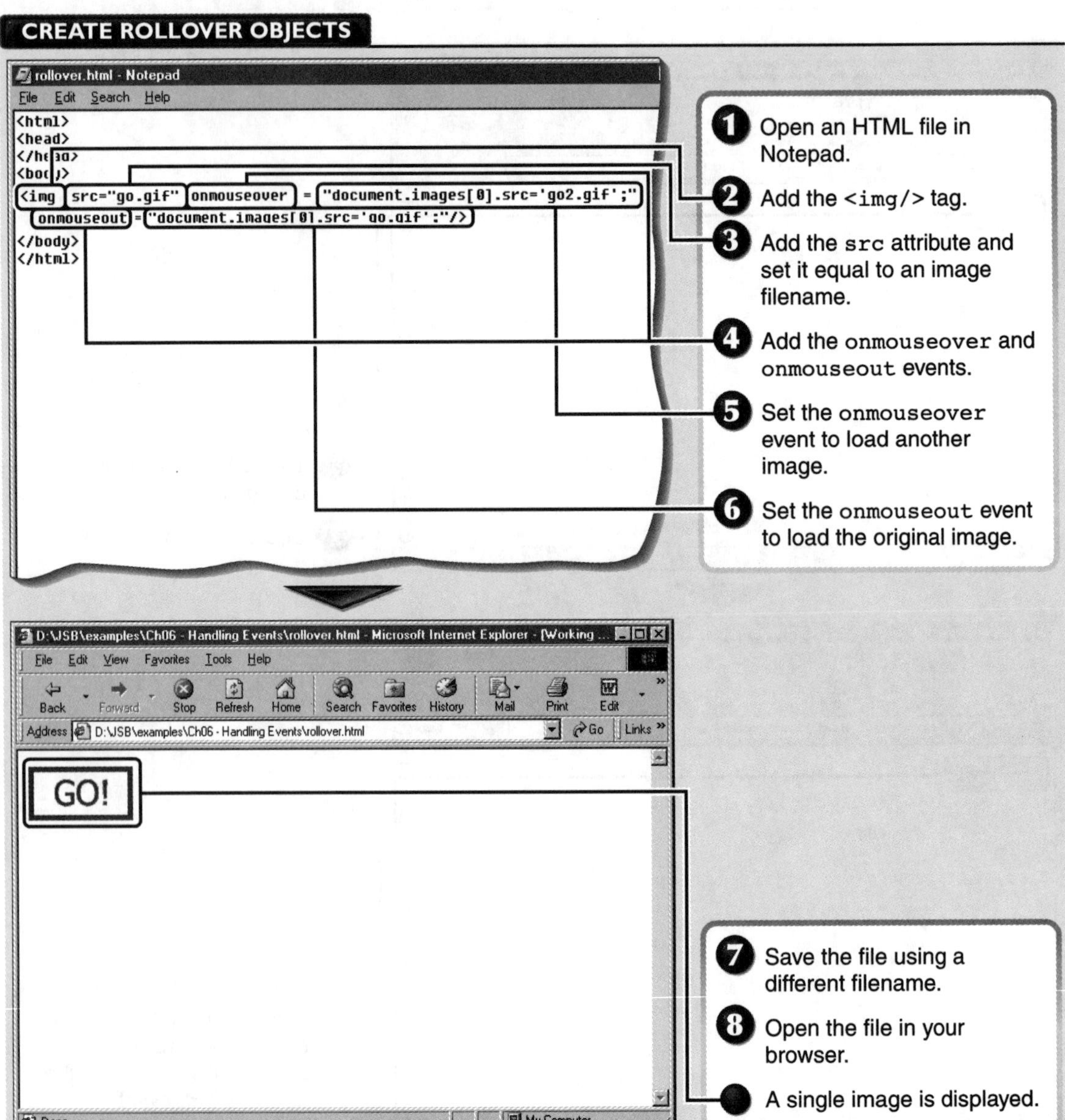

rollover.html - Notepad
File Edit Search Help
<html>
<head>
</head>
<body>
<img src="go.gif" onmouseover = "document.images[0].src='go2.gif';"
onmouseout="document.images[0].src='go.gif';"/>
</body>
</html>
D:\JSB\examples\Ch06 - Handling Events\rollover.html - Microsoft Internet Explorer - [Working ...
File Edit View Favorites Tools Help
Back Forward Stop Refresh Home Search Favorites History Mail Print Edit
Address D:\JSB\examples\Ch06 - Handling Events\rollover.html
Go Links
GO!
Done
My Computer

1. Open an HTML file in Notepad.
2. Add the `<img/>` tag.
3. Add the `src` attribute and set it equal to an image filename.
4. Add the `onmouseover` and `onmouseout` events.
5. Set the `onmouseover` event to load another image.
6. Set the `onmouseout` event to load the original image.
7. Save the file using a different filename.
8. Open the file in your browser.

- A single image is displayed.

in an instant

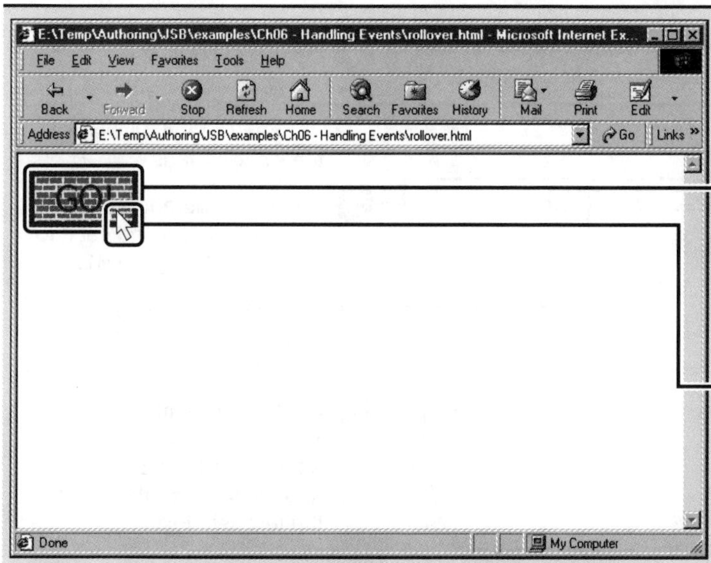

E:\Temp\Authoring\JSB\examples\Ch06 - Handling Events\rollover.html - Microsoft Internet Ex...

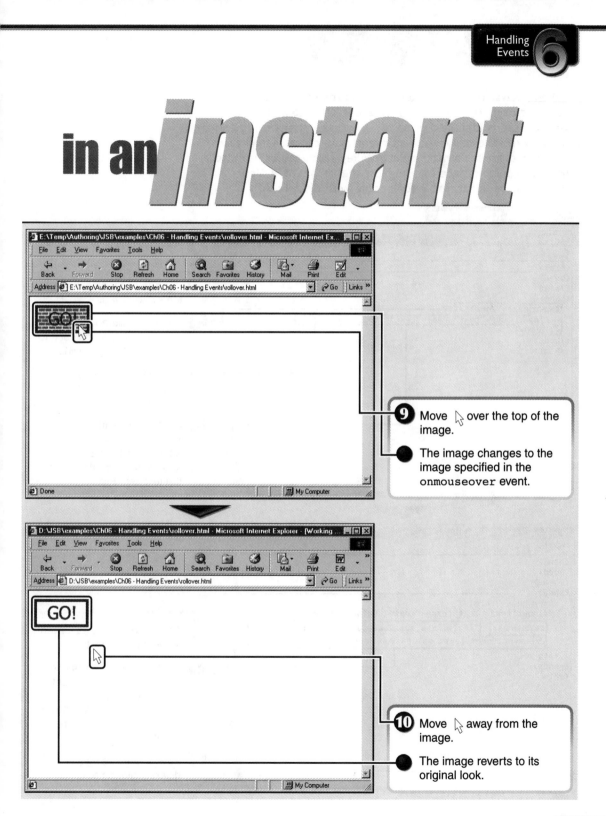

9 Move ⇖ over the top of the image.

- The image changes to the image specified in the `onmouseover` event.

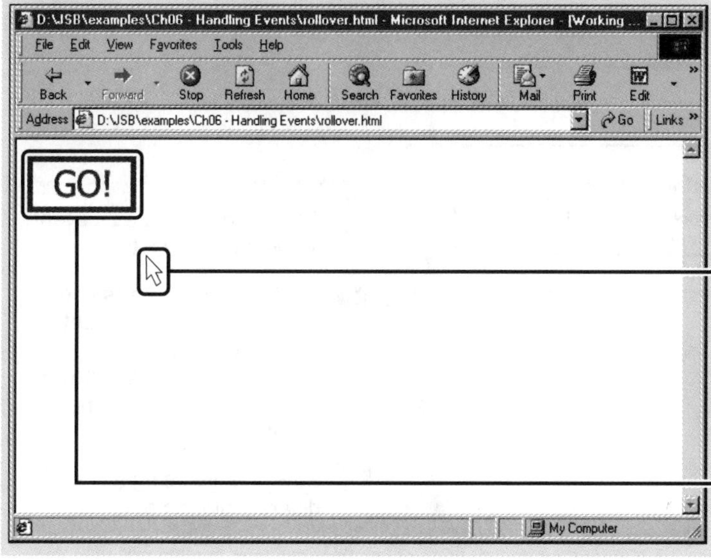

D:\JSB\examples\Ch06 - Handling Events\rollover.html - Microsoft Internet Explorer - [Working ...

10 Move ⇖ away from the image.

- The image reverts to its original look.

DETECT A KEY PRESS

When a keystroke on the keyboard is pressed, it can be detected using the `onkeypress` event. The actual key that was pressed is identified using the `window.event.keyCode` object. With the `onkeypress` events, you can assign all your interface elements a quick selection key. This enables users to navigate your interface by using just the keyboard. It also makes your site accessible for people with disabilities.

DETECT A KEY PRESS

skeleton.html - Notepad

```
<html>
<head>
</head>
<body>
  <form name="form1">
    <input type="text" name="text1" value="Hello"/>
  </form>
</body>
</html>
```

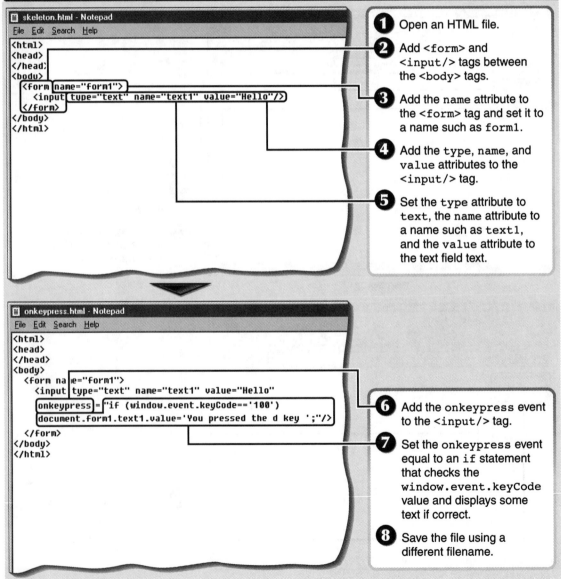

1. Open an HTML file.
2. Add `<form>` and `<input/>` tags between the `<body>` tags.
3. Add the `name` attribute to the `<form>` tag and set it to a name such as `form1`.
4. Add the `type`, `name`, and `value` attributes to the `<input/>` tag.
5. Set the `type` attribute to `text`, the `name` attribute to a name such as `text1`, and the `value` attribute to the text field text.

onkeypress.html - Notepad

```
<html>
<head>
</head>
<body>
  <form name="form1">
    <input type="text" name="text1" value="Hello"
    onkeypress="if (window.event.keyCode=='100')
    document.form1.text1.value='You pressed the d key ';"/>
  </form>
</body>
</html>
```

6. Add the `onkeypress` event to the `<input/>` tag.
7. Set the `onkeypress` event equal to an `if` statement that checks the `window.event.keyCode` value and displays some text if correct.
8. Save the file using a different filename.

in an instant

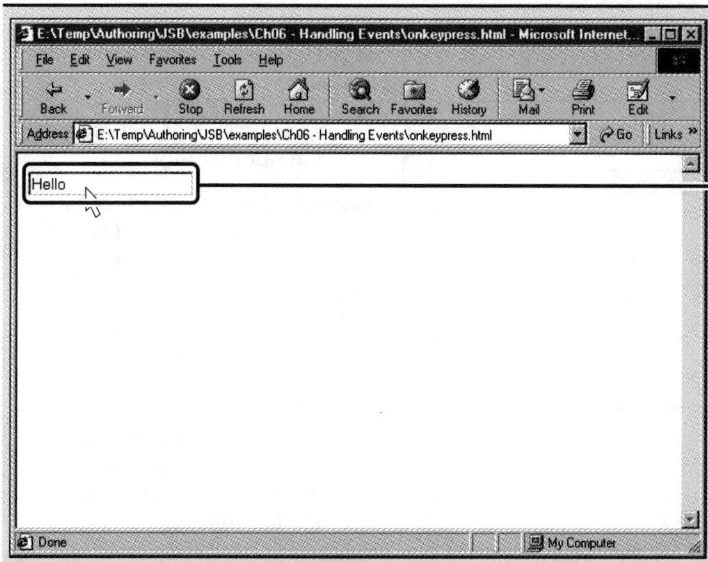

E:\Temp\Authoring\JSB\examples\Ch06 - Handling Events\onkeypress.html - Microsoft Internet...

Hello

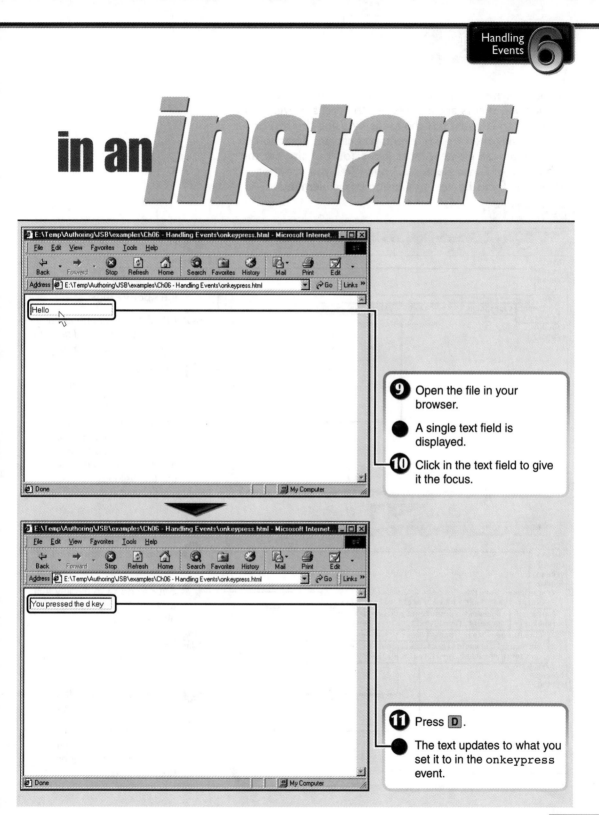

9 Open the file in your browser.

• A single text field is displayed.

10 Click in the text field to give it the focus.

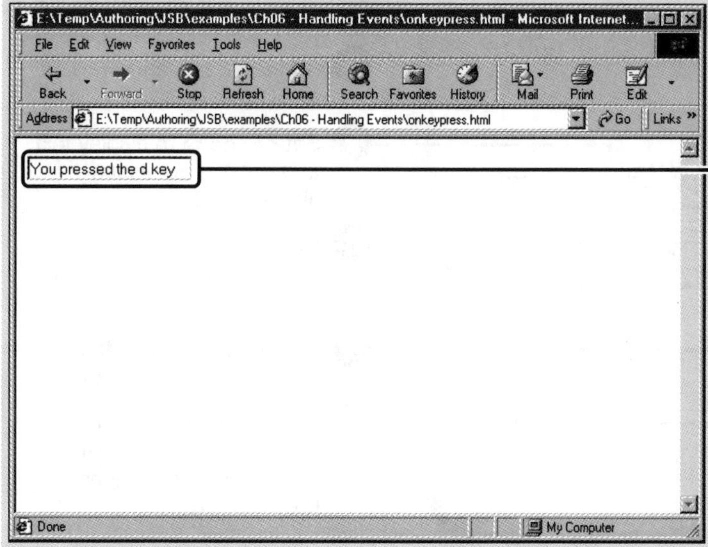

E:\Temp\Authoring\JSB\examples\Ch06 - Handling Events\onkeypress.html - Microsoft Internet...

You pressed the d key

11 Press D.

• The text updates to what you set it to in the `onkeypress` event.

SET FOCUS

Focus determines which `form` element will be affected if the keyboard keys are pressed. As the focus moves, you can detect if an element has the focus by using the `onfocus` event. Using the `onblur` event, you can set an action to occur when an element loses focus. You can also set the tab order of `form` elements. Using Tab, you can then move the focus between different `form` elements.

SET FOCUS

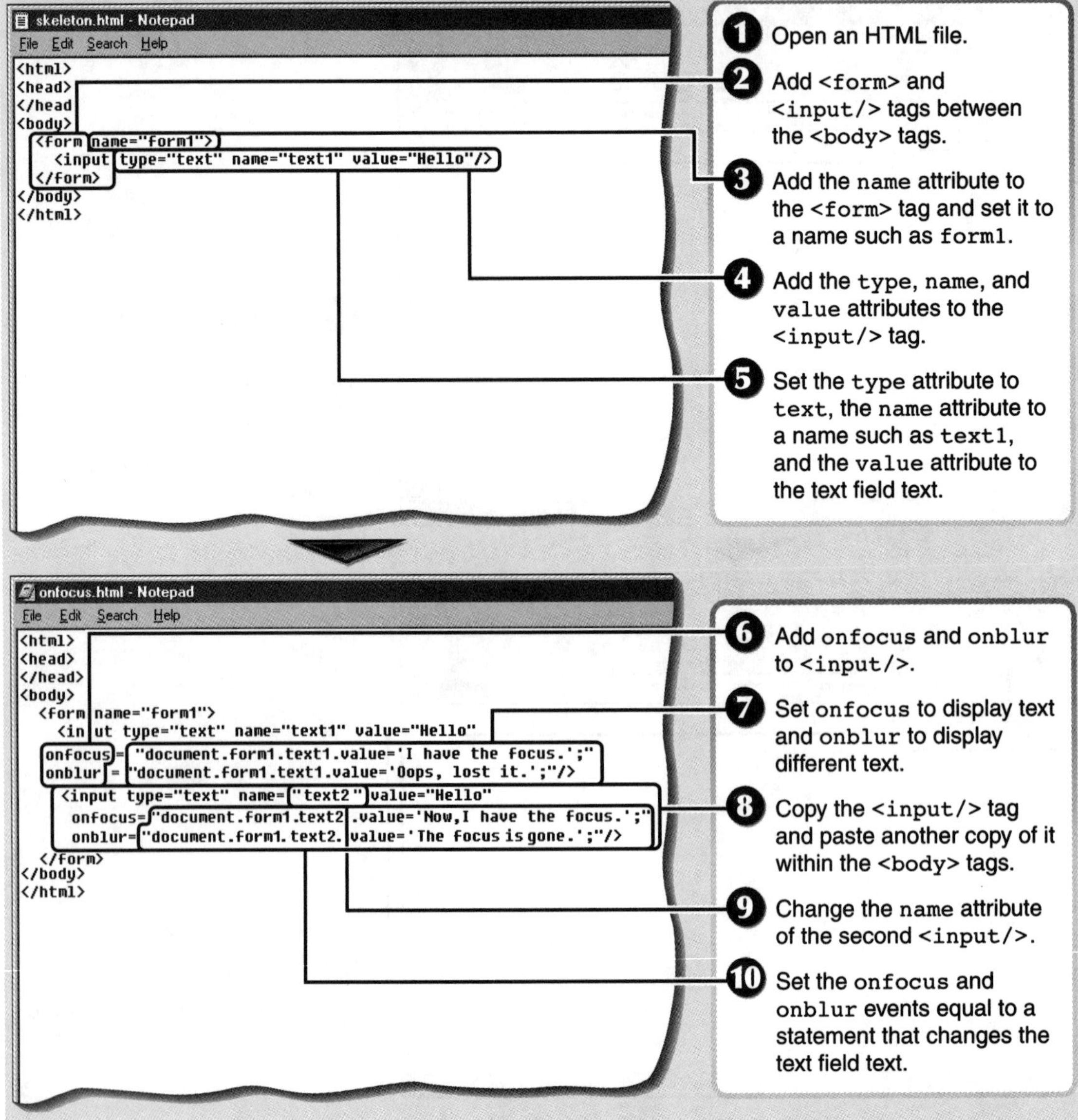

skeleton.html - Notepad
File Edit Search Help
<html>
<head>
</head>
<body>
<form name="form1">
<input type="text" name="text1" value="Hello"/>
</form>
</body>
</html>
onfocus.html - Notepad
File Edit Search Help
<html>
<head>
</head>
<body>
<form name="form1">
<input type="text" name="text1" value="Hello"
onfocus= "document.form1.text1.value='I have the focus.';"
onblur = "document.form1.text1.value='Oops, lost it.';"/>
<input type="text" name="text2" value="Hello"
onfocus="document.form1.text2.value='Now,I have the focus.';"
onblur="document.form1.text2.value='The focus is gone.';"/>
</form>
</body>
</html>

1. Open an HTML file.
2. Add `<form>` and `<input/>` tags between the <body> tags.
3. Add the `name` attribute to the `<form>` tag and set it to a name such as `form1`.
4. Add the `type`, `name`, and `value` attributes to the `<input/>` tag.
5. Set the `type` attribute to `text`, the `name` attribute to a name such as `text1`, and the `value` attribute to the text field text.
6. Add `onfocus` and `onblur` to `<input/>`.
7. Set `onfocus` to display text and `onblur` to display different text.
8. Copy the `<input/>` tag and paste another copy of it within the <body> tags.
9. Change the `name` attribute of the second `<input/>`.
10. Set the `onfocus` and `onblur` events equal to a statement that changes the text field text.

in an instant

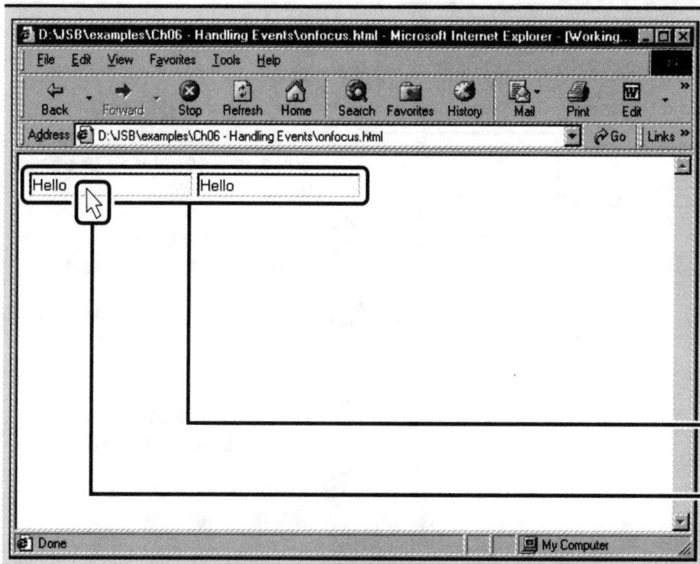

D:\JSB\examples\Ch06 - Handling Events\onfocus.html - Microsoft Internet Explorer - [Working...
File Edit View Favorites Tools Help
Back Forward Stop Refresh Home Search Favorites History Mail Print Edit
Address D:\JSB\examples\Ch06 - Handling Events\onfocus.html
Go Links
Hello
Hello
Done
My Computer

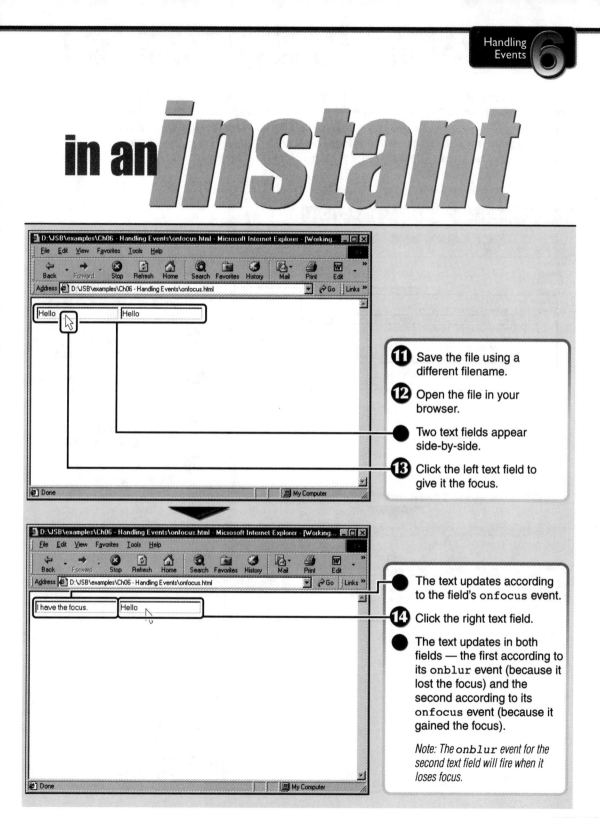

11. Save the file using a different filename.

12. Open the file in your browser.

- Two text fields appear side-by-side.

13. Click the left text field to give it the focus.

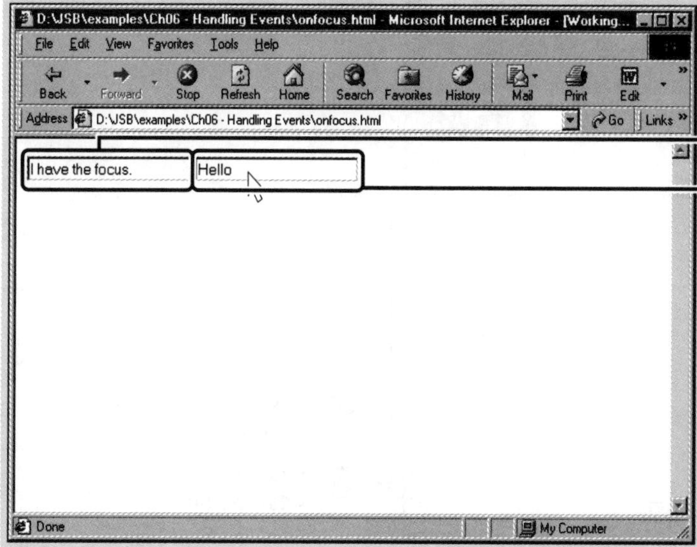

D:\JSB\examples\Ch06 - Handling Events\onfocus.html - Microsoft Internet Explorer - [Working...
File Edit View Favorites Tools Help
Back Forward Stop Refresh Home Search Favorites History Mail Print Edit
Address D:\JSB\examples\Ch06 - Handling Events\onfocus.html
Go Links
I have the focus.
Hello
Done
My Computer

- The text updates according to the field's `onfocus` event.

14. Click the right text field.

- The text updates in both fields — the first according to its `onblur` event (because it lost the focus) and the second according to its `onfocus` event (because it gained the focus).

Note: The `onblur` event for the second text field will fire when it loses focus.

DETECT A PULL-DOWN MENU SELECTION

You can create selection lists within a form by using the `<select>` tag. You can create each separate list item by using the `<option>` tags within the `<select>` tags. Using the `onchange` event, you can detect when a list item is selected. The `onchange` event can detect when a form element changes. The `onchange` event can be used with the `<select>`, `<input/>`, and `<textarea>` tags.

DETECT A PULL-DOWN MENU SELECTION

onchange.html - Notepad

```
<html>
<head>
</head>
<body>
  <form name="form1">
    <select name="select1" size="4"
      onchange="document.form1.text1.value='$3.95';">
      <option>raspberry torte</option>
      <option>chocolate mousse</option>
      <option>pralines truffle</option>
      <option>strawberry shortcake</option>
    </select>
    <input type="text" name="text1" value="Hello"/>
  </form>
</body>
</html>
```

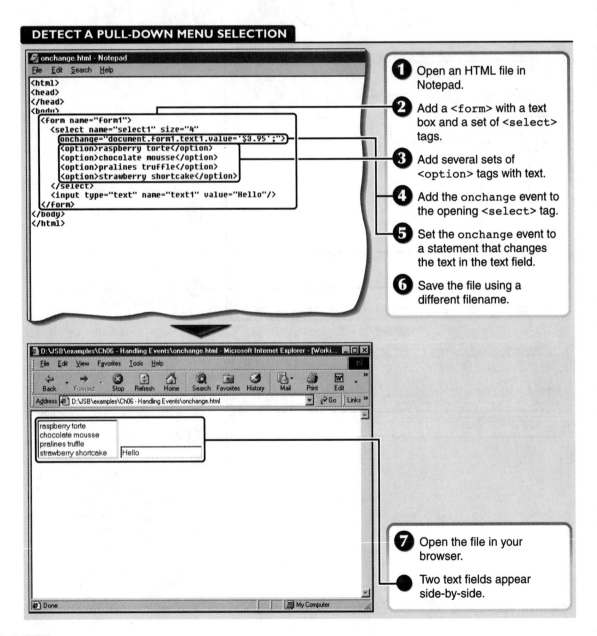

1. Open an HTML file in Notepad.
2. Add a `<form>` with a text box and a set of `<select>` tags.
3. Add several sets of `<option>` tags with text.
4. Add the `onchange` event to the opening `<select>` tag.
5. Set the `onchange` event to a statement that changes the text in the text field.
6. Save the file using a different filename.

D:\JSB\examples\Ch06 - Handling Events\onchange.html - Microsoft Internet Explorer - [Worki...

raspberry torte
chocolate mousse
pralines truffle
strawberry shortcake
Hello

7. Open the file in your browser.

- Two text fields appear side-by-side.

in an instant

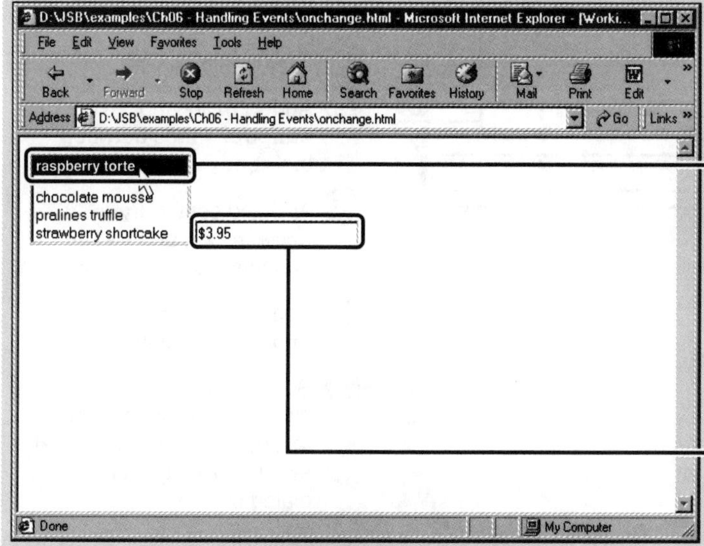

D:\JSB\examples\Ch06 - Handling Events\onchange.html - Microsoft Internet Explorer

raspberry torte
chocolate mousse
pralines truffle
strawberry shortcake
$3.95

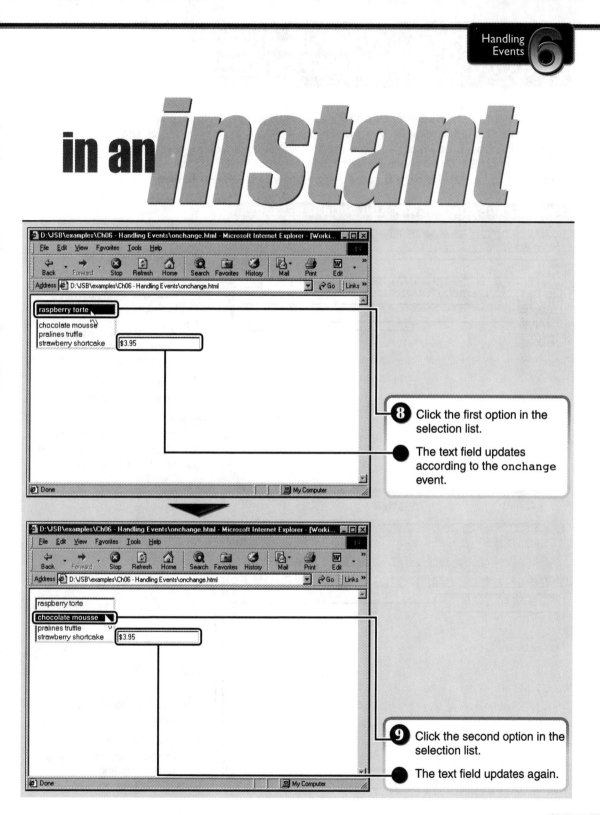

8 Click the first option in the selection list.

- The text field updates according to the `onchange` event.

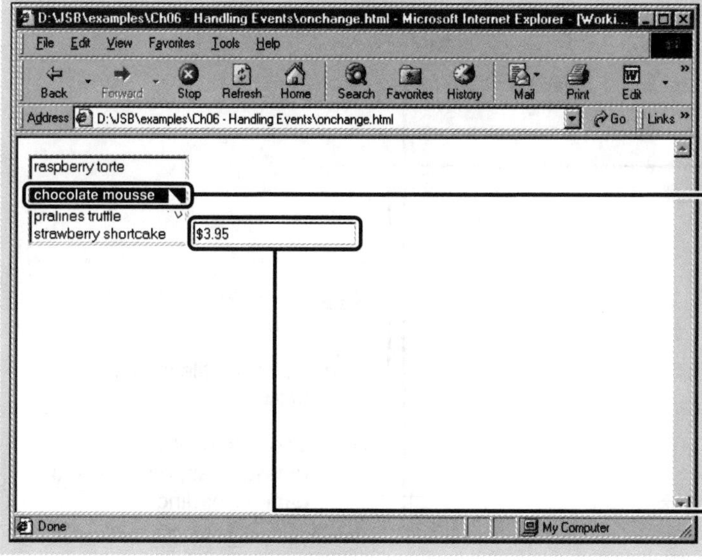

raspberry torte
chocolate mousse
pralines truffle
strawberry shortcake
$3.95

9 Click the second option in the selection list.

- The text field updates again.

CREATE PAGE LOADING AND UNLOADING MESSAGES

You can use the `onload` event to notify the user that the Web page has completely finished loading. This event can also be used to ensure that all the graphics have been downloaded from the server before executing a script on the page. A similar event is `onunload`, which happens when the current page is left or when the page is reset using a browser's Refresh button.

CREATE PAGE LOADING AND UNLOADING MESSAGES

onload.html - Notepad

```
<html>
<head>
</head>
<body onload="document.form1.text1.value='Page Load Complete';"
  onunload="alert('Goodbye, please come again.');">
  <form name="form1">
    <input type="text" name="text1" size="30" value="Page Loading, Please
Wait"/>
  </form>
</body>
</html>
```

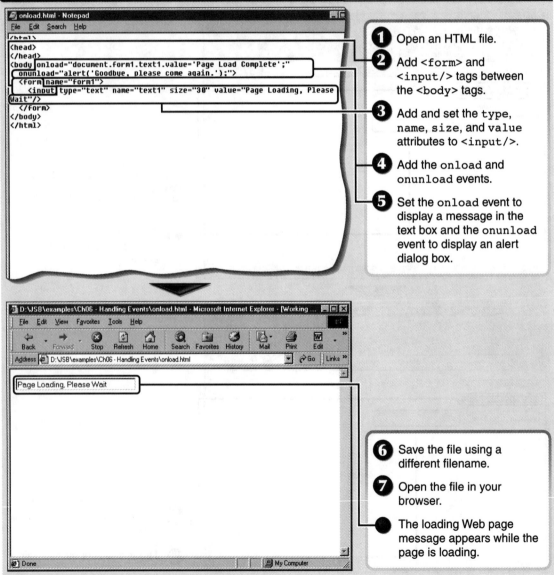

1. Open an HTML file.
2. Add <form> and <input/> tags between the <body> tags.
3. Add and set the `type`, `name`, `size`, and `value` attributes to <input/>.
4. Add the `onload` and `onunload` events.
5. Set the `onload` event to display a message in the text box and the `onunload` event to display an alert dialog box.

D:\JSB\examples\Ch06 - Handling Events\onload.html - Microsoft Internet Explorer - [Working ...

Page Loading, Please Wait

6. Save the file using a different filename.
7. Open the file in your browser.

- The loading Web page message appears while the page is loading.

in an instant

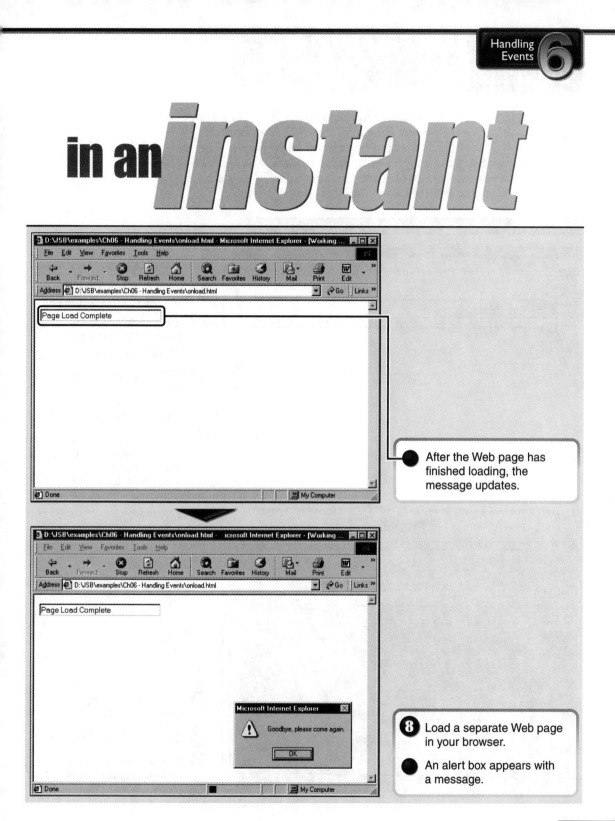

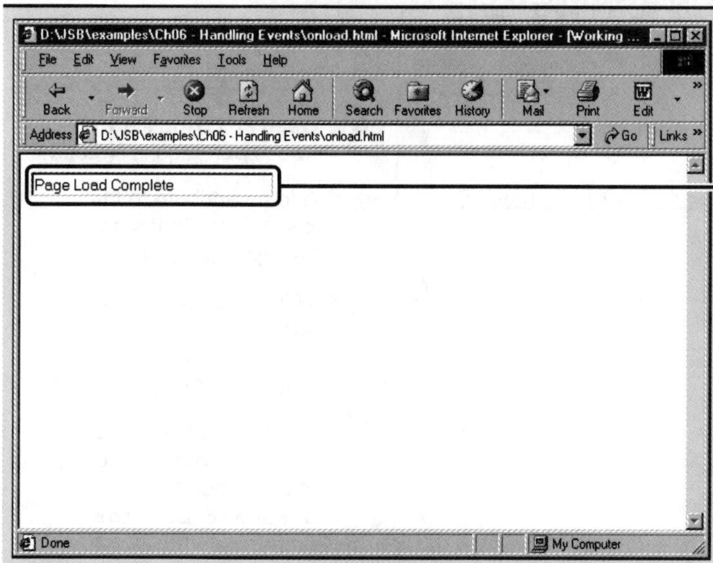

- After the Web page has finished loading, the message updates.

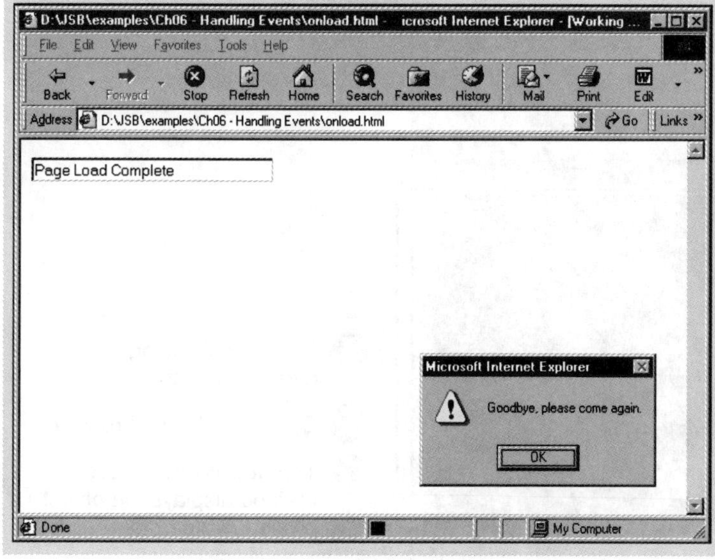

8. Load a separate Web page in your browser.

- An alert box appears with a message.

UNDERSTAND OBJECTS, PROPERTIES, AND METHODS

An *object* is an abstract container that holds data. This data can be a single number or a complex data structure. *Properties* provide information about objects and can be referenced by placing a period between the object and property name, as in `document.title`. Objects can have *methods,* which are functions specific to the object that perform a task and are referenced just like properties.

UNDERSTAND OBJECTS, PROPERTIES, AND METHODS

```
<html>
<head>
</head>
<body bgcolor="green">
  <script language="javascript">
    document.write("The background color is :" + document.bgColor);
  </script>
</body>
</html>
```

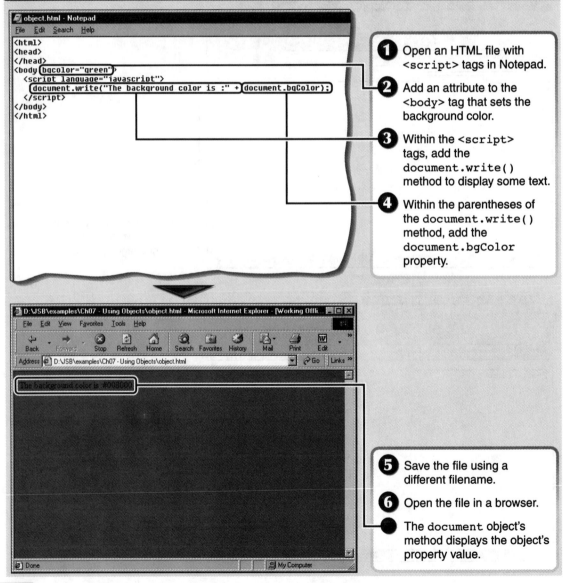

1. Open an HTML file with `<script>` tags in Notepad.
2. Add an attribute to the `<body>` tag that sets the background color.
3. Within the `<script>` tags, add the `document.write()` method to display some text.
4. Within the parentheses of the `document.write()` method, add the `document.bgColor` property.

D:\JSB\examples\Ch07 - Using Objects\object.html - Microsoft Internet Explorer - [Working Offli...
The background color is :#008000

5. Save the file using a different filename.
6. Open the file in a browser.

- The `document` object's method displays the object's property value.

in an instant

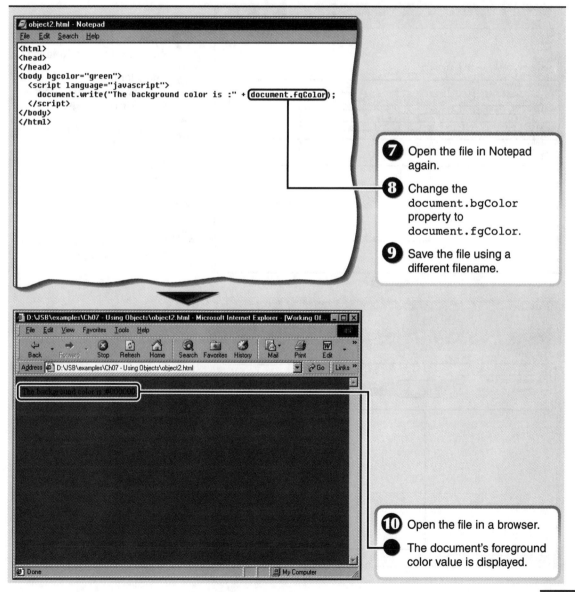

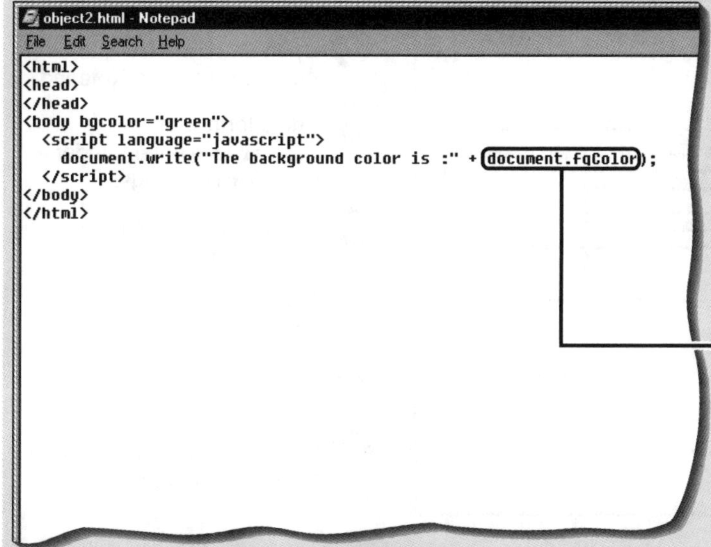

```
<html>
<head>
</head>
<body bgcolor="green">
  <script language="javascript">
    document.write("The background color is :" + document.fgColor);
  </script>
</body>
</html>
```

7 Open the file in Notepad again.

8 Change the `document.bgColor` property to `document.fgColor`.

9 Save the file using a different filename.

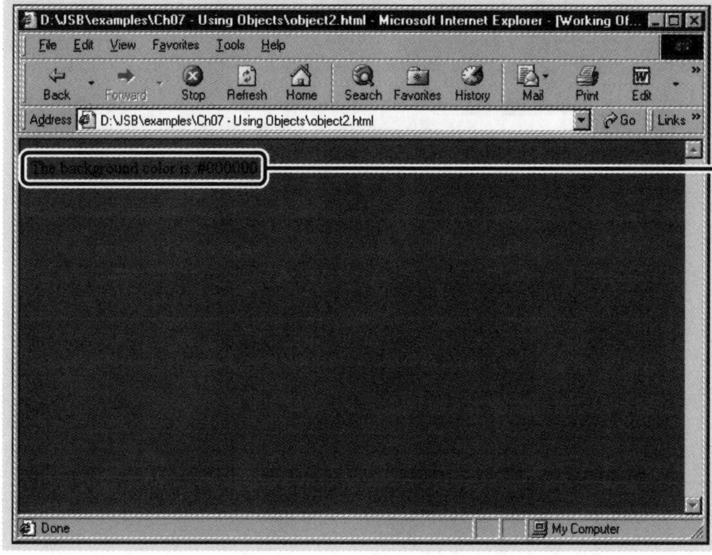

10 Open the file in a browser.

- The document's foreground color value is displayed.

USING WEB PAGE ELEMENT OBJECTS

The complete collection of JavaScript objects that refer to Web page elements is called the *Document Object Model* (DOM). The top object of the DOM is the `window` object. This object includes everything that deals with the browser window. The `window` object also includes the `document` object, which includes all the elements that make up the Web page, such as links, images, and forms.

USING WEB PAGE ELEMENT OBJECTS

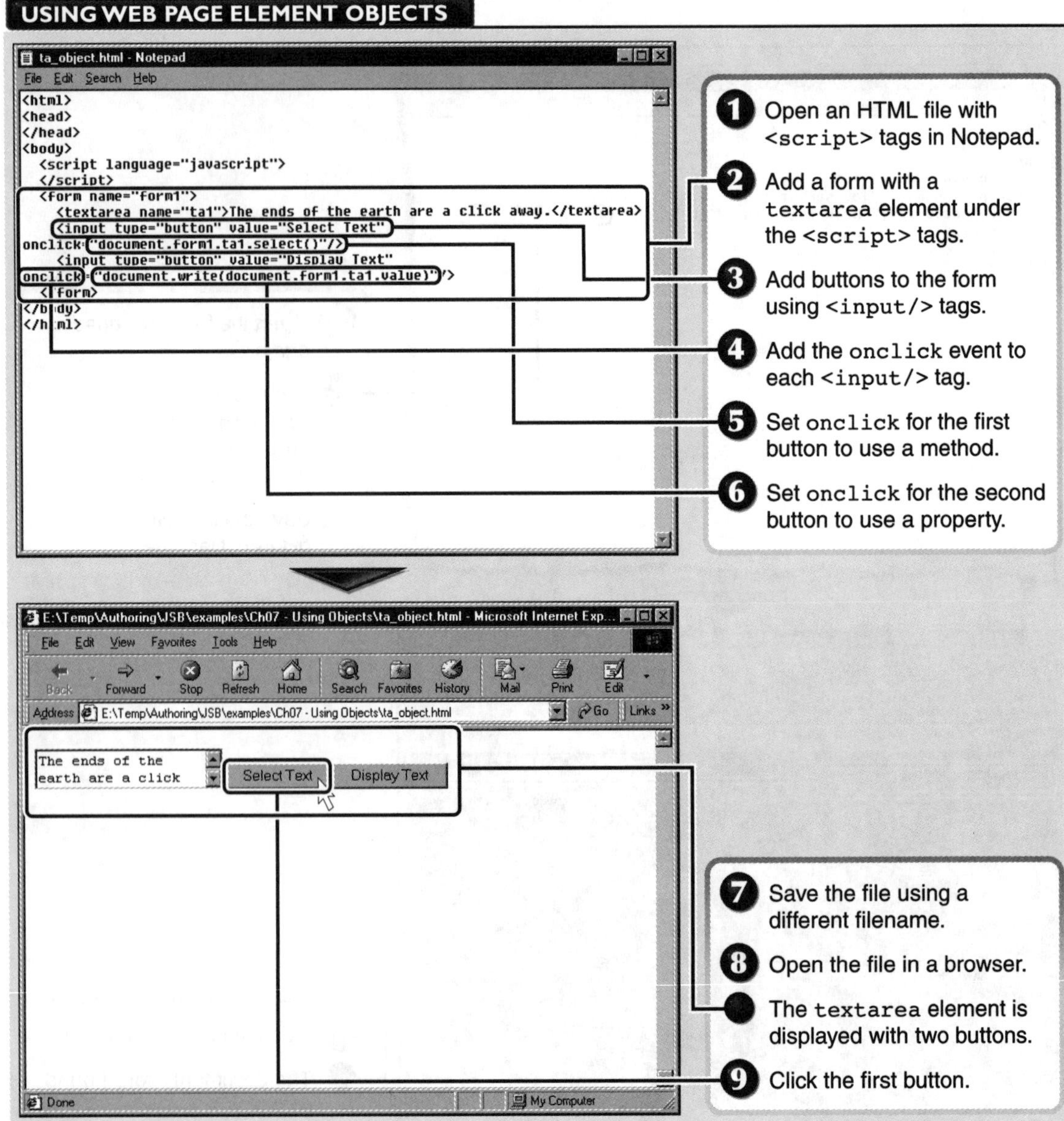

ta_object.html - Notepad
<html>
<head>
</head>
<body>
<script language="javascript">
</script>
<form name="form1">
<textarea name="ta1">The ends of the earth are a click away.</textarea>
<input type="button" value="Select Text"
onclick="document.form1.ta1.select()"/>
<input type="button" value="Display Text"
onclick="document.write(document.form1.ta1.value)"/>
</form>
</body>
</html>
E:\Temp\Authoring\JSB\examples\Ch07 - Using Objects\ta_object.html - Microsoft Internet Exp...
The ends of the earth are a click
Select Text
Display Text
Done
My Computer

1. Open an HTML file with `<script>` tags in Notepad.
2. Add a form with a `textarea` element under the `<script>` tags.
3. Add buttons to the form using `<input/>` tags.
4. Add the `onclick` event to each `<input/>` tag.
5. Set `onclick` for the first button to use a method.
6. Set `onclick` for the second button to use a property.
7. Save the file using a different filename.
8. Open the file in a browser.

- The `textarea` element is displayed with two buttons.

9. Click the first button.

in an instant

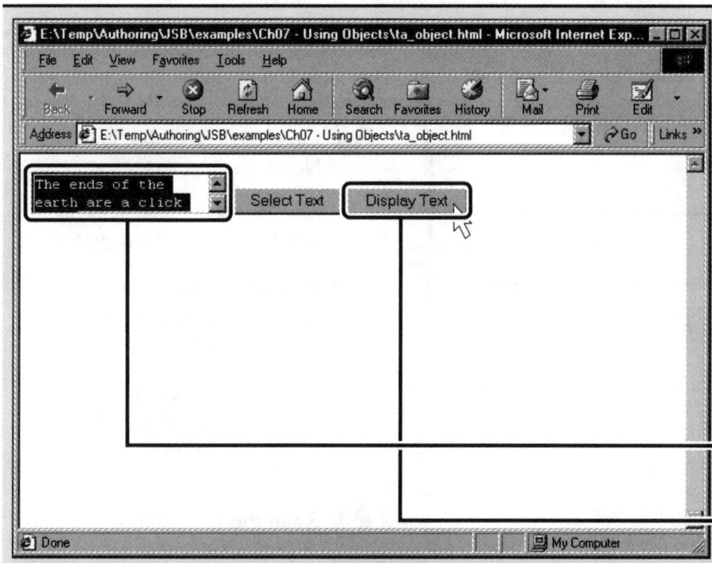

E:\Temp\Authoring\JSB\examples\Ch07 - Using Objects\ta_object.html - Microsoft Internet Exp...
The ends of the earth are a click
Select Text
Display Text

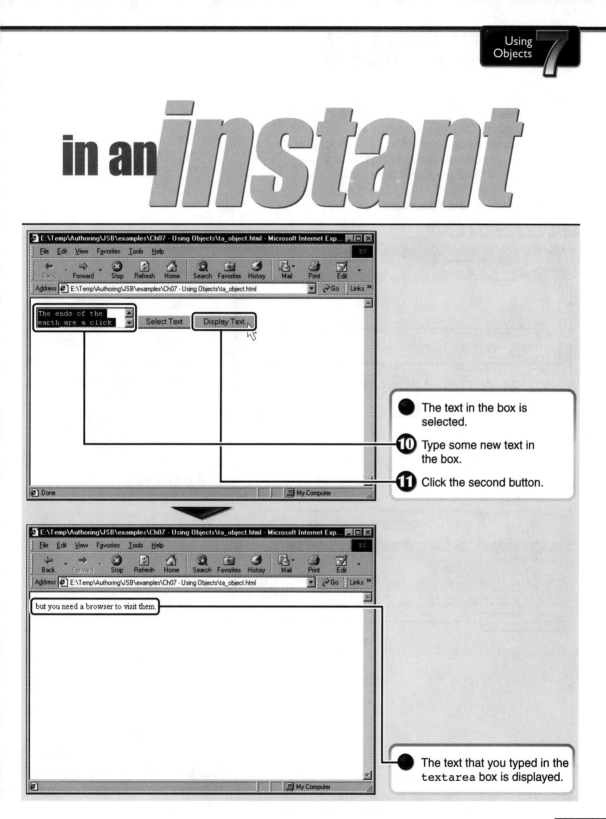

- The text in the box is selected.
- 10 Type some new text in the box.
- 11 Click the second button.

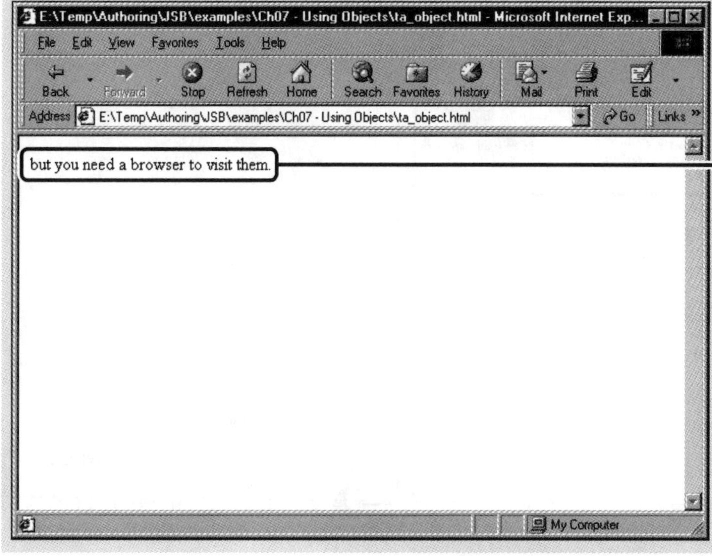

E:\Temp\Authoring\JSB\examples\Ch07 - Using Objects\ta_object.html - Microsoft Internet Exp...
but you need a browser to visit them.

- The text that you typed in the `textarea` box is displayed.

USING SUBOBJECTS

You can nest objects in a hierarchy. Objects that are contained within another object are referred to as *subobjects*. Object properties and methods are referenced using a period (.). For example, `document.bgColor` is the background color property for a Web page, and the method `document.write("hello")` writes the word *hello* to the Web page.

CHANGE A TEXT FIELD

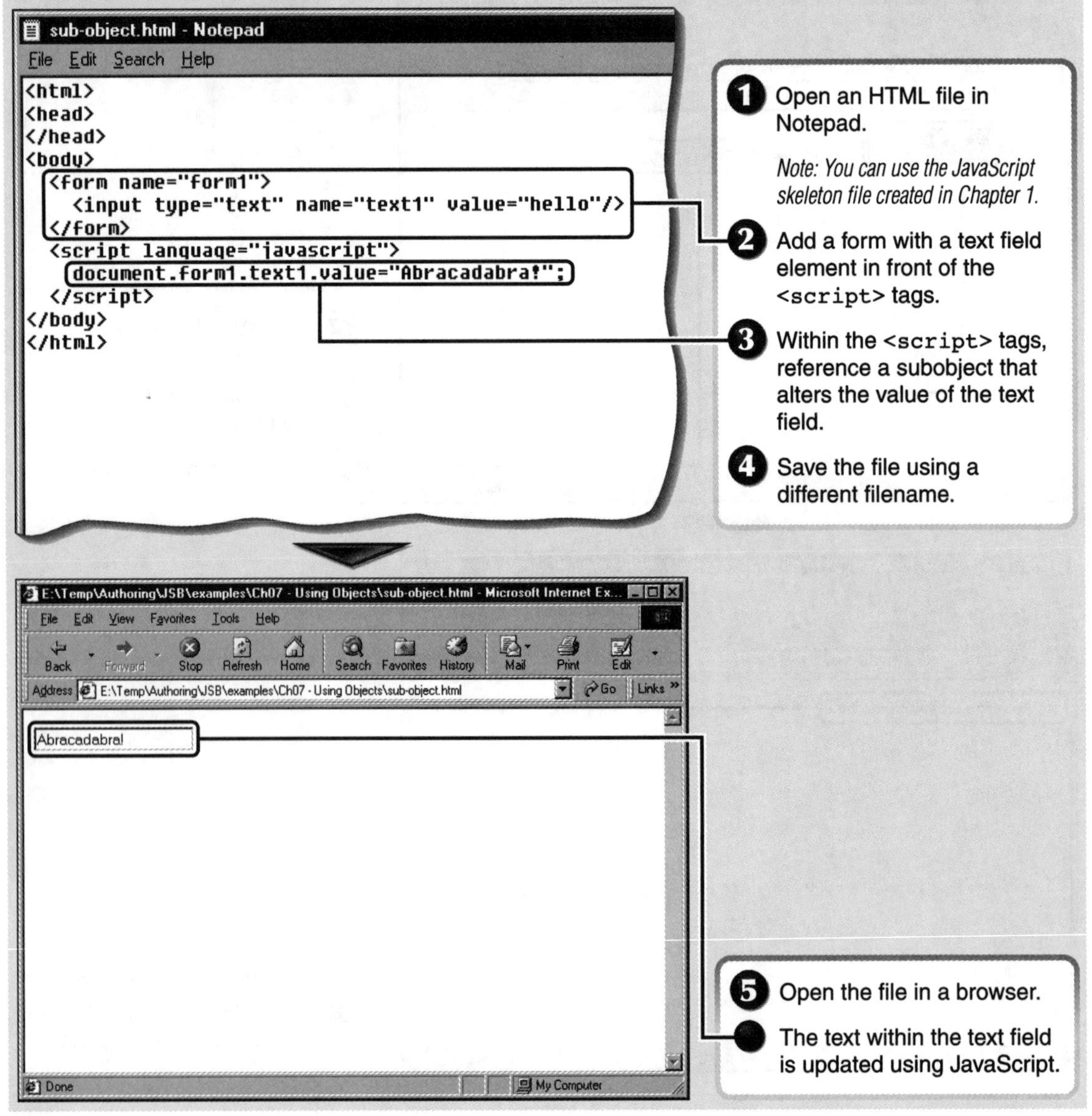

sub-object.html - Notepad
File Edit Search Help
<html>
<head>
</head>
<body>
<form name="form1">
<input type="text" name="text1" value="hello"/>
</form>
<script language="javascript">
document.form1.text1.value="Abracadabra!";
</script>
</body>
</html>
E:\Temp\Authoring\JSB\examples\Ch07 - Using Objects\sub-object.html - Microsoft Internet Ex...
File Edit View Favorites Tools Help
Back Forward Stop Refresh Home Search Favorites History Mail Print Edit
Address E:\Temp\Authoring\JSB\examples\Ch07 - Using Objects\sub-object.html
Go Links
Abracadabra!
Done
My Computer

1. Open an HTML file in Notepad.

   Note: You can use the JavaScript skeleton file created in Chapter 1.

2. Add a form with a text field element in front of the `<script>` tags.
3. Within the `<script>` tags, reference a subobject that alters the value of the text field.
4. Save the file using a different filename.
5. Open the file in a browser.

- The text within the text field is updated using JavaScript.

in an instant

CHECK A RADIO BUTTON

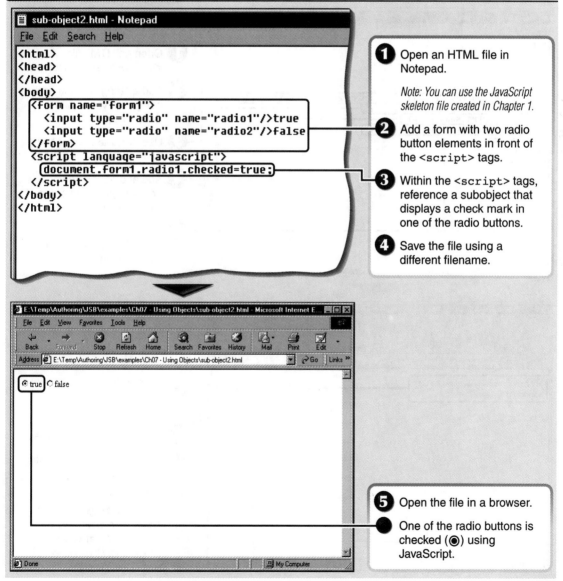

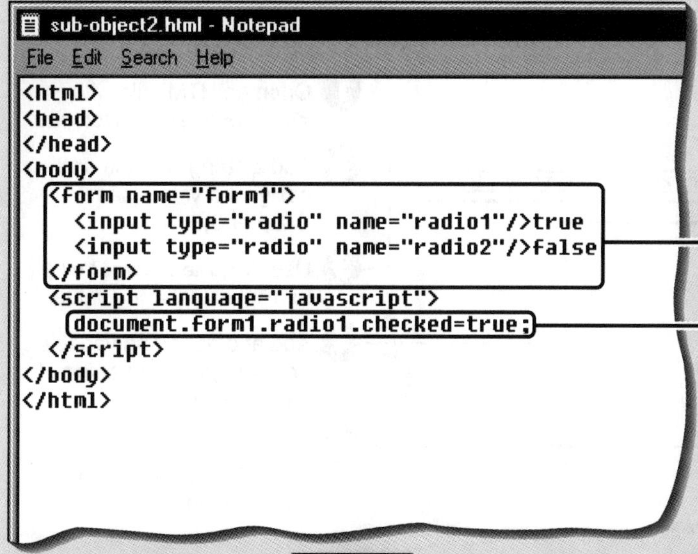

sub-object2.html - Notepad

```
<html>
<head>
</head>
<body>
  <form name="form1">
    <input type="radio" name="radio1"/>true
    <input type="radio" name="radio2"/>false
  </form>
  <script language="javascript">
    document.form1.radio1.checked=true;
  </script>
</body>
</html>
```

1. Open an HTML file in Notepad.

   Note: You can use the JavaScript skeleton file created in Chapter 1.

2. Add a form with two radio button elements in front of the `<script>` tags.
3. Within the `<script>` tags, reference a subobject that displays a check mark in one of the radio buttons.
4. Save the file using a different filename.

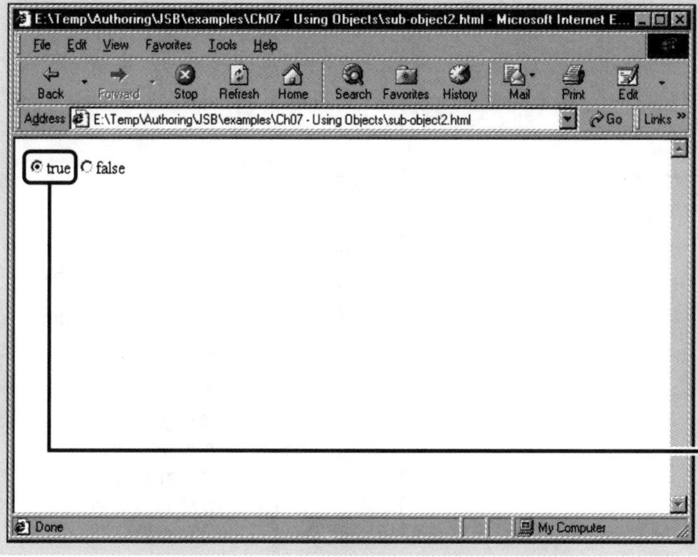

E:\Temp\Authoring\JSB\examples\Ch07 - Using Objects\sub-object2.html - Microsoft Internet E...

true false

5. Open the file in a browser.

- One of the radio buttons is checked (◉) using JavaScript.

USING PREDEFINED OBJECTS

JavaScript's predefined objects include useful objects for working with dates and mathematical functions, as well as objects for interacting with all the various elements of a Web page. Each of these objects has properties and methods that can be used to get information about the object or to perform a certain task.

USING THE STRING OBJECT

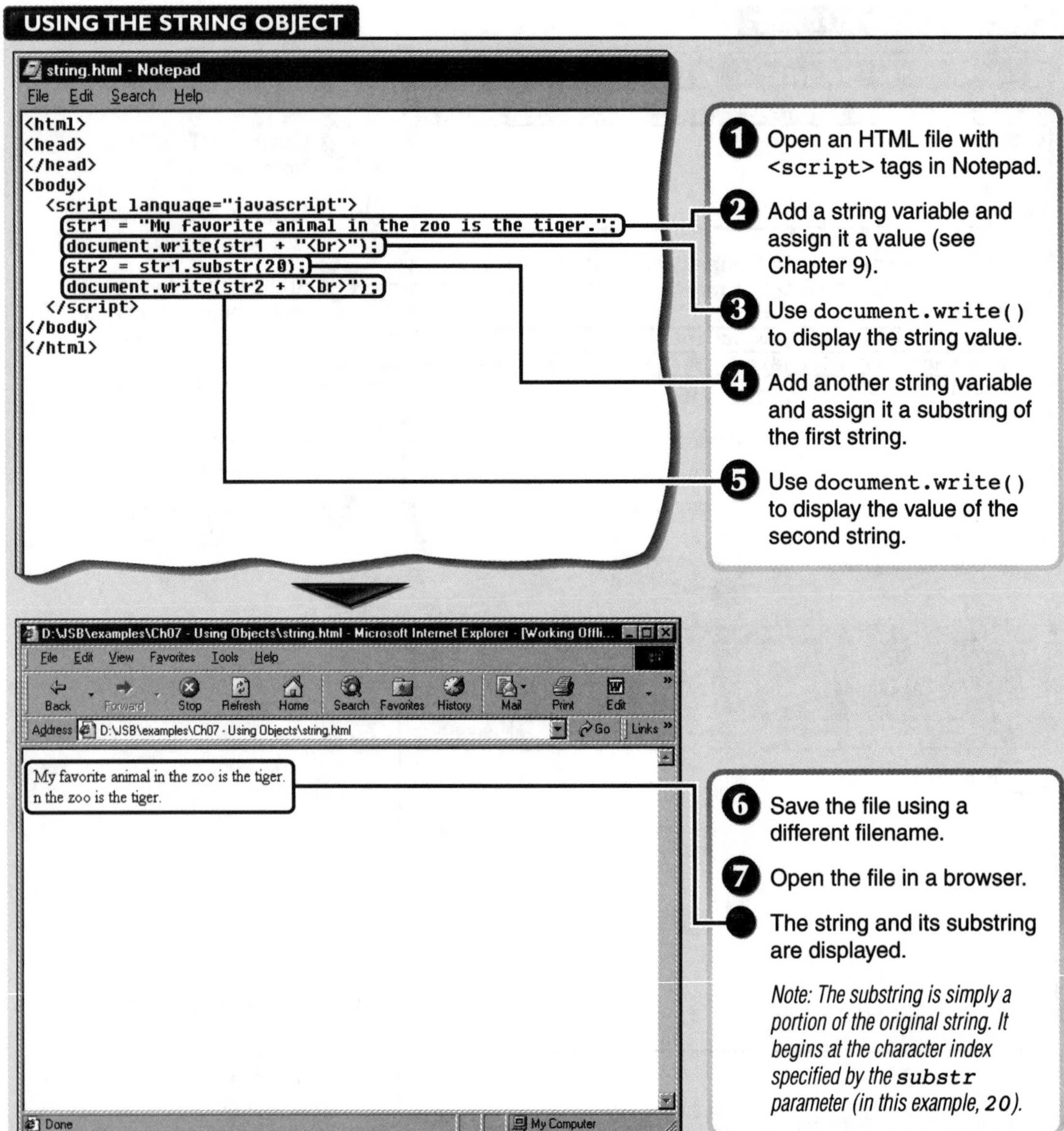

string.html - Notepad
File Edit Search Help
<html>
<head>
</head>
<body>
<script language="javascript">
str1 = "My favorite animal in the zoo is the tiger.";
document.write(str1 + "<br>");
str2 = str1.substr(20);
document.write(str2 + "<br>");
</script>
</body>
</html>
D:\JSB\examples\Ch07 - Using Objects\string.html - Microsoft Internet Explorer - [Working Offli...
My favorite animal in the zoo is the tiger.
n the zoo is the tiger.
Done
My Computer

1. Open an HTML file with `<script>` tags in Notepad.
2. Add a string variable and assign it a value (see Chapter 9).
3. Use `document.write()` to display the string value.
4. Add another string variable and assign it a substring of the first string.
5. Use `document.write()` to display the value of the second string.
6. Save the file using a different filename.
7. Open the file in a browser.

- The string and its substring are displayed.

Note: The substring is simply a portion of the original string. It begins at the character index specified by the `substr` parameter (in this example, `20`).

Using
Objects
7

in an instant

USING THE MATH OBJECT

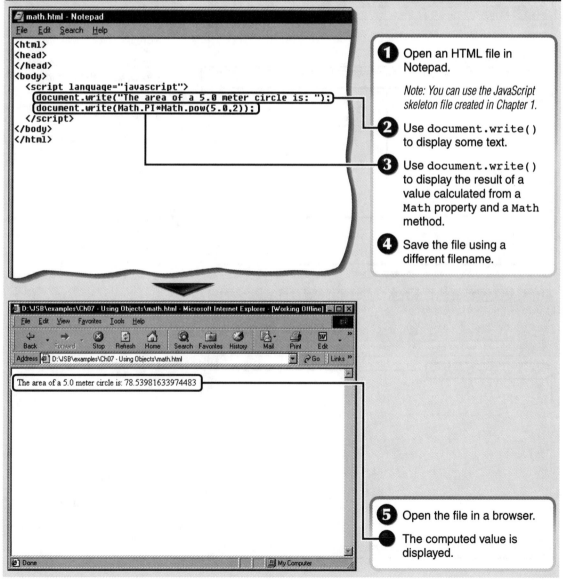

math.html - Notepad

```
<html>
<head>
</head>
<body>
  <script language="javascript">
    document.write("The area of a 5.0 meter circle is: ");
    document.write(Math.PI*Math.pow(5.0,2));
  </script>
</body>
</html>
```

1. Open an HTML file in Notepad.

   Note: You can use the JavaScript skeleton file created in Chapter 1.

2. Use `document.write()` to display some text.
3. Use `document.write()` to display the result of a value calculated from a `Math` property and a `Math` method.
4. Save the file using a different filename.

D:\JSB\examples\Ch07 - Using Objects\math.html - Microsoft Internet Explorer - [Working Offline]

The area of a 5.0 meter circle is: 78.53981633974483

5. Open the file in a browser.

- The computed value is displayed.

CREATE NEW OBJECTS

Some objects are created implicitly whenever a string is declared. Other objects need to be created using the `new` keyword and a function constructor. The `new` keyword, when used with the `Object()` constructor, can be used to create user-defined objects.

CREATE NEW OBJECTS

new.html - Notepad

```
<html>
<head>
</head>
<body>
  <script language="javascript">
    today = new Date();
    document.write("Today is day number " + today.getDate() + " of month " +
(today.getMonth()+1));
  </script>
</body>
</html>
```

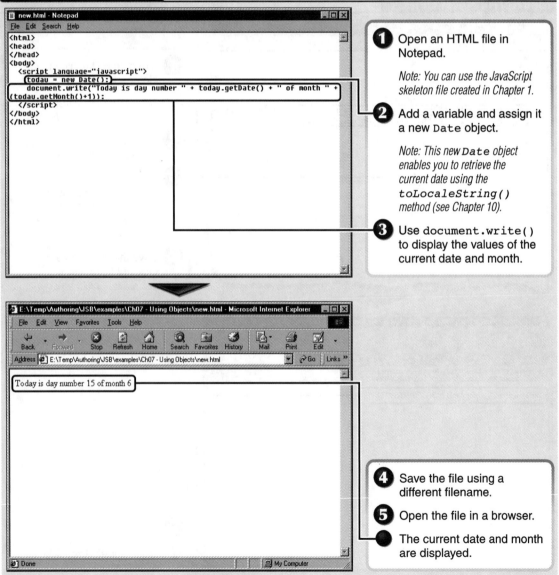

1 Open an HTML file in Notepad.

Note: You can use the JavaScript skeleton file created in Chapter 1.

2 Add a variable and assign it a new `Date` object.

Note: This new `Date` *object enables you to retrieve the current date using the* `toLocaleString()` *method (see Chapter 10).*

3 Use `document.write()` to display the values of the current date and month.

E:\Temp\Authoring\JSB\examples\Ch07 - Using Objects\new.html - Microsoft Internet Explorer

Today is day number 15 of month 6

4 Save the file using a different filename.

5 Open the file in a browser.

- The current date and month are displayed.

in an instant

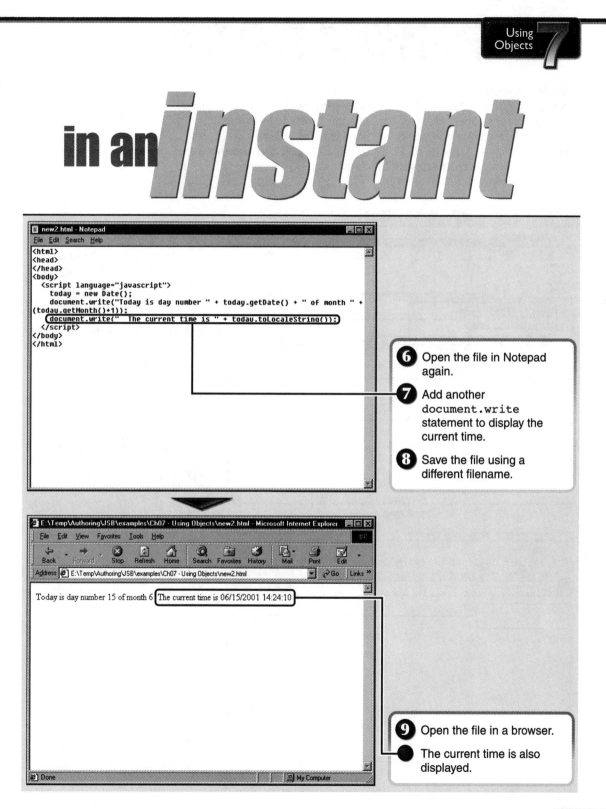

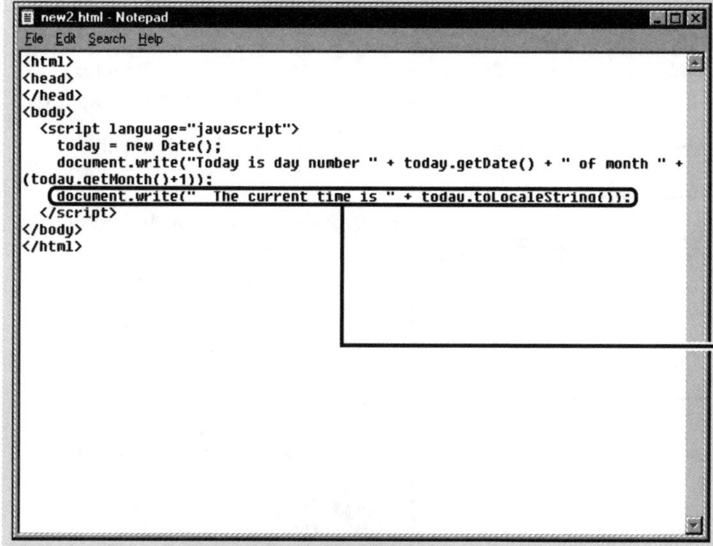

new2.html - Notepad

```
<html>
<head>
</head>
<body>
  <script language="javascript">
    today = new Date();
    document.write("Today is day number " + today.getDate() + " of month " +
(today.getMonth()+1));
    document.write("  The current time is " + today.toLocaleString());
  </script>
</body>
</html>
```

6 Open the file in Notepad again.

7 Add another `document.write` statement to display the current time.

8 Save the file using a different filename.

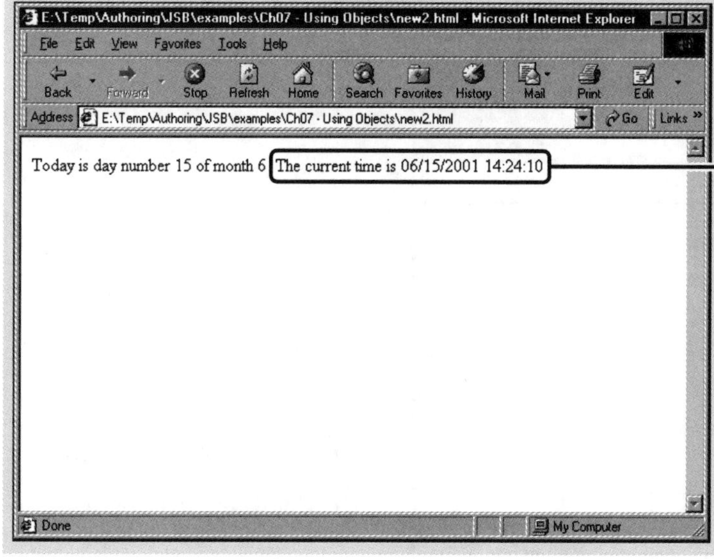

E:\Temp\Authoring\JSB\examples\Ch07 - Using Objects\new2.html - Microsoft Internet Explorer

Today is day number 15 of month 6 The current time is 06/15/2001 14:24:10

9 Open the file in a browser.

- The current time is also displayed.

REFER TO THE CURRENT OBJECT

JavaScript includes a keyword that you can use to reference the current object — `this`. The `this` keyword can be placed in place of the object's parent but can be used only within the current function. For example, if you are using variables passed to a function, such as `function hello(str1)`, you can use the `this` keyword to refer to these variables, such as `this.name = str1`.

IDENTIFY OBJECT PROPERTIES

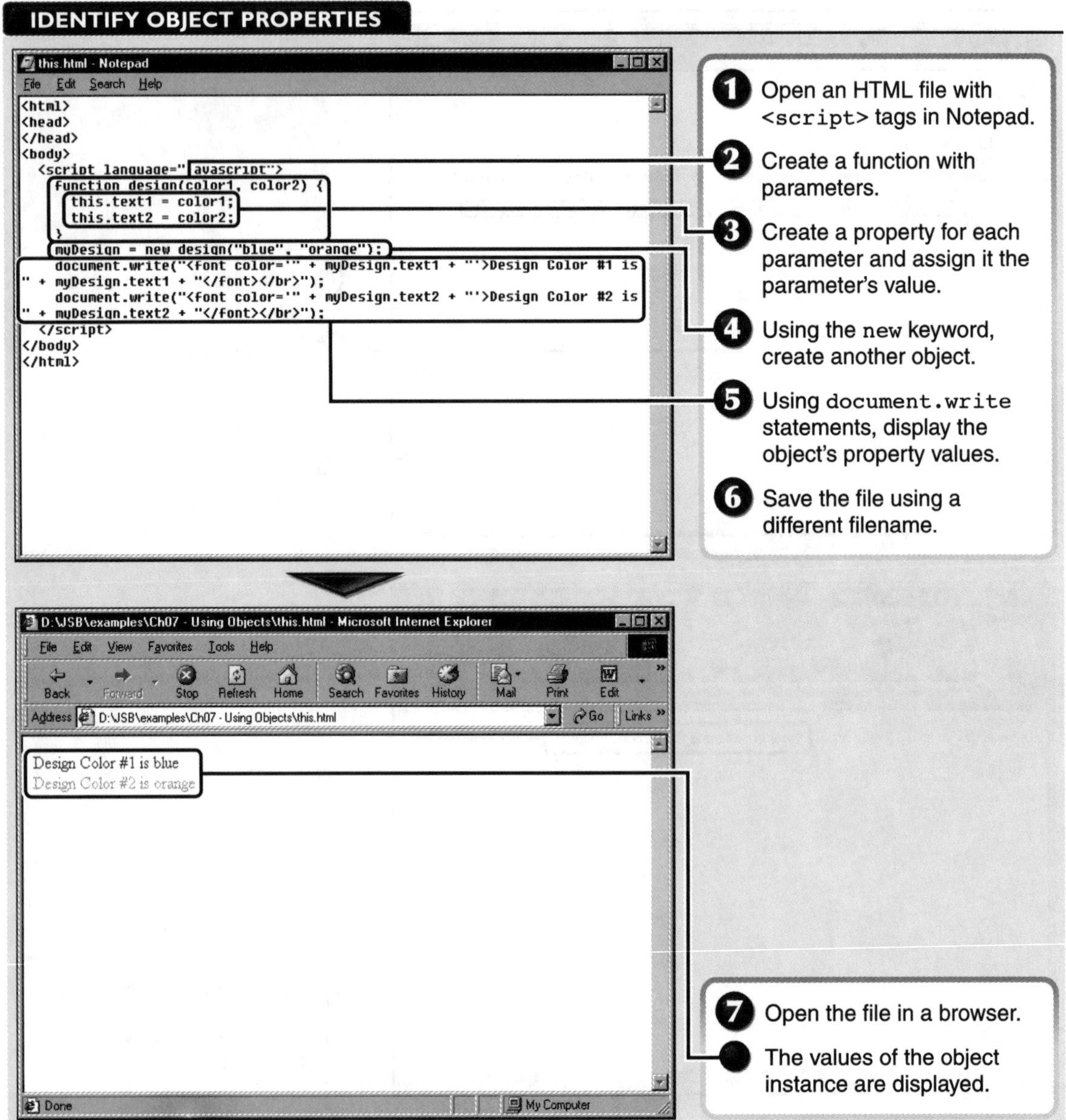

this.html - Notepad
File Edit Search Help
<html>
<head>
</head>
<body>
<script language="javascript">
function design(color1, color2) {
this.text1 = color1;
this.text2 = color2;
}
myDesign = new design("blue", "orange");
document.write("<font color='" + myDesign.text1 + "'>Design Color #1 is " + myDesign.text1 + "</font></br>");
document.write("<font color='" + myDesign.text2 + "'>Design Color #2 is " + myDesign.text2 + "</font></br>");
</script>
</body>
</html>
D:\JSB\examples\Ch07 - Using Objects\this.html - Microsoft Internet Explorer
Design Color #1 is blue
Design Color #2 is orange
Done
My Computer

1. Open an HTML file with `<script>` tags in Notepad.
2. Create a function with parameters.
3. Create a property for each parameter and assign it the parameter's value.
4. Using the `new` keyword, create another object.
5. Using `document.write` statements, display the object's property values.
6. Save the file using a different filename.
7. Open the file in a browser.

- The values of the object instance are displayed.

in an instant

REFER TO THE CURRENT WEB PAGE ELEMENT

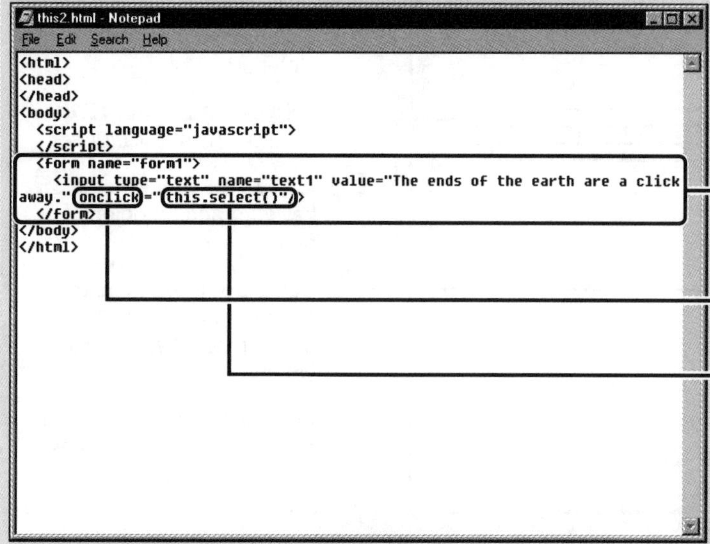

```
<html>
<head>
</head>
<body>
  <script language="javascript">
  </script>
  <form name="form1">
    <input type="text" name="text1" value="The ends of the earth are a click
away." onclick="this.select()">
  </form>
</body>
</html>
```

1. Open an HTML file in Notepad.

   Note: You can use the JavaScript skeleton file created in Chapter 1.

2. Add a form with a text field to the page.
3. Add the `onclick` event to the text field.
4. Set the `onclick` event equal to the `this.select()` method.
5. Save the file using a different filename.

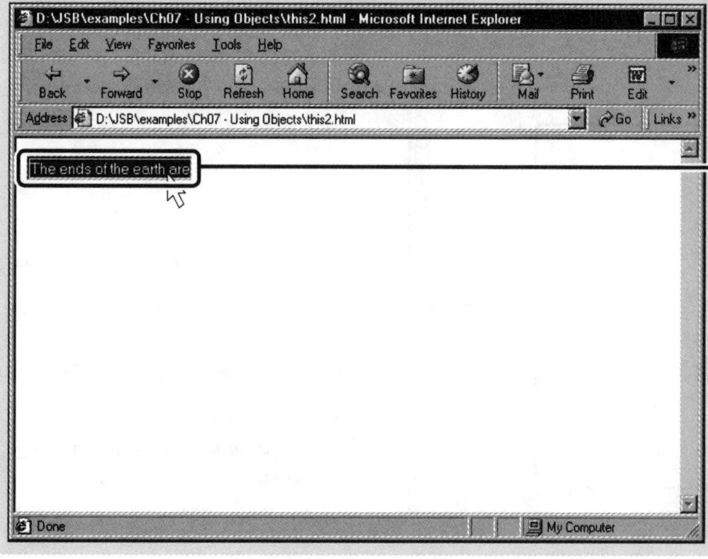

6. Open the file in a browser.
7. Click the text field.

- The text in the text field is selected.

VIEW OBJECT PROPERTIES

You can use JavaScript to list an object's properties. A special version of the `for` loop can be used to look into the object and view all its properties. This `for` loop includes the `in` keyword and the object name. These statements can be used only on objects that have been defined. If an object does not exist, no properties are displayed.

VIEW OBJECT PROPERTIES

```
<html>
<head>
</head>
<body>
  <script language="javascript">
   for (prop in window) {
    document.write("window." + prop + " = " + window[prop] + "<br>");
   }
  </script>
</body>
</html>
```

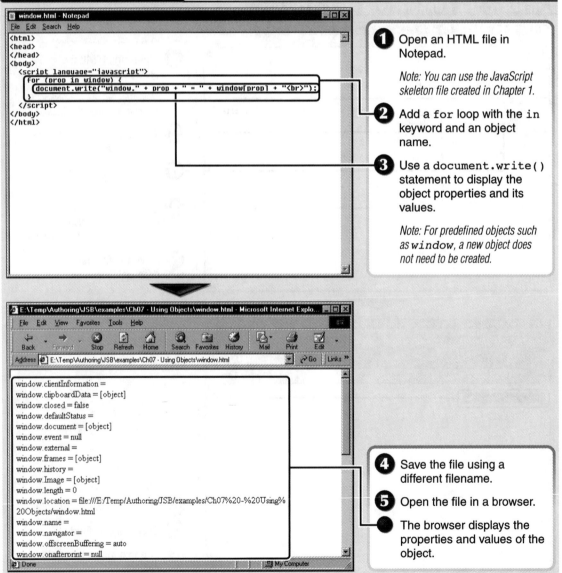

1. Open an HTML file in Notepad.

   Note: You can use the JavaScript skeleton file created in Chapter 1.

2. Add a `for` loop with the `in` keyword and an object name.

3. Use a `document.write()` statement to display the object properties and its values.

   Note: For predefined objects such as `window`, a new object does not need to be created.

```
window.clientInformation =
window.clipboardData = [object]
window.closed = false
window.defaultStatus =
window.document = [object]
window.event = null
window.external =
window.frames = [object]
window.history =
window.Image = [object]
window.length = 0
window.location = file:///E:/Temp/Authoring/JSB/examples/Ch07%20-%20Using%20Objects/window.html
window.name =
window.navigator =
window.offscreenBuffering = auto
window.onafterprint = null
```

4. Save the file using a different filename.

5. Open the file in a browser.

- The browser displays the properties and values of the object.

in an instant

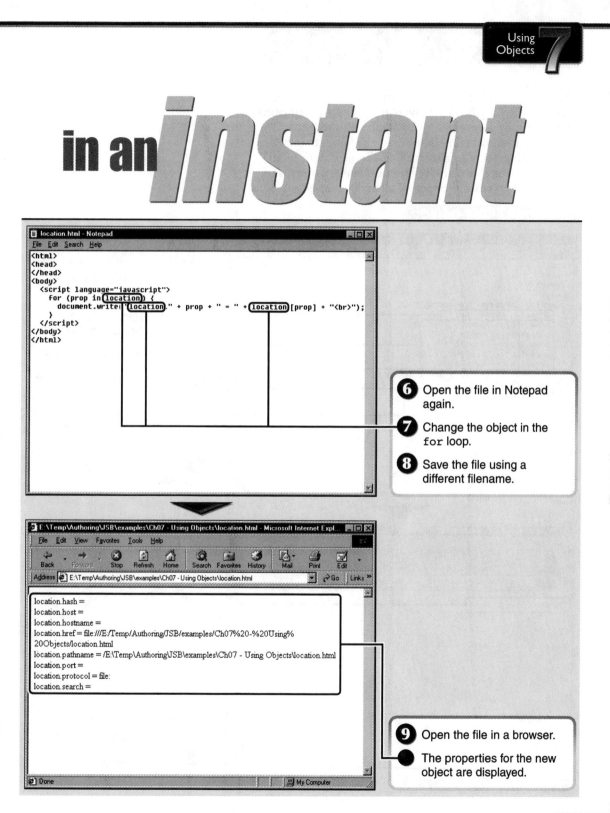

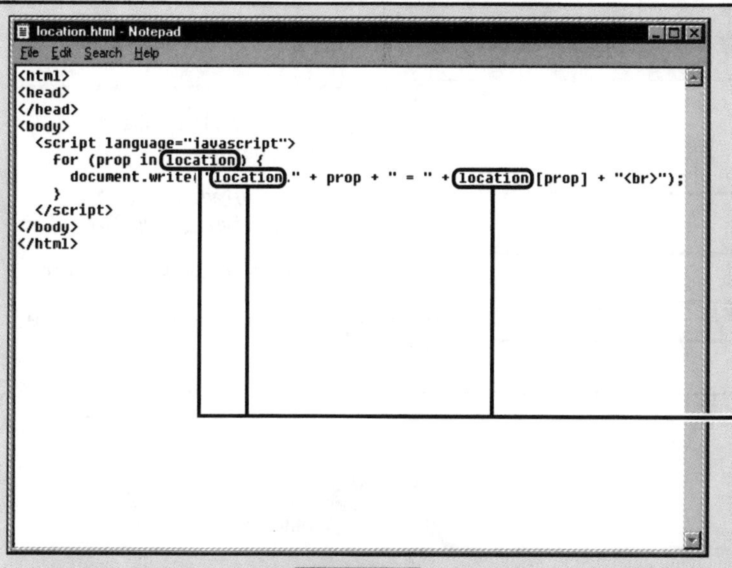
location.html - Notepad
File Edit Search Help
<html>
<head>
</head>
<body>
<script language="javascript">
for (prop in location) {
document.write("location." + prop + " = " + location[prop] + "<br>");
}
</script>
</body>
</html>

6. Open the file in Notepad again.
7. Change the object in the `for` loop.
8. Save the file using a different filename.

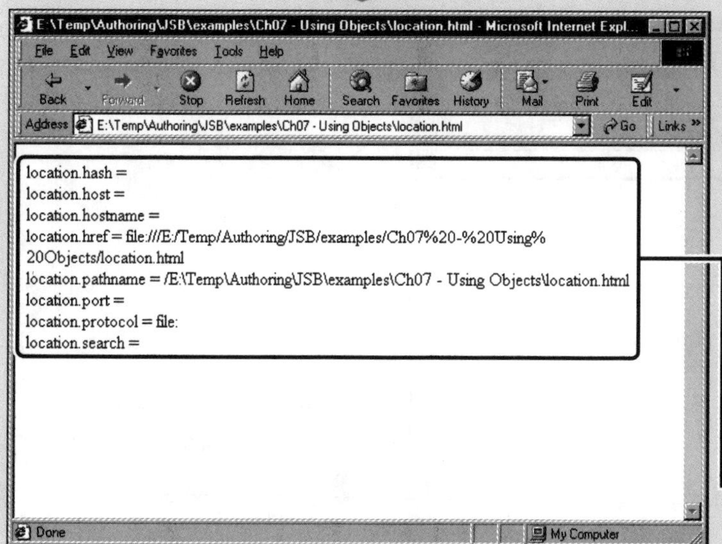
E:\Temp\Authoring\JSB\examples\Ch07 - Using Objects\location.html - Microsoft Internet Expl...
File Edit View Favorites Tools Help
Back Forward Stop Refresh Home Search Favorites History Mail Print Edit
Address E:\Temp\Authoring\JSB\examples\Ch07 - Using Objects\location.html
Go Links
location.hash =
location.host =
location.hostname =
location.href = file:///E:/Temp/Authoring/JSB/examples/Ch07%20-%20Using%20Objects/location.html
location.pathname = /E:\Temp\Authoring\JSB\examples\Ch07 - Using Objects\location.html
location.port =
location.protocol = file:
location.search =
Done
My Computer

9. Open the file in a browser.
- The properties for the new object are displayed.

USING THE ARRAY OBJECT

The `Array` object has a property called `length` that returns the length of the given array. The `Array` object also includes several array manipulation methods. The `join()` method combines all array elements into a single string. You can also sort all the elements of an array by using the `sort()` method. The `reverse()` method reverses the order of all array elements.

USING THE ARRAY OBJECT

array.html - Notepad

```
<html>
<head>
</head>
<body>
  <script language="javascript">
    array1 = new Array();
    array1[0] = "bark";
    array1[1] = "apple";
    array1[2] = "nebula";
    array1[3] = "cookie";
    array1[4] = "technology";
    document.write("This array includes " + array1.length + "
elements<br>");
  </script>
</body>
</html>
```

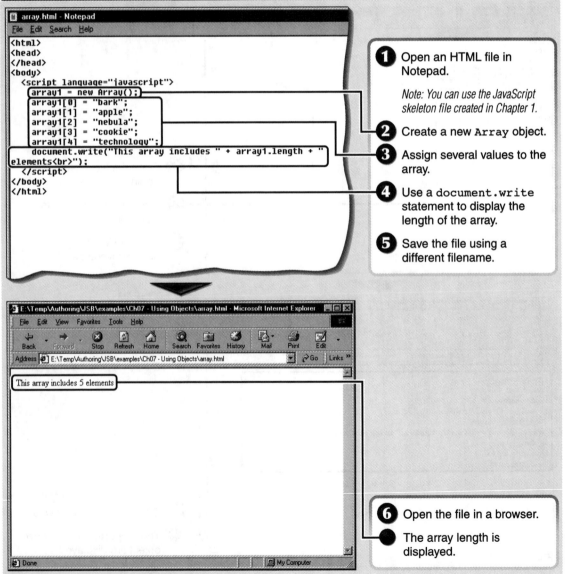

1. Open an HTML file in Notepad.

   Note: You can use the JavaScript skeleton file created in Chapter 1.

2. Create a new `Array` object.
3. Assign several values to the array.
4. Use a `document.write` statement to display the length of the array.
5. Save the file using a different filename.

E:\Temp\Authoring\JSB\examples\Ch07 - Using Objects\array.html - Microsoft Internet Explorer

This array includes 5 elements

6. Open the file in a browser.

- The array length is displayed.

in an instant

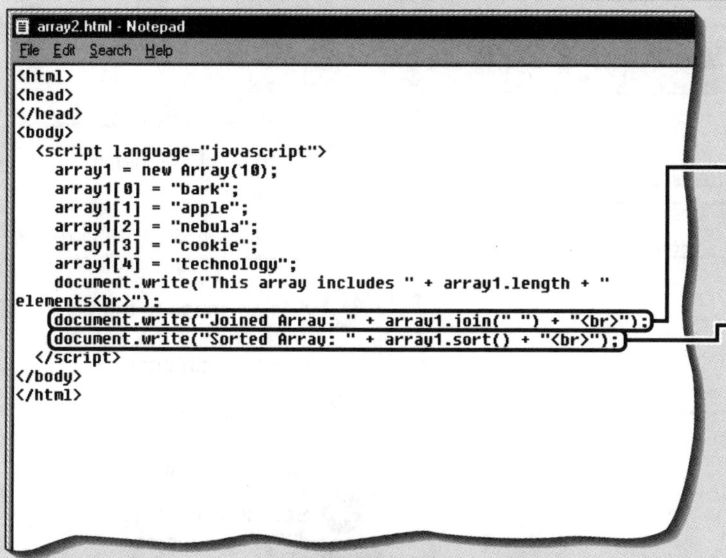

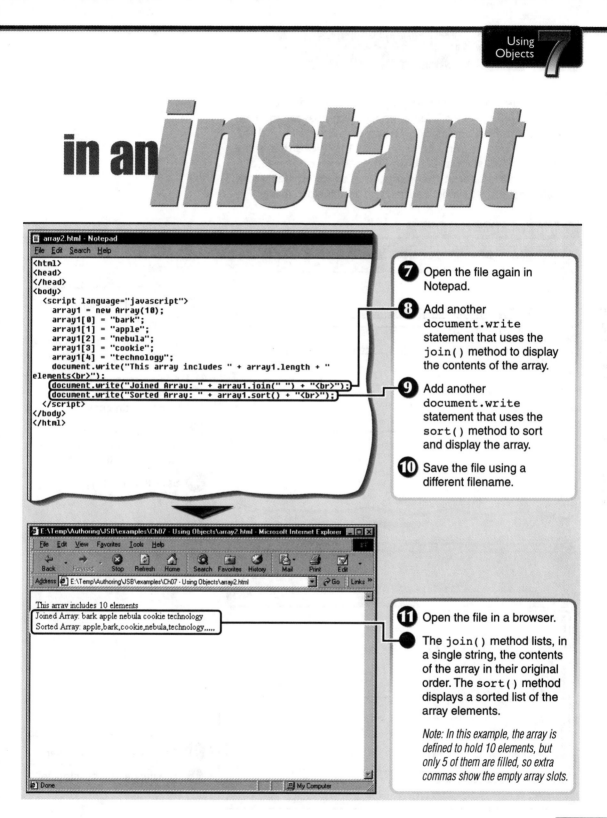

array2.html - Notepad
File Edit Search Help
<html>
<head>
</head>
<body>
<script language="javascript">
array1 = new Array(10);
array1[0] = "bark";
array1[1] = "apple";
array1[2] = "nebula";
array1[3] = "cookie";
array1[4] = "technology";
document.write("This array includes " + array1.length + " elements
");
document.write("Joined Array: " + array1.join(" ") + "<br>");
document.write("Sorted Array: " + array1.sort() + "<br>");
</script>
</body>
</html>

7. Open the file again in Notepad.
8. Add another `document.write` statement that uses the `join()` method to display the contents of the array.
9. Add another `document.write` statement that uses the `sort()` method to sort and display the array.
10. Save the file using a different filename.

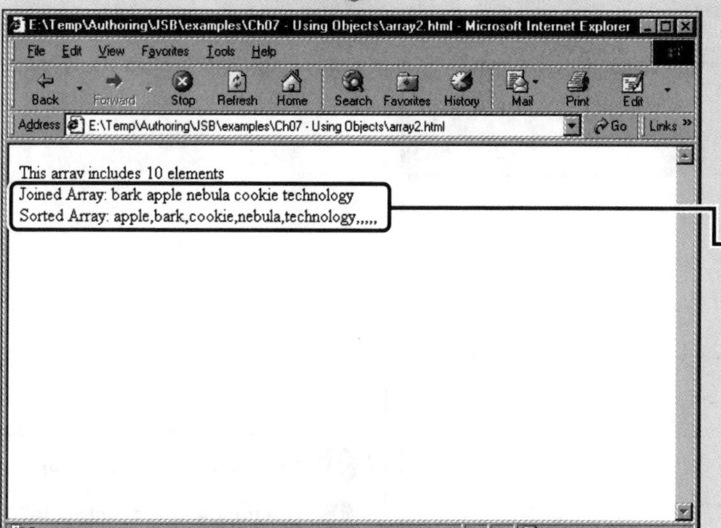

E:\Temp\Authoring\JSB\examples\Ch07 - Using Objects\array2.html - Microsoft Internet Explorer
File Edit View Favorites Tools Help
Back Forward Stop Refresh Home Search Favorites History Mail Print Edit
Address E:\Temp\Authoring\JSB\examples\Ch07 - Using Objects\array2.html
Go Links
This array includes 10 elements
Joined Array: bark apple nebula cookie technology
Sorted Array: apple,bark,cookie,nebula,technology,,,,,
Done
My Computer

11. Open the file in a browser.

- The `join()` method lists, in a single string, the contents of the array in their original order. The `sort()` method displays a sorted list of the array elements.

Note: In this example, the array is defined to hold 10 elements, but only 5 of them are filled, so extra commas show the empty array slots.

USING THE IMAGE OBJECT

The `image` object exists for any Web page that includes at least one image. If a Web page has two images, you can refer to the first one as `document.images[0]` and the second one as `document.images[1]`. (Note that array indexes always start at 0.) Using the index, you can find out information about the image, such as its border width, its dimensions, its name, source, and spacing attributes.

USING THE IMAGE OBJECT

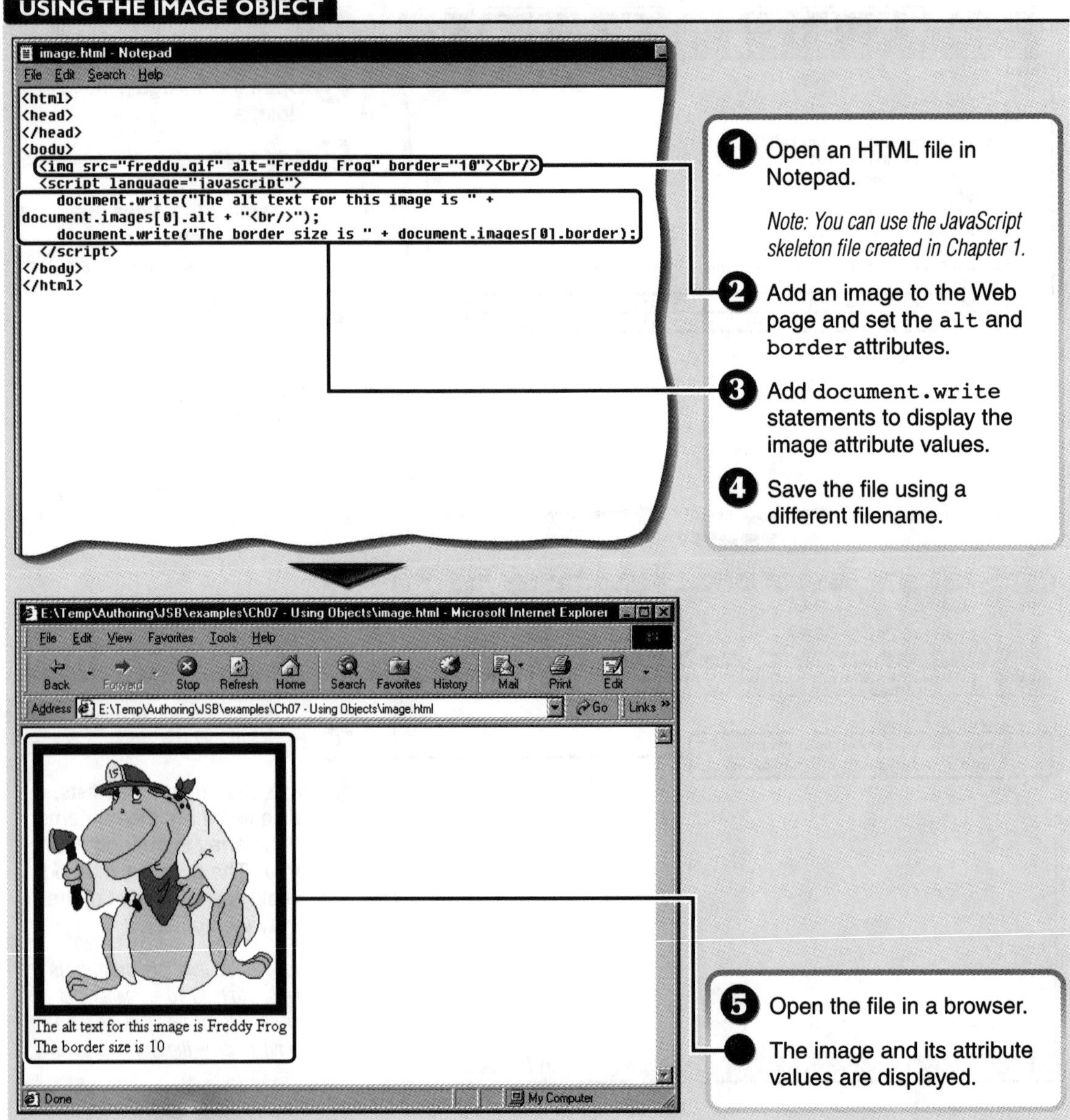

image.html - Notepad
File Edit Search Help
<html>
<head>
</head>
<body>
<img src="freddy.gif" alt="Freddy Frog" border="10">
<script language="javascript">
document.write("The alt text for this image is " +
document.images[0].alt + "<br/>");
document.write("The border size is " + document.images[0].border);
</script>
</body>
</html>
E:\Temp\Authoring\JSB\examples\Ch07 - Using Objects\image.html - Microsoft Internet Explorer
The alt text for this image is Freddy Frog
The border size is 10
Done
My Computer

1. Open an HTML file in Notepad.

   Note: You can use the JavaScript skeleton file created in Chapter 1.

2. Add an image to the Web page and set the `alt` and `border` attributes.
3. Add `document.write` statements to display the image attribute values.
4. Save the file using a different filename.
5. Open the file in a browser.

- The image and its attribute values are displayed.

PRELOAD IMAGES

Using a new `image` object, you can preload an image into memory while the page initially loads. After the image is preloaded, JavaScript can reference the `image` object and display it immediately. To create a new `image` object, you need to specify an image name and use the `new` keyword — for example, `myImage = newImage()`.

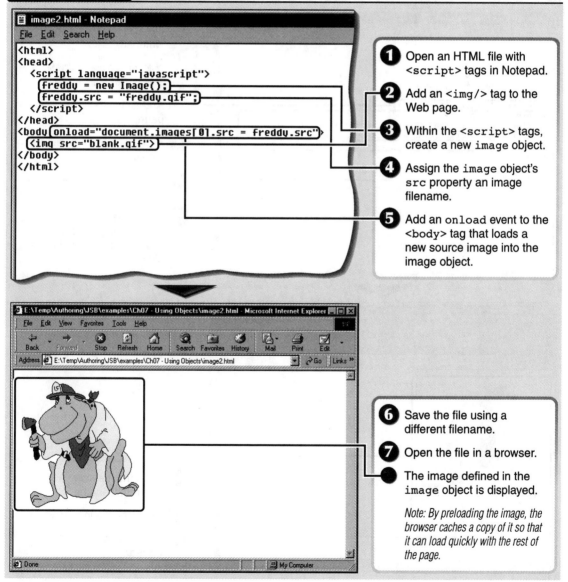

PRELOAD IMAGES

```
<html>
<head>
  <script language="javascript">
    freddy = new Image();
    freddy.src = "freddy.gif";
  </script>
</head>
<body onload="document.images[0].src = freddy.src">
  <img src="blank.gif">
</body>
</html>
```

1 Open an HTML file with `<script>` tags in Notepad.

2 Add an `<img/>` tag to the Web page.

3 Within the `<script>` tags, create a new `image` object.

4 Assign the `image` object's `src` property an image filename.

5 Add an `onload` event to the `<body>` tag that loads a new source image into the image object.

6 Save the file using a different filename.

7 Open the file in a browser.

- The image defined in the `image` object is displayed.

Note: By preloading the image, the browser caches a copy of it so that it can load quickly with the rest of the page.

CHANGE IMAGES

Many of the `image` object properties are the same as the attributes of the HTML `<img/>` tag. When these properties are changed using JavaScript, the Web page image is changed dynamically. Setting the image's `src` attribute to a new value can change the image loaded into a Web page. Before changing images, you should preload the new image so that the image is immediately available.

CHANGE IMAGES

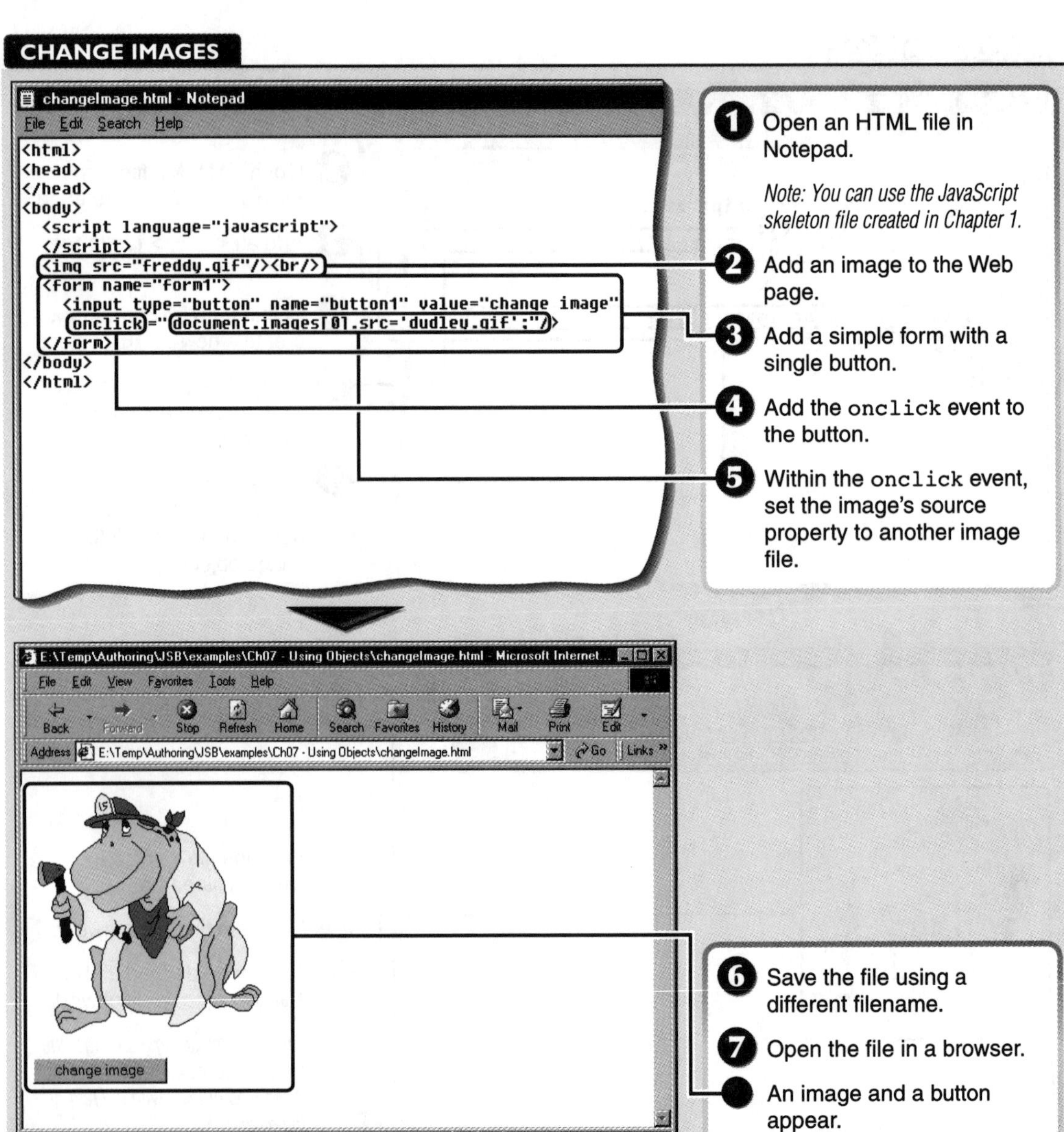

changeImage.html - Notepad
File Edit Search Help
<html>
<head>
</head>
<body>
<script language="javascript">
</script>
<img src="freddy.gif"/>
<form name="form1">
<input type="button" name="button1" value="change image"
onclick="document.images[0].src='dudley.gif';"/>
</form>
</body>
</html>
change image
Done
My Computer

1. Open an HTML file in Notepad.

   Note: You can use the JavaScript skeleton file created in Chapter 1.

2. Add an image to the Web page.
3. Add a simple form with a single button.
4. Add the `onclick` event to the button.
5. Within the `onclick` event, set the image's source property to another image file.
6. Save the file using a different filename.
7. Open the file in a browser.

- An image and a button appear.

in an instant

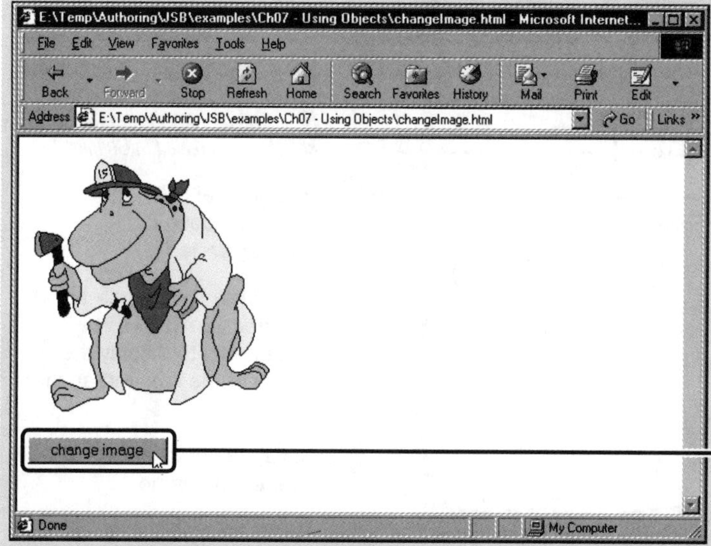

E:\Temp\Authoring\JSB\examples\Ch07 - Using Objects\changeImage.html - Microsoft Internet...
File Edit View Favorites Tools Help
Back Forward Stop Refresh Home Search Favorites History Mail Print Edit
Address E:\Temp\Authoring\JSB\examples\Ch07 - Using Objects\changeImage.html
Go Links
change image
Done
My Computer

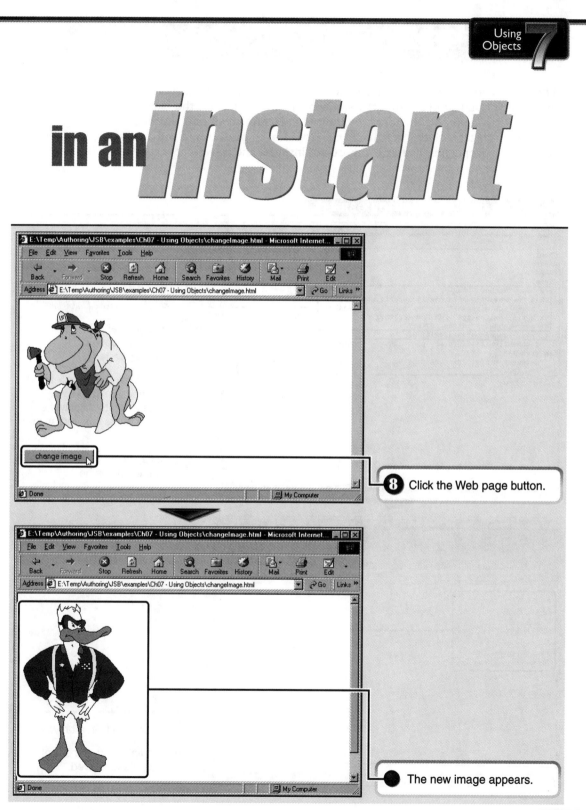

8 Click the Web page button.

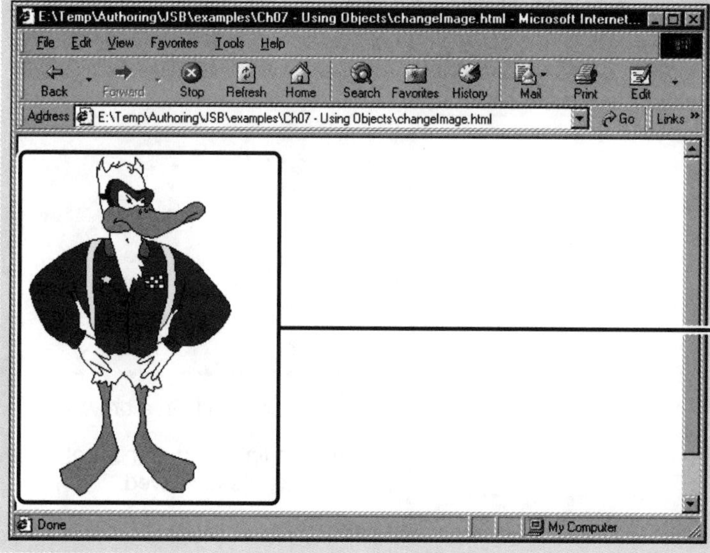

E:\Temp\Authoring\JSB\examples\Ch07 - Using Objects\changeImage.html - Microsoft Internet...
File Edit View Favorites Tools Help
Back Forward Stop Refresh Home Search Favorites History Mail Print Edit
Address E:\Temp\Authoring\JSB\examples\Ch07 - Using Objects\changeImage.html
Go Links
Done
My Computer

- The new image appears.

USING THE LINK AND ANCHOR OBJECTS

The `link` and `anchor` objects are included in an array for reference using JavaScript. The order that the link appears on the page is the index for the array. Links and anchors are counted independent of one another. The `link` object includes the `href`, `target`, `host`, `protocol`, and `pathname` properties. The `anchor` object includes the `name` property.

USING THE LINK AND ANCHOR OBJECTS

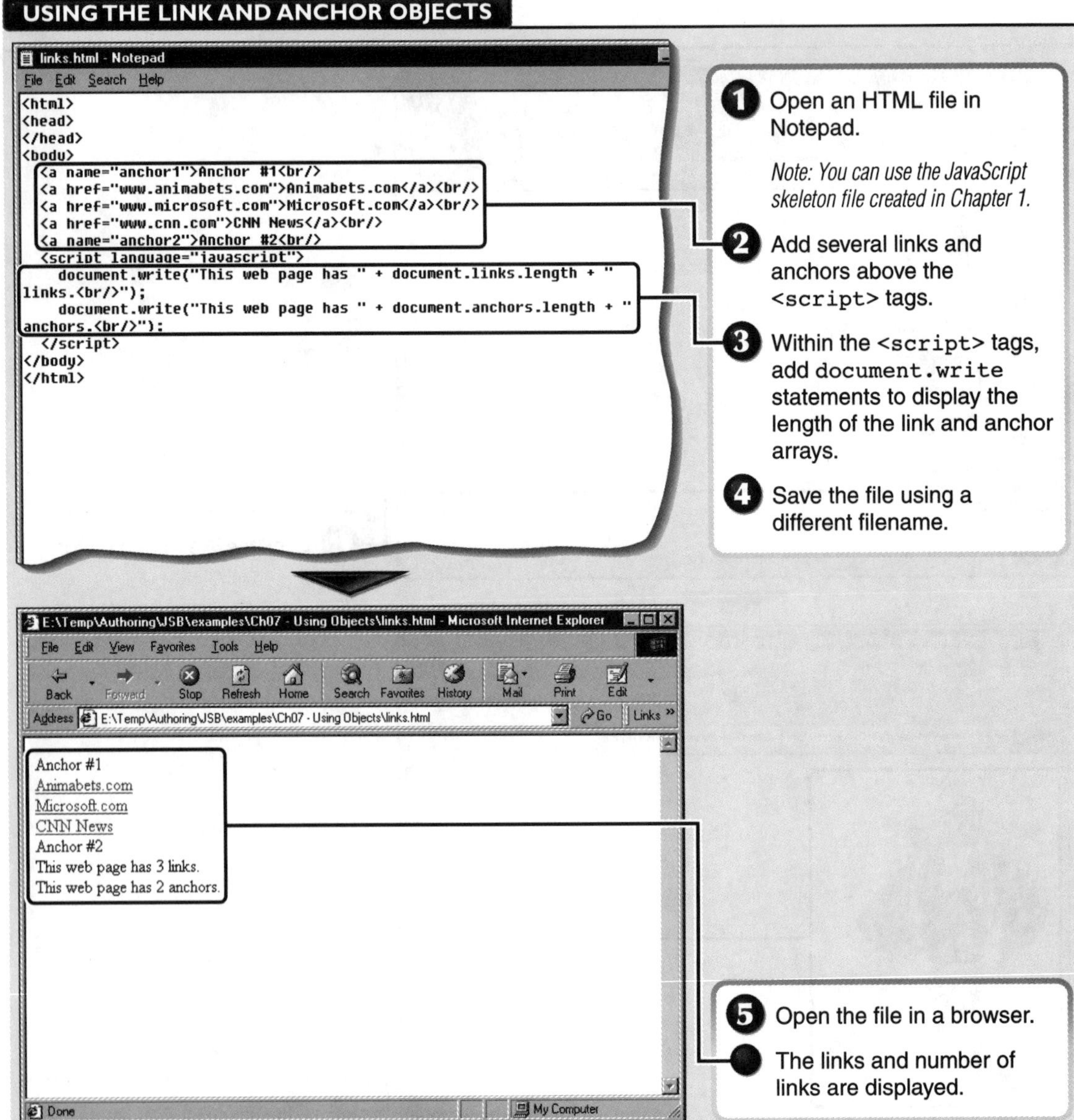

links.html - Notepad
File Edit Search Help
<html>
<head>
</head>
<body>
<a name="anchor1">Anchor #1
<a href="www.animabets.com">Animabets.com</a>
<a href="www.microsoft.com">Microsoft.com</a>
<a href="www.cnn.com">CNN News</a>
<a name="anchor2">Anchor #2
<script language="javascript">
document.write("This web page has " + document.links.length + " links.
");
document.write("This web page has " + document.anchors.length + " anchors.
");
</script>
</body>
</html>
E:\Temp\Authoring\JSB\examples\Ch07 - Using Objects\links.html - Microsoft Internet Explorer
File Edit View Favorites Tools Help
Back Forward Stop Refresh Home Search Favorites History Mail Print Edit
Address E:\Temp\Authoring\JSB\examples\Ch07 - Using Objects\links.html Go Links
Anchor #1
Animabets.com
Microsoft.com
CNN News
Anchor #2
This web page has 3 links.
This web page has 2 anchors.
Done My Computer

1. Open an HTML file in Notepad.

   Note: You can use the JavaScript skeleton file created in Chapter 1.

2. Add several links and anchors above the `<script>` tags.

3. Within the `<script>` tags, add `document.write` statements to display the length of the link and anchor arrays.

4. Save the file using a different filename.

5. Open the file in a browser.

- The links and number of links are displayed.

in an instant

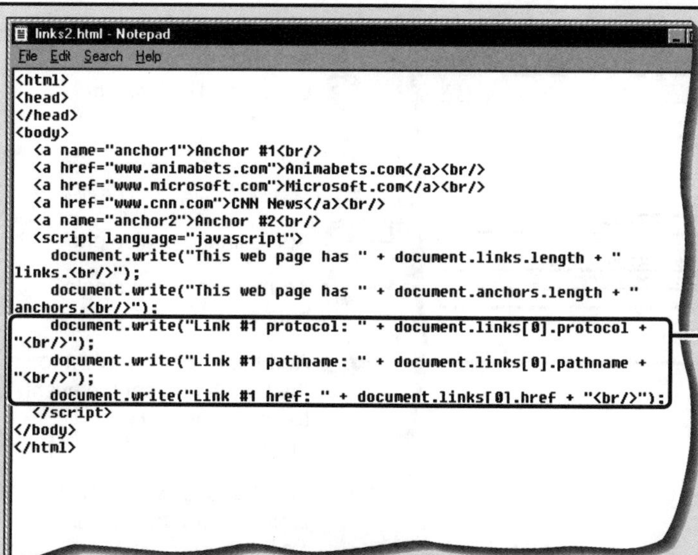

links2.html - Notepad
File Edit Search Help
<html>
<head>
</head>
<body>
<a name="anchor1">Anchor #1
<a href="www.animabets.com">Animabets.com</a>
<a href="www.microsoft.com">Microsoft.com</a>
<a href="www.cnn.com">CNN News</a>
<a name="anchor2">Anchor #2
<script language="javascript">
document.write("This web page has " + document.links.length + " links.
");
document.write("This web page has " + document.anchors.length + " anchors.
");
document.write("Link #1 protocol: " + document.links[0].protocol + "<br/>");
document.write("Link #1 pathname: " + document.links[0].pathname + "<br/>");
document.write("Link #1 href: " + document.links[0].href + "<br/>");
</script>
</body>
</html>

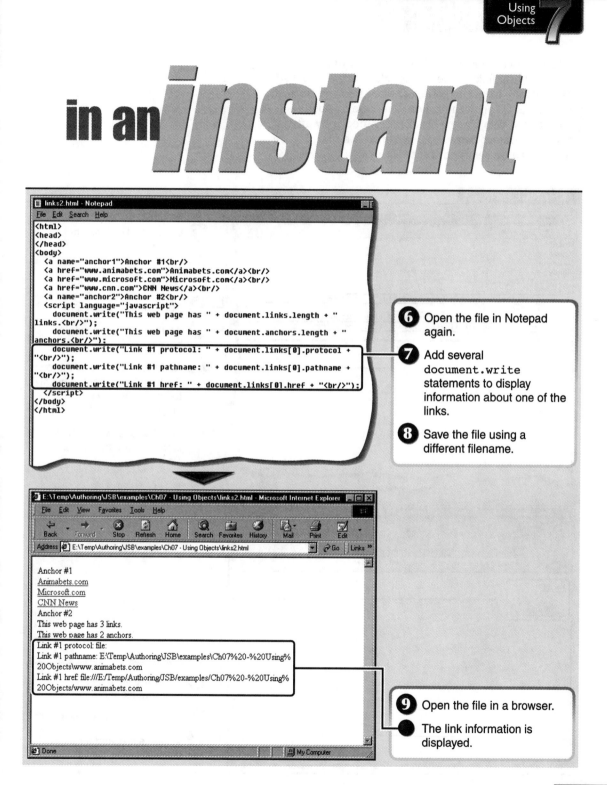

6. Open the file in Notepad again.

7. Add several `document.write` statements to display information about one of the links.

8. Save the file using a different filename.

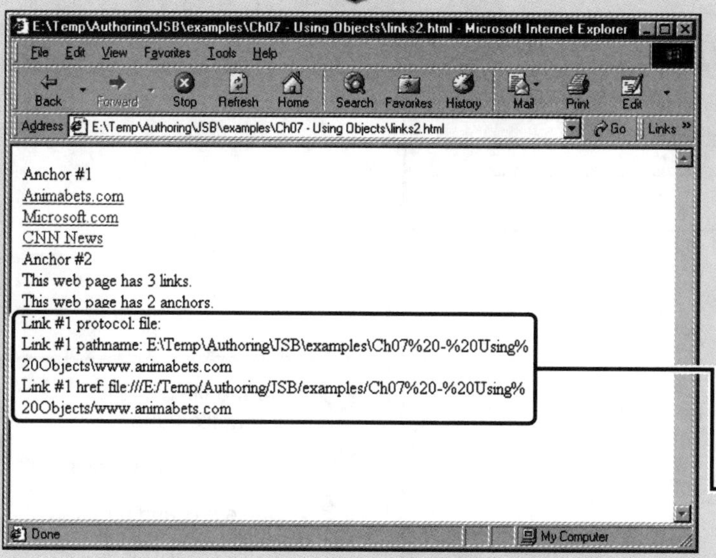

E:\Temp\Authoring\JSB\examples\Ch07 - Using Objects\links2.html - Microsoft Internet Explorer
File Edit View Favorites Tools Help
Back Forward Stop Refresh Home Search Favorites History Mail Print Edit
Address E:\Temp\Authoring\JSB\examples\Ch07 - Using Objects\links2.html
Go Links
Anchor #1
Animabets.com
Microsoft.com
CNN News
Anchor #2
This web page has 3 links.
This web page has 2 anchors.
Link #1 protocol: file:
Link #1 pathname: E:\Temp\Authoring\JSB\examples\Ch07%20-%20Using%20Objects\www.animabets.com
Link #1 href: file:///E:/Temp/Authoring/JSB/examples/Ch07%20-%20Using%20Objects/www.animabets.com
Done
My Computer

9. Open the file in a browser.

- The link information is displayed.

CHANGE LINKS

You can locate individual links by specifying the index value for the link. These index values are numbered sequentially from the top of the page to the bottom, starting at 0 for the first link. The index value is specified within square brackets immediately after the link's object name. For example, the first link on a page can be referred to as `document.links[0]`.

CHANGE LINKS

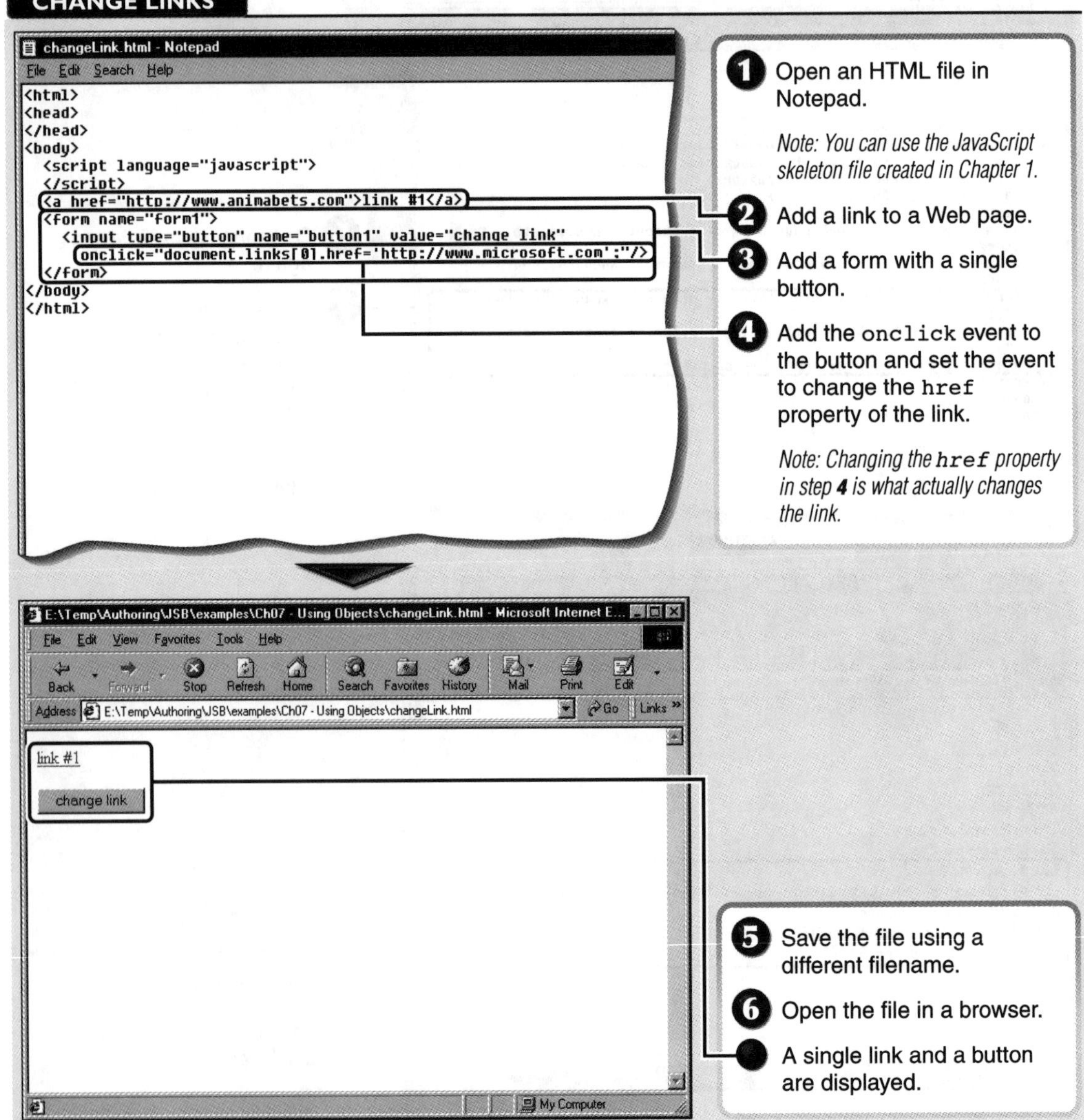
changeLink.html - Notepad
<html>
<head>
</head>
<body>
<script language="javascript">
</script>
<a href="http://www.animabets.com">link #1</a>
<form name="form1">
<input type="button" name="button1" value="change link"
onclick="document.links[0].href='http://www.microsoft.com';"/>
</form>
</body>
</html>
E:\Temp\Authoring\JSB\examples\Ch07 - Using Objects\changeLink.html - Microsoft Internet E...
link #1
change link

1. Open an HTML file in Notepad.

   Note: You can use the JavaScript skeleton file created in Chapter 1.

2. Add a link to a Web page.

3. Add a form with a single button.

4. Add the `onclick` event to the button and set the event to change the `href` property of the link.

   *Note: Changing the `href` property in step **4** is what actually changes the link.*

5. Save the file using a different filename.

6. Open the file in a browser.

- A single link and a button are displayed.

in an instant

E:\Temp\Authoring\JSB\examples\Ch07 - Using Objects\changeLink.html - Microsoft Internet E...
link #1
change link
http://www.animabets.com/
My Computer

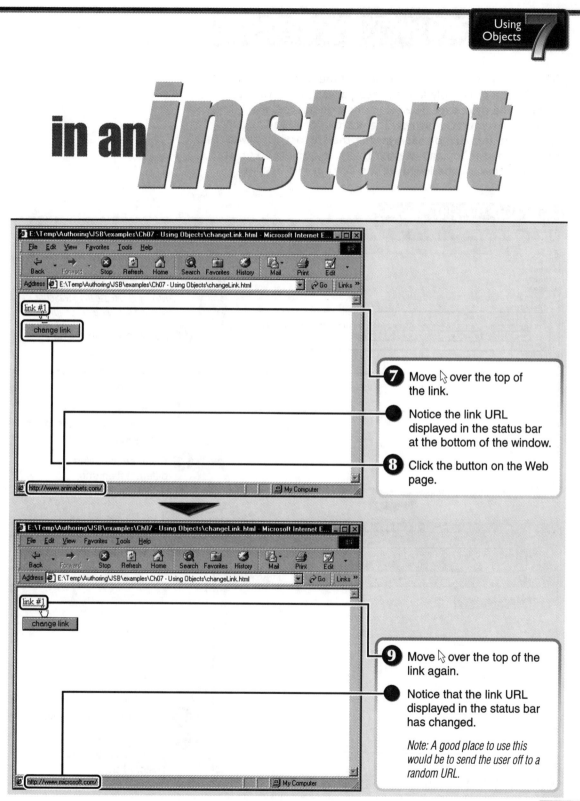

7 Move ⇖ over the top of the link.

- Notice the link URL displayed in the status bar at the bottom of the window.

8 Click the button on the Web page.

E:\Temp\Authoring\JSB\examples\Ch07 - Using Objects\changeLink.html - Microsoft Internet E...
link #1
change link
http://www.microsoft.com/
My Computer

9 Move ⇖ over the top of the link again.

- Notice that the link URL displayed in the status bar has changed.

Note: A good place to use this would be to send the user off to a random URL.

USING THE HISTORY OBJECT

The `history` object includes several methods: `back()` displays the previously loaded Web page, and `forward()` displays the next page. The `go()` method accepts a number parameter, which can be positive or negative, and moves you forward or backward in the History list saved by the browser. You can use the `history` object's `length` property to view the length of the current History list.

USING THE HISTORY OBJECT

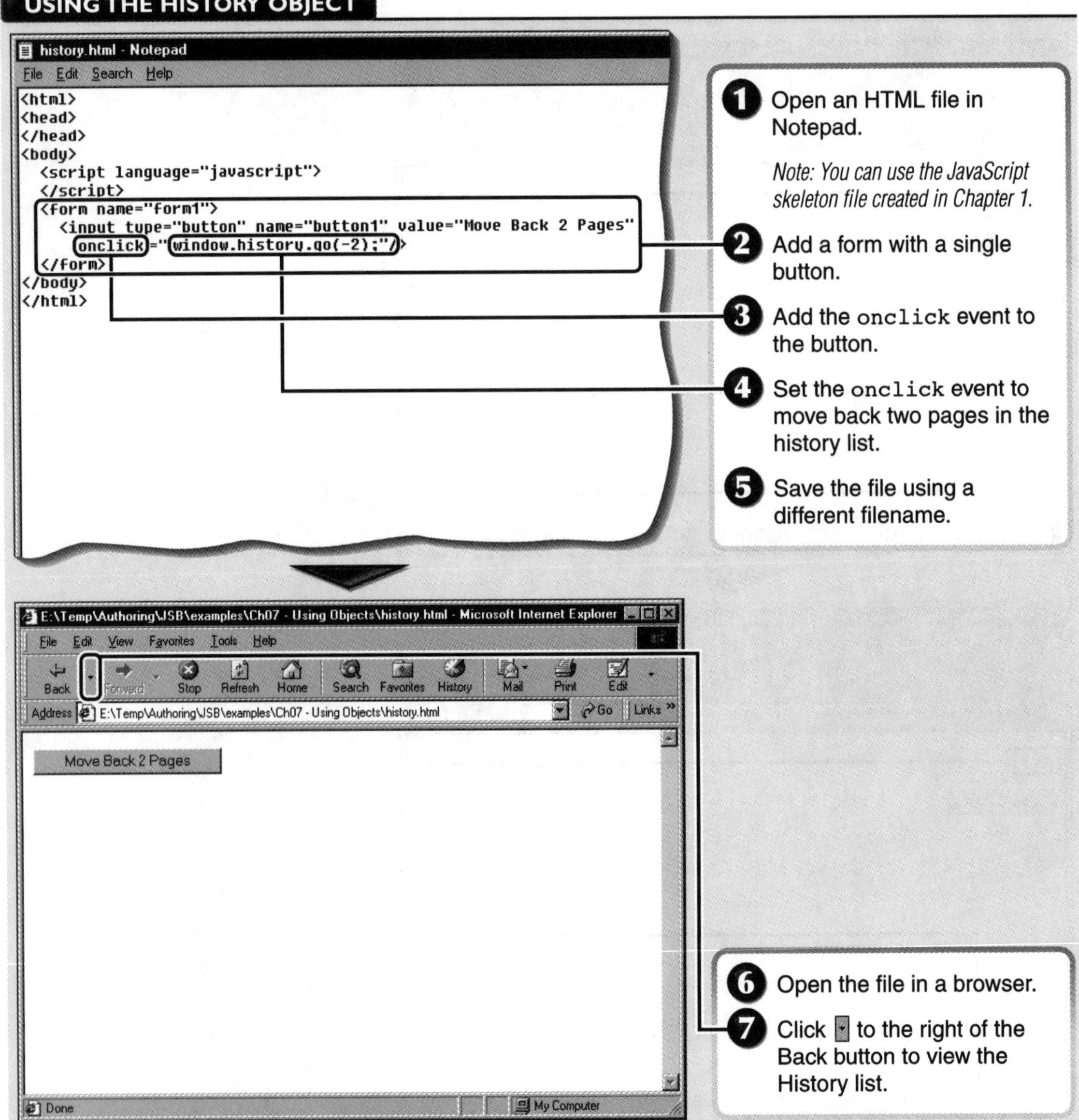
history.html - Notepad
File Edit Search Help
<html>
<head>
</head>
<body>
<script language="javascript">
</script>
<form name="form1">
<input type="button" name="button1" value="Move Back 2 Pages"
onclick="window.history.go(-2);"/>
</form>
</body>
</html>
E:\Temp\Authoring\JSB\examples\Ch07 - Using Objects\history.html - Microsoft Internet Explorer
File Edit View Favorites Tools Help
Back Forward Stop Refresh Home Search Favorites History Mail Print Edit
Address E:\Temp\Authoring\JSB\examples\Ch07 - Using Objects\history.html
Go Links
Move Back 2 Pages
Done
My Computer

1. Open an HTML file in Notepad.

   Note: You can use the JavaScript skeleton file created in Chapter 1.

2. Add a form with a single button.
3. Add the `onclick` event to the button.
4. Set the `onclick` event to move back two pages in the history list.
5. Save the file using a different filename.
6. Open the file in a browser.
7. Click ▾ to the right of the Back button to view the History list.

in an instant

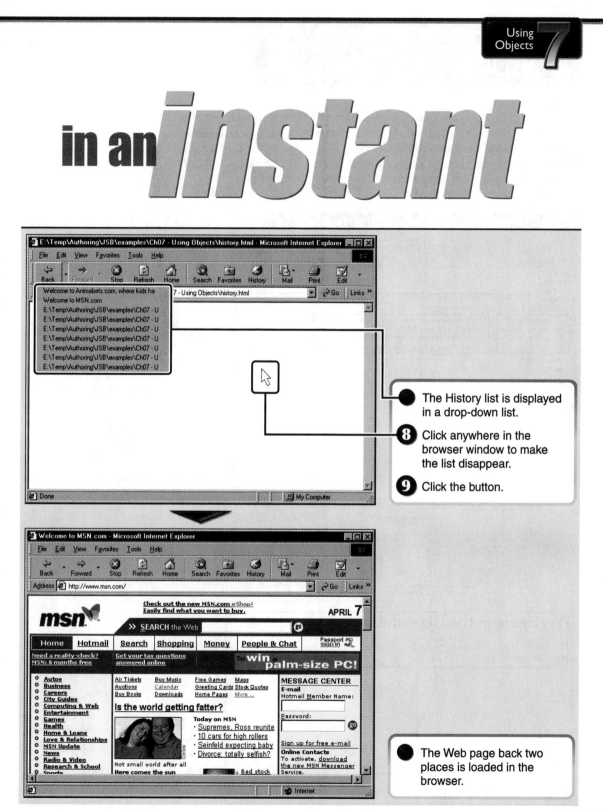

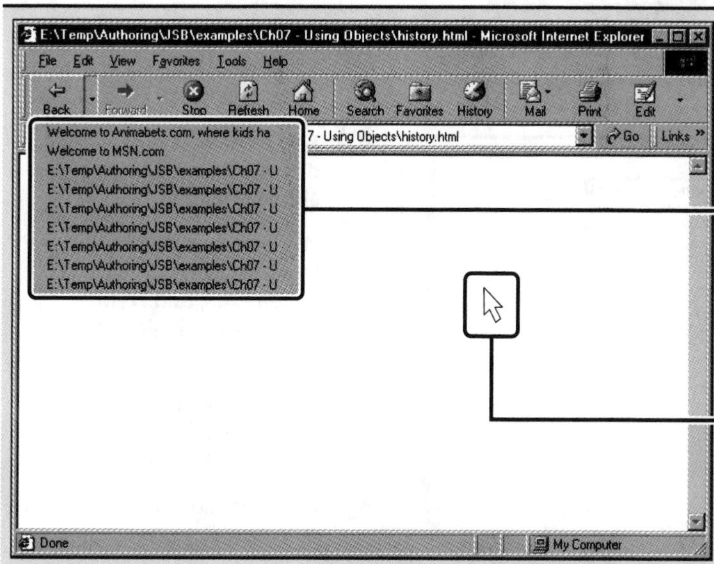

- The History list is displayed in a drop-down list.

8 Click anywhere in the browser window to make the list disappear.

9 Click the button.

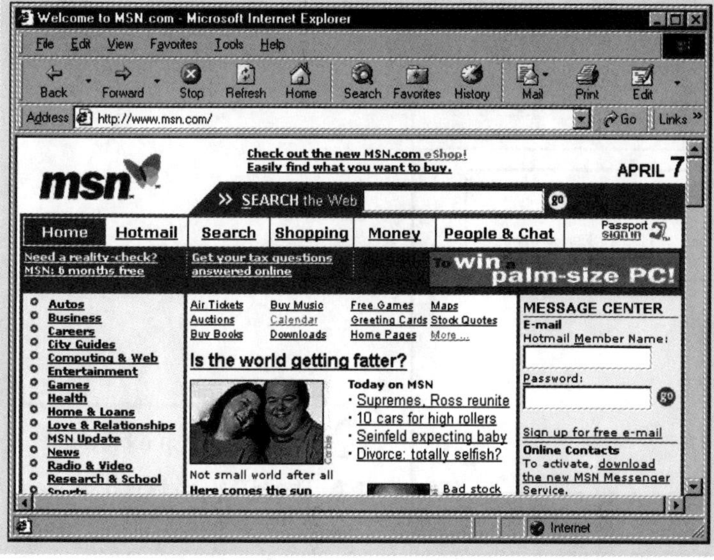

- The Web page back two places is loaded in the browser.

USING THE WINDOW AND DOCUMENT OBJECTS

The `window` object is the top-level parent object and includes the `document`, `location`, and `history` objects. `window` also includes properties and methods for controlling the external look of a browser window. The `document` object allows access to the various elements that make up a Web page. One of its object methods is `write()`, which is used to output text and HTML to the browser window.

USING THE WINDOW AND DOCUMENT OBJECTS

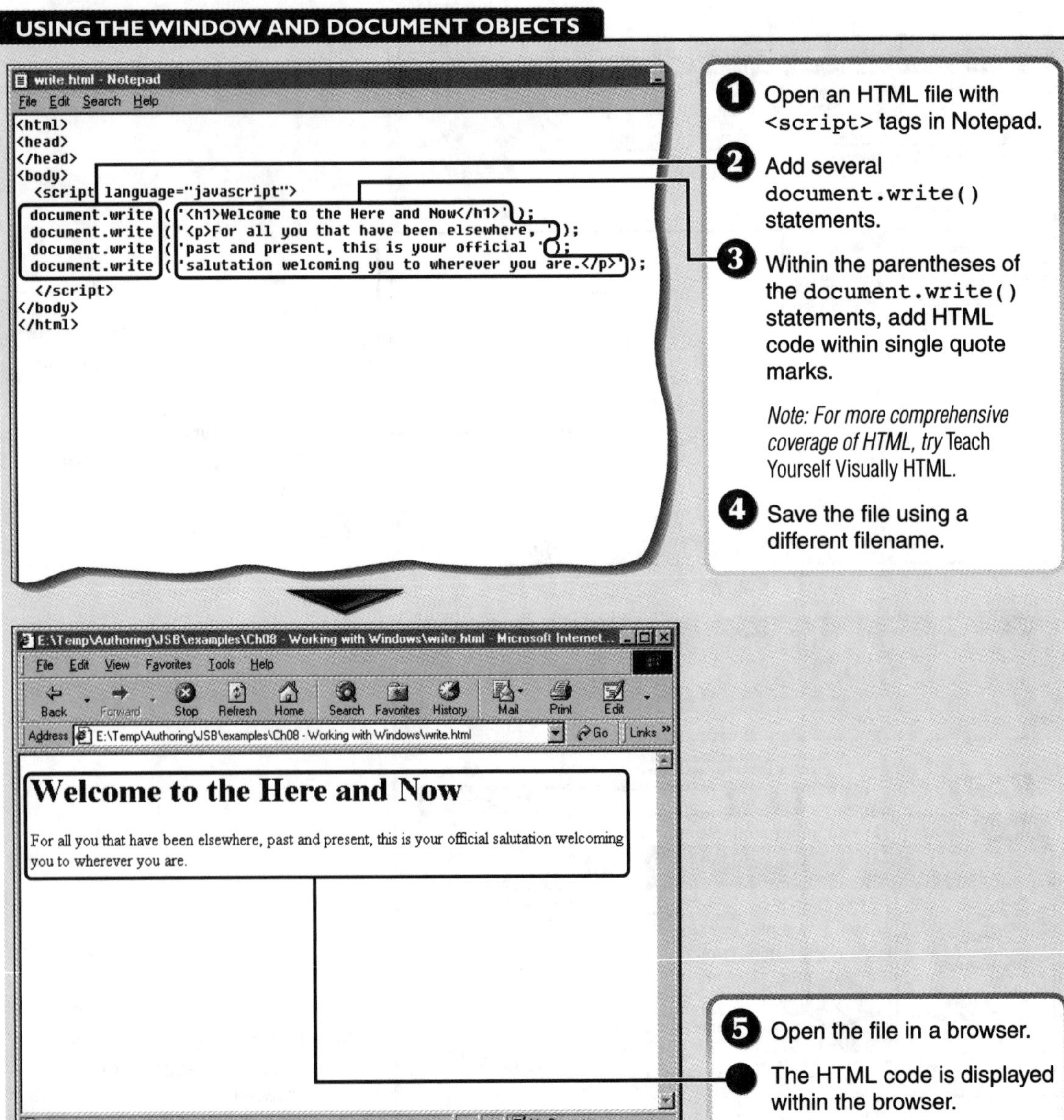

write.html - Notepad
File Edit Search Help
<html>
<head>
</head>
<body>
<script language="javascript">
document.write('<h1>Welcome to the Here and Now</h1>');
document.write('<p>For all you that have been elsewhere, ');
document.write('past and present, this is your official ');
document.write('salutation welcoming you to wherever you are.</p>');
</script>
</body>
</html>
E:\Temp\Authoring\JSB\examples\Ch08 - Working with Windows\write.html - Microsoft Internet...
File Edit View Favorites Tools Help
Back Forward Stop Refresh Home Search Favorites History Mail Print Edit
Address E:\Temp\Authoring\JSB\examples\Ch08 - Working with Windows\write.html
Go Links
Welcome to the Here and Now
For all you that have been elsewhere, past and present, this is your official salutation welcoming you to wherever you are.
Done
My Computer

1. Open an HTML file with `<script>` tags in Notepad.
2. Add several `document.write()` statements.
3. Within the parentheses of the `document.write()` statements, add HTML code within single quote marks.

Note: For more comprehensive coverage of HTML, try Teach Yourself Visually HTML.

4. Save the file using a different filename.
5. Open the file in a browser.

- The HTML code is displayed within the browser.

in an instant

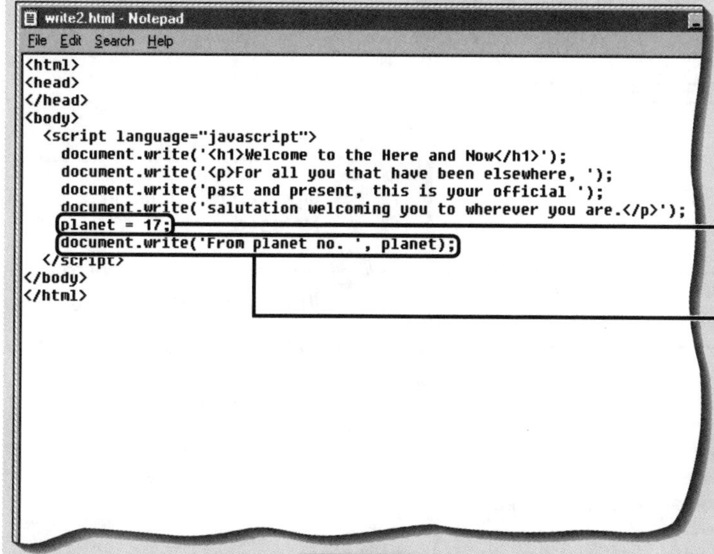

write2.html - Notepad

File Edit Search Help

```
<html>
<head>
</head>
<body>
  <script language="javascript">
    document.write('<h1>Welcome to the Here and Now</h1>');
    document.write('<p>For all you that have been elsewhere, ');
    document.write('past and present, this is your official ');
    document.write('salutation welcoming you to wherever you are.</p>');
    planet = 17;
    document.write('From planet no. ', planet);
  </script>
</body>
</html>
```

ADD A VARIABLE

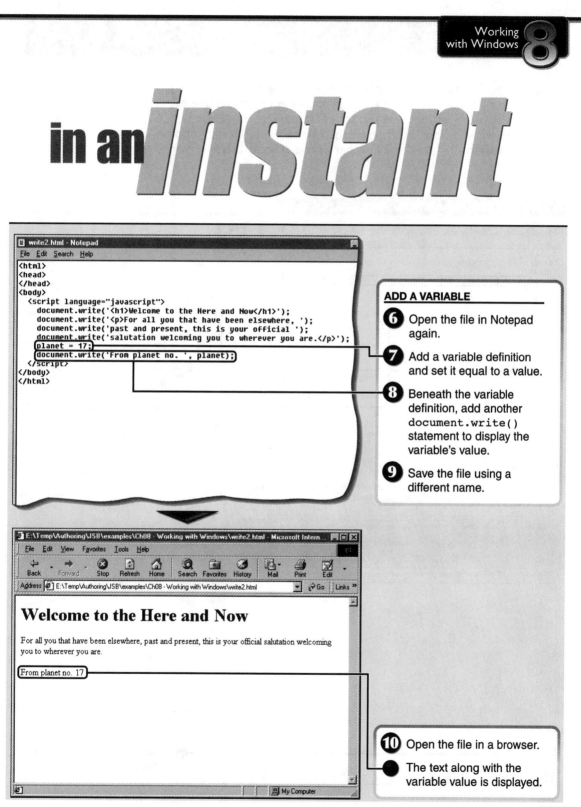

6 Open the file in Notepad again.

7 Add a variable definition and set it equal to a value.

8 Beneath the variable definition, add another `document.write()` statement to display the variable's value.

9 Save the file using a different name.

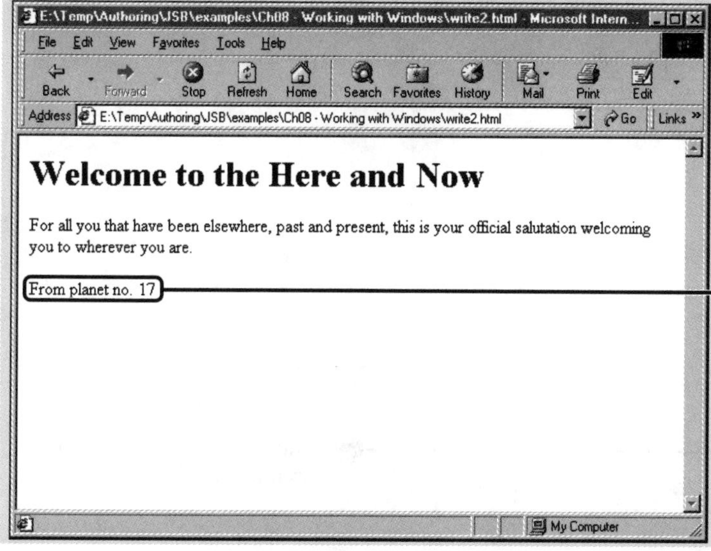

E:\Temp\Authoring\JSB\examples\Ch08 - Working with Windows\write2.html - Microsoft Intern...

File Edit View Favorites Tools Help

Back Forward Stop Refresh Home Search Favorites History Mail Print Edit

Address E:\Temp\Authoring\JSB\examples\Ch08 - Working with Windows\write2.html Go Links

Welcome to the Here and Now

For all you that have been elsewhere, past and present, this is your official salutation welcoming you to wherever you are.

From planet no. 17

My Computer

10 Open the file in a browser.

- The text along with the variable value is displayed.

DISPLAY TEXT ON A BROWSER'S STATUS BAR

You can set the text that is displayed on a browser's status bar by simply setting the `window.status` property equal to the line of text. This text can also include JavaScript statements. For example, the statement `window.status="hello and welcome"` displays "hello and welcome" on the status bar of the current browser window.

DISPLAY TEXT ON A BROWSER'S STATUS BAR

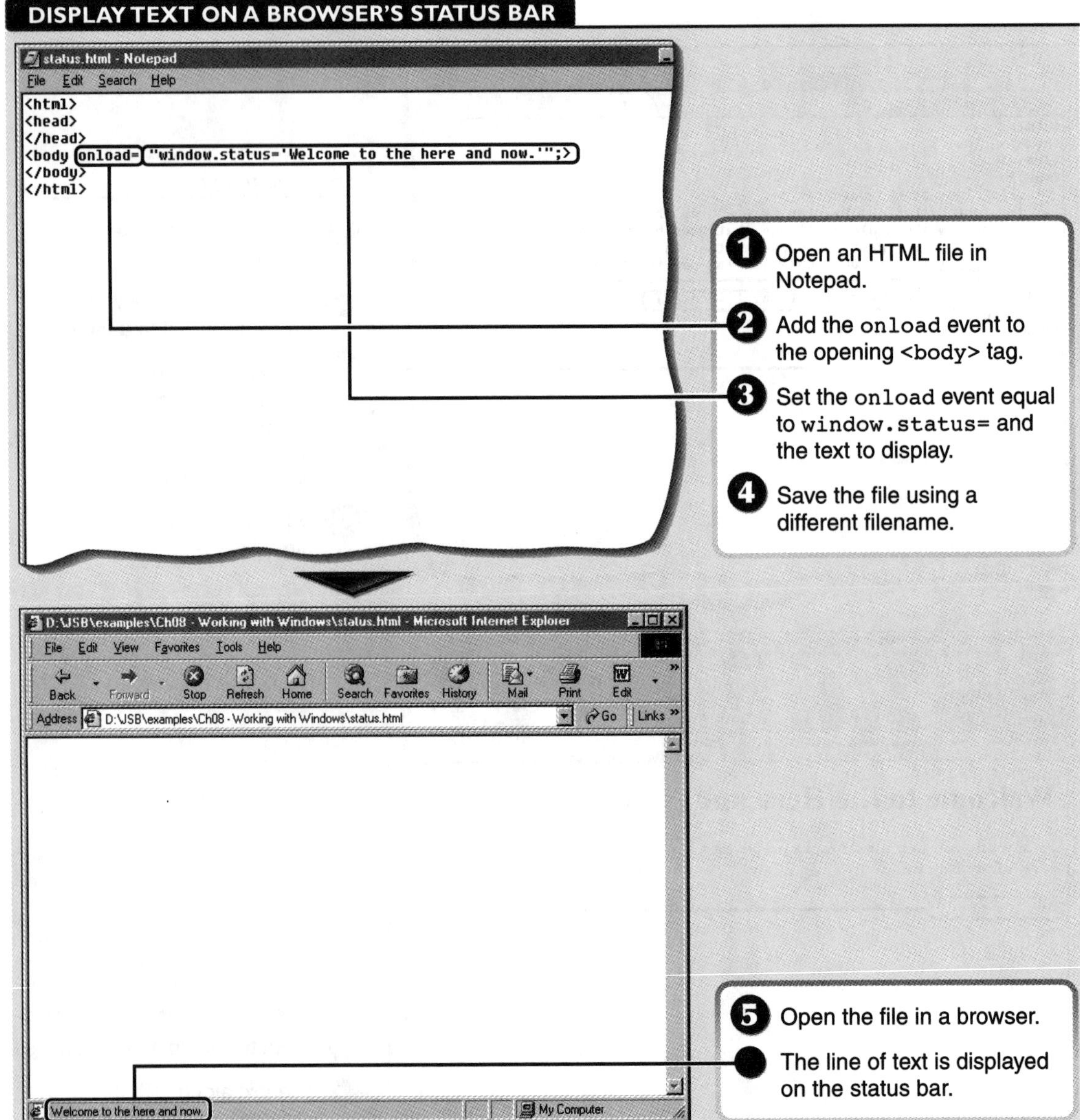

status.html - Notepad
File Edit Search Help
<html>
<head>
</head>
<body onload="window.status='Welcome to the here and now.'";>
</body>
</html>
D:\JSB\examples\Ch08 - Working with Windows\status.html - Microsoft Internet Explorer
File Edit View Favorites Tools Help
Back Forward Stop Refresh Home Search Favorites History Mail Print Edit
Address D:\JSB\examples\Ch08 - Working with Windows\status.html
Go Links
Welcome to the here and now.
My Computer

1. Open an HTML file in Notepad.
2. Add the `onload` event to the opening `<body>` tag.
3. Set the `onload` event equal to `window.status=` and the text to display.
4. Save the file using a different filename.
5. Open the file in a browser.

- The line of text is displayed on the status bar.

in an instant

status2.html - Notepad
File Edit Search Help
<html>
<head>
</head>
<body onload="window.status='Welcome to the here and now.'";>
<a href="www.animabets.com">Animabets.com</a>
</body>
</html>

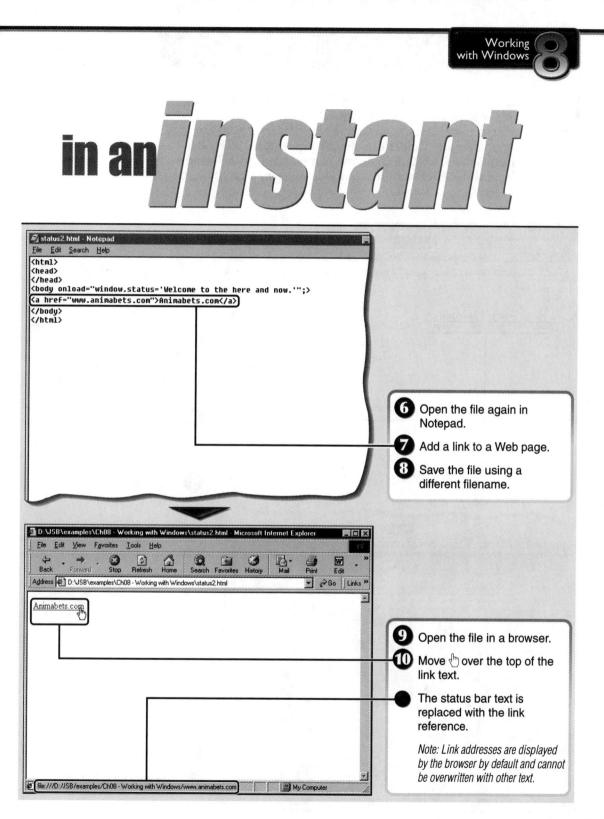

6 Open the file again in Notepad.

7 Add a link to a Web page.

8 Save the file using a different filename.

D:\JSB\examples\Ch08 - Working with Windows\status2.html - Microsoft Internet Explorer
Animabets.com
file:///D:/JSB/examples/Ch08 - Working with Windows/www.animabets.com
My Computer

9 Open the file in a browser.

10 Move the pointer over the top of the link text.

- The status bar text is replaced with the link reference.

Note: Link addresses are displayed by the browser by default and cannot be overwritten with other text.

CHANGE BACKGROUND COLORS

The `document.bgColor` object property holds the current background color, or if you assign this object a color, you can set the background color. Color values can be color names such as `red`, `blue`, or `orange`. Colors can also be represented as RGB hexadecimal numbers, which include the number sign (#) followed by the hexadecimal values of red, green, and blue ranging from `00` to `FF`.

CHANGE BACKGROUND COLORS

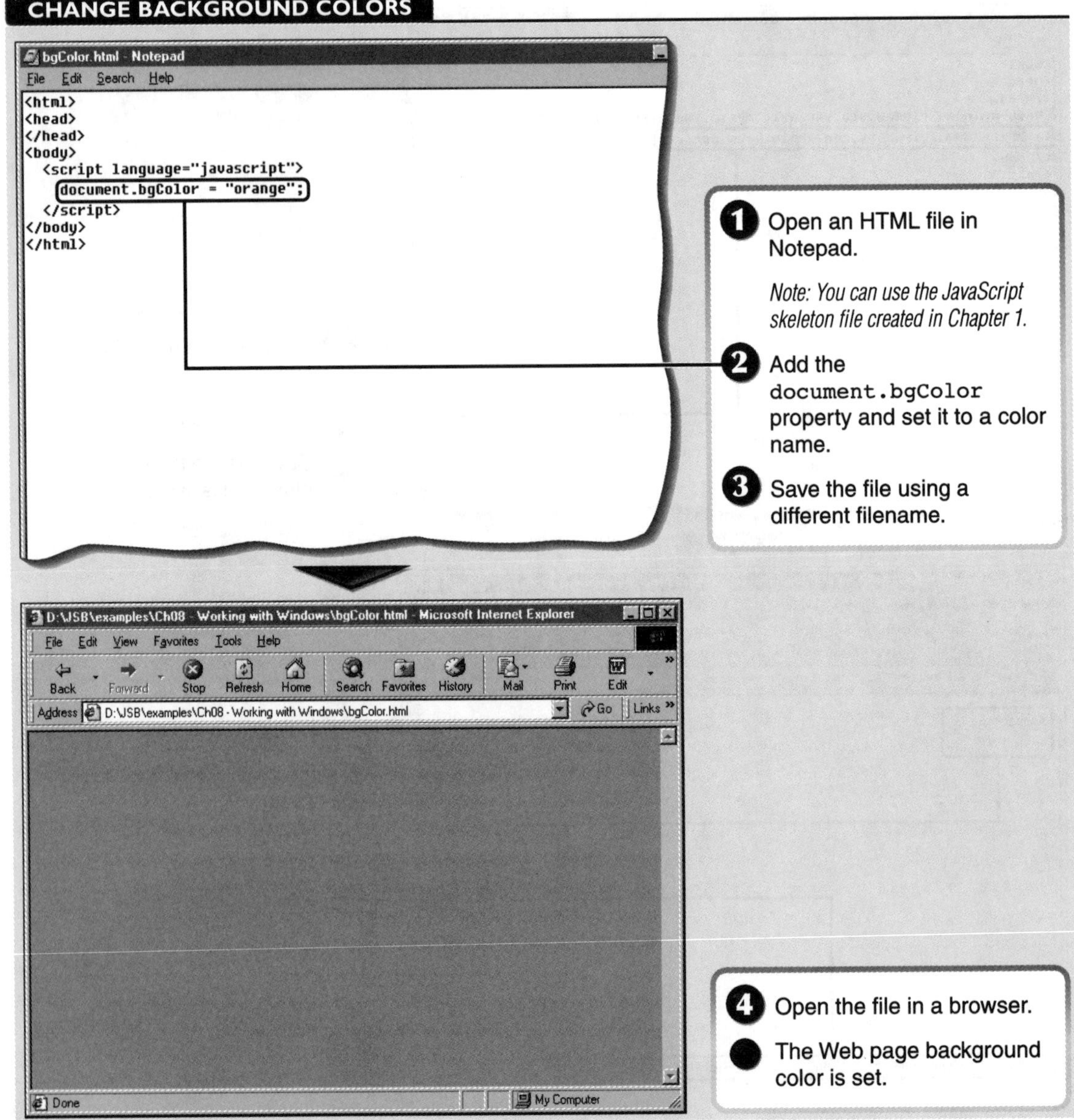
bgColor.html - Notepad
File Edit Search Help
<html>
<head>
</head>
<body>
<script language="javascript">
document.bgColor = "orange";
</script>
</body>
</html>
D:\JSB\examples\Ch08 - Working with Windows\bgColor.html - Microsoft Internet Explorer
File Edit View Favorites Tools Help
Back Forward Stop Refresh Home Search Favorites History Mail Print Edit
Address D:\JSB\examples\Ch08 - Working with Windows\bgColor.html
Go Links
Done
My Computer

1. Open an HTML file in Notepad.

   Note: You can use the JavaScript skeleton file created in Chapter 1.

2. Add the `document.bgColor` property and set it to a color name.

3. Save the file using a different filename.

4. Open the file in a browser.

- The Web page background color is set.

in an instant

LIST THE BACKGROUND COLOR

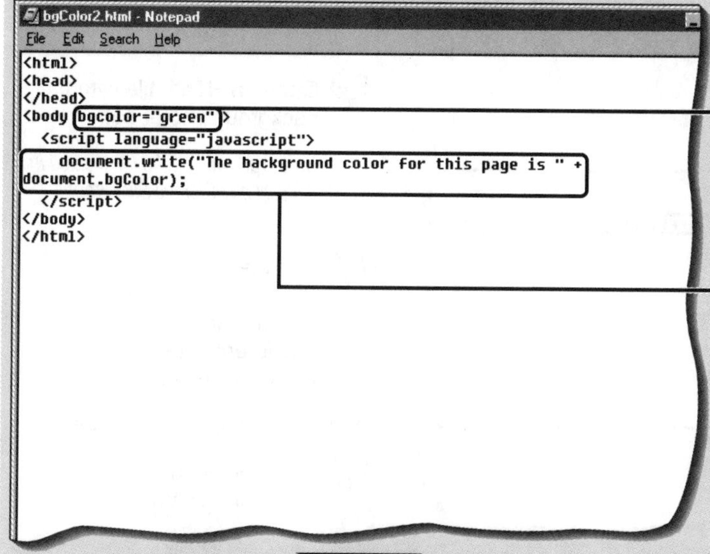

```
<html>
<head>
</head>
<body bgcolor="green">
  <script language="javascript">
    document.write("The background color for this page is " +
document.bgColor);
  </script>
</body>
</html>
```

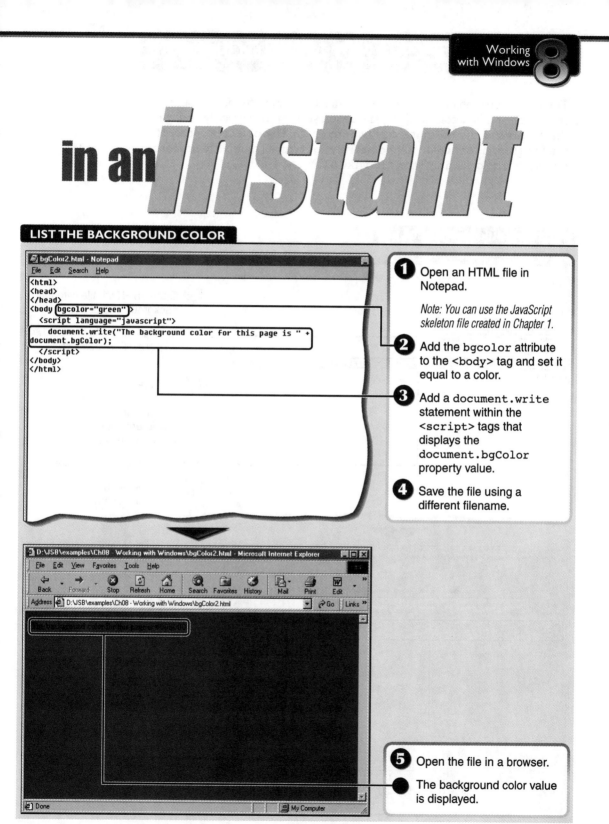

1. Open an HTML file in Notepad.

   Note: You can use the JavaScript skeleton file created in Chapter 1.

2. Add the `bgcolor` attribute to the <body> tag and set it equal to a color.
3. Add a `document.write` statement within the `<script>` tags that displays the `document.bgColor` property value.
4. Save the file using a different filename. 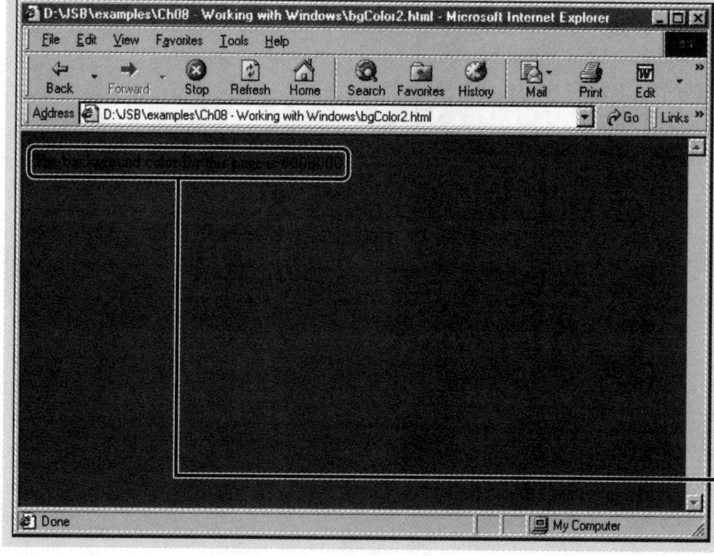
5. Open the file in a browser.

- The background color value is displayed.

CHANGE TEXT AND LINK COLORS

The `document` object includes properties for setting the foreground text color and link colors. Using JavaScript, you can dynamically change these colors as the user interacts with the page. The object property for the foreground text color is `document.fgColor`. The object property for the link color is `document.linkColor`.

SET THE FOREGROUND COLOR

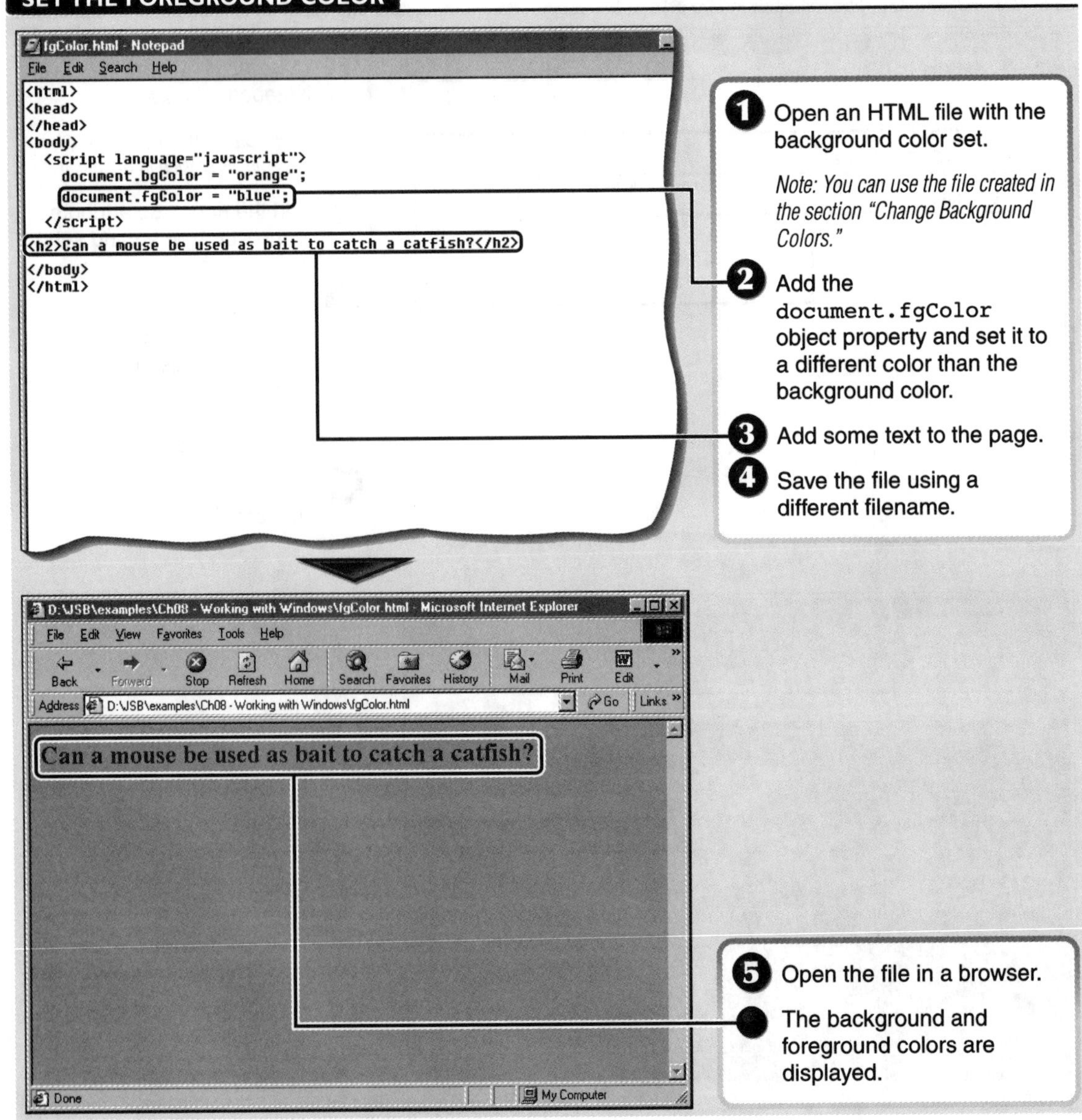

fgColor.html - Notepad
File Edit Search Help
<html>
<head>
</head>
<body>
<script language="javascript">
document.bgColor = "orange";
document.fgColor = "blue";
</script>
<h2>Can a mouse be used as bait to catch a catfish?</h2>
</body>
</html>
1 Open an HTML file with the background color set.
Note: You can use the file created in the section "Change Background Colors."
2 Add the document.fgColor object property and set it to a different color than the background color.
3 Add some text to the page.
4 Save the file using a different filename.
D:\JSB\examples\Ch08 - Working with Windows\fgColor.html - Microsoft Internet Explorer
Can a mouse be used as bait to catch a catfish?
Done
My Computer
5 Open the file in a browser.
The background and foreground colors are displayed.

in an instant

SET THE LINK COLOR

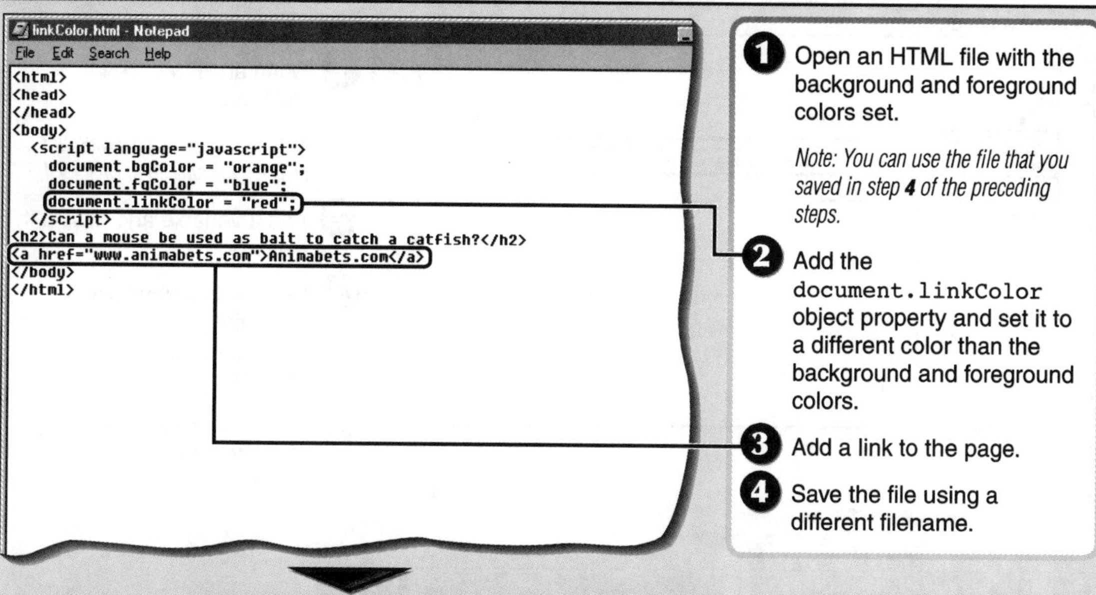
linkColor.html - Notepad
File Edit Search Help
<html>
<head>
</head>
<body>
<script language="javascript">
document.bgColor = "orange";
document.fgColor = "blue";
document.linkColor = "red";
</script>
<h2>Can a mouse be used as bait to catch a catfish?</h2>
<a href="www.animabets.com">Animabets.com</a>
</body>
</html>

1. Open an HTML file with the background and foreground colors set.

   *Note: You can use the file that you saved in step **4** of the preceding steps.*

2. Add the `document.linkColor` object property and set it to a different color than the background and foreground colors.
3. Add a link to the page.
4. Save the file using a different filename.

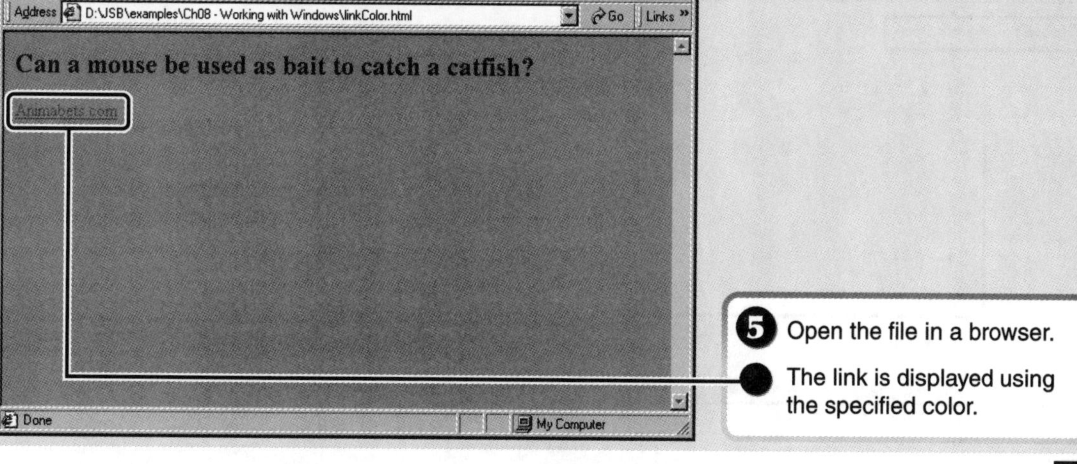
D:\JSB\examples\Ch08 - Working with Windows\linkColor.html - Microsoft Internet Explorer
File Edit View Favorites Tools Help
Back Forward Stop Refresh Home Search Favorites History Mail Print Edit
Address D:\JSB\examples\Ch08 - Working with Windows\linkColor.html
Go Links
Can a mouse be used as bait to catch a catfish?
Animabets.com
Done
My Computer

5. Open the file in a browser.

- The link is displayed using the specified color.

CHANGE THE DOCUMENT TITLE

The `document.title` property holds the current document title, or it can be set to a new value that appears when the page is loaded. For example, to set the title of a document to "Welcome to Joe's," you could set a `name` variable equal to `Joe's` and then set the `document.title` property equal to `"Welcome to " + name`, which would dynamically generate the title for the current document.

CHANGE THE DOCUMENT TITLE

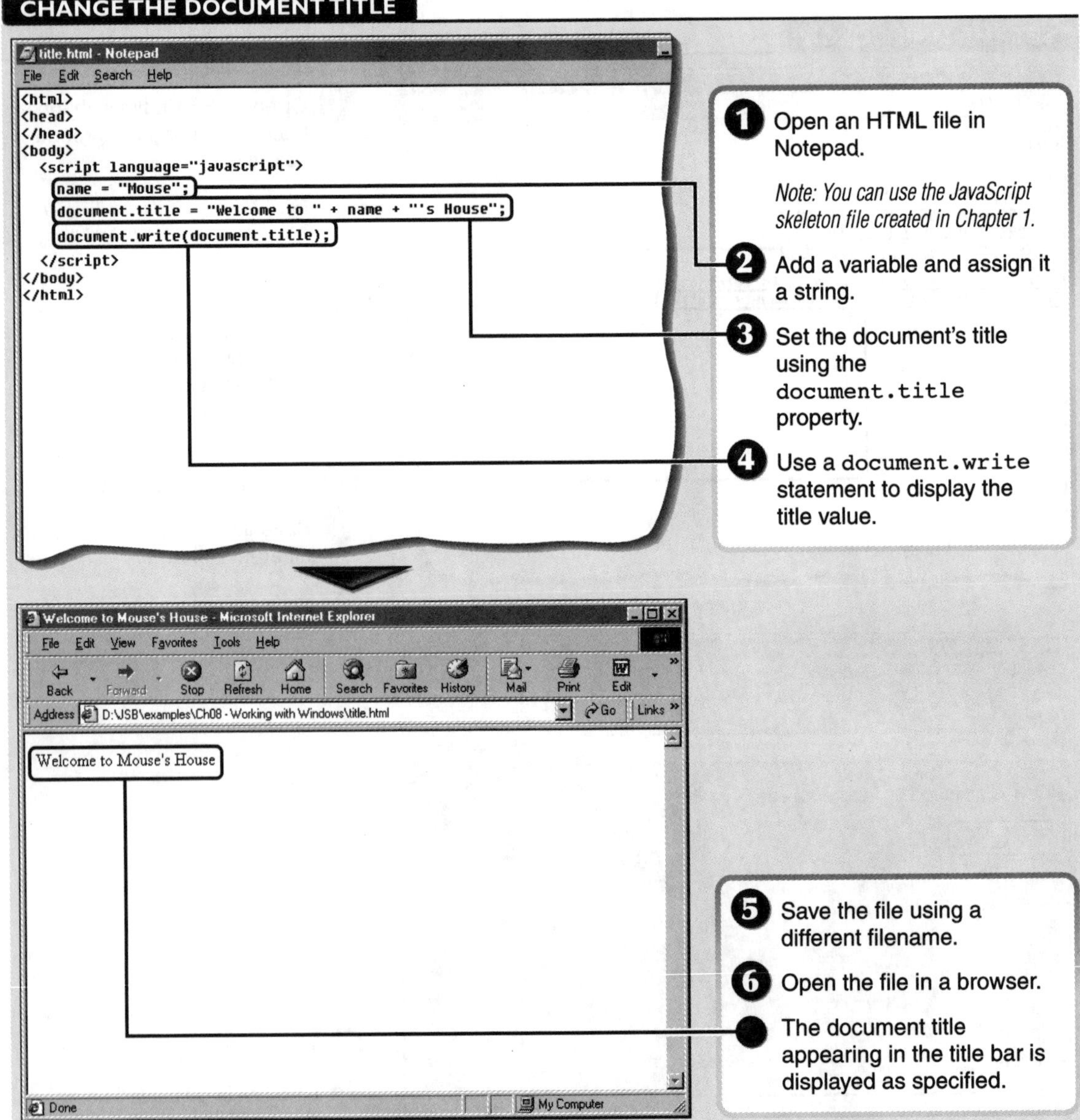

title.html - Notepad
File Edit Search Help
<html>
<head>
</head>
<body>
<script language="javascript">
name = "Mouse";
document.title = "Welcome to " + name + "'s House";
document.write(document.title);
</script>
</body>
</html>
1 Open an HTML file in Notepad.
Note: You can use the JavaScript skeleton file created in Chapter 1.
2 Add a variable and assign it a string.
3 Set the document's title using the document.title property.
4 Use a document.write statement to display the title value.
Welcome to Mouse's House - Microsoft Internet Explorer
File Edit View Favorites Tools Help
Back Forward Stop Refresh Home Search Favorites History Mail Print Edit
Address D:\JSB\examples\Ch08 - Working with Windows\title.html
Go Links
Welcome to Mouse's House
Done
My Computer
5 Save the file using a different filename.
6 Open the file in a browser.
The document title appearing in the title bar is displayed as specified.

DISPLAY THE MODIFICATION DATE

The `document.lastModified` property displays the date when a document was last modified. The format of the modification date includes the month, date, and year, along with the time. In Chapter 10, the `Date` object is covered in more detail.

DISPLAY THE MODIFICATION DATE

lastModified.html - Notepad

```
<html>
<head>
</head>
<body>
  <script language="javascript">
    document.write("This page was last modified on " +
document.lastModified);
  </script>
</body>
</html>
```

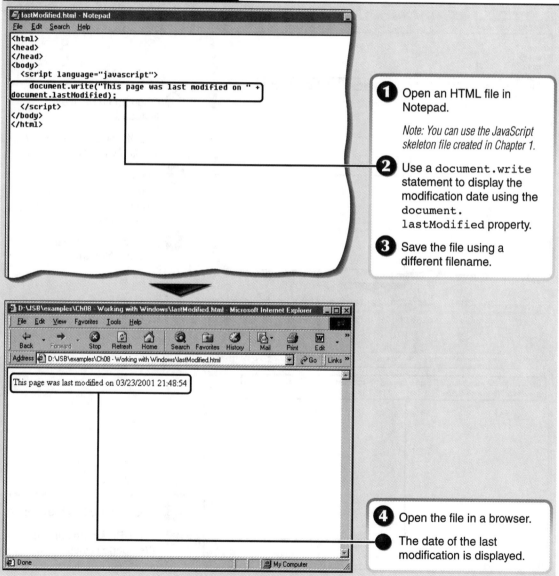

1. Open an HTML file in Notepad.

   Note: You can use the JavaScript skeleton file created in Chapter 1.

2. Use a `document.write` statement to display the modification date using the `document.lastModified` property.

3. Save the file using a different filename.

D:\JSB\examples\Ch08 - Working with Windows\lastModified.html - Microsoft Internet Explorer

This page was last modified on 03/23/2001 21:48:54

4. Open the file in a browser.

- The date of the last modification is displayed.

VIEW THE URL OF THE CURRENT DOCUMENT

You can place the current URL at the bottom of every Web page by using the `URL` property, which is part of the `document` object, in the form of the statement `document.URL`. This property is a read-only property; you cannot use `URL` to change the URL for the current Web page.

VIEW THE URL OF THE CURRENT DOCUMENT

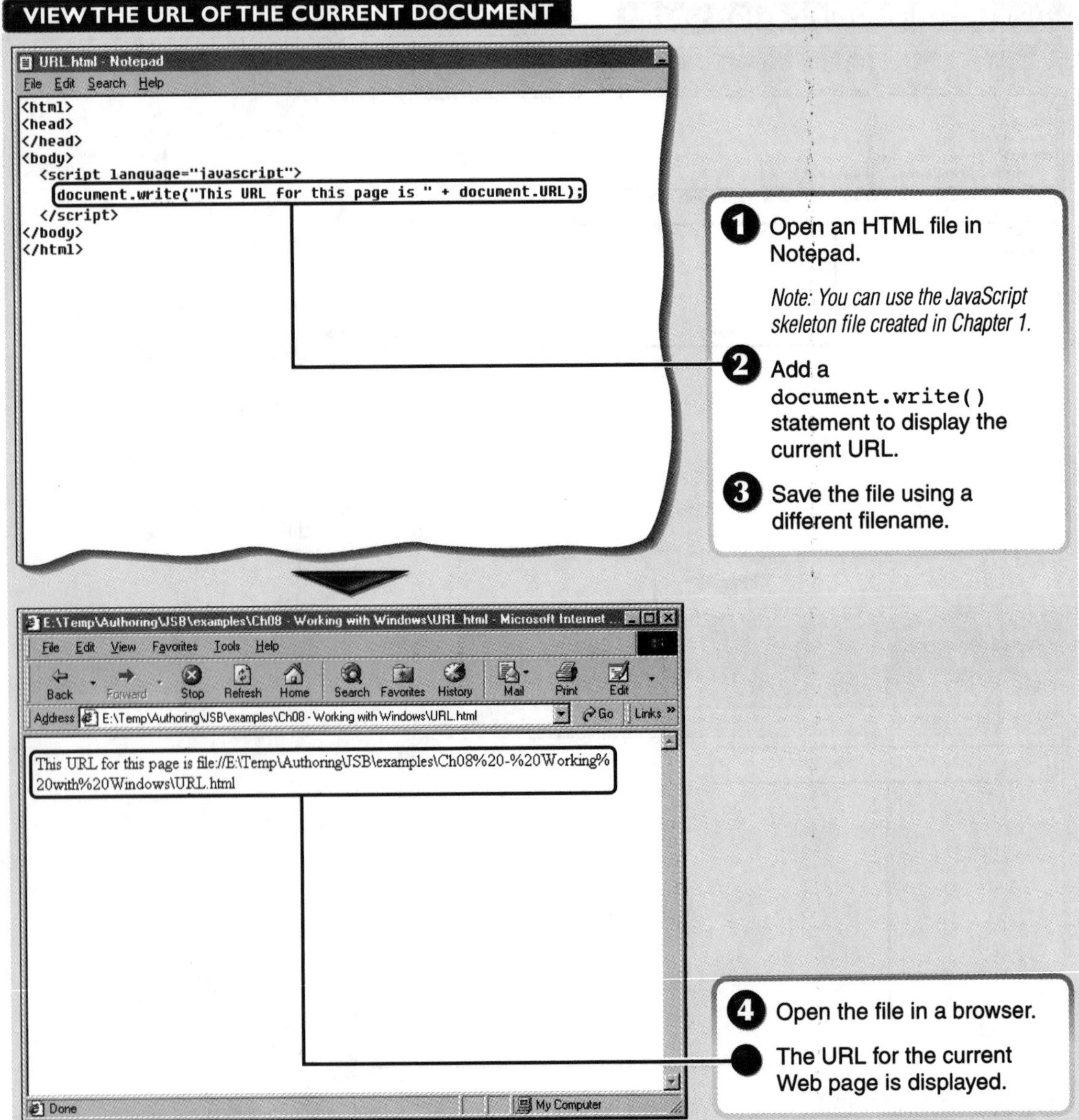

URL.html - Notepad
File Edit Search Help
<html>
<head>
</head>
<body>
<script language="javascript">
document.write("This URL for this page is " + document.URL);
</script>
</body>
</html>
E:\Temp\Authoring\JSB\examples\Ch08 - Working with Windows\URL.html - Microsoft Internet ...
File Edit View Favorites Tools Help
Back Forward Stop Refresh Home Search Favorites History Mail Print Edit
Address E:\Temp\Authoring\JSB\examples\Ch08 - Working with Windows\URL.html
Go Links
This URL for this page is file://E:\Temp\Authoring\JSB\examples\Ch08%20-%20Working%20with%20Windows\URL.html
Done
My Computer

1. Open an HTML file in Notepad.

   Note: You can use the JavaScript skeleton file created in Chapter 1.

2. Add a `document.write()` statement to display the current URL.

3. Save the file using a different filename.

4. Open the file in a browser.

- The URL for the current Web page is displayed.

VIEW THE REFERRING PAGE

Working
with Windows
8

The `document` object includes a property that can be used to view the referring Web page — `referrer`. This property displays the referring URL, which will be URL encoded. Using `document.referrer`, you can determine the link that was used to send the user to your Web page.

VIEW THE REFERRING PAGE

referrer.html - Notepad

```
<html>
<head>
</head>
<body>
  <script language="javascript">
   document.write("This URL for this page is " + document.referrer);
  </script>
</body>
</html>
```

E:\Temp\Authoring\JSB\examples\Ch08 - Working with Windows\referrer.html - Microsoft Inter...

This URL for this page is file://E:\Temp\Authoring\JSB\examples\Ch08%20-%20Working%20with%20Windows\reflink.html

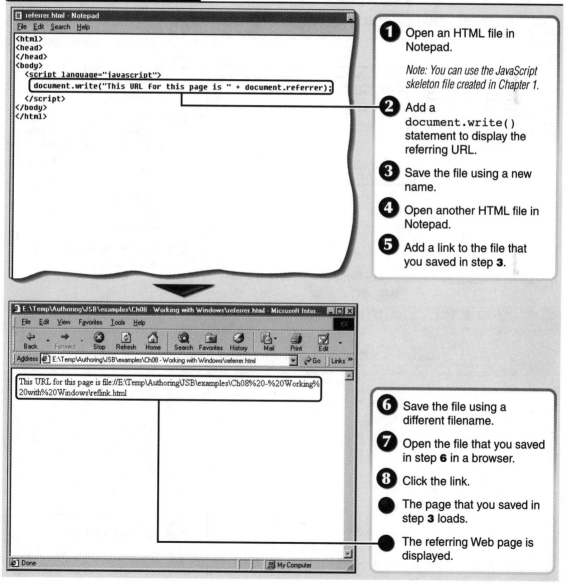

1. Open an HTML file in Notepad.

   Note: You can use the JavaScript skeleton file created in Chapter 1.

2. Add a `document.write()` statement to display the referring URL.
3. Save the file using a new name.
4. Open another HTML file in Notepad.
5. Add a link to the file that you saved in step **3**.
6. Save the file using a different filename.
7. Open the file that you saved in step **6** in a browser.
8. Click the link.

- The page that you saved in step **3** loads.
- The referring Web page is displayed.

OPEN A NEW BROWSER WINDOW

You can have a page open a new browser window by using the `window.open()` method, which accepts three parameters. The first is the new URL. The second is the new window name. The third defines the features of the window, for which you can set the following attributes: `width`, `height`, `toolbar`, `status`, `menubar`, `scrollbars`, and `resizable`. All but the first two of these can be set to `yes` or `no`.

OPEN A NEW BROWSER WINDOW

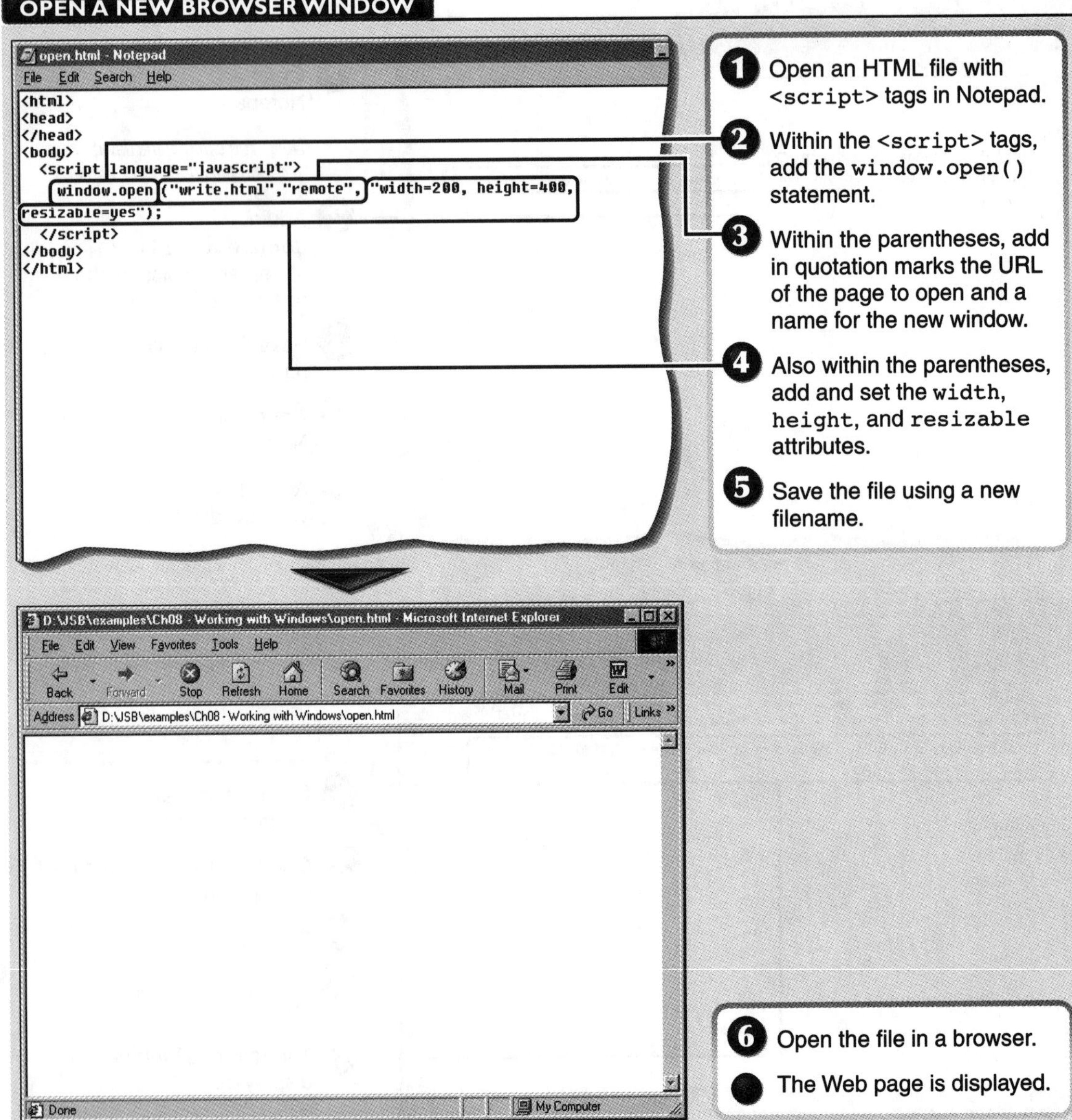

open.html - Notepad
File Edit Search Help
<html>
<head>
</head>
<body>
<script language="javascript">
window.open("write.html","remote","width=200, height=400,
resizable=yes");
</script>
</body>
</html>
D:\JSB\examples\Ch08 - Working with Windows\open.html - Microsoft Internet Explorer
File Edit View Favorites Tools Help
Back Forward Stop Refresh Home Search Favorites History Mail Print Edit
Address D:\JSB\examples\Ch08 - Working with Windows\open.html
Go Links
Done
My Computer

1. Open an HTML file with `<script>` tags in Notepad.
2. Within the `<script>` tags, add the `window.open()` statement.
3. Within the parentheses, add in quotation marks the URL of the page to open and a name for the new window.
4. Also within the parentheses, add and set the `width`, `height`, and `resizable` attributes.
5. Save the file using a new filename.
6. Open the file in a browser.

- The Web page is displayed.

in an instant

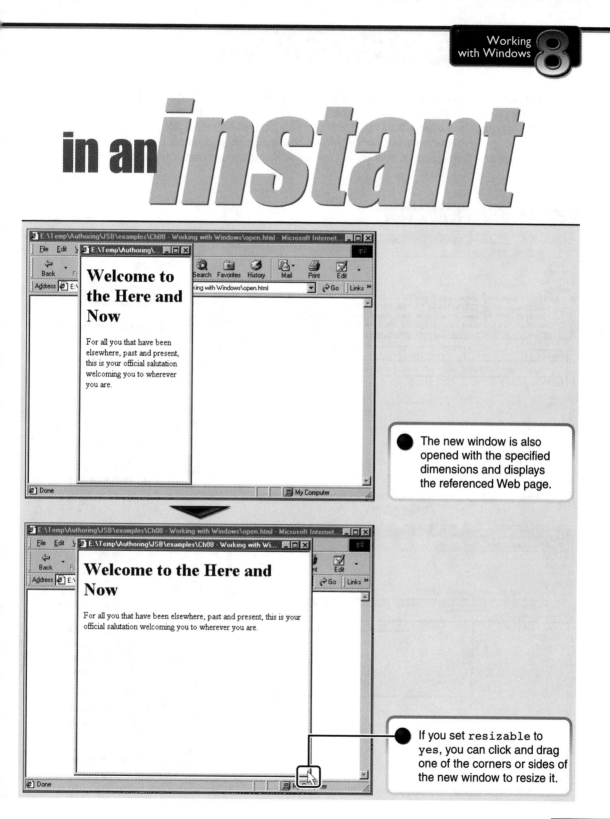

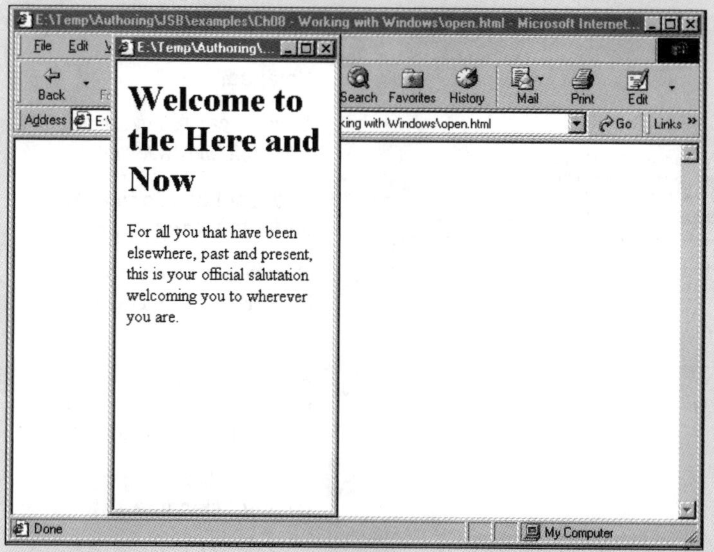

- The new window is also opened with the specified dimensions and displays the referenced Web page.

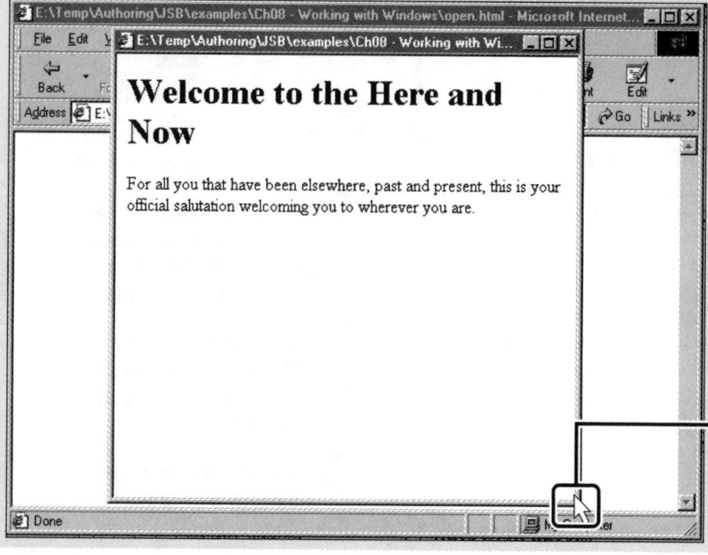

- If you set `resizable` to `yes`, you can click and drag one of the corners or sides of the new window to resize it.

CLOSE A REMOTE WINDOW

To close a remote window, you can use the `window.close()` function. This closes the current remote window. If the `window.close()` function is used to close the original browser window, an alert dialog box will appear, asking if you want to close the browser window. Windows that have been opened using the `window.open()` function automatically close without a confirmation dialog box.

CLOSE A REMOTE WINDOW

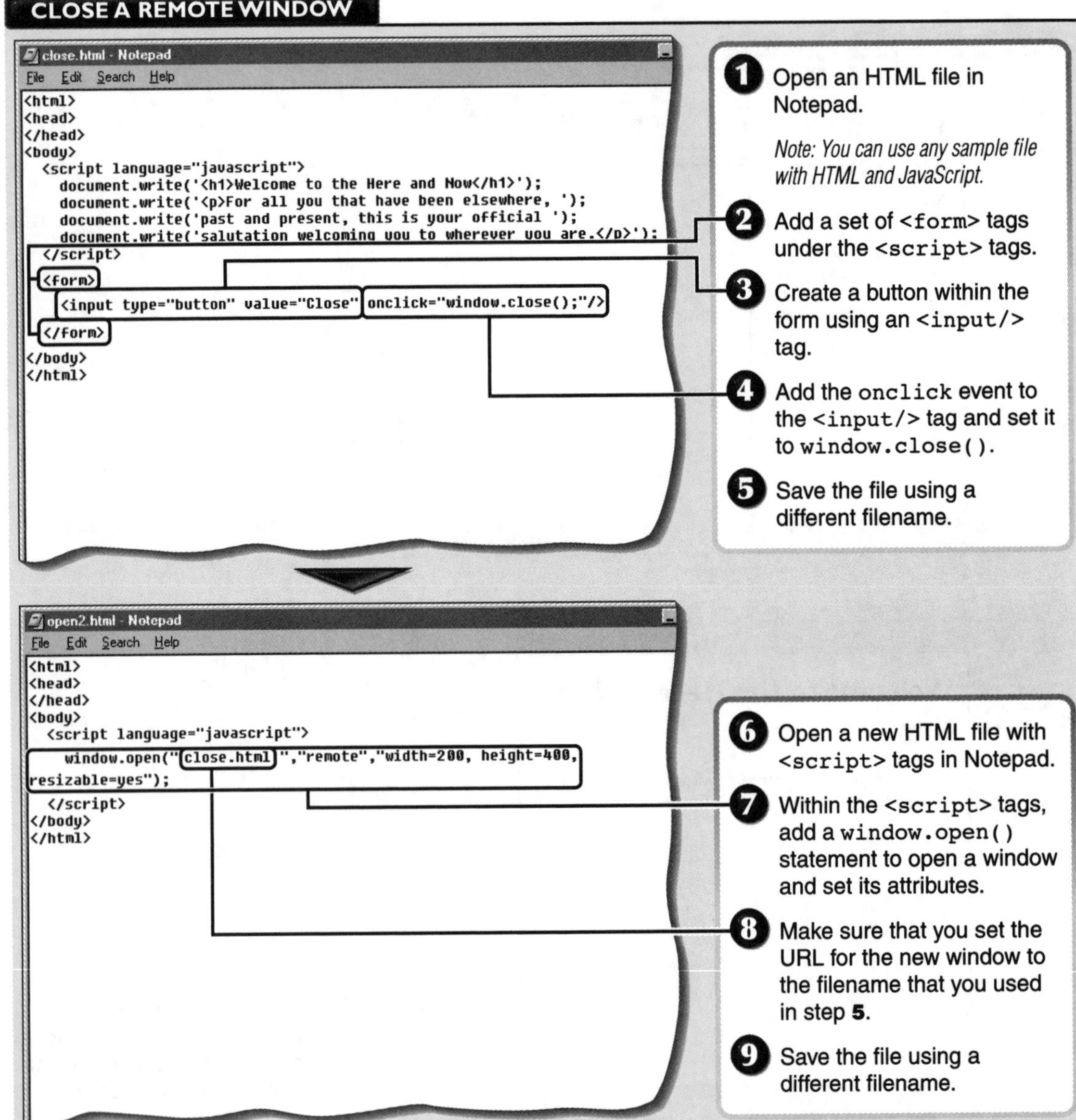

close.html - Notepad
File Edit Search Help
<html>
<head>
</head>
<body>
<script language="javascript">
document.write('<h1>Welcome to the Here and Now</h1>');
document.write('<p>For all you that have been elsewhere, ');
document.write('past and present, this is your official ');
document.write('salutation welcoming you to wherever you are.</p>');
</script>
<form>
<input type="button" value="Close" onclick="window.close();"/>
</form>
</body>
</html>
open2.html - Notepad
File Edit Search Help
<html>
<head>
</head>
<body>
<script language="javascript">
window.open("close.html","remote","width=200, height=400, resizable=yes");
</script>
</body>
</html>

1. Open an HTML file in Notepad.

   Note: You can use any sample file with HTML and JavaScript.

2. Add a set of `<form>` tags under the `<script>` tags.
3. Create a button within the form using an `<input/>` tag.
4. Add the `onclick` event to the `<input/>` tag and set it to `window.close()`.
5. Save the file using a different filename.
6. Open a new HTML file with `<script>` tags in Notepad.
7. Within the `<script>` tags, add a `window.open()` statement to open a window and set its attributes.
8. Make sure that you set the URL for the new window to the filename that you used in step **5**.
9. Save the file using a different filename.

in an instant

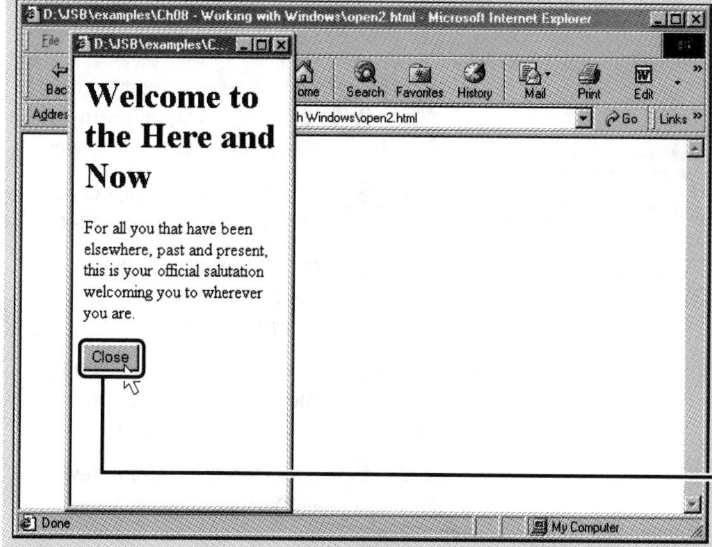

D:\JSB\examples\Ch08 - Working with Windows\open2.html - Microsoft Internet Explorer
Welcome to the Here and Now
For all you that have been elsewhere, past and present, this is your official salutation welcoming you to wherever you are.
Close

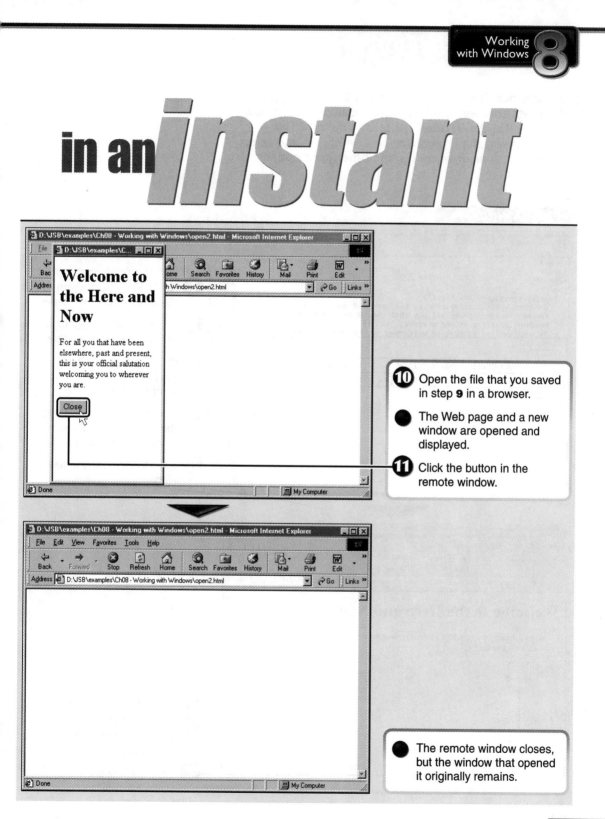

10 Open the file that you saved in step **9** in a browser.

- The Web page and a new window are opened and displayed.

11 Click the button in the remote window.

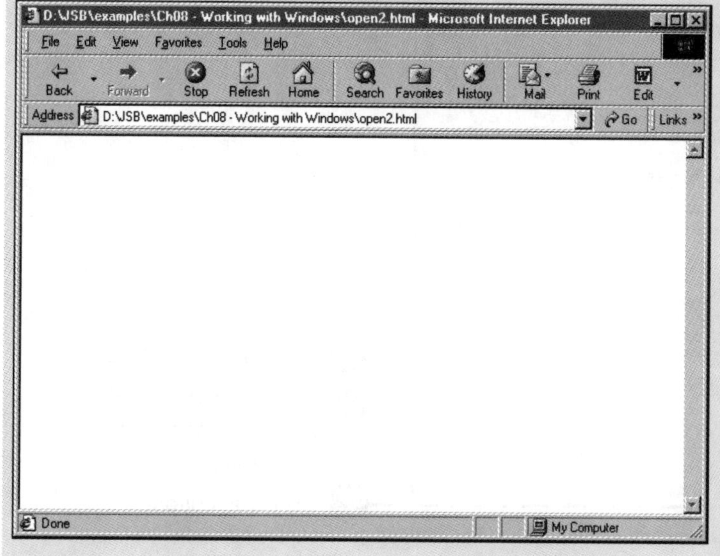

D:\JSB\examples\Ch08 - Working with Windows\open2.html - Microsoft Internet Explorer

- The remote window closes, but the window that opened it originally remains.

PRINT A WINDOW

You can include an element such as a button on your Web page that will enable the user to print the current page by using the `window.print()` method. This method opens the Print dialog box, which lets you select the printer, number of copies, and other print options.

PRINT A WINDOW

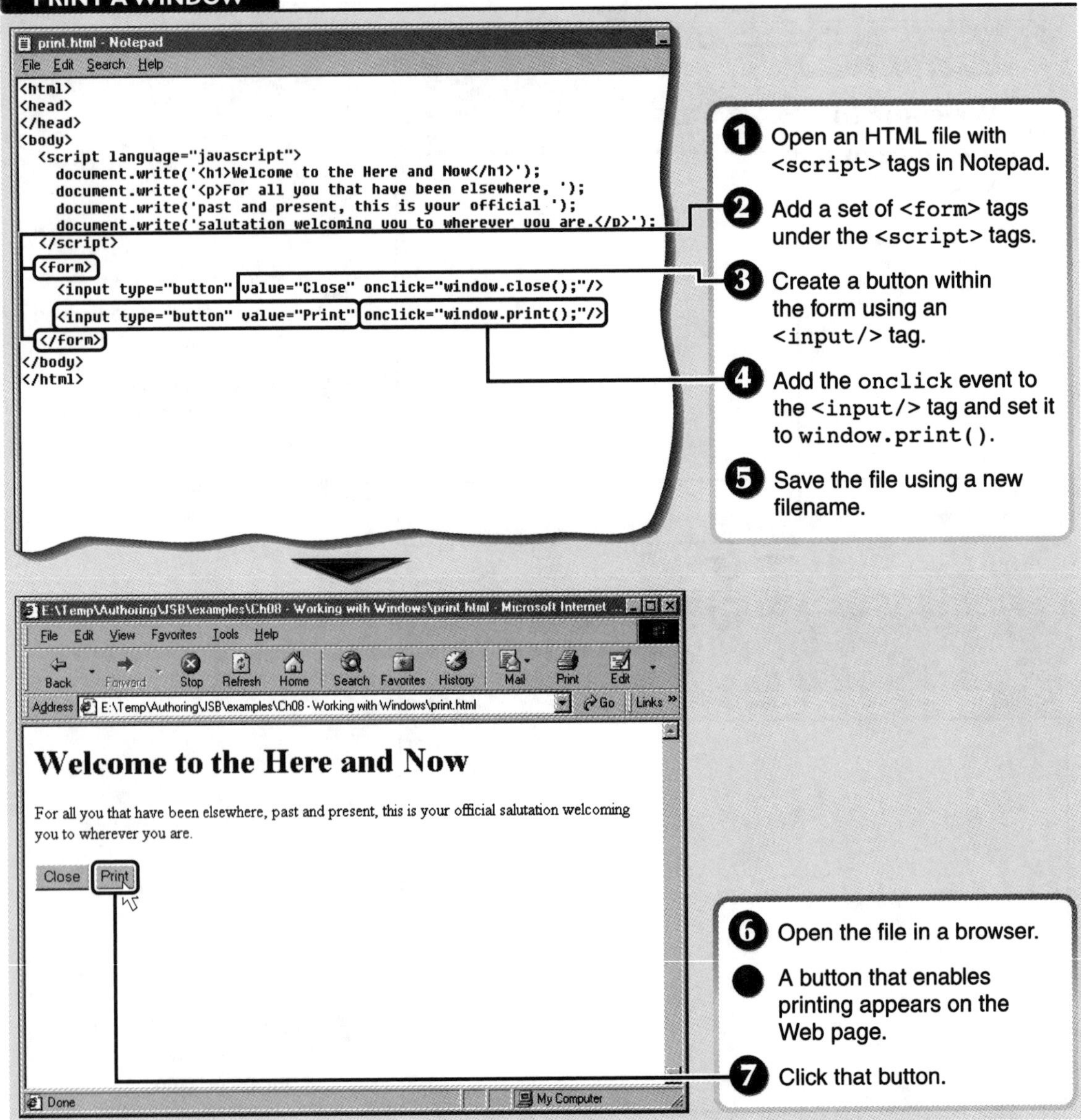

print.html - Notepad
File Edit Search Help
<html>
<head>
</head>
<body>
<script language="javascript">
document.write('<h1>Welcome to the Here and Now</h1>');
document.write('<p>For all you that have been elsewhere, ');
document.write('past and present, this is your official ');
document.write('salutation welcoming you to wherever you are.</p>');
</script>
<form>
<input type="button" value="Close" onclick="window.close();"/>
<input type="button" value="Print" onclick="window.print();"/>
</form>
</body>
</html>
E:\Temp\Authoring\JSB\examples\Ch08 - Working with Windows\print.html - Microsoft Internet ...
File Edit View Favorites Tools Help
Back Forward Stop Refresh Home Search Favorites History Mail Print Edit
Address E:\Temp\Authoring\JSB\examples\Ch08 - Working with Windows\print.html
Go Links
Welcome to the Here and Now
For all you that have been elsewhere, past and present, this is your official salutation welcoming you to wherever you are.
Close
Print
Done
My Computer

1 Open an HTML file with `<script>` tags in Notepad.

2 Add a set of `<form>` tags under the `<script>` tags.

3 Create a button within the form using an `<input/>` tag.

4 Add the `onclick` event to the `<input/>` tag and set it to `window.print()`.

5 Save the file using a new filename.

6 Open the file in a browser.

- A button that enables printing appears on the Web page.

7 Click that button.

in an instant

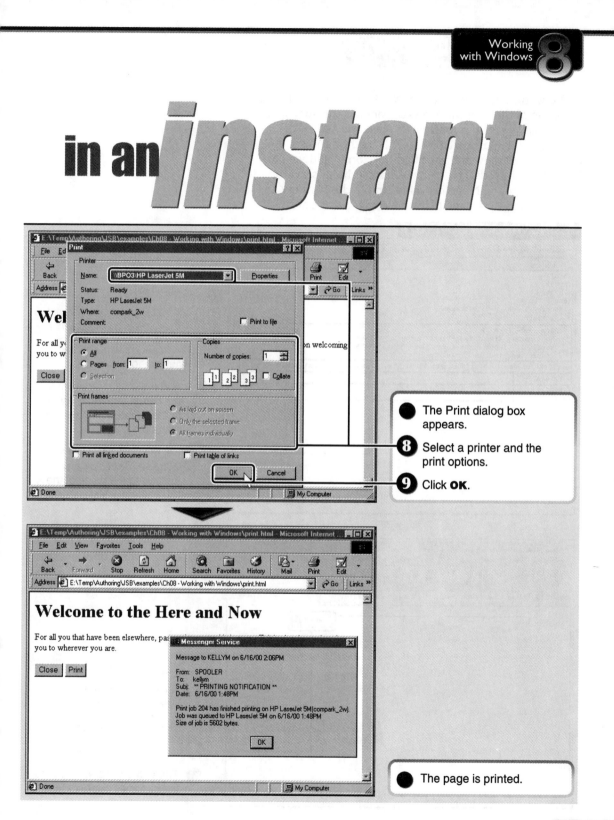

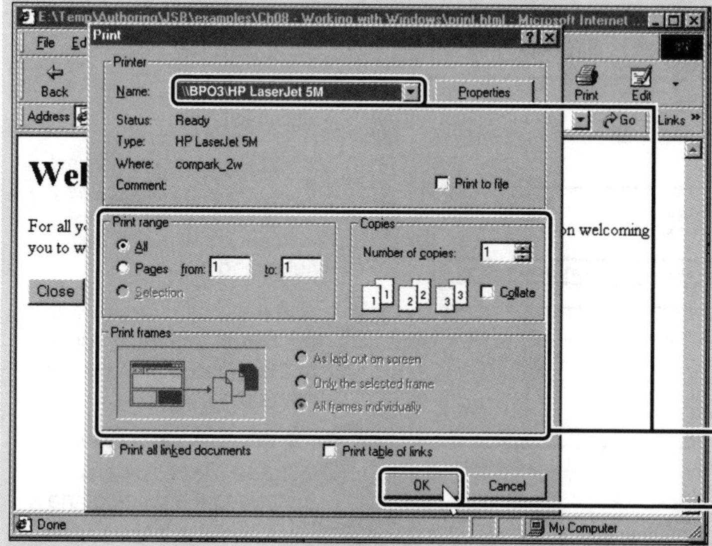

- The Print dialog box appears.

8 Select a printer and the print options.

9 Click **OK**.

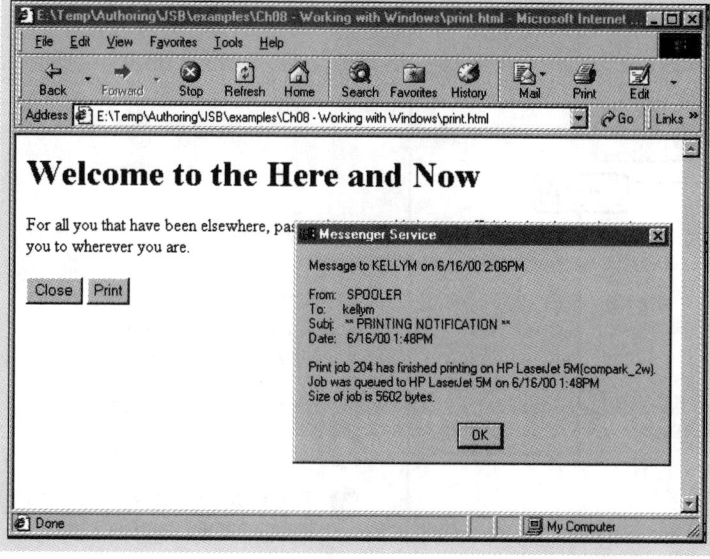

- The page is printed.

MOVE A WINDOW

The `window.moveTo()` method moves the upper-left corner of the current browser window the specified distance in pixels from the left edge and top of the screen. The `window.moveBy()` method moves the browser window the specified horizontal and vertical number of pixels. The parameters can be positive or negative values. Negative values move the window to the left and up rather than to the right and down.

USING WINDOW.MOVETO()

```
<html>
<head>
</head>
<body>
  <script language="javascript">
  </script>
  <form name="form1">
    horizontal: <input type="text" name="x" value="20"/>
    vertical: <input type="text" name="y" value="50"/>
    <input type="button" value="moveTo"
onclick="window.moveTo(document.form1.x.value,document.form1.y.value);"/>
  </form>
</body>
</html>
```

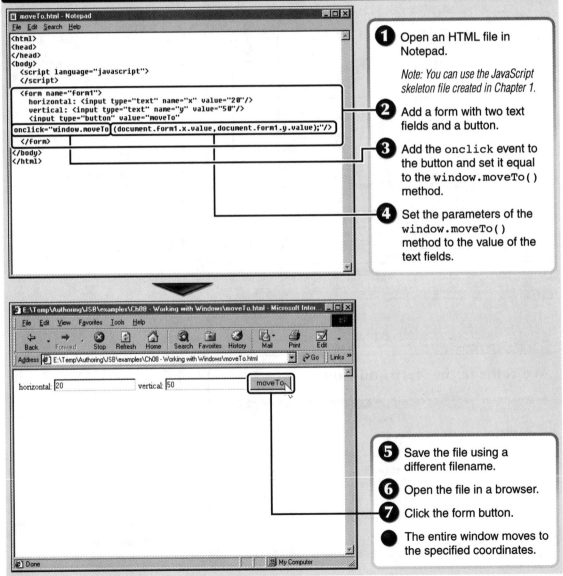

1. Open an HTML file in Notepad.

   Note: You can use the JavaScript skeleton file created in Chapter 1.

2. Add a form with two text fields and a button.
3. Add the `onclick` event to the button and set it equal to the `window.moveTo()` method.
4. Set the parameters of the `window.moveTo()` method to the value of the text fields.

horizontal: 20 vertical: 50 moveTo

5. Save the file using a different filename.
6. Open the file in a browser.
7. Click the form button.

- The entire window moves to the specified coordinates.

in an instant

USING WINDOW.MOVEBY()

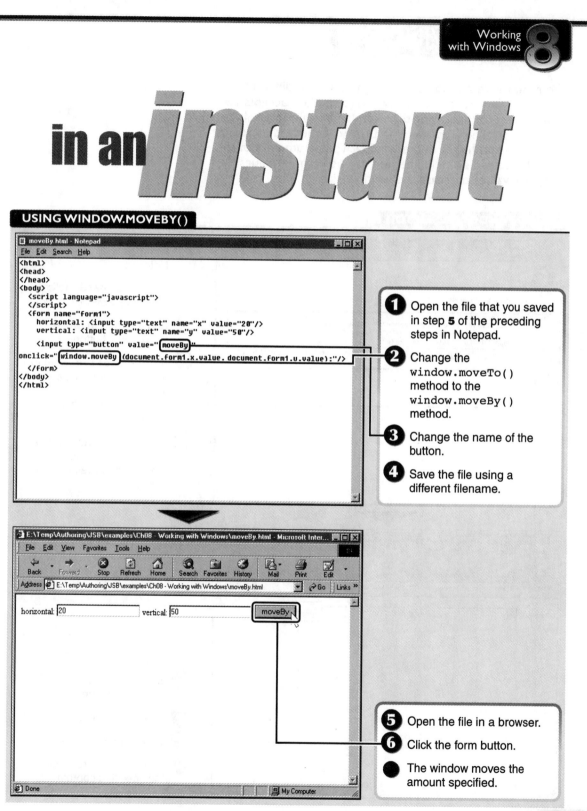

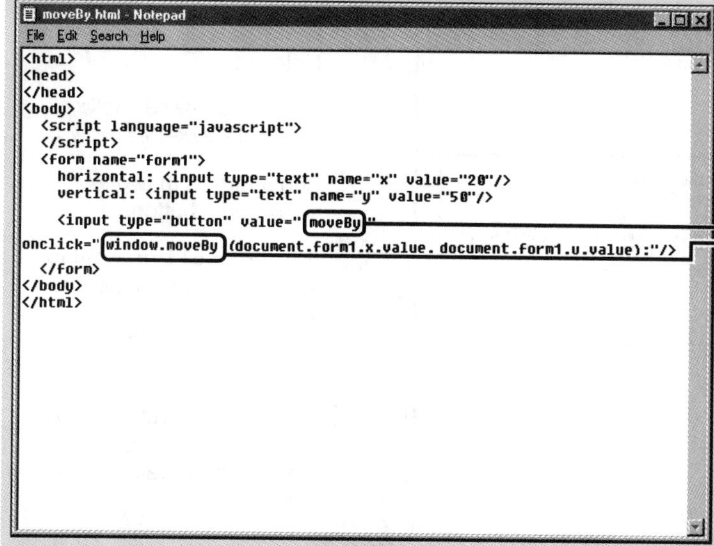

moveBy.html - Notepad

```
<html>
<head>
</head>
<body>
  <script language="javascript">
  </script>
  <form name="form1">
    horizontal: <input type="text" name="x" value="20"/>
    vertical: <input type="text" name="y" value="50"/>
    <input type="button" value="moveBy"
onclick="window.moveBy(document.form1.x.value, document.form1.y.value);"/>
  </form>
</body>
</html>
```

1. Open the file that you saved in step **5** of the preceding steps in Notepad.
2. Change the `window.moveTo()` method to the `window.moveBy()` method.
3. Change the name of the button.
4. Save the file using a different filename.

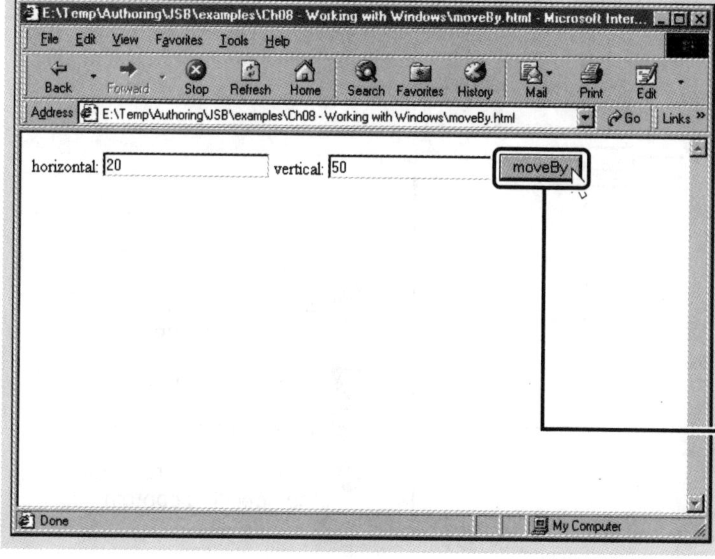

E:\Temp\Authoring\JSB\examples\Ch08 - Working with Windows\moveBy.html - Microsoft Inter...

horizontal: 20 vertical: 50 moveBy

5. Open the file in a browser.
6. Click the form button.

- The window moves the amount specified.

RESIZE A WINDOW

You can resize a window by using a couple of different methods. The `window.resizeTo()` method accepts two parameters for specifying the width and height in pixels of the window. The `window.resizeBy()` method increases the width and height of the window. The parameters of the `window.resizeBy()` method can be negative values; negative values decrease the window size.

USING WINDOW.RESIZETO()

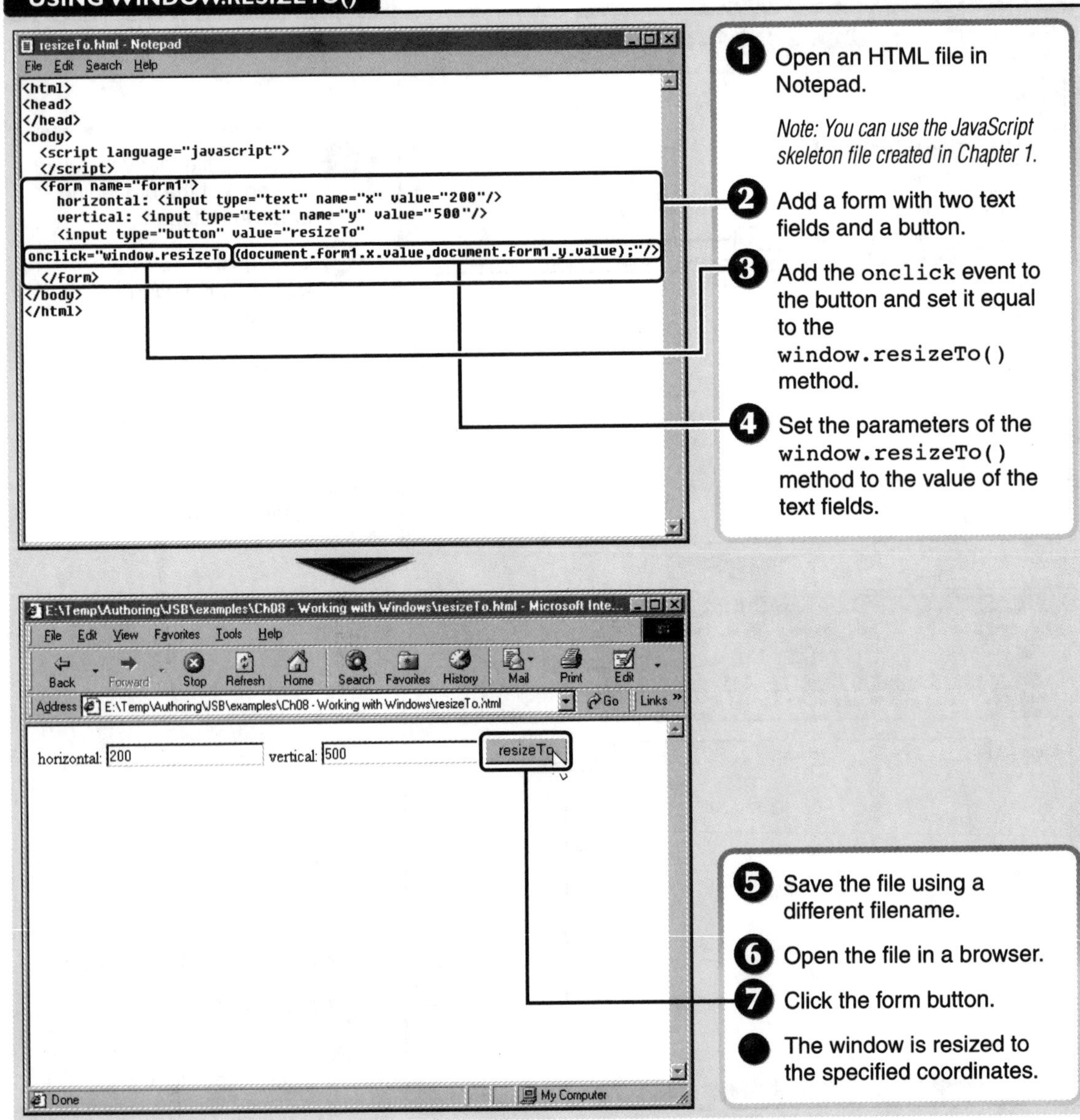

resizeTo.html - Notepad
File Edit Search Help
<html>
<head>
</head>
<body>
<script language="javascript">
</script>
<form name="form1">
horizontal: <input type="text" name="x" value="200"/>
vertical: <input type="text" name="y" value="500"/>
<input type="button" value="resizeTo"
onclick="window.resizeTo(document.form1.x.value,document.form1.y.value);"/>
</form>
</body>
</html>
E:\Temp\Authoring\JSB\examples\Ch08 - Working with Windows\resizeTo.html - Microsoft Inte...
File Edit View Favorites Tools Help
Back Forward Stop Refresh Home Search Favorites History Mail Print Edit
Address E:\Temp\Authoring\JSB\examples\Ch08 - Working with Windows\resizeTo.html
Go Links
horizontal: 200 vertical: 500 resizeTo
Done
My Computer

1. Open an HTML file in Notepad.

   Note: You can use the JavaScript skeleton file created in Chapter 1.

2. Add a form with two text fields and a button.
3. Add the `onclick` event to the button and set it equal to the `window.resizeTo()` method.
4. Set the parameters of the `window.resizeTo()` method to the value of the text fields.
5. Save the file using a different filename.
6. Open the file in a browser.
7. Click the form button.

- The window is resized to the specified coordinates.

in an instant

USING WINDOW.RESIZEBY()

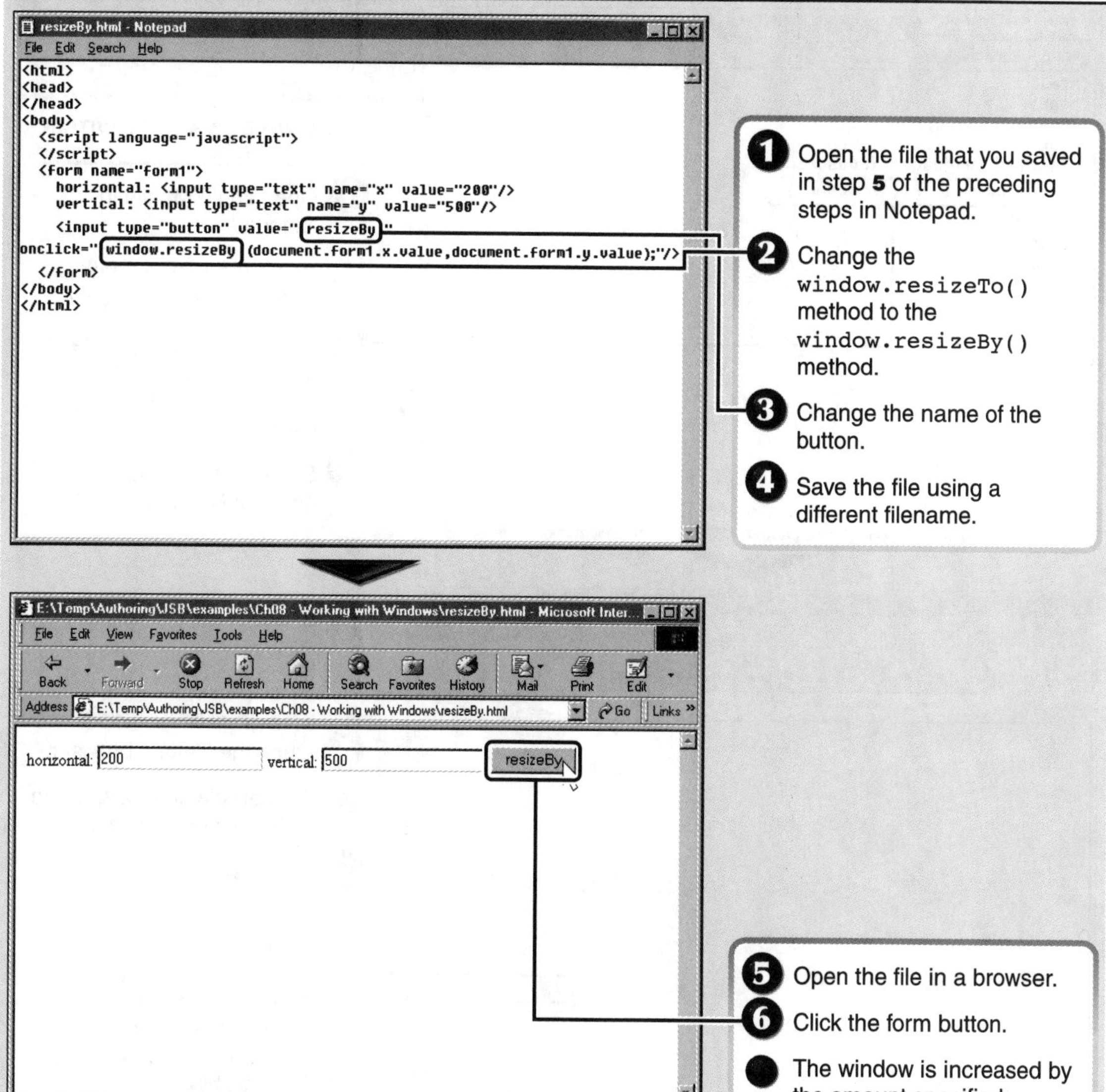
resizeBy.html - Notepad
File Edit Search Help
<html>
<head>
</head>
<body>
<script language="javascript">
</script>
<form name="form1">
horizontal: <input type="text" name="x" value="200"/>
vertical: <input type="text" name="y" value="500"/>
<input type="button" value="resizeBy"
onclick="window.resizeBy(document.form1.x.value,document.form1.y.value);"/>
</form>
</body>
</html>
E:\Temp\Authoring\JSB\examples\Ch08 - Working with Windows\resizeBy.html - Microsoft Inter...
File Edit View Favorites Tools Help
Back Forward Stop Refresh Home Search Favorites History Mail Print Edit
Address E:\Temp\Authoring\JSB\examples\Ch08 - Working with Windows\resizeBy.html
Go Links
horizontal: 200 vertical: 500 resizeBy
Done
My Computer

1. Open the file that you saved in step **5** of the preceding steps in Notepad.
2. Change the `window.resizeTo()` method to the `window.resizeBy()` method.
3. Change the name of the button.
4. Save the file using a different filename.
5. Open the file in a browser.
6. Click the form button.

- The window is increased by the amount specified.

INFORM THE USER WITH AN ALERT DIALOG BOX

JavaScript includes three different types of dialog boxes: alert, prompt, and confirm. All these dialog boxes are `window` object methods. The simplest dialog box is an alert dialog box. This dialog box presents a text message to the user and includes a single OK button. The message is defined in quotation marks as a parameter of the `alert()` method.

INFORM THE USER WITH AN ALERT DIALOG BOX

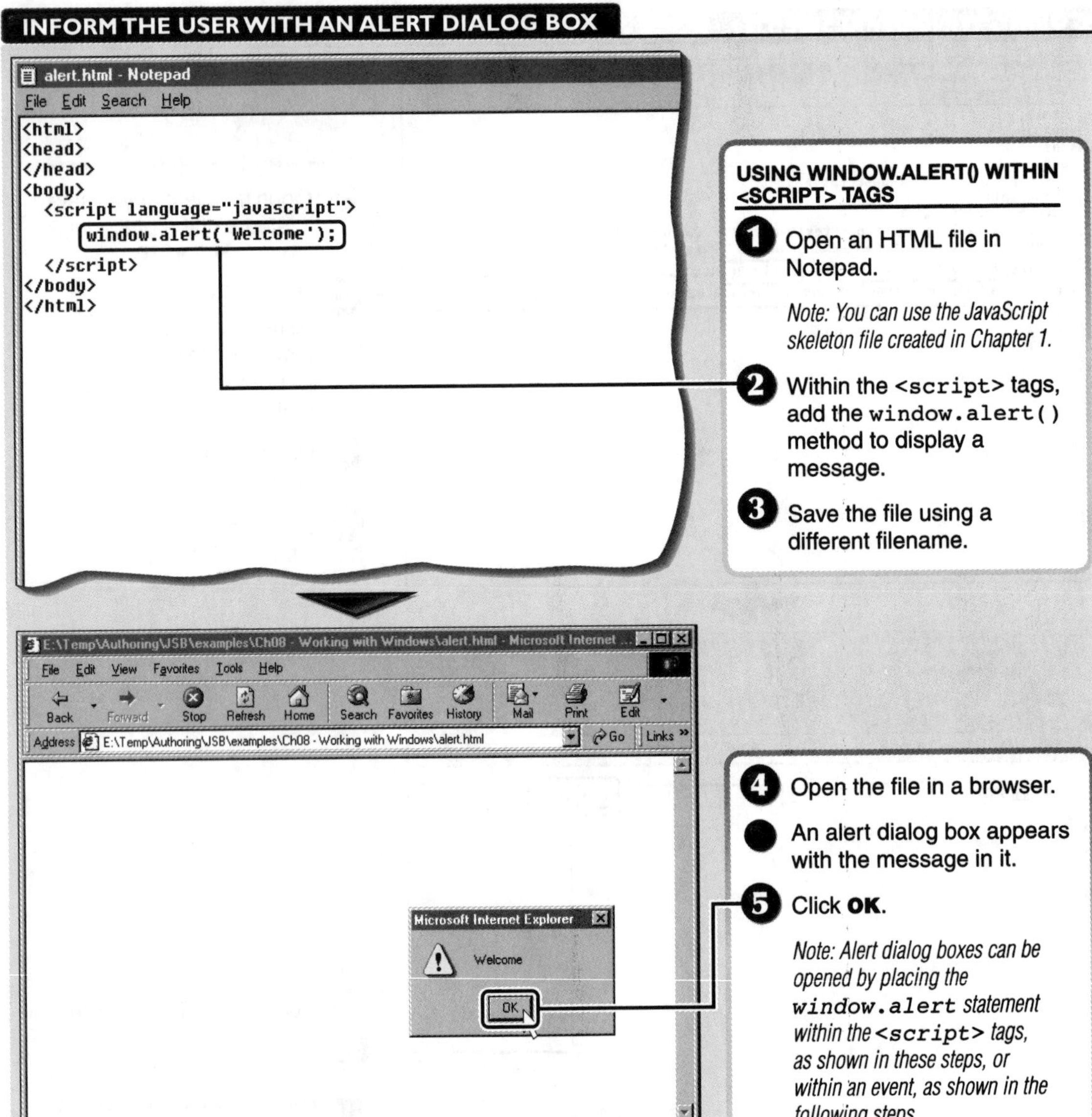
alert.html - Notepad
File Edit Search Help
<html>
<head>
</head>
<body>
<script language="javascript">
window.alert('Welcome');
</script>
</body>
</html>
E:\Temp\Authoring\JSB\examples\Ch08 - Working with Windows\alert.html - Microsoft Internet ...
File Edit View Favorites Tools Help
Back Forward Stop Refresh Home Search Favorites History Mail Print Edit
Address E:\Temp\Authoring\JSB\examples\Ch08 - Working with Windows\alert.html
Go Links
Microsoft Internet Explorer
Welcome
OK
Opening page file://E:\Temp\Authoring\JSB\examples\Ch08 -
My Computer

USING WINDOW.ALERT() WITHIN <SCRIPT> TAGS

1. Open an HTML file in Notepad.

   Note: You can use the JavaScript skeleton file created in Chapter 1.

2. Within the `<script>` tags, add the `window.alert()` method to display a message.

3. Save the file using a different filename.

4. Open the file in a browser.

- An alert dialog box appears with the message in it.

5. Click **OK**.

   Note: Alert dialog boxes can be opened by placing the `window.alert` statement within the `<script>` tags, as shown in these steps, or within an event, as shown in the following steps.

in an instant

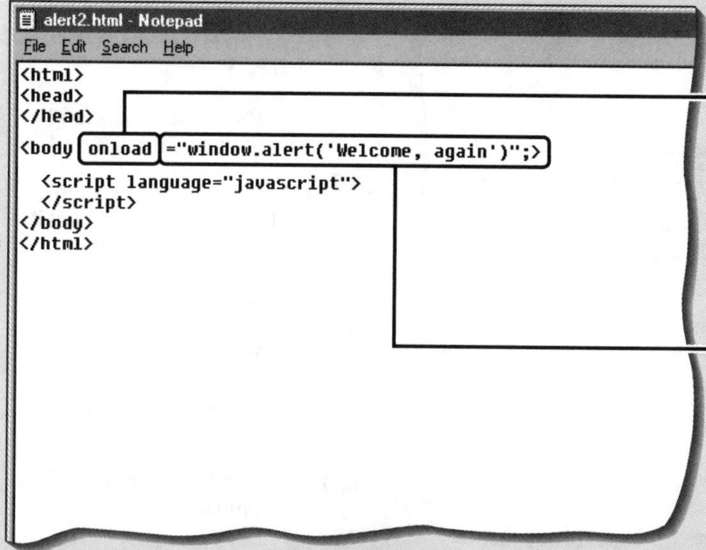

```
<html>
<head>
</head>
<body onload ="window.alert('Welcome, again')";>
  <script language="javascript">
  </script>
</body>
</html>
```

USING WINDOW.ALERT() WITHIN AN EVENT

1. Open a new HTML file in Notepad.

   Note: You can use the JavaScript skeleton file created in Chapter 1.

2. Within the `<body>` tags, add an `onload` event.

3. Set the `onload` event equal to the `window.alert()` method to display a message.

4. Save the file using a different filename.

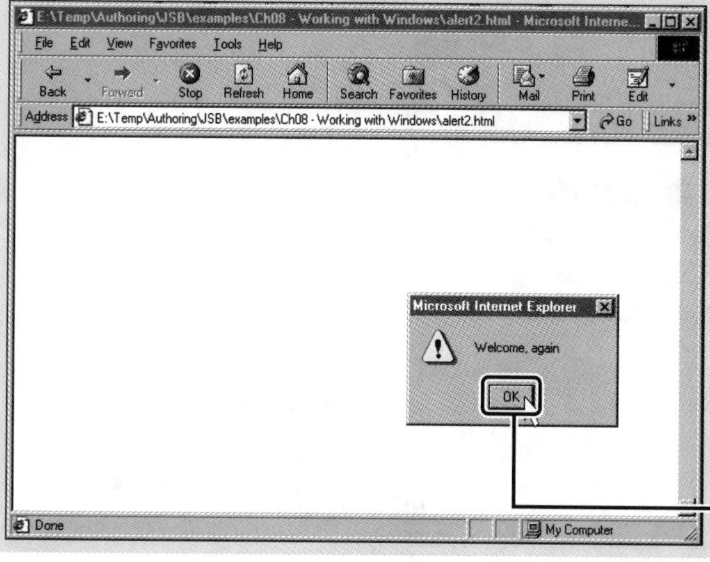

5. Open the file in a browser.

   - An alert dialog box appears with the message in it.

6. Click **OK**.

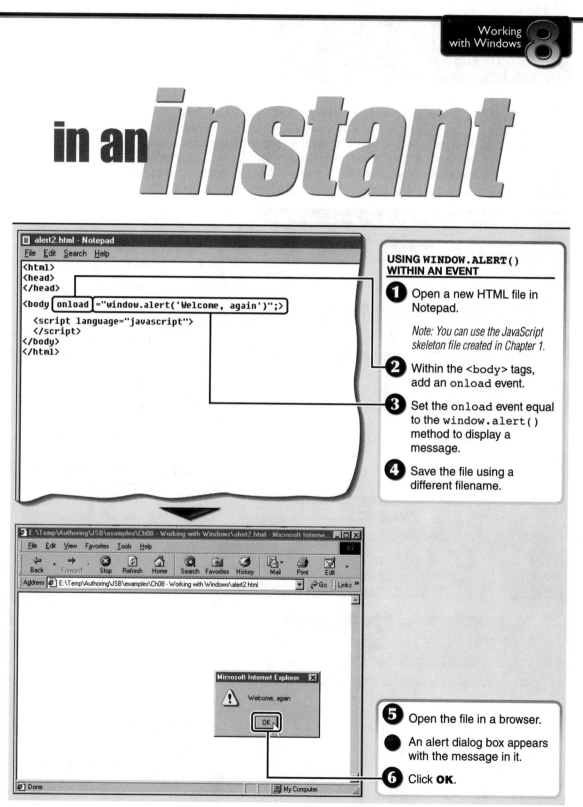

ACCEPT INPUT WITH A PROMPT DIALOG BOX

A prompt dialog box enables a user to enter text into a text field. You can create a prompt dialog box by using the `prompt()` method, which accepts two parameters: The first defines the message text to be displayed, and the second defines the default text for the text field. When OK is clicked, the text in the text field is returned to the script. You can capture this text by assigning the `prompt()` method to a variable.

ACCEPT INPUT WITH A PROMPT DIALOG BOX

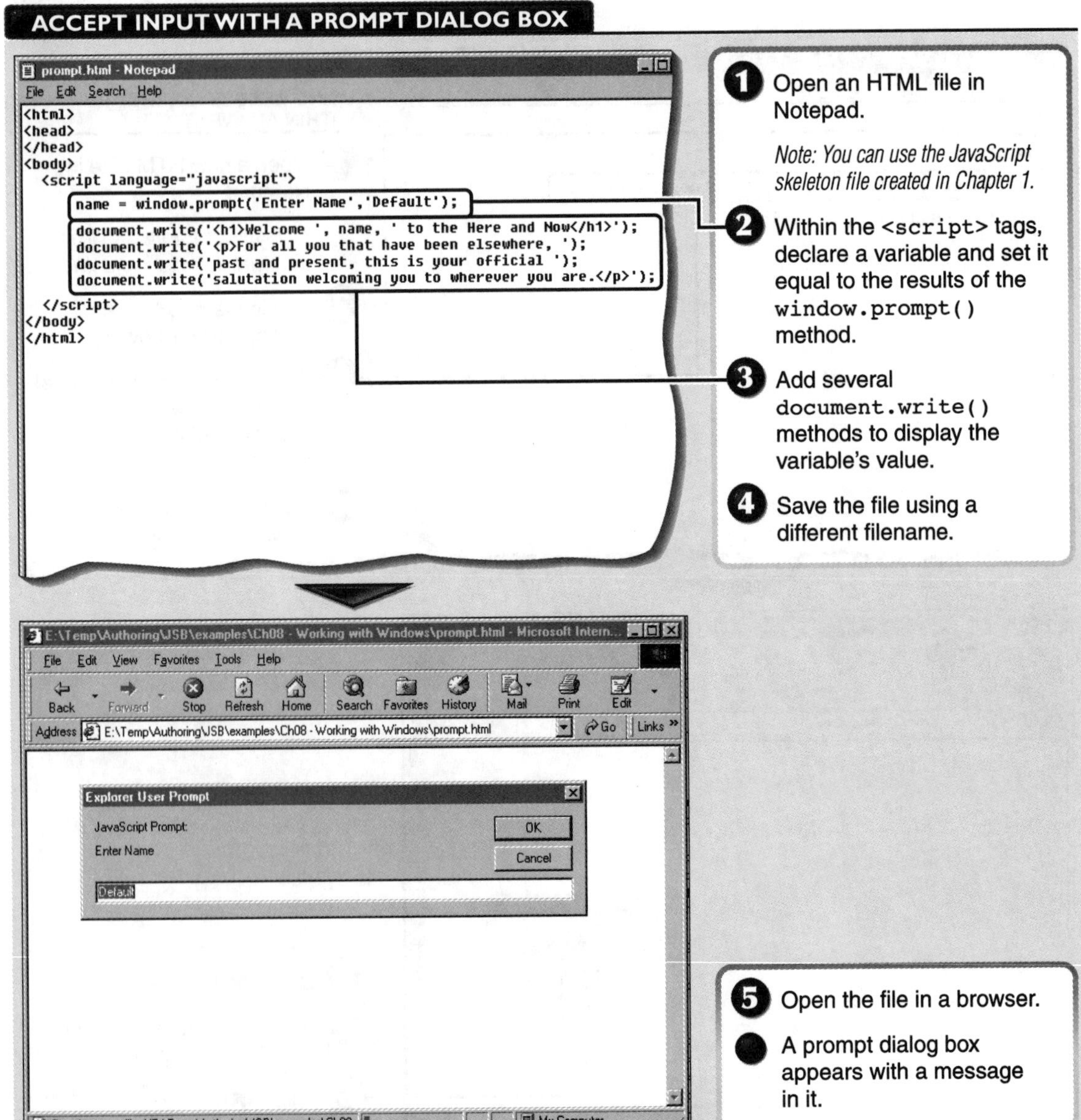

prompt.html - Notepad
File Edit Search Help
<html>
<head>
</head>
<body>
<script language="javascript">
name = window.prompt('Enter Name','Default');
document.write('<h1>Welcome ', name, ' to the Here and Now</h1>');
document.write('<p>For all you that have been elsewhere, ');
document.write('past and present, this is your official ');
document.write('salutation welcoming you to wherever you are.</p>');
</script>
</body>
</html>
E:\Temp\Authoring\JSB\examples\Ch08 - Working with Windows\prompt.html - Microsoft Intern...
Explorer User Prompt
JavaScript Prompt:
Enter Name
OK
Cancel
Default
Opening page file://E:\Temp\Authoring\JSB\examples\Ch08 -
My Computer

1. Open an HTML file in Notepad.

   Note: You can use the JavaScript skeleton file created in Chapter 1.

2. Within the `<script>` tags, declare a variable and set it equal to the results of the `window.prompt()` method.

3. Add several `document.write()` methods to display the variable's value.

4. Save the file using a different filename.

5. Open the file in a browser.

- A prompt dialog box appears with a message in it.

in an instant

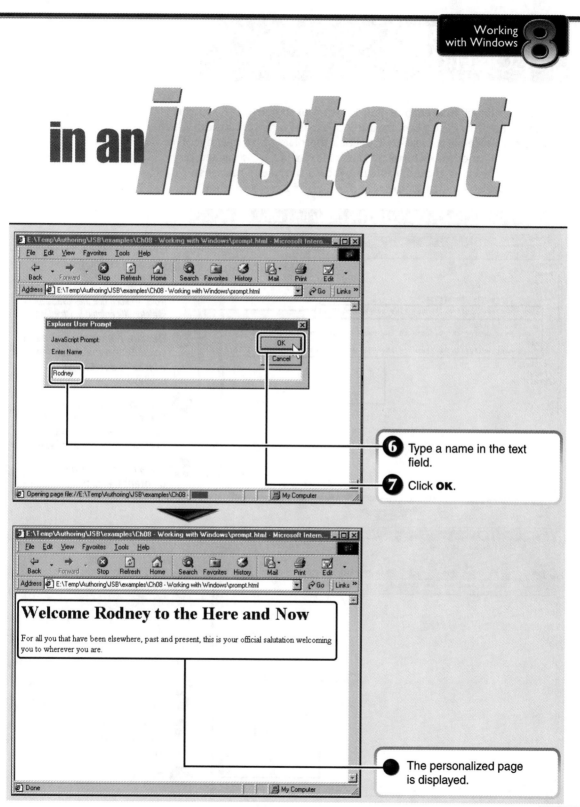

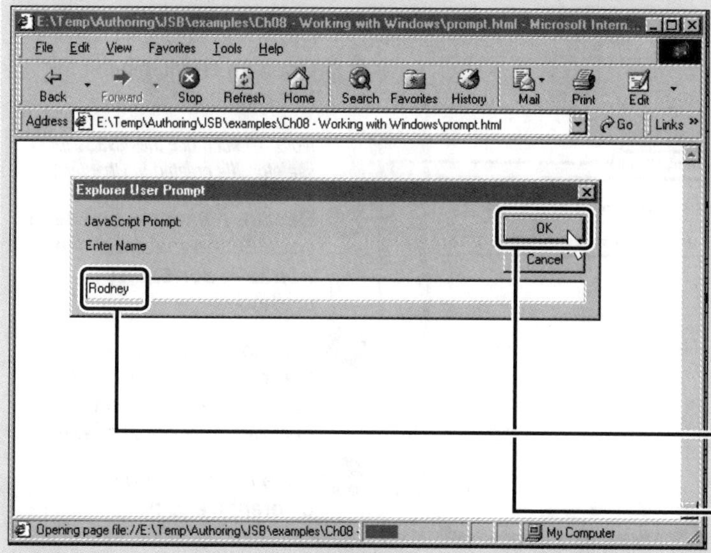

6 Type a name in the text field.

7 Click **OK**.

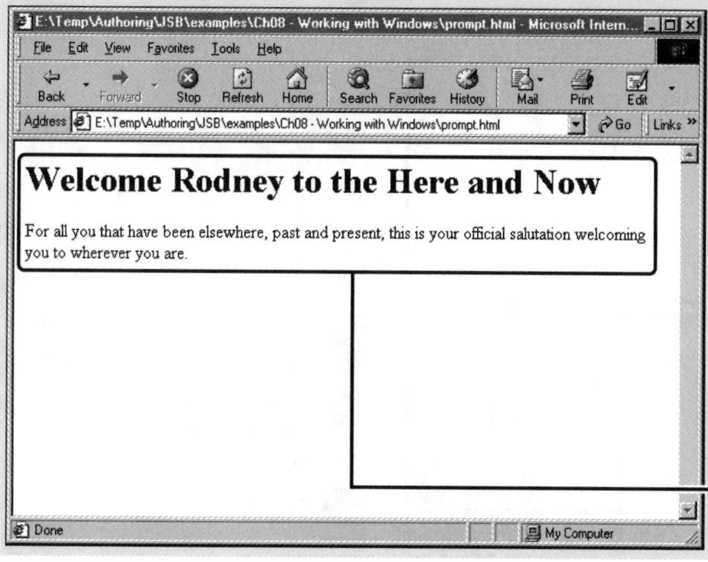

- The personalized page is displayed.

ENABLE USER DECISIONS WITH A CONFIRM DIALOG BOX

A confirm dialog box enables you to ask a user questions. You can create a confirm dialog box by using the `confirm()` method, which accepts a single parameter that defines the dialog box message. The `confirm()` method returns a value of `true` if OK is clicked or `false` if Cancel is clicked. You can capture the user's response by setting a variable equal to the `window.confirm()` method.

ENABLE USER DECISIONS WITH A CONFIRM DIALOG BOX

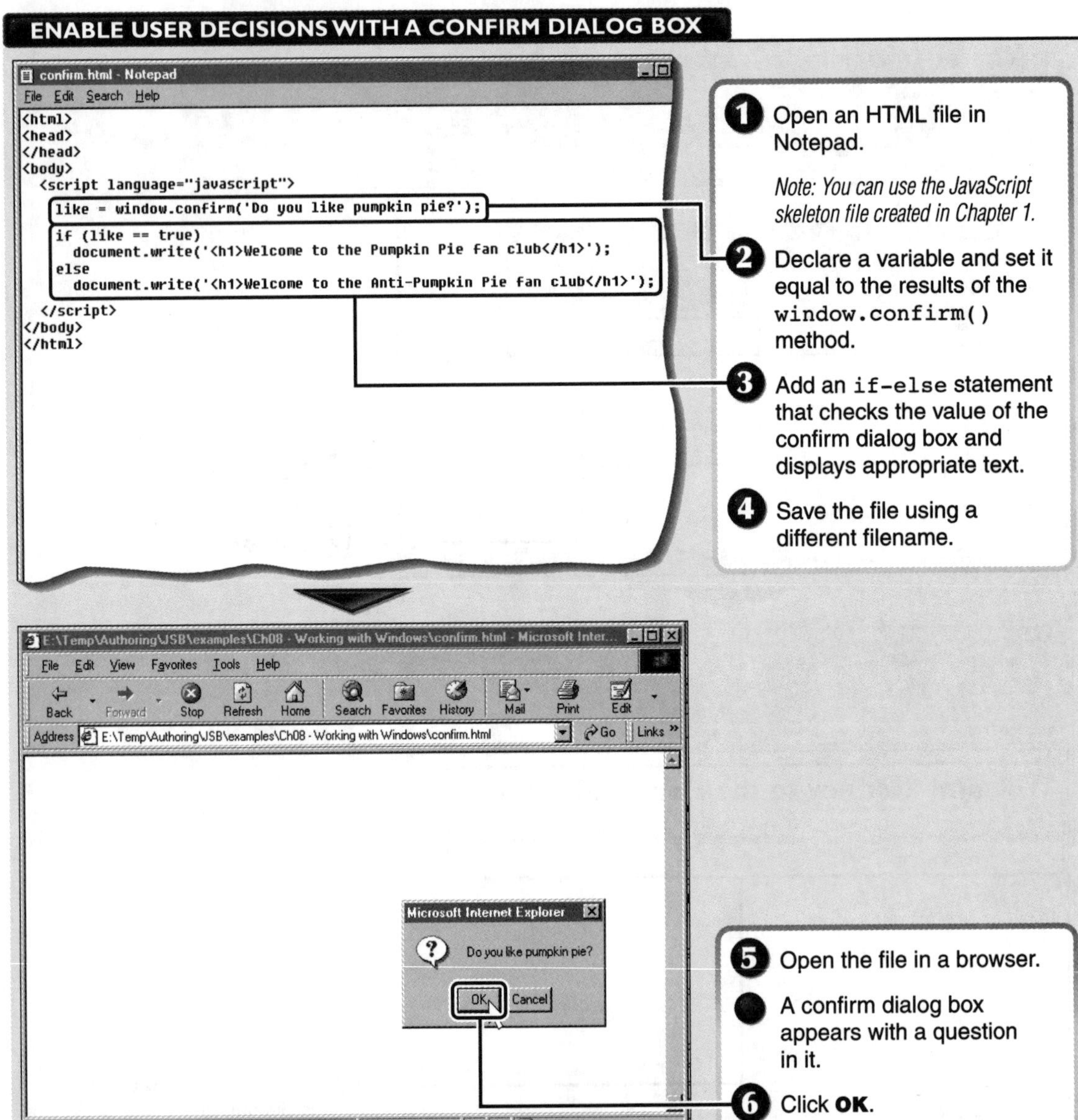

confirm.html - Notepad
File Edit Search Help
<html>
<head>
</head>
<body>
<script language="javascript">
like = window.confirm('Do you like pumpkin pie?');
if (like == true)
document.write('<h1>Welcome to the Pumpkin Pie fan club</h1>');
else
document.write('<h1>Welcome to the Anti-Pumpkin Pie fan club</h1>');
</script>
</body>
</html>
E:\Temp\Authoring\JSB\examples\Ch08 - Working with Windows\confirm.html - Microsoft Inter...
File Edit View Favorites Tools Help
Back Forward Stop Refresh Home Search Favorites History Mail Print Edit
Address E:\Temp\Authoring\JSB\examples\Ch08 - Working with Windows\confirm.html
Go Links
Microsoft Internet Explorer
Do you like pumpkin pie?
OK Cancel
Opening page file://E:\Temp\Authoring\JSB\examples\Ch08 -
My Computer

1. Open an HTML file in Notepad.

   Note: You can use the JavaScript skeleton file created in Chapter 1.

2. Declare a variable and set it equal to the results of the `window.confirm()` method.

3. Add an `if-else` statement that checks the value of the confirm dialog box and displays appropriate text.

4. Save the file using a different filename.

5. Open the file in a browser.

- A confirm dialog box appears with a question in it.

6. Click **OK**.

in an instant

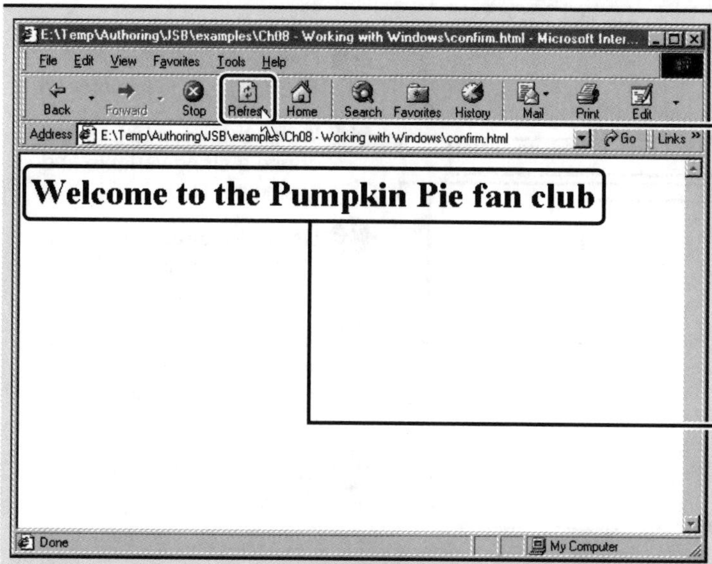

![screenshot]

Welcome to the Pumpkin Pie fan club

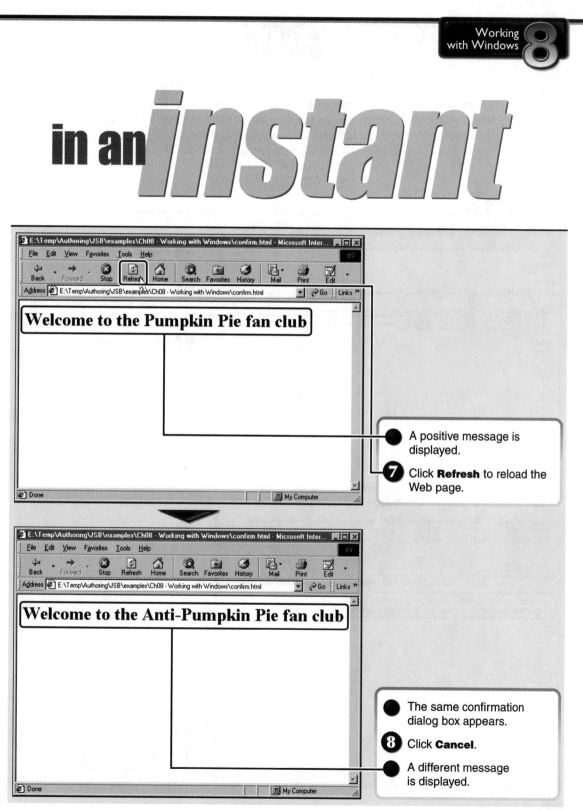

- A positive message is displayed.
- **7** Click **Refresh** to reload the Web page.

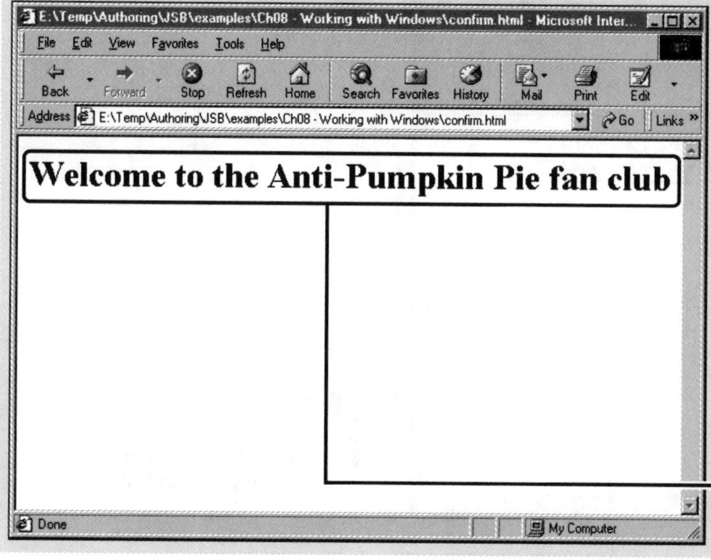

Welcome to the Anti-Pumpkin Pie fan club

- The same confirmation dialog box appears.
- **8** Click **Cancel**.
- A different message is displayed.

USING THE STRING OBJECT

The `string` object has a single property — `length` — which returns the number of characters in the string. `string` has several methods that can be applied to text, a number of which can be used to format the text with HTML tags. String-formatting methods include `bold()`, `big()`, `fontColor(color)`, `fontSize(size)`, `italics()`, `link(href)`, `small()`, `strike()`, `sub()`, `sup()`, `toLowerCase()`, and `toUpperCase()`.

FORMAT TEXT

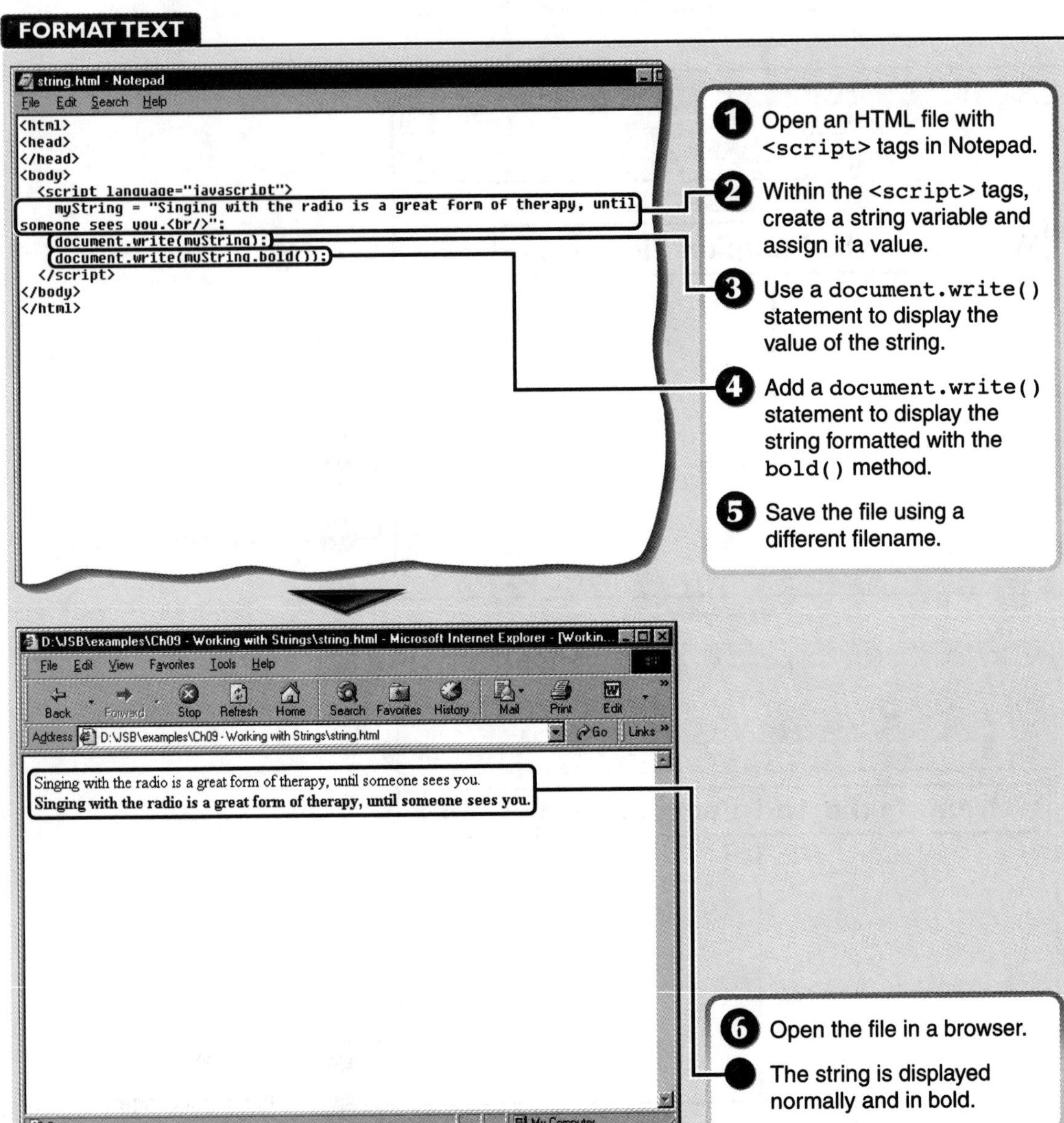

string.html - Notepad
File Edit Search Help
<html>
<head>
</head>
<body>
<script language="javascript">
myString = "Singing with the radio is a great form of therapy, until someone sees you.
";
document.write(myString);
document.write(myString.bold());
</script>
</body>
</html>
D:\JSB\examples\Ch09 - Working with Strings\string.html - Microsoft Internet Explorer - [Workin...
File Edit View Favorites Tools Help
Back Forward Stop Refresh Home Search Favorites History Mail Print Edit
Address D:\JSB\examples\Ch09 - Working with Strings\string.html
Go Links
Singing with the radio is a great form of therapy, until someone sees you.
Singing with the radio is a great form of therapy, until someone sees you.
Done
My Computer

1. Open an HTML file with `<script>` tags in Notepad.
2. Within the `<script>` tags, create a string variable and assign it a value.
3. Use a `document.write()` statement to display the value of the string.
4. Add a `document.write()` statement to display the string formatted with the `bold()` method.
5. Save the file using a different filename.
6. Open the file in a browser.

- The string is displayed normally and in bold.

in an instant

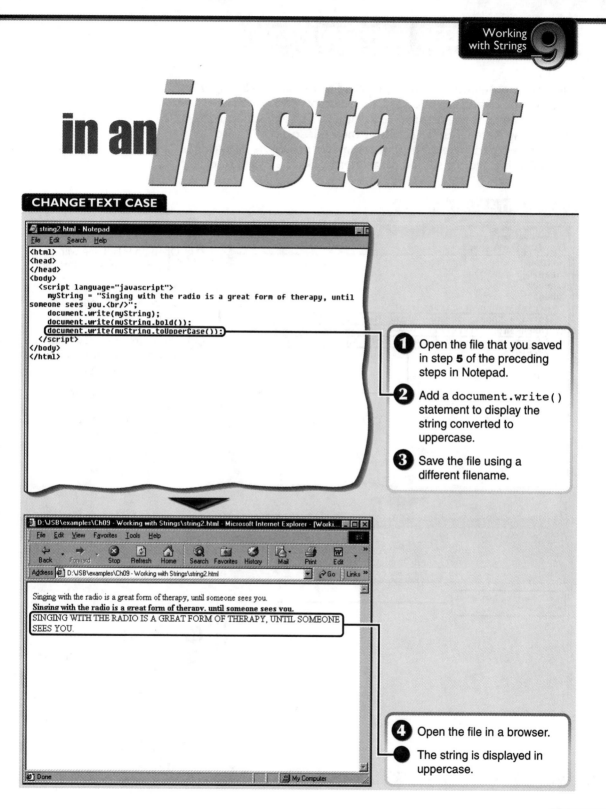

CHANGE TEXT CASE

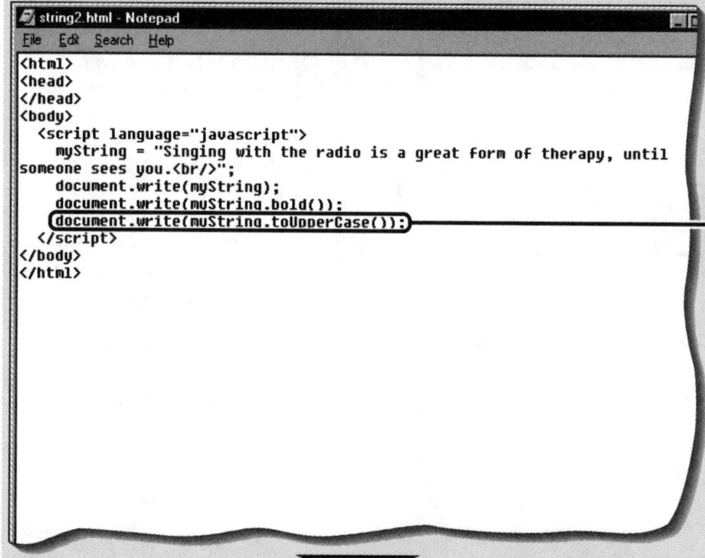

```
<html>
<head>
</head>
<body>
  <script language="javascript">
    myString = "Singing with the radio is a great form of therapy, until
someone sees you.<br/>";
    document.write(myString);
    document.write(myString.bold());
    document.write(myString.toUpperCase());
  </script>
</body>
</html>
```

1. Open the file that you saved in step **5** of the preceding steps in Notepad.
2. Add a `document.write()` statement to display the string converted to uppercase.
3. Save the file using a different filename.

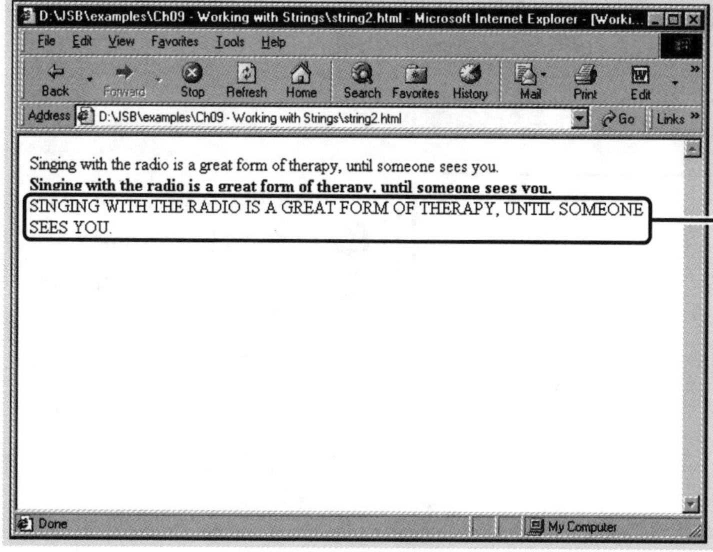

Singing with the radio is a great form of therapy, until someone sees you.
Singing with the radio is a great form of therapy, until someone sees you.
SINGING WITH THE RADIO IS A GREAT FORM OF THERAPY, UNTIL SOMEONE SEES YOU.

4. Open the file in a browser.

- The string is displayed in uppercase.

WORK WITH SUBSTRINGS

You can use the `substring()` method to extract a *substring,* which is a portion of a string. `substring()` accepts two parameters, corresponding to the first and last characters to extract from the base string. Another useful substring method, `substr()`, also accepts two parameters. The first parameter marks the beginning of the substring, and the second parameter marks the length to extract.

WORK WITH SUBSTRINGS

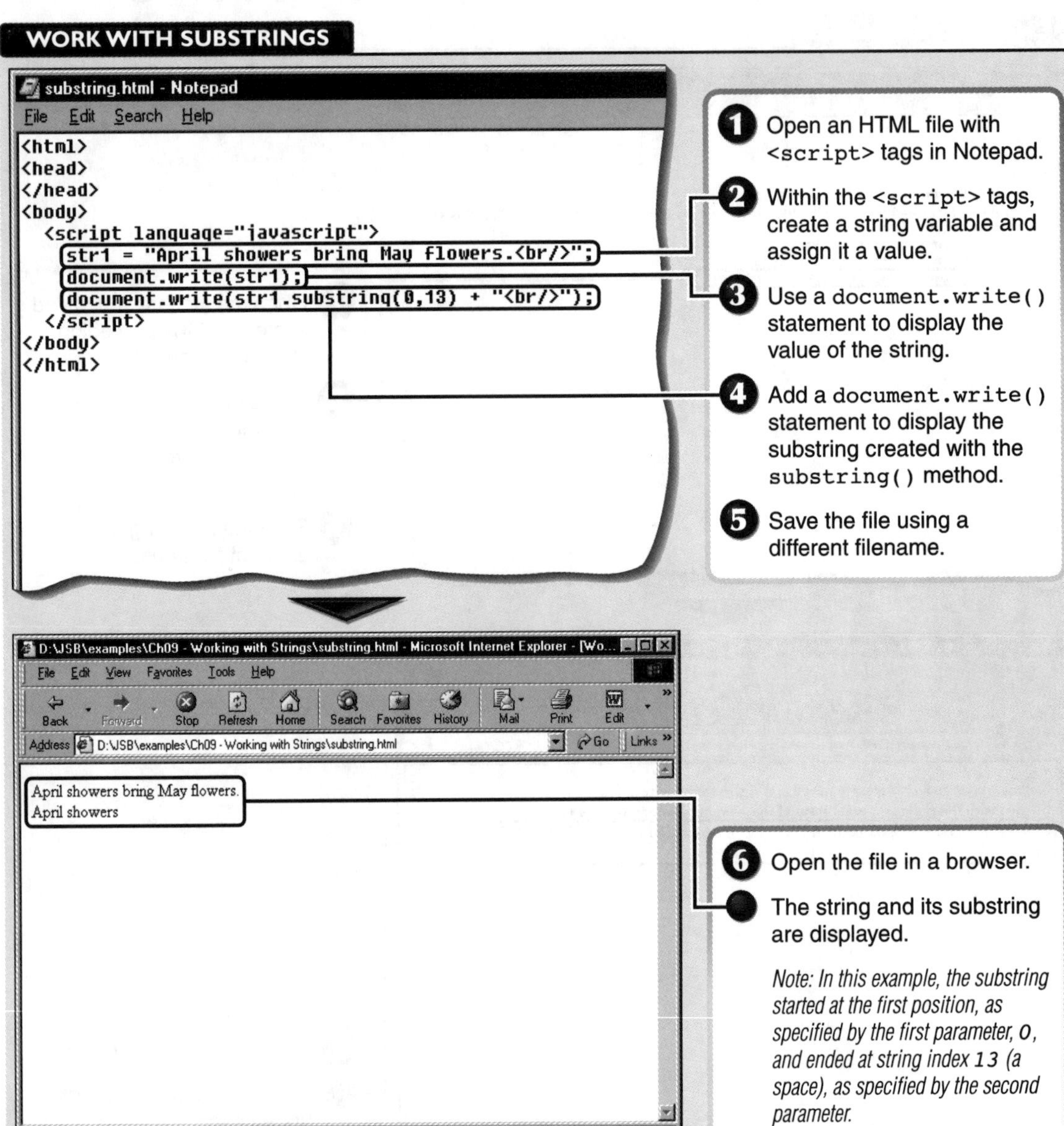

substring.html - Notepad
File Edit Search Help
<html>
<head>
</head>
<body>
<script language="javascript">
str1 = "April showers bring May flowers.
";
document.write(str1);
document.write(str1.substring(0,13) + "<br/>");
</script>
</body>
</html>
D:\JSB\examples\Ch09 - Working with Strings\substring.html - Microsoft Internet Explorer - [Wo...
File Edit View Favorites Tools Help
Back Forward Stop Refresh Home Search Favorites History Mail Print Edit
Address D:\JSB\examples\Ch09 - Working with Strings\substring.html
Go Links
April showers bring May flowers.
April showers
Done
My Computer

1. Open an HTML file with `<script>` tags in Notepad.
2. Within the `<script>` tags, create a string variable and assign it a value.
3. Use a `document.write()` statement to display the value of the string.
4. Add a `document.write()` statement to display the substring created with the `substring()` method.
5. Save the file using a different filename.
6. Open the file in a browser.

- The string and its substring are displayed.

Note: In this example, the substring started at the first position, as specified by the first parameter, `0`*, and ended at string index* `13` *(a space), as specified by the second parameter.*

in an instant

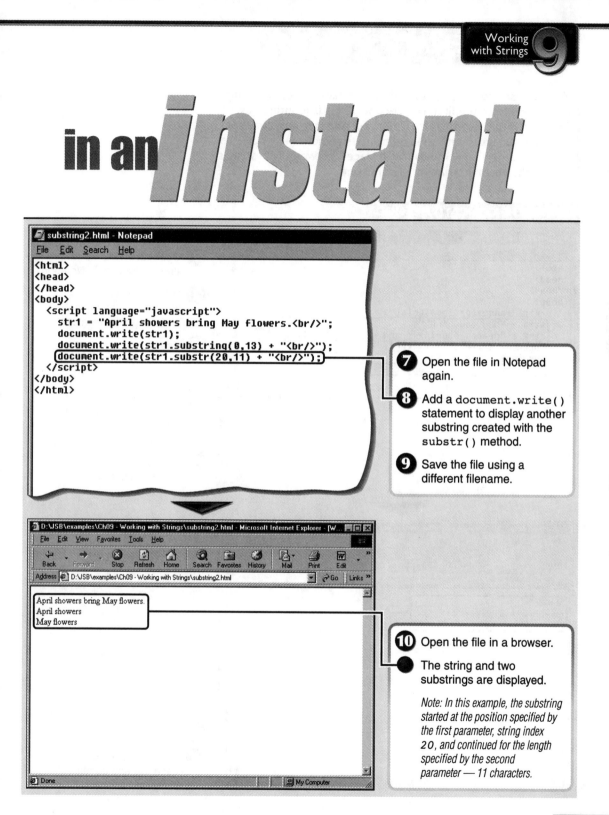

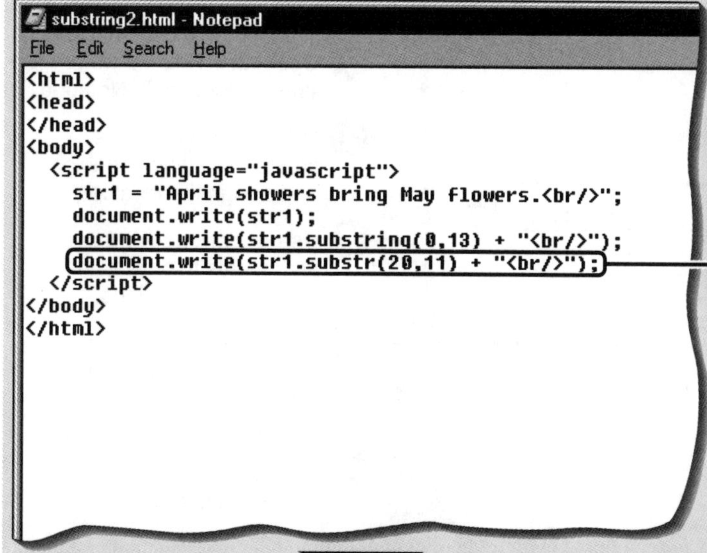

substring2.html - Notepad

```
<html>
<head>
</head>
<body>
  <script language="javascript">
    str1 = "April showers bring May flowers.<br/>";
    document.write(str1);
    document.write(str1.substring(0,13) + "<br/>");
    document.write(str1.substr(20,11) + "<br/>");
  </script>
</body>
</html>
```

7. Open the file in Notepad again.
8. Add a `document.write()` statement to display another substring created with the `substr()` method.
9. Save the file using a different filename.

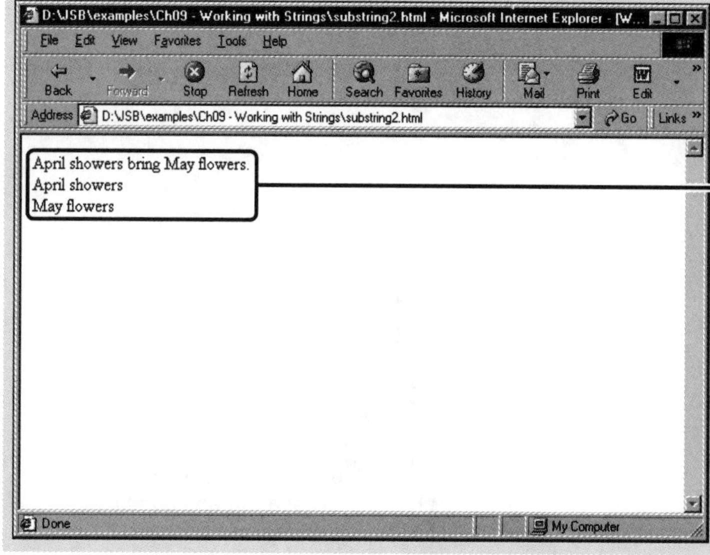

D:\JSB\examples\Ch09 - Working with Strings\substring2.html - Microsoft Internet Explorer

April showers bring May flowers.
April showers
May flowers

10. Open the file in a browser.

- The string and two substrings are displayed.

Note: In this example, the substring started at the position specified by the first parameter, string index `20`*, and continued for the length specified by the second parameter — 11 characters.*

CONCATENATE STRINGS

You can use the `concat()` method to tack a second string onto the end of the first. The second string is identified as a parameter to the `concat()` method. Another easy way to combine strings is with the addition assignment (+=) operator. This operator simply needs to be placed between two strings to add the second string to the first one.

USING THE CONCAT() METHOD

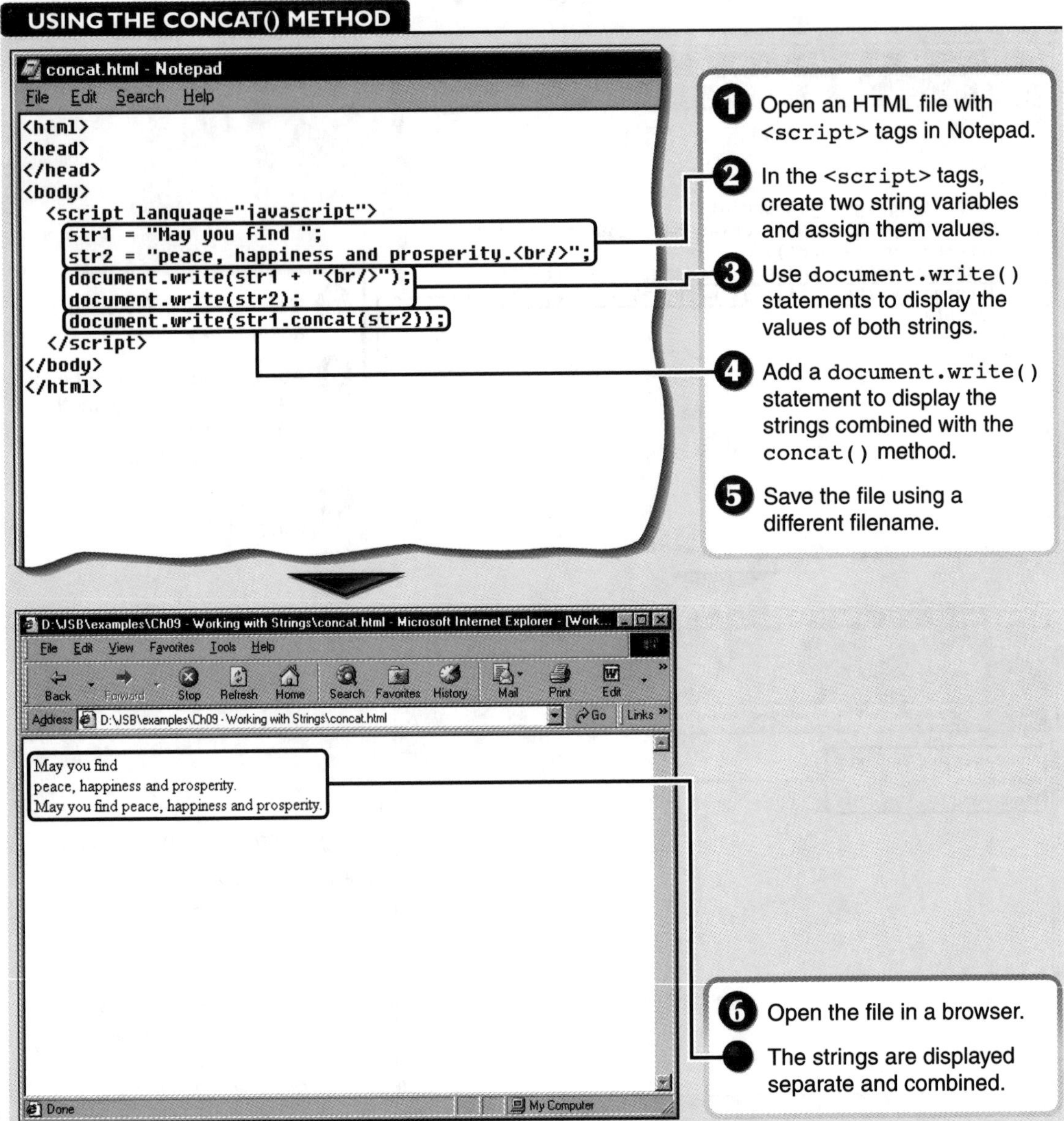

concat.html - Notepad
File Edit Search Help
<html>
<head>
</head>
<body>
<script language="javascript">
str1 = "May you find ";
str2 = "peace, happiness and prosperity.
";
document.write(str1 + "<br/>");
document.write(str2);
document.write(str1.concat(str2));
</script>
</body>
</html>
1 Open an HTML file with <script> tags in Notepad.
2 In the <script> tags, create two string variables and assign them values.
3 Use document.write() statements to display the values of both strings.
4 Add a document.write() statement to display the strings combined with the concat() method.
5 Save the file using a different filename.
D:\JSB\examples\Ch09 - Working with Strings\concat.html - Microsoft Internet Explorer - [Work...
File Edit View Favorites Tools Help
Back Forward Stop Refresh Home Search Favorites History Mail Print Edit
Address D:\JSB\examples\Ch09 - Working with Strings\concat.html Go Links
May you find
peace, happiness and prosperity.
May you find peace, happiness and prosperity.
Done
My Computer
6 Open the file in a browser.
The strings are displayed separate and combined.

in an instant

USING THE ADDITION ASSIGNMENT OPERATOR

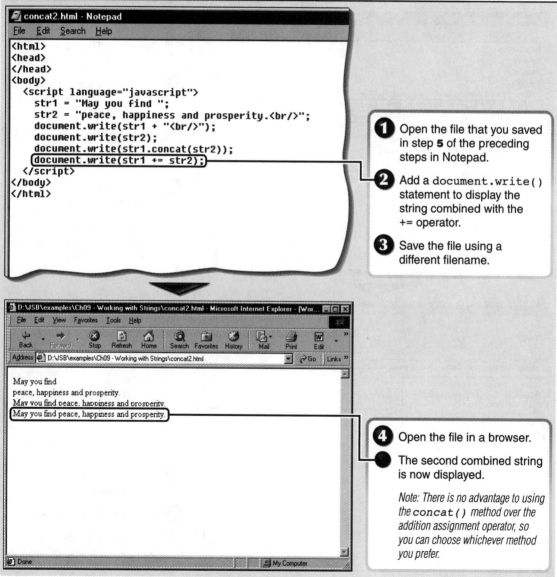

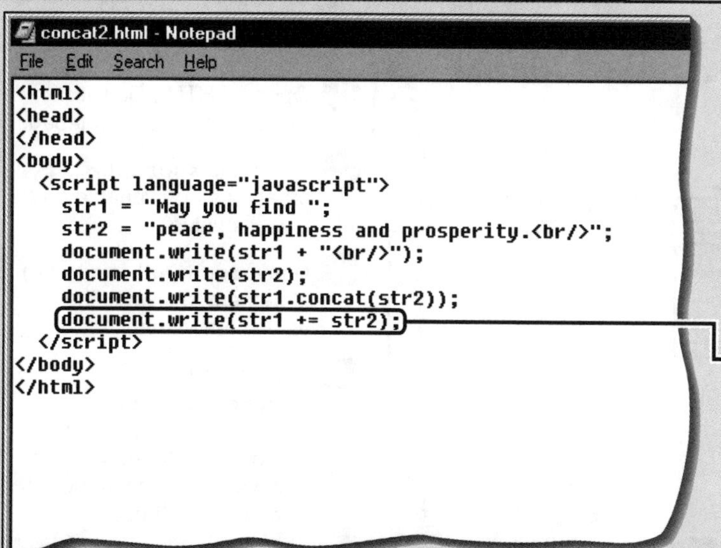

```
<html>
<head>
</head>
<body>
  <script language="javascript">
    str1 = "May you find ";
    str2 = "peace, happiness and prosperity.<br/>";
    document.write(str1 + "<br/>");
    document.write(str2);
    document.write(str1.concat(str2));
    document.write(str1 += str2);
  </script>
</body>
</html>
```

1. Open the file that you saved in step **5** of the preceding steps in Notepad.
2. Add a `document.write()` statement to display the string combined with the += operator.
3. Save the file using a different filename.

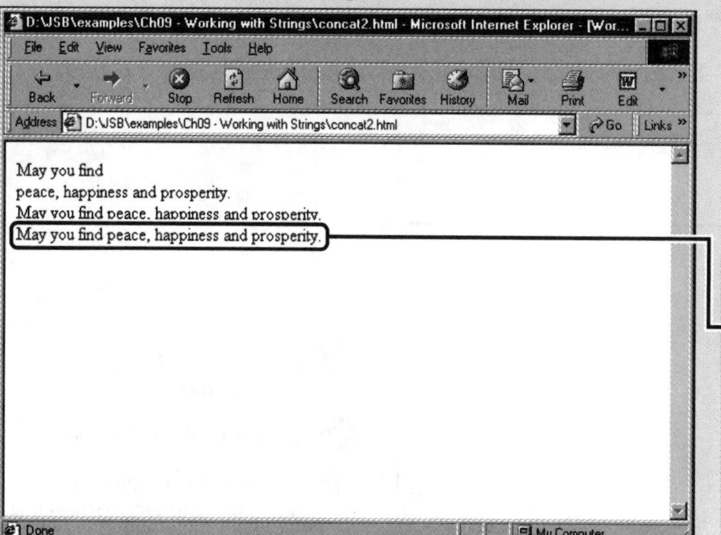
May you find
peace, happiness and prosperity.
May you find peace, happiness and prosperity.
May you find peace, happiness and prosperity.

4. Open the file in a browser.

- The second combined string is now displayed.

Note: There is no advantage to using the `concat()` *method over the addition assignment operator, so you can choose whichever method you prefer.*

FORMAT STRING VARIABLES

Many basic formatting options are available as methods of the `string` object. These string-formatting methods simply add the correct formatting tags to the beginning and end of the string. String-formatting methods include `big()`, `bold()`, `italics()`, `small()`, `strike()`, `sub()`, and `sup()`. You can also change the font size using the `fontsize()` method and set font color with the `fontcolor()` method.

FORMAT STRING VARIABLES

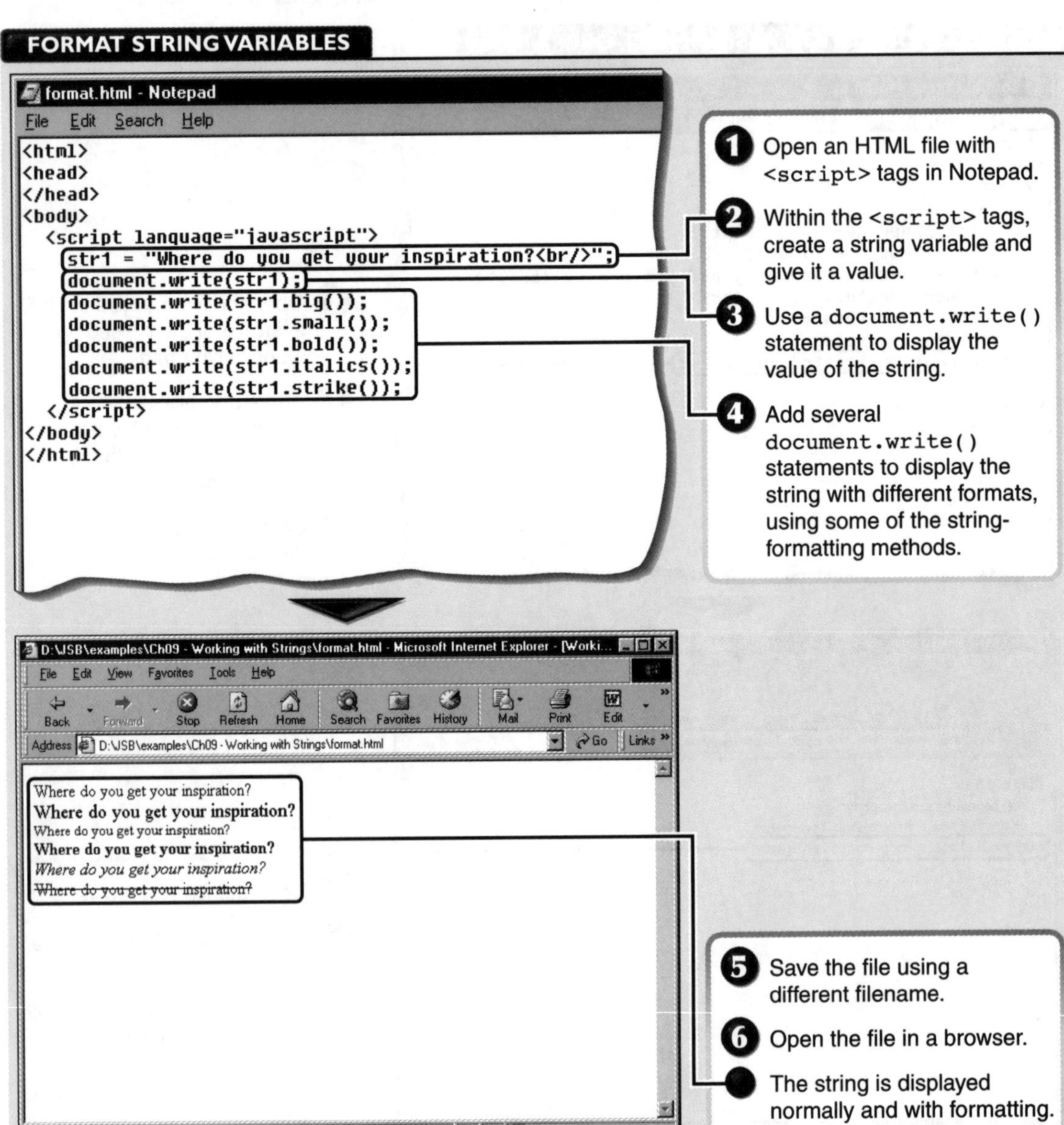

format.html - Notepad
File Edit Search Help
<html>
<head>
</head>
<body>
<script language="javascript">
str1 = "Where do you get your inspiration?
";
document.write(str1);
document.write(str1.big());
document.write(str1.small());
document.write(str1.bold());
document.write(str1.italics());
document.write(str1.strike());
</script>
</body>
</html>
D:\JSB\examples\Ch09 - Working with Strings\format.html - Microsoft Internet Explorer - [Worki...
File Edit View Favorites Tools Help
Back Forward Stop Refresh Home Search Favorites History Mail Print Edit
Address D:\JSB\examples\Ch09 - Working with Strings\format.html
Go Links
Where do you get your inspiration?
Where do you get your inspiration?
Where do you get your inspiration?
Where do you get your inspiration?
Where do you get your inspiration?
Where do you get your inspiration?
Done
My Computer

1. Open an HTML file with `<script>` tags in Notepad.
2. Within the `<script>` tags, create a string variable and give it a value.
3. Use a `document.write()` statement to display the value of the string.
4. Add several `document.write()` statements to display the string with different formats, using some of the string-formatting methods.
5. Save the file using a different filename.
6. Open the file in a browser.

- The string is displayed normally and with formatting.

in an instant

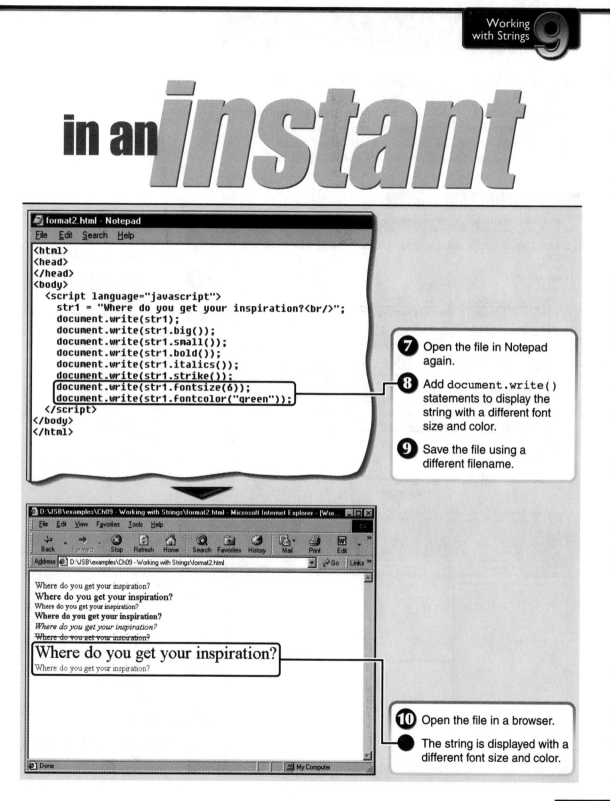

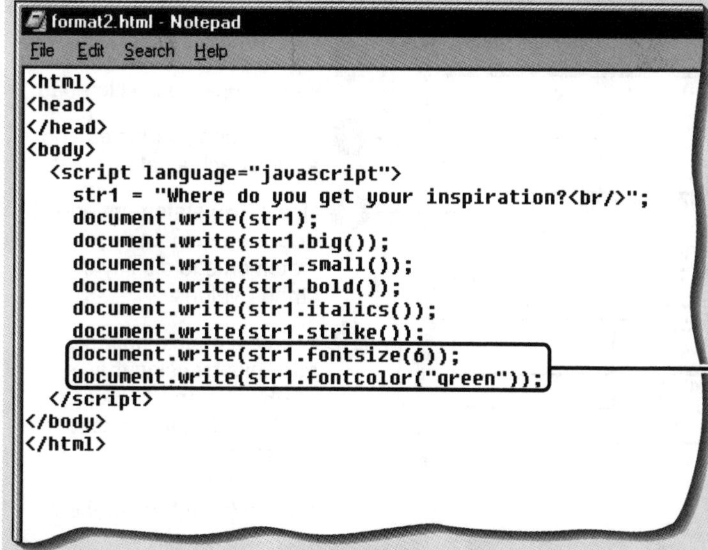

format2.html - Notepad

```
<html>
<head>
</head>
<body>
  <script language="javascript">
    str1 = "Where do you get your inspiration?<br/>";
    document.write(str1);
    document.write(str1.big());
    document.write(str1.small());
    document.write(str1.bold());
    document.write(str1.italics());
    document.write(str1.strike());
    document.write(str1.fontsize(6));
    document.write(str1.fontcolor("green"));
  </script>
</body>
</html>
```

7. Open the file in Notepad again.
8. Add `document.write()` statements to display the string with a different font size and color.
9. Save the file using a different filename.

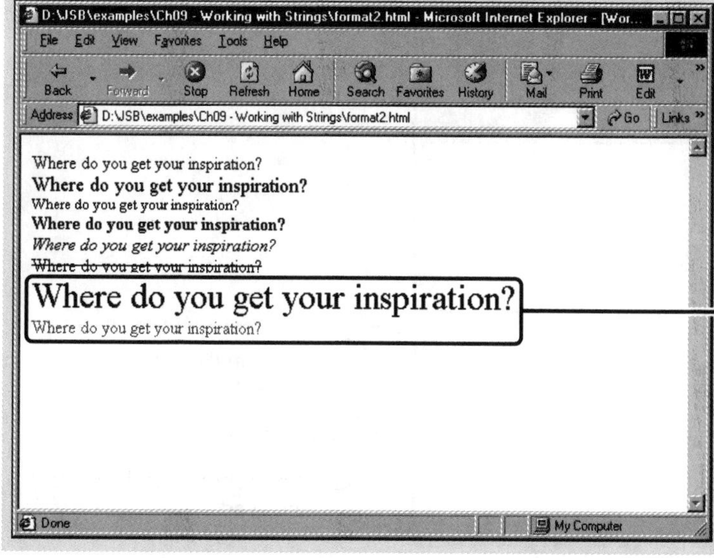

D:\JSB\examples\Ch09 - Working with Strings\format2.html - Microsoft Internet Explorer

Where do you get your inspiration?
Where do you get your inspiration?
Where do you get your inspiration?
Where do you get your inspiration?
Where do you get your inspiration?
~~Where do you get your inspiration?~~
Where do you get your inspiration?
Where do you get your inspiration?

10. Open the file in a browser.

- The string is displayed with a different font size and color.

BUILD ANCHORS AND LINKS

Any defined `string` object can be changed into an anchor or a link by using the `anchor()` and `link()` methods of the `string` object. The `anchor()` method accepts a name parameter that is used to specify the name of the anchor. The `link()` method accepts an `href` parameter that defines where the link points.

BUILD ANCHORS AND LINKS

link.html - Notepad

```
<html>
<head>
</head>
<body>
  <script language="javascript">
    str1 = "This is the beginning of the page.<br/>";
    str2 = ". . .<br/>";
    str3 = "This is the end of the page.<br/>";
    str4 = "link to the start<br/>";
    str5 = "link to the end<br/>";
    document.write(str1.anchor("start"));
    for (i=0;i<10;i++)
      document.write(str2);
    document.write(str3.anchor("end"));
    document.write(str4.link("#start"));
    document.write(str5.link("#end"));
  </script>
</body>
</html>
```

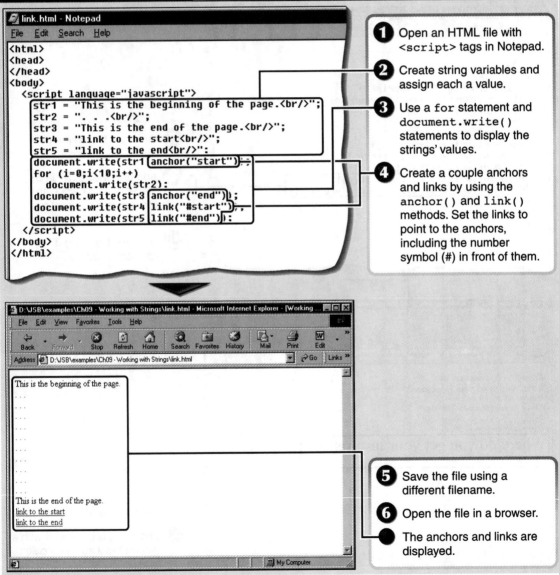

1. Open an HTML file with `<script>` tags in Notepad.
2. Create string variables and assign each a value.
3. Use a `for` statement and `document.write()` statements to display the strings' values.
4. Create a couple anchors and links by using the `anchor()` and `link()` methods. Set the links to point to the anchors, including the number symbol (#) in front of them.

D:\JSB\examples\Ch09 - Working with Strings\link.html - Microsoft Internet Explorer

This is the beginning of the page.
. . .
. . .
. . .
. . .
. . .
. . .
. . .
. . .
. . .
. . .
This is the end of the page.
link to the start
link to the end

5. Save the file using a different filename.
6. Open the file in a browser.

- The anchors and links are displayed.

in an instant

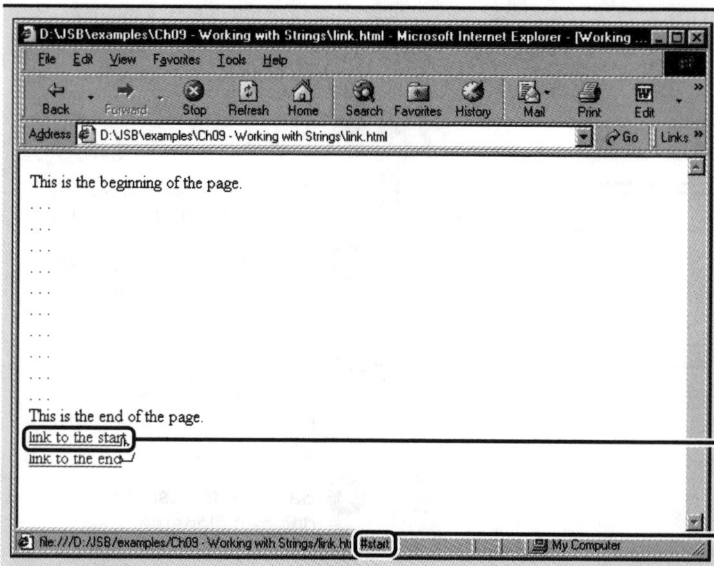

D:\JSB\examples\Ch09 - Working with Strings\link.html - Microsoft Internet Explorer - [Working ...

File Edit View Favorites Tools Help

Back Forward Stop Refresh Home Search Favorites History Mail Print Edit

Address D:\JSB\examples\Ch09 - Working with Strings\link.html Go Links

This is the beginning of the page.
...
...
...
...
...
...
...
...
...
...
This is the end of the page.
link to the start
link to the end

file:///D:/JSB/examples/Ch09 - Working with Strings/link.htm#start My Computer

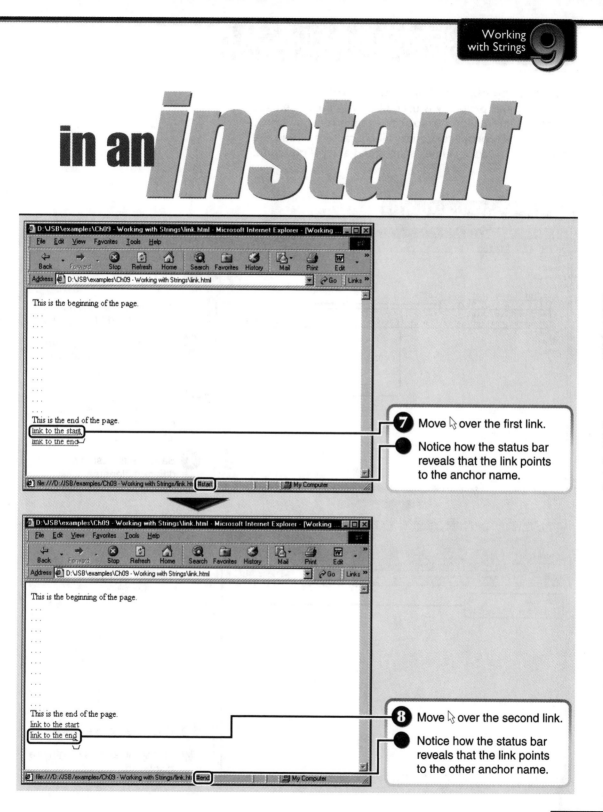

7 Move over the first link.

- Notice how the status bar reveals that the link points to the anchor name.

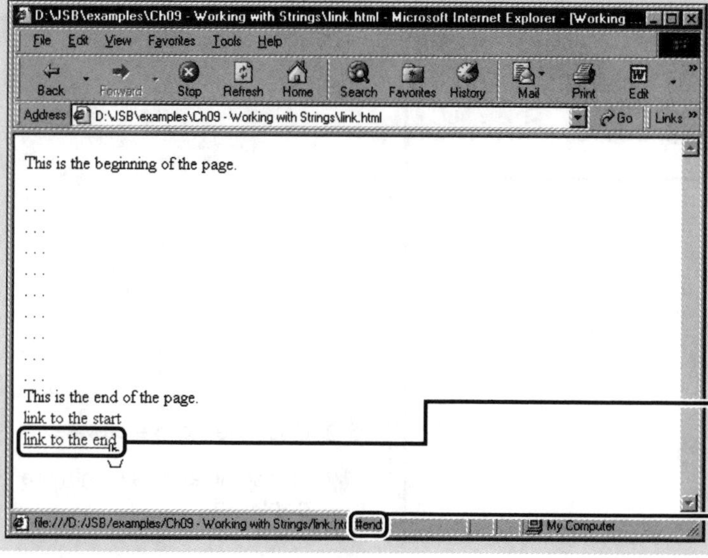

D:\JSB\examples\Ch09 - Working with Strings\link.html - Microsoft Internet Explorer - [Working ...

File Edit View Favorites Tools Help

Back Forward Stop Refresh Home Search Favorites History Mail Print Edit

Address D:\JSB\examples\Ch09 - Working with Strings\link.html Go Links

This is the beginning of the page.
...
...
...
...
...
...
...
...
...
...
This is the end of the page.
link to the start
link to the end

file:///D:/JSB/examples/Ch09 - Working with Strings/link.htm#end My Computer

8 Move over the second link.

- Notice how the status bar reveals that the link points to the other anchor name.

DETERMINE STRING LENGTH

The `string` object includes a single property — `length`. This property is useful because it can be used as part of a `for` loop to look at each letter in a string. The `length` property counts all characters within the quotation marks including spaces and any HTML code.

DETERMINE STRING LENGTH

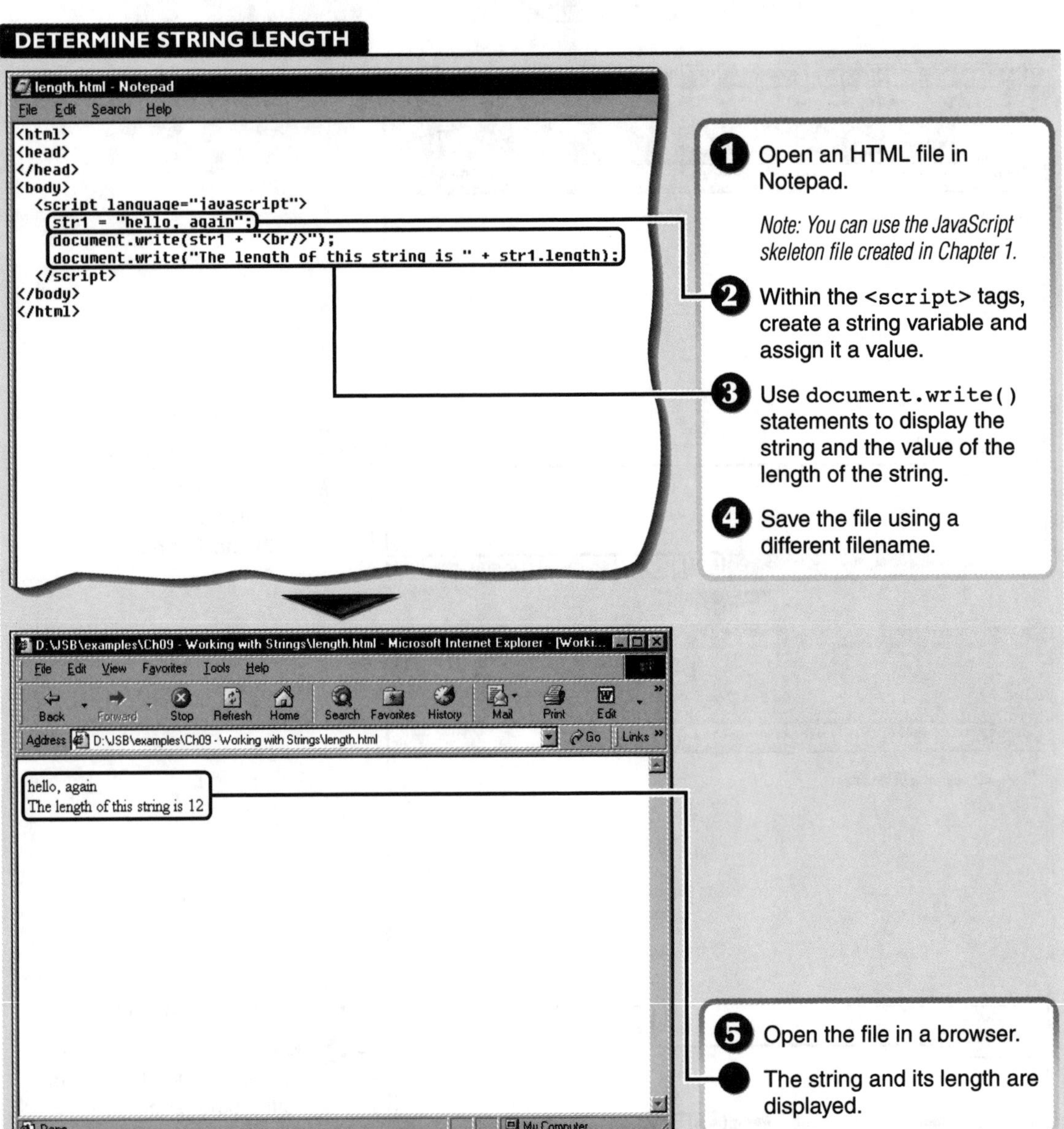

length.html - Notepad
File Edit Search Help
<html>
<head>
</head>
<body>
<script language="javascript">
str1 = "hello, again";
document.write(str1 + "<br/>");
document.write("The length of this string is " + str1.length);
</script>
</body>
</html>
1 Open an HTML file in Notepad.
Note: You can use the JavaScript skeleton file created in Chapter 1.
2 Within the <script> tags, create a string variable and assign it a value.
3 Use document.write() statements to display the string and the value of the length of the string.
4 Save the file using a different filename.
D:\JSB\examples\Ch09 - Working with Strings\length.html - Microsoft Internet Explorer
hello, again
The length of this string is 12
5 Open the file in a browser.
The string and its length are displayed.

CHANGE CASE

You can use the toLowerCase() method to convert a string to all lowercase letters. Remember that even initial capitals (the first letter of each word is capitalized) are changed to lowercase. You can use the toUpperCase() method to convert a string to all capital letters.

CHANGE CASE

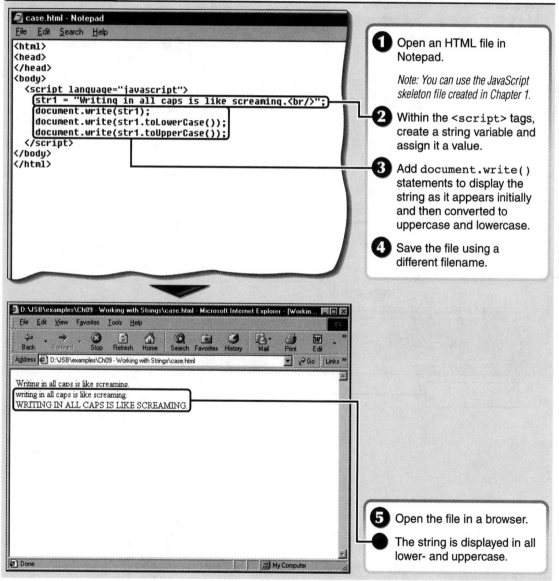

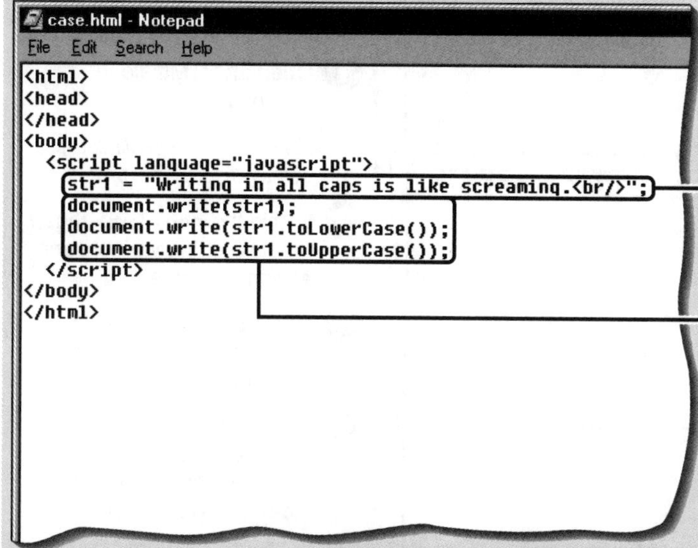

case.html - Notepad

```
<html>
<head>
</head>
<body>
  <script language="javascript">
    str1 = "Writing in all caps is like screaming.<br/>";
    document.write(str1);
    document.write(str1.toLowerCase());
    document.write(str1.toUpperCase());
  </script>
</body>
</html>
```

1. Open an HTML file in Notepad.

   Note: You can use the JavaScript skeleton file created in Chapter 1.

2. Within the <script> tags, create a string variable and assign it a value.

3. Add document.write() statements to display the string as it appears initially and then converted to uppercase and lowercase.

4. Save the file using a different filename.

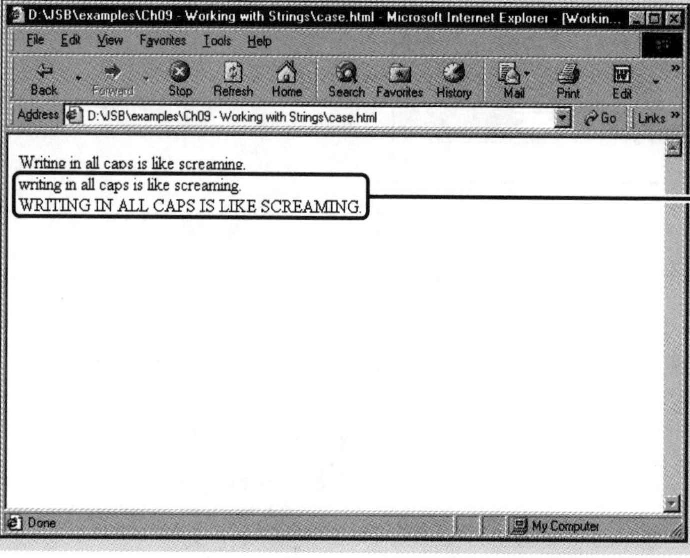

D:\JSB\examples\Ch09 - Working with Strings\case.html - Microsoft Internet Explorer

Writing in all caps is like screaming.
writing in all caps is like screaming.
WRITING IN ALL CAPS IS LIKE SCREAMING.

5. Open the file in a browser.

- The string is displayed in all lower- and uppercase.

SEARCH WITHIN A STRING

You can use the `string` object method `search()` to search within a string for a section of text. The parameter for this method is the string for which you are searching. The method returns the index for the position of the search string. If the search string cannot be found within the string, the method returns a value of `-1`.

SEARCH WITHIN A STRING

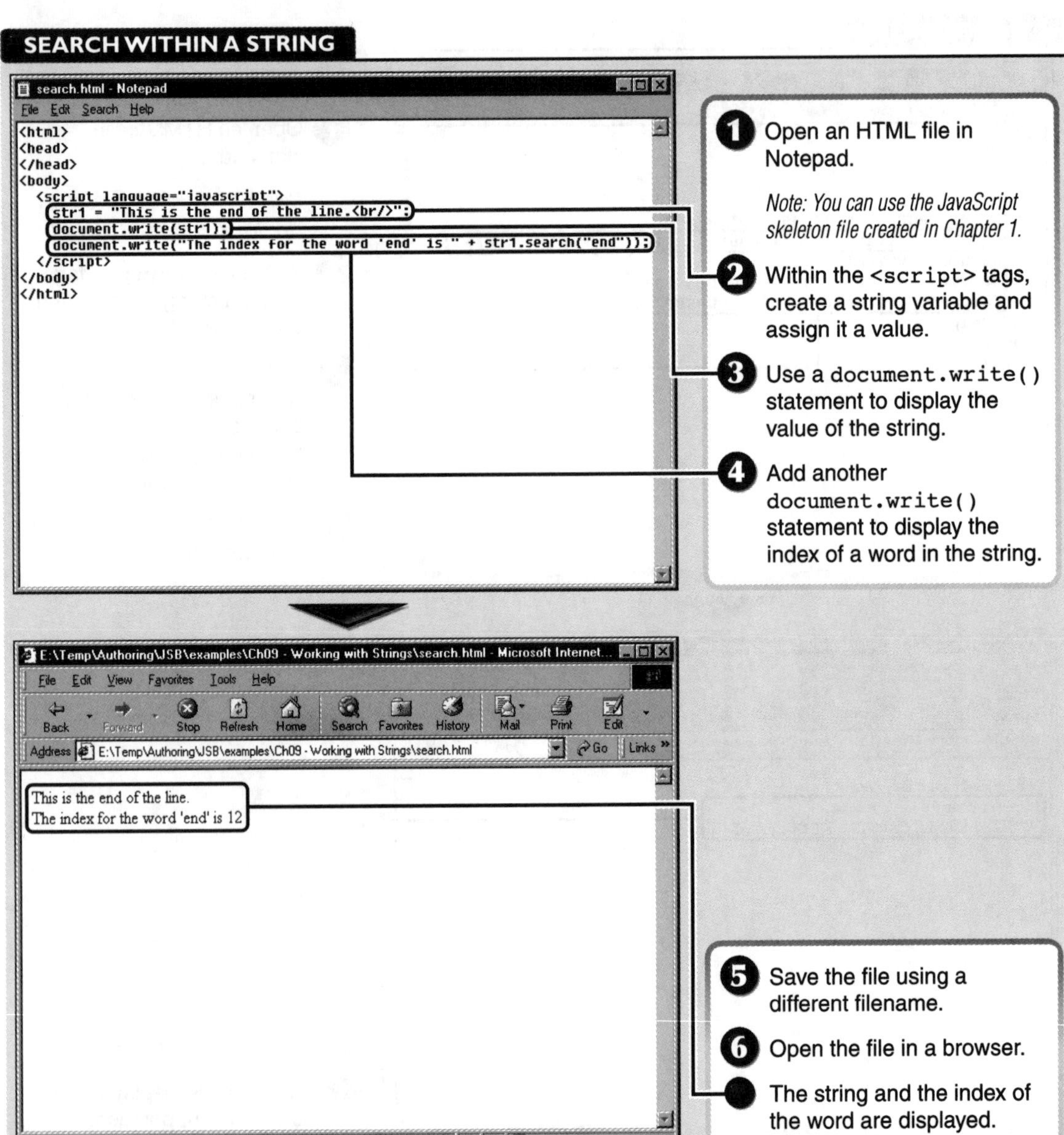

search.html - Notepad
File Edit Search Help
<html>
<head>
</head>
<body>
<script language="javascript">
str1 = "This is the end of the line.
";
document.write(str1);
document.write("The index for the word 'end' is " + str1.search("end"));
</script>
</body>
</html>
E:\Temp\Authoring\JSB\examples\Ch09 - Working with Strings\search.html - Microsoft Internet...
This is the end of the line.
The index for the word 'end' is 12

1. Open an HTML file in Notepad.

   Note: You can use the JavaScript skeleton file created in Chapter 1.

2. Within the `<script>` tags, create a string variable and assign it a value.
3. Use a `document.write()` statement to display the value of the string.
4. Add another `document.write()` statement to display the index of a word in the string.
5. Save the file using a different filename.
6. Open the file in a browser.

- The string and the index of the word are displayed.

in an instant

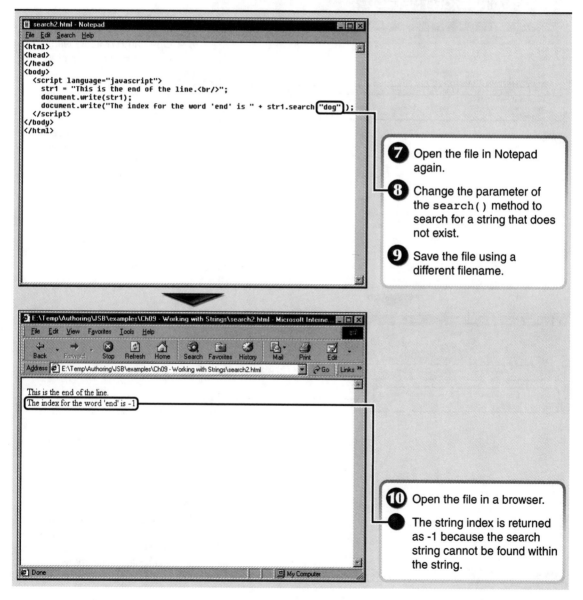

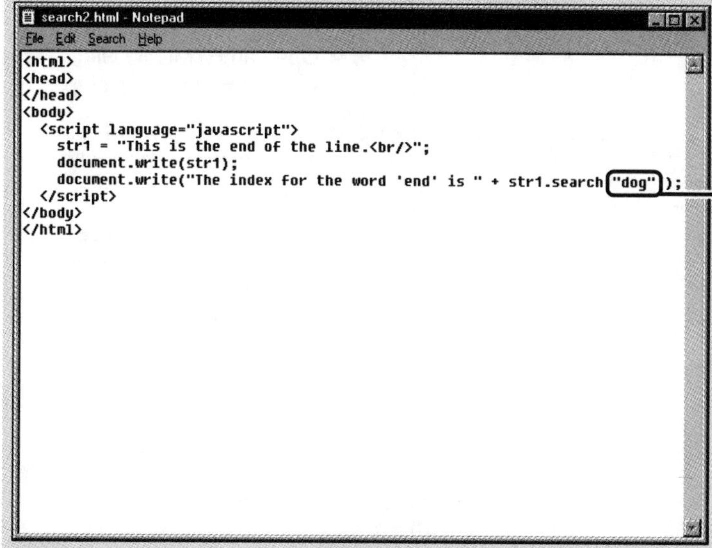

```
<html>
<head>
</head>
<body>
  <script language="javascript">
    str1 = "This is the end of the line.<br/>";
    document.write(str1);
    document.write("The index for the word 'end' is " + str1.search("dog"));
  </script>
</body>
</html>
```

7. Open the file in Notepad again.
8. Change the parameter of the `search()` method to search for a string that does not exist.
9. Save the file using a different filename.

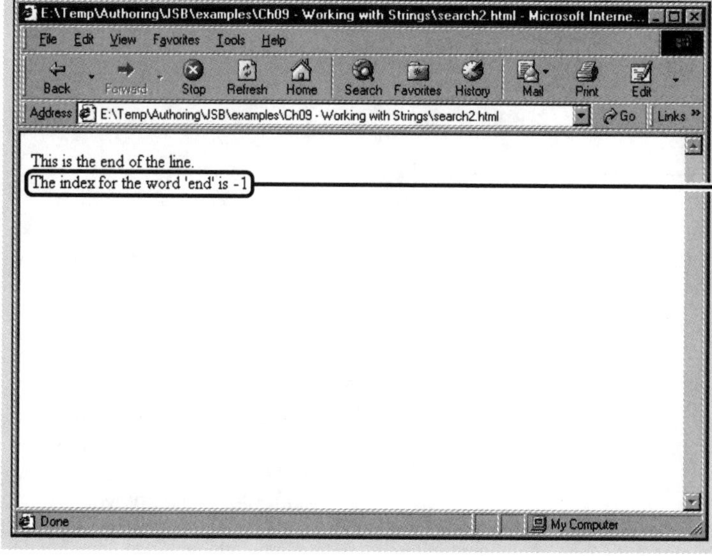

This is the end of the line.
The index for the word 'end' is -1

10. Open the file in a browser.
- The string index is returned as -1 because the search string cannot be found within the string.

LOCATE CHARACTERS IN A STRING

You can use the `indexOf()` method, like `search()`, to locate the first occurrence of a string, but you can specify where `indexOf()` begins looking. You can also search from the end of the string by using the `lastIndexOf()` method. If you provide a second parameter to this method, it searches backward toward the beginning of the string from the index specified in the second parameter.

USING THE INDEXOF() METHOD

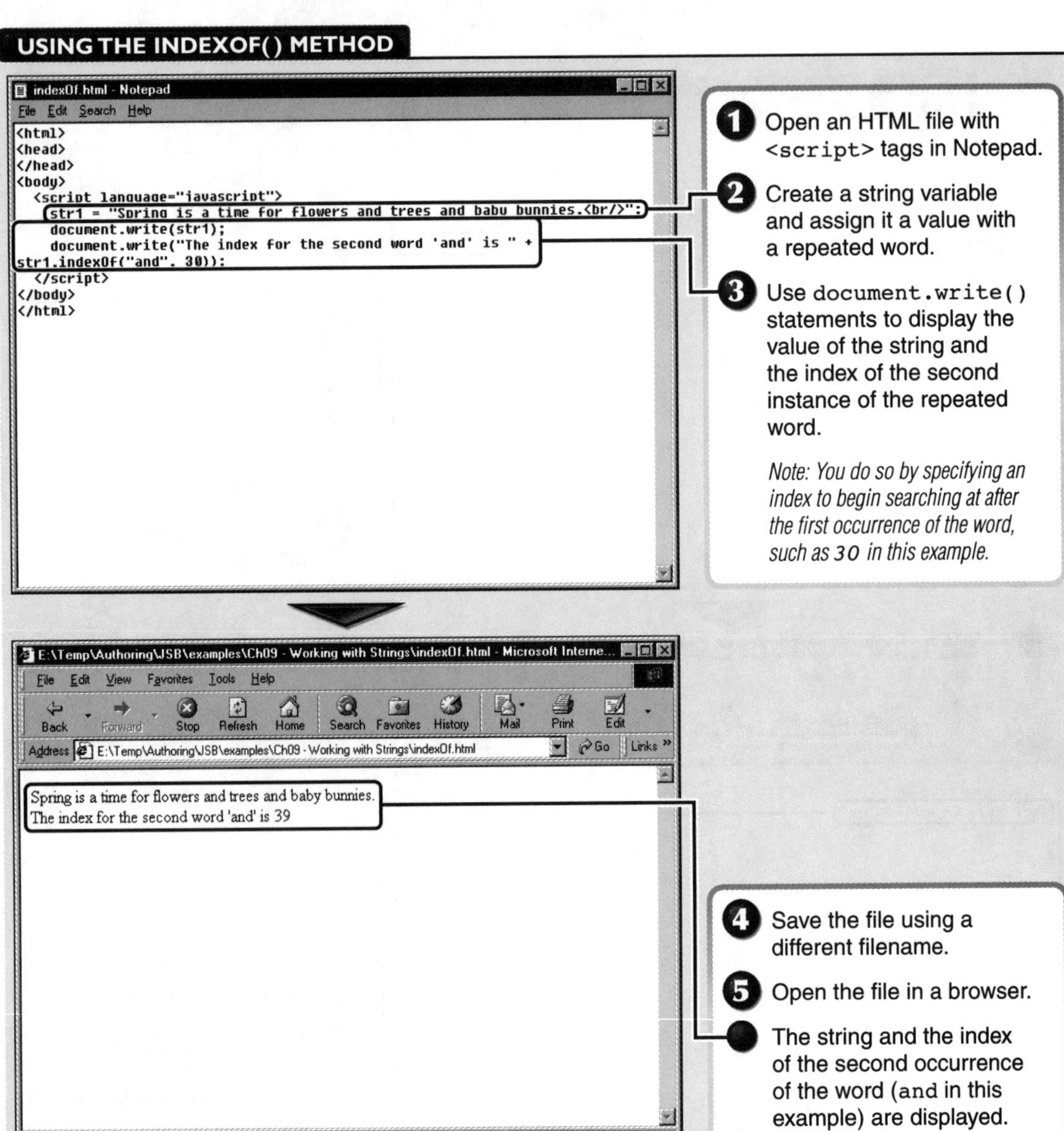

indexOf.html - Notepad
File Edit Search Help
<html>
<head>
</head>
<body>
<script language="javascript">
str1 = "Spring is a time for flowers and trees and baby bunnies.
";
document.write(str1);
document.write("The index for the second word 'and' is " +
str1.indexOf("and", 30));
</script>
</body>
</html>
E:\Temp\Authoring\JSB\examples\Ch09 - Working with Strings\indexOf.html - Microsoft Interne...
File Edit View Favorites Tools Help
Back Forward Stop Refresh Home Search Favorites History Mail Print Edit
Address E:\Temp\Authoring\JSB\examples\Ch09 - Working with Strings\indexOf.html
Go Links
Spring is a time for flowers and trees and baby bunnies.
The index for the second word 'and' is 39
Done
My Computer

1. Open an HTML file with `<script>` tags in Notepad.
2. Create a string variable and assign it a value with a repeated word.
3. Use `document.write()` statements to display the value of the string and the index of the second instance of the repeated word.

Note: You do so by specifying an index to begin searching at after the first occurrence of the word, such as `30` in this example.

4. Save the file using a different filename.
5. Open the file in a browser.

- The string and the index of the second occurrence of the word (`and` in this example) are displayed.

in an instant

USING THE LASTINDEXOF() METHOD

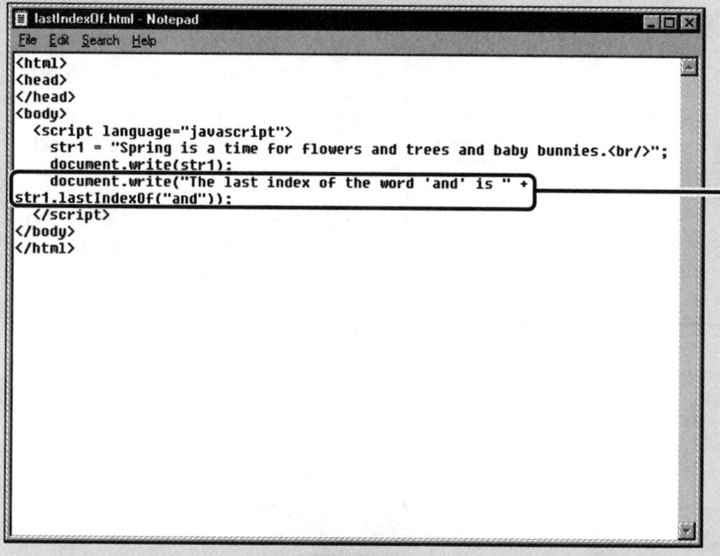
lastIndexOf.html - Notepad
File Edit Search Help
<html>
<head>
</head>
<body>
<script language="javascript">
str1 = "Spring is a time for flowers and trees and baby bunnies.
";
document.write(str1);
document.write("The last index of the word 'and' is " +
str1.lastIndexOf("and"));
</script>
</body>
</html>

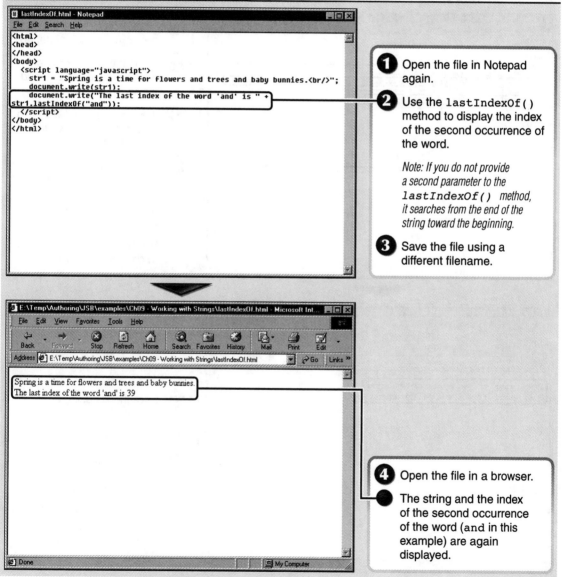

1. Open the file in Notepad again.
2. Use the `lastIndexOf()` method to display the index of the second occurrence of the word.

Note: If you do not provide a second parameter to the `lastIndexOf()` method, it searches from the end of the string toward the beginning.

3. Save the file using a different filename.

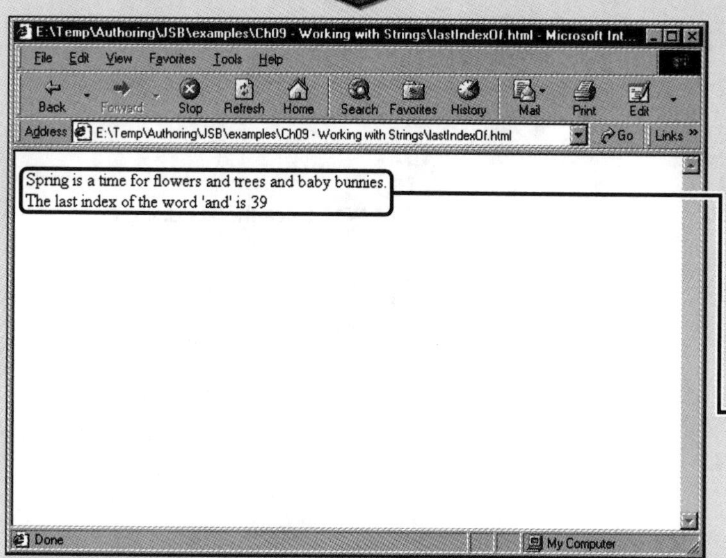
E:\Temp\Authoring\JSB\examples\Ch09 - Working with Strings\lastIndexOf.html - Microsoft Int...
File Edit View Favorites Tools Help
Back Forward Stop Refresh Home Search Favorites History Mail Print Edit
Address E:\Temp\Authoring\JSB\examples\Ch09 - Working with Strings\lastIndexOf.html
Go Links
Spring is a time for flowers and trees and baby bunnies.
The last index of the word 'and' is 39
Done
My Computer

4. Open the file in a browser.

- The string and the index of the second occurrence of the word (`and` in this example) are again displayed.

REPLACE TEXT IN A STRING

You can use the replace() method to replace one string with another. The replace() method accepts the string to search for as its first parameter. The second parameter is the replacement string. This method replaces only a single instance of the search string, not all instances in the entire string. To replace all instances, you need to use the method several times.

REPLACE TEXT IN A STRING

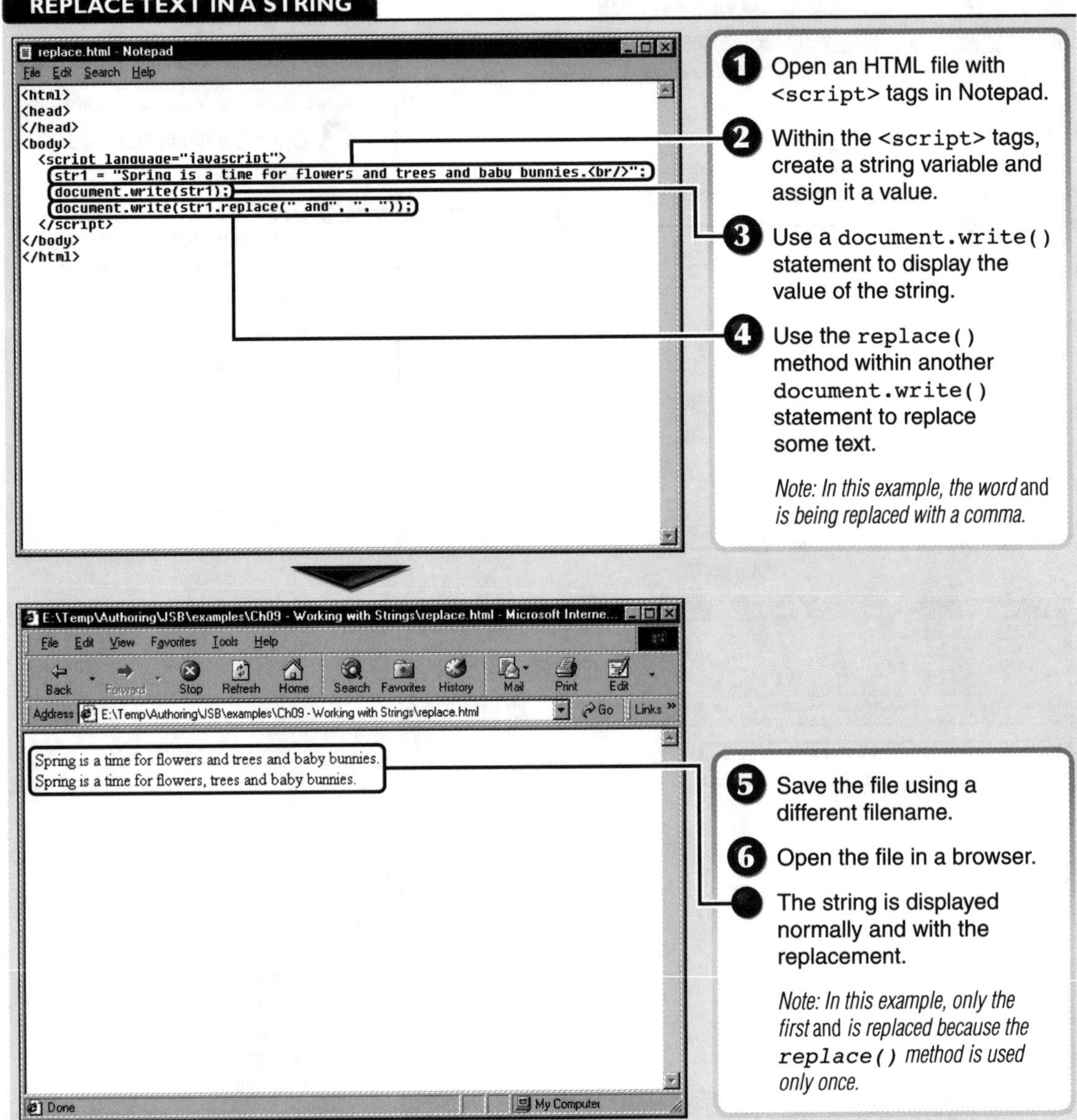

replace.html - Notepad
File Edit Search Help
<html>
<head>
</head>
<body>
<script language="javascript">
str1 = "Spring is a time for flowers and trees and baby bunnies.
";
document.write(str1);
document.write(str1.replace(" and", ","));
</script>
</body>
</html>
E:\Temp\Authoring\JSB\examples\Ch09 - Working with Strings\replace.html - Microsoft Interne...
File Edit View Favorites Tools Help
Back Forward Stop Refresh Home Search Favorites History Mail Print Edit
Address E:\Temp\Authoring\JSB\examples\Ch09 - Working with Strings\replace.html
Go Links
Spring is a time for flowers and trees and baby bunnies.
Spring is a time for flowers, trees and baby bunnies.
Done
My Computer

1. Open an HTML file with <script> tags in Notepad.
2. Within the <script> tags, create a string variable and assign it a value.
3. Use a document.write() statement to display the value of the string.
4. Use the replace() method within another document.write() statement to replace some text.

Note: In this example, the word and *is being replaced with a comma.*

5. Save the file using a different filename.
6. Open the file in a browser.

- The string is displayed normally and with the replacement.

Note: In this example, only the first and *is replaced because the* replace() *method is used only once.*

in an instant

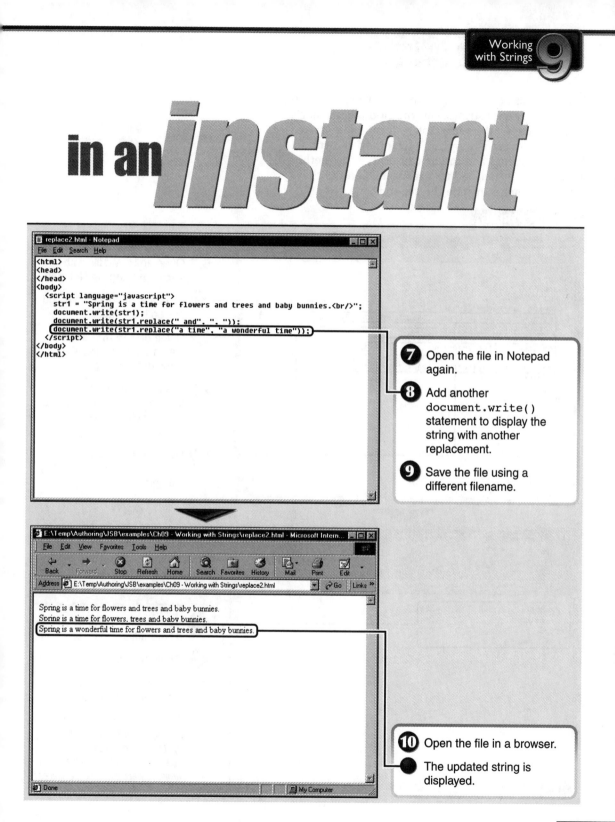

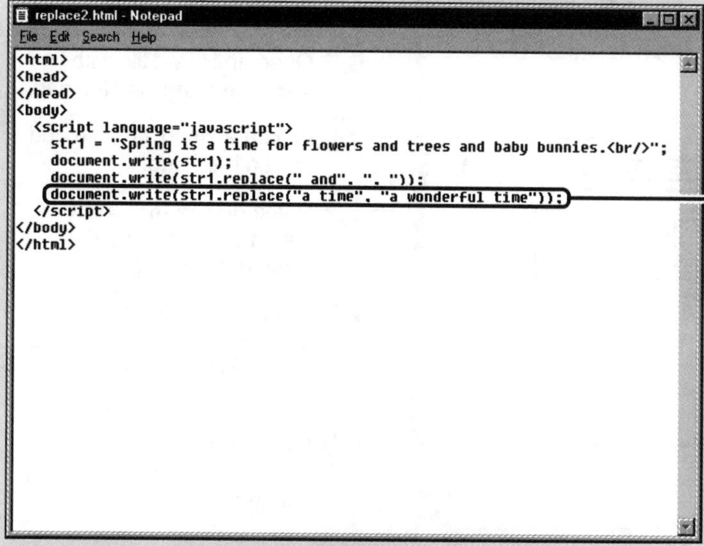

replace2.html - Notepad

File Edit Search Help

```
<html>
<head>
</head>
<body>
  <script language="javascript">
    str1 = "Spring is a time for flowers and trees and baby bunnies.<br/>";
    document.write(str1);
    document.write(str1.replace(" and", ","));
    document.write(str1.replace("a time", "a wonderful time"));
  </script>
</body>
</html>
```

7 Open the file in Notepad again.

8 Add another `document.write()` statement to display the string with another replacement.

9 Save the file using a different filename.

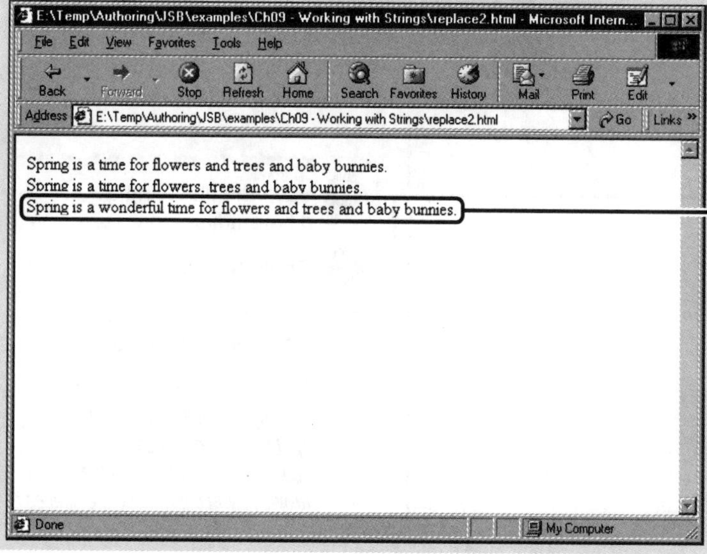

E:\Temp\Authoring\JSB\examples\Ch09 - Working with Strings\replace2.html - Microsoft Intern...

File Edit View Favorites Tools Help

Back Forward Stop Refresh Home Search Favorites History Mail Print Edit

Address E:\Temp\Authoring\JSB\examples\Ch09 - Working with Strings\replace2.html Go Links

Spring is a time for flowers and trees and baby bunnies.
Spring is a time for flowers, trees and baby bunnies.
Spring is a wonderful time for flowers and trees and baby bunnies.

Done My Computer

10 Open the file in a browser.

- The updated string is displayed.

SPLIT A STRING

You can use the `split()` method to split a string into an array of strings. This method takes a single parameter — the separator to locate and use to split the string. The `split()` method returns an array of strings and can be captured if the method statement is assigned to a variable. None of the array elements include the separator.

SPLIT A STRING

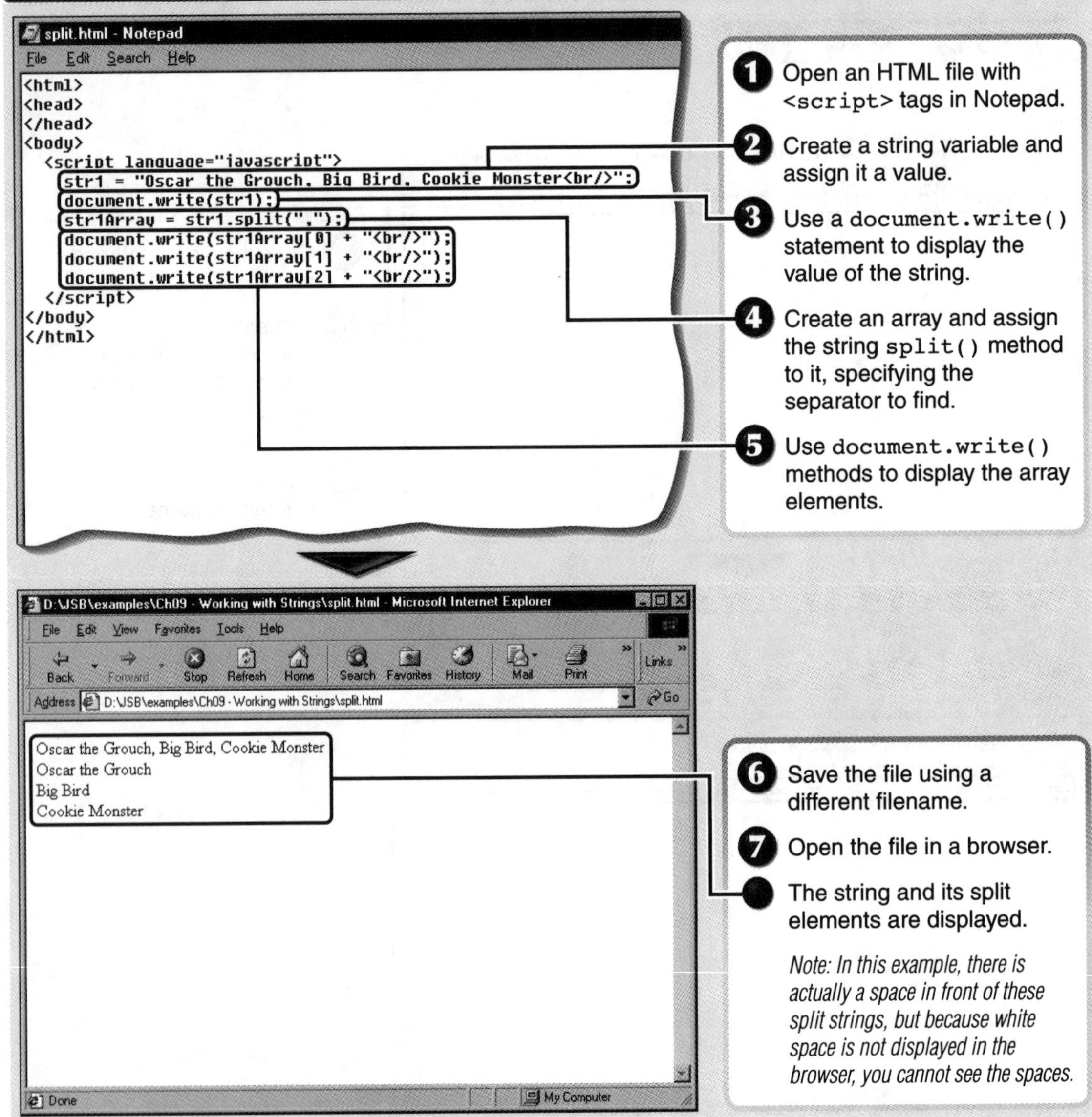

split.html - Notepad
File Edit Search Help
<html>
<head>
</head>
<body>
<script language="javascript">
str1 = "Oscar the Grouch, Big Bird, Cookie Monster
";
document.write(str1);
str1Array = str1.split(",");
document.write(str1Array[0] + "<br/>");
document.write(str1Array[1] + "<br/>");
document.write(str1Array[2] + "<br/>");
</script>
</body>
</html>
D:\JSB\examples\Ch09 - Working with Strings\split.html - Microsoft Internet Explorer
File Edit View Favorites Tools Help
Back Forward Stop Refresh Home Search Favorites History Mail Print
Links
Address D:\JSB\examples\Ch09 - Working with Strings\split.html
Go
Oscar the Grouch, Big Bird, Cookie Monster
Oscar the Grouch
Big Bird
Cookie Monster
Done
My Computer

1. Open an HTML file with `<script>` tags in Notepad.
2. Create a string variable and assign it a value.
3. Use a `document.write()` statement to display the value of the string.
4. Create an array and assign the string `split()` method to it, specifying the separator to find.
5. Use `document.write()` methods to display the array elements.
6. Save the file using a different filename.
7. Open the file in a browser.

- The string and its split elements are displayed.

Note: In this example, there is actually a space in front of these split strings, but because white space is not displayed in the browser, you cannot see the spaces.

in an instant

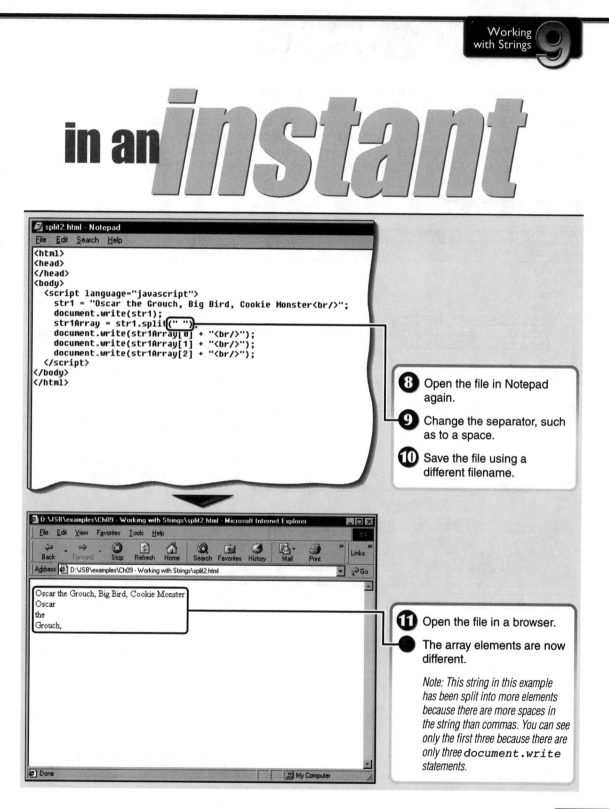

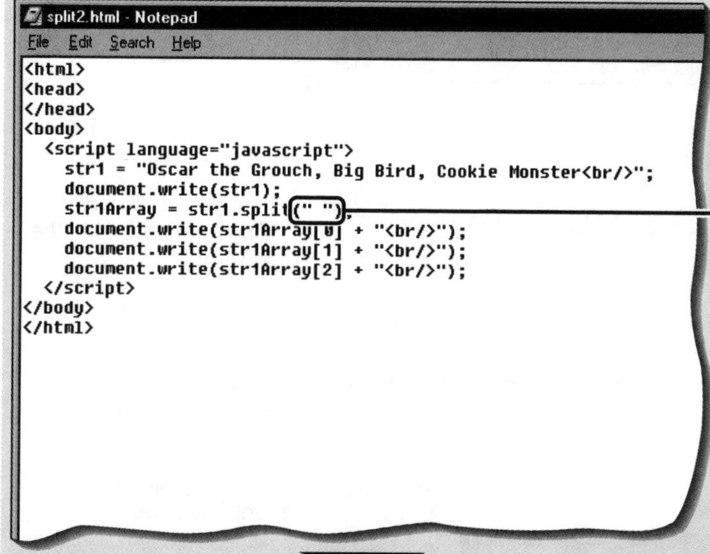

```
<html>
<head>
</head>
<body>
  <script language="javascript">
    str1 = "Oscar the Grouch, Big Bird, Cookie Monster<br/>";
    document.write(str1);
    str1Array = str1.split(" ");
    document.write(str1Array[0] + "<br/>");
    document.write(str1Array[1] + "<br/>");
    document.write(str1Array[2] + "<br/>");
  </script>
</body>
</html>
```

8 Open the file in Notepad again.

9 Change the separator, such as to a space.

10 Save the file using a different filename.

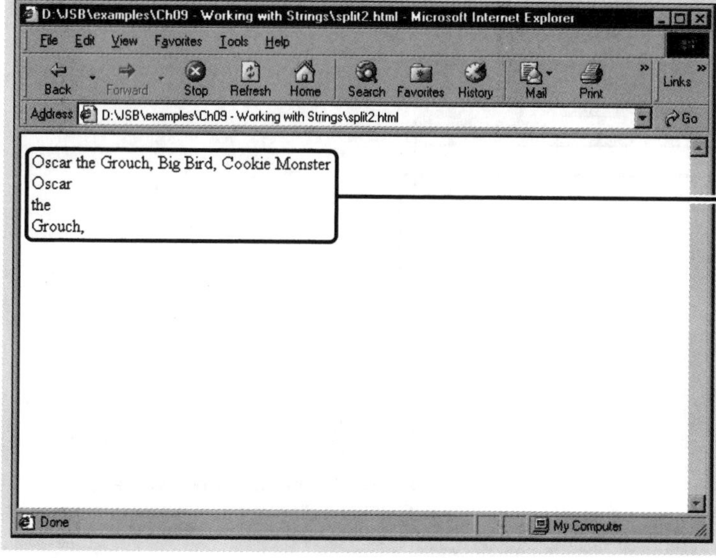

Oscar the Grouch, Big Bird, Cookie Monster
Oscar
the
Grouch,

11 Open the file in a browser.

- The array elements are now different.

Note: This string in this example has been split into more elements because there are more spaces in the string than commas. You can see only the first three because there are only three `document.write` *statements.*

USING THE DATE OBJECT

To use the date object, you must first create it by giving it a variable name and setting that equal to new followed by Date(). You can set the date format by defining a parameter to Date() using one of three definitions: The first is placed in quotes and includes "month day, year hours:minutes: seconds." The second includes just numbers for the year, month, and day. The third is like the second but also includes hours, minutes, and seconds.

USING THE DATE OBJECT

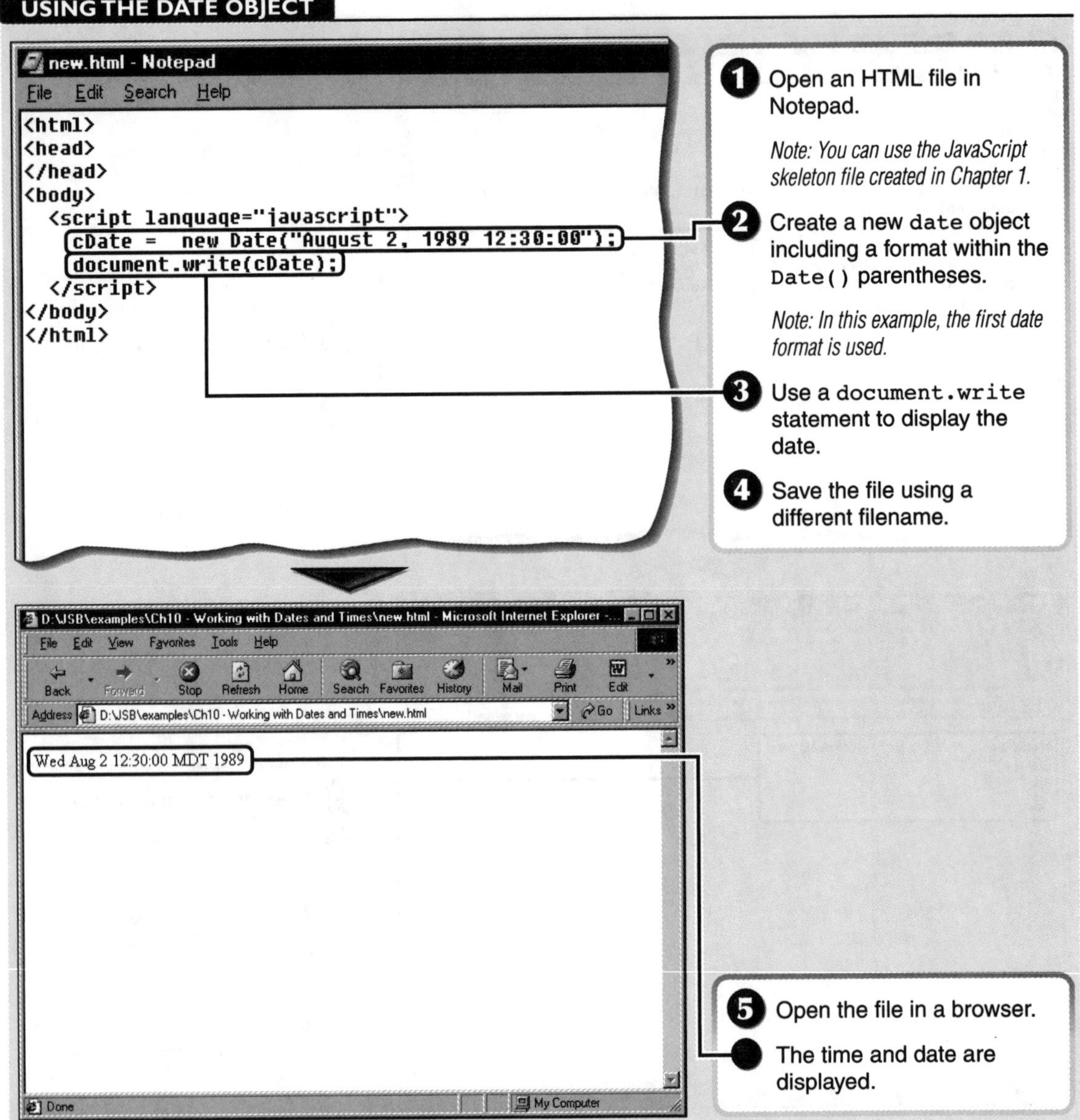

new.html - Notepad
File Edit Search Help
<html>
<head>
</head>
<body>
<script language="javascript">
cDate = new Date("August 2, 1989 12:30:00");
document.write(cDate);
</script>
</body>
</html>
D:\JSB\examples\Ch10 - Working with Dates and Times\new.html - Microsoft Internet Explorer
File Edit View Favorites Tools Help
Back Forward Stop Refresh Home Search Favorites History Mail Print Edit
Address D:\JSB\examples\Ch10 - Working with Dates and Times\new.html
Go Links
Wed Aug 2 12:30:00 MDT 1989
Done
My Computer

1. Open an HTML file in Notepad.

   Note: You can use the JavaScript skeleton file created in Chapter 1.

2. Create a new date object including a format within the Date() parentheses.

   Note: In this example, the first date format is used.

3. Use a document.write statement to display the date.

4. Save the file using a different filename.

5. Open the file in a browser.

- The time and date are displayed.

in an instant

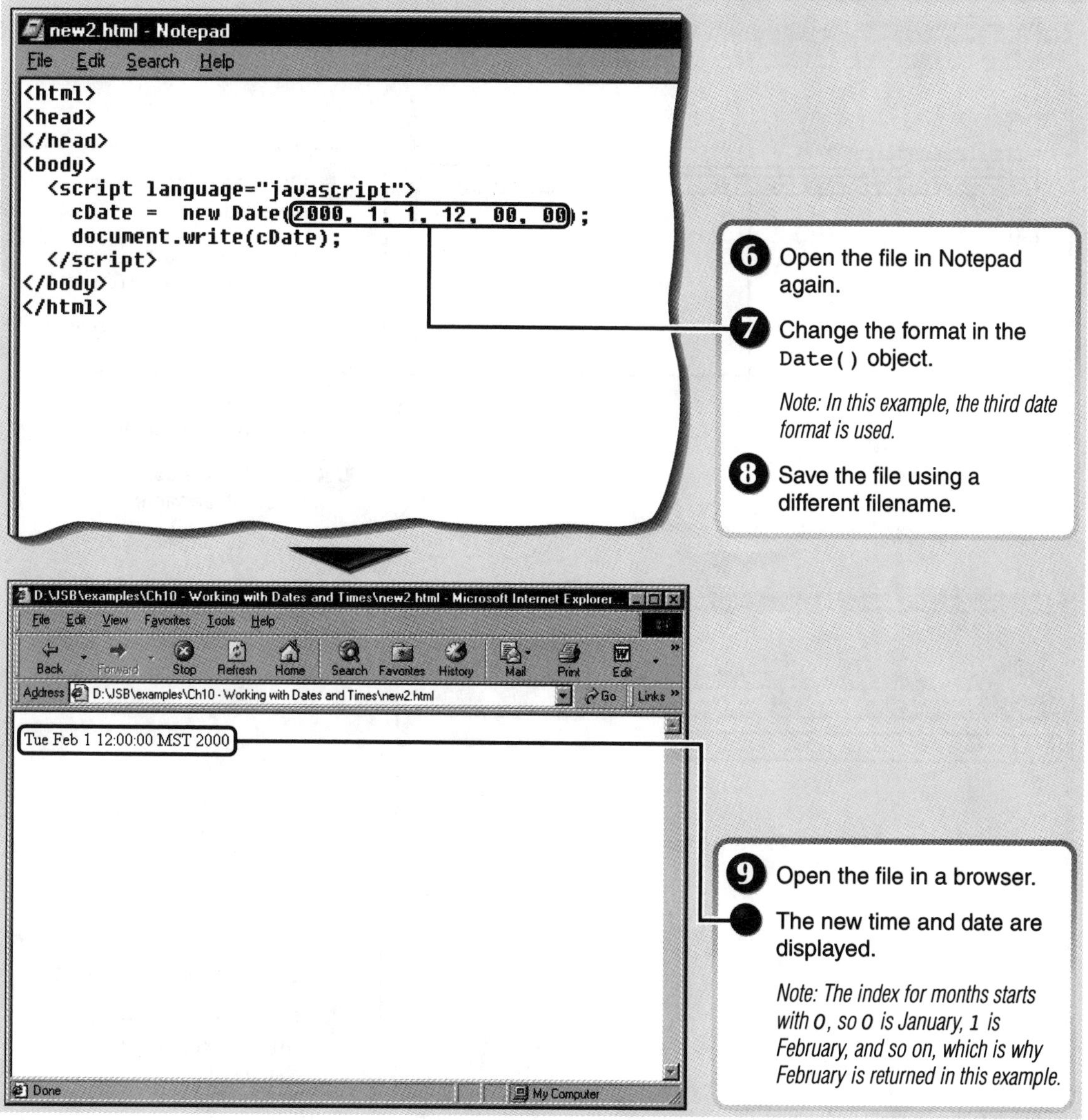
new2.html - Notepad
File Edit Search Help
<html>
<head>
</head>
<body>
<script language="javascript">
cDate = new Date(2000, 1, 1, 12, 00, 00);
document.write(cDate);
</script>
</body>
</html>
D:\JSB\examples\Ch10 - Working with Dates and Times\new2.html - Microsoft Internet Explorer
Tue Feb 1 12:00:00 MST 2000
Done
My Computer

6 Open the file in Notepad again.

7 Change the format in the `Date()` object.

Note: In this example, the third date format is used.

8 Save the file using a different filename.

9 Open the file in a browser.

- The new time and date are displayed.

Note: The index for months starts with `0`, so `0` is January, `1` is February, and so on, which is why February is returned in this example.

DISPLAY THE TIME AND DATE

You can use the toGMTString() method to return the current Greenwich mean time (GMT). You can use the toLocaleString() method to return the current date and time for the local time zone. The format for these dates and times lists the day, the date, the month, and then the year. After the year come the hours, minutes, and seconds, and finally the time zone.

DISPLAY GREENWICH MEAN TIME

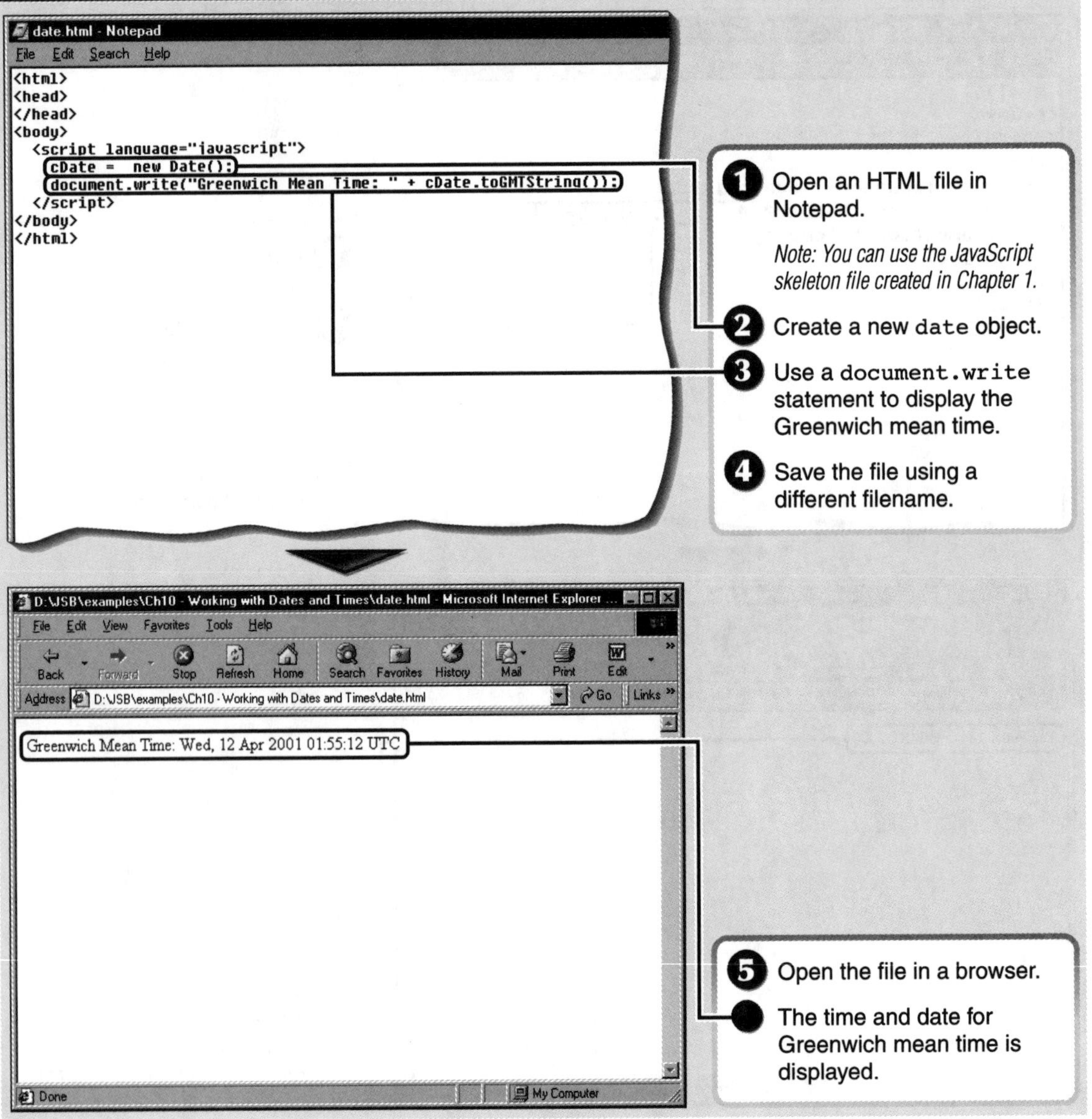

date.html - Notepad
File Edit Search Help
<html>
<head>
</head>
<body>
<script language="javascript">
cDate = new Date();
document.write("Greenwich Mean Time: " + cDate.toGMTString());
</script>
</body>
</html>
D:\JSB\examples\Ch10 - Working with Dates and Times\date.html - Microsoft Internet Explorer
Greenwich Mean Time: Wed, 12 Apr 2001 01:55:12 UTC
Done
My Computer

1. Open an HTML file in Notepad.

   Note: You can use the JavaScript skeleton file created in Chapter 1.

2. Create a new date object.
3. Use a document.write statement to display the Greenwich mean time.
4. Save the file using a different filename.
5. Open the file in a browser.

- The time and date for Greenwich mean time is displayed.

in an instant

DISPLAY THE LOCAL TIME AND DATE

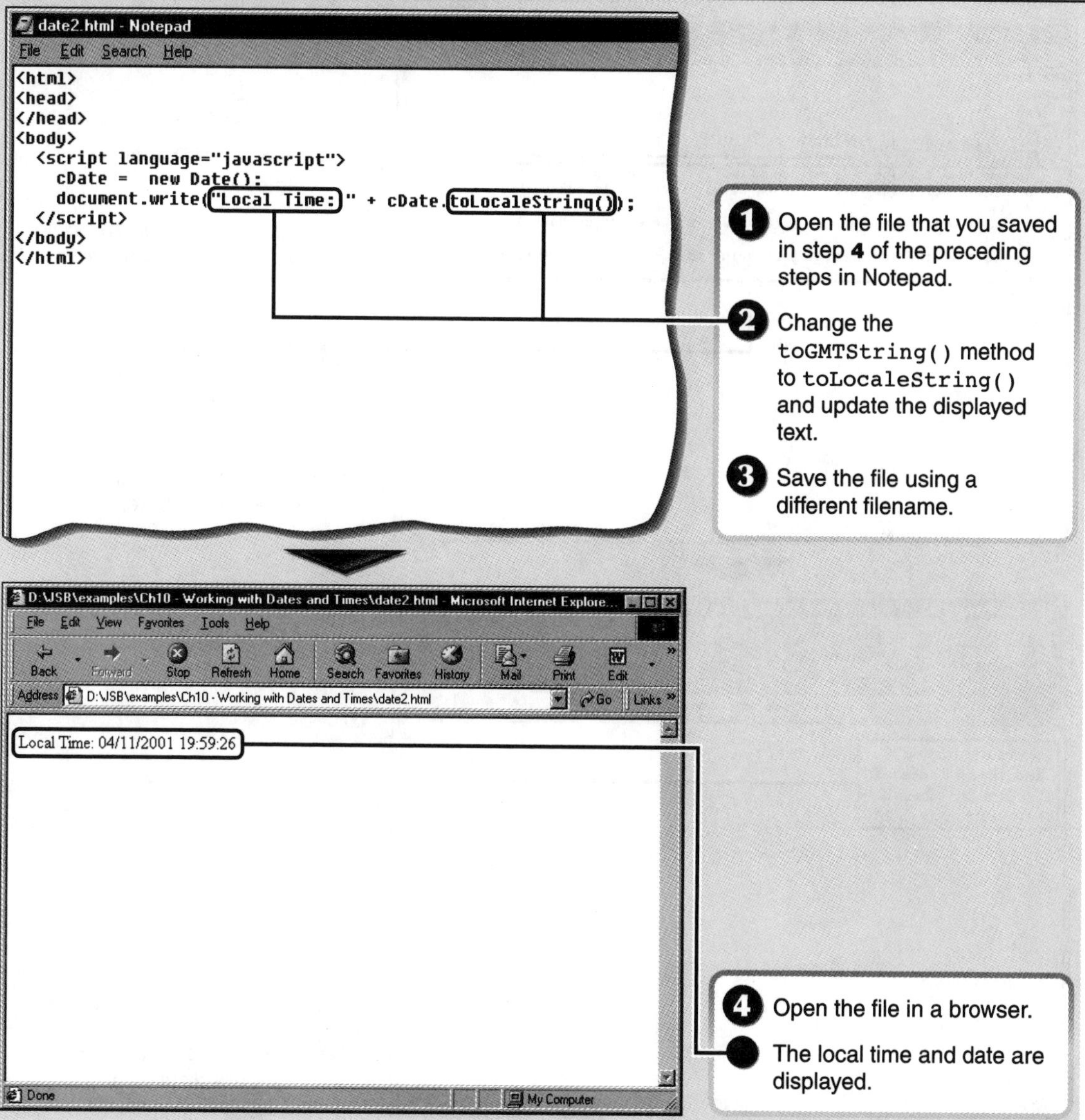
date2.html - Notepad
File Edit Search Help
<html>
<head>
</head>
<body>
<script language="javascript">
cDate = new Date();
document.write("Local Time: " + cDate.toLocaleString());
</script>
</body>
</html>
D:\JSB\examples\Ch10 - Working with Dates and Times\date2.html - Microsoft Internet Explore...
Address D:\JSB\examples\Ch10 - Working with Dates and Times\date2.html
Local Time: 04/11/2001 19:59:26
Done
My Computer

1. Open the file that you saved in step **4** of the preceding steps in Notepad.
2. Change the `toGMTString()` method to `toLocaleString()` and update the displayed text.
3. Save the file using a different filename.

4. Open the file in a browser.

- The local time and date are displayed.

GET DATE AND TIME VALUES

The `getDate()` method returns the current date. `getDay()` returns an integer representing the day of the week (with 1 for Monday). `getHours()` returns the hour in 24-hour military time format. The `getMinutes()` and `getSeconds()` methods return the number of minutes and seconds. The `getMonth()` method returns an integer representing the month of the year, starting with 0 for January.

GET DATE VALUES

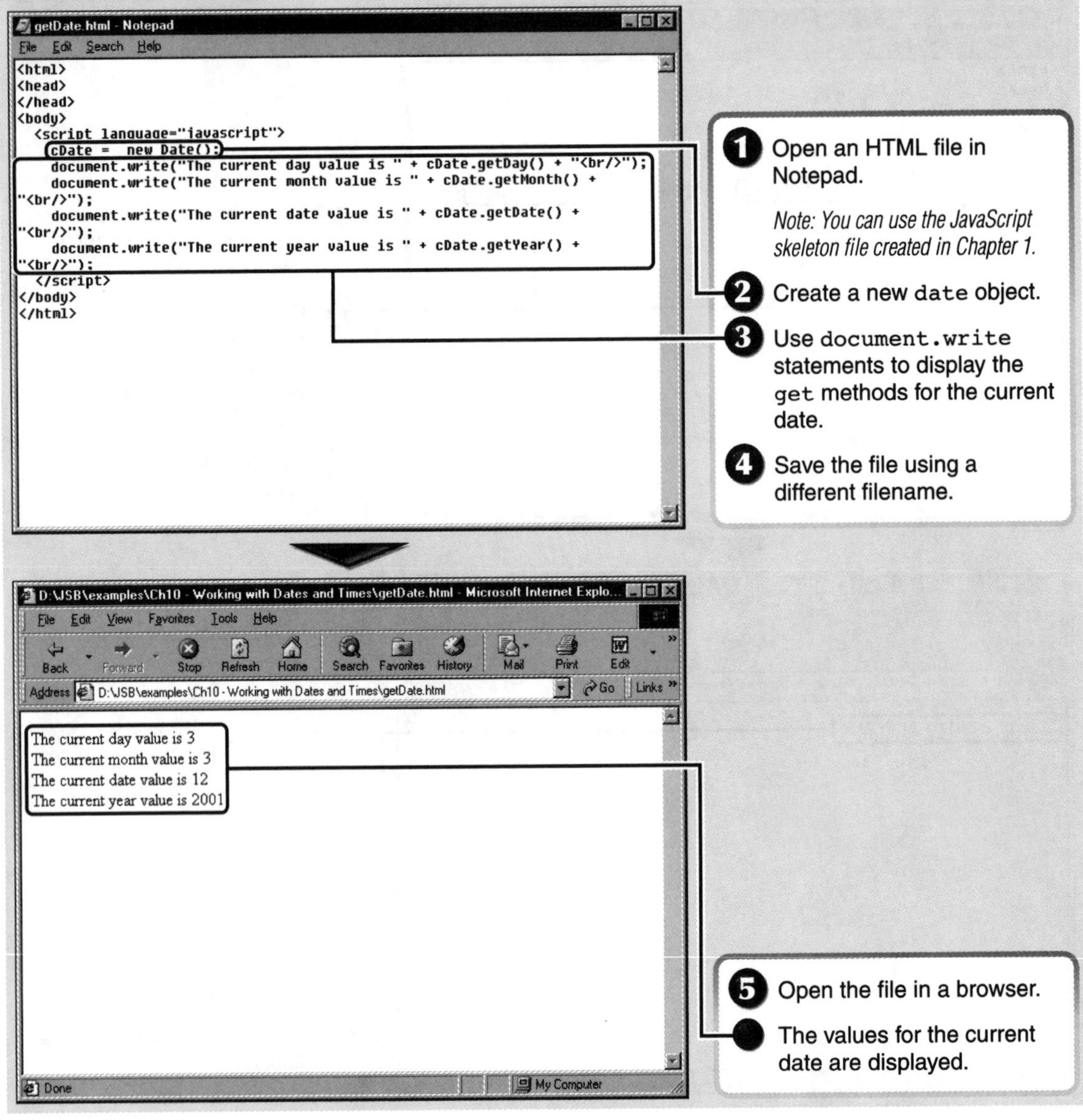
getDate.html - Notepad
File Edit Search Help
<html>
<head>
</head>
<body>
<script language="javascript">
cDate = new Date();
document.write("The current day value is " + cDate.getDay() + "<br/>");
document.write("The current month value is " + cDate.getMonth() + "<br/>");
document.write("The current date value is " + cDate.getDate() + "<br/>");
document.write("The current year value is " + cDate.getYear() + "<br/>");
</script>
</body>
</html>
1 Open an HTML file in Notepad.
Note: You can use the JavaScript skeleton file created in Chapter 1.
2 Create a new date object.
3 Use document.write statements to display the get methods for the current date.
4 Save the file using a different filename.
D:\JSB\examples\Ch10 - Working with Dates and Times\getDate.html - Microsoft Internet Explo...
File Edit View Favorites Tools Help
Back Forward Stop Refresh Home Search Favorites History Mail Print Edit
Address D:\JSB\examples\Ch10 - Working with Dates and Times\getDate.html
Go Links
The current day value is 3
The current month value is 3
The current date value is 12
The current year value is 2001
Done
My Computer
5 Open the file in a browser.
The values for the current date are displayed.

in an instant

GET TIME VALUES

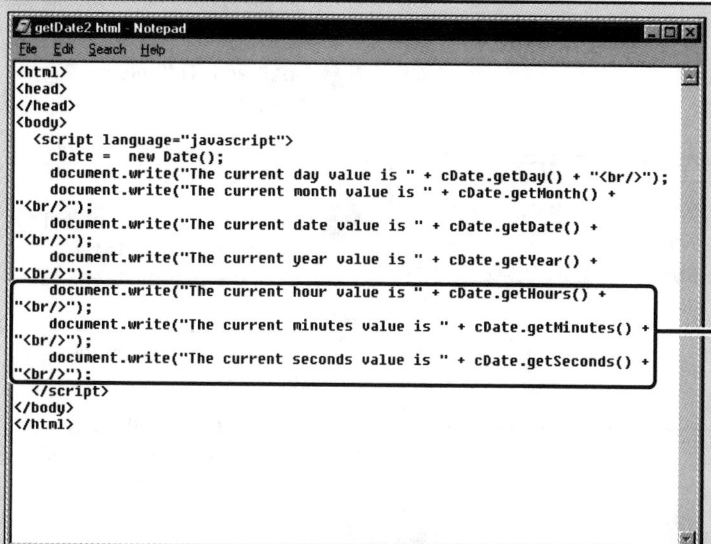
getDate2.html - Notepad
File Edit Search Help
<html>
<head>
</head>
<body>
<script language="javascript">
cDate = new Date();
document.write("The current day value is " + cDate.getDay() + "<br/>");
document.write("The current month value is " + cDate.getMonth() + "<br/>");
document.write("The current date value is " + cDate.getDate() + "<br/>");
document.write("The current year value is " + cDate.getYear() + "<br/>");
document.write("The current hour value is " + cDate.getHours() + "<br/>");
document.write("The current minutes value is " + cDate.getMinutes() + "<br/>");
document.write("The current seconds value is " + cDate.getSeconds() + "<br/>");
</script>
</body>
</html>

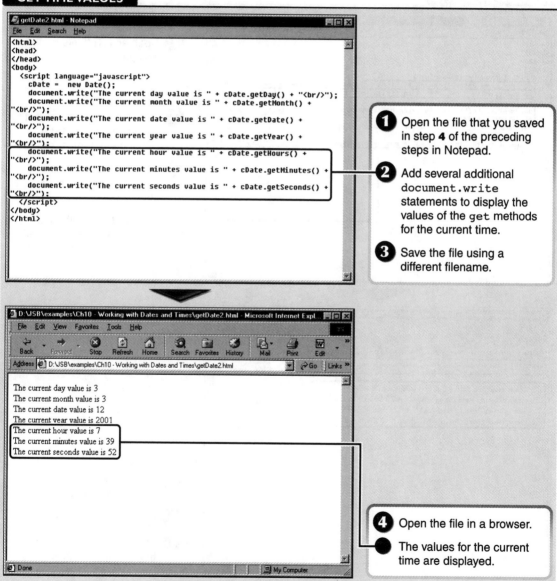

1. Open the file that you saved in step **4** of the preceding steps in Notepad.
2. Add several additional `document.write` statements to display the values of the `get` methods for the current time.
3. Save the file using a different filename.

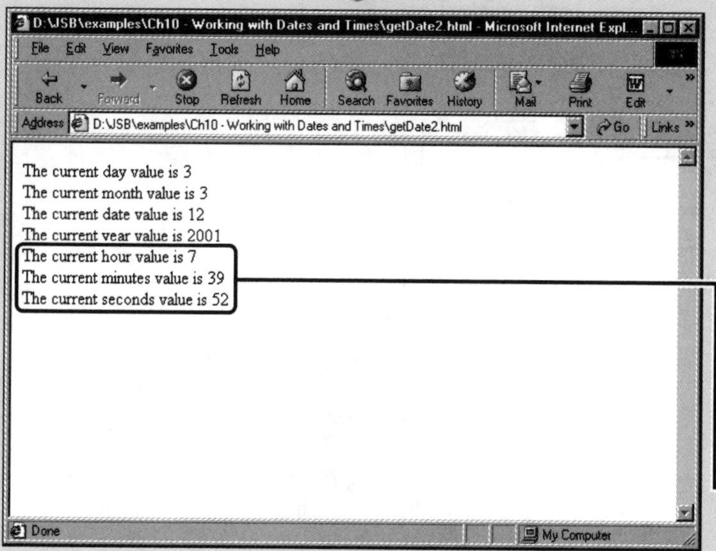
D:\JSB\examples\Ch10 - Working with Dates and Times\getDate2.html - Microsoft Internet Expl...
File Edit View Favorites Tools Help
Back Forward Stop Refresh Home Search Favorites History Mail Print Edit
Address D:\JSB\examples\Ch10 - Working with Dates and Times\getDate2.html Go Links
The current day value is 3
The current month value is 3
The current date value is 12
The current year value is 2001
The current hour value is 7
The current minutes value is 39
The current seconds value is 52
Done
My Computer

4. Open the file in a browser.

- The values for the current time are displayed.

SET DATE AND TIME VALUES

The `setDate()` method sets the date as a value between 1 and 31. `setMonth()` sets the month as a value between 0 and 11, with 0 for January. `setYear()` accepts a two-digit or four-digit year value. The `setHours()` method sets the hour of day in 24-hour military time format. The `setMinutes()` and `setSeconds()` methods set the number of minutes and seconds.

SET DATE VALUES

setDate.html - Notepad

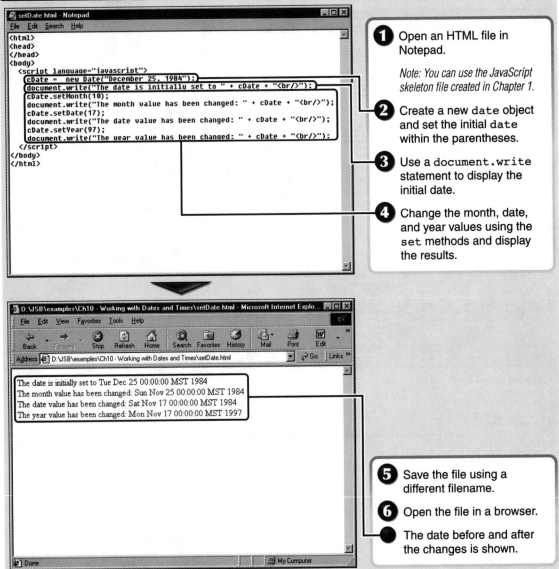

```
<html>
<head>
</head>
<body>
  <script language="javascript">
   cDate =  new Date("December 25, 1984");
   document.write("The date is initially set to " + cDate + "<br/>");
   cDate.setMonth(10);
   document.write("The month value has been changed: " + cDate + "<br/>");
   cDate.setDate(17);
   document.write("The date value has been changed: " + cDate + "<br/>");
   cDate.setYear(97);
   document.write("The year value has been changed: " + cDate + "<br/>");
  </script>
</body>
</html>
```

1. Open an HTML file in Notepad.

   Note: You can use the JavaScript skeleton file created in Chapter 1.

2. Create a new `date` object and set the initial `date` within the parentheses.

3. Use a `document.write` statement to display the initial date.

4. Change the month, date, and year values using the `set` methods and display the results.

D:\JSB\examples\Ch10 - Working with Dates and Times\setDate.html - Microsoft Internet Explorer

```
The date is initially set to Tue Dec 25 00:00:00 MST 1984
The month value has been changed: Sun Nov 25 00:00:00 MST 1984
The date value has been changed: Sat Nov 17 00:00:00 MST 1984
The year value has been changed: Mon Nov 17 00:00:00 MST 1997
```

5. Save the file using a different filename.

6. Open the file in a browser.

- The date before and after the changes is shown.

in an instant

SET TIME VALUES

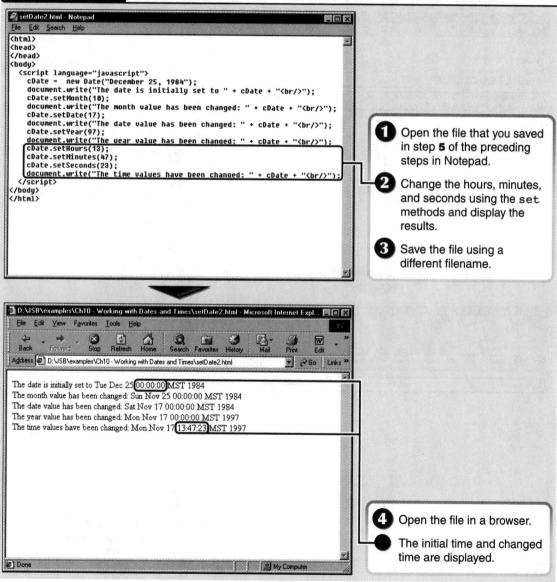

setDate2.html - Notepad

```
<html>
<head>
</head>
<body>
  <script language="javascript">
    cDate =  new Date("December 25, 1984");
    document.write("The date is initially set to " + cDate + "<br/>");
    cDate.setMonth(10);
    document.write("The month value has been changed: " + cDate + "<br/>");
    cDate.setDate(17);
    document.write("The date value has been changed: " + cDate + "<br/>");
    cDate.setYear(97);
    document.write("The year value has been changed: " + cDate + "<br/>");
    cDate.setHours(13);
    cDate.setMinutes(47);
    cDate.setSeconds(23);
    document.write("The time values have been changed: " + cDate + "<br/>");
  </script>
</body>
</html>
```

1. Open the file that you saved in step **5** of the preceding steps in Notepad.
2. Change the hours, minutes, and seconds using the `set` methods and display the results.
3. Save the file using a different filename.

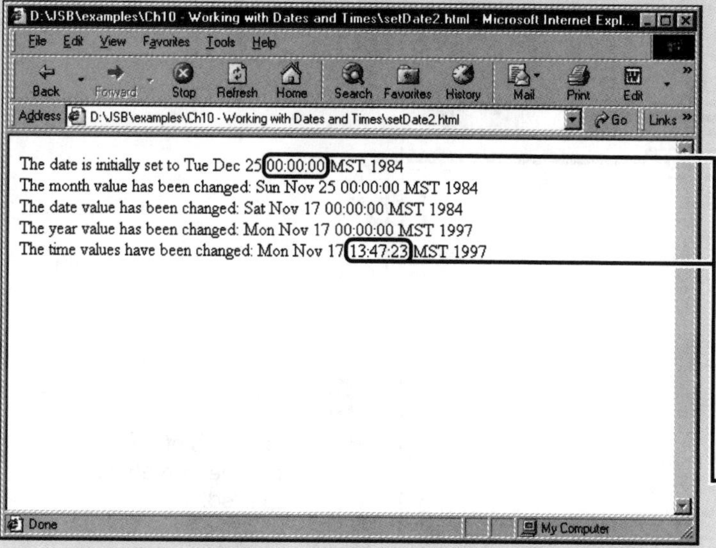
D:\JSB\examples\Ch10 - Working with Dates and Times\setDate2.html - Microsoft Internet Expl...
The date is initially set to Tue Dec 25 00:00:00 MST 1984
The month value has been changed: Sun Nov 25 00:00:00 MST 1984
The date value has been changed: Sat Nov 17 00:00:00 MST 1984
The year value has been changed: Mon Nov 17 00:00:00 MST 1997
The time values have been changed: Mon Nov 17 13:47:23 MST 1997

4. Open the file in a browser.

- The initial time and changed time are displayed.

WORK WITH TIME

The `getTime()` method returns an integer value equal to the milliseconds that have passed since January 1, 1970. You can also change a date into this standard format using the `Date.parse()` method. This method accepts a month, date, and year such as February 14, 1980 and returns the number of milliseconds since January 1, 1970.

WORK WITH TIME

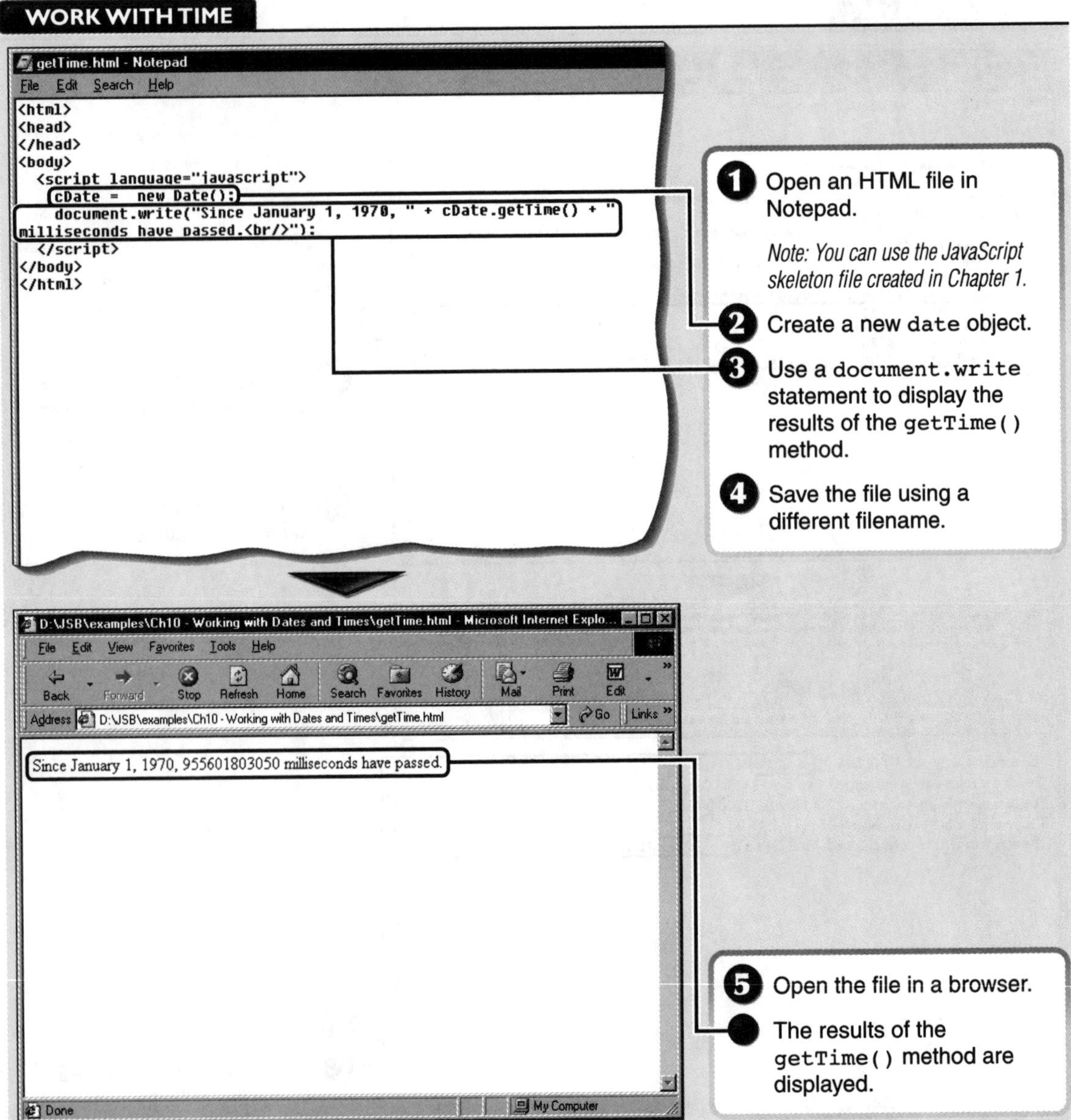

getTime.html - Notepad
File Edit Search Help
<html>
<head>
</head>
<body>
<script language="javascript">
cDate = new Date();
document.write("Since January 1, 1970, " + cDate.getTime() + " milliseconds have passed.
");
</script>
</body>
</html>
D:\JSB\examples\Ch10 - Working with Dates and Times\getTime.html - Microsoft Internet Explo...
File Edit View Favorites Tools Help
Back Forward Stop Refresh Home Search Favorites History Mail Print Edit
Address D:\JSB\examples\Ch10 - Working with Dates and Times\getTime.html
Go Links
Since January 1, 1970, 955601803050 milliseconds have passed.
Done
My Computer

1. Open an HTML file in Notepad.

   Note: You can use the JavaScript skeleton file created in Chapter 1.

2. Create a new `date` object.

3. Use a `document.write` statement to display the results of the `getTime()` method.

4. Save the file using a different filename.

5. Open the file in a browser.

- The results of the `getTime()` method are displayed.

in an instant

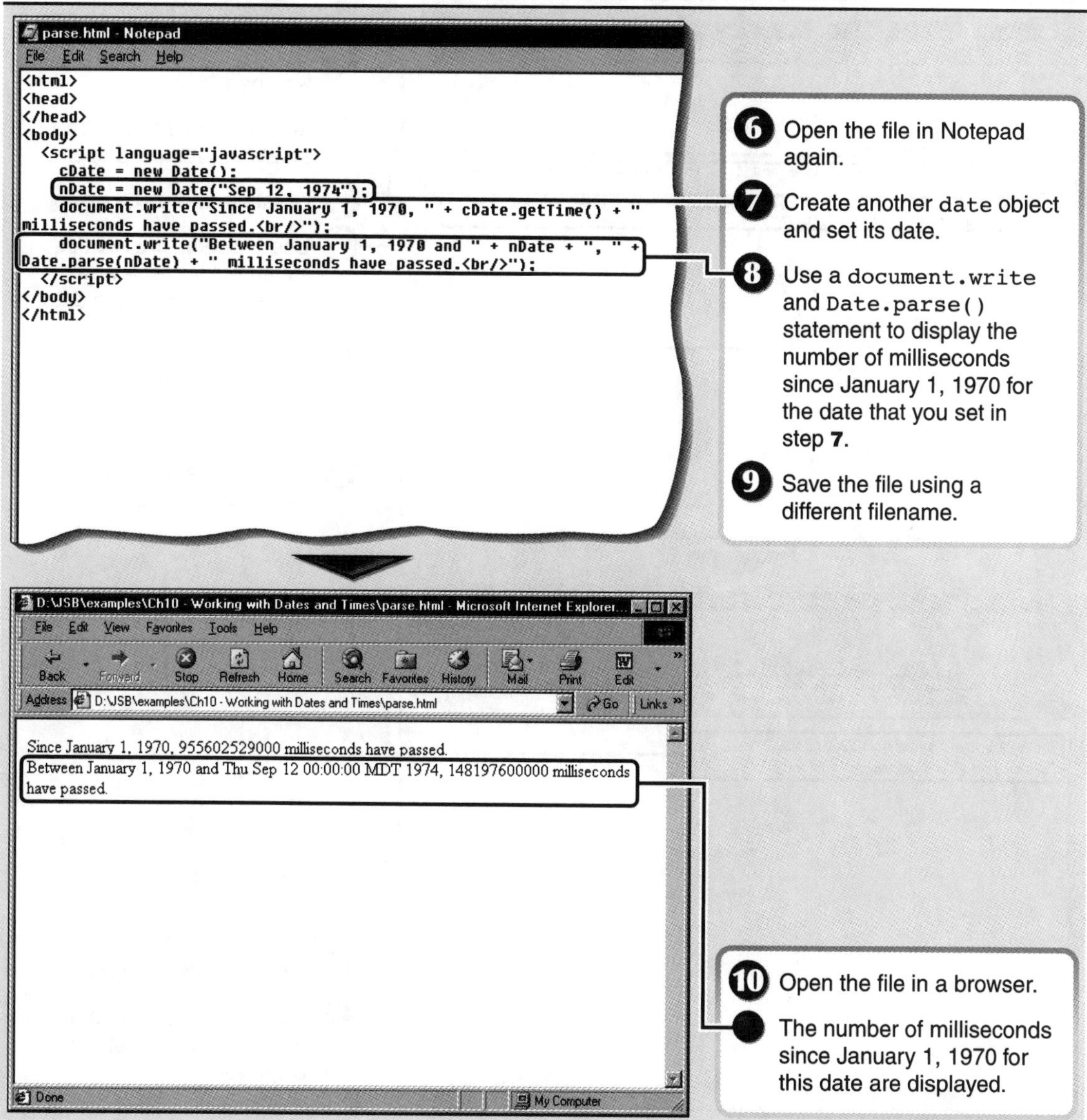
parse.html - Notepad
File Edit Search Help
<html>
<head>
</head>
<body>
<script language="javascript">
cDate = new Date();
nDate = new Date("Sep 12, 1974");
document.write("Since January 1, 1970, " + cDate.getTime() + " milliseconds have passed.
");
document.write("Between January 1, 1970 and " + nDate + ", " + Date.parse(nDate) + " milliseconds have passed.
");
</script>
</body>
</html>
D:\JSB\examples\Ch10 - Working with Dates and Times\parse.html - Microsoft Internet Explorer...
Since January 1, 1970, 955602529000 milliseconds have passed.
Between January 1, 1970 and Thu Sep 12 00:00:00 MDT 1974, 148197600000 milliseconds have passed.
Done
My Computer

6 Open the file in Notepad again.

7 Create another `date` object and set its date.

8 Use a `document.write` and `Date.parse()` statement to display the number of milliseconds since January 1, 1970 for the date that you set in step **7**.

9 Save the file using a different filename.

10 Open the file in a browser.

- The number of milliseconds since January 1, 1970 for this date are displayed.

WORK WITH TIME ZONES

The `getTimezoneOffset()` method returns the number of minutes between GMT and the local time zone. The returned value can be positive or negative, depending on whether the time zone is ahead of or behind GMT. For example, in the Pacific time zone, for the date object `myDate`, the statement `myDate.getTimezoneOffset()` returns a value of `480` (an offset of 8 hours from GMT).

WORK WITH TIME ZONES

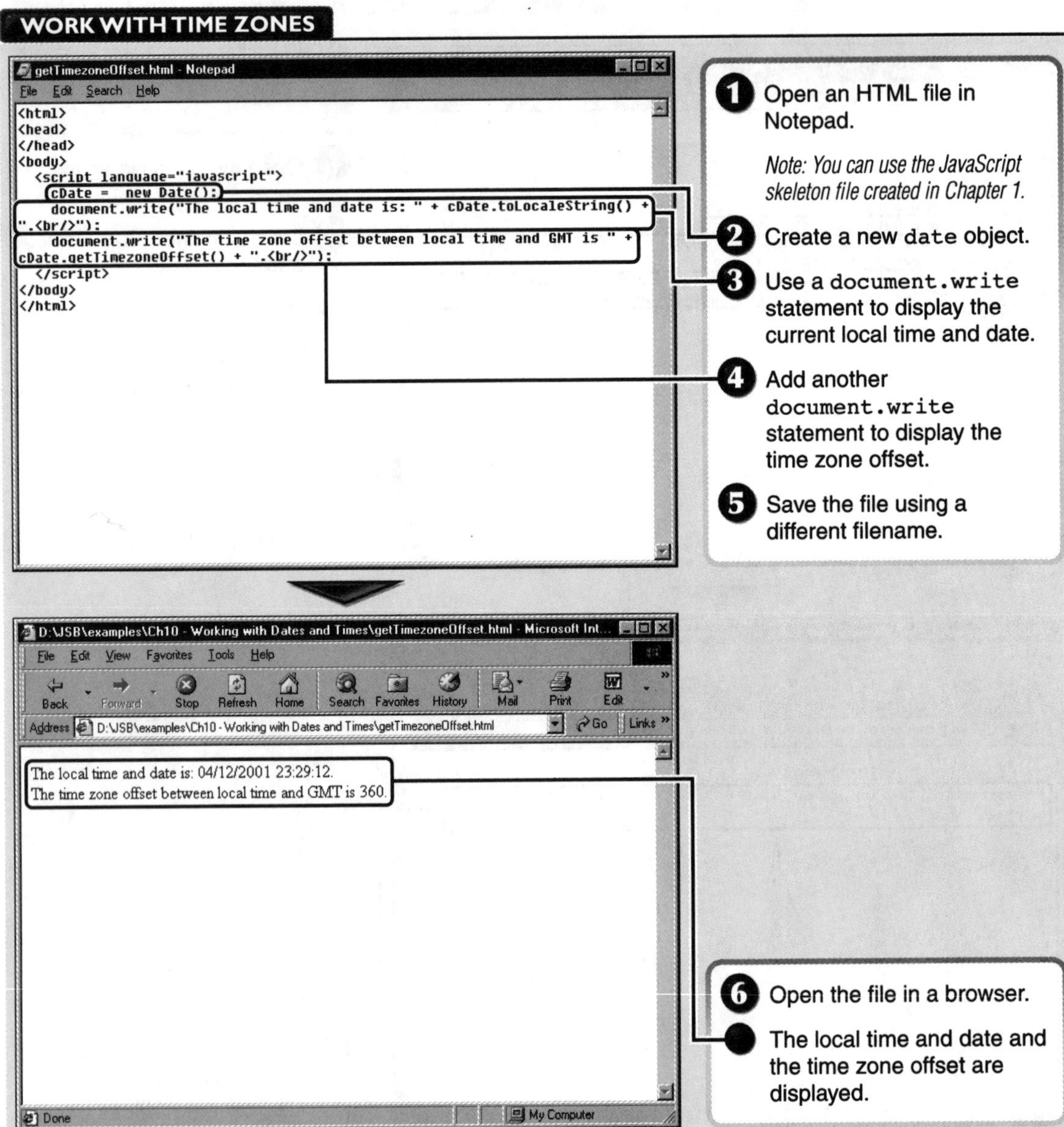

getTimezoneOffset.html - Notepad
File Edit Search Help
<html>
<head>
</head>
<body>
<script language="javascript">
cDate = new Date();
document.write("The local time and date is: " + cDate.toLocaleString() + ".
");
document.write("The time zone offset between local time and GMT is " + cDate.getTimezoneOffset() + ".
");
</script>
</body>
</html>
D:\JSB\examples\Ch10 - Working with Dates and Times\getTimezoneOffset.html - Microsoft Int...
File Edit View Favorites Tools Help
Back Forward Stop Refresh Home Search Favorites History Mail Print Edit
Address D:\JSB\examples\Ch10 - Working with Dates and Times\getTimezoneOffset.html
Go Links
The local time and date is: 04/12/2001 23:29:12.
The time zone offset between local time and GMT is 360.
Done
My Computer

1. Open an HTML file in Notepad.

   Note: You can use the JavaScript skeleton file created in Chapter 1.

2. Create a new `date` object.
3. Use a `document.write` statement to display the current local time and date.
4. Add another `document.write` statement to display the time zone offset.
5. Save the file using a different filename.
6. Open the file in a browser.

- The local time and date and the time zone offset are displayed.

in an instant

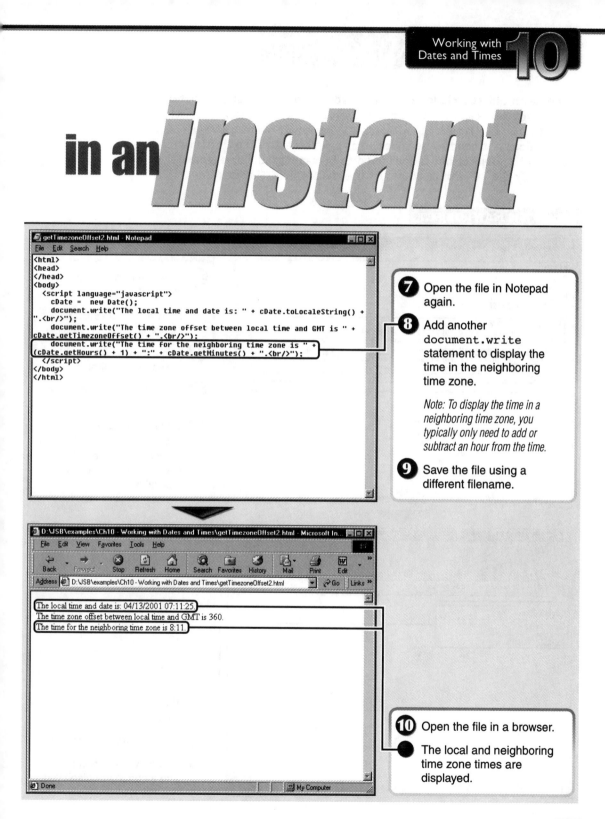

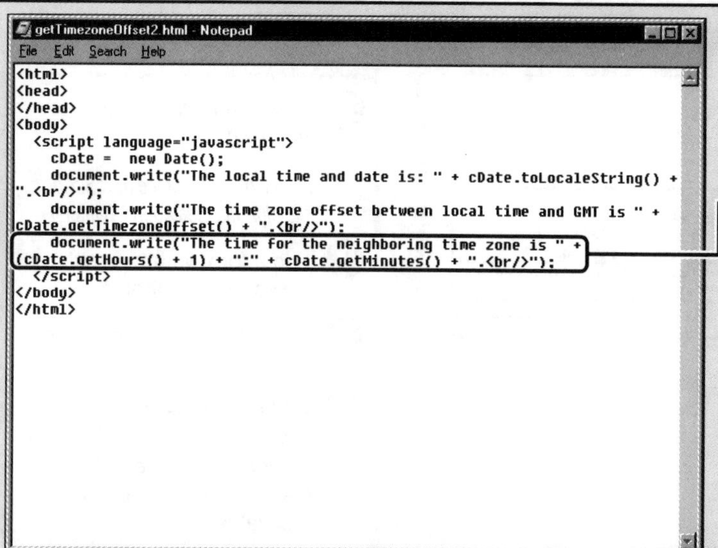
getTimezoneOffset2.html - Notepad
File Edit Search Help
<html>
<head>
</head>
<body>
<script language="javascript">
cDate = new Date();
document.write("The local time and date is: " + cDate.toLocaleString() + ".
");
document.write("The time zone offset between local time and GMT is " + cDate.getTimezoneOffset() + ".
");
document.write("The time for the neighboring time zone is " + (cDate.getHours() + 1) + ":" + cDate.getMinutes() + ".
");
</script>
</body>
</html>

7. Open the file in Notepad again.

8. Add another `document.write` statement to display the time in the neighboring time zone.

   Note: To display the time in a neighboring time zone, you typically only need to add or subtract an hour from the time.

9. Save the file using a different filename.

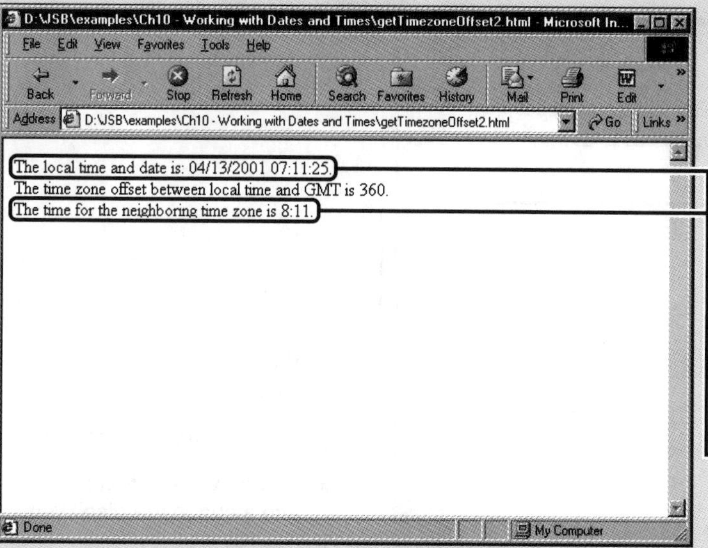
D:\JSB\examples\Ch10 - Working with Dates and Times\getTimezoneOffset2.html - Microsoft In...
File Edit View Favorites Tools Help
Back Forward Stop Refresh Home Search Favorites History Mail Print Edit
Address D:\JSB\examples\Ch10 - Working with Dates and Times\getTimezoneOffset2.html
Go Links
The local time and date is: 04/13/2001 07:11:25.
The time zone offset between local time and GMT is 360.
The time for the neighboring time zone is 8:11.
Done
My Computer

10. Open the file in a browser.

- The local and neighboring time zone times are displayed.

USING THE MATH OBJECT

The `Math` object includes a variety of advanced mathematical functions, including `abs(x)`, `ceil(x)`, `floor(x)`, `sin(x)`, `cos(x)`, `tan(x)`, `log(x)`, `min(x)`, `max(x)`, `pow(x,y)`, `random()`, and `sqrt(x)`. `Math` does not need to be specified as a subobject of the `document` or `window` objects, but it does need to be capitalized. For example, to specify the value of pi, you must use the `Math.PI` syntax.

USING THE MATH OBJECT

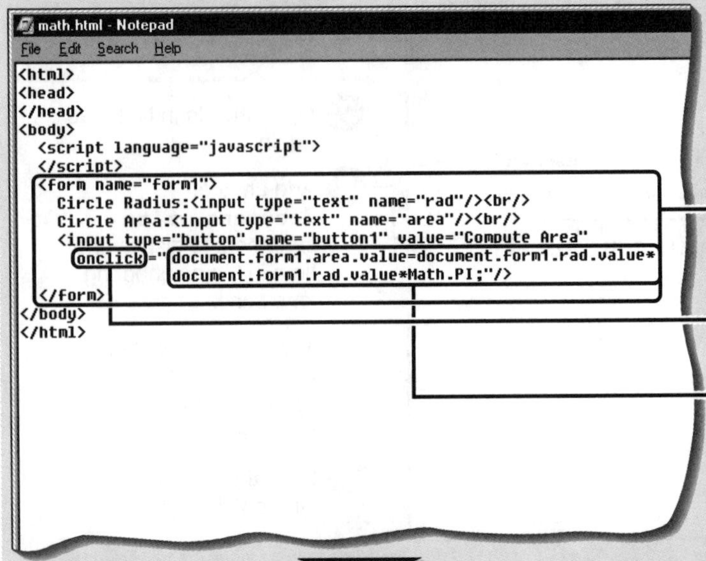

math.html - Notepad

```
<html>
<head>
</head>
<body>
  <script language="javascript">
  </script>
  <form name="form1">
    Circle Radius:<input type="text" name="rad"/><br/>
    Circle Area:<input type="text" name="area"/><br/>
    <input type="button" name="button1" value="Compute Area"
      onclick="document.form1.area.value=document.form1.rad.value*
      document.form1.rad.value*Math.PI;"/>
  </form>
</body>
</html>
```

1. Open an HTML file in Notepad.

   Note: You can use the JavaScript skeleton file created in Chapter 1.

2. Add a form with two text boxes and a button.
3. Add the `onclick` event to the button.
4. Add a statement for the `onclick` event that computes the area of a circle based on the text box value.

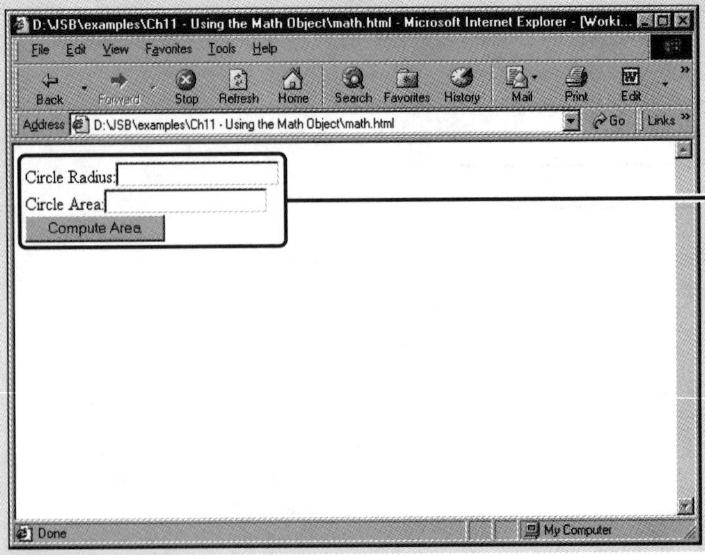

D:\JSB\examples\Ch11 - Using the Math Object\math.html - Microsoft Internet Explorer

Circle Radius:
Circle Area:
Compute Area

5. Save the file using a different filename.
6. Open the file in a browser.

- A form with two text boxes and a button are displayed.

in an instant

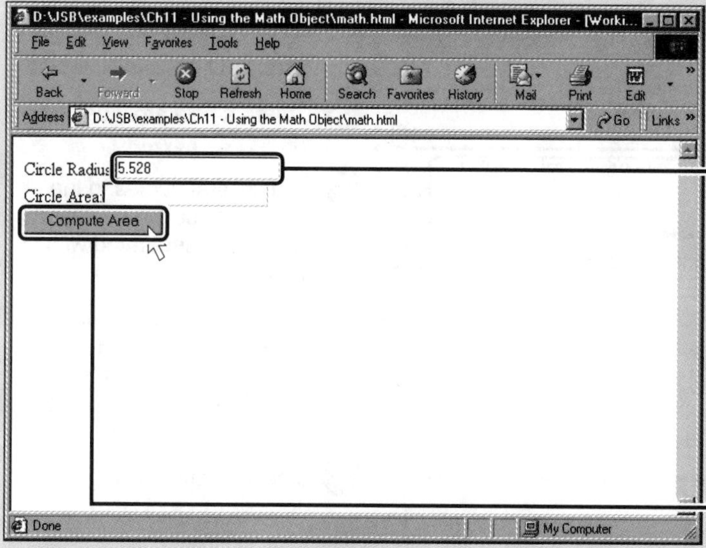

D:\JSB\examples\Ch11 - Using the Math Object\math.html - Microsoft Internet Explorer - [Worki...

Circle Radius: 5.528

Circle Area:

Compute Area

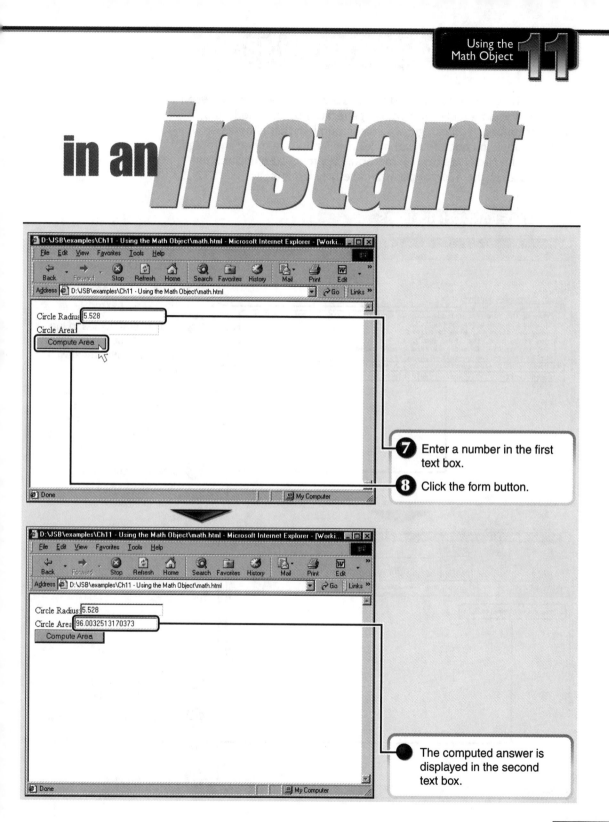

7 Enter a number in the first text box.

8 Click the form button.

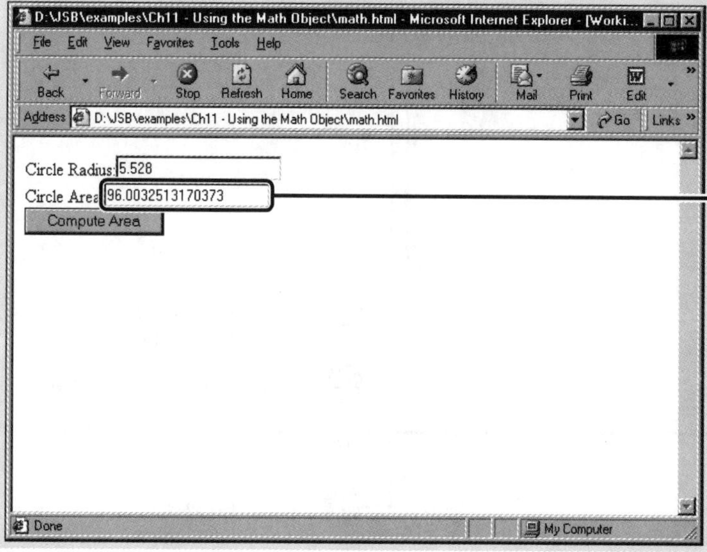

D:\JSB\examples\Ch11 - Using the Math Object\math.html - Microsoft Internet Explorer - [Worki...

Circle Radius: 5.528

Circle Area: 96.0032513170373

Compute Area

● The computed answer is displayed in the second text box.

GENERATE RANDOM NUMBERS

The `Math.random()` method returns a random number between 0 and 1. If you multiply the number generated by this method by another number, you can get a random number that is between 0 and the other number. You can make the random number an integer by using the `Math.floor()` method. This method truncates the numbers after the decimal point and returns an integer.

GENERATE RANDOM NUMBERS

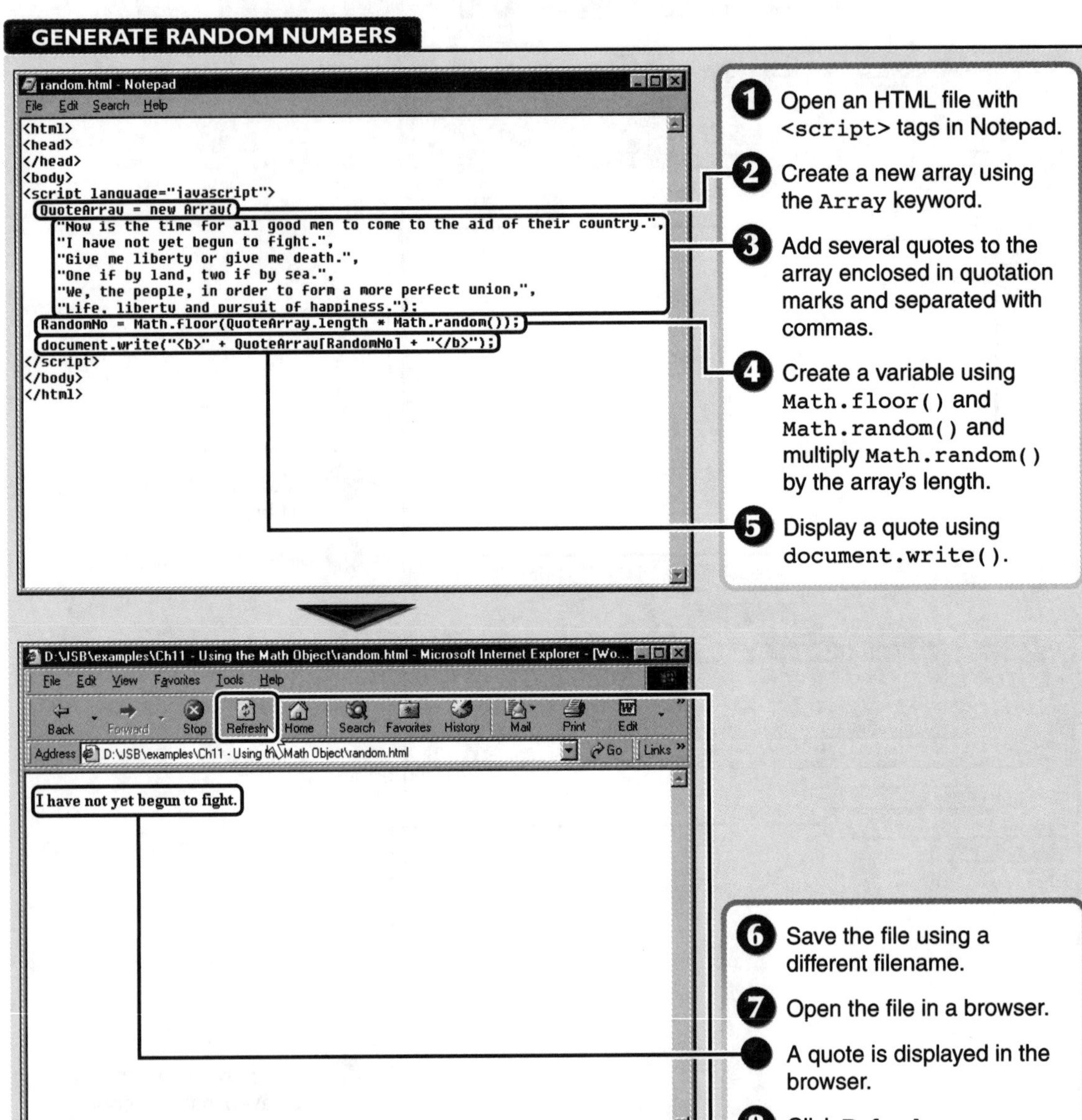

random.html - Notepad
File Edit Search Help
<html>
<head>
</head>
<body>
<script language="javascript">
QuoteArray = new Array(
"Now is the time for all good men to come to the aid of their country.",
"I have not yet begun to fight.",
"Give me liberty or give me death.",
"One if by land, two if by sea.",
"We, the people, in order to form a more perfect union,",
"Life, liberty and pursuit of happiness.");
RandomNo = Math.floor(QuoteArray.length * Math.random());
document.write("<b>" + QuoteArray[RandomNo] + "</b>");
</script>
</body>
</html>
D:\JSB\examples\Ch11 - Using the Math Object\random.html - Microsoft Internet Explorer
File Edit View Favorites Tools Help
Back Forward Stop Refresh Home Search Favorites History Mail Print Edit
Address D:\JSB\examples\Ch11 - Using the Math Object\random.html
Go Links
I have not yet begun to fight.
Done
My Computer

1. Open an HTML file with `<script>` tags in Notepad.
2. Create a new array using the `Array` keyword.
3. Add several quotes to the array enclosed in quotation marks and separated with commas.
4. Create a variable using `Math.floor()` and `Math.random()` and multiply `Math.random()` by the array's length.
5. Display a quote using `document.write()`.
6. Save the file using a different filename.
7. Open the file in a browser.

- A quote is displayed in the browser.

8. Click **Refresh**.

in an instant

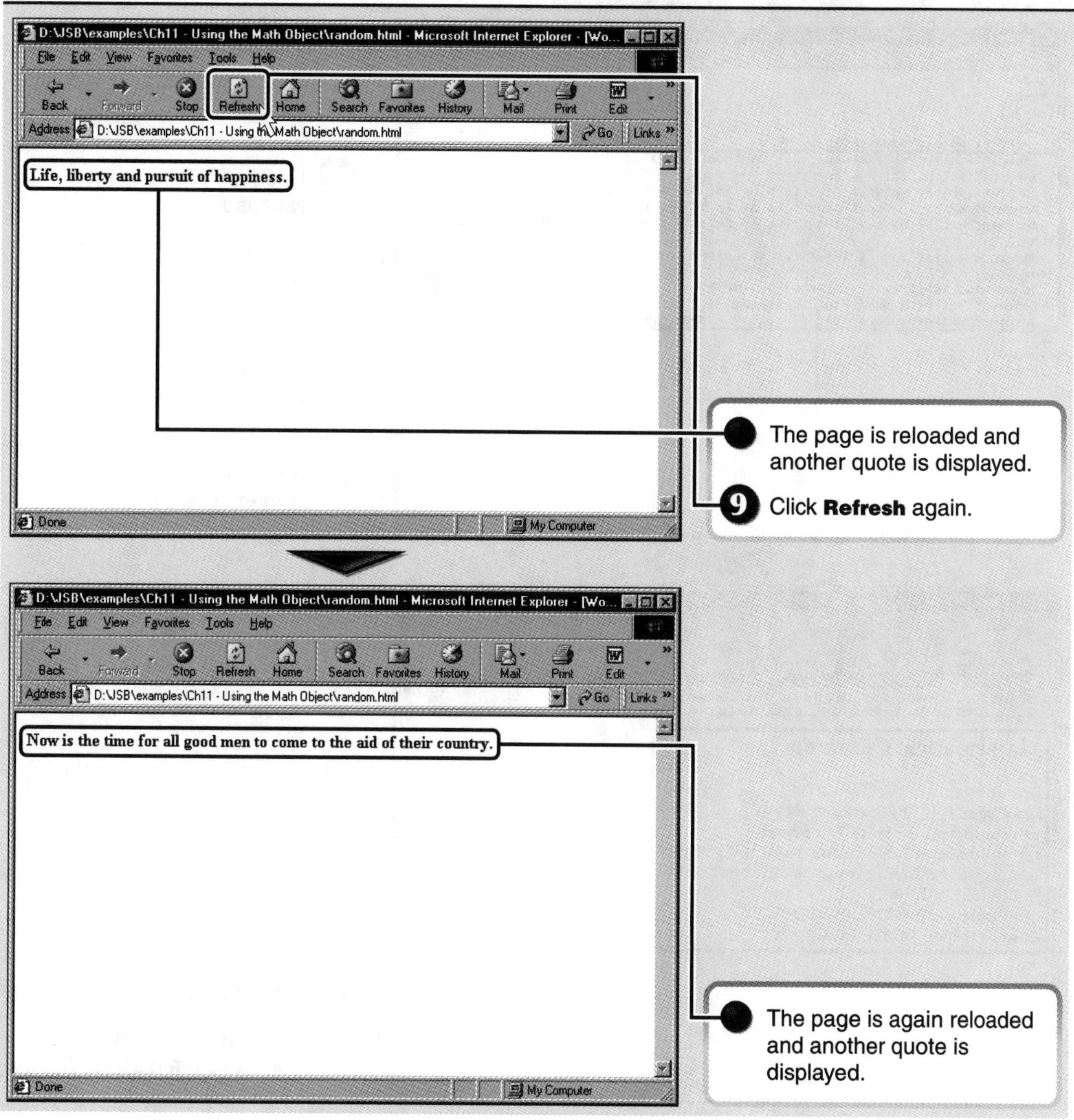
D:\JSB\examples\Ch11 - Using the Math Object\random.html - Microsoft Internet Explorer - [Wo...
File Edit View Favorites Tools Help
Back Forward Stop Refresh Home Search Favorites History Mail Print Edit
Address D:\JSB\examples\Ch11 - Using the Math Object\random.html
Go Links
Life, liberty and pursuit of happiness.
Done
My Computer
Now is the time for all good men to come to the aid of their country.

- The page is reloaded and another quote is displayed.

9 Click **Refresh** again.

- The page is again reloaded and another quote is displayed.

USING MATHEMATICAL CONSTANTS

The properties of the `Math` object are used to represent several standard mathematical constants. These properties can be inserted wherever the constant would normally appear in the equation. JavaScript computes the value of the constant to roughly 17 digits. Using these constants enables a high level of accuracy without having to type in all the digits.

DISPLAY THE MATH OBJECT CONSTANTS

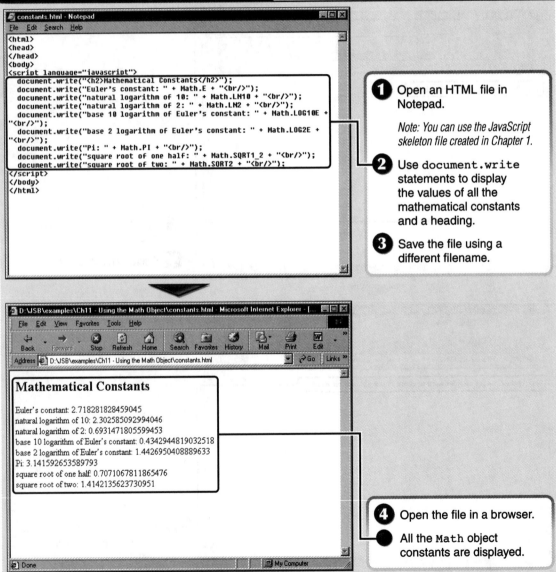

constants.html - Notepad

```
<html>
<head>
</head>
<body>
<script language="javascript">
  document.write("<h2>Mathematical Constants</h2>");
  document.write("Euler's constant: " + Math.E + "<br/>");
  document.write("natural logarithm of 10: " + Math.LN10 + "<br/>");
  document.write("natural logarithm of 2: " + Math.LN2 + "<br/>");
  document.write("base 10 logarithm of Euler's constant: " + Math.LOG10E +
"<br/>");
  document.write("base 2 logarithm of Euler's constant: " + Math.LOG2E +
"<br/>");
  document.write("Pi: " + Math.PI + "<br/>");
  document.write("square root of one half: " + Math.SQRT1_2 + "<br/>");
  document.write("square root of two: " + Math.SQRT2 + "<br/>");
</script>
</body>
</html>
```

1. Open an HTML file in Notepad.

   Note: You can use the JavaScript skeleton file created in Chapter 1.

2. Use `document.write` statements to display the values of all the mathematical constants and a heading.

3. Save the file using a different filename.

D:\JSB\examples\Ch11 - Using the Math Object\constants.html - Microsoft Internet Explorer

Mathematical Constants

Euler's constant: 2.718281828459045
natural logarithm of 10: 2.302585092994046
natural logarithm of 2: 0.6931471805599453
base 10 logarithm of Euler's constant: 0.4342944819032518
base 2 logarithm of Euler's constant: 1.4426950408889633
Pi: 3.141592653589793
square root of one half: 0.7071067811865476
square root of two: 1.4142135623730951

4. Open the file in a browser.

- All the `Math` object constants are displayed.

in an instant

USING THE MATH.PI CONSTANT

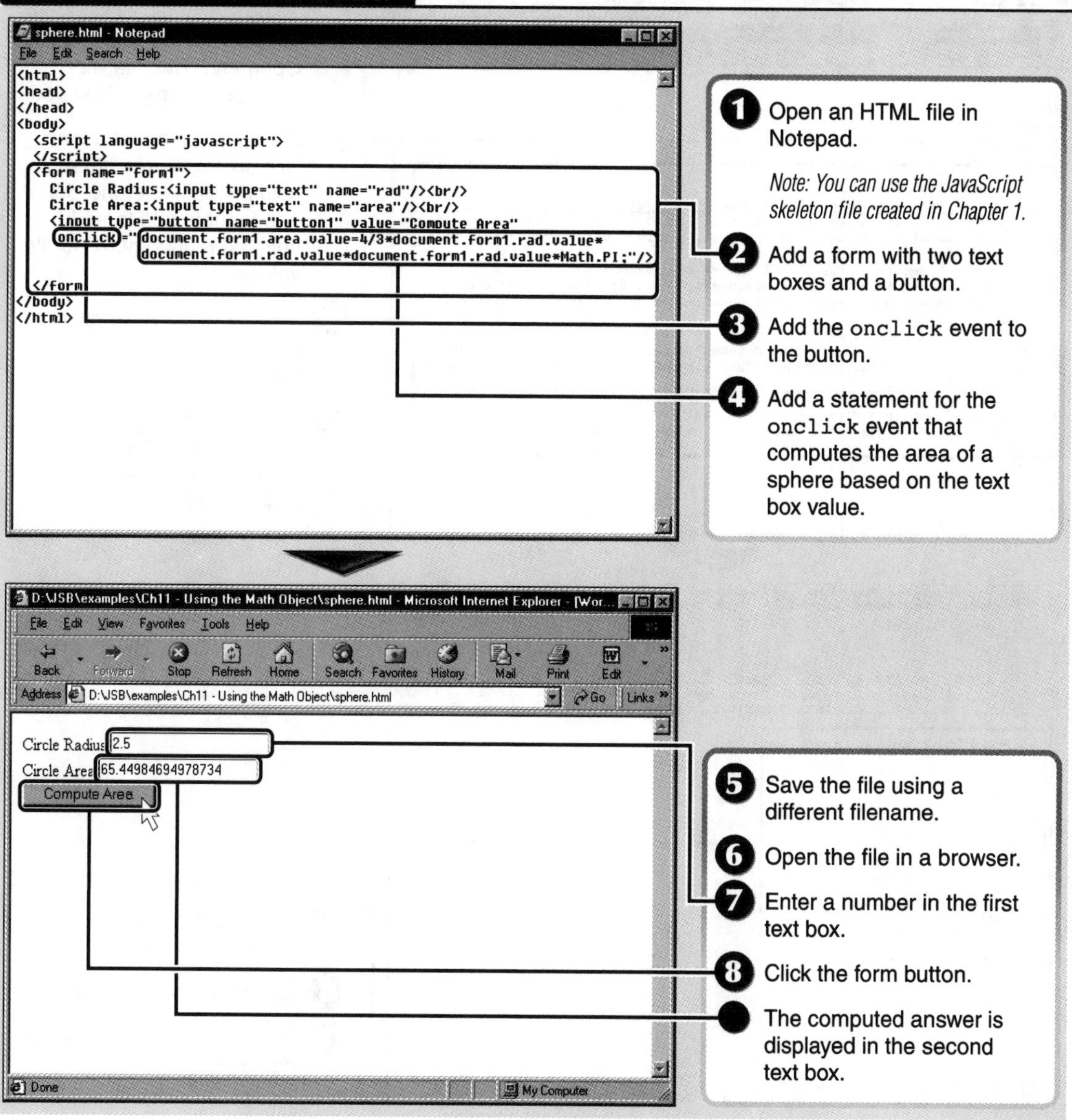
sphere.html - Notepad
<html>
<head>
</head>
<body>
<script language="javascript">
</script>
<form name="form1">
Circle Radius:<input type="text" name="rad"/>
Circle Area:<input type="text" name="area"/>
<input type="button" name="button1" value="Compute Area"
onclick="document.form1.area.value=4/3*document.form1.rad.value*
document.form1.rad.value*document.form1.rad.value*Math.PI;"/>
</form>
</body>
</html>
1 Open an HTML file in Notepad.
Note: You can use the JavaScript skeleton file created in Chapter 1.
2 Add a form with two text boxes and a button.
3 Add the onclick event to the button.
4 Add a statement for the onclick event that computes the area of a sphere based on the text box value.
D:\JSB\examples\Ch11 - Using the Math Object\sphere.html - Microsoft Internet Explorer
Circle Radius 2.5
Circle Area 65.44984694978734
Compute Area
5 Save the file using a different filename.
6 Open the file in a browser.
7 Enter a number in the first text box.
8 Click the form button.
The computed answer is displayed in the second text box.

USING TRIGONOMETRIC FUNCTIONS

JavaScript supports trigonometric functions as methods of the `Math` object, including `cos()`, `sin()`, `tan()`, `acos()`, `asin()`, and `atan()`. These functions take a single parameter value and return an angular value in radians. JavaScript also includes a trigonometric method that can convert standard *x* and *y* coordinate values to an angular measurement — `atan2()`, which takes two coordinate values as parameters.

USING TRIGONOMETRIC FUNCTIONS

trig.html - Notepad

```
<html>
<head>
</head>
<body>
  <script language="javascript">
  </script>
  <h2>For a right angle triangle</h2>
  <form name="form1">
    Opposite Side:<input type="text" name="opp" value="0"
onchange="document.form1.sin.value=document.form1.opp.value/document.form1.h
yp.value;document.form1.tan.value=document.form1.opp.value/document.form1.ad
j.value;"/><br/>
    Adjacent Side:<input type="text" name="adj" value="0"
onchange="document.form1.cos.value=document.form1.adj.value/document.form1.h
yp.value;document.form1.tan.value=document.form1.opp.value/document.form1.ad
j.value;"/><br/>
    Hypotenuse:<input type="text" name="hyp" value="0"
onchange="document.form1.sin.value=document.form1.opp.value/document.form1.h
yp.value;document.form1.cos.value=document.form1.adj.value/document.form1.hy
p.value;"/><br/><br/>
    Sine:<input type="text" name="sin" value="0"/><br/>
    Cosine:<input type="text" name="cos" value="0"/><br/>
    Tangent:<input type="text" name="tan" value="0"/><br/>
  </form>
</body>
</html>
```

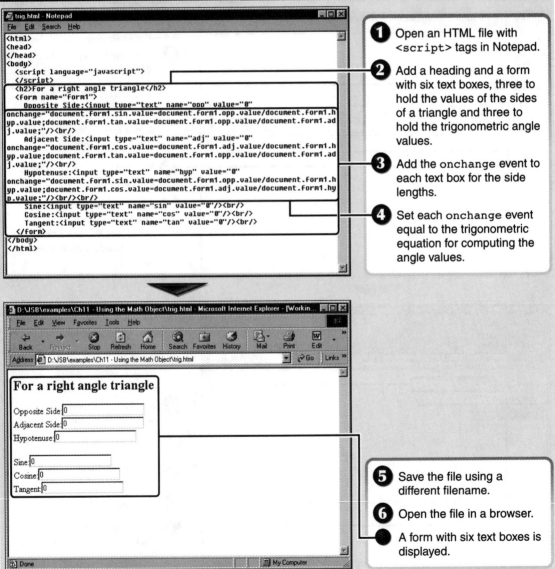

1. Open an HTML file with `<script>` tags in Notepad.
2. Add a heading and a form with six text boxes, three to hold the values of the sides of a triangle and three to hold the trigonometric angle values.
3. Add the `onchange` event to each text box for the side lengths.
4. Set each `onchange` event equal to the trigonometric equation for computing the angle values.

D:\JSB\examples\Ch11 - Using the Math Object\trig.html - Microsoft Internet Explorer - [Workin...

File Edit View Favorites Tools Help

Back Forward Stop Refresh Home Search Favorites History Mail Print Edit

Address D:\JSB\examples\Ch11 - Using the Math Object\trig.html Go Links

For a right angle triangle

Opposite Side: 0
Adjacent Side: 0
Hypotenuse: 0

Sine: 0
Cosine: 0
Tangent: 0

Done | My Computer

5. Save the file using a different filename.
6. Open the file in a browser.

- A form with six text boxes is displayed.

in an instant

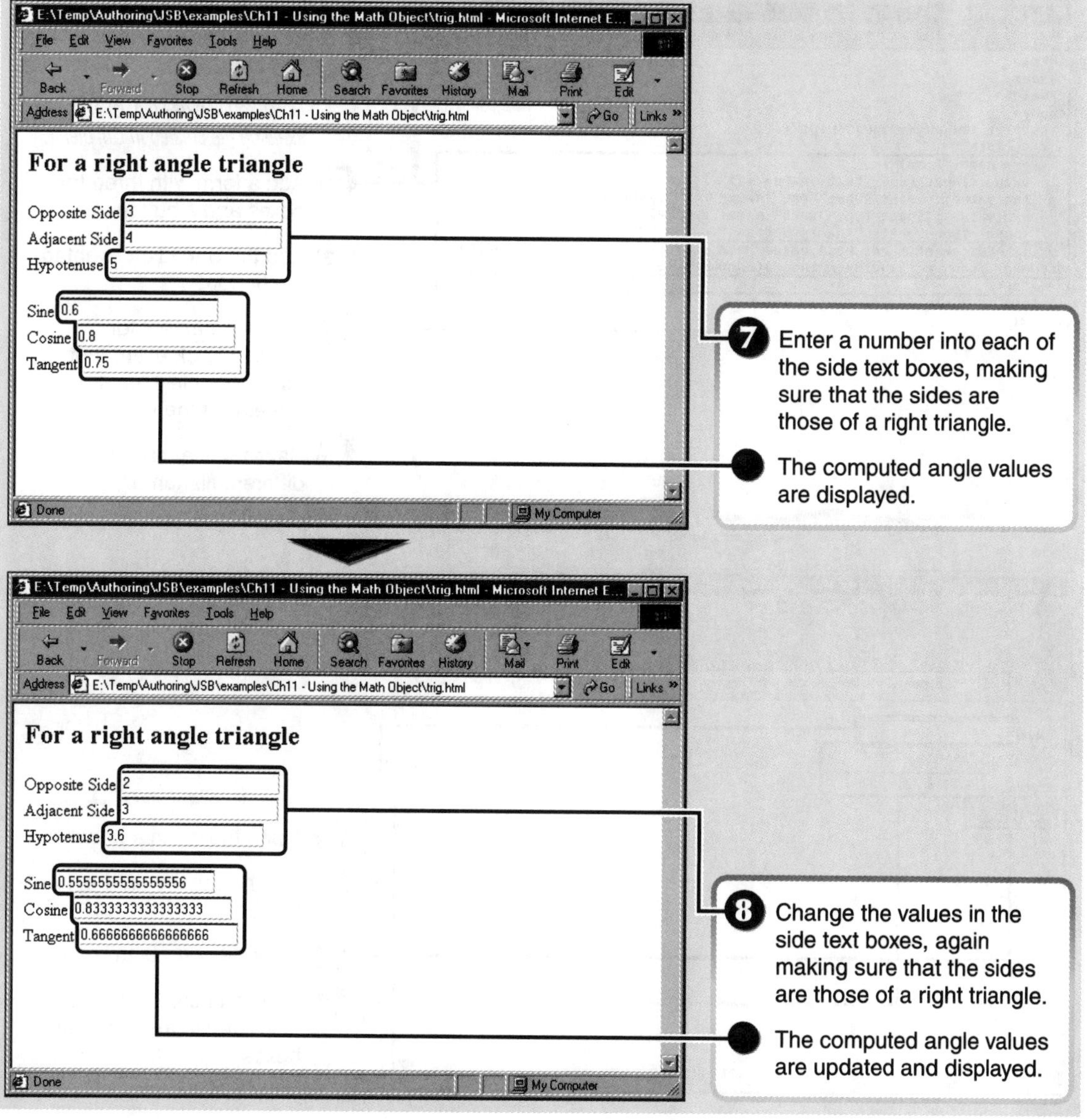
E:\Temp\Authoring\JSB\examples\Ch11 - Using the Math Object\trig.html - Microsoft Internet E...
For a right angle triangle
Opposite Side 3
Adjacent Side 4
Hypotenuse 5
Sine 0.6
Cosine 0.8
Tangent 0.75
For a right angle triangle
Opposite Side 2
Adjacent Side 3
Hypotenuse 3.6
Sine 0.5555555555555556
Cosine 0.8333333333333333
Tangent 0.6666666666666666

7 Enter a number into each of the side text boxes, making sure that the sides are those of a right triangle.

- The computed angle values are displayed.

8 Change the values in the side text boxes, again making sure that the sides are those of a right triangle.

- The computed angle values are updated and displayed.

USING LOGARITHMIC AND EXPONENTIAL METHODS

JavaScript includes two methods for working with natural logarithms and exponentials based on Euler's constant. The `log()` method takes a number as a parameter and returns the natural logarithm (base e) of the number. The `exp()` method takes a number as a parameter and returns the value of Euler's constant raised to the power of the number.

USING LOGARITHMIC AND EXPONENTIAL METHODS

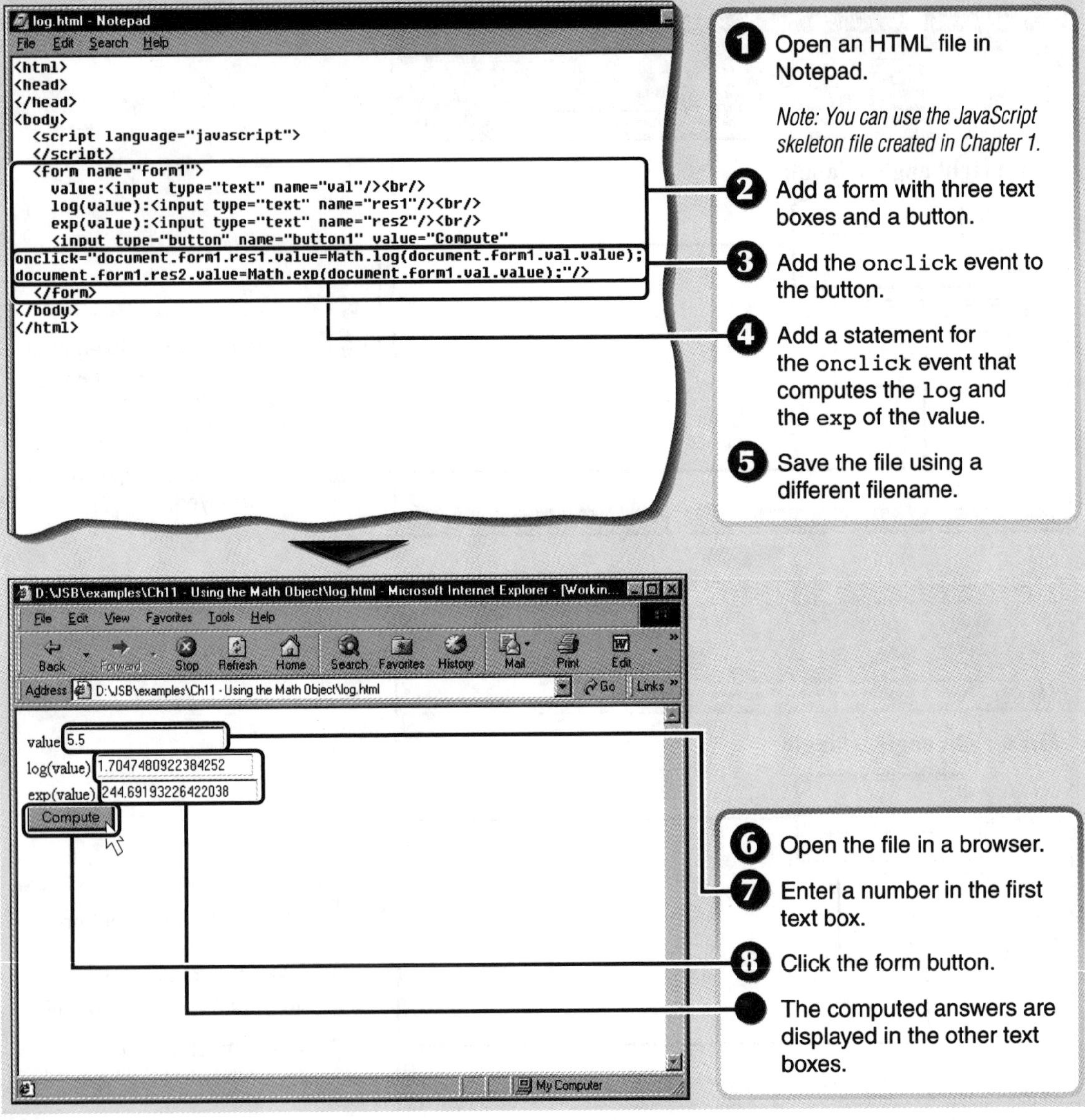
log.html - Notepad
File Edit Search Help
<html>
<head>
</head>
<body>
<script language="javascript">
</script>
<form name="form1">
value:<input type="text" name="val"/>
log(value):<input type="text" name="res1"/>
exp(value):<input type="text" name="res2"/>
<input type="button" name="button1" value="Compute"
onclick="document.form1.res1.value=Math.log(document.form1.val.value);
document.form1.res2.value=Math.exp(document.form1.val.value);"/>
</form>
</body>
</html>
1 Open an HTML file in Notepad.
Note: You can use the JavaScript skeleton file created in Chapter 1.
2 Add a form with three text boxes and a button.
3 Add the onclick event to the button.
4 Add a statement for the onclick event that computes the log and the exp of the value.
5 Save the file using a different filename.
D:\JSB\examples\Ch11 - Using the Math Object\log.html - Microsoft Internet Explorer - [Workin...
File Edit View Favorites Tools Help
Back Forward Stop Refresh Home Search Favorites History Mail Print Edit
Address D:\JSB\examples\Ch11 - Using the Math Object\log.html
Go Links
value 5.5
log(value) 1.7047480922384252
exp(value) 244.69193226422038
Compute
My Computer
6 Open the file in a browser.
7 Enter a number in the first text box.
8 Click the form button.
The computed answers are displayed in the other text boxes.

USING THE SQUARE ROOT METHOD

Using the
Math Object
11

You can use the sqrt() method to compute the square root of a number. sqrt() receives a number as a parameter and returns its square root. An example of using sqrt() is in computing the Pythagorean theorem (the square of two sides of a right triangle equals the square of the hypotenuse).

USING THE SQUARE ROOT METHOD

```
<html>
<head>
</head>
<body>
  <script language="javascript">
  </script>
  <form name="form1">
    value:<input type="text" name="val"/><br/>
    sqrt(value):<input type="text" name="sqrt"/><br/>
    <input type="button" name="button1" value="Compute"
onclick="document.form1.sqrt.value=Math.sqrt(document.form1.val.value);"/>
  </form>
</body>
</html>
```

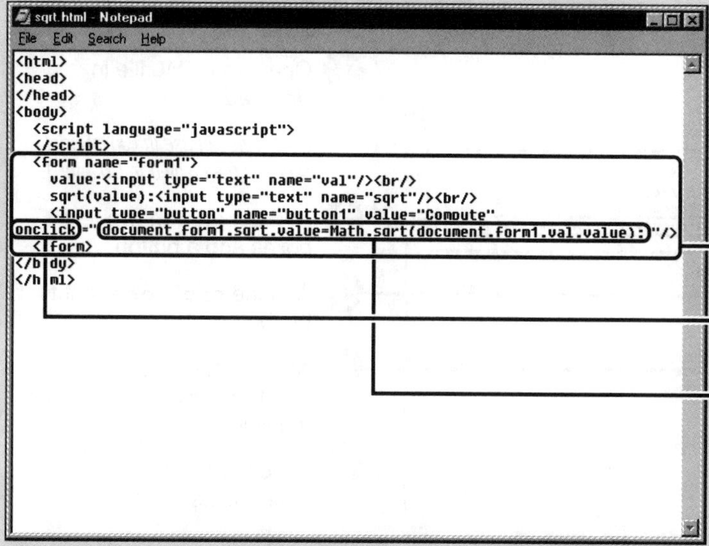

1. Open an HTML file in Notepad.

   Note: You can use the JavaScript skeleton file created in Chapter 1.

2. Add a form with two text boxes and a button.
3. Add the onclick event to the button.
4. Add a statement for the onclick event that computes the square root of the value in the first text box.

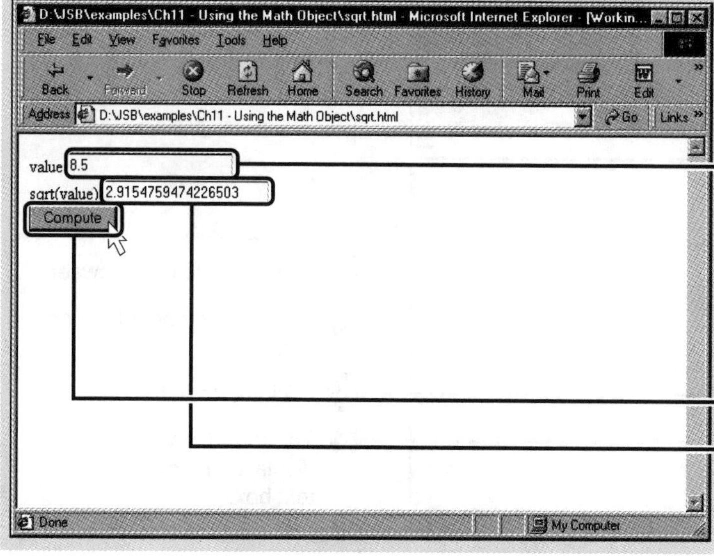

value 8.5

sqrt(value) 2.9154759474226503

Compute

5. Save the file using a different filename.
6. Open the file in a browser.
7. Enter a number in the first text box.
8. Click the form button.

- The computed value is displayed in the second text box.

ROUND NUMBERS

If you are working with floating-point numbers that include a decimal point, you can eliminate the numbers after the decimal point by using the `round()` method. Any decimal value less than 0.5 converts the number to the closest lower integer value. Any decimal value greater than or equal to 0.5 rounds up to the next greatest integer.

ROUND NUMBERS

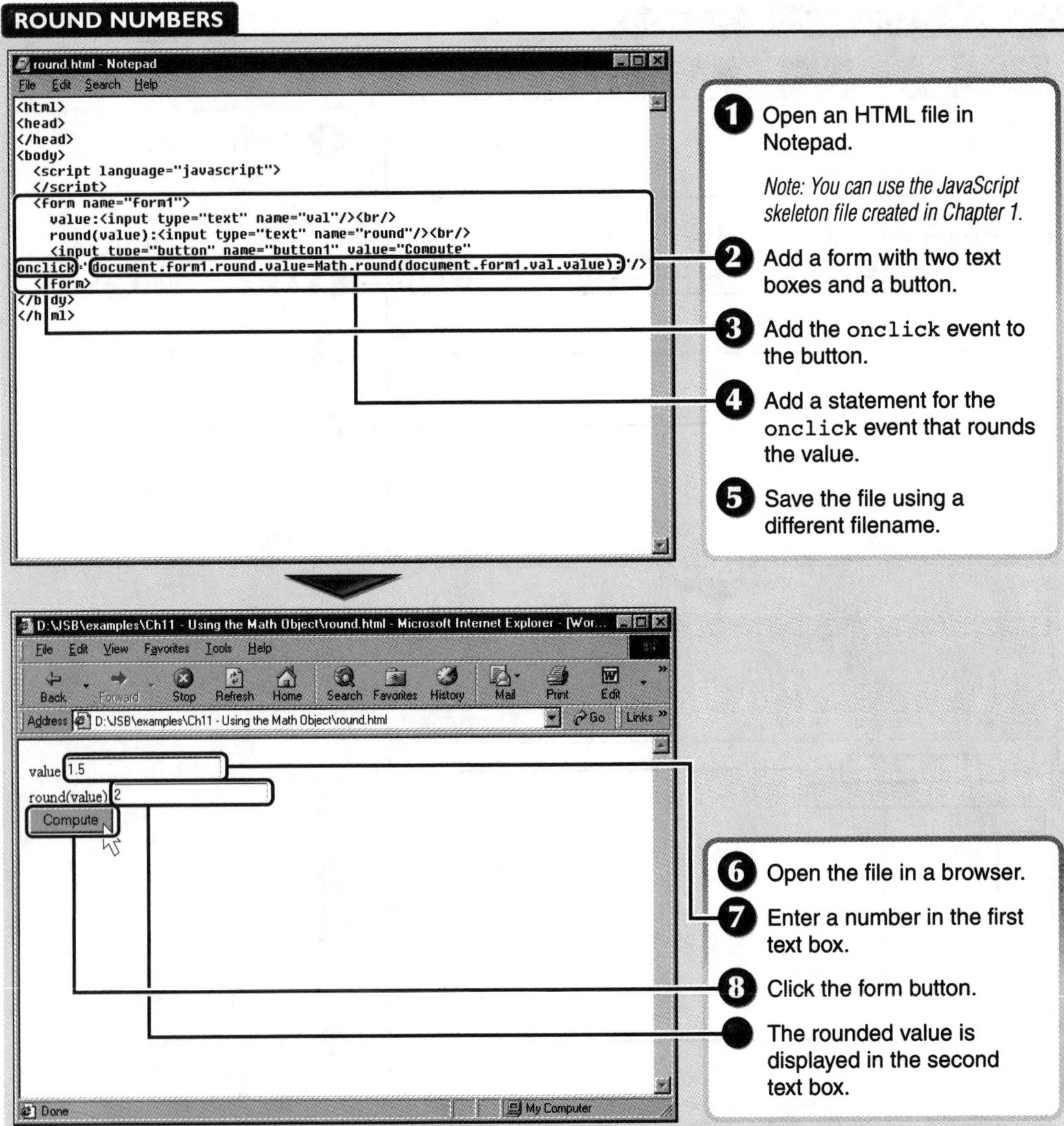

round.html - Notepad
<html>
<head>
</head>
<body>
<script language="javascript">
</script>
<form name="form1">
value:<input type="text" name="val"/>
round(value):<input type="text" name="round"/>
<input type="button" name="button1" value="Compute"
onclick='document.form1.round.value=Math.round(document.form1.val.value);'/>
</form>
</body>
</html>
D:\JSB\examples\Ch11 - Using the Math Object\round.html - Microsoft Internet Explorer
value 1.5
round(value) 2
Compute

1. Open an HTML file in Notepad.

   Note: You can use the JavaScript skeleton file created in Chapter 1.

2. Add a form with two text boxes and a button.
3. Add the `onclick` event to the button.
4. Add a statement for the `onclick` event that rounds the value.
5. Save the file using a different filename.
6. Open the file in a browser.
7. Enter a number in the first text box.
8. Click the form button.

- The rounded value is displayed in the second text box.

RAISE NUMBERS TO A POWER

You can use the pow() method to raise one number to the power of another. pow() accepts two parameters: The first is the number, and the second is the power that the number is raised to. For example, the statement Math.pow(5, 2) raises the number 5 to the power of 2, resulting in a value of 25.

RAISE NUMBERS TO A POWER

```
<html>
<head>
</head>
<body>
  <script language="javascript">
  </script>
  <form name="form1">
    value:<input type="text" name="val"/><br/>
    power:<input type="text" name="power"/><br/>
    result:<input type="text" name="result"/><br/>
    <input type="button" name="button1" value="Compute"
onclick="document.form1.result.value=Math.pow(document.form1.val.value,document.form1.power.value);"/>
  </form>
</body>
</html>
```

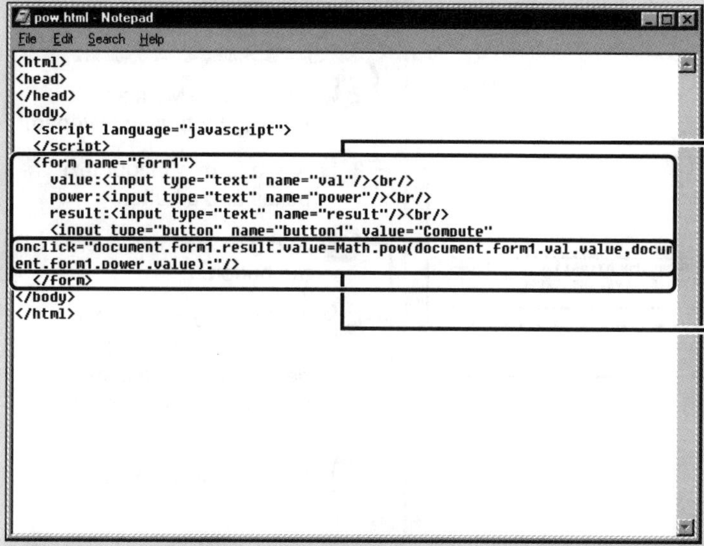

1. Open an HTML file with <script> tags in Notepad.
2. Add a form with three text boxes and a button.
3. Add the onclick event to the button.
4. Add a statement for the onclick event that computes the value of the first text box raised to the power of the second text box.
5. Save the file using a different filename.

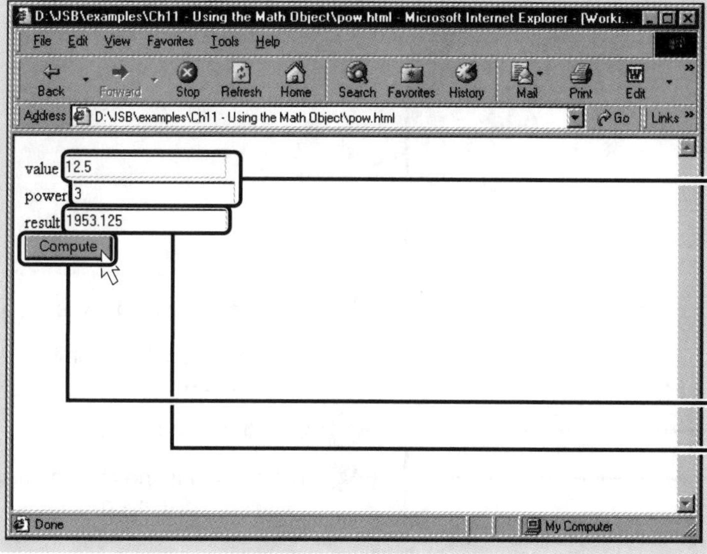

value 12.5
power 3
result 1953.125
Compute

6. Open the file in a browser.
7. Enter numbers in the first two text boxes.
8. Click the form button.

- The resulting value is displayed in the third text box.

FIND MINIMUM AND MAXIMUM VALUES

You can use the min() and max() methods to determine if one number is greater than another. These Math object methods accept two parameters and return the number that is smaller or greater, depending on the method used. For example, min (3, 4) returns 3 because 3 is the smaller number of the two, whereas max(3, 4) returns 4.

FIND MINIMUM AND MAXIMUM VALUES

```
<html>
<head>
</head>
<body>
  <script language="javascript">
  </script>
  <form name="form1">
    value1:<input type="text" name="val1"/><br/>
    value2:<input type="text" name="val2"/><br/>
    minimum:<input type="text" name="min"/><br/>
    maximum:<input type="text" name="max"/><br/>
    <input type="button" name="button1" value="Compute"
onclick="document.form1.min.value=Math.min(document.form1.val1.value,document.form1.val2.value);document.form1.max.value=Math.max(document.form1.val1.value,document.form1.val2.value);"/>
  </form>
</body>
</html>
```

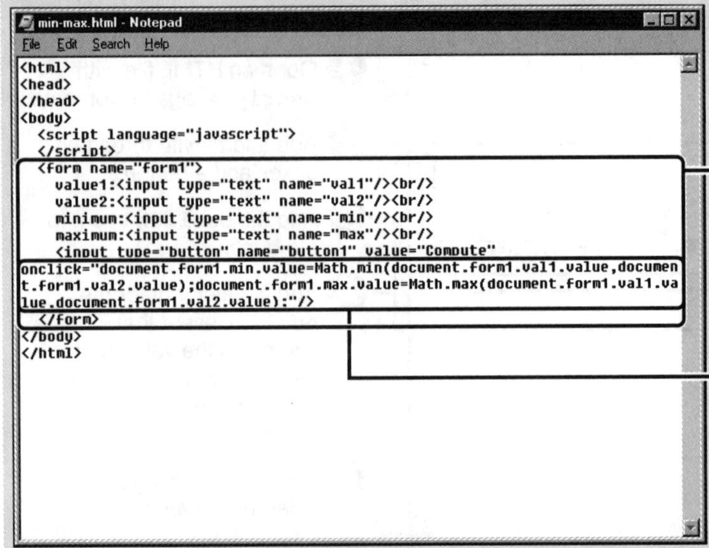

1 Open an HTML file with <script> tags in Notepad.

2 Add a form with four text boxes and a button.

3 Add the onclick event to the button.

4 Add a statement for the onclick event that determines the minimum and maximum values in the first two text boxes.

5 Save the file using a different filename.

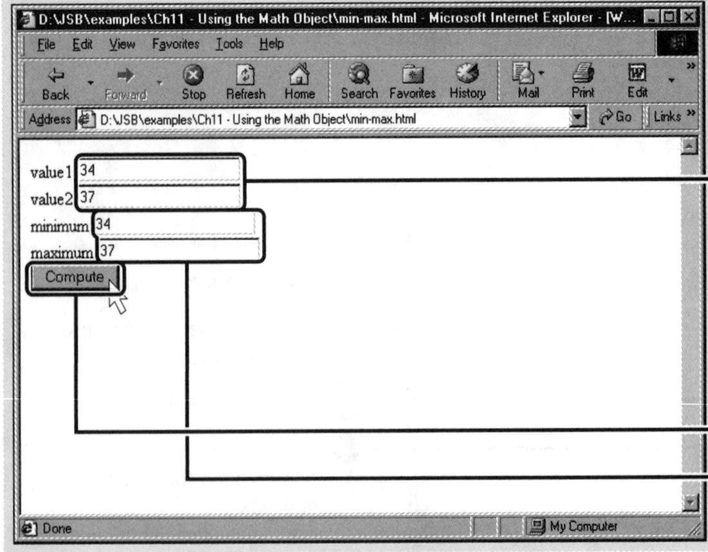

6 Open the file in a browser.

7 Enter numbers in the first two text boxes.

8 Click the form button.

- The minimum and maximum values are displayed.

USING ABSOLUTE VALUES

You can use the `abs()` method to return the absolute value of a number. Absolute value ensures that a number is positive. If a negative number is sent, the negative sign is removed, and the positive value is returned. For example, `Math.abs(-25)` returns a positive value of `25`.

USING ABSOLUTE VALUES

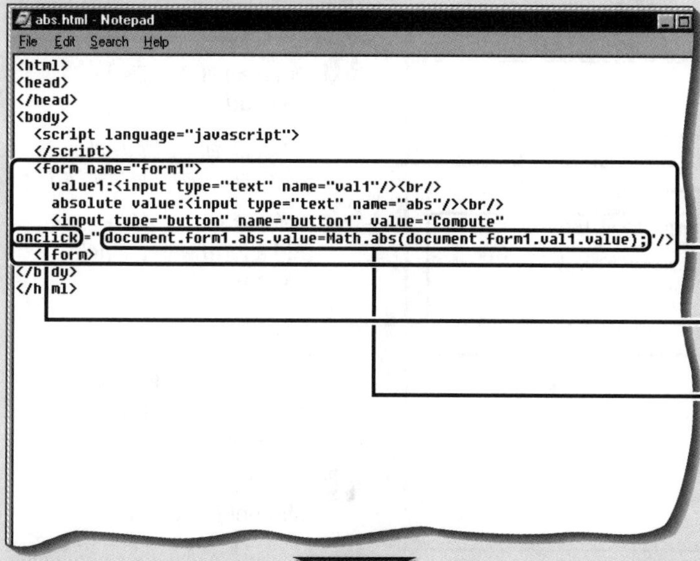

```
<html>
<head>
</head>
<body>
  <script language="javascript">
  </script>
  <form name="form1">
    value1:<input type="text" name="val1"/><br/>
    absolute value:<input type="text" name="abs"/><br/>
    <input type="button" name="button1" value="Compute"
onclick="document.form1.abs.value=Math.abs(document.form1.val1.value);"/>
  </form>
</body>
</html>
```

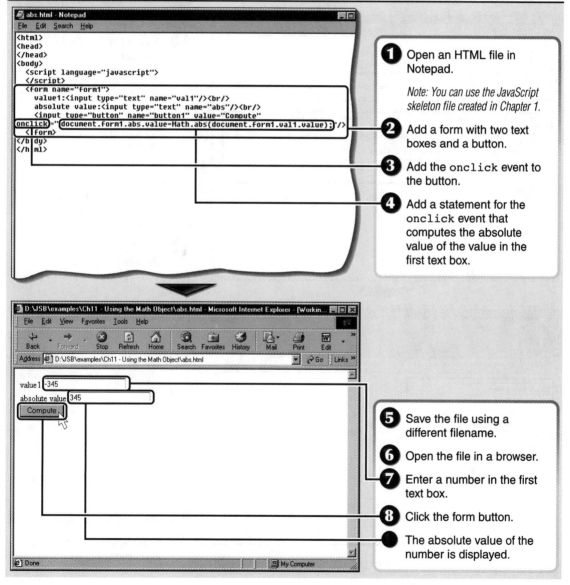

1. Open an HTML file in Notepad.

   Note: You can use the JavaScript skeleton file created in Chapter 1.

2. Add a form with two text boxes and a button.
3. Add the `onclick` event to the button.
4. Add a statement for the `onclick` event that computes the absolute value of the value in the first text box.

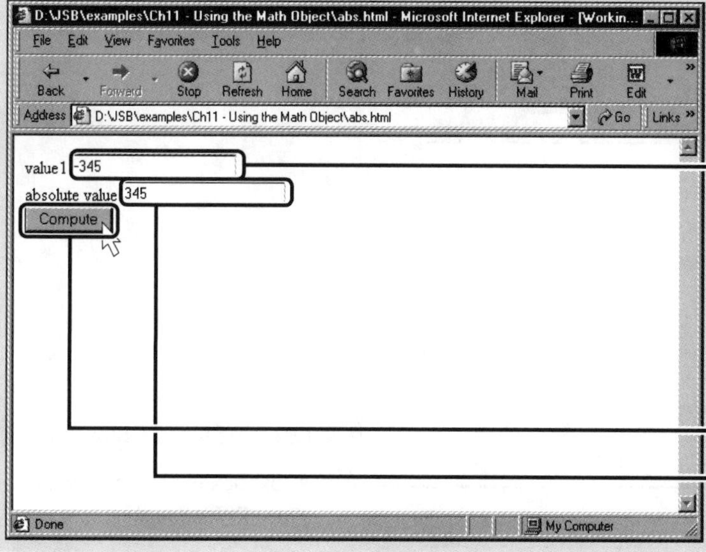

D:\JSB\examples\Ch11 - Using the Math Object\abs.html - Microsoft Internet Explorer

value1 -345
absolute value 345
Compute

5. Save the file using a different filename.
6. Open the file in a browser.
7. Enter a number in the first text box.
8. Click the form button.

- The absolute value of the number is displayed.

USING TEXT BOXES

To reference a text box in JavaScript, you need to refer to the form name and the text box name. For example, you can get the value of a text box named `text1` within a form named `form1` by using `document.form1.text1.value`. Properties for the text box object include `defaultValue`, `enabled`, `form`, `name`, `size`, `type`, and `value`. The methods include `focus()`, `blur()`, and `select()`.

DISPLAY TEXT BOX OBJECT PROPERTIES

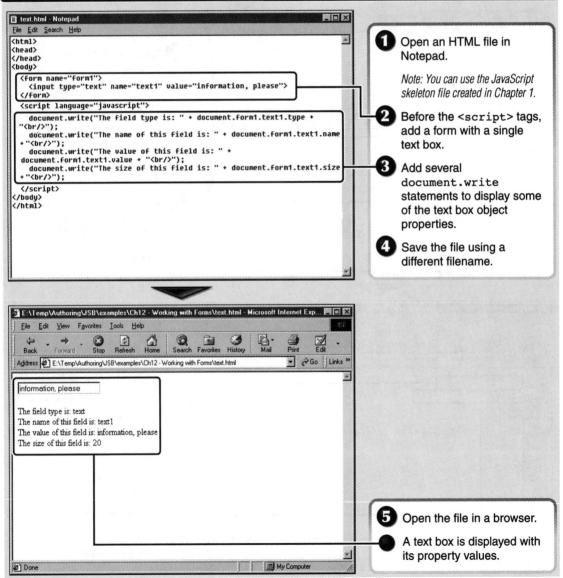

text.html - Notepad

```
<html>
<head>
</head>
<body>
  <form name="form1">
    <input type="text" name="text1" value="information, please">
  </form>
  <script language="javascript">
    document.write("The field type is: " + document.form1.text1.type +
"<br/>");
    document.write("The name of this field is: " + document.form1.text1.name
+ "<br/>");
    document.write("The value of this field is: " +
document.form1.text1.value + "<br/>");
    document.write("The size of this field is: " + document.form1.text1.size
+ "<br/>");
  </script>
</body>
</html>
```

1. Open an HTML file in Notepad.

   Note: You can use the JavaScript skeleton file created in Chapter 1.

2. Before the `<script>` tags, add a form with a single text box.
3. Add several `document.write` statements to display some of the text box object properties.
4. Save the file using a different filename.

E:\Temp\Authoring\JSB\examples\Ch12 - Working with Forms\text.html - Microsoft Internet Exp...

information, please

The field type is: text
The name of this field is: text1
The value of this field is: information, please
The size of this field is: 20

5. Open the file in a browser.

- A text box is displayed with its property values.

in an instant

USING TEXT BOX OBJECT METHODS

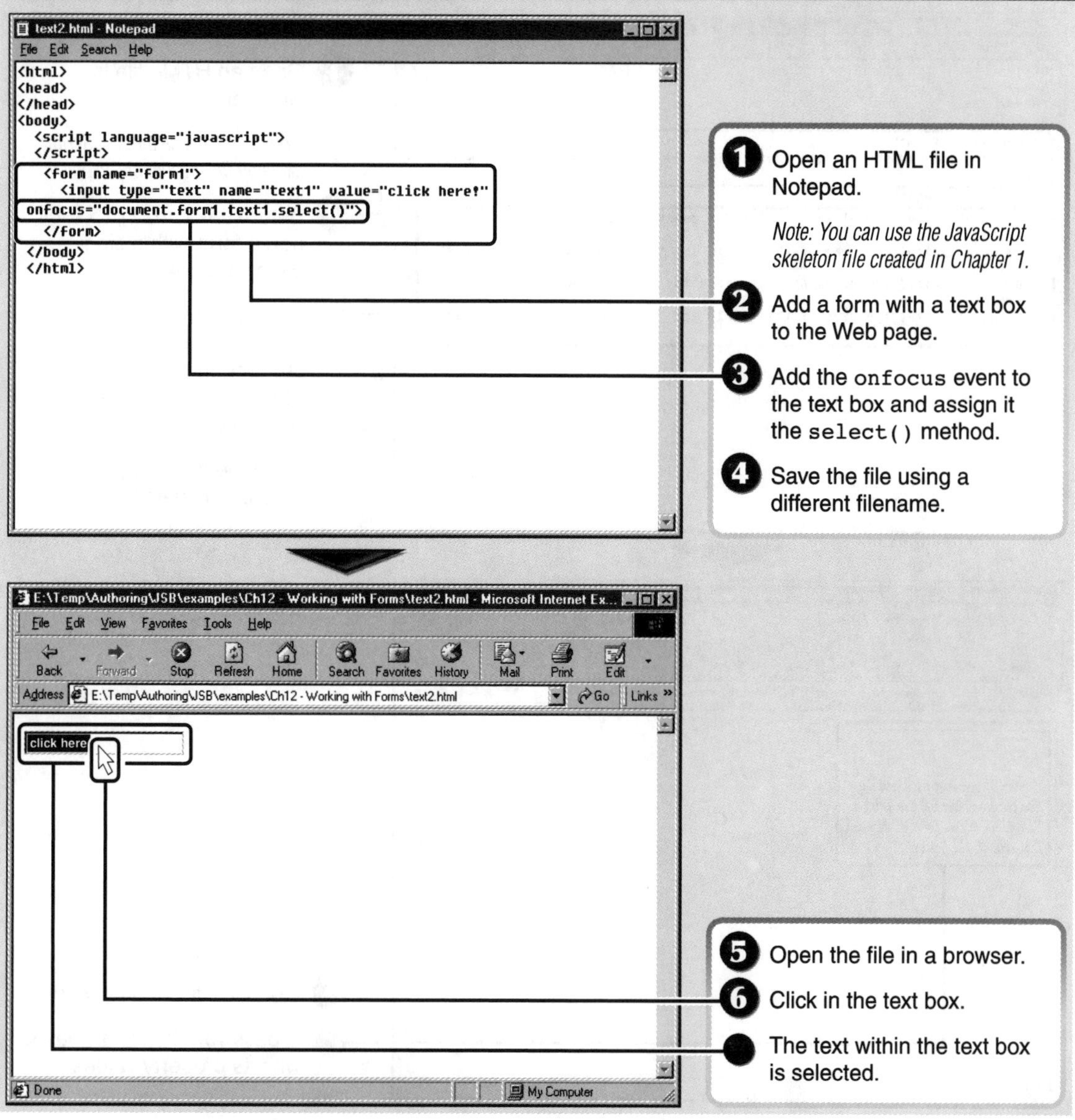
text2.html - Notepad
File Edit Search Help
<html>
<head>
</head>
<body>
<script language="javascript">
</script>
<form name="form1">
<input type="text" name="text1" value="click here!"
onfocus="document.form1.text1.select()">
</form>
</body>
</html>
E:\Temp\Authoring\JSB\examples\Ch12 - Working with Forms\text2.html - Microsoft Internet Ex...
File Edit View Favorites Tools Help
Back Forward Stop Refresh Home Search Favorites History Mail Print Edit
Address E:\Temp\Authoring\JSB\examples\Ch12 - Working with Forms\text2.html
Go Links
click here
Done
My Computer

1. Open an HTML file in Notepad.

   Note: You can use the JavaScript skeleton file created in Chapter 1.

2. Add a form with a text box to the Web page.
3. Add the `onfocus` event to the text box and assign it the `select()` method.
4. Save the file using a different filename.
5. Open the file in a browser.
6. Click in the text box.

- The text within the text box is selected.

WORK WITH PASSWORD BOXES

Password boxes are similar to text boxes, except all characters typed in are displayed as asterisks (*). This masking is useful for inputting sensitive information such as a password without revealing it to anyone nearby. The password box object includes properties for `defaultValue`, `enabled`, `form`, `name`, `size`, `type`, and `value`. It also includes methods for `focus()`, `blur()`, and `select()`.

WORK WITH PASSWORD BOXES

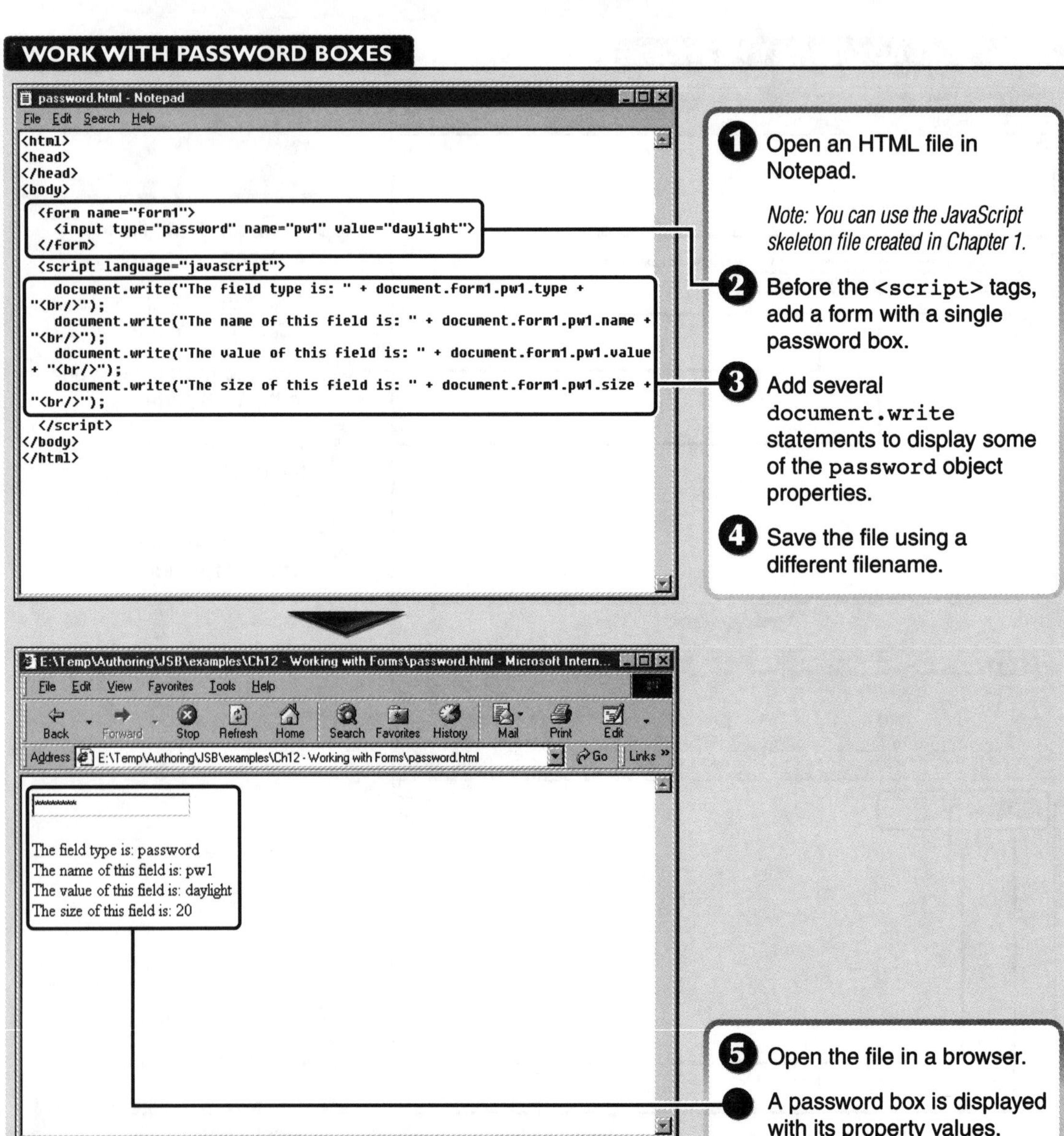

password.html - Notepad
File Edit Search Help
<html>
<head>
</head>
<body>
<form name="form1">
<input type="password" name="pw1" value="daylight">
</form>
<script language="javascript">
document.write("The field type is: " + document.form1.pw1.type + "<br/>");
document.write("The name of this field is: " + document.form1.pw1.name + "<br/>");
document.write("The value of this field is: " + document.form1.pw1.value + "<br/>");
document.write("The size of this field is: " + document.form1.pw1.size + "<br/>");
</script>
</body>
</html>
E:\Temp\Authoring\JSB\examples\Ch12 - Working with Forms\password.html - Microsoft Intern...
File Edit View Favorites Tools Help
Back Forward Stop Refresh Home Search Favorites History Mail Print Edit
Address E:\Temp\Authoring\JSB\examples\Ch12 - Working with Forms\password.html
Go Links
****
The field type is: password
The name of this field is: pw1
The value of this field is: daylight
The size of this field is: 20
Done
My Computer

1. Open an HTML file in Notepad.

   Note: You can use the JavaScript skeleton file created in Chapter 1.

2. Before the `<script>` tags, add a form with a single password box.
3. Add several `document.write` statements to display some of the `password` object properties.
4. Save the file using a different filename.
5. Open the file in a browser.

- A password box is displayed with its property values.

WORK WITH HIDDEN FIELDS

Hidden fields are a special type of form element. You create them by using the `<input/>` tag with the `type` attribute set to `hidden`. Hidden fields do not display anything within a browser but can be used to pass data to the form-processing script. The `hidden` object includes only three properties — `name`, `type`, and `value` — and no methods.

WORK WITH HIDDEN FIELDS

```
<html>
<head>
</head>
<body>
  <form name="form1">
    <input type="hidden" name="hid1" value="pieces of eight">
  </form>
  <script language="javascript">
    document.write("The field type is: " + document.form1.hid1.type +
"<br/>");
    document.write("The name of this field is: " + document.form1.hid1.name
+ "<br/>");
    document.write("The value of this field is: " +
document.form1.hid1.value + "<br/>");
  </script>
</body>
</html>
```

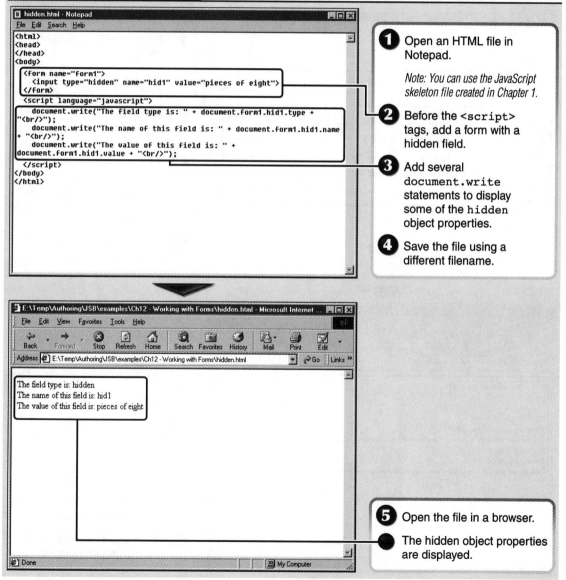

1. Open an HTML file in Notepad.

   Note: You can use the JavaScript skeleton file created in Chapter 1.

2. Before the `<script>` tags, add a form with a hidden field.
3. Add several `document.write` statements to display some of the `hidden` object properties.
4. Save the file using a different filename.

The field type is: hidden
The name of this field is: hid1
The value of this field is: pieces of eight

5. Open the file in a browser.

- The hidden object properties are displayed.

WORK WITH TEXTAREA BOXES

Textarea boxes are like multiple-line text boxes. You can specify the size of a textarea box by using the `rows` and `cols` attributes. The `textarea` object is similar to the `text` object. It includes properties for identifying `defaultValue`, `enabled`, `form`, `name`, `rows`, `cols`, `type`, and `value` and methods for `focus()`, `blur()`, and `select()`.

DISPLAY TEXTAREA BOX PROPERTIES

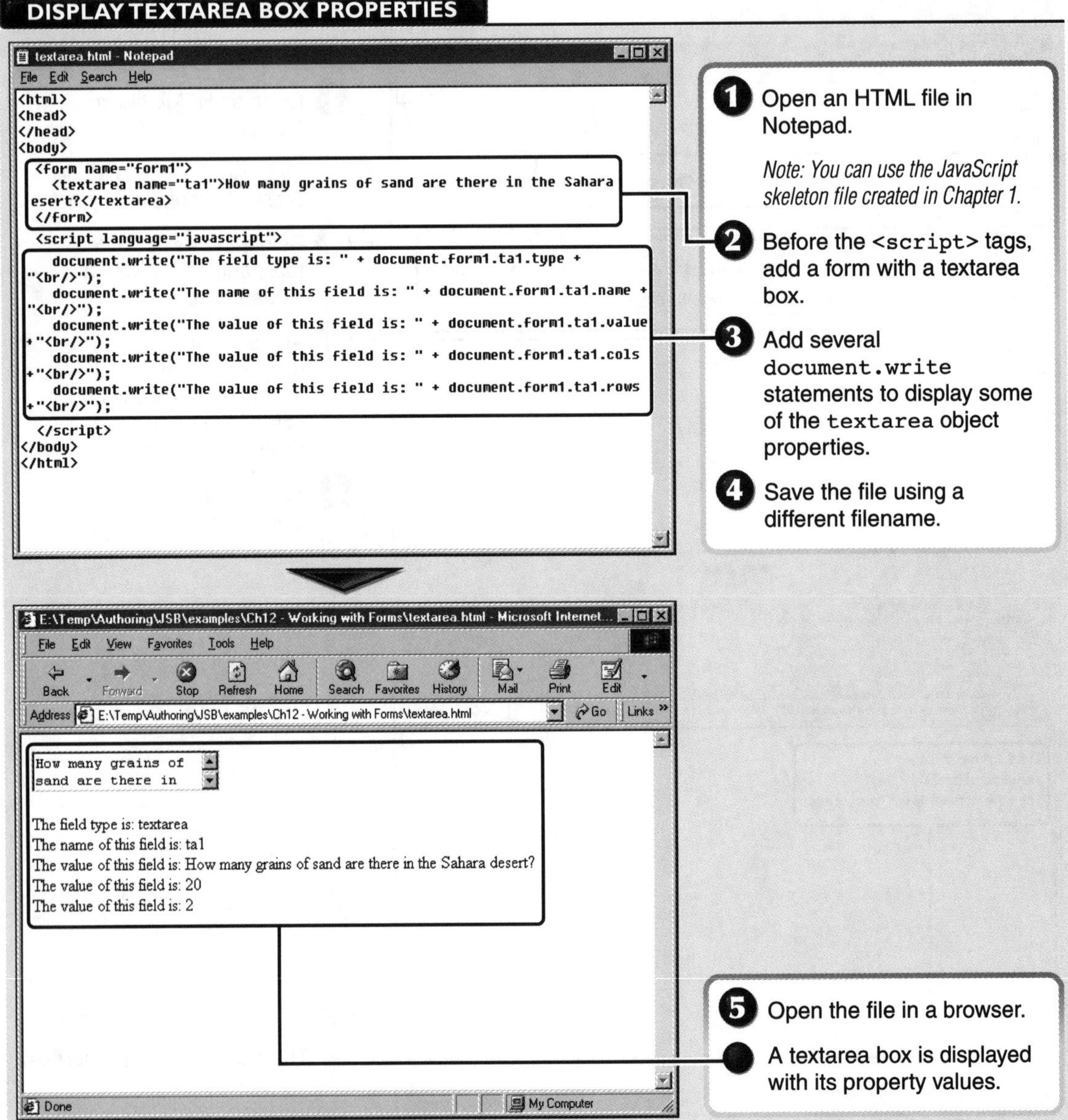

textarea.html - Notepad
File Edit Search Help
<html>
<head>
</head>
<body>
<form name="form1">
<textarea name="ta1">How many grains of sand are there in the Sahara
esert?</textarea>
</form>
<script language="javascript">
document.write("The field type is: " + document.form1.ta1.type +
"<br/>");
document.write("The name of this field is: " + document.form1.ta1.name +
"<br/>");
document.write("The value of this field is: " + document.form1.ta1.value
+"<br/>");
document.write("The value of this field is: " + document.form1.ta1.cols
+"<br/>");
document.write("The value of this field is: " + document.form1.ta1.rows
+"<br/>");
</script>
</body>
</html>
E:\Temp\Authoring\JSB\examples\Ch12 - Working with Forms\textarea.html - Microsoft Internet...
File Edit View Favorites Tools Help
Back Forward Stop Refresh Home Search Favorites History Mail Print Edit
Address E:\Temp\Authoring\JSB\examples\Ch12 - Working with Forms\textarea.html
Go Links
How many grains of
sand are there in
The field type is: textarea
The name of this field is: ta1
The value of this field is: How many grains of sand are there in the Sahara desert?
The value of this field is: 20
The value of this field is: 2
Done
My Computer

1. Open an HTML file in Notepad.

   Note: You can use the JavaScript skeleton file created in Chapter 1.

2. Before the `<script>` tags, add a form with a textarea box.

3. Add several `document.write` statements to display some of the `textarea` object properties.

4. Save the file using a different filename.

5. Open the file in a browser.

- A textarea box is displayed with its property values.

in an instant

USING A TEXTAREA BOX OBJECT METHOD

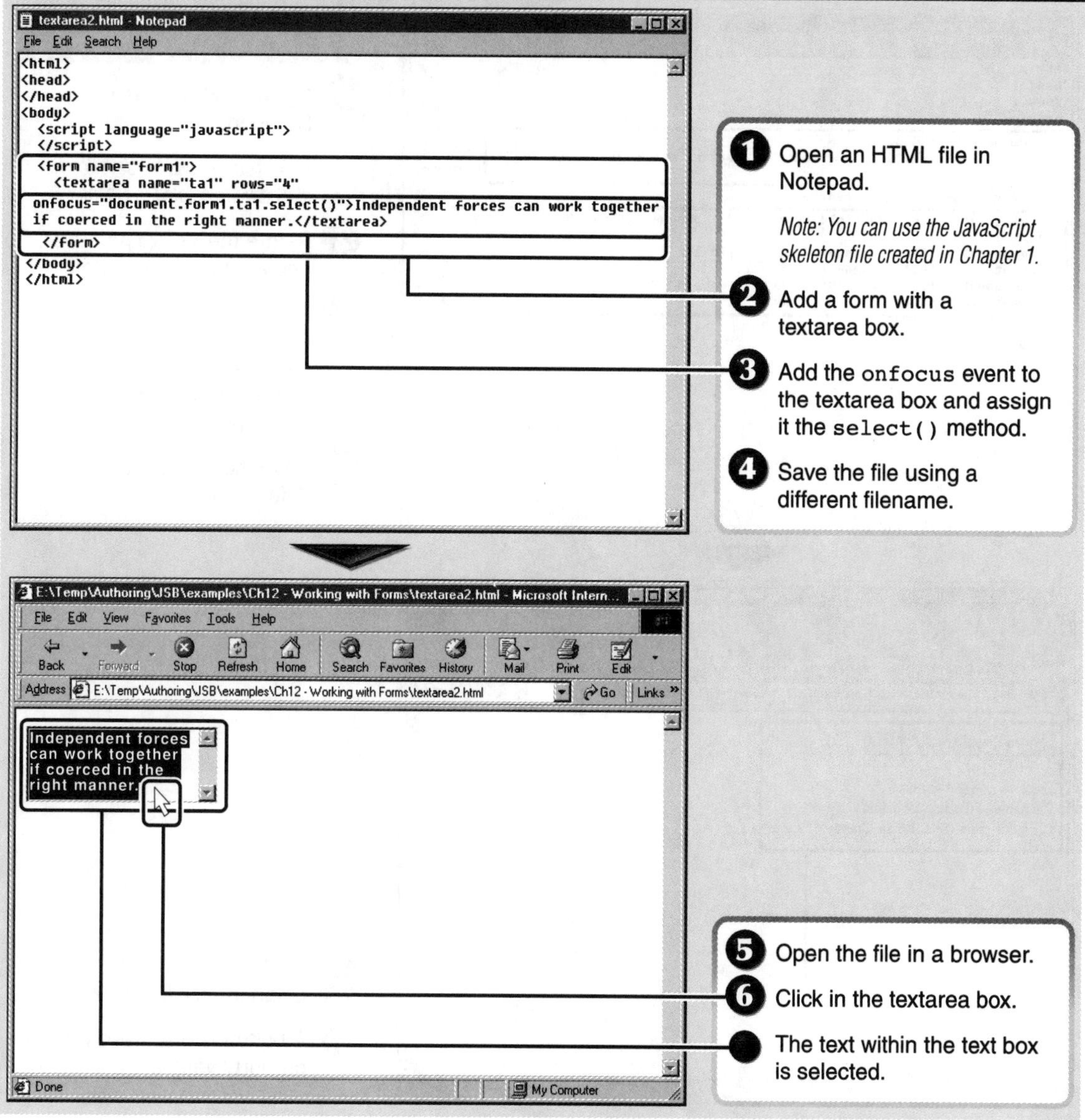
textarea2.html - Notepad
File Edit Search Help
<html>
<head>
</head>
<body>
<script language="javascript">
</script>
<form name="form1">
<textarea name="ta1" rows="4"
onfocus="document.form1.ta1.select()">Independent forces can work together
if coerced in the right manner.</textarea>
</form>
</body>
</html>
E:\Temp\Authoring\JSB\examples\Ch12 - Working with Forms\textarea2.html - Microsoft Intern...
Address E:\Temp\Authoring\JSB\examples\Ch12 - Working with Forms\textarea2.html
Independent forces can work together if coerced in the right manner.
Done
My Computer

1. Open an HTML file in Notepad.

   Note: You can use the JavaScript skeleton file created in Chapter 1.

2. Add a form with a textarea box.
3. Add the `onfocus` event to the textarea box and assign it the `select()` method.
4. Save the file using a different filename.
5. Open the file in a browser.
6. Click in the textarea box.

- The text within the text box is selected.

USING BUTTONS

JavaScript includes a `button` object that includes properties and methods for controlling form buttons. `button` properties include `enabled`, `form`, `name`, `type`, and `value`. The `value` attribute determines the text that appears on the surface of the button. The `button` object methods include `click()` and `focus()`. Using the `click()` method, you can simulate the user clicking the button.

DISPLAY BUTTON OBJECT PROPERTIES

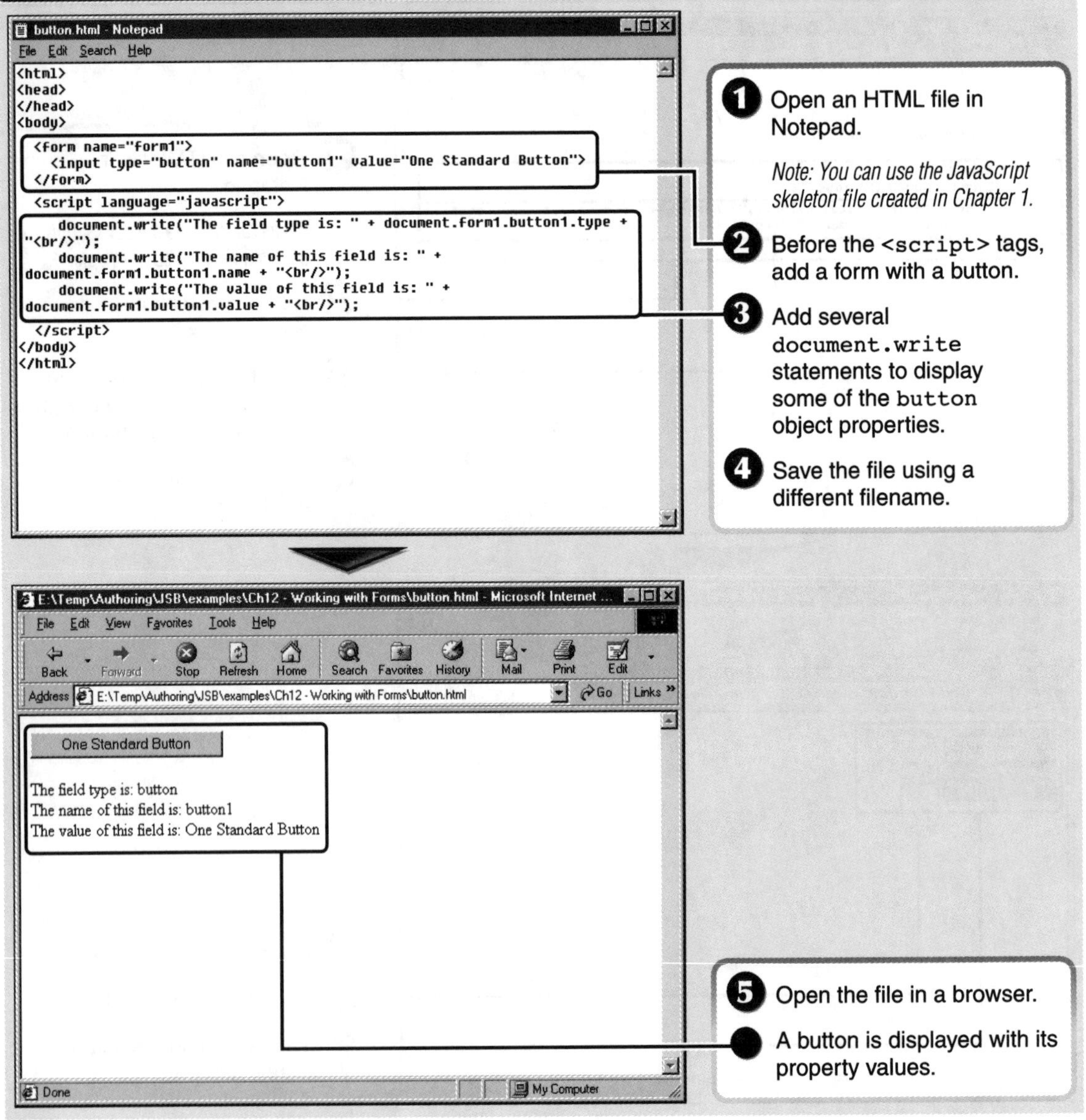
button.html - Notepad
File Edit Search Help
<html>
<head>
</head>
<body>
<form name="form1">
<input type="button" name="button1" value="One Standard Button">
</form>
<script language="javascript">
document.write("The field type is: " + document.form1.button1.type + "<br/>");
document.write("The name of this field is: " + document.form1.button1.name + "<br/>");
document.write("The value of this field is: " + document.form1.button1.value + "<br/>");
</script>
</body>
</html>
E:\Temp\Authoring\JSB\examples\Ch12 - Working with Forms\button.html - Microsoft Internet ...
File Edit View Favorites Tools Help
Back Forward Stop Refresh Home Search Favorites History Mail Print Edit
Address E:\Temp\Authoring\JSB\examples\Ch12 - Working with Forms\button.html
Go Links
One Standard Button
The field type is: button
The name of this field is: button1
The value of this field is: One Standard Button
Done
My Computer

1. Open an HTML file in Notepad.

   Note: You can use the JavaScript skeleton file created in Chapter 1.

2. Before the `<script>` tags, add a form with a button.
3. Add several `document.write` statements to display some of the `button` object properties.
4. Save the file using a different filename.
5. Open the file in a browser.

- A button is displayed with its property values.

in an instant

REACT TO A CLICK EVENT

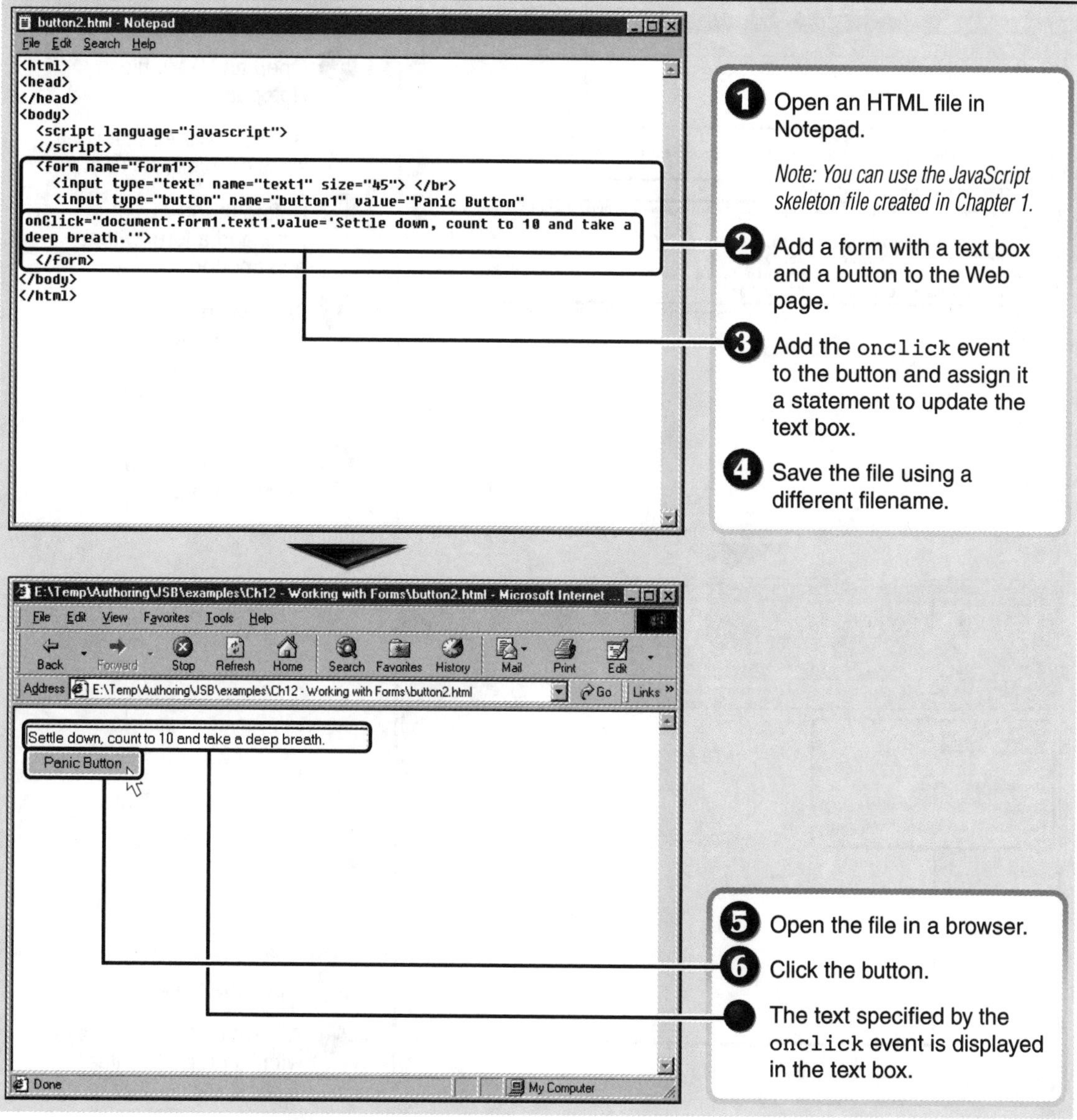
button2.html - Notepad
File Edit Search Help
<html>
<head>
</head>
<body>
<script language="javascript">
</script>
<form name="form1">
<input type="text" name="text1" size="45"> </br>
<input type="button" name="button1" value="Panic Button"
onClick="document.form1.text1.value='Settle down, count to 10 and take a deep breath.'">
</form>
</body>
</html>
E:\Temp\Authoring\JSB\examples\Ch12 - Working with Forms\button2.html - Microsoft Internet ...
File Edit View Favorites Tools Help
Back Forward Stop Refresh Home Search Favorites History Mail Print Edit
Address E:\Temp\Authoring\JSB\examples\Ch12 - Working with Forms\button2.html
Go Links
Settle down, count to 10 and take a deep breath.
Panic Button
Done
My Computer

1. Open an HTML file in Notepad.

   Note: You can use the JavaScript skeleton file created in Chapter 1.

2. Add a form with a text box and a button to the Web page.
3. Add the `onclick` event to the button and assign it a statement to update the text box.
4. Save the file using a different filename.
5. Open the file in a browser.
6. Click the button.

- The text specified by the `onclick` event is displayed in the text box.

USING A RESET BUTTON

A *reset button* is a special type of button that resets all the form elements to their initial default values. You can create a reset button by using the `<input/>` tag with the `type` attribute set to `reset`. The `reset` object includes properties for `enabled`, `form`, `name`, and `value`. Just like the `button` object, it also includes `click()` and `focus()` methods.

USING A RESET BUTTON

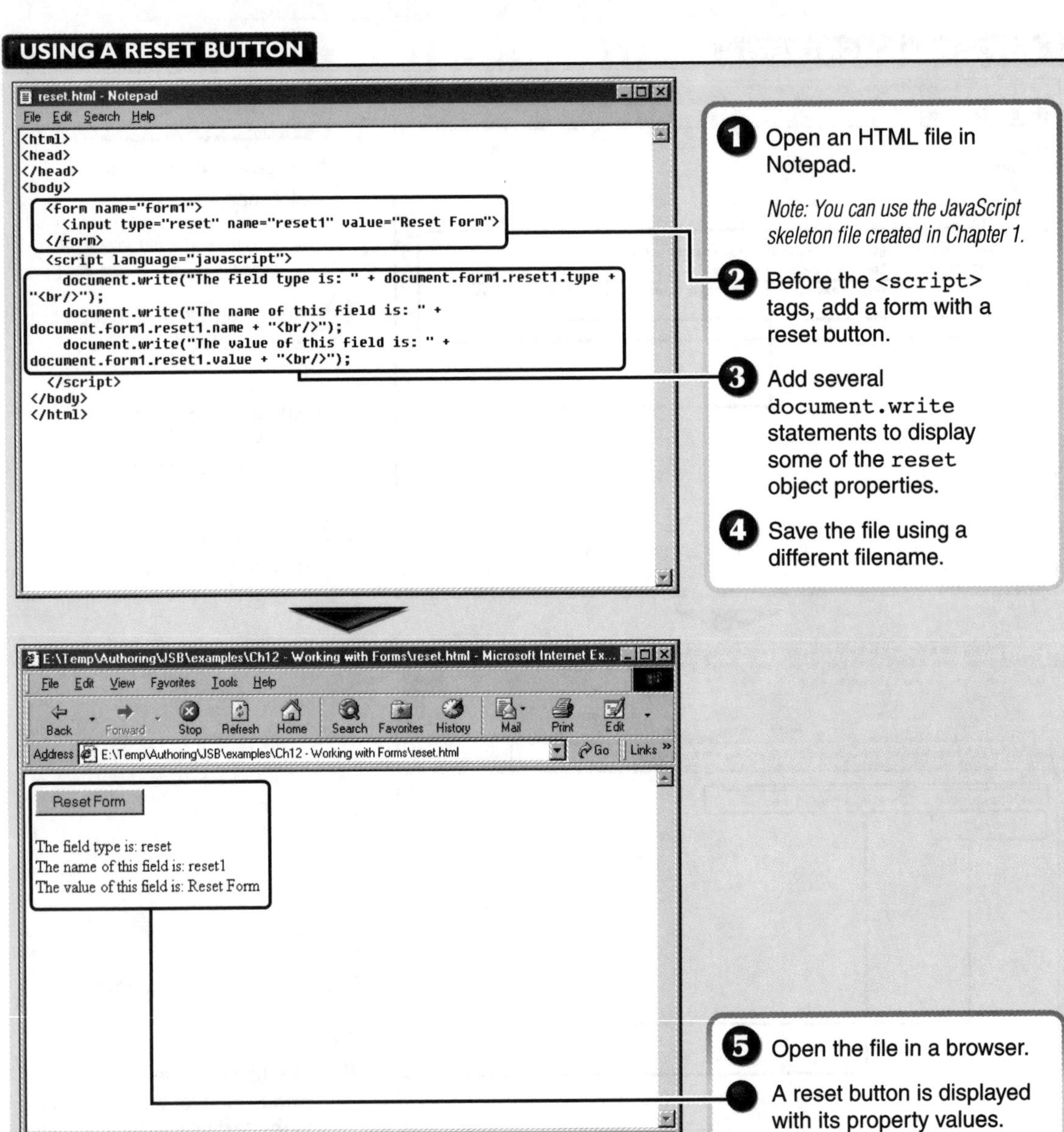
reset.html - Notepad
File Edit Search Help
<html>
<head>
</head>
<body>
<form name="form1">
<input type="reset" name="reset1" value="Reset Form">
</form>
<script language="javascript">
document.write("The field type is: " + document.form1.reset1.type + "<br/>");
document.write("The name of this field is: " + document.form1.reset1.name + "<br/>");
document.write("The value of this field is: " + document.form1.reset1.value + "<br/>");
</script>
</body>
</html>
1 Open an HTML file in Notepad.
Note: You can use the JavaScript skeleton file created in Chapter 1.
2 Before the <script> tags, add a form with a reset button.
3 Add several document.write statements to display some of the reset object properties.
4 Save the file using a different filename.
E:\Temp\Authoring\JSB\examples\Ch12 - Working with Forms\reset.html - Microsoft Internet Ex...
File Edit View Favorites Tools Help
Back Forward Stop Refresh Home Search Favorites History Mail Print Edit
Address E:\Temp\Authoring\JSB\examples\Ch12 - Working with Forms\reset.html
Go Links
Reset Form
The field type is: reset
The name of this field is: reset1
The value of this field is: Reset Form
Done
My Computer
5 Open the file in a browser.
A reset button is displayed with its property values.

USING A SUBMIT BUTTON

A *submit button* sends form data to the server. Where the data is sent is determined by the `<form>` tag's `action` attribute. You can create a submit button by using the `<input/>` tag with the `type` attribute set to `submit`. The `submit` object includes properties for `enabled`, `form`, `name`, and `value`, as well as the `click()` and `focus()` methods.

USING A SUBMIT BUTTON

```
<html>
<head>
</head>
<body>
  <form name="form1">
    <input type="submit" name="submit1" value="Submit Form">
  </form>
  <script language="javascript">
     document.write("The field type is: " + document.form1.submit1.type +
"<br/>");
     document.write("The name of this field is: " +
document.form1.submit1.name + "<br/>");
     document.write("The value of this field is: " +
document.form1.submit1.value + "<br/>");
   </script>
  </body>
  </html>
```

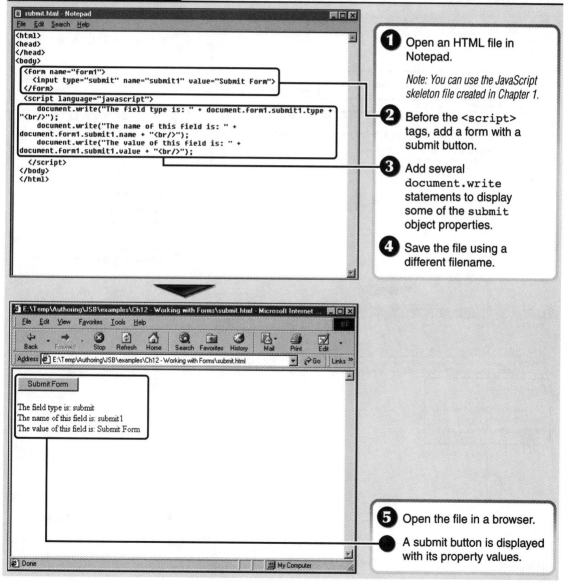

1. Open an HTML file in Notepad.

   Note: You can use the JavaScript skeleton file created in Chapter 1.

2. Before the `<script>` tags, add a form with a submit button.
3. Add several `document.write` statements to display some of the `submit` object properties.
4. Save the file using a different filename.

```
Submit Form

The field type is: submit
The name of this field is: submit1
The value of this field is: Submit Form
```

5. Open the file in a browser.

- A submit button is displayed with its property values.

USING CHECK BOX BUTTONS

You can create a check box by using an `<input/>` tag with the `type` attribute set to `checkbox`. The `checkbox` object identifies each element by its `name` attribute. `checkbox` properties include `checked`, `defaultChecked`, `enabled`, `form`, `name`, `type`, and `value`. `checked` is a Boolean value that is set to `true` if the check box is checked. The methods for `checkbox` are `click()` and `focus()`.

DISPLAY CHECK BOX OBJECT PROPERTIES

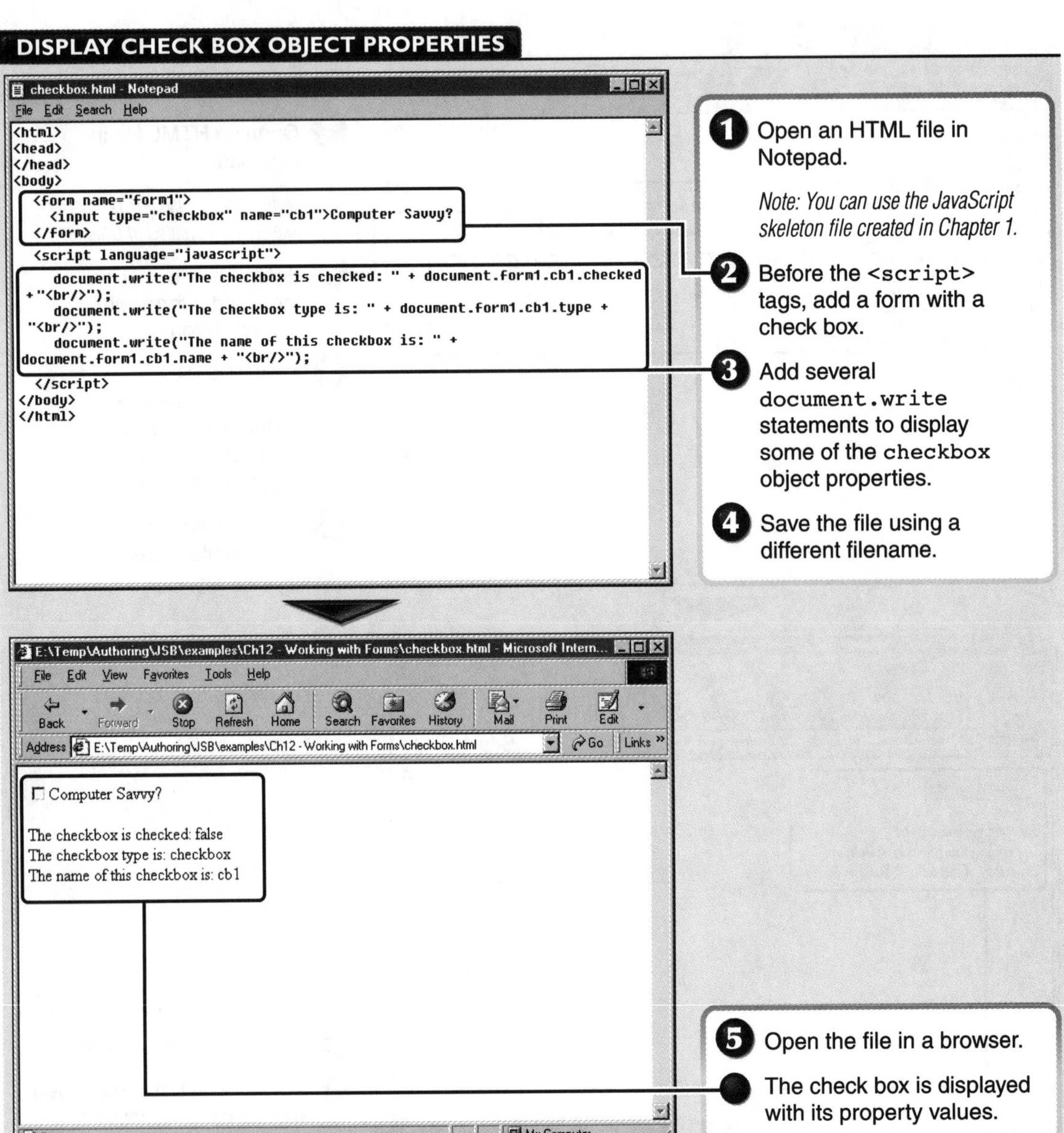

checkbox.html - Notepad
File Edit Search Help
<html>
<head>
</head>
<body>
<form name="form1">
<input type="checkbox" name="cb1">Computer Savvy?
</form>
<script language="javascript">
document.write("The checkbox is checked: " + document.form1.cb1.checked + "<br/>");
document.write("The checkbox type is: " + document.form1.cb1.type + "<br/>");
document.write("The name of this checkbox is: " + document.form1.cb1.name + "<br/>");
</script>
</body>
</html>
E:\Temp\Authoring\JSB\examples\Ch12 - Working with Forms\checkbox.html - Microsoft Intern...
File Edit View Favorites Tools Help
Back Forward Stop Refresh Home Search Favorites History Mail Print Edit
Address E:\Temp\Authoring\JSB\examples\Ch12 - Working with Forms\checkbox.html
Go Links
Computer Savvy?
The checkbox is checked: false
The checkbox type is: checkbox
The name of this checkbox is: cb1
Done
My Computer

1. Open an HTML file in Notepad.

   Note: You can use the JavaScript skeleton file created in Chapter 1.

2. Before the `<script>` tags, add a form with a check box.
3. Add several `document.write` statements to display some of the `checkbox` object properties.
4. Save the file using a different filename.
5. Open the file in a browser.

- The check box is displayed with its property values.

in an instant

CHECK MULTIPLE CHECK BOXES

checkbox2.html - Notepad

```
<html>
<head>
</head>
<body>
  <form name="form1">
    <input type="checkbox" name="cb1">Computer Savvy?
    <input type="checkbox" name="cb2">Web Savvy?
    <input type="checkbox" name="cb3">Email Savvy?
    <input type="checkbox" name="cb4">Internet Savvy?<br/>
    <input type="button" name="button1" value="Check All"
onclick="document.form1.cb1.checked=true;document.form1.cb2.checked=true;doc
ument.form1.cb3.checked=true;document.form1.cb4.checked=true;">
  </form>
  <script language="javascript">
  </script>
</body>
</html>
```

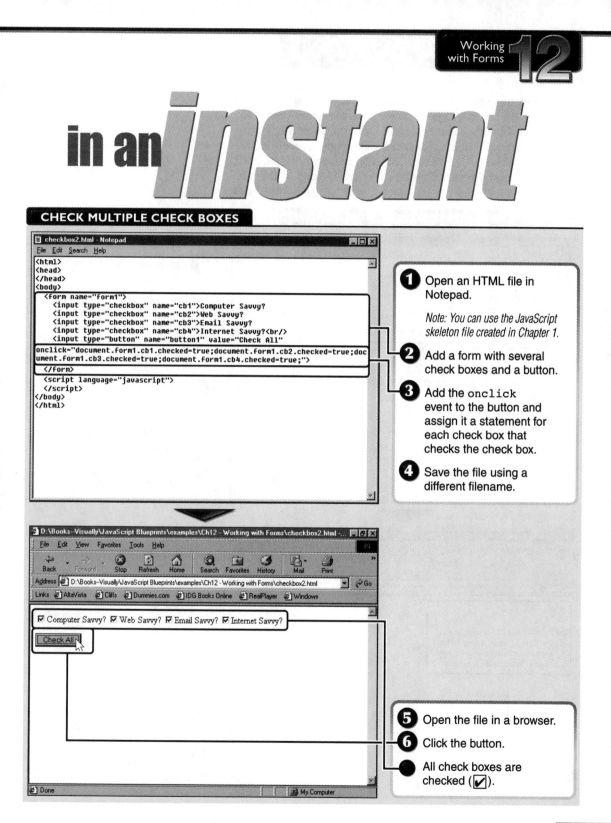

1. Open an HTML file in Notepad.

   Note: You can use the JavaScript skeleton file created in Chapter 1.

2. Add a form with several check boxes and a button.
3. Add the `onclick` event to the button and assign it a statement for each check box that checks the check box.
4. Save the file using a different filename.

D:\Books--Visually\JavaScript Blueprints\examples\Ch12 - Working with Forms\checkbox2.html

☑ Computer Savvy? ☑ Web Savvy? ☑ Email Savvy? ☑ Internet Savvy?

Check All

5. Open the file in a browser.
6. Click the button.

- All check boxes are checked (☑).

USING RADIO BUTTONS

Radio buttons come in sets. Only one button can be selected at a time. All the buttons in a set share the same name but are indexed by appearance order. The first button has an index of `0`. `radio` object properties include `checked`, `defaultChecked`, `enabled`, `form`, `length`, `name`, and `value`. `length` returns the number of buttons in the set. `radio` also includes the `click()` and `focus()` methods.

DISPLAY RADIO BUTTON OBJECT PROPERTIES

```
<html>
<head>
</head>
<body>
  <form name="form1">
    <input type="radio" name="radio1">Male
    <input type="radio" name="radio1">Female
  </form>
  <script language="javascript">
    document.write("The first radio button is selected: " +
document.form1.radio1[0].checked + "<br/>");
    document.write("The second radio button is selected: " +
document.form1.radio1[1].checked + "<br/>");
    document.write("The name of this radio button set is: " +
document.form1.radio1[0].name + "<br/>");
    document.write("The length of this radio button set is: " +
document.form1.radio1.length + "<br/>");
  </script>
 </body>
 </html>
```

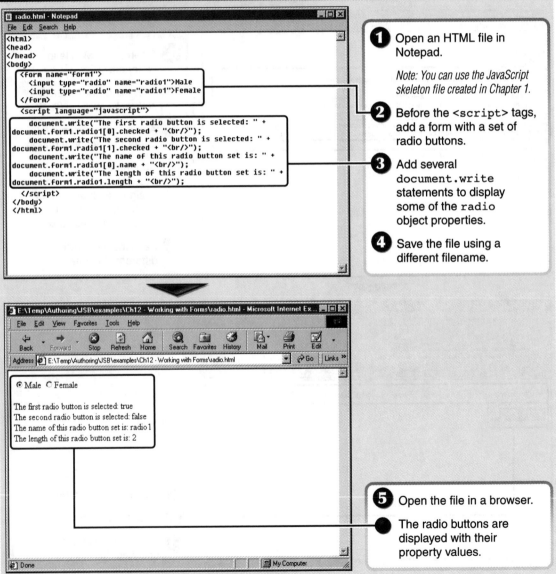

1. Open an HTML file in Notepad.

   Note: You can use the JavaScript skeleton file created in Chapter 1.

2. Before the `<script>` tags, add a form with a set of radio buttons.
3. Add several `document.write` statements to display some of the `radio` object properties.
4. Save the file using a different filename.

E:\Temp\Authoring\JSB\examples\Ch12 - Working with Forms\radio.html - Microsoft Internet Ex...
Male Female
The first radio button is selected: true
The second radio button is selected: false
The name of this radio button set is: radio1
The length of this radio button set is: 2

5. Open the file in a browser.

- The radio buttons are displayed with their property values.

in an instant

RESPOND TO A RADIO BUTTON SELECTION

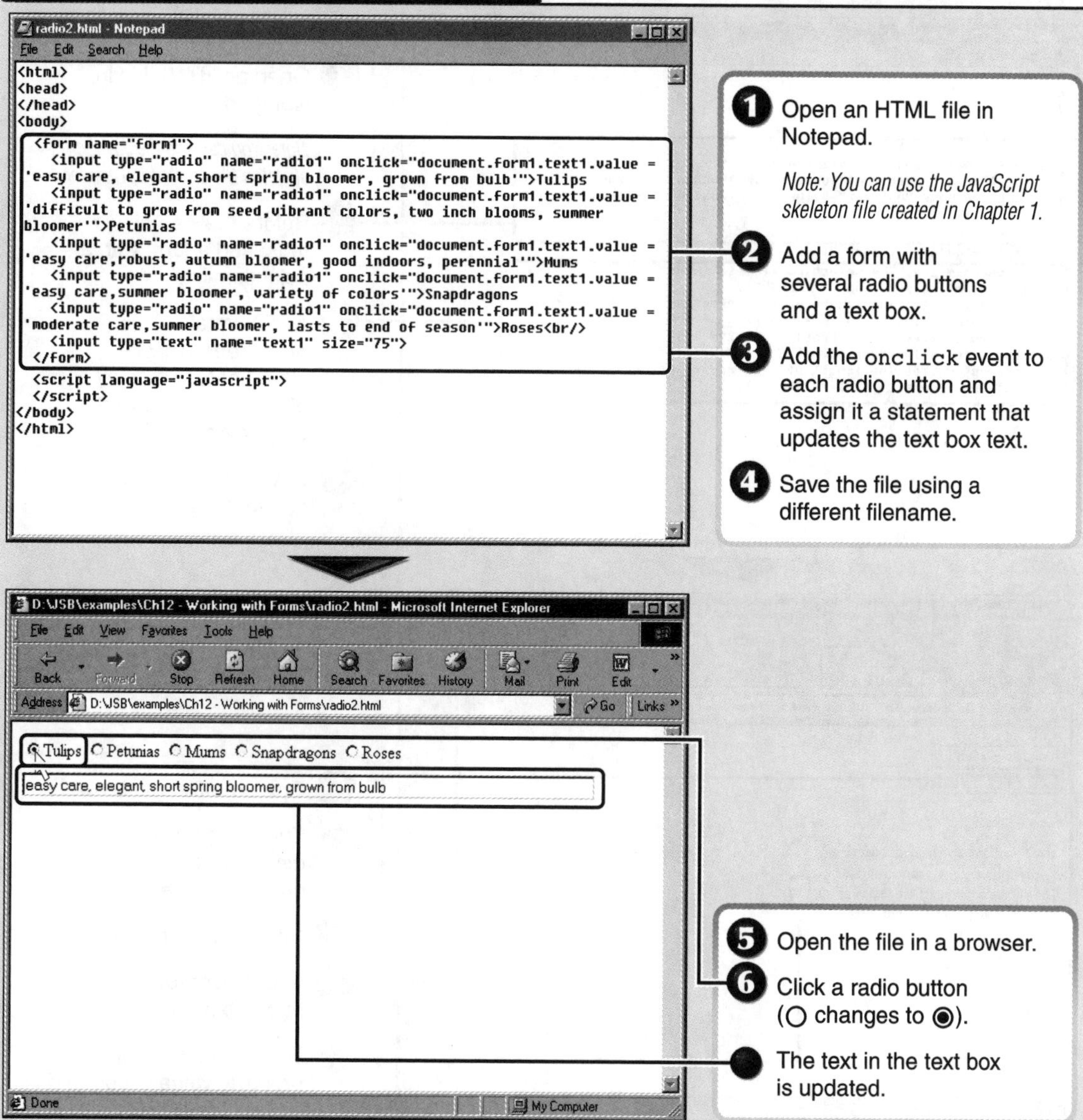
radio2.html - Notepad
File Edit Search Help
<html>
<head>
</head>
<body>
<form name="form1">
<input type="radio" name="radio1" onclick="document.form1.text1.value = 'easy care, elegant,short spring bloomer, grown from bulb'">Tulips
<input type="radio" name="radio1" onclick="document.form1.text1.value = 'difficult to grow from seed,vibrant colors, two inch blooms, summer bloomer'">Petunias
<input type="radio" name="radio1" onclick="document.form1.text1.value = 'easy care,robust, autumn bloomer, good indoors, perennial'">Mums
<input type="radio" name="radio1" onclick="document.form1.text1.value = 'easy care,summer bloomer, variety of colors'">Snapdragons
<input type="radio" name="radio1" onclick="document.form1.text1.value = 'moderate care,summer bloomer, lasts to end of season'">Roses
<input type="text" name="text1" size="75">
</form>
<script language="javascript">
</script>
</body>
</html>
D:\JSB\examples\Ch12 - Working with Forms\radio2.html - Microsoft Internet Explorer
Tulips Petunias Mums Snapdragons Roses
easy care, elegant, short spring bloomer, grown from bulb
Done
My Computer

1. Open an HTML file in Notepad.

   Note: You can use the JavaScript skeleton file created in Chapter 1.

2. Add a form with several radio buttons and a text box.

3. Add the `onclick` event to each radio button and assign it a statement that updates the text box text.

4. Save the file using a different filename.

5. Open the file in a browser.

6. Click a radio button (○ changes to ◉).

- The text in the text box is updated.

WORK WITH SELECTION LISTS

The `select` object is used to create selection lists and includes the `name`, `length`, `size`, and `selectedIndex` properties. `length` returns the number of list options, and `selectedIndex` holds the selected list item index. `select` also includes the `blur()` and `focus()` methods. Each option of a selection list can be referred to by using its index value (with `0` being the first option).

DISPLAY SELECT OBJECT PROPERTIES

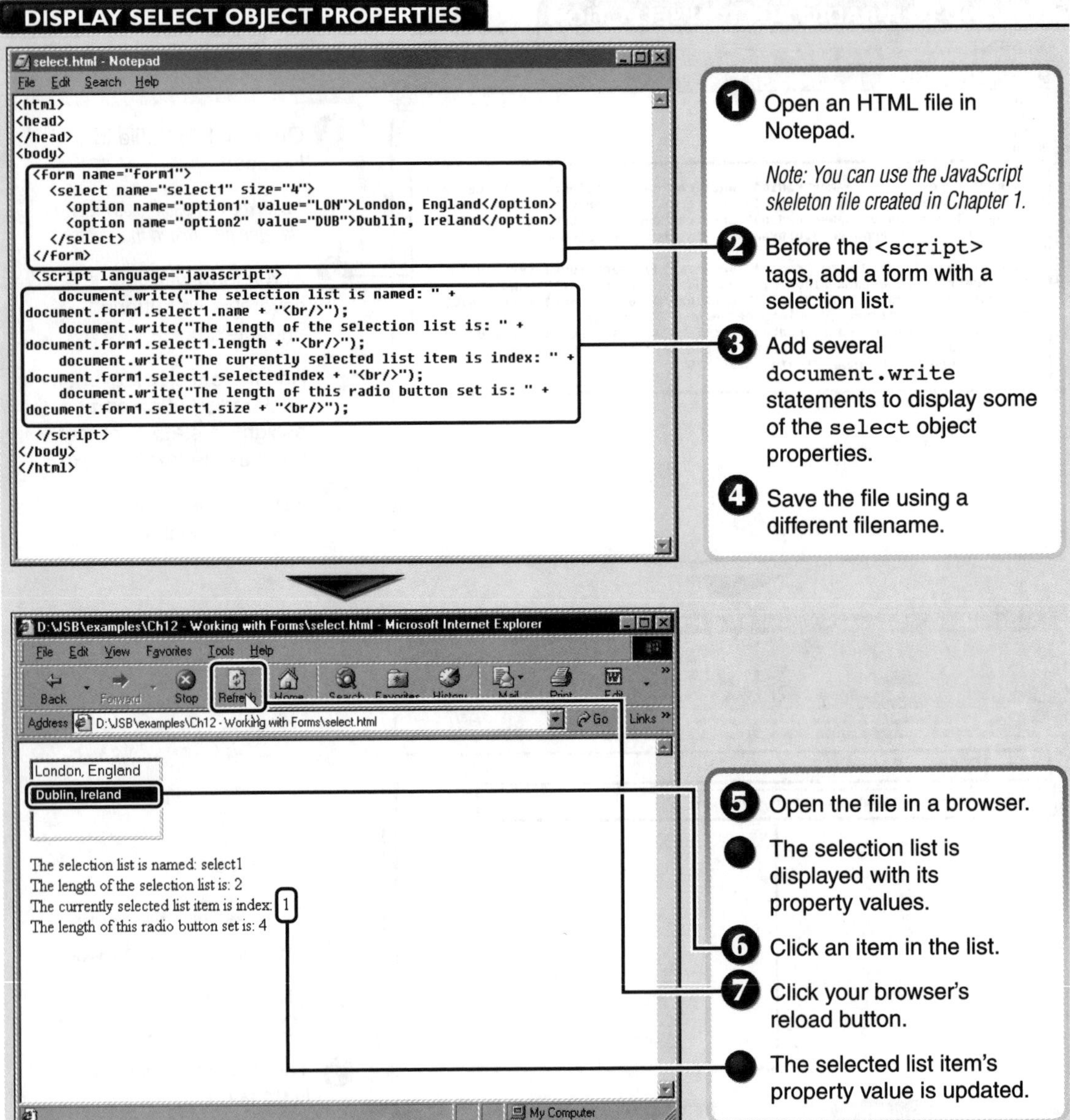
select.html - Notepad
File Edit Search Help
<html>
<head>
</head>
<body>
<form name="form1">
<select name="select1" size="4">
<option name="option1" value="LON">London, England</option>
<option name="option2" value="DUB">Dublin, Ireland</option>
</select>
</form>
<script language="javascript">
document.write("The selection list is named: " + document.form1.select1.name + "<br/>");
document.write("The length of the selection list is: " + document.form1.select1.length + "<br/>");
document.write("The currently selected list item is index: " + document.form1.select1.selectedIndex + "<br/>");
document.write("The length of this radio button set is: " + document.form1.select1.size + "<br/>");
</script>
</body>
</html>
D:\JSB\examples\Ch12 - Working with Forms\select.html - Microsoft Internet Explorer
London, England
Dublin, Ireland
The selection list is named: select1
The length of the selection list is: 2
The currently selected list item is index: 1
The length of this radio button set is: 4
My Computer

1. Open an HTML file in Notepad.

   Note: You can use the JavaScript skeleton file created in Chapter 1.

2. Before the `<script>` tags, add a form with a selection list.

3. Add several `document.write` statements to display some of the `select` object properties.

4. Save the file using a different filename.

5. Open the file in a browser.

- The selection list is displayed with its property values.

6. Click an item in the list.

7. Click your browser's reload button.

- The selected list item's property value is updated.

in an instant

RESPOND TO A LIST SELECTION

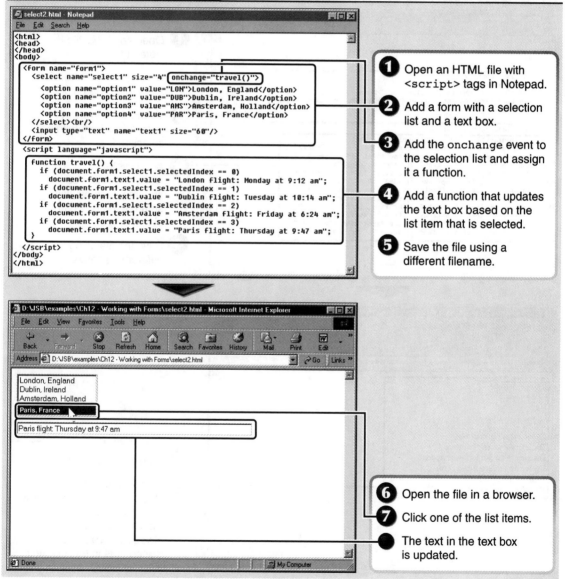

```
<html>
<head>
</head>
<body>
  <form name="form1">
    <select name="select1" size="4" onchange="travel()">
      <option name="option1" value="LON">London, England</option>
      <option name="option2" value="DUB">Dublin, Ireland</option>
      <option name="option3" value="AMS">Amsterdam, Holland</option>
      <option name="option4" value="PAR">Paris, France</option>
    </select><br/>
    <input type="text" name="text1" size="60"/>
  </form>
  <script language="javascript">
   function travel() {
     if (document.form1.select1.selectedIndex == 0)
       document.form1.text1.value = "London flight: Monday at 9:12 am";
     if (document.form1.select1.selectedIndex == 1)
       document.form1.text1.value = "Dublin flight: Tuesday at 10:14 am";
     if (document.form1.select1.selectedIndex == 2)
       document.form1.text1.value = "Amsterdam flight: Friday at 6:24 am";
     if (document.form1.select1.selectedIndex == 3)
       document.form1.text1.value = "Paris flight: Thursday at 9:47 am";
   }
  </script>
</body>
</html>
```

1. Open an HTML file with `<script>` tags in Notepad.
2. Add a form with a selection list and a text box.
3. Add the `onchange` event to the selection list and assign it a function.
4. Add a function that updates the text box based on the list item that is selected.
5. Save the file using a different filename.

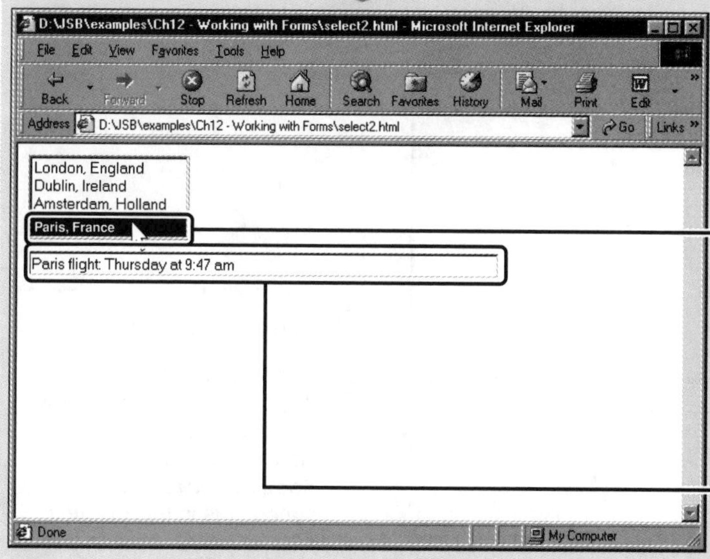

Browser window (D:\JSB\examples\Ch12 - Working with Forms\select2.html - Microsoft Internet Explorer):

London, England
Dublin, Ireland
Amsterdam, Holland
Paris, France

Paris flight: Thursday at 9:47 am

6. Open the file in a browser.
7. Click one of the list items.

- The text in the text box is updated.

WORK WITH SEPARATE SELECTION LIST ITEMS

The `option` object is a subobject of `select` and includes the properties `defaultSelected`, `index`, `length`, `name`, `selected`, `selectedIndex`, `text`, and `value`. `defaultSelected` returns the default selected item index. `selectedIndex` identifies the currently selected item. `selected` is a Boolean that identifies if the current item is selected. `text` returns the text between the `<option>` tags. The `option` object does not include any methods.

DISPLAY OPTION OBJECT PROPERTIES

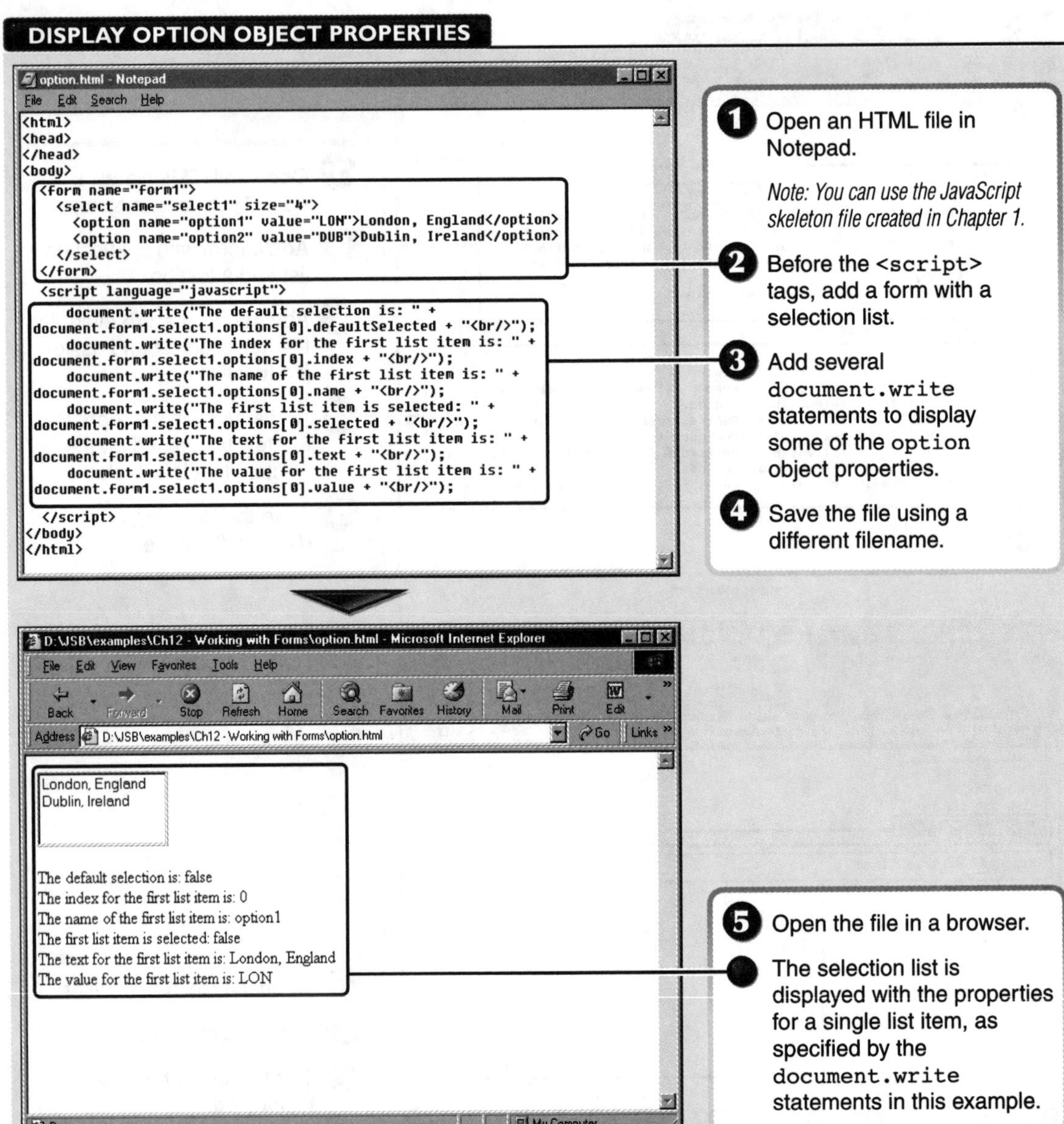

option.html - Notepad
File Edit Search Help
<html>
<head>
</head>
<body>
<form name="form1">
<select name="select1" size="4">
<option name="option1" value="LON">London, England</option>
<option name="option2" value="DUB">Dublin, Ireland</option>
</select>
</form>
<script language="javascript">
document.write("The default selection is: " + document.form1.select1.options[0].defaultSelected + "<br/>");
document.write("The index for the first list item is: " + document.form1.select1.options[0].index + "<br/>");
document.write("The name of the first list item is: " + document.form1.select1.options[0].name + "<br/>");
document.write("The first list item is selected: " + document.form1.select1.options[0].selected + "<br/>");
document.write("The text for the first list item is: " + document.form1.select1.options[0].text + "<br/>");
document.write("The value for the first list item is: " + document.form1.select1.options[0].value + "<br/>");
</script>
</body>
</html>
D:\JSB\examples\Ch12 - Working with Forms\option.html - Microsoft Internet Explorer
File Edit View Favorites Tools Help
Back Forward Stop Refresh Home Search Favorites History Mail Print Edit
Address D:\JSB\examples\Ch12 - Working with Forms\option.html
Go Links
London, England
Dublin, Ireland
The default selection is: false
The index for the first list item is: 0
The name of the first list item is: option1
The first list item is selected: false
The text for the first list item is: London, England
The value for the first list item is: LON
Done
My Computer

1. Open an HTML file in Notepad.

   Note: You can use the JavaScript skeleton file created in Chapter 1.

2. Before the `<script>` tags, add a form with a selection list.
3. Add several `document.write` statements to display some of the `option` object properties.
4. Save the file using a different filename.
5. Open the file in a browser.

- The selection list is displayed with the properties for a single list item, as specified by the `document.write` statements in this example.

in an instant

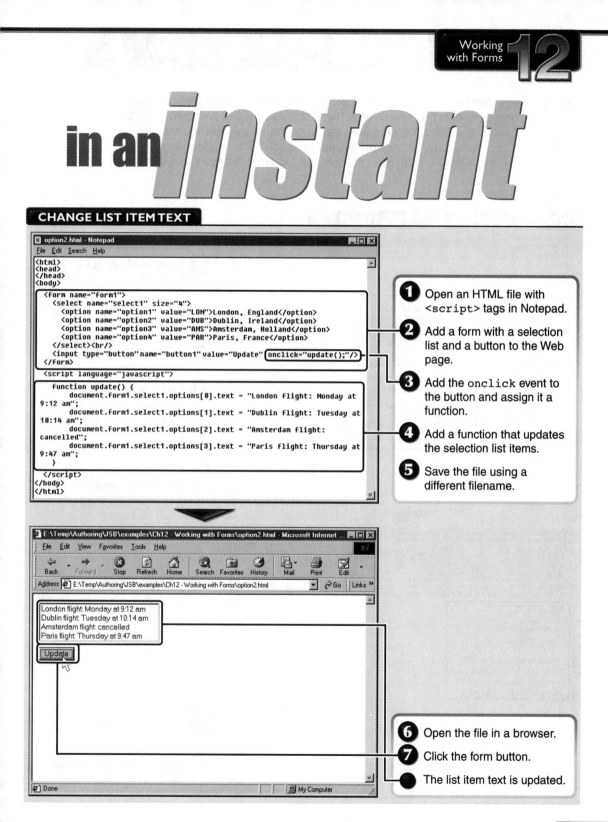

CHANGE LIST ITEM TEXT

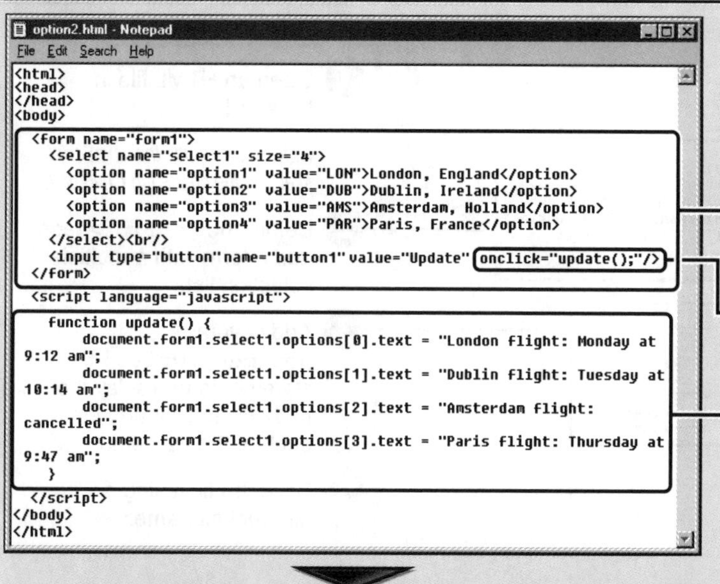
option2.html - Notepad
File Edit Search Help
<html>
<head>
</head>
<body>
<form name="form1">
<select name="select1" size="4">
<option name="option1" value="LON">London, England</option>
<option name="option2" value="DUB">Dublin, Ireland</option>
<option name="option3" value="AMS">Amsterdam, Holland</option>
<option name="option4" value="PAR">Paris, France</option>
</select>
<input type="button" name="button1" value="Update" onclick="update();"/>
</form>
<script language="javascript">
function update() {
document.form1.select1.options[0].text = "London flight: Monday at 9:12 am";
document.form1.select1.options[1].text = "Dublin flight: Tuesday at 10:14 am";
document.form1.select1.options[2].text = "Amsterdam flight: cancelled";
document.form1.select1.options[3].text = "Paris flight: Thursday at 9:47 am";
}
</script>
</body>
</html>

1. Open an HTML file with `<script>` tags in Notepad.
2. Add a form with a selection list and a button to the Web page.
3. Add the `onclick` event to the button and assign it a function.
4. Add a function that updates the selection list items.
5. Save the file using a different filename.

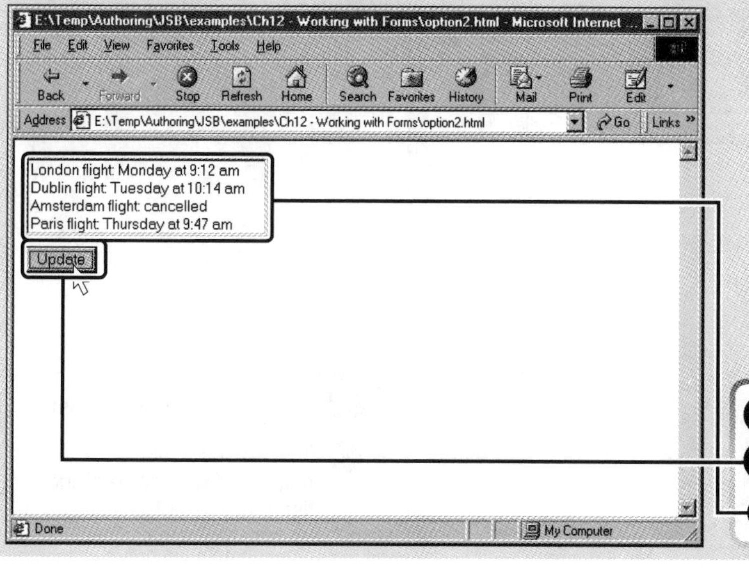
E:\Temp\Authoring\JSB\examples\Ch12 - Working with Forms\option2.html - Microsoft Internet ...
File Edit View Favorites Tools Help
Back Forward Stop Refresh Home Search Favorites History Mail Print Edit
Address E:\Temp\Authoring\JSB\examples\Ch12 - Working with Forms\option2.html
Go Links
London flight: Monday at 9:12 am
Dublin flight: Tuesday at 10:14 am
Amsterdam flight: cancelled
Paris flight: Thursday at 9:47 am
Update
Done
My Computer

6. Open the file in a browser.
7. Click the form button.

- The list item text is updated.

WORK WITH A MULTIPLE-SELECTION LIST

You can set selection list boxes to accept multiple selections by including the `multiple` attribute in the `<select>` tag. The `select` and `option` object properties work the same for multiple selection lists as they do for a single selection lists. The `selectedIndex` property, which for a single selection lists the index of the selected item, returns only the index of the lowest selected item.

WORK WITH A MULTIPLE-SELECTION LIST

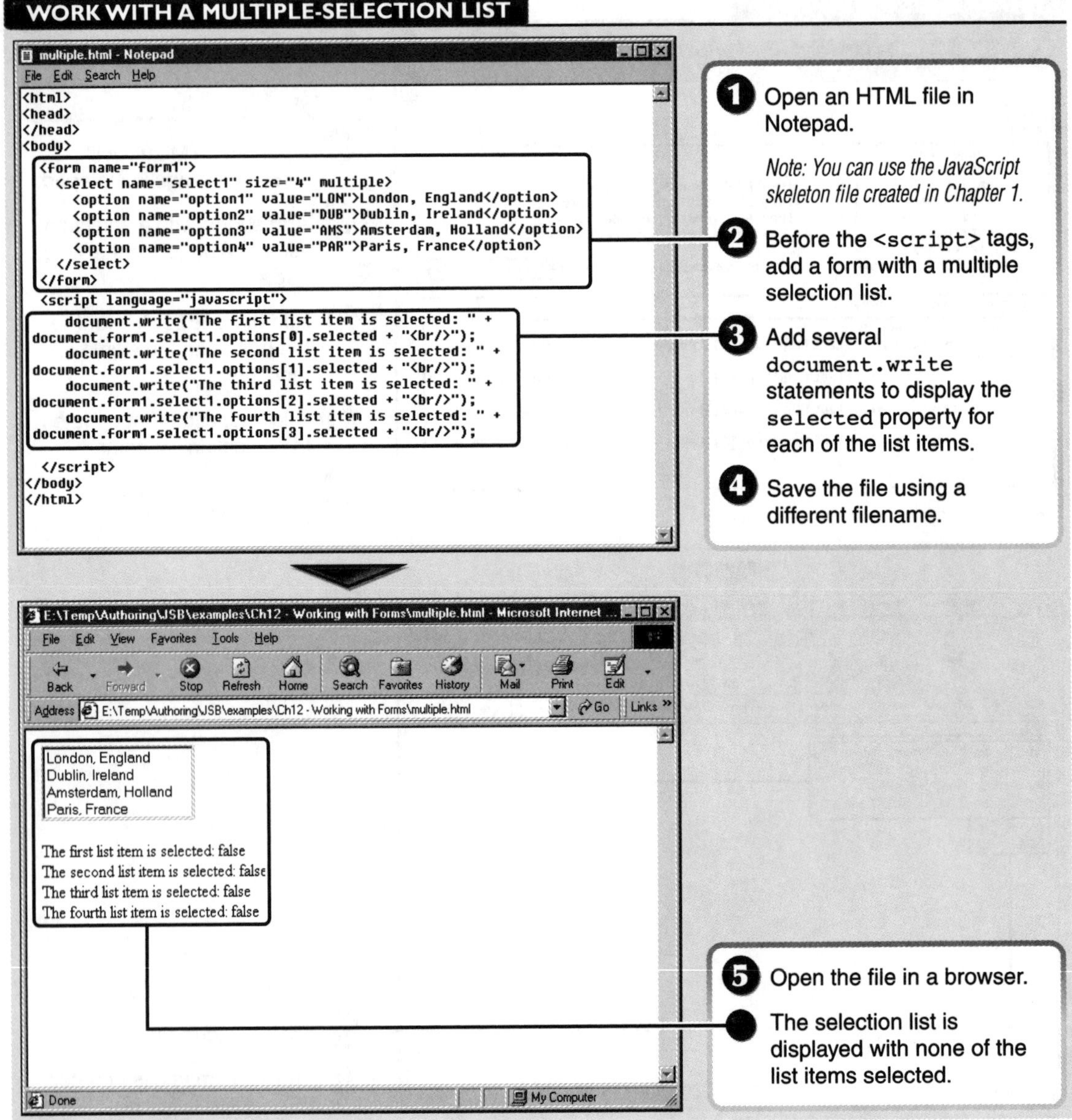

multiple.html - Notepad
File Edit Search Help
<html>
<head>
</head>
<body>
<form name="form1">
<select name="select1" size="4" multiple>
<option name="option1" value="LON">London, England</option>
<option name="option2" value="DUB">Dublin, Ireland</option>
<option name="option3" value="AMS">Amsterdam, Holland</option>
<option name="option4" value="PAR">Paris, France</option>
</select>
</form>
<script language="javascript">
document.write("The first list item is selected: " + document.form1.select1.options[0].selected + "<br/>");
document.write("The second list item is selected: " + document.form1.select1.options[1].selected + "<br/>");
document.write("The third list item is selected: " + document.form1.select1.options[2].selected + "<br/>");
document.write("The fourth list item is selected: " + document.form1.select1.options[3].selected + "<br/>");
</script>
</body>
</html>
E:\Temp\Authoring\JSB\examples\Ch12 - Working with Forms\multiple.html - Microsoft Internet ...
File Edit View Favorites Tools Help
Back Forward Stop Refresh Home Search Favorites History Mail Print Edit
Address E:\Temp\Authoring\JSB\examples\Ch12 - Working with Forms\multiple.html
Go Links
London, England
Dublin, Ireland
Amsterdam, Holland
Paris, France
The first list item is selected: false
The second list item is selected: false
The third list item is selected: false
The fourth list item is selected: false
Done
My Computer

1. Open an HTML file in Notepad.

   Note: You can use the JavaScript skeleton file created in Chapter 1.

2. Before the `<script>` tags, add a form with a multiple selection list.

3. Add several `document.write` statements to display the `selected` property for each of the list items.

4. Save the file using a different filename.

5. Open the file in a browser.

- The selection list is displayed with none of the list items selected.

in an instant

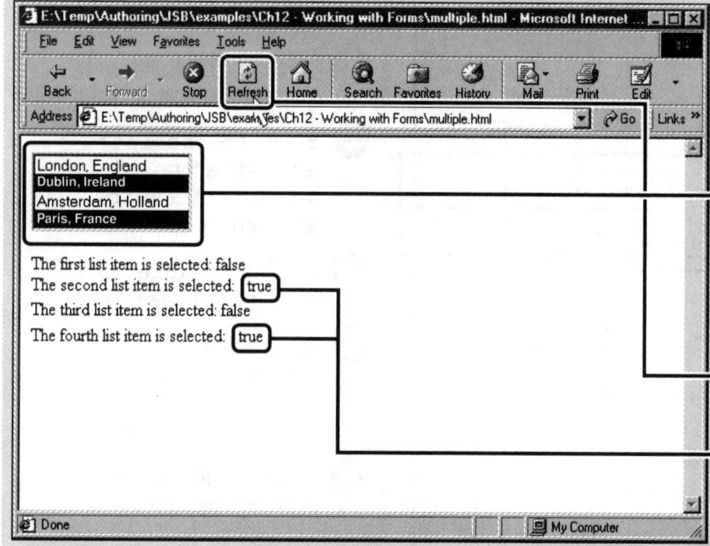

E:\Temp\Authoring\JSB\examples\Ch12 - Working with Forms\multiple.html - Microsoft Internet ...
London, England
Dublin, Ireland
Amsterdam, Holland
Paris, France
The first list item is selected: false
The second list item is selected: true
The third list item is selected: false
The fourth list item is selected: true

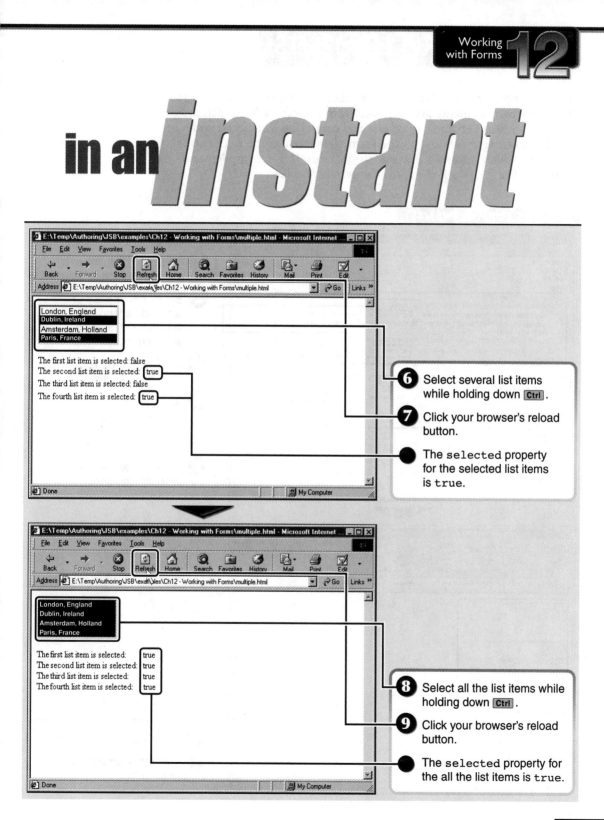

6. Select several list items while holding down Ctrl.
7. Click your browser's reload button.

- The `selected` property for the selected list items is `true`.

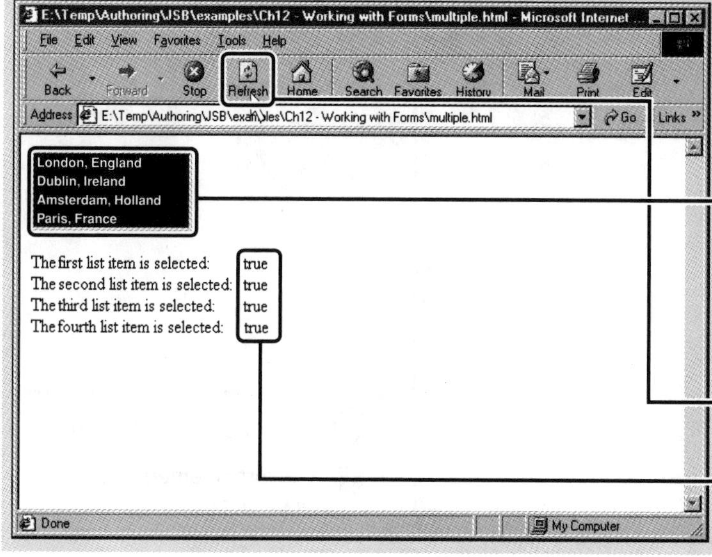

E:\Temp\Authoring\JSB\examples\Ch12 - Working with Forms\multiple.html - Microsoft Internet ...
London, England
Dublin, Ireland
Amsterdam, Holland
Paris, France
The first list item is selected: true
The second list item is selected: true
The third list item is selected: true
The fourth list item is selected: true

8. Select all the list items while holding down Ctrl.
9. Click your browser's reload button.

- The `selected` property for the all the list items is `true`.

DISABLE FORM ELEMENTS

Form elements can be disabled if the `disabled` attribute is included. Disabled form elements are removed from the tab order, which assigns focus. They also become grayed out and cannot be interacted with until enabled again. Almost all the form elements include a `disabled` property, which returns a Boolean value: `true` if the form element is disabled or `false` if the form element is enabled.

DISABLE FORM ELEMENTS

disabled.html - Notepad

```
<html>
<head>
</head>
<body>
  <form name="form1">
    <select name="select1" size="4" disabled >
      <option name="option1" value="LON">London, England</option>
      <option name="option2" value="DUB">Dublin, Ireland</option>
    </select><br/>
    <input type="text" name="text1" value="Update" disabled /><br/>
    <input type="checkbox" name="cb1" disabled >Computer Savvy?
  </form>
  <script language="javascript">
    document.write("The selection list is disabled: " +
document.form1.select1.disabled + "<br/>");
    document.write("The text field is disabled: " +
document.form1.text1.disabled + "<br/>");
    document.write("The checkbox is disabled: " +
document.form1.cb1.disabled + "<br/>");
  </script>
</body>
</html>
```

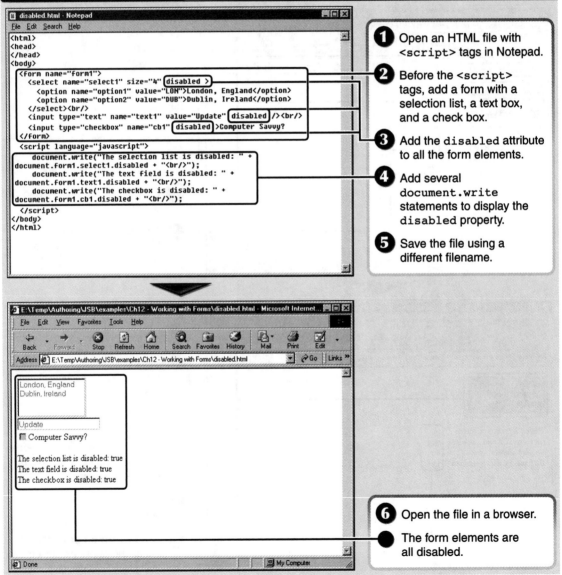

1. Open an HTML file with `<script>` tags in Notepad.
2. Before the `<script>` tags, add a form with a selection list, a text box, and a check box.
3. Add the `disabled` attribute to all the form elements.
4. Add several `document.write` statements to display the `disabled` property.
5. Save the file using a different filename.

E:\Temp\Authoring\JSB\examples\Ch12 - Working with Forms\disabled.html - Microsoft Internet...

London, England
Dublin, Ireland
Update
Computer Savvy?

The selection list is disabled: true
The text field is disabled: true
The checkbox is disabled: true

6. Open the file in a browser.

- The form elements are all disabled.

in an instant

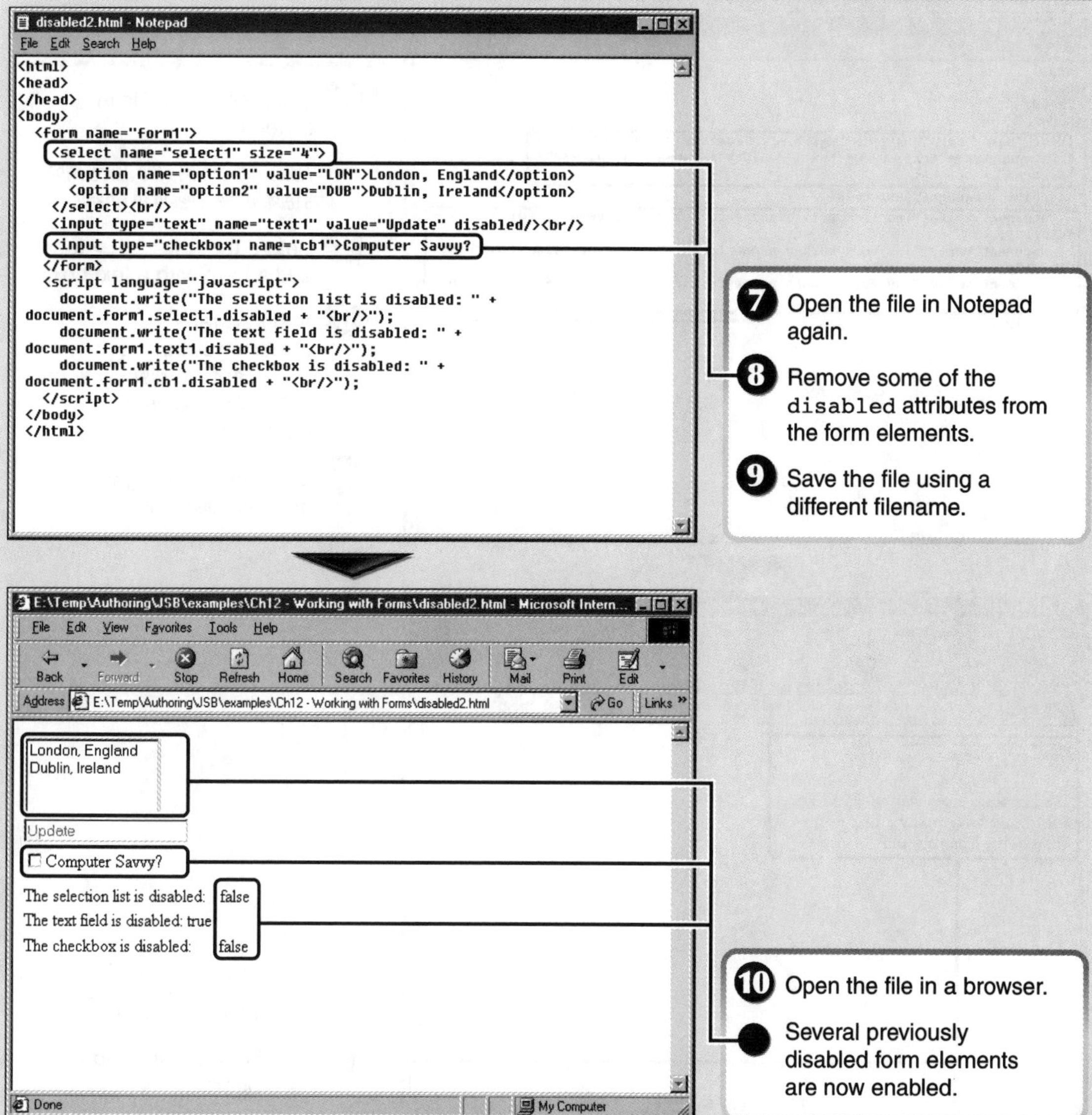

disabled2.html - Notepad
File Edit Search Help
<html>
<head>
</head>
<body>
<form name="form1">
<select name="select1" size="4">
<option name="option1" value="LON">London, England</option>
<option name="option2" value="DUB">Dublin, Ireland</option>
</select>
<input type="text" name="text1" value="Update" disabled/>
<input type="checkbox" name="cb1">Computer Savvy?
</form>
<script language="javascript">
document.write("The selection list is disabled: " + document.form1.select1.disabled + "<br/>");
document.write("The text field is disabled: " + document.form1.text1.disabled + "<br/>");
document.write("The checkbox is disabled: " + document.form1.cb1.disabled + "<br/>");
</script>
</body>
</html>
E:\Temp\Authoring\JSB\examples\Ch12 - Working with Forms\disabled2.html - Microsoft Intern...
File Edit View Favorites Tools Help
Back Forward Stop Refresh Home Search Favorites History Mail Print Edit
Address E:\Temp\Authoring\JSB\examples\Ch12 - Working with Forms\disabled2.html
Go Links
London, England
Dublin, Ireland
Update
Computer Savvy?
The selection list is disabled: false
The text field is disabled: true
The checkbox is disabled: false
Done
My Computer

7. Open the file in Notepad again.
8. Remove some of the `disabled` attributes from the form elements.
9. Save the file using a different filename.
10. Open the file in a browser.

- Several previously disabled form elements are now enabled.

WORK WITH FORMS

The form object properties include action, elements, length, method, and target. The action and method properties determine where and how the form data gets passed to the server. The form object methods that reset and send the form data to the server are reset() and submit(). Using these methods, you can reset or submit the form data using any JavaScript event.

DISPLAY FORM OBJECT PROPERTIES

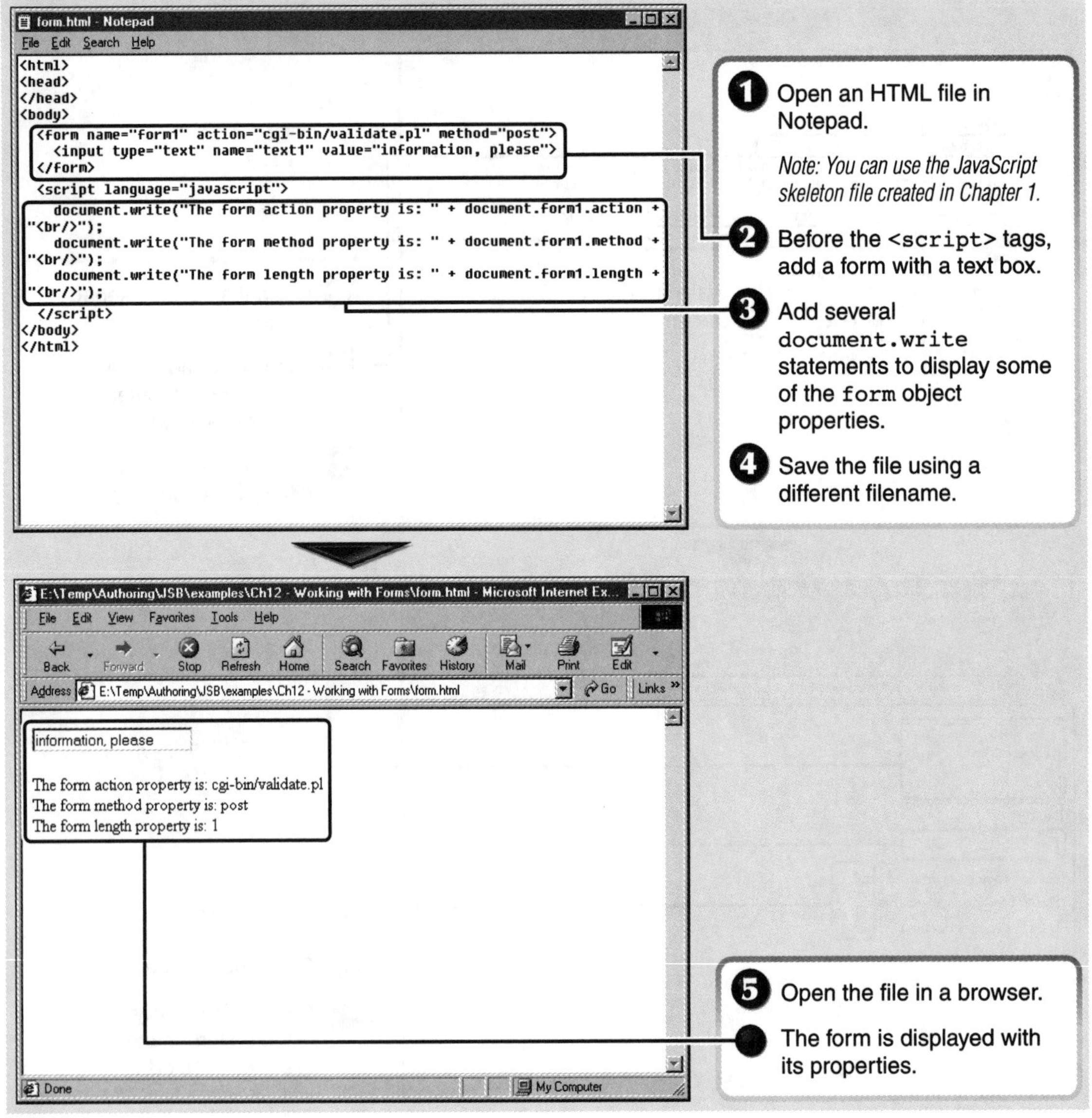

form.html - Notepad
File Edit Search Help
<html>
<head>
</head>
<body>
<form name="form1" action="cgi-bin/validate.pl" method="post">
<input type="text" name="text1" value="information, please">
</form>
<script language="javascript">
document.write("The form action property is: " + document.form1.action + "<br/>");
document.write("The form method property is: " + document.form1.method + "<br/>");
document.write("The form length property is: " + document.form1.length + "<br/>");
</script>
</body>
</html>
E:\Temp\Authoring\JSB\examples\Ch12 - Working with Forms\form.html - Microsoft Internet Ex...
information, please
The form action property is: cgi-bin/validate.pl
The form method property is: post
The form length property is: 1
Done
My Computer

1. Open an HTML file in Notepad.

   Note: You can use the JavaScript skeleton file created in Chapter 1.

2. Before the <script> tags, add a form with a text box.
3. Add several document.write statements to display some of the form object properties.
4. Save the file using a different filename.
5. Open the file in a browser.

- The form is displayed with its properties.

in an instant

DISPLAY FORM ELEMENT PROPERTIES

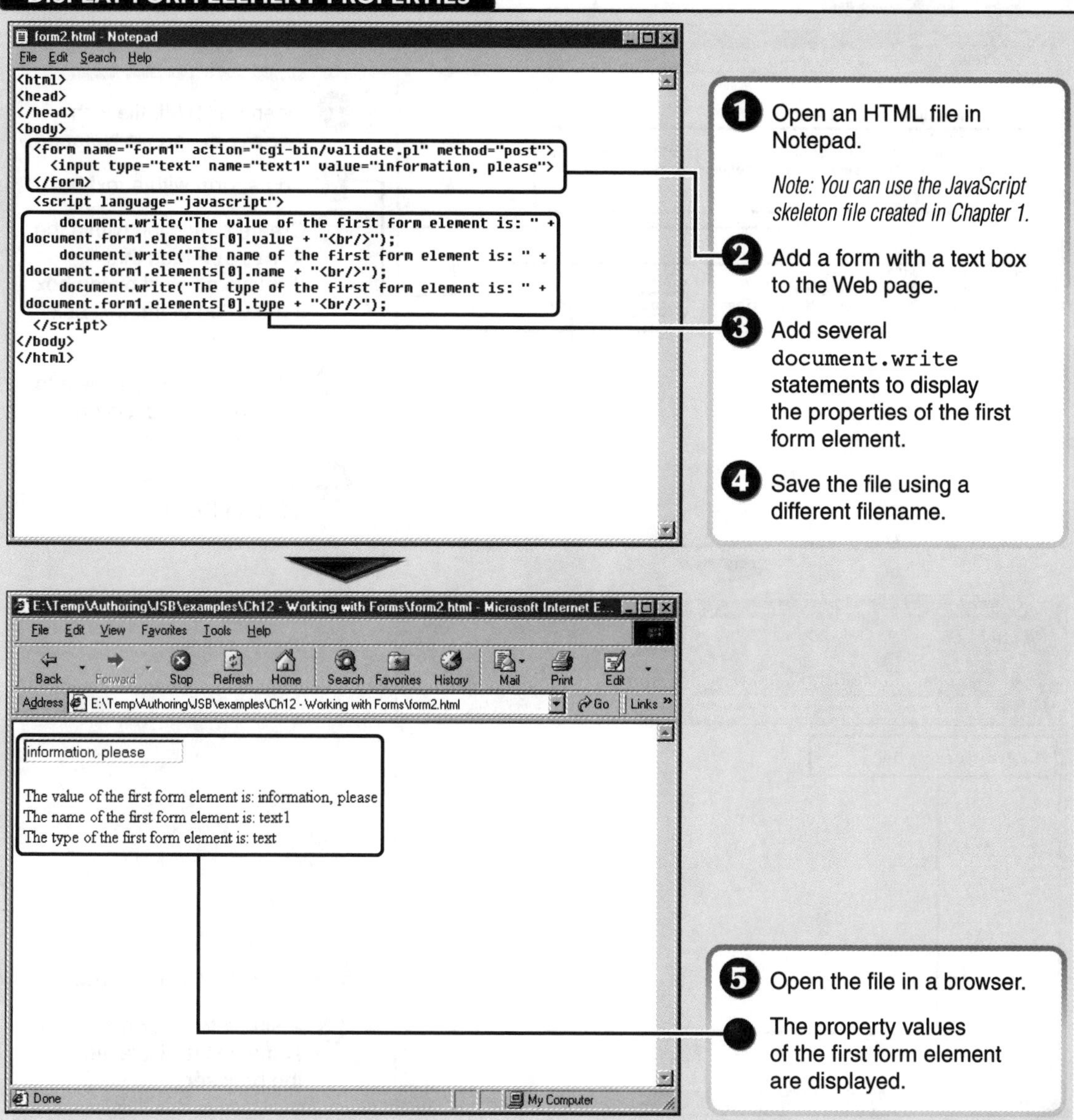
form2.html - Notepad
File Edit Search Help
<html>
<head>
</head>
<body>
<form name="form1" action="cgi-bin/validate.pl" method="post">
<input type="text" name="text1" value="information, please">
</form>
<script language="javascript">
document.write("The value of the first form element is: " + document.form1.elements[0].value + "<br/>");
document.write("The name of the first form element is: " + document.form1.elements[0].name + "<br/>");
document.write("The type of the first form element is: " + document.form1.elements[0].type + "<br/>");
</script>
</body>
</html>
E:\Temp\Authoring\JSB\examples\Ch12 - Working with Forms\form2.html - Microsoft Internet E...
File Edit View Favorites Tools Help
Back Forward Stop Refresh Home Search Favorites History Mail Print Edit
Address E:\Temp\Authoring\JSB\examples\Ch12 - Working with Forms\form2.html
Go Links
information, please
The value of the first form element is: information, please
The name of the first form element is: text1
The type of the first form element is: text
Done
My Computer

1. Open an HTML file in Notepad.

   Note: You can use the JavaScript skeleton file created in Chapter 1.

2. Add a form with a text box to the Web page.
3. Add several `document.write` statements to display the properties of the first form element.
4. Save the file using a different filename.
5. Open the file in a browser.

- The property values of the first form element are displayed.

VALIDATE FORMS

You can use JavaScript to validate form data before it is sent to the server. If invalid values are identified and corrected before making a server request, many unnecessary server requests can be eliminated. The way to validate form data is different for every type of data, but JavaScript includes many operators that help you customize the validation routines.

VALIDATE FORMS

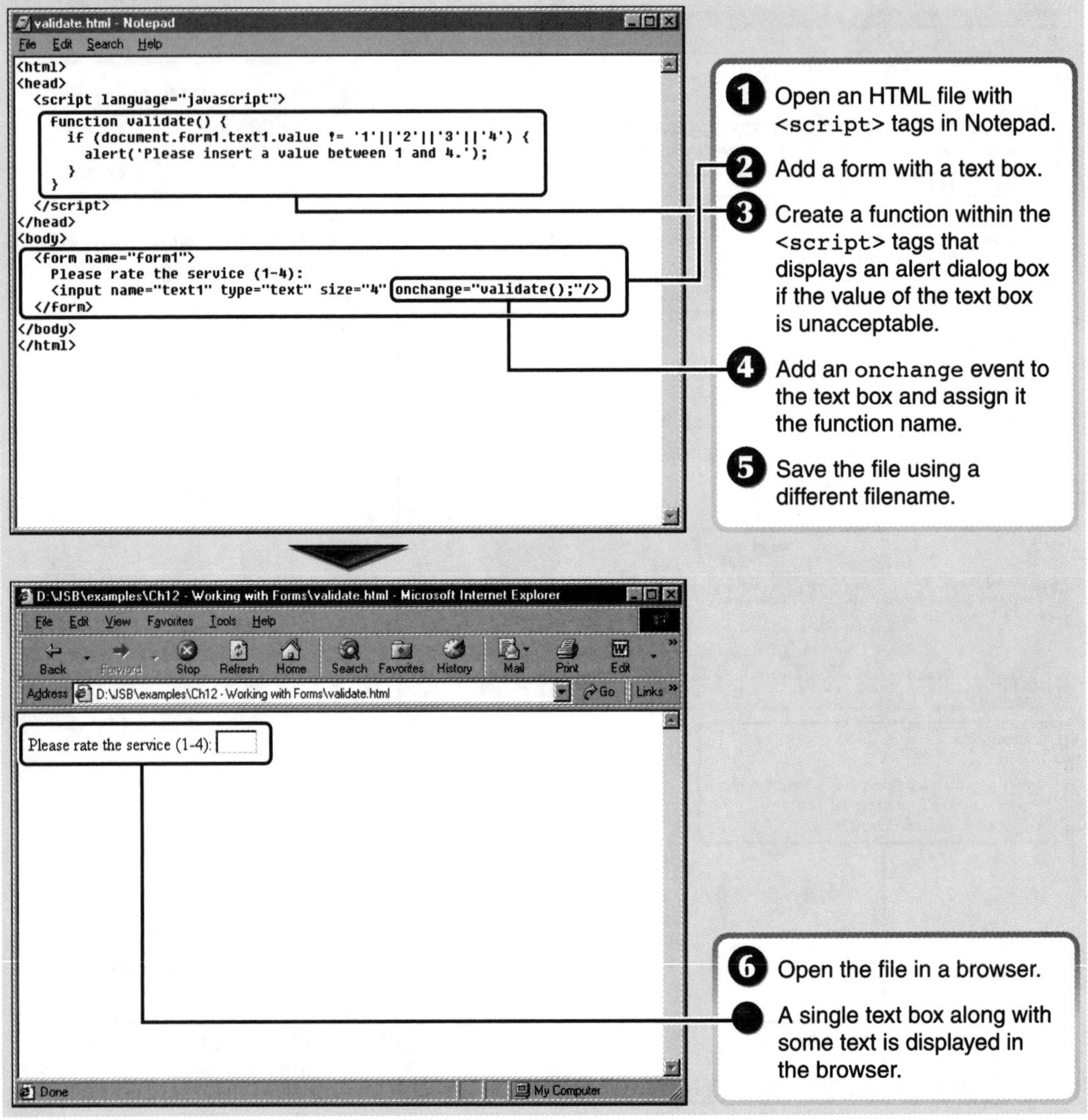
validate.html - Notepad
<html>
<head>
<script language="javascript">
function validate() {
if (document.form1.text1.value != '1'||'2'||'3'||'4') {
alert('Please insert a value between 1 and 4.');
}
}
</script>
</head>
<body>
<form name="form1">
Please rate the service (1-4):
<input name="text1" type="text" size="4" onchange="validate();"/>
</form>
</body>
</html>
1 Open an HTML file with <script> tags in Notepad.
2 Add a form with a text box.
3 Create a function within the <script> tags that displays an alert dialog box if the value of the text box is unacceptable.
4 Add an onchange event to the text box and assign it the function name.
5 Save the file using a different filename.
D:\JSB\examples\Ch12 - Working with Forms\validate.html - Microsoft Internet Explorer
Please rate the service (1-4):
6 Open the file in a browser.
A single text box along with some text is displayed in the browser.

in an instant

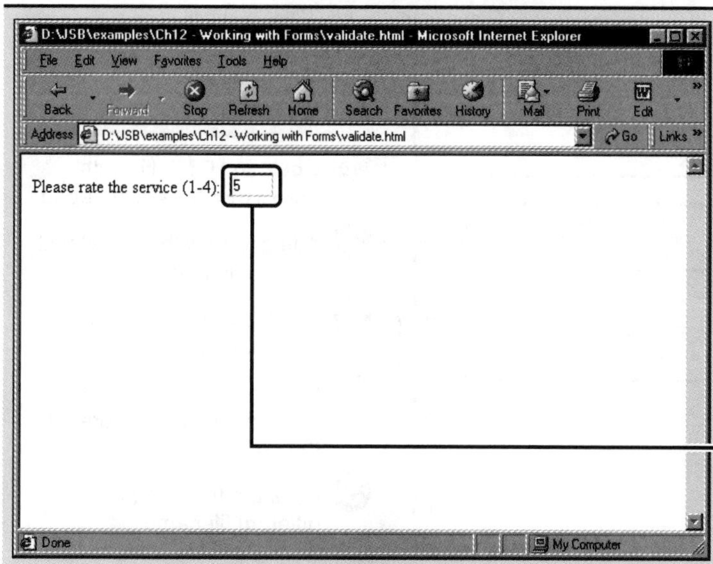

Please rate the service (1-4): 5

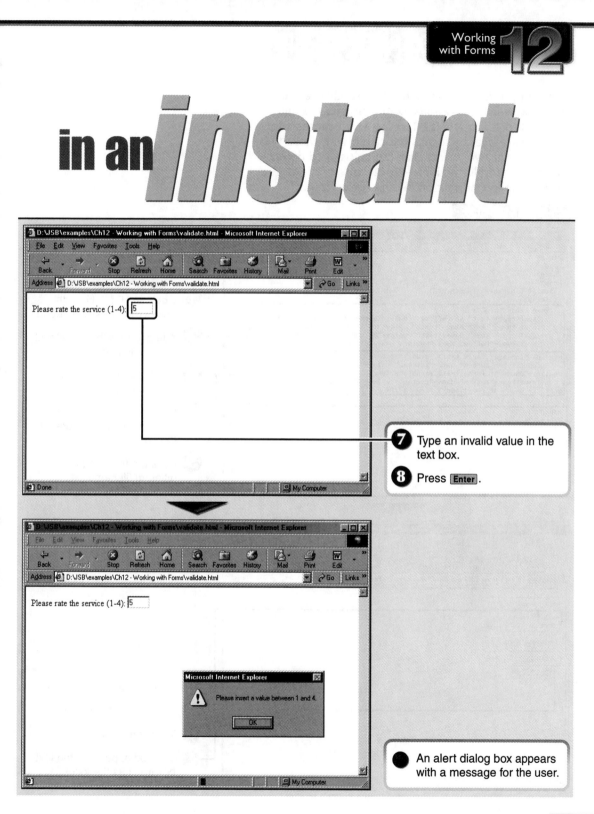

7. Type an invalid value in the text box.

8. Press Enter.

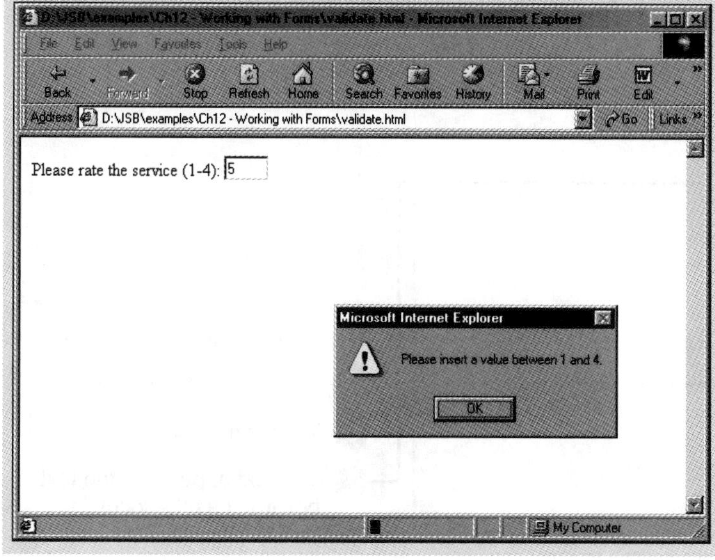

Please rate the service (1-4): 5

Microsoft Internet Explorer

Please insert a value between 1 and 4.

OK

- An alert dialog box appears with a message for the user.

CONTROL FORM FOCUS

You can use the focus() method to change the focus between the various form elements. A similar method to focus() is blur(), which causes a form element to lose the focus. Associated with these two methods are two events that can be used to detect the focus and blur actions — onFocus and onBlur (see the following section, "Using Focus Events").

CHANGE FOCUS

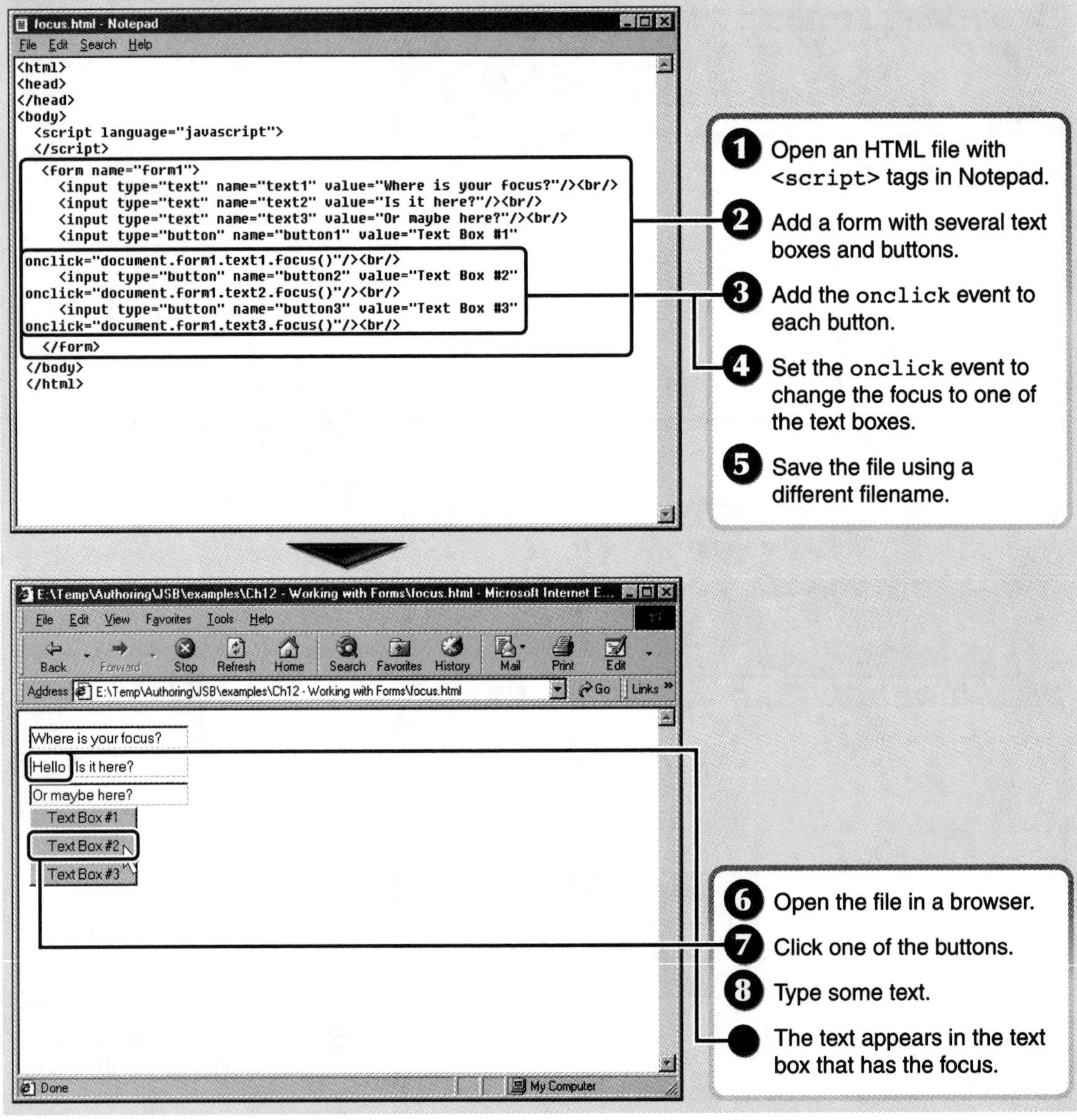

focus.html - Notepad
File Edit Search Help
<html>
<head>
</head>
<body>
<script language="javascript">
</script>
<form name="form1">
<input type="text" name="text1" value="Where is your focus?"/>
<input type="text" name="text2" value="Is it here?"/>
<input type="text" name="text3" value="Or maybe here?"/>
<input type="button" name="button1" value="Text Box #1"
onclick="document.form1.text1.focus()"/>
<input type="button" name="button2" value="Text Box #2"
onclick="document.form1.text2.focus()"/>
<input type="button" name="button3" value="Text Box #3"
onclick="document.form1.text3.focus()"/>
</form>
</body>
</html>
1 Open an HTML file with <script> tags in Notepad.
2 Add a form with several text boxes and buttons.
3 Add the onclick event to each button.
4 Set the onclick event to change the focus to one of the text boxes.
5 Save the file using a different filename.
E:\Temp\Authoring\JSB\examples\Ch12 - Working with Forms\focus.html - Microsoft Internet E...
File Edit View Favorites Tools Help
Back Forward Stop Refresh Home Search Favorites History Mail Print Edit
Address E:\Temp\Authoring\JSB\examples\Ch12 - Working with Forms\focus.html
Go Links
Where is your focus?
Hello Is it here?
Or maybe here?
Text Box #1
Text Box #2
Text Box #3
Done
My Computer
6 Open the file in a browser.
7 Click one of the buttons.
8 Type some text.
The text appears in the text box that has the focus.

in an instant

USING BLUR

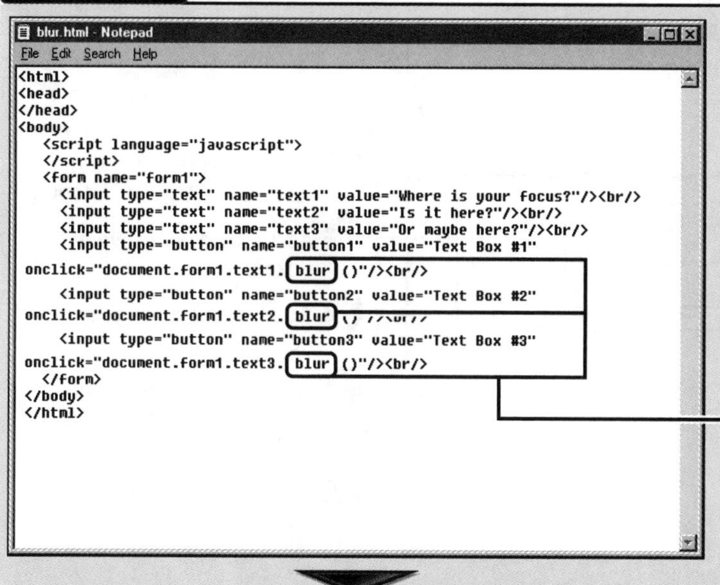
blur.html - Notepad
File Edit Search Help
<html>
<head>
</head>
<body>
<script language="javascript">
</script>
<form name="form1">
<input type="text" name="text1" value="Where is your focus?"/>
<input type="text" name="text2" value="Is it here?"/>
<input type="text" name="text3" value="Or maybe here?"/>
<input type="button" name="button1" value="Text Box #1"
onclick="document.form1.text1.blur()"/>
<input type="button" name="button2" value="Text Box #2"
onclick="document.form1.text2.blur
<input type="button" name="button3" value="Text Box #3"
onclick="document.form1.text3.blur()"/>
</form>
</body>
</html>

1. Open the file that you saved in step **5** of the preceding steps in Notepad.
2. Change the `focus()` methods to `blur()`.
3. Save the file using a different filename.

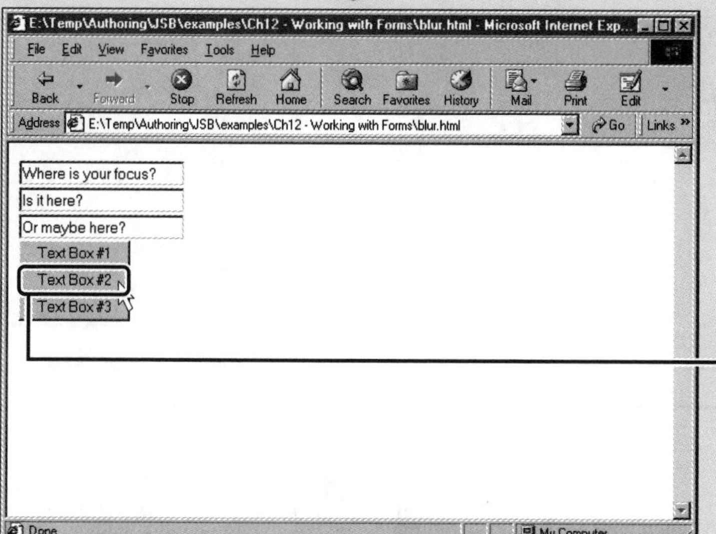
E:\Temp\Authoring\JSB\examples\Ch12 - Working with Forms\blur.html - Microsoft Internet Exp...
File Edit View Favorites Tools Help
Back Forward Stop Refresh Home Search Favorites History Mail Print Edit
Address E:\Temp\Authoring\JSB\examples\Ch12 - Working with Forms\blur.html Go Links
Where is your focus?
Is it here?
Or maybe here?
Text Box #1
Text Box #2
Text Box #3
Done
My Computer

4. Open the file in a browser.
5. Click one of the buttons.
6. Type some text.

- No text appears in any of the text boxes because they have lost the focus.

USING FOCUS EVENTS

You can set the order that each form element receives the focus by using the `tabindex` attribute. You can also detect when a form element receives or loses the focus by using the `onFocus` and `onBlur` events. The `onFocus` event can be used on every form element, but `onBlur` can be used only with the `select`, `option`, `text`, `password`, and `textarea` form elements.

DETECT FOCUS

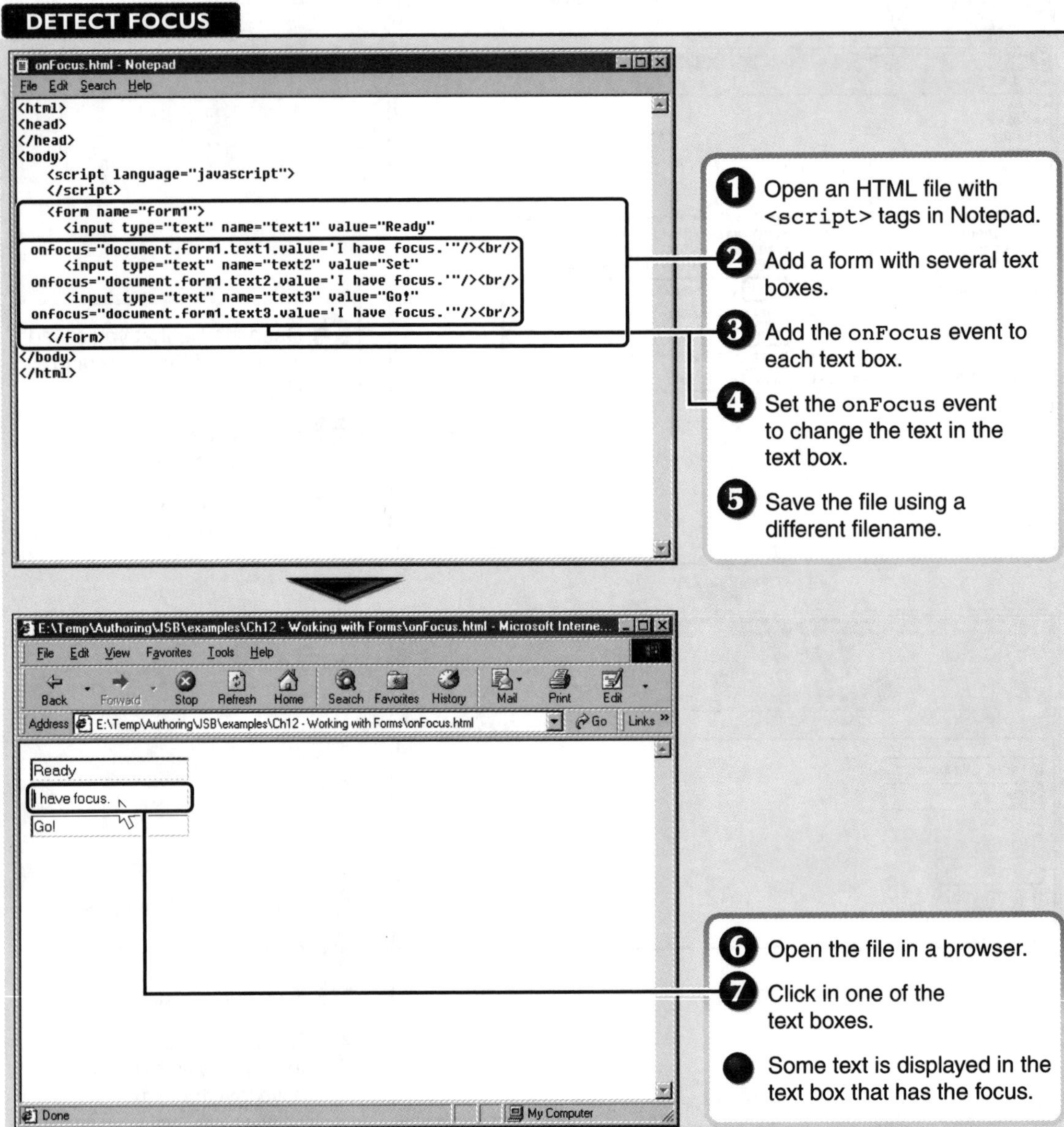

```
<html>
<head>
</head>
<body>
   <script language="javascript">
   </script>
   <form name="form1">
     <input type="text" name="text1" value="Ready"
 onfocus="document.form1.text1.value='I have focus.'"/><br/>
     <input type="text" name="text2" value="Set"
 onfocus="document.form1.text2.value='I have focus.'"/><br/>
     <input type="text" name="text3" value="Go!"
 onfocus="document.form1.text3.value='I have focus.'"/><br/>
   </form>
</body>
</html>
```

onFocus.html - Notepad
File Edit Search Help
E:\Temp\Authoring\JSB\examples\Ch12 - Working with Forms\onFocus.html - Microsoft Interne...
File Edit View Favorites Tools Help
Back Forward Stop Refresh Home Search Favorites History Mail Print Edit
Address E:\Temp\Authoring\JSB\examples\Ch12 - Working with Forms\onFocus.html
Go Links
Ready
I have focus.
Go!
Done
My Computer

1. Open an HTML file with `<script>` tags in Notepad.
2. Add a form with several text boxes.
3. Add the `onFocus` event to each text box.
4. Set the `onFocus` event to change the text in the text box.
5. Save the file using a different filename.
6. Open the file in a browser.
7. Click in one of the text boxes.

- Some text is displayed in the text box that has the focus.

in an instant

DETECT BLUR

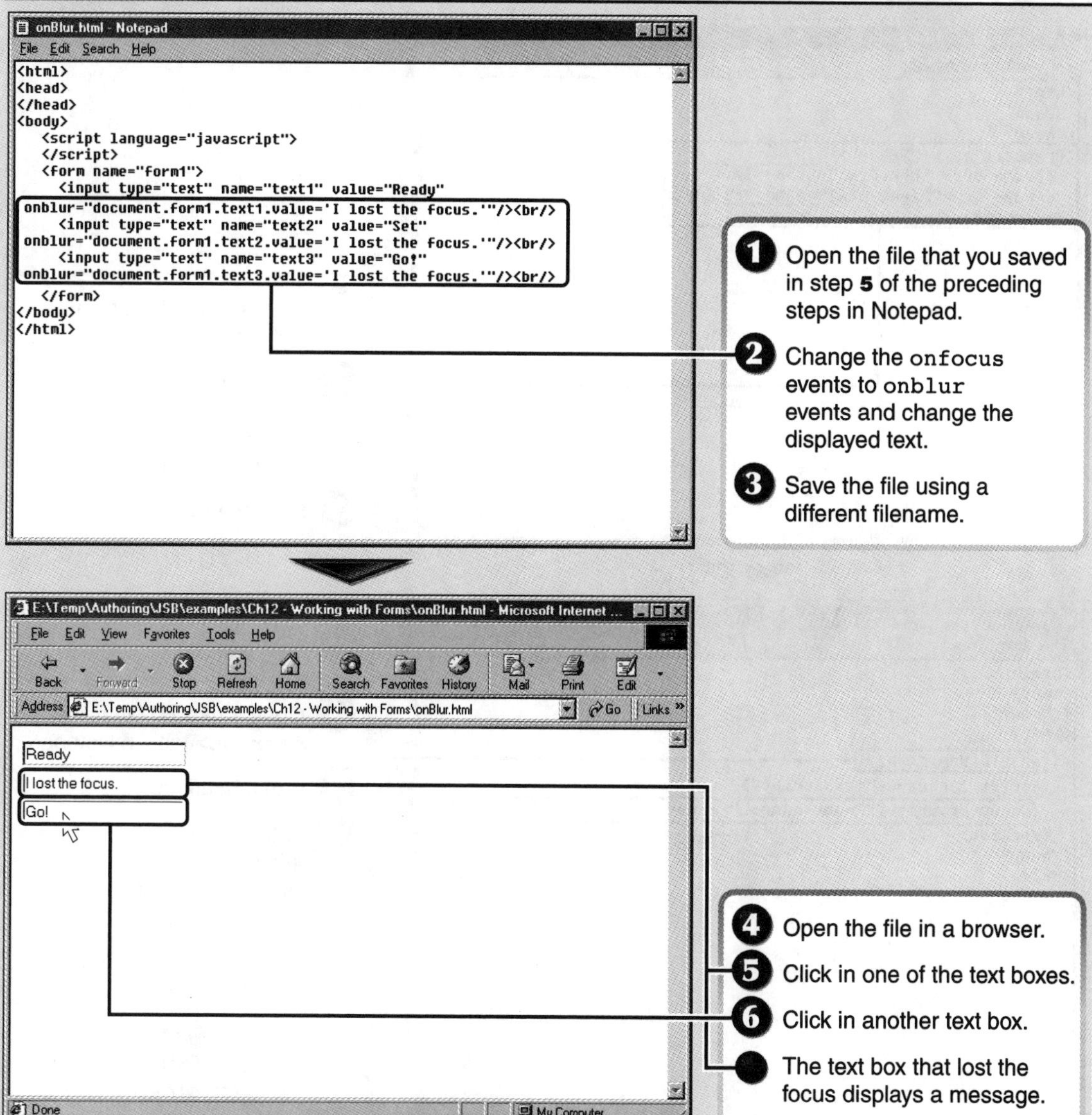
onBlur.html - Notepad
File Edit Search Help
```
<html>
<head>
</head>
<body>
<script language="javascript">
</script>
<form name="form1">
<input type="text" name="text1" value="Ready"
onblur="document.form1.text1.value='I lost the focus.'"/><br/>
<input type="text" name="text2" value="Set"
onblur="document.form1.text2.value='I lost the focus.'"/><br/>
<input type="text" name="text3" value="Go!"
onblur="document.form1.text3.value='I lost the focus.'"/><br/>
</form>
</body>
</html>
```
1 Open the file that you saved in step 5 of the preceding steps in Notepad.
2 Change the onfocus events to onblur events and change the displayed text.
3 Save the file using a different filename.
E:\Temp\Authoring\JSB\examples\Ch12 - Working with Forms\onBlur.html - Microsoft Internet ...
File Edit View Favorites Tools Help
Back Forward Stop Refresh Home Search Favorites History Mail Print Edit
Address E:\Temp\Authoring\JSB\examples\Ch12 - Working with Forms\onBlur.html Go Links
Ready
I lost the focus.
Go!
Done
My Computer
4 Open the file in a browser.
5 Click in one of the text boxes.
6 Click in another text box.
The text box that lost the focus displays a message.

WORK WITH THE FRAME OBJECT

The `frame` object includes the properties `frames`, `onBlur`, `onFocus`, `parent`, `self`, `top`, and `window`. The `frames` property is an array of all the frames in a frameset. You can reference the frames by an index value that matches the order that they appear in the HTML file. The `frame` object also includes methods such as `open()` and `close()`, which are the same as for the `document` object.

WORK WITH THE FRAME OBJECT

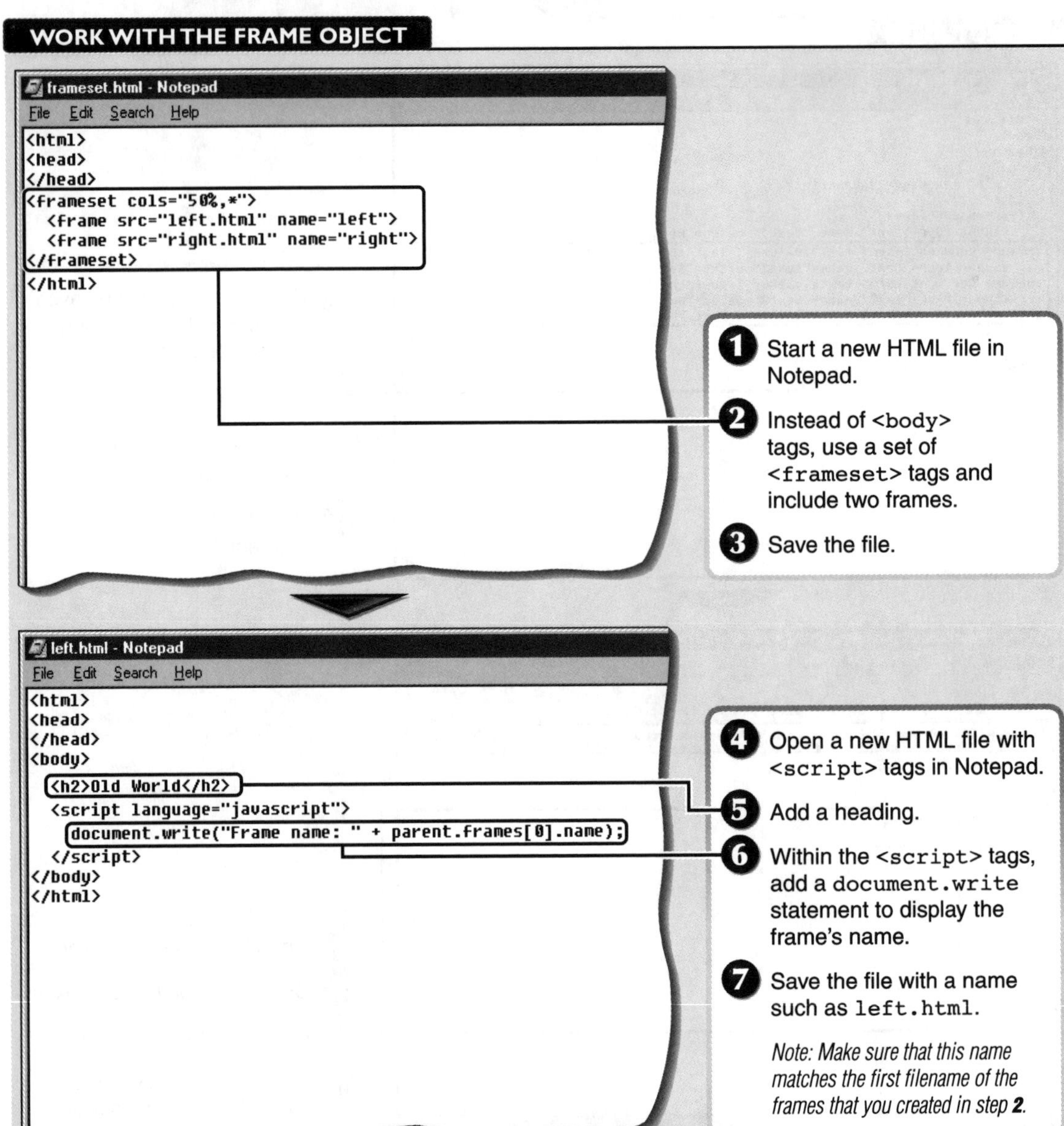

frameset.html - Notepad
File Edit Search Help
<html>
<head>
</head>
<frameset cols="50%,*">
<frame src="left.html" name="left">
<frame src="right.html" name="right">
</frameset>
</html>
left.html - Notepad
File Edit Search Help
<html>
<head>
</head>
<body>
<h2>Old World</h2>
<script language="javascript">
document.write("Frame name: " + parent.frames[0].name);
</script>
</body>
</html>

1. Start a new HTML file in Notepad.
2. Instead of `<body>` tags, use a set of `<frameset>` tags and include two frames.
3. Save the file.
4. Open a new HTML file with `<script>` tags in Notepad.
5. Add a heading.
6. Within the `<script>` tags, add a `document.write` statement to display the frame's name.
7. Save the file with a name such as `left.html`.

*Note: Make sure that this name matches the first filename of the frames that you created in step **2**.*

in an instant

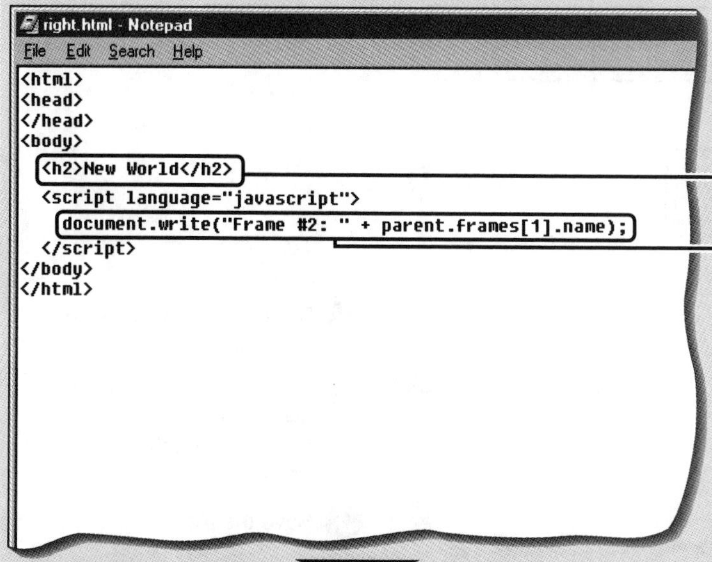

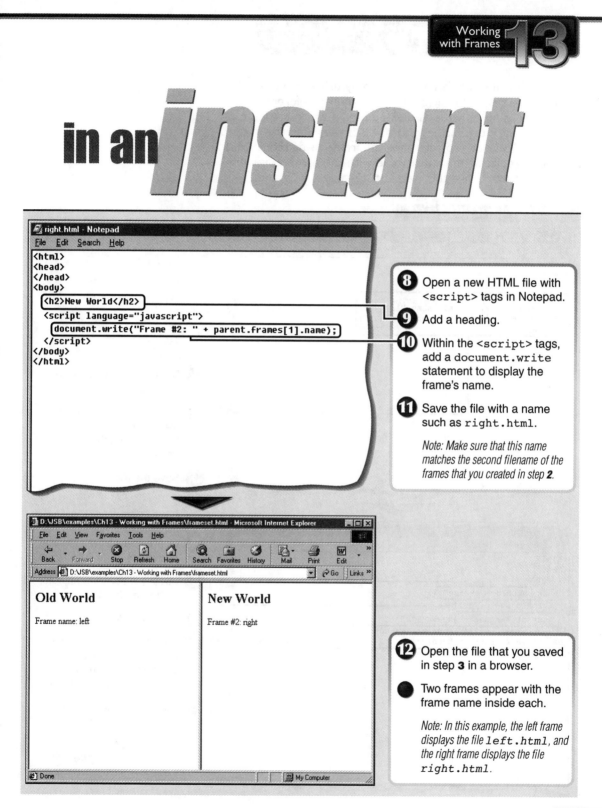

right.html - Notepad
File Edit Search Help
<html>
<head>
</head>
<body>
<h2>New World</h2>
<script language="javascript">
document.write("Frame #2: " + parent.frames[1].name);
</script>
</body>
</html>

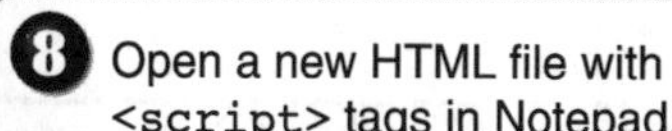

8 Open a new HTML file with `<script>` tags in Notepad.

9 Add a heading.

10 Within the `<script>` tags, add a `document.write` statement to display the frame's name.

11 Save the file with a name such as `right.html`.

*Note: Make sure that this name matches the second filename of the frames that you created in step **2**.*

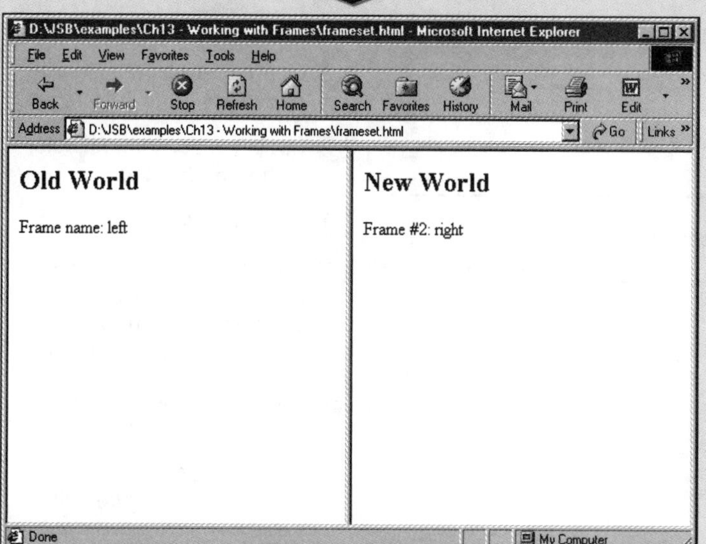

D:\JSB\examples\Ch13 - Working with Frames\frameset.html - Microsoft Internet Explorer
File Edit View Favorites Tools Help
Back Forward Stop Refresh Home Search Favorites History Mail Print Edit
Address D:\JSB\examples\Ch13 - Working with Frames\frameset.html
Go Links
Old World
Frame name: left
New World
Frame #2: right
Done
My Computer

12 Open the file that you saved in step **3** in a browser.

- Two frames appear with the frame name inside each.

Note: In this example, the left frame displays the file `left.html`, and the right frame displays the file `right.html`.

ACCESS FRAMES BY NAME

Although you can reference a frame by using its index value, such as `parent.frames[0]`, you can also reference a frame by using its name as defined by the `name` attribute of the `<frame>` tag, such as `parent.frame1` for the frame `frame1`. You can also reference the frame using the `frames` array by replacing the index value with the name value in quotation marks like this: `parent.frames["frame1"]`.

ACCESS FRAMES BY NAME

frameset2.html - Notepad

File Edit Search Help

```
<html>
<head>
</head>
<frameset cols="50%,*">
  <frame src="left2.html" name="left">
  <frame src="right2.html" name="right">
</frameset>
</html>
```

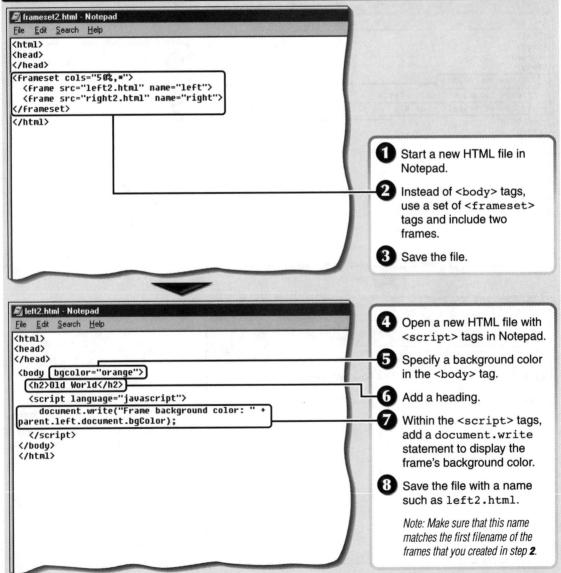

1. Start a new HTML file in Notepad.
2. Instead of `<body>` tags, use a set of `<frameset>` tags and include two frames.
3. Save the file.

left2.html - Notepad

File Edit Search Help

```
<html>
<head>
</head>
 <body bgcolor="orange">
  <h2>Old World</h2>
  <script language="javascript">
    document.write("Frame background color: " +
parent.left.document.bgColor);
  </script>
 </body>
 </html>
```

4. Open a new HTML file with `<script>` tags in Notepad.
5. Specify a background color in the `<body>` tag.
6. Add a heading.
7. Within the `<script>` tags, add a `document.write` statement to display the frame's background color.
8. Save the file with a name such as `left2.html`.

*Note: Make sure that this name matches the first filename of the frames that you created in step **2**.*

in an instant

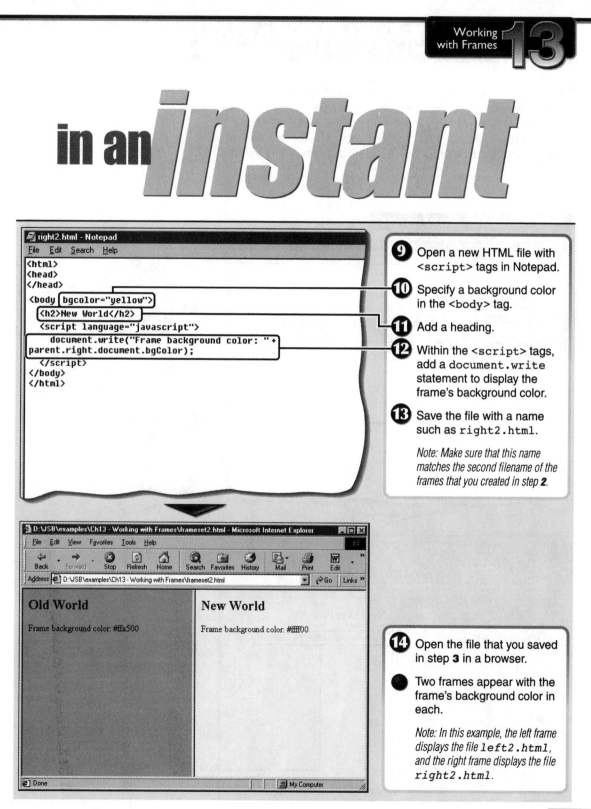

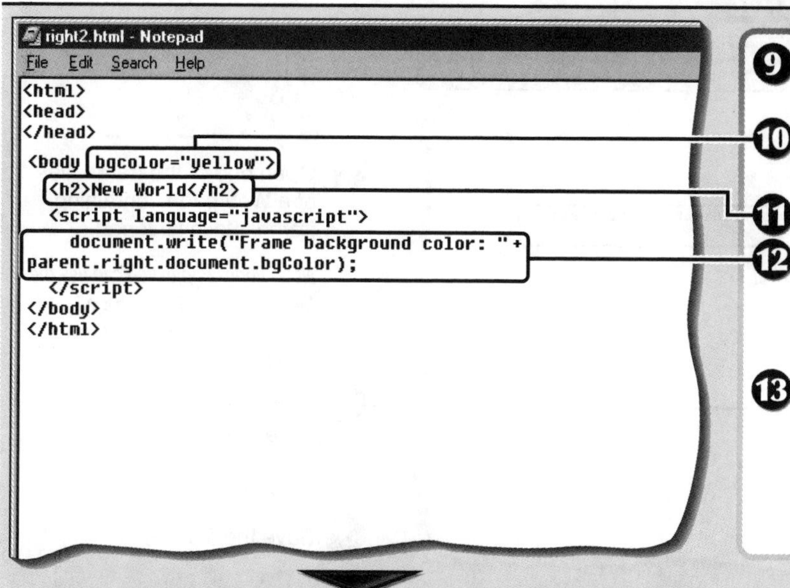
right2.html - Notepad
File Edit Search Help
<html>
<head>
</head>
<body bgcolor="yellow">
<h2>New World</h2>
<script language="javascript">
document.write("Frame background color: " +
parent.right.document.bgColor);
</script>
</body>
</html>

9. Open a new HTML file with <script> tags in Notepad.
10. Specify a background color in the <body> tag.
11. Add a heading.
12. Within the <script> tags, add a `document.write` statement to display the frame's background color.
13. Save the file with a name such as `right2.html`.

*Note: Make sure that this name matches the second filename of the frames that you created in step **2**.*

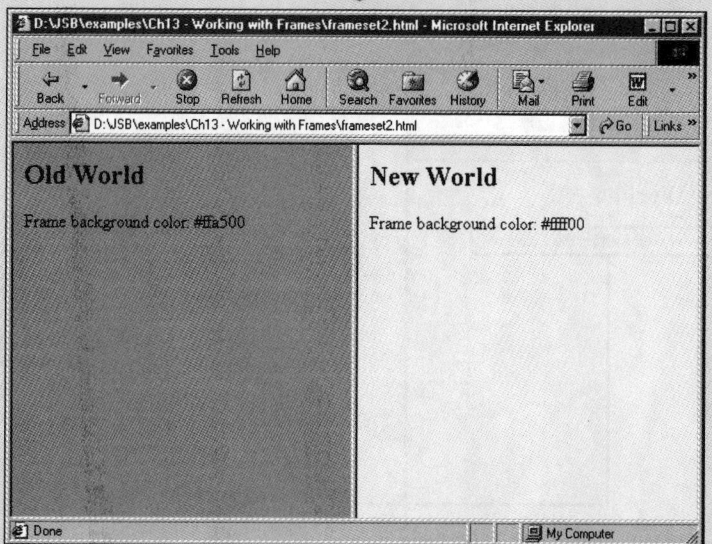
D:\JSB\examples\Ch13 - Working with Frames\frameset2.html - Microsoft Internet Explorer
File Edit View Favorites Tools Help
Back Forward Stop Refresh Home Search Favorites History Mail Print Edit
Address D:\JSB\examples\Ch13 - Working with Frames\frameset2.html Go Links
Old World
Frame background color: #ffa500
New World
Frame background color: #ffff00
Done
My Computer

14. Open the file that you saved in step **3** in a browser.

- Two frames appear with the frame's background color in each.

Note: In this example, the left frame displays the file `left2.html`, and the right frame displays the file `right2.html`.

FIND THE NUMBER OF FRAMES

For a given frameset, you can determine the number of frames that it includes by using the `length` property. You can reference this property from the parent object. The `length` property returns the number of frames. For example, for a frameset with three frames, `parent.frames.length` returns a value of `3`.

FIND THE NUMBER OF FRAMES

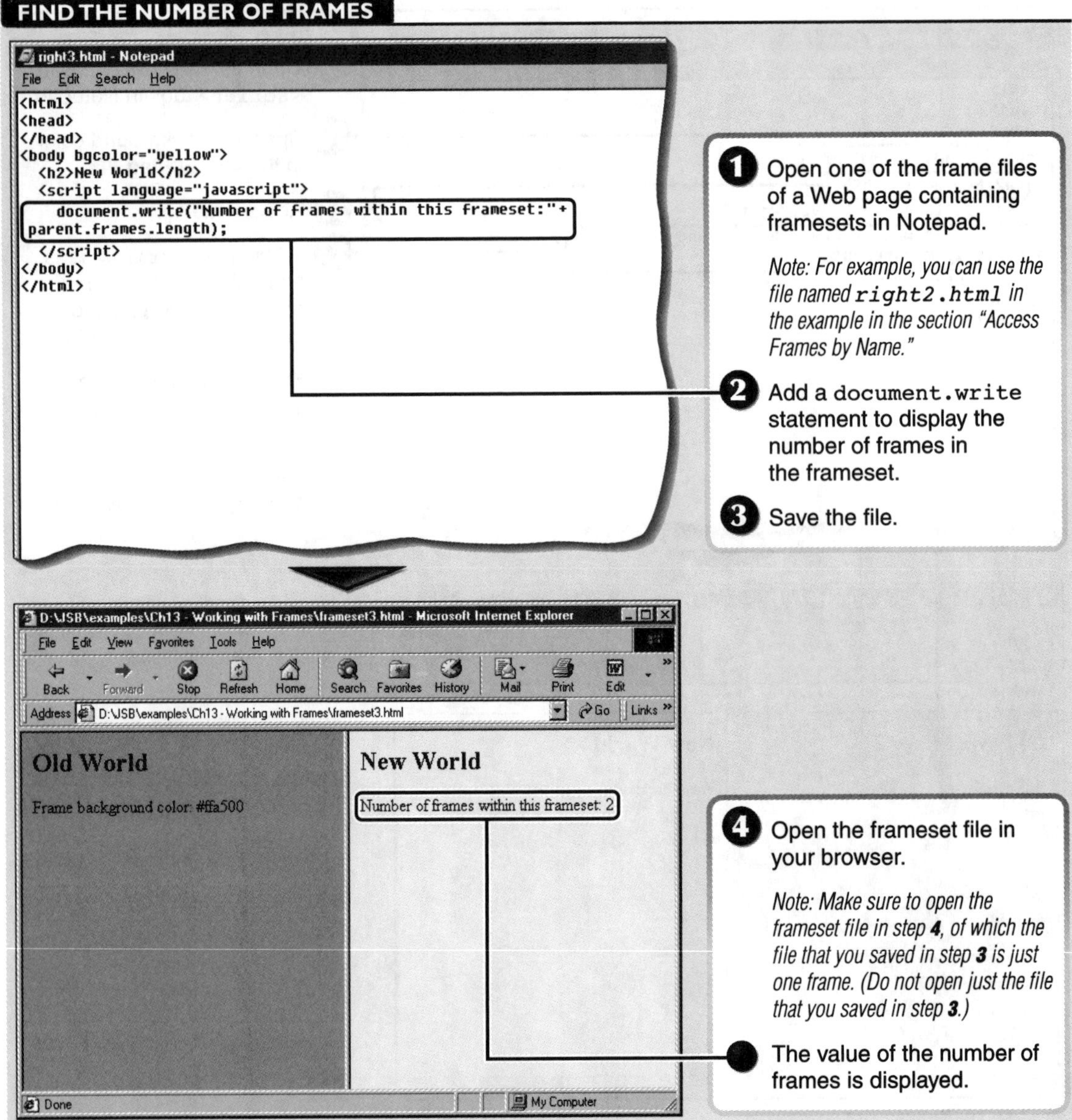

right3.html - Notepad
File Edit Search Help
<html>
<head>
</head>
<body bgcolor="yellow">
<h2>New World</h2>
<script language="javascript">
document.write("Number of frames within this frameset:"+
parent.frames.length);
</script>
</body>
</html>
D:\JSB\examples\Ch13 - Working with Frames\frameset3.html - Microsoft Internet Explorer
Old World
Frame background color: #ffa500
New World
Number of frames within this frameset: 2
Done
My Computer

1. Open one of the frame files of a Web page containing framesets in Notepad.

   Note: For example, you can use the file named `right2.html` *in the example in the section "Access Frames by Name."*

2. Add a `document.write` statement to display the number of frames in the frameset.

3. Save the file.

4. Open the frameset file in your browser.

   *Note: Make sure to open the frameset file in step **4**, of which the file that you saved in step **3** is just one frame. (Do not open just the file that you saved in step **3**.)*

- The value of the number of frames is displayed.

REFERENCE THE CURRENT FRAME

You can always reference the current frame by using the `self` object. The `parent` object refers to the `frameset` object that calls the current frame, but the `self` object refers to the current frame. For example, if you have a frame named `frame1`, you can refer to the title of the frame using `self.document.title` rather than `parent.frame1.document.title`.

REFERENCE THE CURRENT FRAME

```
<html>
<head>
</head>
<body bgcolor="orange">
  <h2>Old World</h2>
  <script language="javascript">
  document.write("Frame background color: " + self.document.bgColor);
  </script>
</body>
</html>
```

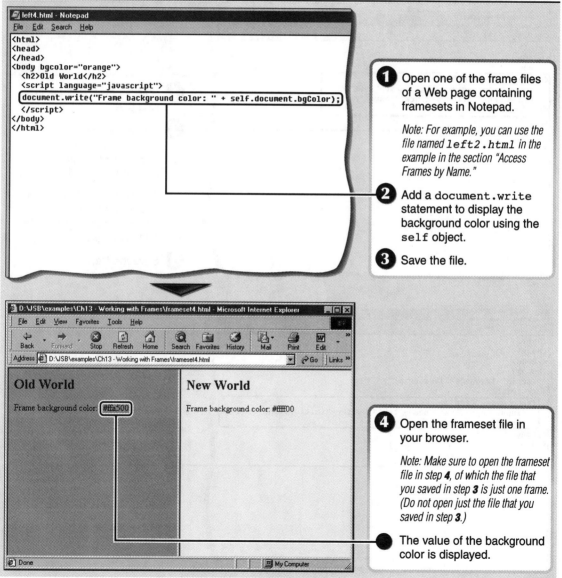

1. Open one of the frame files of a Web page containing framesets in Notepad.

   Note: For example, you can use the file named `left2.html` in the example in the section "Access Frames by Name."

2. Add a `document.write` statement to display the background color using the `self` object.

3. Save the file.

Old World

Frame background color: #ffa500

New World

Frame background color: #ffff00

4. Open the frameset file in your browser.

   *Note: Make sure to open the frameset file in step **4**, of which the file that you saved in step **3** is just one frame. (Do not open just the file that you saved in step **3**.)*

- The value of the background color is displayed.

REFERENCE ACROSS FRAMES

You can access elements in a separate frame by using the frame's array. For example, you reference a text box in `frame1` from `frame2` with `parent.frame1.document.forms[0].text1.value`. For nested framesets, to access frames in the same frameset, use `parent`, which contains all thechild frames. To access frames outside the current frameset, use `top` to get to the topmost frameset. From the top frameset, you can access the child frames.

REFERENCE ACROSS FRAMES

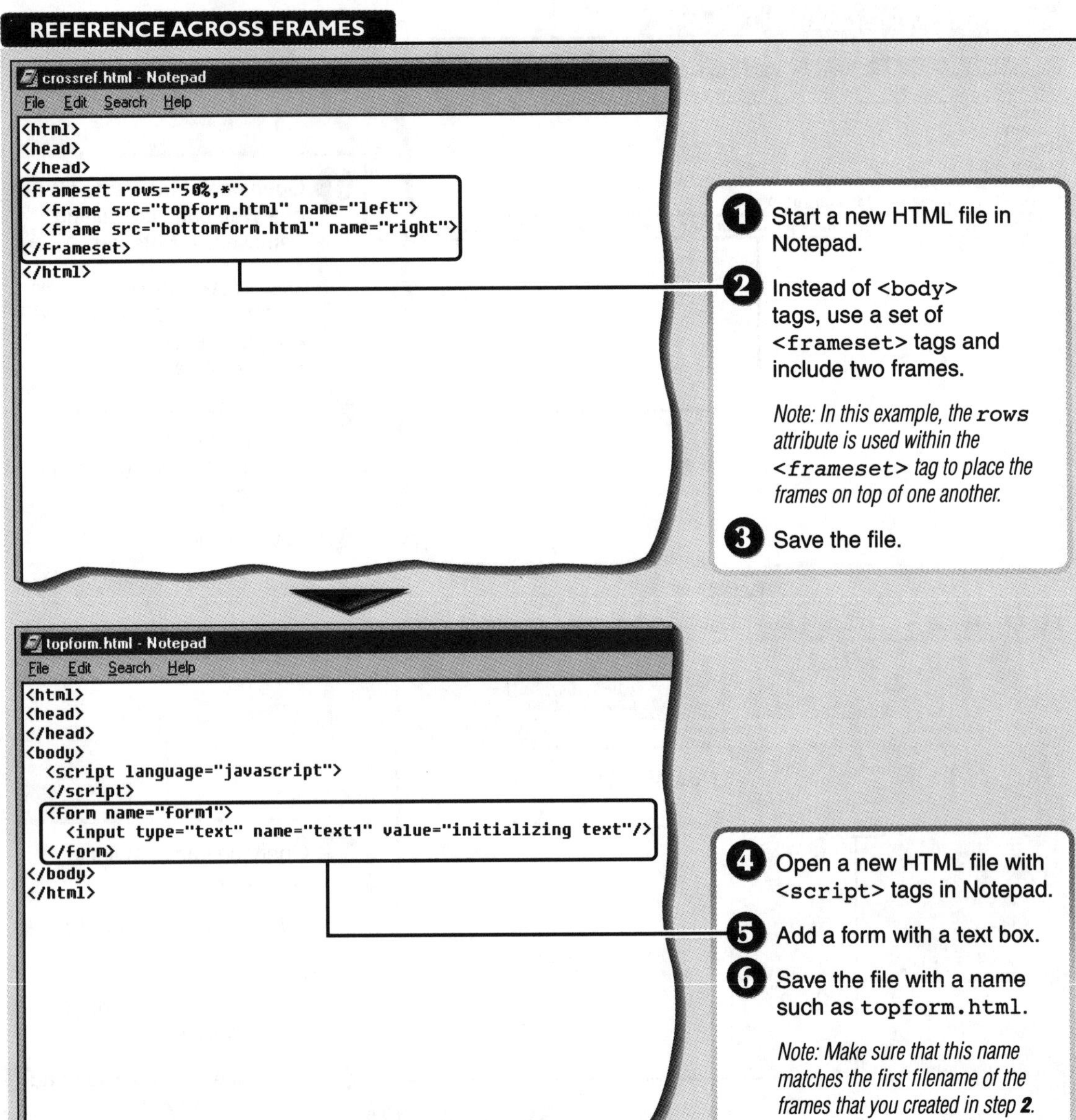
crossref.html - Notepad
File Edit Search Help
<html>
<head>
</head>
<frameset rows="50%,*">
<frame src="topform.html" name="left">
<frame src="bottomform.html" name="right">
</frameset>
</html>
1 Start a new HTML file in Notepad.
2 Instead of <body> tags, use a set of <frameset> tags and include two frames.
Note: In this example, the rows attribute is used within the <frameset> tag to place the frames on top of one another.
3 Save the file.
topform.html - Notepad
File Edit Search Help
<html>
<head>
</head>
<body>
<script language="javascript">
</script>
<form name="form1">
<input type="text" name="text1" value="initializing text"/>
</form>
</body>
</html>
4 Open a new HTML file with <script> tags in Notepad.
5 Add a form with a text box.
6 Save the file with a name such as topform.html.
Note: Make sure that this name matches the first filename of the frames that you created in step 2.

in an instant

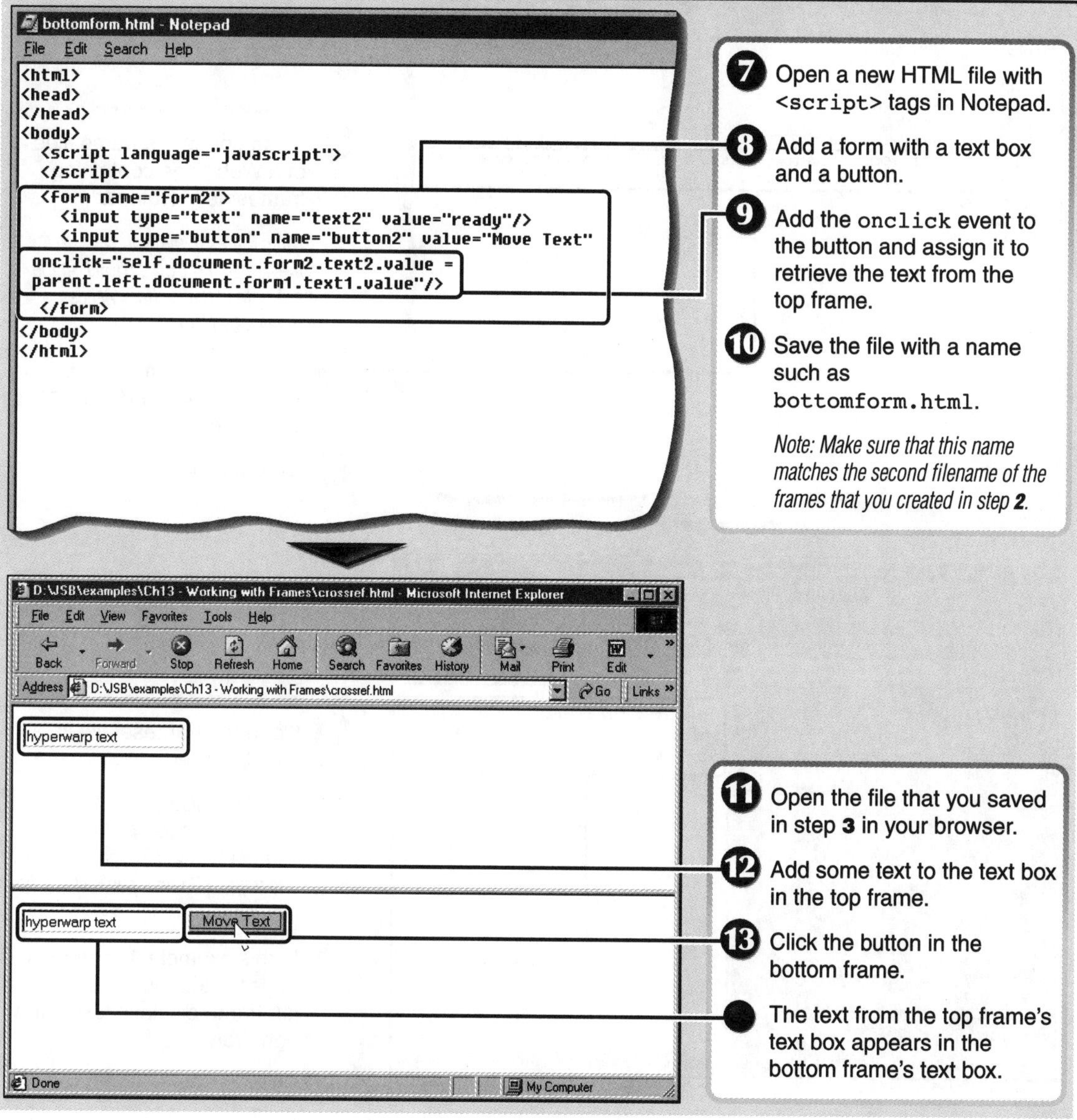
bottomform.html - Notepad
File Edit Search Help
<html>
<head>
</head>
<body>
<script language="javascript">
</script>
<form name="form2">
<input type="text" name="text2" value="ready"/>
<input type="button" name="button2" value="Move Text"
onclick="self.document.form2.text2.value =
parent.left.document.form1.text1.value"/>
</form>
</body>
</html>
D:\JSB\examples\Ch13 - Working with Frames\crossref.html - Microsoft Internet Explorer
File Edit View Favorites Tools Help
Back Forward Stop Refresh Home Search Favorites History Mail Print Edit
Address D:\JSB\examples\Ch13 - Working with Frames\crossref.html
Go Links
hyperwarp text
hyperwarp text
Move Text
Done
My Computer

7. Open a new HTML file with `<script>` tags in Notepad.
8. Add a form with a text box and a button.
9. Add the `onclick` event to the button and assign it to retrieve the text from the top frame.
10. Save the file with a name such as `bottomform.html`.

    *Note: Make sure that this name matches the second filename of the frames that you created in step **2**.*

11. Open the file that you saved in step **3** in your browser.
12. Add some text to the text box in the top frame.
13. Click the button in the bottom frame.

- The text from the top frame's text box appears in the bottom frame's text box.

WRITE TO A SEPARATE FRAME

You can use the `document.write` statement to display text within the current document window, but by using frame references, you can also use it to write text to another window. For example, you can write the word *welcome* in the second frame (`frame2`) by adding the following to the first frame (`frame1`): `parent.frame2.document.write("welcome")`.

WRITE TO A SEPARATE FRAME

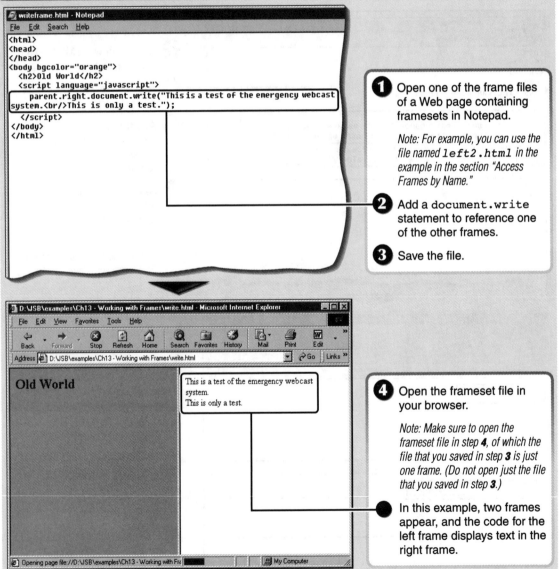

```
<html>
<head>
</head>
<body bgcolor="orange">
  <h2>Old World</h2>
  <script language="javascript">
    parent.right.document.write("This is a test of the emergency webcast
system.<br/>This is only a test.");
  </script>
</body>
</html>
```

1. Open one of the frame files of a Web page containing framesets in Notepad.

   Note: For example, you can use the file named `left2.html` *in the example in the section "Access Frames by Name."*

2. Add a `document.write` statement to reference one of the other frames.

3. Save the file.

4. Open the frameset file in your browser.

   *Note: Make sure to open the frameset file in step **4**, of which the file that you saved in step **3** is just one frame. (Do not open just the file that you saved in step **3**.)*

- In this example, two frames appear, and the code for the left frame displays text in the right frame.

DETECT FRAME RESIZING

The `frame` object identifies standard events, including `onBlur` and `onFocus`. It also can be used with two unique events — `onMove` and `onResize`. These events can be added to the `<frame>` tags within the frameset file. When referencing frames from the frameset file, you need to use `self` and the name of the frame because the frameset file is the parent.

DETECT FRAME RESIZING

```
<html>
<head>
</head>
<frameset cols="50%,*">
  <frame src="left2.html" name="left"
onResize="self.left.document.write('Hey,quit pushing!')">
  <frame src="right2.html" name="right">
</frameset>
</html>
```

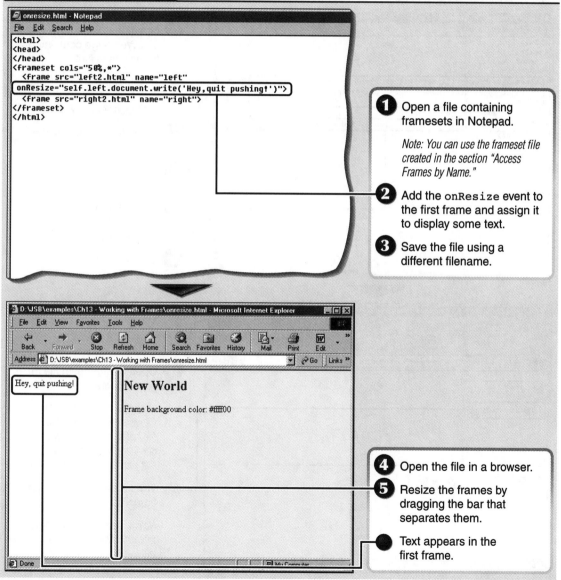

1. Open a file containing framesets in Notepad.

   Note: You can use the frameset file created in the section "Access Frames by Name."

2. Add the `onResize` event to the first frame and assign it to display some text.
3. Save the file using a different filename.

Hey, quit pushing!

New World

Frame background color: #ffff00

4. Open the file in a browser.
5. Resize the frames by dragging the bar that separates them.

- Text appears in the first frame.

SET THE TARGET FRAME

Web page elements including forms and links can include a `target` attribute. This attribute is the name of a frame where the results of the form or the link should be displayed. Using JavaScript, you can view the `target` value using the `target` property of the `frame` object. You can also set the `target` value dynamically.

SET THE TARGET FRAME

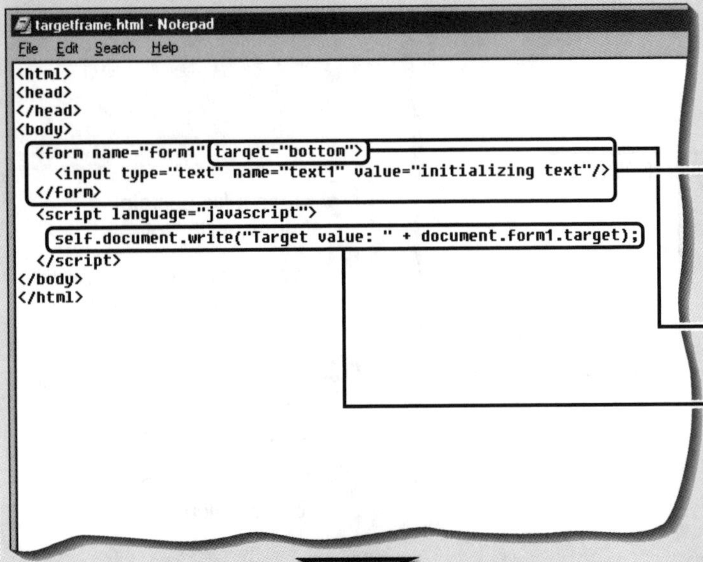

targetframe.html - Notepad

```
<html>
<head>
</head>
<body>
  <form name="form1" target="bottom">
    <input type="text" name="text1" value="initializing text"/>
  </form>
  <script language="javascript">
    self.document.write("Target value: " + document.form1.target);
  </script>
</body>
</html>
```

1. Open one of the frame files of a Web page containing framesets in Notepad.

   Note: You can use the file named `topform.html` *in the example in "Reference across Frames."*

2. Move the form above the `<script>` tags.
3. Add the `target` attribute to the form.
4. Add a `document.write` statement to display the `target` value.
5. Save the file.

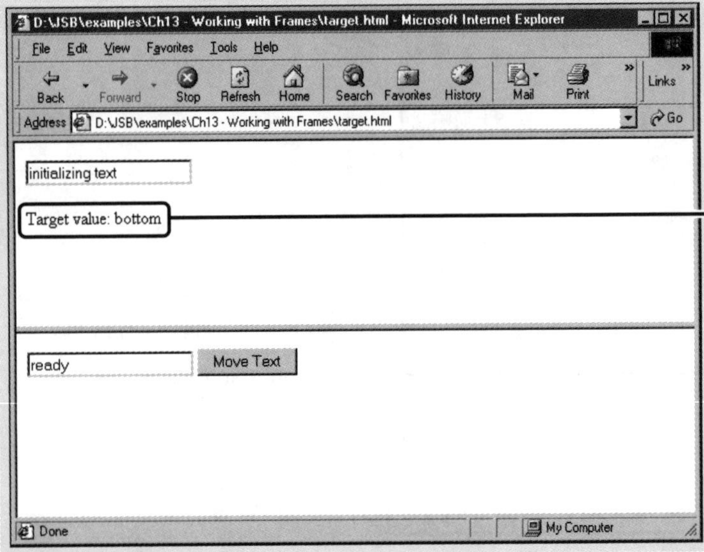

D:\JSB\examples\Ch13 - Working with Frames\target.html - Microsoft Internet Explorer

initializing text

Target value: bottom

ready | Move Text

6. Open the frameset file in your browser.

   *Note: Make sure to open the frameset file in step **6**, of which the file that you saved in step **5** is just one frame. (Do not open just the file that you saved in step **5**.)*

- The frames and the target name appear.

  Note: The target name identifies where the linked Web page will load.

PRINT A FRAME

Another useful method of the `frame` object is the `print()` method. This method enables you to print a single frame. The `print()` method opens the Print dialog box for your computer system. You need to click **OK** in this dialog box to actually send the page to the printer.

PRINT A FRAME

```
<html>
<head>
</head>
<body>
  <script language="javascript">
  </script>
  <form name="form2">
    <input type="text" name="text2" value="ready"/>
    <input type="button" name="button2" value=" Print Frame "
onclick  =" parent.right.print() "/>
  </form>
</body>
</html>
```

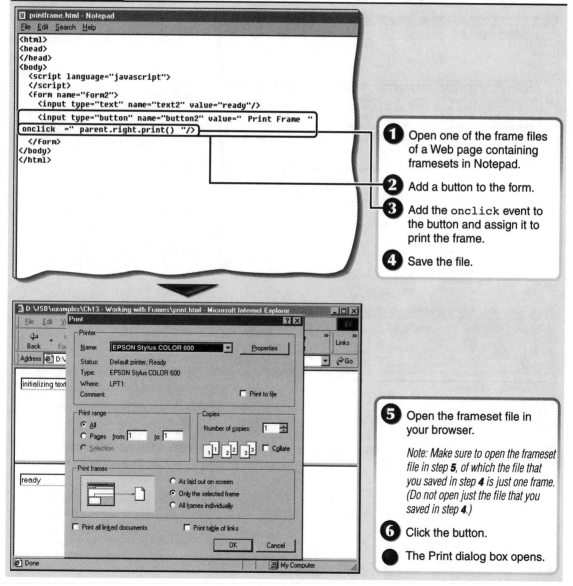

1 Open one of the frame files of a Web page containing framesets in Notepad.

2 Add a button to the form.

3 Add the `onclick` event to the button and assign it to print the frame.

4 Save the file.

5 Open the frameset file in your browser.

*Note: Make sure to open the frameset file in step **5**, of which the file that you saved in step **4** is just one frame. (Do not open just the file that you saved in step **4**.)*

6 Click the button.

- The Print dialog box opens.

USING THE NAVIGATOR OBJECT

The `navigator` object includes many properties and methods required to determine the user's system. The `navigator` object properties include `appCodeName`, `appName`, `appVersion`, `platform`, and `userAgent`. The `navigator` object method is `javaEnabled()`. The properties of the `navigator` object are described in the section "Detect a User's Browser."

USING THE NAVIGATOR OBJECT

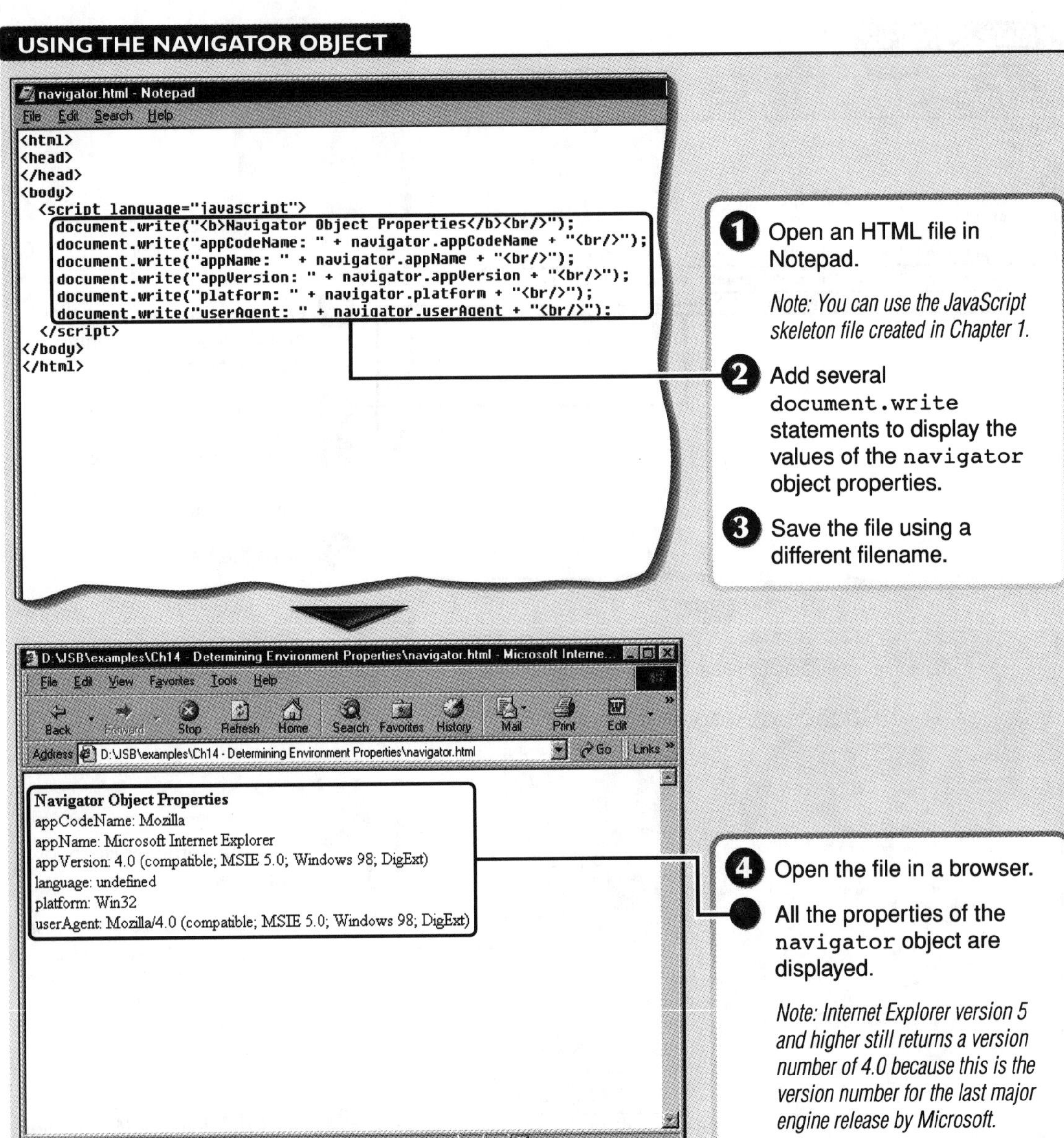

navigator.html - Notepad
File Edit Search Help
<html>
<head>
</head>
<body>
<script language="javascript">
document.write("<b>Navigator Object Properties</b>
");
document.write("appCodeName: " + navigator.appCodeName + "<br/>");
document.write("appName: " + navigator.appName + "<br/>");
document.write("appVersion: " + navigator.appVersion + "<br/>");
document.write("platform: " + navigator.platform + "<br/>");
document.write("userAgent: " + navigator.userAgent + "<br/>");
</script>
</body>
</html>
D:\JSB\examples\Ch14 - Determining Environment Properties\navigator.html - Microsoft Interne...
File Edit View Favorites Tools Help
Back Forward Stop Refresh Home Search Favorites History Mail Print Edit
Address D:\JSB\examples\Ch14 - Determining Environment Properties\navigator.html
Go Links
Navigator Object Properties
appCodeName: Mozilla
appName: Microsoft Internet Explorer
appVersion: 4.0 (compatible; MSIE 5.0; Windows 98; DigExt)
language: undefined
platform: Win32
userAgent: Mozilla/4.0 (compatible; MSIE 5.0; Windows 98; DigExt)
Done
My Computer

1. Open an HTML file in Notepad.

   Note: You can use the JavaScript skeleton file created in Chapter 1.

2. Add several `document.write` statements to display the values of the `navigator` object properties.

3. Save the file using a different filename.

4. Open the file in a browser.

- All the properties of the `navigator` object are displayed.

Note: Internet Explorer version 5 and higher still returns a version number of 4.0 because this is the version number for the last major engine release by Microsoft.

in an instant

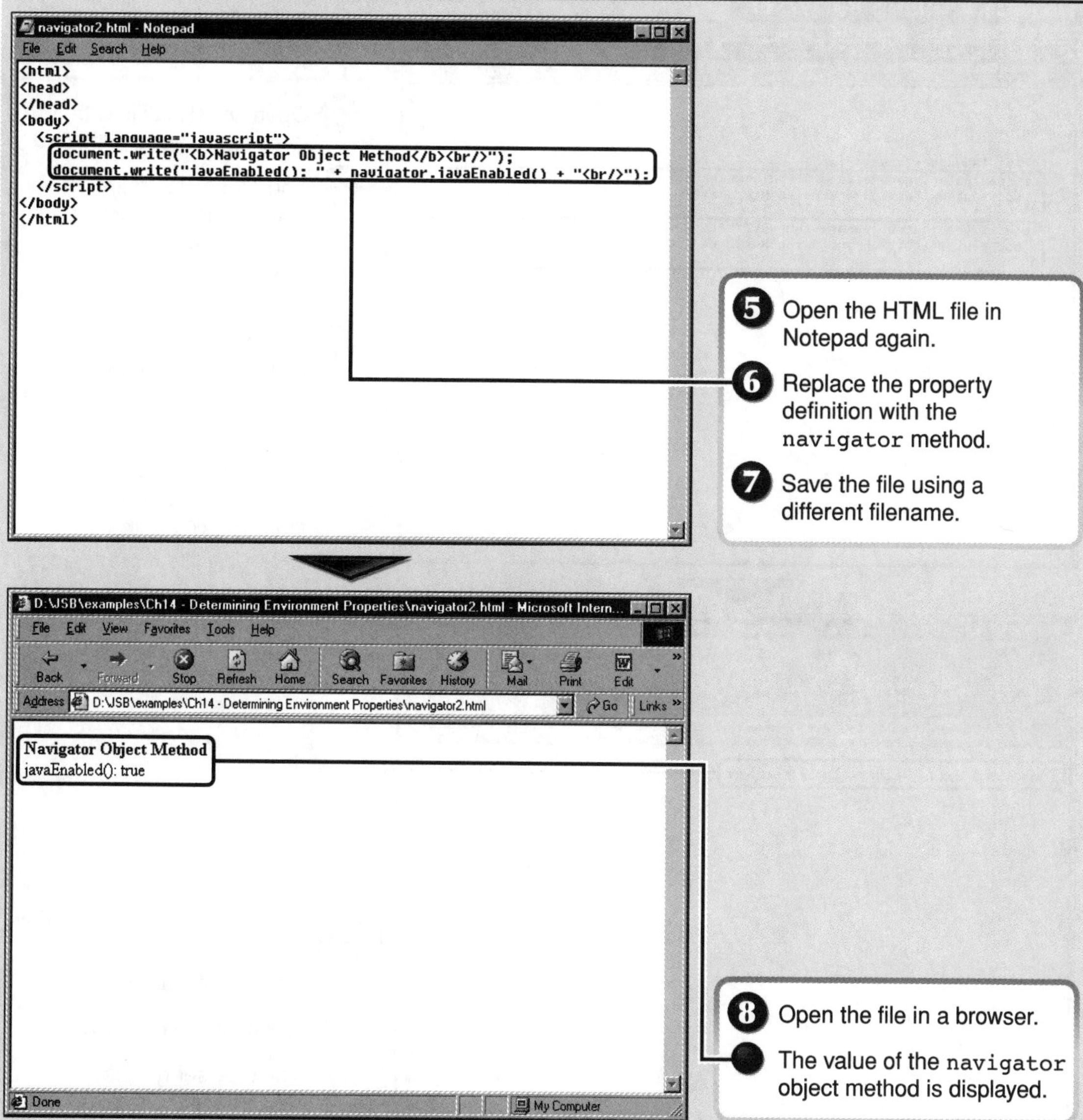
navigator2.html - Notepad
File Edit Search Help
<html>
<head>
</head>
<body>
<script language="javascript">
document.write("<b>Navigator Object Method</b>
");
document.write("javaEnabled(): " + navigator.javaEnabled() + "<br/>");
</script>
</body>
</html>
D:\JSB\examples\Ch14 - Determining Environment Properties\navigator2.html - Microsoft Intern...
File Edit View Favorites Tools Help
Back Forward Stop Refresh Home Search Favorites History Mail Print Edit
Address D:\JSB\examples\Ch14 - Determining Environment Properties\navigator2.html
Go Links
Navigator Object Method
javaEnabled(): true
Done
My Computer

5 Open the HTML file in Notepad again.

6 Replace the property definition with the `navigator` method.

7 Save the file using a different filename.

8 Open the file in a browser.

- The value of the `navigator` object method is displayed.

DETECT A USER'S BROWSER

The `navigator` object includes three properties that return the type of browser. The `appCodeName` property returns the code name of the current browser. This is typically `Mozilla`, which is the standard code base. `appName` returns the actual browser name, such as Microsoft Internet Explorer. `appVersion` returns the version information or number for the browser, such as `5.0`.

DETECT A USER'S BROWSER

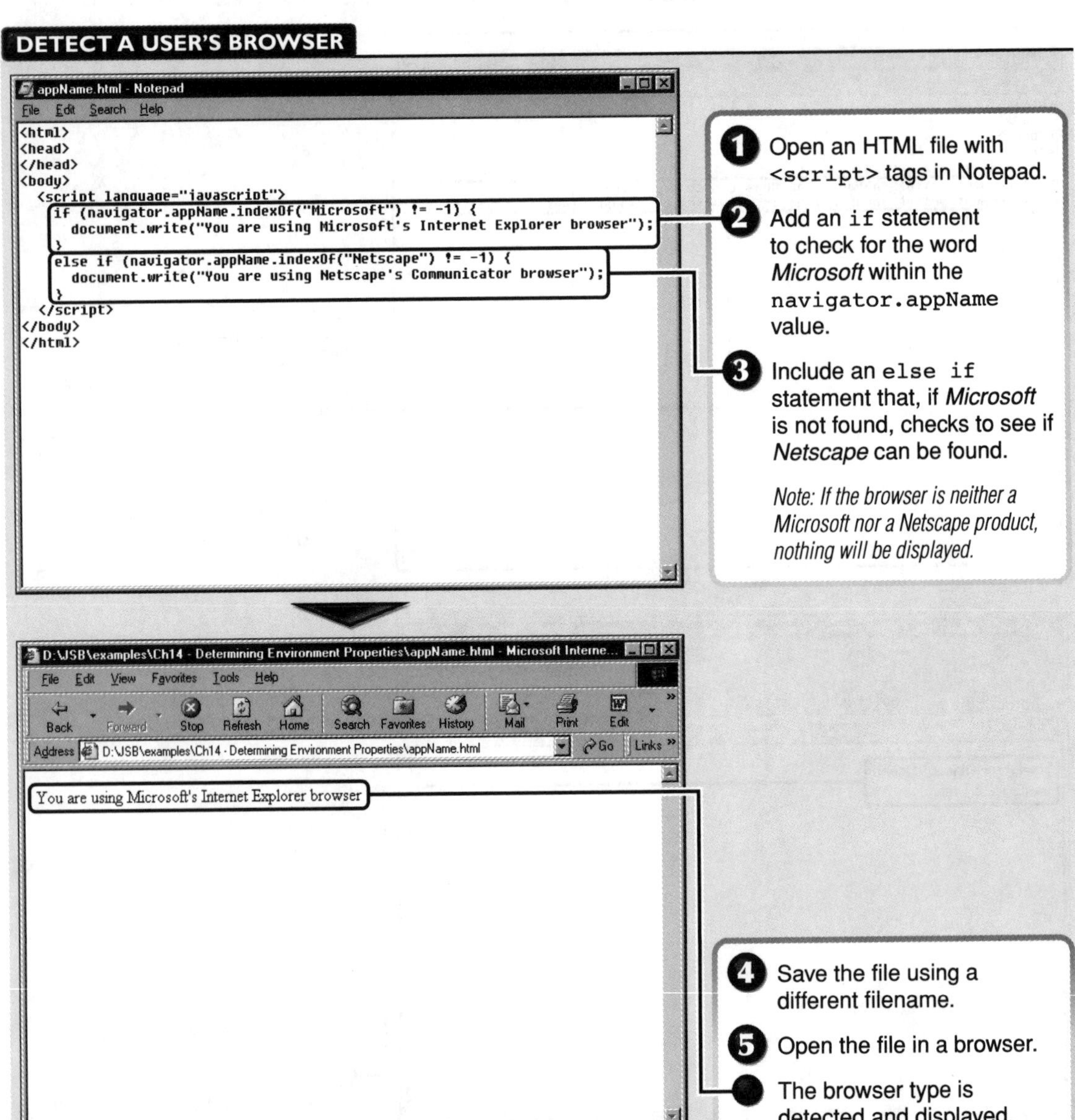

appName.html - Notepad
File Edit Search Help
<html>
<head>
</head>
<body>
<script language="javascript">
if (navigator.appName.indexOf("Microsoft") != -1) {
document.write("You are using Microsoft's Internet Explorer browser");
}
else if (navigator.appName.indexOf("Netscape") != -1) {
document.write("You are using Netscape's Communicator browser");
}
</script>
</body>
</html>
D:\JSB\examples\Ch14 - Determining Environment Properties\appName.html - Microsoft Interne...
File Edit View Favorites Tools Help
Back Forward Stop Refresh Home Search Favorites History Mail Print Edit
Address D:\JSB\examples\Ch14 - Determining Environment Properties\appName.html
Go Links
You are using Microsoft's Internet Explorer browser
Done
My Computer

1. Open an HTML file with `<script>` tags in Notepad.
2. Add an `if` statement to check for the word *Microsoft* within the `navigator.appName` value.
3. Include an `else if` statement that, if *Microsoft* is not found, checks to see if *Netscape* can be found.

Note: If the browser is neither a Microsoft nor a Netscape product, nothing will be displayed.

4. Save the file using a different filename.
5. Open the file in a browser.

- The browser type is detected and displayed.

DETECT THE BROWSER'S VERSION

Different browsers support differing levels of HTML. For example, the early 3 browser versions supported only HTML version 3.2. Later versions supported later HTML specifications. If you use a feature in a later HTML version with a browser that does not support it, the results can be unexpected. To eliminate any problems, you can check for the current browser version number by using the `navigator.appVersion` property.

DETECT THE BROWSER'S VERSION

```
<html>
<head>
</head>
<body>
  <script language="javascript">
   if (navigator.appVersion.indexOf("4.0") != -1) {
     document.write("You are using a version 4.0 compatible browser.");
   }
   else {
     document.write("This browser is not 4.0 compliant.");
   }
  </script>
</body>
</html>
```

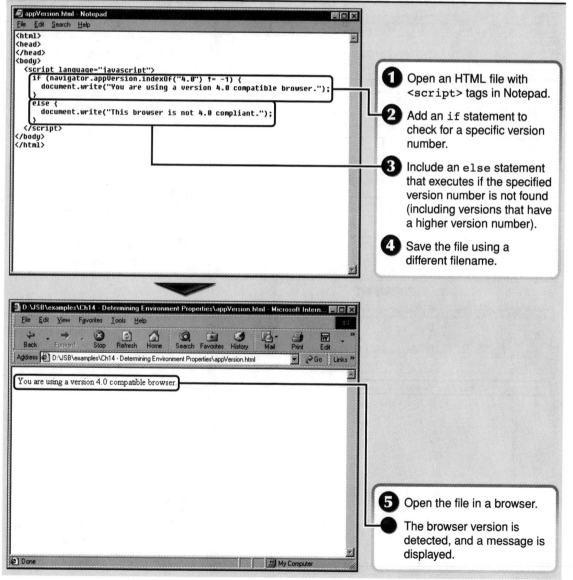

1. Open an HTML file with `<script>` tags in Notepad.
2. Add an `if` statement to check for a specific version number.
3. Include an `else` statement that executes if the specified version number is not found (including versions that have a higher version number).
4. Save the file using a different filename.

You are using a version 4.0 compatible browser.

5. Open the file in a browser.

- The browser version is detected, and a message is displayed.

DETECT A USER'S OPERATING SYSTEM

Understanding the user's operating system helps you know what type of interfaces he or she is most comfortable with. For example, Macintosh interfaces are different from Windows and UNIX interfaces. You can detect a user's operating system by using the `platform` propertyof the `navigator` object. This property returns the platform for which the browser was compiled.

DETECT A USER'S OPERATING SYSTEM

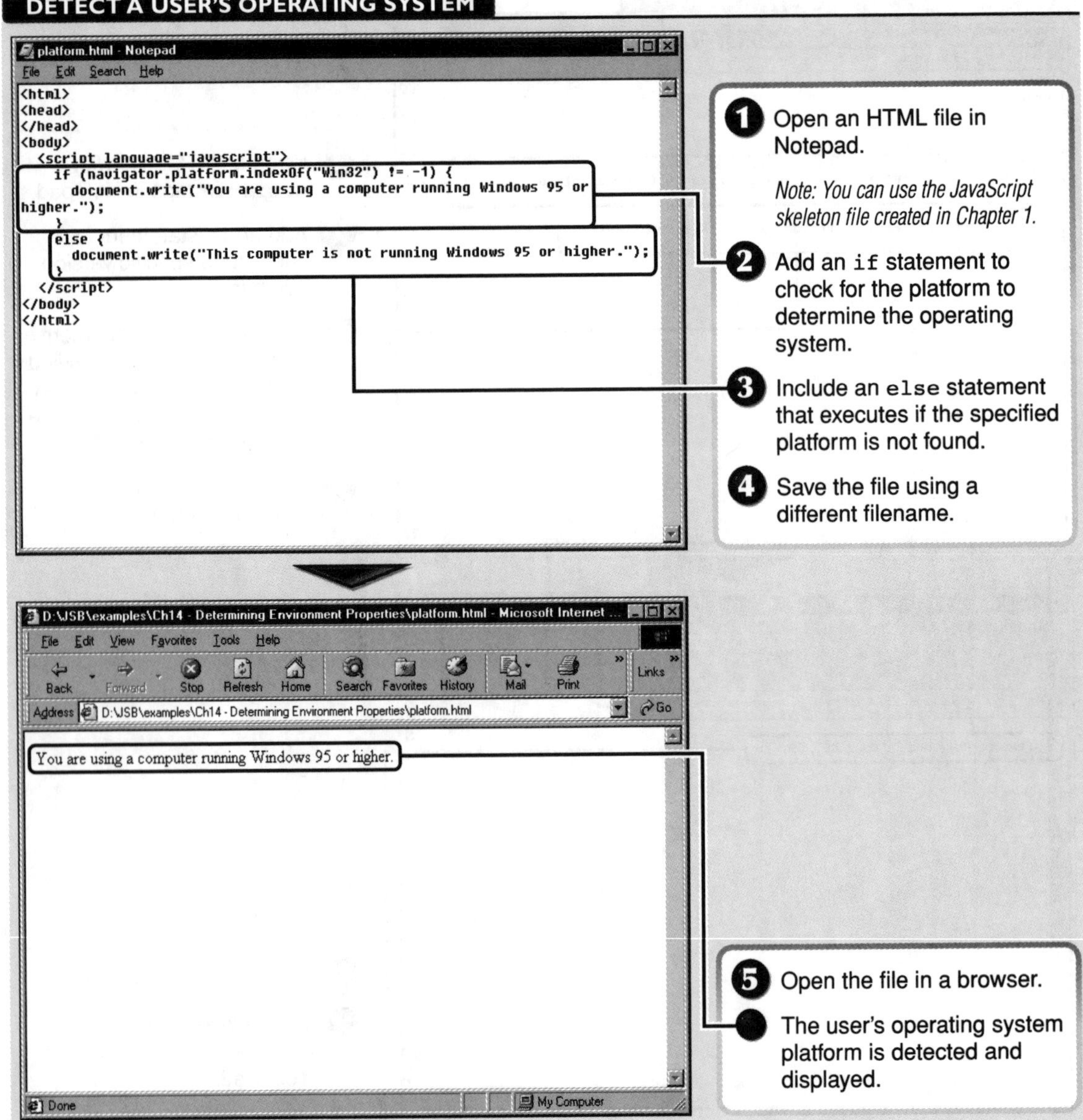

platform.html - Notepad
File Edit Search Help
<html>
<head>
</head>
<body>
<script language="javascript">
if (navigator.platform.indexOf("Win32") != -1) {
document.write("You are using a computer running Windows 95 or higher.");
}
else {
document.write("This computer is not running Windows 95 or higher.");
}
</script>
</body>
</html>
D:\JSB\examples\Ch14 - Determining Environment Properties\platform.html - Microsoft Internet ...
File Edit View Favorites Tools Help
Back Forward Stop Refresh Home Search Favorites History Mail Print
Links
Address D:\JSB\examples\Ch14 - Determining Environment Properties\platform.html
Go
You are using a computer running Windows 95 or higher.
Done
My Computer

1. Open an HTML file in Notepad.

   Note: You can use the JavaScript skeleton file created in Chapter 1.

2. Add an `if` statement to check for the platform to determine the operating system.
3. Include an `else` statement that executes if the specified platform is not found.
4. Save the file using a different filename.
5. Open the file in a browser.

- The user's operating system platform is detected and displayed.

UNDERSTAND A USER AGENT

The `userAgent` property of the `navigator` object returns the header information that is sent to the server during a request by the browser. The information in the header includes the same information in the `appVersion` property plus the information from the `appCodeName` property.

UNDERSTAND A USER AGENT

```
<html>
<head>
</head>
<body>
  <script language="javascript">
    if ((navigator.userAgent.indexOf("MSIE") != -1) &&
(navigator.userAgent.indexOf("Windows 98") != -1)) {
      document.write("You are using Microsoft Internet Explorer on a Windows
98 computer.");
    }
    else {
      document.write("This computer is not running Internet Explorer
on Windows 98.");
    }
  </script>
</body>
</html>
```

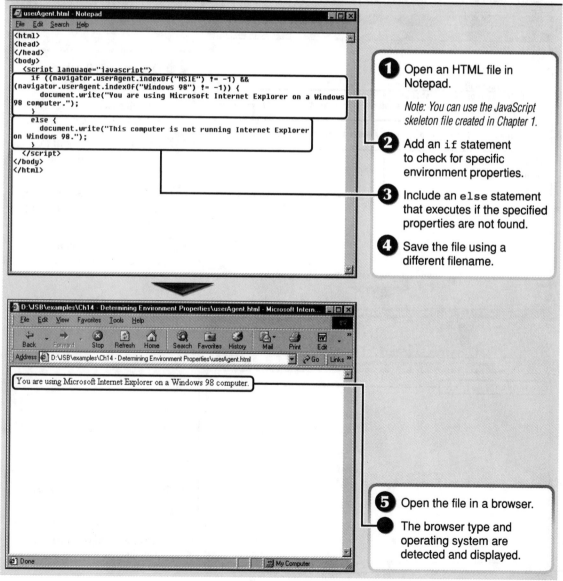

1. Open an HTML file in Notepad.

   Note: You can use the JavaScript skeleton file created in Chapter 1.

2. Add an `if` statement to check for specific environment properties.
3. Include an `else` statement that executes if the specified properties are not found.
4. Save the file using a different filename.

D:\JSB\examples\Ch14 - Determining Environment Properties\userAgent.html - Microsoft Intern...

You are using Microsoft Internet Explorer on a Windows 98 computer.

5. Open the file in a browser.

- The browser type and operating system are detected and displayed.

DETERMINE WHETHER JAVA IS ENABLED

Browsers have an option to allow users to enable or disable Java. If Java is disabled, no Java content will run within the browser. The `navigator` object includes a method for determining whether Java is enabled for the browser. This method is `javaEnabled()`. It returns either a `true` or a `false` value.

DETERMINE WHETHER JAVA IS ENABLED

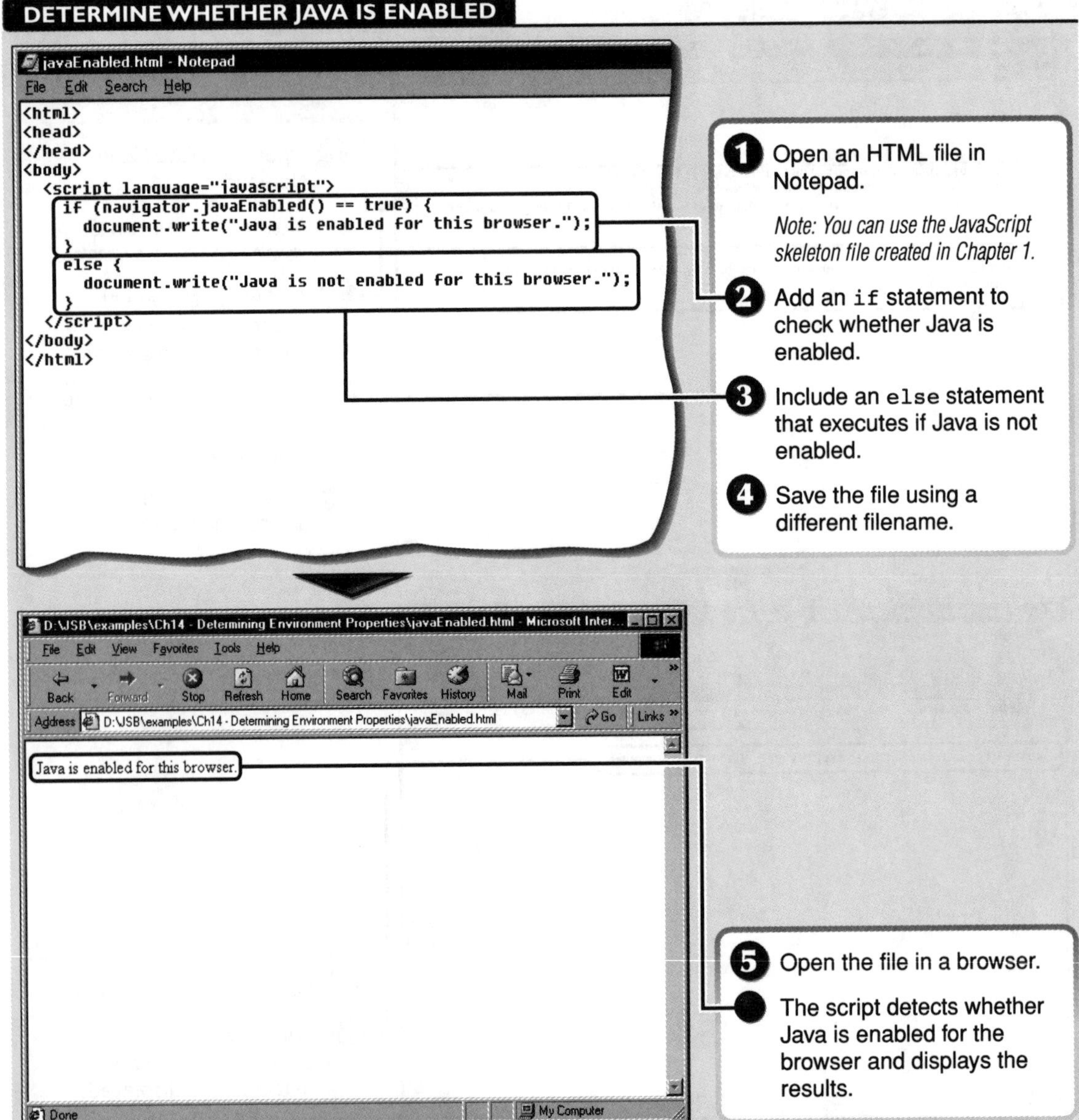

javaEnabled.html - Notepad
File Edit Search Help
<html>
<head>
</head>
<body>
<script language="javascript">
if (navigator.javaEnabled() == true) {
document.write("Java is enabled for this browser.");
}
else {
document.write("Java is not enabled for this browser.");
}
</script>
</body>
</html>
D:\JSB\examples\Ch14 - Determining Environment Properties\javaEnabled.html - Microsoft Inter...
File Edit View Favorites Tools Help
Back Forward Stop Refresh Home Search Favorites History Mail Print Edit
Address D:\JSB\examples\Ch14 - Determining Environment Properties\javaEnabled.html
Go Links
Java is enabled for this browser.
Done
My Computer

1. Open an HTML file in Notepad.

   Note: You can use the JavaScript skeleton file created in Chapter 1.

2. Add an `if` statement to check whether Java is enabled.

3. Include an `else` statement that executes if Java is not enabled.

4. Save the file using a different filename.

5. Open the file in a browser.

- The script detects whether Java is enabled for the browser and displays the results.

DETERMINE THE CODE NAME

The appCodeName property returns the name of the code used by the browser. This value represents a baseline of functionality. Both Microsoft Internet Explorer and Netscape Navigator return Mozilla for this value. This is the developer's name for the browser code.

DETERMINE THE CODE NAME

```
<html>
<head>
</head>
<body>
  <script language="javascript">
    if (navigator.appVersion.indexOf("Mozilla") != -1) {
      document.write("The code name for this browser is Mozilla.");
    }
    else {
      document.write("This code name for this browser isn't Mozilla.");
    }
  </script>
</body>
</html>
```

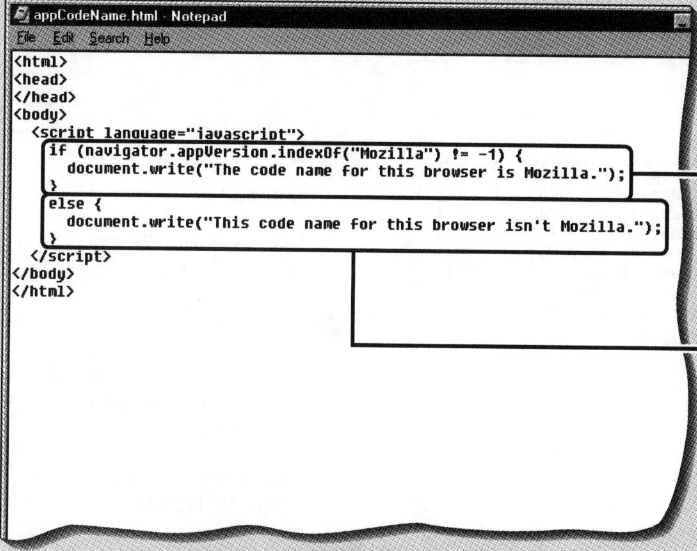

1. Open an HTML file in Notepad.

   Note: You can use the JavaScript skeleton file created in Chapter 1.

2. Add an if statement to check the code name.
3. Include an else statement that executes if the specified code name is not found.
4. Save the file using a different filename.

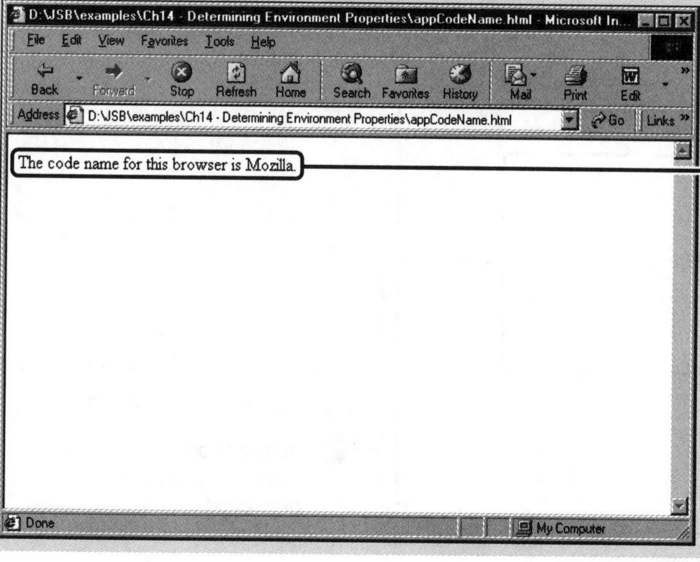

The code name for this browser is Mozilla.

5. Open the file in a browser.

- The script detects and displays the code name.

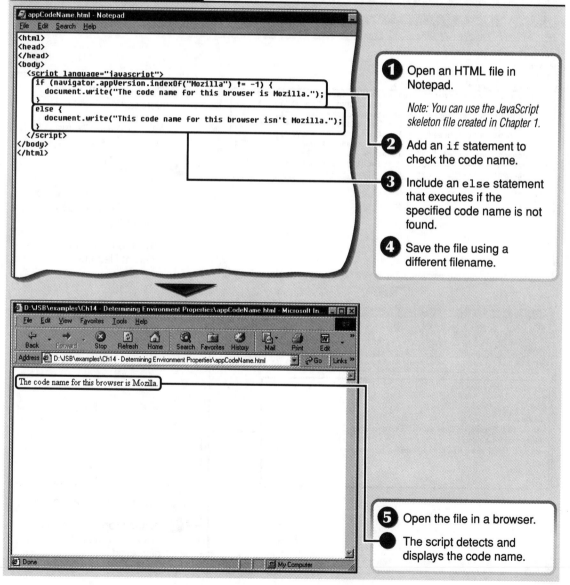

USING THE LOCATION OBJECT

The `location` object includes properties that hold every piece of information that make up a URL. These properties are similar to the `link` object properties and include `hash`, `host`, `hostname`, `href`, `pathname`, `port`, `protocol`, and `search`. All these properties return information about the current URL. The `location` object also includes the `reload()` method, which reloads the current URL.

DISPLAY THE LOCATION OBJECT PROPERTIES

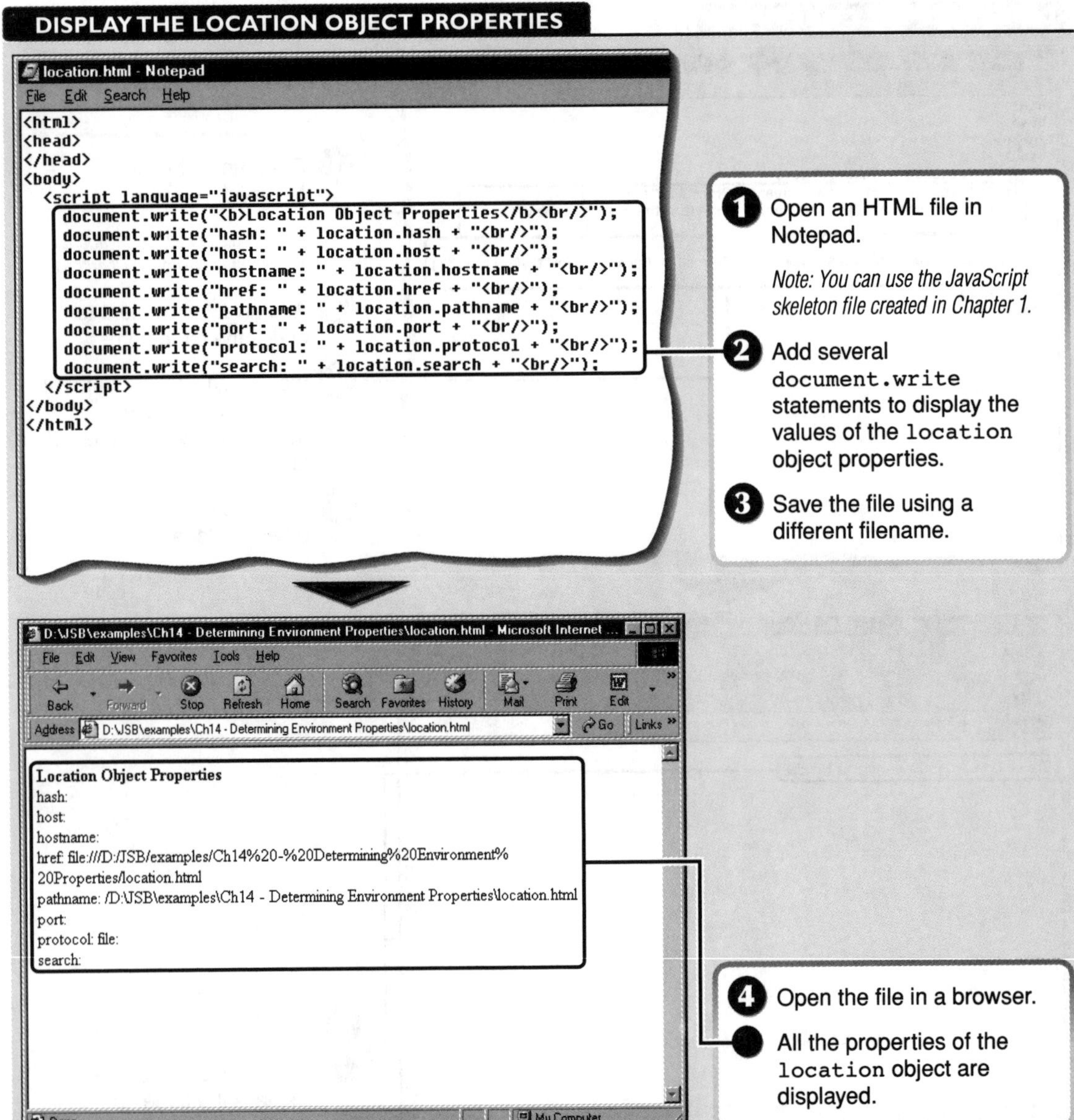

location.html - Notepad
File Edit Search Help
<html>
<head>
</head>
<body>
<script language="javascript">
document.write("<b>Location Object Properties</b>
");
document.write("hash: " + location.hash + "<br/>");
document.write("host: " + location.host + "<br/>");
document.write("hostname: " + location.hostname + "<br/>");
document.write("href: " + location.href + "<br/>");
document.write("pathname: " + location.pathname + "<br/>");
document.write("port: " + location.port + "<br/>");
document.write("protocol: " + location.protocol + "<br/>");
document.write("search: " + location.search + "<br/>");
</script>
</body>
</html>
D:\JSB\examples\Ch14 - Determining Environment Properties\location.html - Microsoft Internet ...
File Edit View Favorites Tools Help
Back Forward Stop Refresh Home Search Favorites History Mail Print Edit
Address D:\JSB\examples\Ch14 - Determining Environment Properties\location.html
Go Links
Location Object Properties
hash:
host:
hostname:
href: file:///D:/JSB/examples/Ch14%20-%20Determining%20Environment%20Properties/location.html
pathname: /D:\JSB\examples\Ch14 - Determining Environment Properties\location.html
port:
protocol: file:
search:
Done
My Computer

1. Open an HTML file in Notepad.

   Note: You can use the JavaScript skeleton file created in Chapter 1.

2. Add several `document.write` statements to display the values of the `location` object properties.

3. Save the file using a different filename.

4. Open the file in a browser.

- All the properties of the `location` object are displayed.

in an instant

RELOAD A PAGE

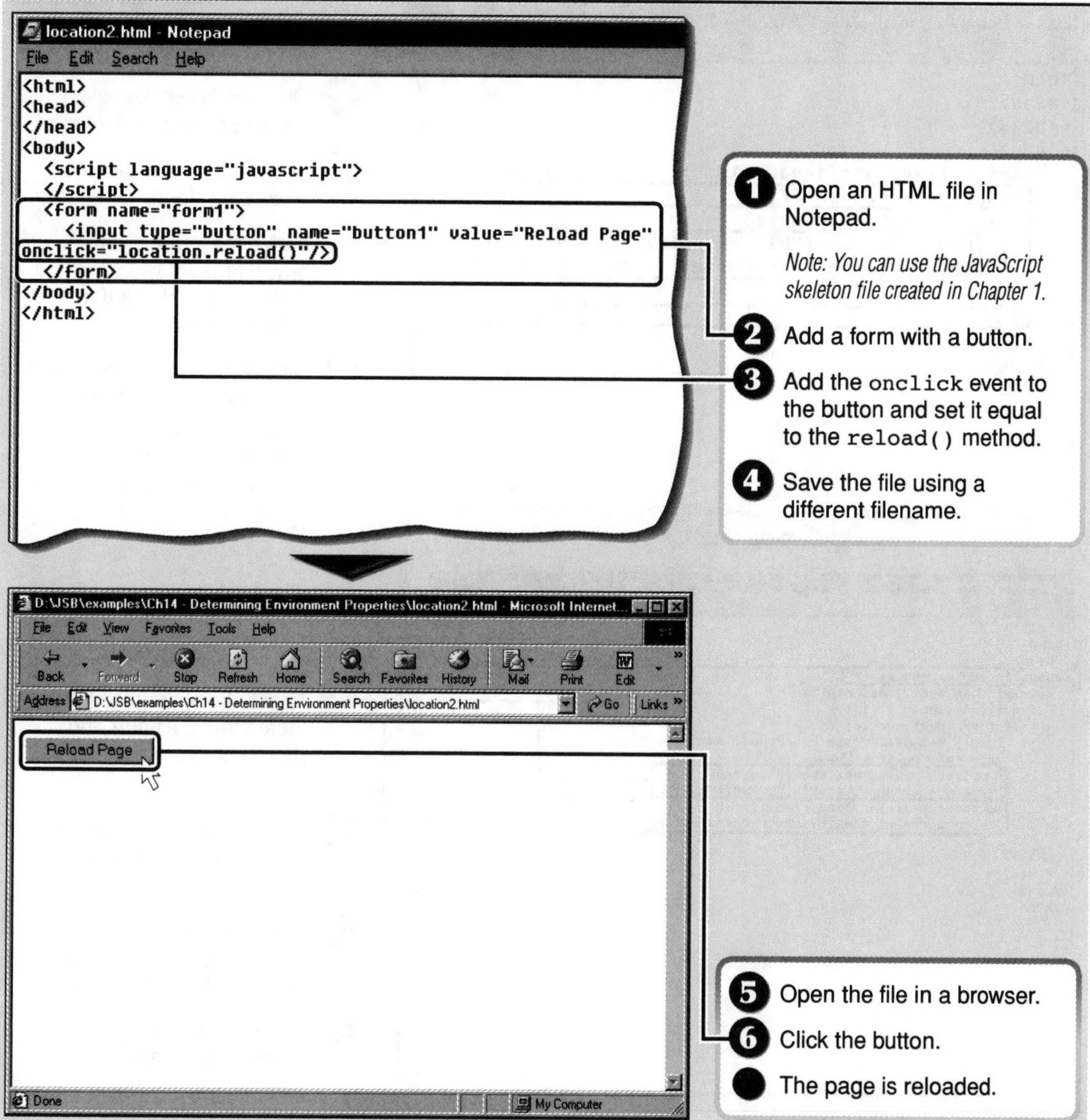
location2.html - Notepad
File Edit Search Help
<html>
<head>
</head>
<body>
<script language="javascript">
</script>
<form name="form1">
<input type="button" name="button1" value="Reload Page"
onclick="location.reload()"/>
</form>
</body>
</html>
D:\JSB\examples\Ch14 - Determining Environment Properties\location2.html - Microsoft Internet...
File Edit View Favorites Tools Help
Back Forward Stop Refresh Home Search Favorites History Mail Print Edit
Address D:\JSB\examples\Ch14 - Determining Environment Properties\location2.html
Go Links
Reload Page
Done
My Computer

1. Open an HTML file in Notepad.

   Note: You can use the JavaScript skeleton file created in Chapter 1.

2. Add a form with a button.
3. Add the `onclick` event to the button and set it equal to the `reload()` method.
4. Save the file using a different filename.
5. Open the file in a browser.
6. Click the button.

- The page is reloaded.

SET AND READ COOKIES

You can use the document.cookie object to create a cookie using JavaScript. Set this object equal to the piece of data that you want to save. The cookie is automatically written to the user's computer. When the user returns later to the site, the data is retrieved and used.

SET AND READ COOKIES

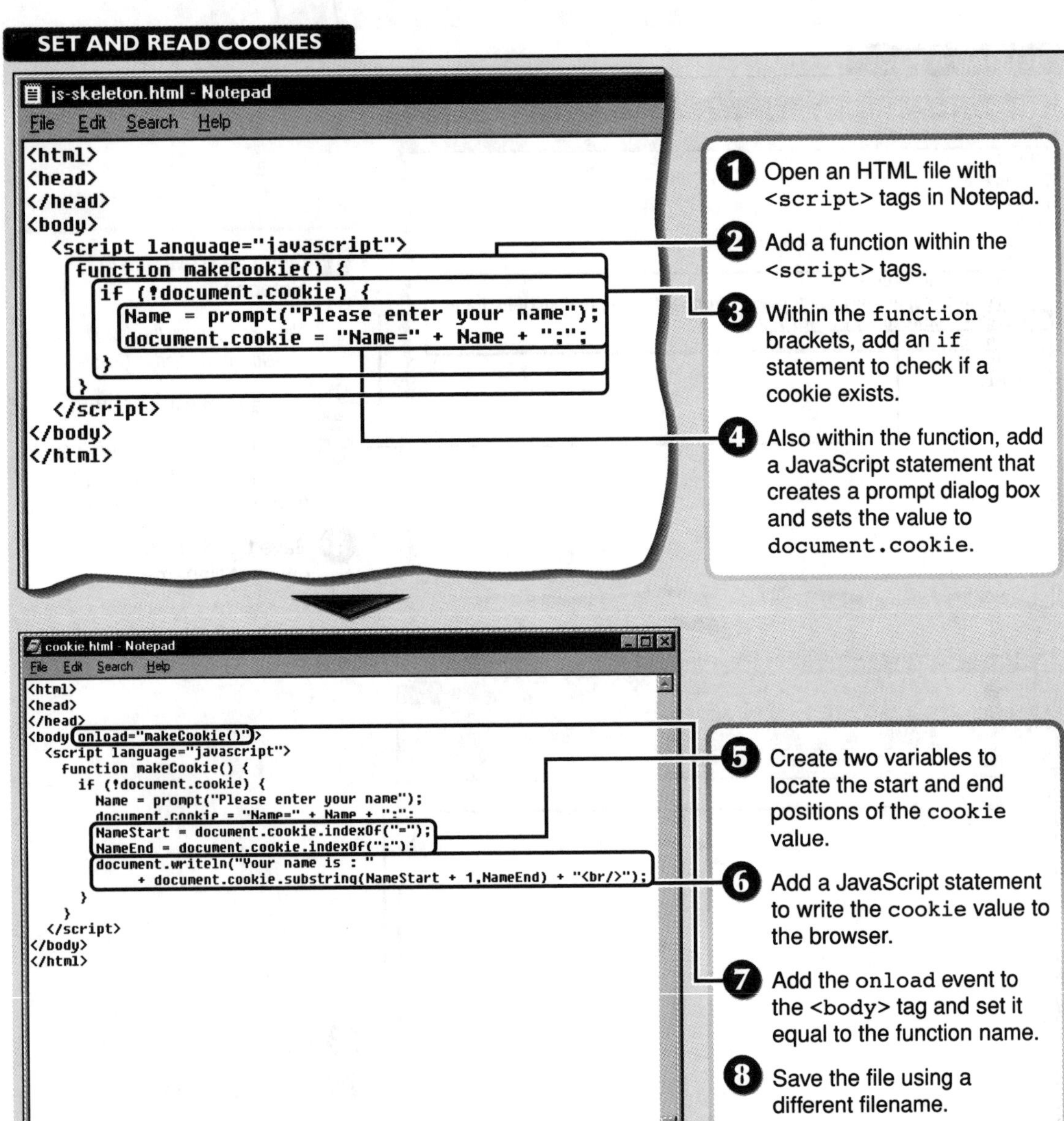

js-skeleton.html - Notepad
File Edit Search Help
<html>
<head>
</head>
<body>
<script language="javascript">
function makeCookie() {
if (!document.cookie) {
Name = prompt("Please enter your name");
document.cookie = "Name=" + Name + ";";
}
}
</script>
</body>
</html>
cookie.html - Notepad
File Edit Search Help
<html>
<head>
</head>
<body onload="makeCookie()">
<script language="javascript">
function makeCookie() {
if (!document.cookie) {
Name = prompt("Please enter your name");
document.cookie = "Name=" + Name + ";";
NameStart = document.cookie.indexOf("=");
NameEnd = document.cookie.indexOf(";");
document.writeln("Your name is : "
+ document.cookie.substring(NameStart + 1,NameEnd) + "<br/>");
}
}
</script>
</body>
</html>

1. Open an HTML file with <script> tags in Notepad.
2. Add a function within the <script> tags.
3. Within the function brackets, add an if statement to check if a cookie exists.
4. Also within the function, add a JavaScript statement that creates a prompt dialog box and sets the value to document.cookie.
5. Create two variables to locate the start and end positions of the cookie value.
6. Add a JavaScript statement to write the cookie value to the browser.
7. Add the onload event to the <body> tag and set it equal to the function name.
8. Save the file using a different filename.

in an instant

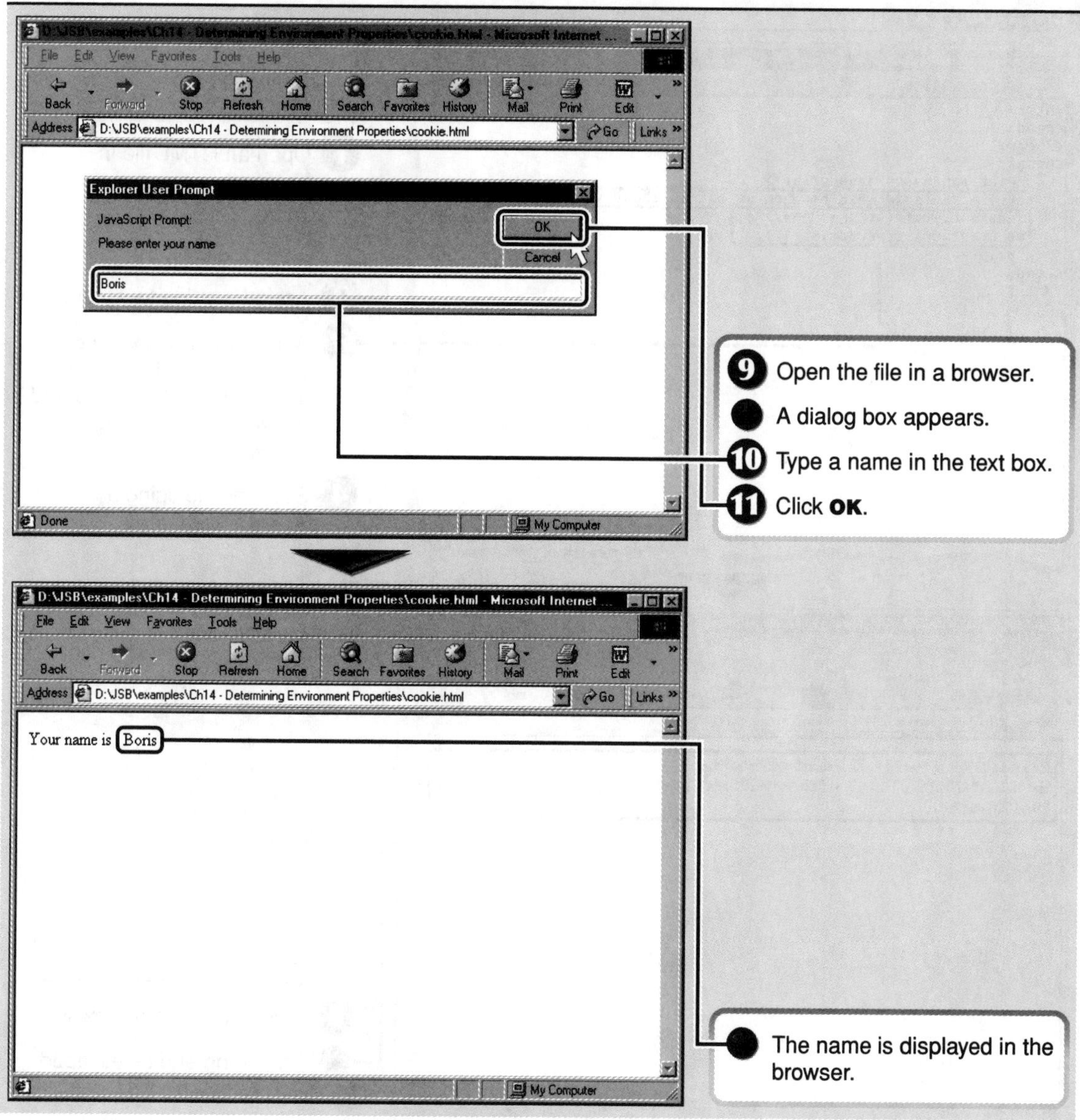
Explorer User Prompt
JavaScript Prompt:
Please enter your name
OK
Cancel
Boris
Your name is Boris

9. Open the file in a browser.
- A dialog box appears.

10. Type a name in the text box.
11. Click **OK**.
- The name is displayed in the browser.

ENCODE CHARACTERS

Some characters can be confused as server commands. This can result in the incorrect processing of data. To ensure the integrity of data, you can encode it, and the server will decode it. You encode a character with `escape()`, which accepts a single string — the text to encode. The text is encoded by converting it to a percentage symbol (`%`) followed by a two-digit ASCII value. Encoded text can be decoded with `unescape()`.

ENCODE TEXT

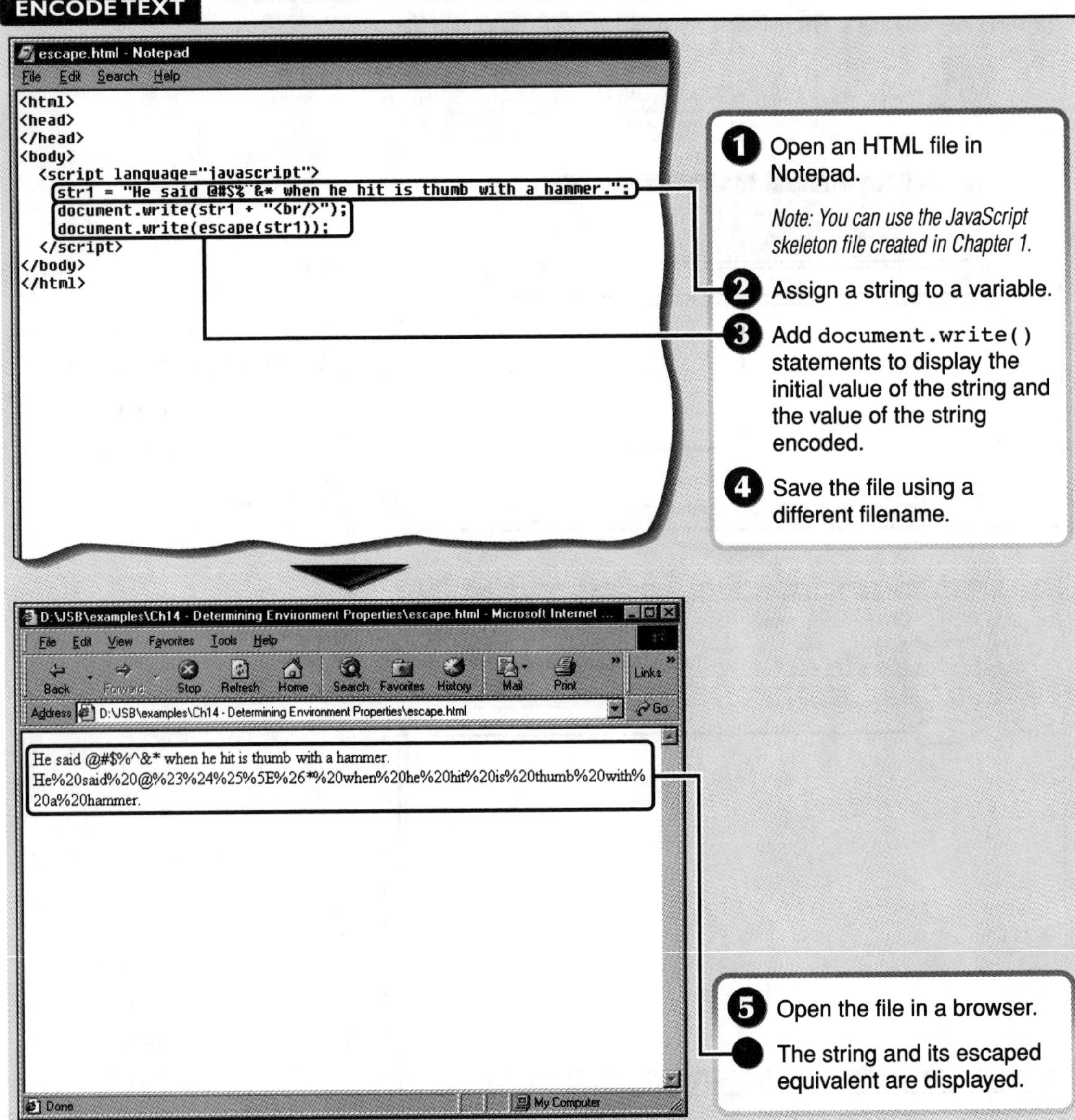

escape.html - Notepad
File Edit Search Help
<html>
<head>
</head>
<body>
<script language="javascript">
str1 = "He said @#$%^&* when he hit is thumb with a hammer.";
document.write(str1 + "<br/>");
document.write(escape(str1));
</script>
</body>
</html>
D:\JSB\examples\Ch14 - Determining Environment Properties\escape.html - Microsoft Internet ...
File Edit View Favorites Tools Help
Back Forward Stop Refresh Home Search Favorites History Mail Print
Links
Address D:\JSB\examples\Ch14 - Determining Environment Properties\escape.html
Go
He said @#$%^&* when he hit is thumb with a hammer.
He%20said%20@%23%24%25%5E%26*%20when%20he%20hit%20is%20thumb%20with%20a%20hammer.
Done
My Computer

1. Open an HTML file in Notepad.

   Note: You can use the JavaScript skeleton file created in Chapter 1.

2. Assign a string to a variable.
3. Add `document.write()` statements to display the initial value of the string and the value of the string encoded.
4. Save the file using a different filename.
5. Open the file in a browser.

- The string and its escaped equivalent are displayed.

in an instant

DECODE TEXT

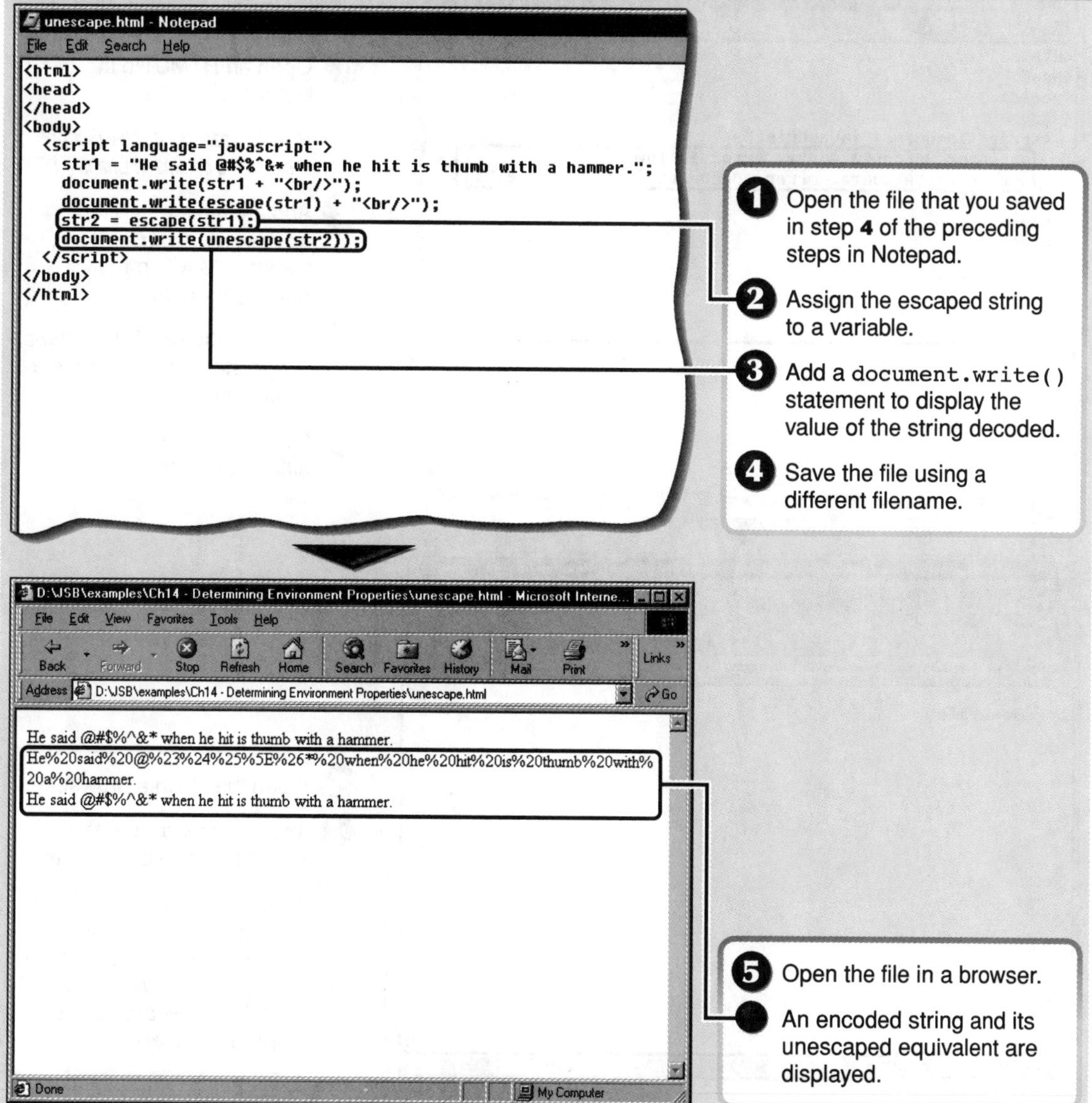
unescape.html - Notepad
File Edit Search Help
<html>
<head>
</head>
<body>
<script language="javascript">
str1 = "He said @#$%^&* when he hit is thumb with a hammer.";
document.write(str1 + "<br/>");
document.write(escape(str1) + "<br/>");
str2 = escape(str1);
document.write(unescape(str2));
</script>
</body>
</html>
D:\JSB\examples\Ch14 - Determining Environment Properties\unescape.html - Microsoft Interne...
File Edit View Favorites Tools Help
Back Forward Stop Refresh Home Search Favorites History Mail Print Links
Address D:\JSB\examples\Ch14 - Determining Environment Properties\unescape.html Go
He said @#$%^&* when he hit is thumb with a hammer.
He%20said%20@%23%24%25%5E%26*%20when%20he%20hit%20is%20thumb%20with%20a%20hammer.
He said @#$%^&* when he hit is thumb with a hammer.
Done
My Computer

1. Open the file that you saved in step **4** of the preceding steps in Notepad.
2. Assign the escaped string to a variable.
3. Add a `document.write()` statement to display the value of the string decoded.
4. Save the file using a different filename.
5. Open the file in a browser.

- An encoded string and its unescaped equivalent are displayed.

DETECT JAVASCRIPT ERRORS

JavaScript *syntax errors* occur when you use syntax that the browser cannot understand. *Runtime errors* occur when the syntax is correct but the program does not do what it should. Syntax errors are the easiest to detect because the browser lets you know that an error has occurred. Runtime errors are harder to find but can be found with some careful debugging techniques.

DETECT JAVASCRIPT ERRORS

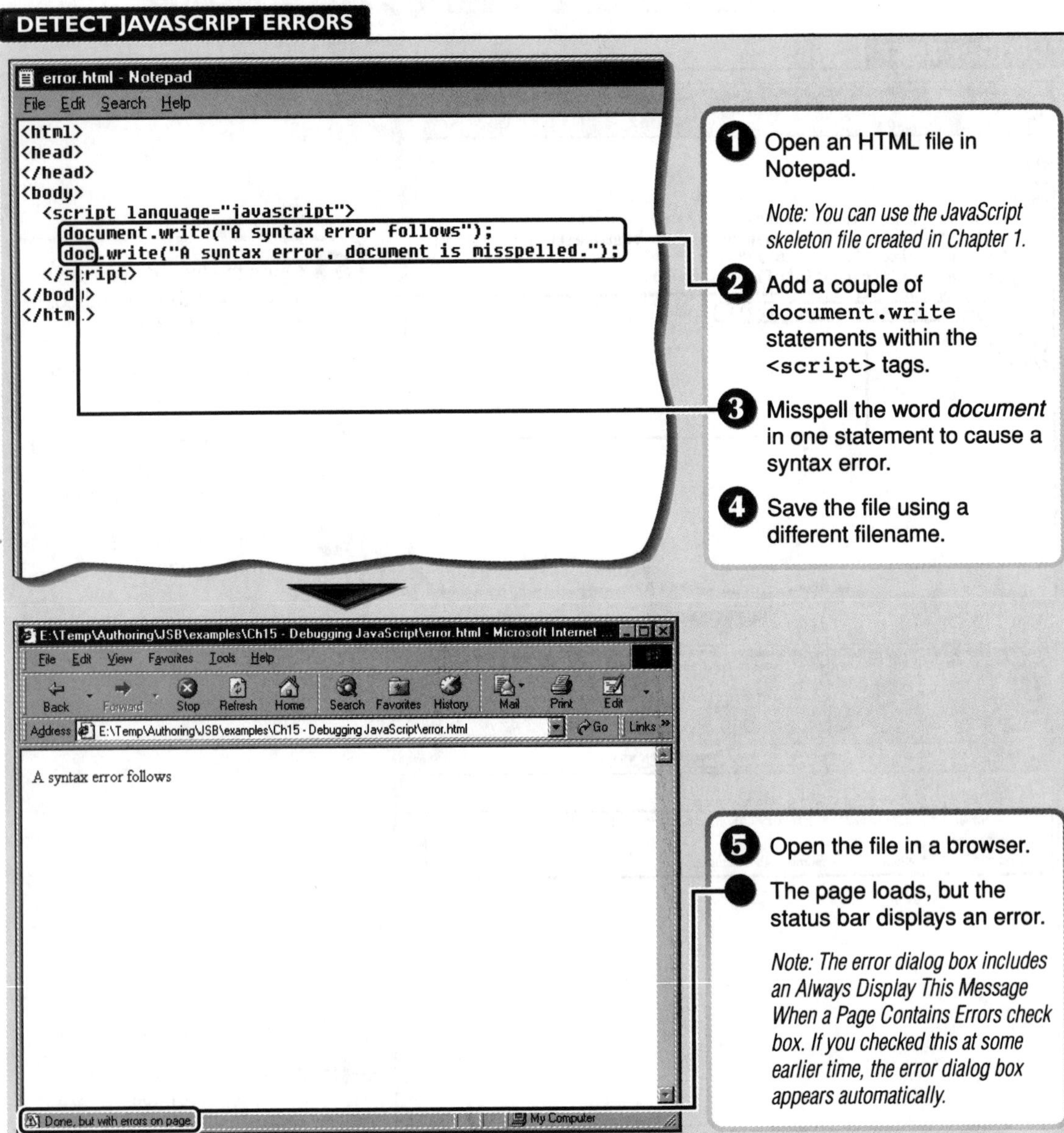
error.html - Notepad
File Edit Search Help
<html>
<head>
</head>
<body>
<script language="javascript">
document.write("A syntax error follows");
doc.write("A syntax error, document is misspelled.");
</script>
</body>
</html>
E:\Temp\Authoring\JSB\examples\Ch15 - Debugging JavaScript\error.html - Microsoft Internet ...
File Edit View Favorites Tools Help
Back Forward Stop Refresh Home Search Favorites History Mail Print Edit
Address E:\Temp\Authoring\JSB\examples\Ch15 - Debugging JavaScript\error.html
Go Links
A syntax error follows
Done, but with errors on page.
My Computer

1. Open an HTML file in Notepad.

   Note: You can use the JavaScript skeleton file created in Chapter 1.

2. Add a couple of `document.write` statements within the `<script>` tags.

3. Misspell the word *document* in one statement to cause a syntax error.

4. Save the file using a different filename.

5. Open the file in a browser.

- The page loads, but the status bar displays an error.

  Note: The error dialog box includes an Always Display This Message When a Page Contains Errors check box. If you checked this at some earlier time, the error dialog box appears automatically.

in an instant

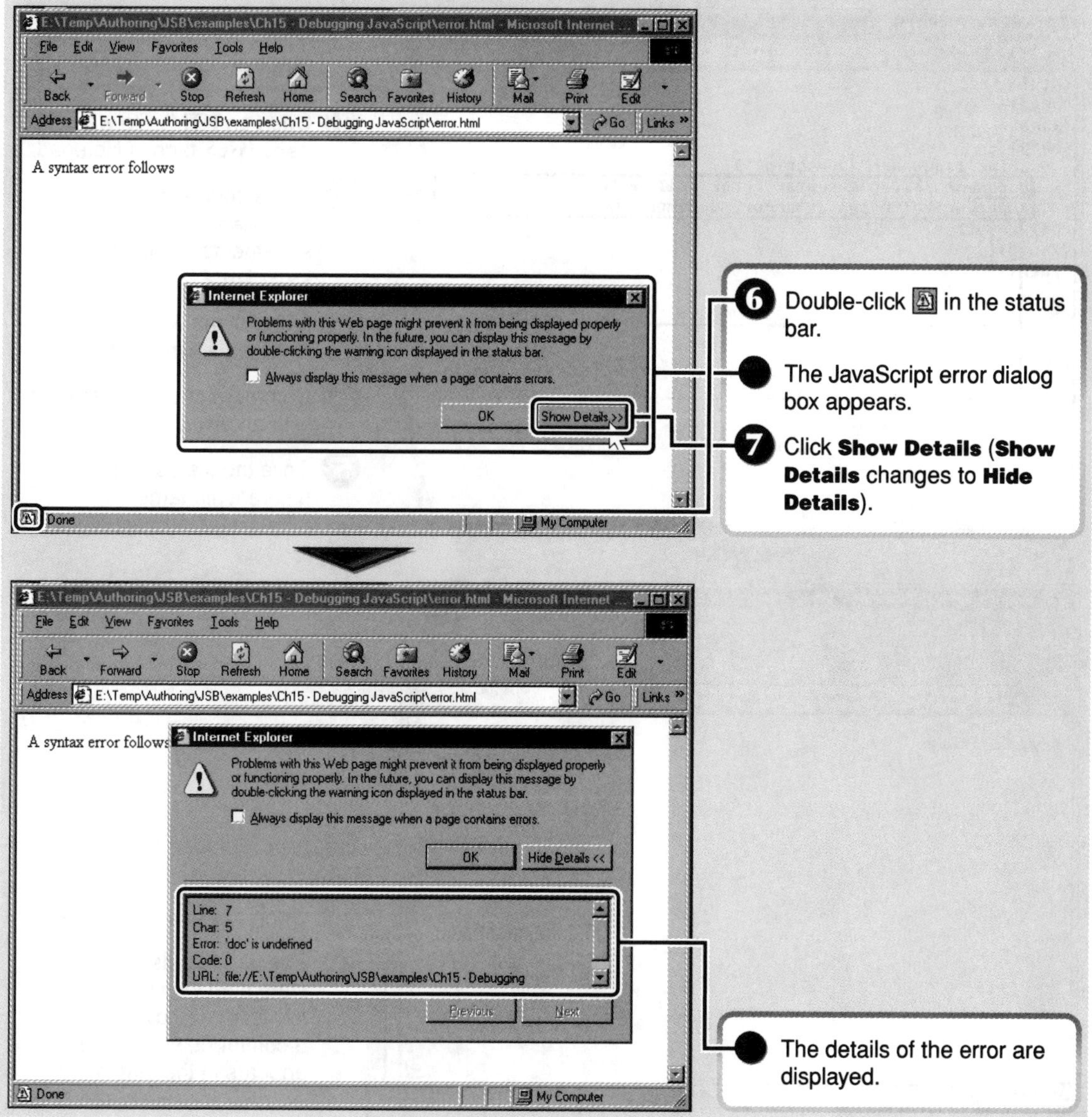
A syntax error follows
Internet Explorer
Problems with this Web page might prevent it from being displayed properly or functioning properly. In the future, you can display this message by double-clicking the warning icon displayed in the status bar.
Always display this message when a page contains errors.
OK
Show Details >>
Done
My Computer
6 Double-click [icon] in the status bar.
The JavaScript error dialog box appears.
7 Click Show Details (Show Details changes to Hide Details).
Hide Details <<
Line: 7
Char: 5
Error: 'doc' is undefined
Code: 0
URL: file://E:\Temp\Authoring\JSB\examples\Ch15 - Debugging
Previous
Next
The details of the error are displayed.

DEBUG WITH COMMENTS

You can use comments to help you identify errors; if you comment out a statement with an error, the rest of the page should work fine. You can add a comment to a single line by placing two slash marks (//) anywhere in the line, and everything after the slashes will be ignored by the browser. The /* and */ marks comment out any statements between them, even over multiple lines.

USING SINGLE-LINE COMMENTS

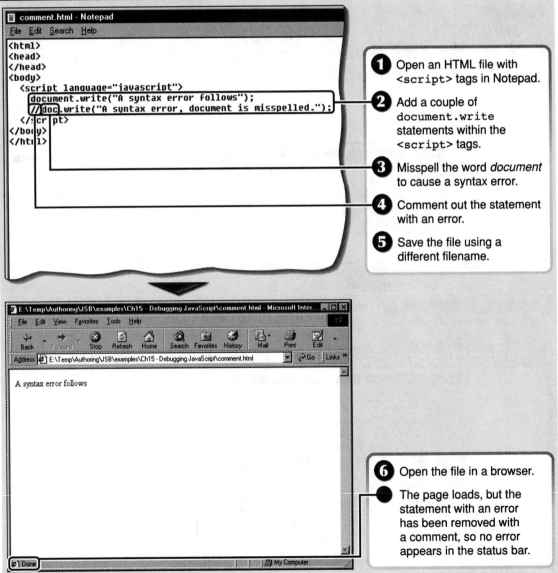

comment.html - Notepad

File Edit Search Help

```
<html>
<head>
</head>
<body>
  <script language="javascript">
    document.write("A syntax error follows");
    //doc.write("A syntax error, document is misspelled.");
  </script>
</body>
</html>
```

1. Open an HTML file with `<script>` tags in Notepad.
2. Add a couple of `document.write` statements within the `<script>` tags.
3. Misspell the word *document* to cause a syntax error.
4. Comment out the statement with an error.
5. Save the file using a different filename.

E:\Temp\Authoring\JSB\examples\Ch15 - Debugging JavaScript\comment.html - Microsoft Inter...

Address E:\Temp\Authoring\JSB\examples\Ch15 - Debugging JavaScript\comment.html

A syntax error follows

Done | My Computer

6. Open the file in a browser.

- The page loads, but the statement with an error has been removed with a comment, so no error appears in the status bar.

in an instant

USING MULTIPLE-LINE COMMENTS

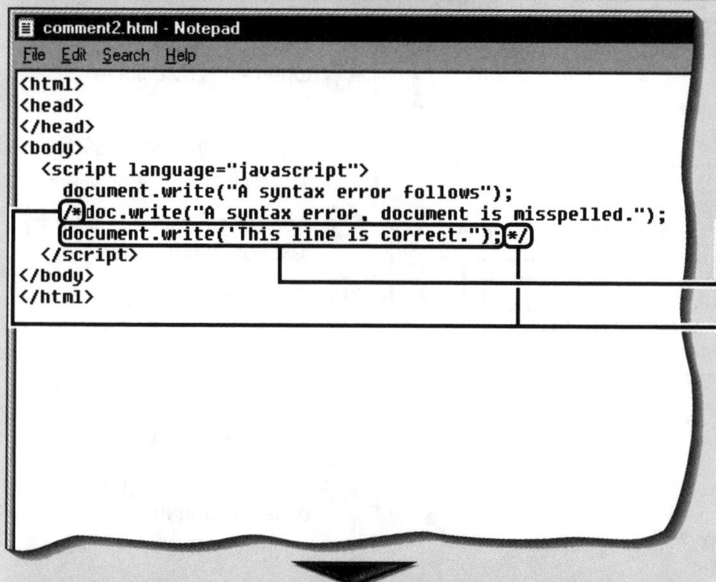
comment2.html - Notepad
File Edit Search Help
<html>
<head>
</head>
<body>
<script language="javascript">
document.write("A syntax error follows");
/*doc.write("A syntax error, document is misspelled.");
document.write('This line is correct.");*/
</script>
</body>
</html>

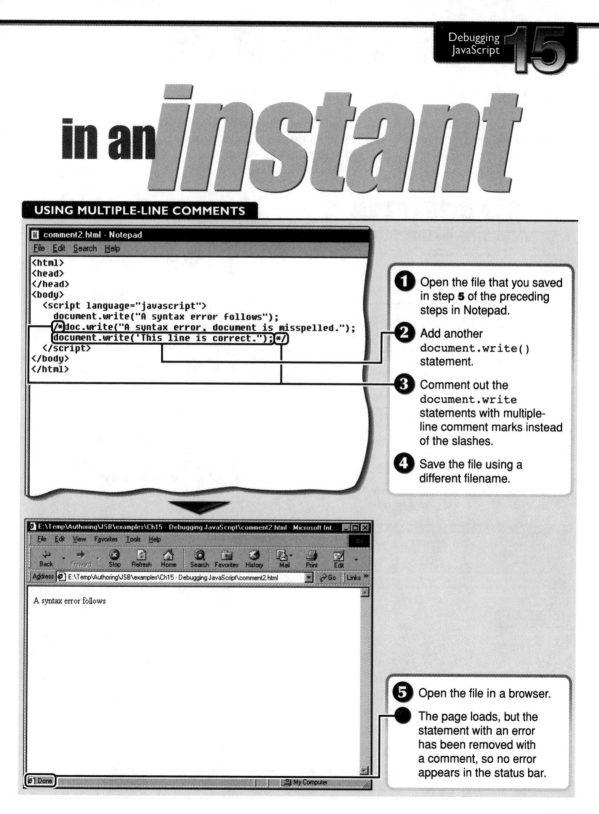

1. Open the file that you saved in step **5** of the preceding steps in Notepad.
2. Add another `document.write()` statement.
3. Comment out the `document.write` statements with multiple-line comment marks instead of the slashes.
4. Save the file using a different filename.

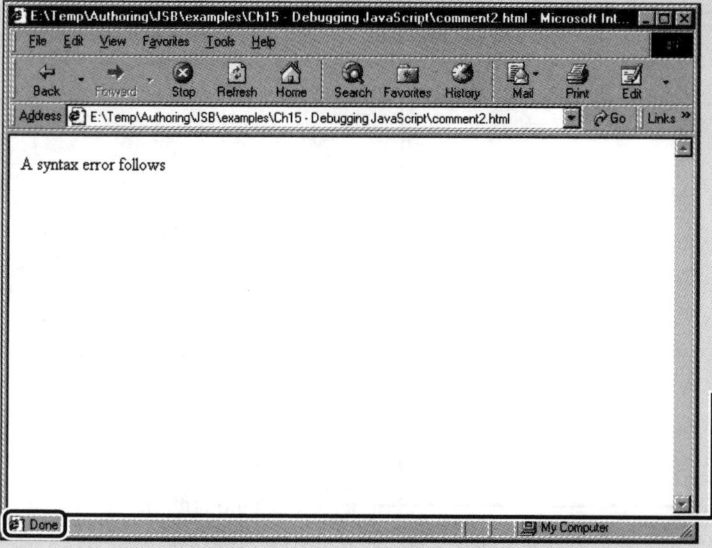
E:\Temp\Authoring\JSB\examples\Ch15 - Debugging JavaScript\comment2.html - Microsoft Int...
File Edit View Favorites Tools Help
Back Forward Stop Refresh Home Search Favorites History Mail Print Edit
Address E:\Temp\Authoring\JSB\examples\Ch15 - Debugging JavaScript\comment2.html
Go Links
A syntax error follows
Done
My Computer

5. Open the file in a browser.

- The page loads, but the statement with an error has been removed with a comment, so no error appears in the status bar.

OUTPUT VALUES TO TEXT BOXES

You can debug JavaScript by outputting the value of the variables that you are working with to a temporary text box. This gives you a chance to examine the value as the script is being executed. Text boxes can be easily included within any form on the page, or a new form can be quickly added to the page to display the values.

OUTPUT VALUES TO TEXT BOXES

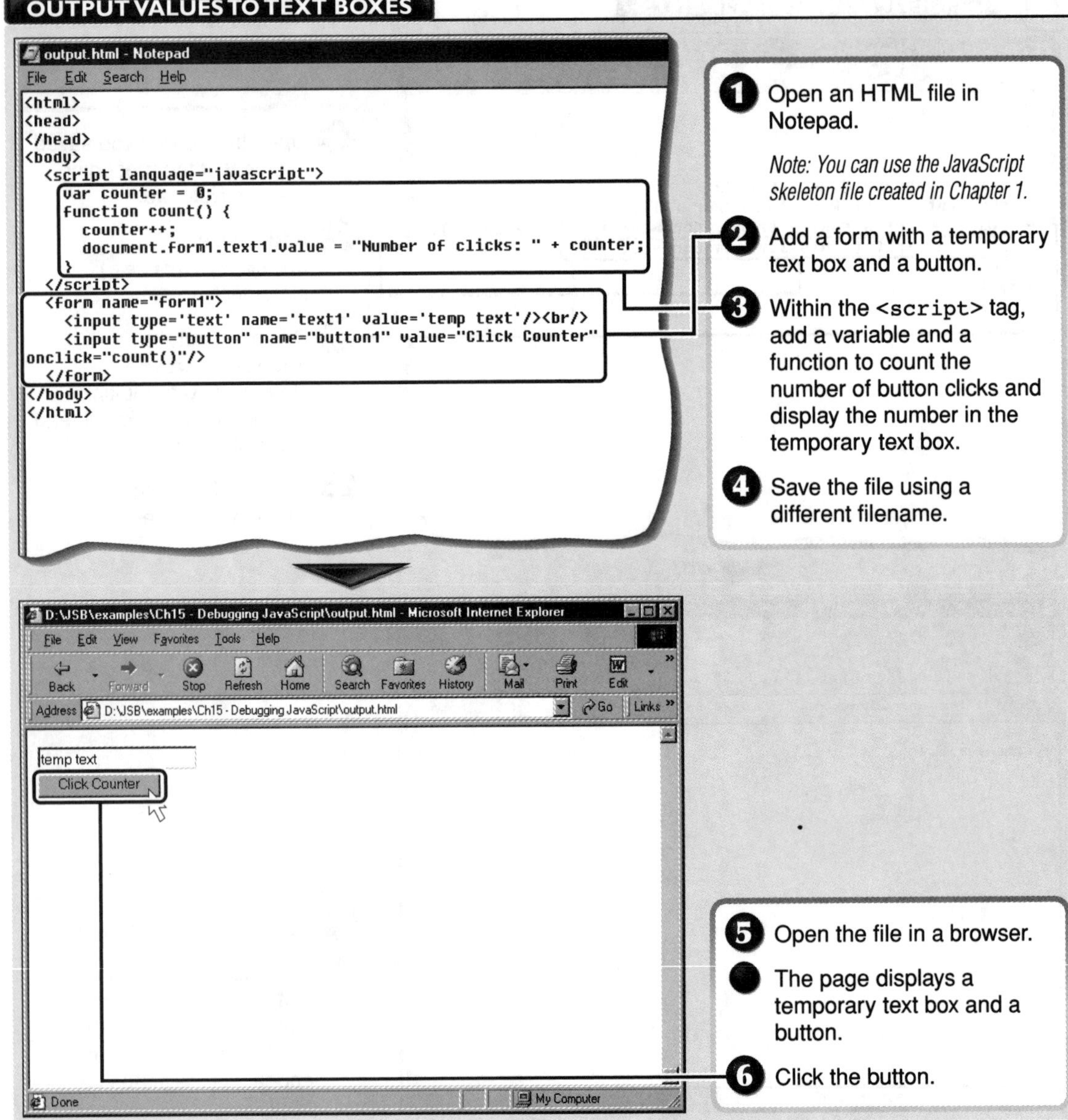

output.html - Notepad
File Edit Search Help
<html>
<head>
</head>
<body>
<script language="javascript">
var counter = 0;
function count() {
counter++;
document.form1.text1.value = "Number of clicks: " + counter;
}
</script>
<form name="form1">
<input type='text' name='text1' value='temp text'/>
<input type="button" name="button1" value="Click Counter"
onclick="count()"/>
</form>
</body>
</html>
D:\JSB\examples\Ch15 - Debugging JavaScript\output.html - Microsoft Internet Explorer
File Edit View Favorites Tools Help
Back Forward Stop Refresh Home Search Favorites History Mail Print Edit
Address D:\JSB\examples\Ch15 - Debugging JavaScript\output.html
Go Links
temp text
Click Counter
Done
My Computer

1. Open an HTML file in Notepad.

   Note: You can use the JavaScript skeleton file created in Chapter 1.

2. Add a form with a temporary text box and a button.

3. Within the `<script>` tag, add a variable and a function to count the number of button clicks and display the number in the temporary text box.

4. Save the file using a different filename.

5. Open the file in a browser.

- The page displays a temporary text box and a button.

6. Click the button.

in an instant

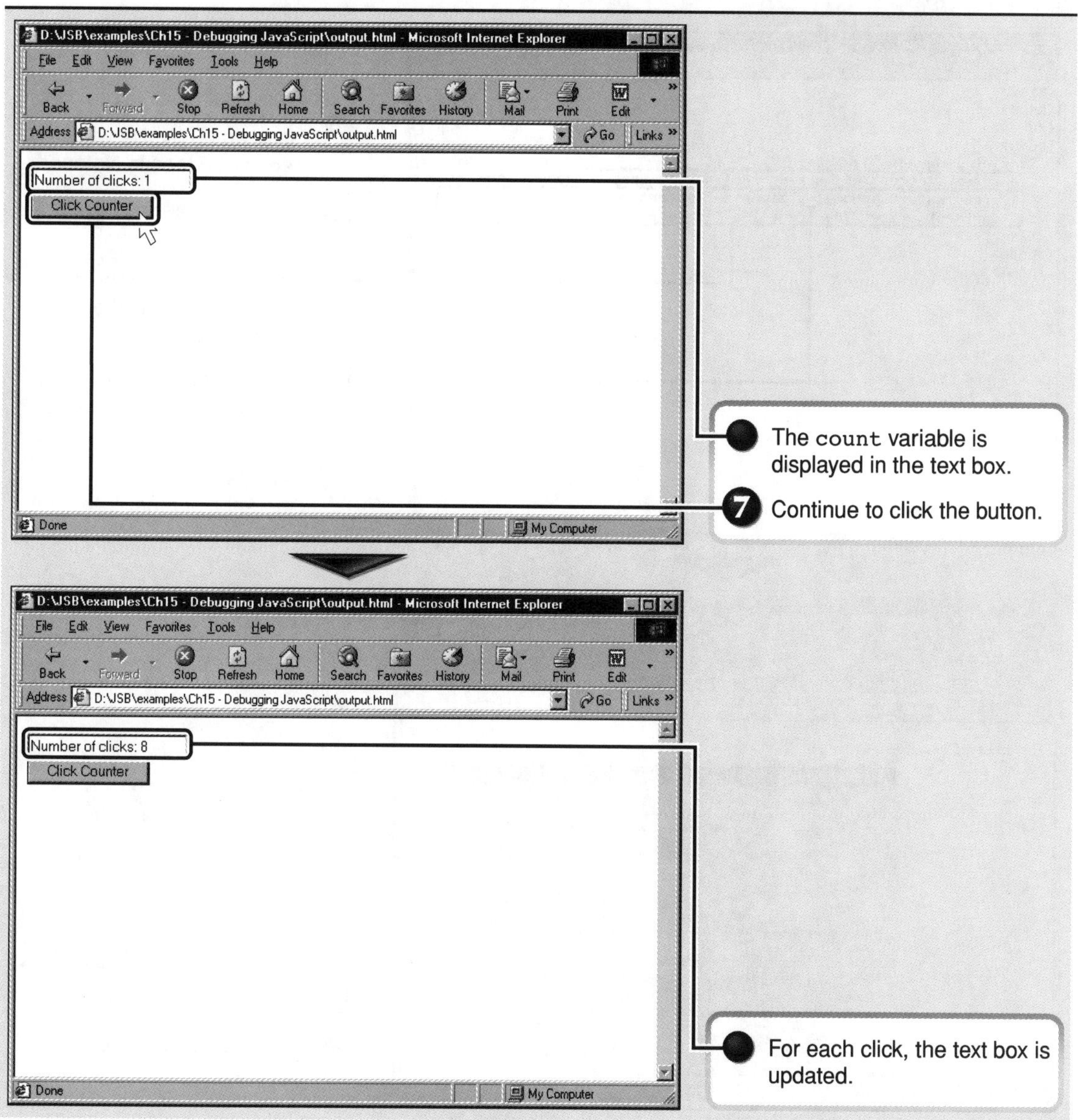
D:\JSB\examples\Ch15 - Debugging JavaScript\output.html - Microsoft Internet Explorer
Number of clicks: 1
Click Counter
Number of clicks: 8
Click Counter

- The `count` variable is displayed in the text box.

7 Continue to click the button.

- For each click, the text box is updated.

COMMON JAVASCRIPT ERRORS

A common error in `if` statements is to use the assignment operator (=) instead of the equality operator (==). Another common error is to mismatch brackets, quote marks, and parentheses. Object properties and methods are case-sensitive, so `bgColor` will not work if you forget to capitalize the *C*. Another common error is to use properties, methods, and events that are not associated with a specific object.

COMMON JAVASCRIPT ERRORS

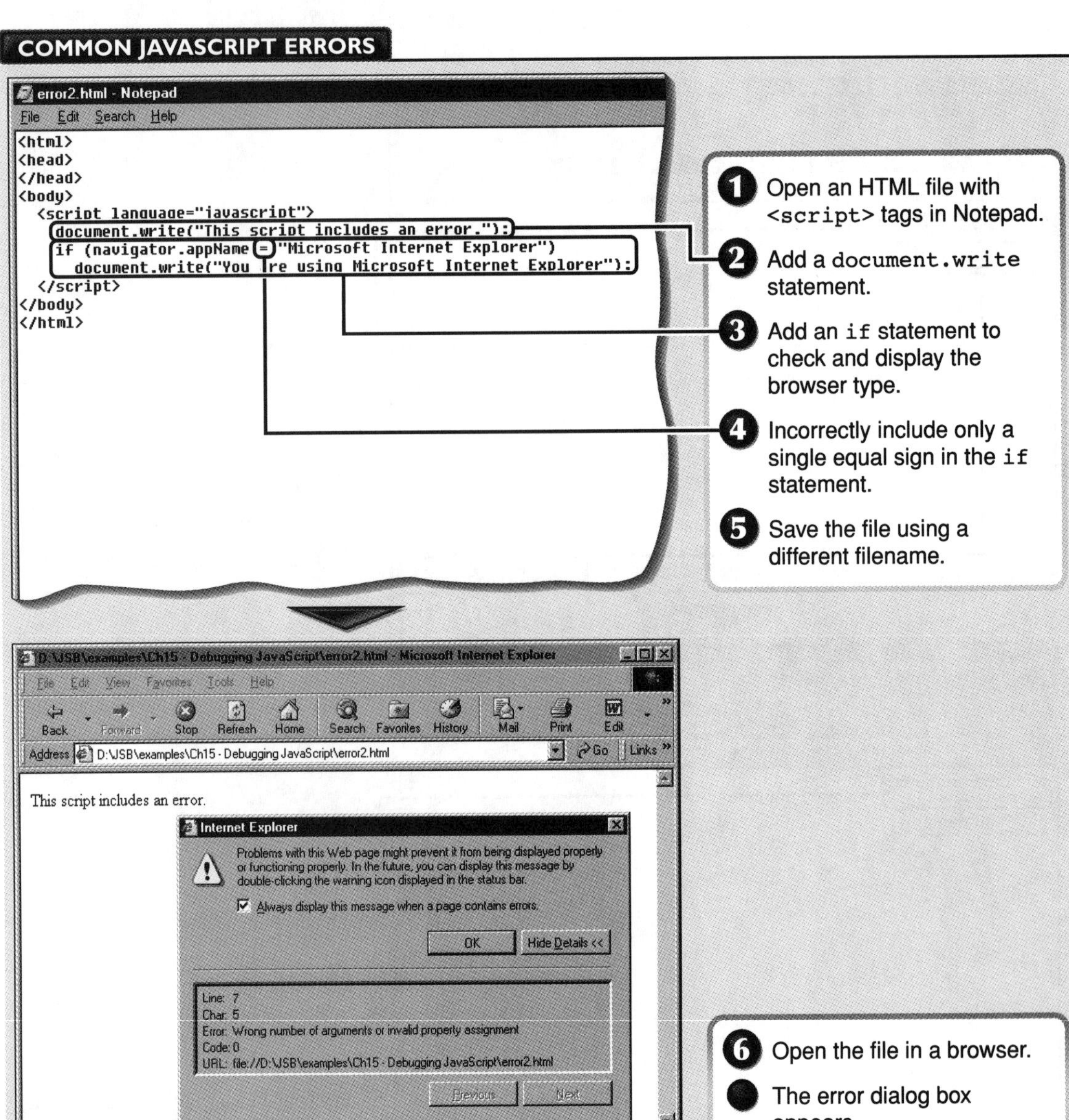

error2.html - Notepad
File Edit Search Help
<html>
<head>
</head>
<body>
<script language="javascript">
document.write("This script includes an error.");
if (navigator.appName = "Microsoft Internet Explorer")
document.write("You are using Microsoft Internet Explorer");
</script>
</body>
</html>
D:\JSB\examples\Ch15 - Debugging JavaScript\error2.html - Microsoft Internet Explorer
This script includes an error.
Internet Explorer
Problems with this Web page might prevent it from being displayed properly or functioning properly. In the future, you can display this message by double-clicking the warning icon displayed in the status bar.
Always display this message when a page contains errors.
OK
Hide Details <<
Line: 7
Char: 5
Error: Wrong number of arguments or invalid property assignment
Code: 0
URL: file://D:\JSB\examples\Ch15 - Debugging JavaScript\error2.html
Previous
Next
Error on page.
My Computer

1. Open an HTML file with `<script>` tags in Notepad.
2. Add a `document.write` statement.
3. Add an `if` statement to check and display the browser type.
4. Incorrectly include only a single equal sign in the `if` statement.
5. Save the file using a different filename.
6. Open the file in a browser.

- The error dialog box appears.

in an instant

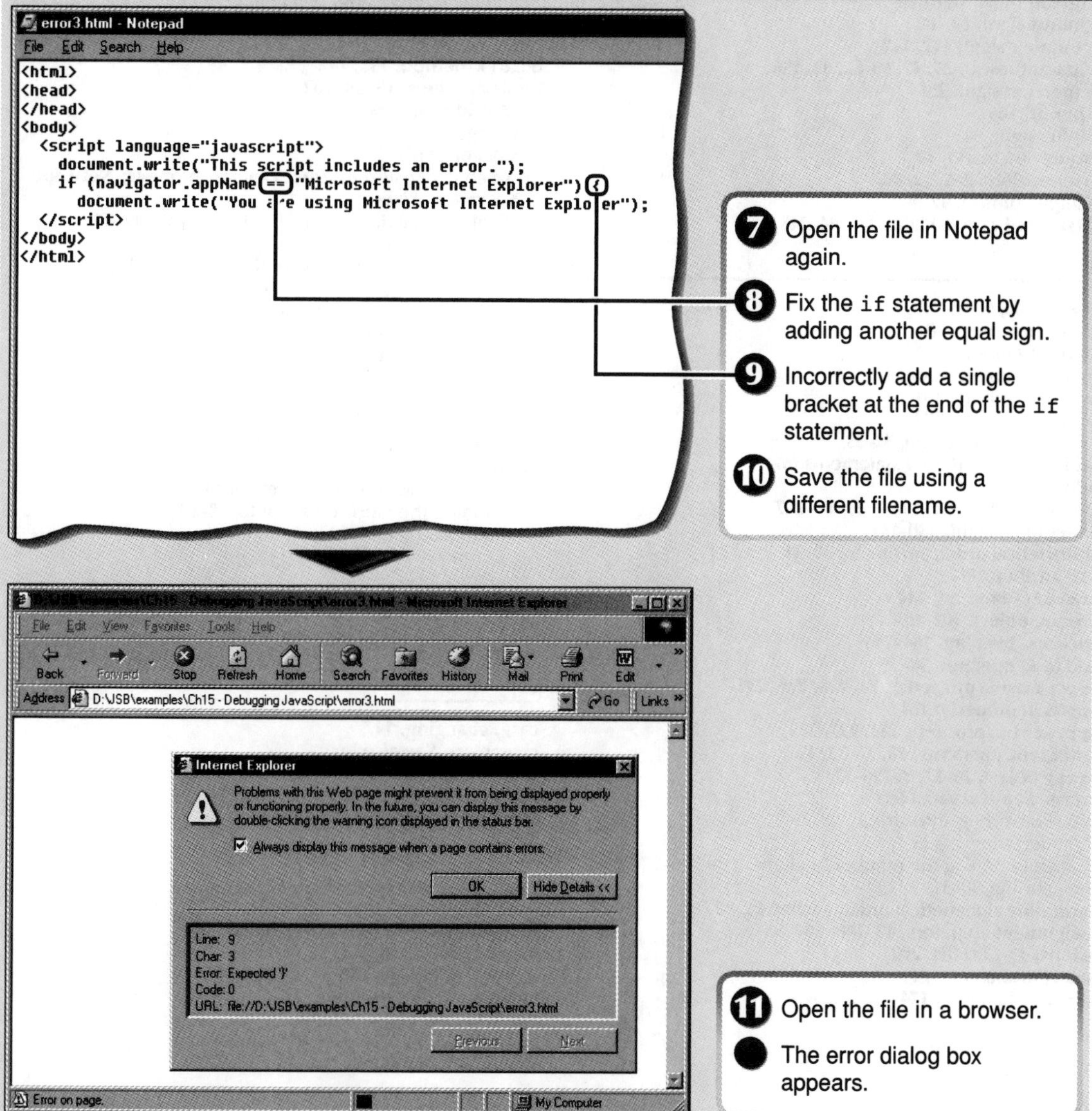
error3.html - Notepad
File Edit Search Help
<html>
<head>
</head>
<body>
<script language="javascript">
document.write("This script includes an error.");
if (navigator.appName == "Microsoft Internet Explorer") {
document.write("You are using Microsoft Internet Explorer");
</script>
</body>
</html>
Internet Explorer
Problems with this Web page might prevent it from being displayed properly or functioning properly. In the future, you can display this message by double-clicking the warning icon displayed in the status bar.
Always display this message when a page contains errors.
OK
Hide Details <<
Line: 9
Char: 3
Error: Expected '}'
Code: 0
URL: file://D:\JSB\examples\Ch15 - Debugging JavaScript\error3.html
Previous
Next
Address D:\JSB\examples\Ch15 - Debugging JavaScript\error3.html
Error on page.
My Computer

7. Open the file in Notepad again.
8. Fix the `if` statement by adding another equal sign.
9. Incorrectly add a single bracket at the end of the `if` statement.
10. Save the file using a different filename.

11. Open the file in a browser.

- The error dialog box appears.

INDEX

D

E

F

INDEX

N

O

P

Q–R

INDEX

U

V

W–Z